BRITAIN SINCE 1918

Also by David Marquand

Ramsay MacDonald
Parliament for Europe
The Unprincipled Society
The Progressive Dilemma
The New Reckoning
Decline of the Public

BRITAIN SINCE 1918

THE STRANGE CAREER OF BRITISH DEMOCRACY

DAVID MARQUAND

Weidenfeld & Nicolson

LONDON

First published in Great Britain in 2008
by Weidenfeld & Nicolson

3 5 7 9 10 8 6 4 2

© 2008 David Marquand

A CIP catalogue record for this book
is available from the British Library.

ISBN-13   978 0 297 64320 3

Typeset by Input Data Services Ltd, Bridgwater, Somerset

Printed in Great Britain by CPI Mackays, Chatham ME5 8TD

Weidenfeld & Nicolson

The Orion Publishing Group Ltd
Orion House
5 Upper Saint Martin's Lane
London, WC2H 9EA

An Hachette Livre UK Company

The Orion Publishing Group's policy is to use papers that
are natural, renewable and recyclable products and made
from wood grown in sustainable forests. The logging and
manufacturing processes are expected to conform to the
environmental regulations of the country of origin.

www.orionbooks.co.uk

For Judith — again

CONTENTS

ILLUSTRATIONS

The photo of R.H. Tawney is reproduced courtesy of Jane Bown/Guardian News &
Media Ltd 1960. The other pictures are supplied by Getty Images.

PREFACE

This book has had a long gestation. I have been preoccupied with the past, present and possible futures of British democracy since I was a Member of Parliament more than thirty years ago, experiencing the grandeurs and servitudes of the 'Westminster Model' at first-hand. I have wrestled with these themes in most of my published work since then. They were present between the lines in my first book, a biography of the first Labour Prime Minister, Ramsay MacDonald; and helped to shape the most recent one, *Decline of the Public*. But I am now taking what is, for me, a new tack. I have increasingly come to believe that it is misleading to think of British democracy as though it were a single monolithic lump to be accepted or rejected en bloc. As John Dunn shows in his brilliant *Setting the People Free*, democracy is plural, not singular; it has taken different forms at different times and means different things to different people.

In the pages that follow I tell the story of democratic politics in Britain since the coming of manhood suffrage and partial female suffrage in 1918, from that perspective. I begin by tracing the long march of British democratisation that culminated in the 'Fourth Reform Act' of that year and then examine the diverse visions of democracy and the democratic state that emerged from it. But I have not sought to contribute to the voluminous theoretical literature about democracy that now spans substantially more than two millennia. My approach is historical, not theoretical: particular, not general.

I have tried to show how politicians, officials and (not least) citizens in my own country of Britain responded to the advent of democracy, came to terms with its dynamics and interpreted its arrival. I am concerned with power and the use of power: with statecraft and the twists and turns of statecraft; with the accidents of personality and the contingencies of fate. But I am concerned most of all with dreams and the traditions that they reflect – with the memories, visions and ideals that have helped to structure the struggle for power, to define the terms on which it has been used, to shape the identities of those who sought and held it, and to mobilise those in whose names they have done so.

I have had a great deal of fun writing this book, and I have also learned a lot. My childhood heroes in the post-war Labour Government (in which my father was a minister) no longer seem quite as heroic as they did – though for the twin giants, Ernest Bevin and Stafford Cripps, my admiration is undimmed. Aneurin Bevan, whose deadly mixture of cutting wit and blazing passion set my pulse racing when I heard him at the great Trafalgar Square anti-Suez protest in 1956, now seems to me a statesman manqué as well as the greatest tribune of the people in his generation. Tony Benn, the *enfant terrible* of dying Labourism, became intoxicated by his own popularity, but the new directions for which he was groping before oratorical inebriation set in seem far more promising to me now than they did at the time.

However, my most surprising discoveries have been on the political right. I used to admire Edward Heath's clumsy, rather grouchy honesty when I sat on the benches opposite him in Parliament. I now see him as a nearly-great and wholly tragic figure, whose downfall testified to his virtues rather than his faults. Enoch Powell, Keith Joseph and Margaret Thatcher – respectively the pathfinders and the pacemaker of the capitalist renaissance of our time – seem to me to have worn much better than their opponents on the left. And Harold Macmillan, that master of irony and specialist in ambiguity, emerges from my story as the nearest thing to a great Prime Minister in the post-war years.

Among the thinkers and practitioners whose narratives still echo through our political culture, the broad sympathies and generous passion of Edmund Burke, like the scarifying prose of the great Lord Salisbury, have been revelations – matched only by the soaring eloquence and fierce invective of John Milton's political writings, the astonishing political creativity of the Levellers, whose call for a democratic English Republic is as stirring now as it was 350 years ago, and Thomas Paine's marvellous optimism. As all this implies, what I have learned above all is that there are more riches in the British political tradition than I dreamed of before I started. But, though I have tried to be fair to all the characters in my rich cast list, I cannot pretend to have been unbiased. History is biased by definition.

I have accumulated a multitude of debts. My written sources can be found in the footnotes and bibliography, but I have also benefited enormously from interviews with Lord Bancroft, Sir Alec Cairncross, Lord Croham, Edmund Dell, Sir Donald MacDougall, James Meade, Lord ('Len') Murray, Max Nicholson, Sir Richard O'Brien, Sir Leo Pliatzky, Lord Plowden, Lord Roll and Lord Sherfield. I am grateful to the Social Sciences Research School at the Australian National University for the award of a Visiting Fellowship and for the stimulating conversations and warm hospitality I enjoyed while I was there. I am also grateful to the Leverhulme Trust for awarding me a research grant, enabling me to take leave of absence from my duties at the University of Sheffield in the critical early stages of my labours.

It would take too long to mention all my intellectual debts, but one or two deserve special attention. I have already mentioned Dunn's *Setting the People Free*. To that I should add Quentin Skinner's analysis of 'Roman liberty' in *Liberty Before Liberalism;* Conor Cruise O'Brien's path-breaking study of Burke, *The Great Melody;* Edmund Dell's mordant study of post-war economic policy-making, *The Chancellors;* Peter Hennessy's rich and zestful *Having It So Good;* John Campbell's biographies of Edward Heath and Margaret Thatcher; Alistair Horne's biography of Harold Macmillan; and Philip Williamson's subtle study of Baldwin's rhetoric and statecraft, *Stanley Baldwin, Conservative Leadership and National Values.*

I should like to thank Anthony Goff, my agent at David Higham Associates, for his invaluable moral support and encouragement. I am immensely grateful to Benjamin Buchan, my long-suffering editor at Weidenfeld and Nicolson, for his forbearance, wisdom and editorial acumen. Nina Fishman, Dick Leonard, Robert Taylor and Andrew Gamble read the manuscript in whole or in part; to all of them I owe a great debt of gratitude. Andrew Gamble's careful and insightful comments were particularly helpful. Some of them caused me sleepless nights, but the book is a much better one than it would have been without them. I salute his tact and thank him for his help. It goes without saying that any remaining errors of fact or interpretation are mine.

My greatest debt of all is to my beloved wife Judith. She has read every page of this book, some of them several times. Her encouragement and support have been indispensable and her advice invaluable. I dedicate the book to her.

David Marquand
Old Headington
November 2007

ACKNOWLEDGEMENTS

I am grateful to the following for permission to quote from copyright material: Argyll Publishing, in respect of an extract from Kenyon Wright, *The People Say Yes: The Making of Scotland's Parliament* (Argyll Publishing, Glendaruel, Argyll, 1997); Cambridge University Press, in respect of an extract from Onora O'Neill, *A Question of Trust* (Cambridge University Press, Cambridge, 2002); Constable & Robinson, in respect of extracts from J. Enoch Powell (ed. John Wood) *Freedom and Reality* (Elliott Right Way Books, paperback edition, Kingswood Surrey, 1969); David Higham Associates in respect of extracts from Aneurin Bevan, *In Place of Fear* (William Heinemann Ltd, London, 1952); the Fabian Society in respect of an extract from *Fabian Essays in Socialism* (ed. G. Bernard Shaw, Fabian Society, London, 1889); A.M. Heath, by permission of Bill Hamilton as the Literary Executor of the Estate of the Late Sonia Brownell Orwell and Secker & Warburg Ltd, in respect of extracts from *Coming Up For Air* (George Orwell, © George Orwell, Secker & Warburg, London, 1948) and from 'The Lion and the Unicorn: Socialism and the English Genius' (George Orwell, © George Orwell) in Sonia Orwell and Ian Angus (eds), *The Collected Essays and Letters of George Orwell*, vol. II, *My Country Right or Left* (Penguin Books, Harmondsworth, 1970); *The New Statesman*, in respect of an extract from a letter of 22 June 1935, by R.H. Tawney (© All Rights reserved with permission, *New Statesman*); The Random House Group Ltd., in respect of extracts from Alastair Campbell, *The Blair Years: extracts from the Alastair Campbell Diaries* (Hutchinson, London, 2007), from Colin Crouch, *The Student Revolt* (The Bodley Head, London, 1970), from Bryan Magee, *Clouds of Glory: A Hoxton Childhood* (Jonathan Cape, London, 2003), from Ferdinand Mount, *The British Constitution Now: Recovery or Decline?* (William Heinemann Ltd., London, 1992) and from Malise Ruthven, *A Satanic Affair: Salman Rushdie and the Wrath of Islam* (Hogarth Press, London, 1991); and Sheil Land Associates, in respect of extracts from Alan Sillitoe, *Saturday Night and Sunday Morning* (© Alan Sillitoe, Pan Books, London, 1960). Every effort has been made to trace copyright holders, but in the event of any omissions the author would be glad to hear from them.

Last, but by no means least, I would like to acknowledge the unfailing courtesy, assiduity and skill of the librarians at Sheffield University Library, the Australian National University Library, the Bodleian Library and the London Library. Without their help this book could not have been written.

1

PROLOGUE

✤

The accursed power which stands on Privilege
(And goes with Women, and Champagne and Bridge)
Broke – and Democracy resumed her reign;
(Which goes with Bridge, and Women and Champagne).

Hilaire Belloc, 'On a Great Election', 1906

✤

Over most of Britain, Thursday 1 May 1997 dawned bright and brisk. Spring was in the air. Strangers grinned at each other on their way to vote in the first general election for five years; outside the polling stations the atmosphere of anticipation and excitement was almost palpable. For Labour and Liberal Democrat supporters (by now, the two categories overlapped so far that it was hard to tell them apart) the night was even better than the day. Gisela Stuart, the German-born Labour candidate for Birmingham Edgbaston, a Conservative seat since 1922, won the constituency with a swing of 10 per cent. In solidly Tory Southgate, the thirty-one-year-old gay Labour candidate, Stephen Twigg, unseated Michael Portillo, the Prince Rupert of the Thatcherite hard core, with a swing of 17.4 per cent.

Some of the seats Labour gained that night, wrote Anthony King, were 'so redolent of Tory England that it was almost impossible to imagine them ever being won by a Labour candidate'. Their names evoked 'shady oaks, mock Tudor villas, well watered lawns and a Jaguar (or at least one of the larger Fords) in every drive'.[1] When the counting was over, Tony Blair's 'New' Labour Party had 419 seats, the largest number Labour had ever won. Its Commons majority was 179, the largest in its history and the largest any party had enjoyed since 1935. The Conservatives were crushed; their share of the vote was lower than at any time since 1832. The Liberal Democrats' share was down, but they had won forty-six seats – more than any third party since 1929. It was more than a landslide, a television commentator declared; it was 'like an asteroid hitting the planet and destroying practically all life on earth'.[2]

The shock waves could still be felt a decade later. In 2001, Labour won another crushing victory. In 2005 it won again, though with a smaller share of a fractionally larger popular vote. Blair was Prime Minister for an uninterrupted total of ten years and two months. Of his twentieth-century predecessors only Thatcher could boast as much. At the start of his term, he displayed a captivating mixture of youthful exuberance and emollient charm. That gave way to crusading bellicosity at the zenith, and to a grim, back-to-the-wall doggedness during the long, sad finale. Yet through all the highs and lows, one theme was constant. Blair epitomised it in a speech to a meeting of European socialist leaders during his first continental foray after becoming Prime Minister. The world, he declared, was experiencing 'a veritable revolution of change'. Technology, trade and travel were transforming our lives; South-East Asia could compete with Europe on equal terms; every day, 'vast amounts' of money were traded across international boundaries. 'New, new, new', he exclaimed, 'everything is new.'[3]

That note survived Blair's departure from office. In June 2007, his Chancellor, Gordon Brown, succeeded him as leader of the Labour Party, before taking over as Prime Minister. In Brown's acceptance speech, there were thirty references to change. For both men, and for much of the party they led, the words 'new' and 'change' had acquired a totemic significance. The world was new, modernity was monolithic and the path to the future, linear. There was one modern condition, to which resistance was vain. The only rational course was to adapt to it. Attempts to resist change, in the name of cherished traditions or inherited values, were spitting into the wind. From it, there was no hiding place; against it, no protection.

There was a germ of truth in the rhetoric. The world was passing through a technological revolution of unprecedented speed. The economy, the culture, the society and the global order had all changed profoundly during the Thatcher years, and they continued to change under Blair. But things were not quite as new as he and Brown imagined. The capitalism foreshadowed by John Maynard Keynes, Henry Ford, Franklin Roosevelt and Ernest Bevin – the stable, organised capitalism of demand management, the mixed economy, giant plants and giant unions – was undeniably a thing of the past. But in fundamentals the restless, masterless, dynamic capitalism of the late twentieth and early twenty-first centuries, with its global scope, gross inequalities, predatory ultra-rich and powerless underclasses, was strikingly reminiscent of the capitalism of 100 years earlier. It would probably have astonished Anthony Crosland, the leading theorist of British social democracy during the high noon of the Keynesian era, but it would not have surprised Karl Marx.

The same was true of the state over which Blair and his colleagues presided. It was a more humdrum and uncertain creature than the war-battered but supremely confident state of the 1940s. Its capacity to manage the economy had sharply declined. Many of its agencies had been forced to adopt unwelcome new methods of working, borrowed from the private sector. But, in a host of ways, it was still an imperial state, with reflexes derived from the days when the Royal Navy policed the world's sea lanes and the City of London dominated its capital markets. By the same token, Britain was still torn between a European vocation, dictated by geography, and an extra-European vocation, derived from a venerable, not to say antiquated, interpretation of her history.

At the core of Blair's response to the shifts in the global order was a fierce determination to assert the largely mythical 'special relationship' between Britain and the United States, which had been the lodestar of almost all British governments for fifty years (though not of American ones). Behind that determination lay the half-conscious assumption that Britain was, in some special sense, an exceptional nation, set apart from the rest of the continent to which she belonged. Blair and his colleagues held essentially the same centralist vision of the democratic state as that held by pioneers of Fabian socialism like Sidney Webb and George Bernard Shaw in the 1880s. Their constitutional changes harked back to the debates over Irish Home Rule, Welsh disestablishment and Lords reform that had preoccupied the Liberal Government before the First World War. The conception of democratic citizenship that lay behind them could be traced back to Renaissance Italy and even to Republican Rome. In the long sweep of British history, Blair's 'revolution of change' was as much a restoration as a revolution. New Labour's path to the future was haunted by ghosts from the past.

Four great questions faced the governments of the 1980s, 1990s and 2000s. What conception of democracy did the famously unwritten British constitution embody – and what conception ought it to embody? Could the democratic promise of political equality be squared with the economic inequality inherent in capitalism, and if so, how? Who were the British, and how did 'Britishness' relate to the much older national identities of the British Isles? Where did Britain fit into the global order and its European subset, and where should she try to fit? To the politicians who groped for answers to them, these questions seemed new, sometimes alarmingly so. Yet similar questions had been asked, in different words, during the convulsive debates that had erupted during the civil wars of the seventeenth century. They had all been asked repeatedly during the long march towards democracy that provides a central theme of British history in the nineteenth and early twentieth centuries, and they were asked at least as insistently in the decades following the belated arrival of manhood suffrage and partial female suffrage in 1918.

Like their predecessors, the Thatcher and Blair governments viewed them through the prism of the evolving British political tradition. They were bound to; it was the only prism they had. In their more exalted moments, both governments liked to depict themselves as the argonauts of a brave new world. In reality, they were the most recent protagonists in a story that had begun more than 300 years before, and whose early chapters had helped to structure the later ones. The tradition that had shaped them was fluid, flexible and, above all, contestable as living traditions always are, but it was also constraining, and its constraints impinged as powerfully on those who were not conscious of them as on those who were. Its roots went a long way back, perhaps even to the centralising monarchs of the Middle Ages. Henry VIII's break with Rome, and his defiant claim that the realm of England was now an 'empire', free of all external authority, was a crucial milestone in its evolution. But the length of its roots is little more than a historical curiosity today. What matters is that it was stamped through and through by the legacy of a long-drawn-out, occasionally violent and always fiercely contested transmutation, through which a pre-democratic state, ruled by a tiny elite, slowly acquired a more or less democratic constitution.

From the vantage point of the twenty-first century, the coming of democracy seems almost inevitable, but it did not seem so while the halting march towards it was in progress. The first serious attempt to establish a democratic polity on British soil was made during the English Revolution that led to the execution of Charles I and the establishment of the Commonwealth. But though the Commonwealth was a republic, it was not a democracy, and those who tried to give it a quasi-democratic suffrage were suppressed. So were the so-called 'British Jacobins' who campaigned for manhood suffrage in the 1790s, and the Chartists who tried to mobilise the nascent working class behind a democratic 'People's Charter' in the 1830s and 1840s. Nearly a century passed between the great Reform Act of 1832, which increased the size of the electorate from 4.5 per cent to 7 per cent of the adult population, and the arrival of manhood suffrage in 1918. Even then, women could not vote in parliamentary elections before the age of thirty.

Plural voting survived until the 1940s. As late as 1945 my own parents had two votes each: one as citizens and one as university graduates. It was not until 1911 that the House of Lords lost its veto powers, and not until 1999 that most (though still not all) hereditary peers lost their seats in it. Though the Commons voted in favour of an elected upper house early in 2007, the House of Lords contained no elected members when this book went to press. As all this implies, the political class viewed the approach of democracy with trepidation, as did much of the intelligentsia. Democracy's many opponents offered stubborn resistance, clothed in telling arguments. Some of its supporters half shared its opponents' assumptions, sometimes without realising the fact. Sturdy working-class radicals, who fought hard for extensions of the suffrage in the 1860s and 1880s, opposed giving votes to the poorest and most dependent of their class, on the grounds that they were not fit for citizenship. The great Liberal leader, Gladstone, opposed female enfranchisement because he thought women were too refined for the hurly-burly of politics.

That history lived on in the reflexes of politicians and voters. There was no single, authoritative narrative of Britain's long march towards democracy. There were several conflicting narratives, reflecting divergent interests and contrasting visions of democratic politics and the democratic state. These narratives, and the visions they reflected, were fundamental to Britain's political culture. They were (and are) embodied at least as powerfully in ritual and iconography as in theories or programmes. To mention only a few examples, the prayers for the monarchy in the Book of Common Prayer, the card votes at the Trade Union Congress, the proud Victorian town halls of the industrial North, and the statues and paintings in the Palace of Westminster did as much as any written text to lodge them in the nation's imagination. Subliminally as well as directly, they told both leaders and led who they were and how they ought to behave. Their implications for statecraft – for the mixtures of rhetoric and policy through which political leaders seek to win and hold power – differed, sometimes radically. In any case, none of them pointed unambiguously in only one direction. There has always been room for argument. But the room has never been unlimited.

In recent years the arguments have been more vigorous than at any time since the First World War, but even today, at the start of the twenty-first century, the protagonists draw on ancient memories of Britain's crablike progress towards democracy and on the visions of democratic politics that helped to determine its course. Yet all too many of them are strangely incurious about the origins and meaning of the memories and visions concerned. The politicians and commentators who dominate the national conversation are the products of a restless, febrile age, when the past is apt to be dismissed as unnecessary baggage, and public debate focuses on surface novelties rather than on the deeper currents of long-term change. In the Westminster village and the media, a strange mixture of amnesia and mythology prevails, impoverishing our understanding of ourselves and nar-rowing the scope of political imagination. Yet, as I hope to show in the rest of this book, the diverse narratives that make up the British political tradition are far richer and more fertile than the constricting common sense of our time admits. 'The tradition of all the dead generations', said Marx, 'weighs like a nightmare on the brain of the living.'[4] The best way to rescue the living from their nightmare is to look again at what the dead actually thought and did.

This book concentrates on British political history since the coming of a more or less democratic suffrage in 1918. One recurrent theme is the disputed identity of Britain and the British as their empire faded. Another is the inevitable tension between democracy and capitalism. A third is the interplay between political, cultural and social change. A fourth is the subtle, often ambiguous relationship between individual character and experience, and political action and belief. My story falls naturally into three phases. Phase One was dominated by the gradual emergence of democratic government on British soil and the narratives that reflected it. The central theme of Phase Two lay in the attempts of governments of all stripes to tame capitalism in the interests of social harmony and democratic inclusion. Phase Three has been dominated by the renaissance of 'untamed' capitalism, and by the strange mixture of ferocious centralism in the polity and hyperindividualism in the culture and economy, that it seems to have brought in its train.

But the British political tradition, and the memories and understandings it encapsulates, loom in the background throughout, like the Chorus in a Greek play. I begin with them.

PART I
AMBLING TO DEMOCRACY

2

SACRED FLAME

And unnatural, irrational, sinful, wicked, unjust, devilish and tyrannical it is, for any man whatsoever ... to appropriate and assume unto himself a power, authority and jurisdiction to rule, govern or reign over any sort of men in the world without their free consent.
John Lilburne, 'The freeman's freedom vindicated', 19 June 1646

For really I think that the poorest he that is in England hath a life to live as the greatest he; and therefore truly, sir, I think it's clear that every man that is to live under a government ought first to put himself under that government; and I do think that the poorest man in England is not at all bound in a strict sense to that government that he hath not had a voice to put himself under.
Colonel Thomas Rainborough at the General Council of the New Model Army, Putney, 29 October 1647

If you want venality, if you want ignorance, if you want drunkenness, and facility for being intimidated. ... Do you go to the top or to the bottom?
Robert Lowe, opposing the 1866 Reform Bill

✣

DEFIANCE FROM BELOW

On 22 May 1917, nearly three years after the start of the First World War, the Lloyd George coalition's Representation of the People Bill, giving votes to all adult men and to women over thirty, received a second reading in the House of Commons. It was a curiously muted occasion. Fourteen million people were about to be enfranchised – easily the biggest extension of the suffrage in British history. The proportion of the adult population with the right to vote in parliamentary elections would be raised from 28 per cent to 78 per cent. Manhood suffrage was no longer a distant dream or an ominous spectre. It was very nearly an accomplished fact. Despite the strange differentiation between the voting ages for men and women, the same was true of female suffrage. But the debate was low-key. Controversy focused on the bill's provisions for the Single Transferable Vote in a limited number of seats, and the Alternative Vote in the rest, both of which were abandoned before the bill passed into law. The historic extension of the suffrage was virtually unopposed.

The opening speech by Sir George Cave, the Unionist Home Secretary (and future Lord Chancellor), typified the mood of the House. In times past, he declared, such a step would have been regarded as a leap in the dark. But experience had shown that extensions of the suffrage fostered 'contentment and stability', and 'added strength' to the throne. Moreover,

> The spirit manifested in this War by all classes of our countrymen has brought us nearer together, has opened men's eyes, and removed mis-understandings on all sides. It has made it, I think, impossible that . . . there should be a revival of the old class feeling which was responsible . . . for the exclusion for a period of so many of our population from the class of electors.[1]

It was a comforting message. Democratic citizenship, as Cave depicted it, was a vehicle for social harmony and a reward for good conduct, rather than a right. New classes had not had to force their way into the political nation, as they had in less happy lands; a statesmanlike elite had gradually admitted them when they had shown that they were ready for the privilege. The purpose of the exercise was to sustain the country's existing institutions; and in this it had succeeded.

These pieties contained an element of truth. The complex process through which Britain eventually acquired a democratic suffrage *was*, at first sight, a decorous affair. Its most obvious hallmarks were incremental change; step-by-step reform; gradual, top-down innovation within a struc-ture of inherited tradition; peaceful accommodation to changing times. But, on closer inspection, decorum dissolves into ambiguity. Incrementalism was the child (or at least the grandchild) of crisis. Most step-by-step reforms were fiercely opposed. Resistance, revolt and repression loomed as large as peaceful accommodation. Tradition was a battlefield as well as an icon.

Long before the process of top-down adaptation culminated in the 1917 bill, defiant demands for more radical change had come from below. Although they had been suppressed without much difficulty, they left an enduring legacy. Running through all of them were the themes of independence, self-respect and scorn for flummery and flunkeyism. Behind them lay a vision of equal, participatory citizenship and popular sovereignty. Though they focused on the polity rather than on the economy, the political egalitarianism that inspired them went hand in hand with a deep-seated suspicion of market power. Irrespective of the religious beliefs of their authors, they were infused with the unbiddable spirit of Protestant dissent. They defied distinctions of rank and status – sometimes at the cost of the liberties and even the lives of those who made them. The language in which they were expressed was sometimes demagogic, inflated and self-righteous, but they empowered the powerless and leavened the lump of time-encrusted deference. As the next chapter will show, the values and hopes that inspired them are an enduring part of the British political tradition.

They also helped to define the terrain on which subsequent gradualist reformers and their opponents battled. Britain's belated acquisition of a more or less democratic suffrage, and the conflicting narratives with which leaders and led made sense of her meandering progress towards it, are incomprehensible if they are left out of the account. The British version of democracy was the product of an interplay between top-down reform and bottom-up defiance. In this chapter, I shall look at both.

❦

The story begins at the dawn of the modern age, during a brief, extraordinary moment in the English civil wars. The defeat and imprisonment, and the subsequent trial and execution of Charles I, the Lord's anointed for most parliamentarians as well as for royalists, shattered the moral foundations of Church and State. The crust of custom was broken and the social world 'turned upside down'.[2] Apocalyptic visions of England as Christ's kingdom proliferated. In one of the most famous passages of his *Areopagitica*, John Milton exclaimed that God had revealed himself 'as His manner is, first to His Englishmen'.[3] Many thought 'the total rooting out of Antichrist' was imminent.[4]

The grim Calvinist doctrine of election, according to which the saved and the damned had been chosen irrevocably before the beginning of time, acquired a potentially revolutionary political dimension. The mighty of this world might be damned in the next; humble craftsmen might be among the saved. Calvinist saints easily became republican citizens, often with swords in their hands. Writers such as the former All Souls' chorister and sometime royalist, Marchamount Nedham; the Northamptonshire country gentleman, James Harrington; and, above all, Milton himself drew on the ideological legacy of Renaissance Italy and ancient Rome to lay the doctrinal foundations of a republican free state, made up of free citizens, in which monarchical tyranny would be no more.

The most extraordinary episode of all occurred between 1647 and 1649, when a coalition made up of radical sectaries, London craftsmen and certain regiments of Cromwell's victorious New Model Army set out the constitutional framework for a secular, democratic republic, and then tried energetically to mobilise support for it. Their most famous leader – the charismatic, disputatious and frequently imprisoned John Lilburne – described them as 'the hobnails, clouted shoes, the private soldiers, the leather and woollen aprons, and the laborious and industrious people in England'.[5] That was over-egging the pudding. Lilburne himself had enlisted in the parliamentary army as a captain and rose to become a lieutenant colonel; the hot-headed and courageous Thomas Rainborough, whose plea for the rights of the 'poorest he' is one of the most resonant political utterances in the language, was also a colonel, and the son of a naval officer to boot.

All the same, Lilburne's description conveys the flavour of the movement. He and his allies were nicknamed 'Levellers', implying that they wished to level estates, but the equality they sought was political, not economic. In October 1647, they produced what amounted to a draft constitution for an English republic, with the explosive title, *An Agreement of the People*. It was put before the General Council of the Army at a three-day series of highly charged meetings in Putney, most of them in the local church. In it, the Levellers demanded equal electoral districts, biennial parliaments, equality before the law, religious toleration and freedom from conscription, in most cases on the grounds that they were natural rights. Nothing quite like the Putney debates had been seen in England before, and nothing quite like them has been seen since. The questions at issue went to the heart of the social and political order; the atmosphere was halfway between a prayer meeting and an embryo constituent assembly. Most of the participants were soldiers, under military discipline, but the debaters spoke as fellow seekers after truth, wrestling with their consciences and their God.

The Leveller representatives made it clear that, in addition to the programme set out in the *Agreement*, they stood for something very close to manhood suffrage.[6] (On the quintessentially republican assumption that those who 'depend upon the will of other men'[7] could not be genuinely free, they would have excluded servants and paupers.) John Wildman's summary of the argument echoes across the centuries:

[W]e have been under slavery; that's acknowledged by all; our very laws were made by our conquerors. ... We are now engaged for our freedom. That's the end of parliaments: not to constitute what is already established but to act according to the just rules of government. Every person in England has as clear a right to elect his representative as the greatest person in England. I conceive that's the undeniable maxim of all government: that all government is in the free consent of the people.[8]

It was too much for Cromwell, the Army grandees and even for the Army at large. The Levellers and the citizen soldiers who had made them a force to be reckoned with gradually parted company. Within a few days of the Putney debates, a small-scale Leveller mutiny was suppressed at Ware. Private Richard Arnold, one of the ringleaders, was shot dead at the head of his regiment. In the tense final weeks of 1648 following the so-called second civil war, and leading up to the king's execution in January 1649, there was a rapprochement between the Levellers and the Army leadership, reflected in a more nuanced second *Agreement*. But the Levellers soon discovered that Cromwell's conservative revolutionaries had as short a way with defiance from below as the monarchy had had. In March 1649, Lilburne and his closest associates were charged with treason and imprisoned in the Tower. On 1 May 1649, they produced a third, more radical *Agreement*, published in the name of the 'free people of England'. Its demands included annual parliaments and a franchise close to manhood suffrage. To safeguard a series of fundamental freedoms from the incursions of arbitrary power, it insisted that there should be 'limits both to our supreme and to all sub-ordinate authority'[9] – in other words, that certain rights should be protected by an unamendable charter, superior in status to ordinary laws.

But by now the Levellers' moment had passed. According to Lilburne, Cromwell had already told the Council of State that the only way to deal with them was 'to break them in pieces'.[10] He did not waste much time. Two weeks after the 1649 *Agreement* was published, a more serious Leveller mutiny was quelled at Burford; the three alleged ringleaders were shot dead in the churchyard, while their followers were forced to watch from the church roof. (A fourth ringleader made such a show of pious repentance that Cromwell forgave him.) The Levellers' revolution was over before it had begun.

⁂

It left a luminous afterglow. In an age when regimes of all stripes pay lip service to democratic principles, it is easy to miss the breathtaking audacity of the Levellers' central claims: that it is tyrannical and unjust to govern without the free consent of the governed; and that consent must come from the propertyless as well as from the propertied. For most of human history, hierarchy and subordination – religious, political, familial and economic – have been sacrosanct as well as customary. The right to govern has come from God, from ancestors, from myth-encrusted lawgivers in a remote and awe-inspiring past. Massive, intimidating structures of custom and belief, sacred as well as secular, underpinning the entire social order and embodied in myth, magic and ritual as well as in laws and doctrines, have carried the habits and values of authority and obedience from one generation to the next. A tiny minority has given the orders; the rest have been born to obey.

This has been as true of European civilisation as of others. Until very recent times, the most distinguished minds of Europe, from Plato and Aristotle onwards, condemned popular government as impious and destructive folly. Protestants as well as Catholics, Presbyterians as well as Anglicans, took it for granted that established authorities were part of a seamless web, spun by the authority of God. The eighteenth-century Anglican devotional manual, *The New Whole Duty of Man*, epitomised the wisdom of millennia: '[W]herever it is placed, authority is a sacred thing, as being a ray and image of the divine majesty, and such as may justly claim honour and reverence from all men: and whoever contemns the lowest degree of it, offers an affront to the highest; for he that resisteth the power resisteth the ordinance of God.'[11]

Before democracy could become feasible a revolution had to take place, in ideas and mentalities even more than in institutions. In eighteenth-century America and France, just such a revolution took place with an explosive force that left a lasting impact on the imagination of the world. That explains the resonance of the world's two great revolutionary 'days' – 4 July and 14 July. Britain has never known an explosion on that scale. Yet the Levellers' abortive challenge to the structures of hierarchy and subordination of seventeenth-century England had more in common with its American and French successors than has anything in later British history.

A yawning chasm of culture and language separated them from the sceptical rationalists who inspired the great Atlantic revolutions of 150 years later, and further still from the liberals and social democrats of our own day. The Levellers had one foot in the modern world, but one in the Middle Ages. To them, God, the devil, salvation and damnation were ever-present realities. They attached at least as much importance to religious freedom as to political. Their vision of a self-governing polity, based on a compact between free and active citizens, reflected their experience of the self-governing radical sects. They were steeped in the intoxicating cadences of the Scriptures, which they took to be divinely inspired. Again and again, their arguments were framed in biblical categories. In his *freeman's freedom vindicated* Lilburne appealed to the book of Genesis; the regimental spokesmen who put the Army's case to General Fairfax on the eve of the Putney debate based their argument on the parable of the talents.[12] Yet across the gulf of time and vocabulary, three themes in the Levellers' challenge to the Army grandees sound as powerfully in the twenty-first century as they did in the seventeenth.

The first was a cry of protest against the ancient link between economic status and political participation. The Putney debates centred on a clash of values and assumptions that has reverberated through the history of capitalism: a clash between the claims of citizenship on the one hand and of property on the other. Cromwell grumbled that although the Levellers might not wish for anarchy, a franchise that gave votes to the propertyless, whose only interest in the country was 'the interest of breathing', must 'end in anarchy'. Grant the principle of equal citizenship, said his brilliant and provocative son-in-law, Henry Ireton, and what would stop the propertyless from applying the same principle to 'meat, drink, clothes' – indeed, to property as such? The propertyless were in a majority of five to one, said Colonel Rich; if they had votes, a law might be passed to destroy property and establish 'an equality of goods and estate'.

The Levellers repeatedly insisted that they were as committed to private property as the grandees. Their concessions to property rights came from the head, however; their hearts spoke a different language. On Rich's assumptions, declared the indefatigable Rainborough, the existing franchise would allow the propertied sixth of the population to 'make hewers of wood and drawers of water of the other five, and so the greatest part of the nation [would] be enslaved'.[13] Liberty trumped property, as surely as it trumped the prerogatives of a self-aggrandising monarch.

The second theme was more explosive still. The Levellers' vision of a democratic republic went beyond politics and tapped emotions to which narrowly political arguments could not do justice. A critic accused them of wanting a society in which 'every Jack shall vie with a gentleman and every gentleman be made a Jack.'[14] There was something in this. 'I am sure there was no man born marked of God above another,' declared the old Leveller, Richard Rumbold, just before he was executed for taking part in the Monmouth rebellion of 1685, 'for no man comes into the world with a saddle on his back, neither any booted and spurred to ride him.'[15] The victorious, war-radicalised young soldiers of the New Model Army insisted that they were not 'a mere mercenary army hired to serve any arbitrary power of a state' but volunteers who had taken up arms 'in judgement and conscience' to defend 'our own and the people's liberties'.[16] Their meaning was plain: they had heads on their shoulders as well as swords in their hands, and they were determined to think for themselves. For them, the elaborate apparatus of status differentiation and moral indoctrination, which their generals still took for granted, no longer had meaning. The soldiers had risked their lives for their birthrights, declared Captain Saxby at Putney, and now the grandees were telling them that only property had rights. Grant that, and 'we were mere mercenary soldiers' – instruments, not free citizens.

The Levellers' constitutional programme spoke to the same stubborn sense of personal autonomy and human dignity, and to a corresponding ethic of republican austerity. In a memorable passage, written on the eve of Charles II's restoration, Milton defined a 'free commonwealth' as one in which

> They who are greatest are perpetual servants and drudges to the public at their own cost and charges; neglect their own affairs; yet are not elevated above their brethren, live soberly in their families, walk the streets as other men, may be spoken to freely, familiarly, without adoration. Whereas a king must be adored like a demigod, with a dissolute and haughty court about him, of vast expense and luxury.

To restore the monarchy, he added in a savage phrase, would be to pay a single person to 'pageant himself up and down in progress among the perpetual bowings and cringings of an abject people'.[17] Milton was no Leveller, but his biting contempt for bowing and cringing epitomised a crucial aspect of the Levellers' vision.

The third theme was the most important. For the Levellers, liberty also trumped tradition. It involved a clean break with the past, inspired by first principles. Though the Levellers shared the then commonplace notion that the Normans had illegitimately usurped ancient Saxon freedoms, that well-worn theme embellished a more original (and more subversive) argument. They based their case for a democratic and secular republic on natural rights, not on history or tradition. Custom and precedent, they insisted, were irrelevant. As Rainborough put it, 'the old law of England', for which both sides had claimed to be fighting when the first civil war broke out, was 'the most tyrannical law under heaven'.[18] In an age in which political argument was structured by precedent, when debate turned on rival interpretations of the wisdom of the ancestors, statements like these were more subversive than any substantive programme. The Levellers were saying that ancestral wisdom carried no special authority; that free citizens, not venerable institutions or time-honoured practices, were the source of political legitimacy. They were the first, and almost the last, significant political movement in British history to insist that a just political order could be built only by making a conscious, deliberate and principled break with constitutional precedent.

For Cromwell – arch-pragmatist as well as Calvinist saint; would-be constitutional conservationist as well as reluctant revolutionary – that was probably their real offence. The *Agreement* seemed plausible, he conceded at the start of the Putney debates, but it involved 'very great alterations in the very government of the kingdom'. What was to stop another group coming forward with equally plausible alterations, and 'not only another, and another, but many of this kind?' If they did, what would the consequences be? 'Would it not be confusion? Would it not be utter confusion? Would it not make England like the Switzerland country, one canton of the Swiss against another, and one county against another?'[19] The alternative to properly constituted authority, in short, was chaos.

ഷ

The second big upsurge of defiance from below took place almost 150 years after the Levellers' defeat. In that century and a half, Britain saw great changes – the return of the monarchy and its 'bowings and cringings' in 1660; the 'Glorious Revolution' of 1688, which drove the Stuarts from the throne; the Act of Union of 1707, which created a new British state in place of the English and Scottish states; victory in a long-drawn-out race for empire against France, only partly tarnished by the loss of the American colonies in 1783; the gradual emergence of a tenacious 'British' identity, centred on the stirring themes of Protestantism, liberty and maritime supremacy; and the beginning of the Industrial Revolution. After the climacteric of 1688, however, the political order changed very little. Throughout the following century, the Anglican landed elite, which had made the Revolution, enjoyed a virtual monopoly of political power. (Protestant dissenters were tolerated, but effectively excluded from the political nation.)

Vigorous political conflicts took place within the elite. In their attacks on the court, the independent gentry of the so-called 'Country Party' drew on a diffuse ideology, stressing civic virtue, manly independence and disdain for Crown-sponsored corruption that harked back to the republicans of Cromwell's time. Popular disturbances were frequent. Disaffected elite politicians – such as the engaging rapscallion and future City alderman, John Wilkes, and the magnetic prince of parliamentary debaters, Charles James Fox – often drew on the country ideology to harness the crowd to their own campaigns against the executive. None of this posed a serious threat to the regime, but after the loss of the American colonies increasingly vociferous demands for parliamentary reform, involving a radical extension of the suffrage and a redistribution of seats, began to call into question the foundations of elite rule.[20]

Then came the French Revolution – a social, political and ideological earthquake whose effects were felt right across Europe, from Moscow to Madrid, and which provokes passionate debate even today. In Britain, its first stages were greeted with acclamation. Charles James Fox spoke for many when he declared that the fall of the Bastille on 14 July 1789 was the 'greatest event' that had ever happened in the world. Yet as events across the Channel gathered pace, opinion in Britain polarised.[21] To an increasingly frightened elite, it seemed that France had plunged into an abyss of anarchy, spoliation and atheism that now gaped before the social and moral order of all Europe. The elite was backed by state repression and surveillance, a flood of loyalist propaganda and, not least, a wave of passionate, anti-revolutionary, popular patriotism. Many moderate reformers – notably Edmund Burke, once one of the staunchest British supporters of the American cause – gave a further push to the anti-revolutionary backlash.

Meanwhile, bold spirits in the reform camp – the Birmingham unitarian, philosopher and scientist, Dr Joseph Priestley; the international revolutionary and pamphleteer, Thomas Paine; the pioneer of women's enfranchisement, Mary Wollstonecraft; the London radical organiser and propagandist, John Horne Tooke; the Scottish shoemaker, Thomas Hardy; and a growing number of radical artisans, small masters, journeymen and tradesmen – looked increasingly to revolutionary France for inspiration. They sang the 'Marsellaise' and 'Ça Ira', sported tricolour cockades, sent fervent addresses of support to the French National Assembly and Convention, corresponded with the Jacobin clubs of Paris and the French provinces, and danced around the Liberty Tree.

They also created a network of democratic societies, published a flood of pamphlets, founded several newspapers and proselytised energetically in the countryside. They spoke the language of liberty and citizenship, not of class, but one of their most important achievements was to construct an ideological framework for the aspirations of the nascent working class, largely derived from Thomas Paine's explosive challenge to prescription and privilege, *Rights of Man*. Their enemies called them 'Jacobins', and in time they wore the label proudly. A comment in 1795 by John Thelwall, radical stalwart, minor poet, ex-tailor and eventual elocution teacher, helps to explain why. He gloried in the French Revolution, he wrote, because

[I]t has been upheld and propagated as a principle of that Revolution, that ancient abuses are not, by their antiquity, converted into virtues; that it has been affirmed and established that man has rights which no statutes or usages can take away ... that one order of society has no right, how many years soever they have been guilty of the pillage, to plunder and oppress the other parts of the community. ... These are the principles that I admire, and that cause me, notwithstanding all its excesses, to exult in the French Revolution.[22]

The curve of British Jacobinism rose quite sharply for a while. Revolution societies set up to commemorate the Glorious Revolution of 1688 became centres of Francophile radicalism. 'Constitutional societies' carried the message of democracy and human rights to East Anglia, the Midlands and the North. (The Sheffield Society, in particular, was a byword for turbulent and defiant agitation.) In January 1792, Thomas Hardy founded the enthusiastic and largely artisan London Corresponding Society, which quickly became the flagship of the movement. But as the tempo of revolution quickened in France, anxiety among the elite, often shared by the masses for whom the British Jacobins thought they spoke, began to verge on panic. A royal proclamation against seditious writings, issued in May 1792, was followed by a second proclamation in December, ordering the embodiment of part of the militia. A loyalist 'Association for the Preservation of Liberty and Property against Republicans and Levellers' set out to intimidate the radical societies, often with the help of local magistrates. Paine, who had been prosecuted for seditious libel in May and had then left for France, was found guilty and outlawed in his absence. In the winter of 1792–3, he was burned in effigy in hundreds of tumultuous popular ceremonies, in places as far apart as Dover and Newcastle.[23]

In 1793 the pace warmed up. In January, Louis XVI was guillotined. On 1 February, the French Republic, which the British Government had refused to recognise, declared war on Britain. The British state was now the linchpin of a Europe-wide, counter-revolutionary alliance, bent on stamping out the French contagion. British Jacobins faced a harsh dilemma. If they stood their ground, they risked being branded as traitors. If they retreated, they would be untrue to themselves and perhaps give a further fillip to reaction.

Most British Jacobins stuck to their guns. Their most spectacular stroke came in November 1793, when they held a British Convention in Edinburgh. The Convention was forcibly dissolved; the ringleaders were sentenced to transportation for fourteen years. In May 1794, habeas corpus was suspended. In October, a number of British Jacobin leaders, including Tooke, Thelwall and Hardy, were charged with high treason. They were acquitted; but in November the Government pushed through a Treasonable Practices Act, widening the definition of treason to cover speeches and writings as well as actions. A Seditious Meetings Act empowered local magistrates to disallow public meetings of more than fifty persons; resistance to their orders to disperse was made punishable by death. These two Acts ran with the grain of the popular loyalism that the Paineites had outraged, and delivered the *coup de grâce* to the movement. It lingered on in a twilight of semi-legality and underground conspiracy but, as a Leeds society reported in October 1797, the 'Sacred flame' that had been kindled in its members' breasts in better days had been extinguished.[24] By the end of the decade, the second serious upsurge of defiance from below had been suppressed as thoroughly as the first.

୶ଡ଼ୡ

'An army of principles will penetrate where an army of soldiers cannot.' Thomas Paine wrote in an ebullient moment in 1797. 'It will march on the horizon of the world and it will conquer.'[25] Paine's phrase could serve as an epigraph for the fate of the British Jacobins. They were quashed as easily as the Levellers had been but, unlike the Levellers, they bequeathed an ideological and moral legacy that entered the bloodstream of popular politics. Unitarian divines, itinerant lecturers and provincial editors played their part in this, as did the cordwainers, cutlers, carpenters and the like who took part in the radical societies' debates. But the lion's share of the credit goes to Paine. Like the Levellers, the British Jacobins challenged the whole edifice of custom, hierarchy and social control on which the British Church and State were based; that was why their enemies in all classes feared and hated them. Paine clothed the challenge in a mixture of passion, invective, irony and sarcasm, expressed in a limpid, demotic prose that can still set the pulse racing.

In the 1790s, his acidulous contempt for the mystique of the British *ancien régime*, the connections that he drew between political subordination and the injustices of everyday life and, most of all perhaps, his exhilarating optimism must have been a revelation. He was not an original or a systematic thinker. His ideas tumbled out, higgledy-piggledy, in the heat of argument; most of them came from the common stock of Atlantic republicanism. But that did not detract from his central message: the people had been robbbed of the liberty that was theirs by right; if they had the determination and courage to construct a new political system, they could regain it. 'For a nation to love liberty, it is sufficient that she knows it; and to be free, it is sufficient that she wills it.'[26]

Paine's success as a propagandist stemmed, in part, from his background. The craftsmen and small masters who formed the backbone of British Jacobinism were his people. In his later years, success as a writer carried him to the heights of political life on two continents. He was an intimate of Thomas Jefferson, a protégé of Benjamin Franklin, and he discussed French plans to invade Britain with Napoleon Bonaparte. (He also fell foul of Robespierre and narrowly escaped the guillotine during the Terror.) However, having been born into the skilled but low-status artisanate, he carried its insecurities, humiliations and stubborn pride in his bones. He was apprenticed to his father's trade of staymaker, but could not settle down.

He was by turns a sailor, a staymaker, a schoolteacher and an exciseman. He had talent, energy, courage and a passion for politics, but there was no outlet for them in the caste society of eighteenth-century England. Success did not come until he emigrated to America in 1774.

During the revolution he became the Americans' most influential propagandist. In Britain, as in America, his success as a writer owed much to the stimulus of the moment. The most influential of all his writings, *Rights of Man*, written after his return to Britain, was a reply to Edmund Burke's volcanic onslaught on the French Revolution and its British supporters, *Reflections on the Revolution in France*. Paine and Burke had been on the same side over the American war. To Paine, it seemed that Burke had now betrayed his past. As the next chapter will show, he was wrong about that: the Burke who had attacked British policy towards the American colonists was also the Burke who excoriated the French revolutionaries. But the mistake gave Paine's reply an edge of passion that helped to make the book a runaway best-seller.

His overriding aim was to make the unthinkable thinkable: to convince his readers that, despite their antiquity, the barriers that excluded the vast majority of adult males from the political nation could be demolished if they were given a hard push. To do that, he had to demystify the hallowed British constitution; to make plain that, far from being the repository of immemorial wisdom, it was a farrago of highfalutin nonsense, and that the elite whose power it sustained was risible rather than awesome. The monarchy was a favourite target. William the Conqueror, from whom the kings of England derived their title to rule, was nothing but a 'French bastard landing with an armed banditti, and establishing himself king of England against the consent of the natives ... in plain terms a very paltry rascally original'.[27] The whole notion of hereditary rule was degrading: 'To inherit a government is to inherit the people, as if they were flocks and herds'.[28] As for the House of Lords, the notion of a hereditary legislator was 'as absurd as an hereditary mathematician, or an hereditary wise man'. The titles that went with it embodied 'a sort of foppery in the human character, which degrades it'. In abolishing them, France had 'outgrown the baby-cloaths of *Count* and *Duke*, and breeched itself in manhood'.

These sallies were the opening salvo of a much more formidable barrage. The British constitution drew its authority from a long chain of precedents binding it to its past. To show that legitimate rule was grounded in the sovereign people and not in custom and prescription, Paine had to take an axe to that chain, demonstrating that the past could not bind the present. The loyalists' faith in precedent, he argued, was akin to the worship of supposedly holy relics with which monks deceived the credulous. The whole notion of governing from beyond the grave was 'the most ridiculous and insolent of all tyrannies'. Besides, reliance on precedent was self-contradictory. Precedents from a hundred or even a thousand years ago could be cancelled out by contrary precedents from an even remoter past. In truth, there was no logical stopping place short of the moment 'when man came from the hand of his Maker ... It is authority against authority all the way, till we come to the divine origin of the rights of man at the creation.'

It followed that all men were born equal, with equal natural rights. That, in turn, meant that only the people, acting through a representative body elected for the purpose, could draw up a constitution. For constitutions were '*antecedent* to government'. A nation's constitution was 'not the act of its government, but of the people constituting a government'. Parliament was not a substitute for the people; it was part of the system that a proper constitution would sweep away. The 'moderate' reform, peddled by aristocratic 'Friends of Liberty', was worse than useless since its purpose was to abandon some abuses in order to hang on to the rest. The conclusions were as obvious as they were shocking: the much-venerated British Constitution was not a constitution at all; the people had 'yet a constitution to form'.

From the elite's point of view, that was bad enough, but more alarming horrors followed. As well as demystifying Britain's *ancien régime*, Paine insisted that the political injustice at its core bred economic and social injustice, and that human rights had an economic and social dimension as well as a political one. 'When, in countries that are called civilized, we see age going to the workhouse and youth to the gallows,' he declared, 'something must be wrong in the system of government.' And, in a passage throbbing with indignation, he asked: 'Why is it that scarcely any are executed but the poor? ... [T]hey are the exposed sacrifice of vice and legal barbarity.'[29] But a new political order would not banish wretchedness all by itself. And so, in a stroke of genius far ahead of its time, Paine called for the redistribution of wealth as well as of political power. Unconditional state payments would go to the elderly and the young, financed by damming up the stream of bribes, pensions, sinecures and inflated official salaries that helped to keep the elite afloat. A progressive property tax would break up the great estates out of which the *ancien régime* was built. The implications were (and are) explosive. Although no enemy to capitalism or the market economy, Paine insisted that huge disparities of wealth were incompatible with equal citizenship and sought to overcome them. His message resonates as loudly in the age of the global super-rich as it did when he wrote it.

The third and last significant episode of bottom-up defiance took place nearly half a century after the second. It drew on the Paineite radicalism of the 1790s, and on memories of the turbulent popular agitation that had followed the French wars, but it is best seen as a riposte to the first big instalment of top-down reform – the 'Great' Reform Act of 1832 – and to the laissez-faire commitments of its authors. The 1832 Act was the first real fissure in the *ancien régime*. It was carried through Parliament by the first Whig Government for forty years, headed by Earl Grey, once a leading 'friend of liberty'. It increased the total electorate from around 500,000 to around 700,000, and has often been seen as the first step towards democracy. That, however, was not how its supporters saw it. It was a classic example of the 'moderate reform' that Paine had scorned. The Whig noblemen who drafted it and steered it on to the statute book had no intention of undermining the power of their own caste or of the property relations on which it depended. They were for change, but only to preserve.

They could see that industrialisation and urbanisation had created important new social interests. They thought these interests would have to be incorporated into the political nation sooner or later, and feared that if they were not incorporated peacefully they would incorporate themselves through revolution. But they wanted to forestall democracy, not to move towards it. In a savage passage in 1829, the young T.B. Macaulay, future doyen of Whig historians and then a rising Whig politician and essayist, had declared that, in a democracy, the rich 'would be pillaged as unmercifully as under a Turkish Pacha' – adding, for good measure, that 'taste, literature, science, commerce, manufactures, everything but the rude arts necessary for the support of animal life' would be swept away.[30] Few Whigs would have disagreed. As they saw it, the question for the government was how to avert the evils that Macaulay had depicted. Their answer was to drive a wedge between the middle class and the working class. The Reform Act was a finely calibrated piece of political engineering, designed to do just that.

The Act had two prongs, both of them much sharper than the political world had expected. First, it redrew the electoral map. The unreformed House of Commons represented an extraordinary patchwork of constituencies of varying sizes, with a bewildering variety of qualifications for the suffrage. The new industrial centres in the North were grossly underrepresented in comparison with small towns and villages in the South. The Reform Act left the patchwork in place, but made it far less flagrant. Fifty-six small boroughs were disfranchised altogether; thirty lost one member apiece. The chief beneficiaries were unrepresented towns, such as Manchester, Birmingham, Leeds and Sheffield. Second, the suffrage was rationalised. Existing voters retained their rights during their lifetimes, but in the boroughs (and the vast majority of MPs sat for boroughs) the right to vote would thereafter be confined to adult males occupying property with an annual value of £10 or more. These £10 householders were assumed to be middle-class. The working class was thought to be safely below the £10 line. The previously unenfranchised sections of the middle class would be allowed into the political nation; the working class would be locked out.

By a cruel paradox, however, working-class support turned out to be essential to the success of the operation. The bill ran into fierce Tory opposition, particularly in the House of Lords. If the struggle had been confined to the political elite, the bill would almost certainly have been lost. It was passed only because its opponents were overawed by a brilliantly organised and massively supported extra-parliamentary agitation, orchestrated by so-called political unions in which working-class organisations and leaders played an indispensable part. Had the working class stood aloof, the spectre of revolution, which did more than anything else to intimidate the bill's opponents, would never have hovered in the Westminster air.

The paradox of 1832 made another upsurge of defiance from below almost inevitable. To a growing number of working-class radicals and their leaders, the moral of the Reform Act seemed obvious. Cross-class collaboration was a treacherous snare. To realise the dream of popular government, and win the disfranchised masses their rightful place in the political nation, the working class would have to do for itself what it had done for the middle class in 1832. From that logic sprang the London Working Men's Association, founded in 1836, with the modest, occasionally morose but steadfastly radical cabinet maker, William Lovett, in the van. The 1838 People's Charter, largely drawn up by Lovett, followed the same logic, as did the subsequent Chartist movement, which mobilised an unprecedented mass following among working people, of all levels of skill and from a huge variety of occupations, for a decade and more.

The Charter's six points – manhood suffrage, annual parliaments, payment of MPs, the secret ballot, equal electoral districts and the end of the property qualification for MPs – were not new. Some of them went back to the Levellers; they were all part of the stock-in-trade of the radical tradition. The ideology behind them was not new either. For the Chartists, as for Paine, politics structured economics. A corrupt state, dominated by the few, was bound to oppress and impoverish the many. Political justice was therefore a precondition of social justice. 'Knaves will tell you that it is because you have no property, you are unrepresented,' declared Bronterre O'Brien, the prickly, unstable but brilliant Chartist pamphleteer and journalist. 'I tell you on the contrary, it is because you are unrepresented that you have no property'.[31]

Schemes for social or economic amelioration were a blind alley. What counted, to quote O'Brien again, was 'POWER, solid, substantial POWER, that the millions must obtain *and retain*, if they would enjoy the produce of their own labour and the privileges of freemen'.[32] And the post-1832 regime was as corrupt and exploitative as the one it had replaced. Before 1832, the labouring classes had been oppressed by the aristocracy. Thanks to the Reform Act, the aristocracy had been joined by the 'Jewocracy, Millocracy, Shopocracy, and every other Ocracy which feeds on human vitals'.[33] Other themes – land reform, currency reform and educational reform – wove in and out of the Chartist message, but they were ancillary to the central, nearly 200-year-old theme of systematic constitutional reconstruction.

However, the moral and emotional texture of Chartism was newer than its ideology. In a sense untrue of previous radical movements, it was defiantly working-class in rhetoric, support and self-understanding – so much so that the young Friedrich Engels saw it as the harbinger of an inevitable proletarian revolution.[34] This did not mean that all Chartists belonged to the working class, or even that they all came from it. The charismatic, wayward, golden-tongued Feargus O'Connor, the best-known and best-loved of all the Chartist leaders, was the scion of a landed Protestant family in County Cork. Ernest Jones, the leading figure in the movement's last phase, was the son of an equerry to the Duke of Cumberland. Both, however, were exceptions that proved the rule. Most Chartists worked with their hands. Though some were skilled artisans, there were plenty from humbler occupations – labourers, spinners, weavers, colliers, nailers and stockingers, to mention only a few.

Distinctions of skill mattered less than a unifying rhetoric and a commonality of feeling. Chartism was, by definition, a movement of the excluded – of those whom the Whigs had judged unfit to join the political nation. It focused on political exclusion, but it also gave voice to a gnawing sense of economic exclusion. The laissez-faire theorists of the time viewed labour as a commodity, like a bale of cotton or a hod of coal, without human meaning. Under the Whigs, these teachings inspired a punitive change in social policy – the so-called New Poor Law of 1834 – designed to expose the poor to the full rigour of the labour market. Previously, starvation wages had been supplemented out of the rates. The 1834 Act decreed that poor relief would go only to those enrolled in prison-like 'workhouses' (soon known as 'Bastilles'), where conditions were to be worse than the worst beyond their walls.

In part the Chartists' appeal was instrumental: votes would enable the propertyless masses to put an end to their economic and social wrongs. But its extraordinary resonance came from deeper sources than that. '[T]he scorn of the rich is pointed towards us,' complained the Chartist women of Newcastle: 'the brand of slavery is on our kindred, and we feel the degradation.'[35] The combination of the Reform Act and the New Poor Law gave new force to the familiar rhetoric of freedom versus slavery. Politically and economically, the labouring poor were demeaned. In place of degradation, the Chartists offered them dignity and self-respect. Once enrolled under the Chartist banner, the 'fustian jackets and unshaven chins' whom O'Connor mobilised were no longer the helpless objects of state policy or employer exploitation. Potentially, at least, they became self-liberating subjects.

But only potentially. The Chartists were astonishingly successful in sustaining the support of their followers through repeated setbacks, but their attempts to overcome the inevitable opposition of the state failed miserably. The supposed parallel with 1832 turned out to be a chimera. Thanks to the Reform Act, the state was far more legitimate and more self-confident than it had been before. There was no chink in the blank wall of property and power surrounding the political nation, and no fissure in the political elite. The Chartists' strategy was to demonstrate overwhelming mass support, in the hope that this would overawe or persuade their opponents in the way that popular agitation had overawed the opponents of the Reform Bill in 1832. The demonstration took place; but it overawed no one.

In 1839, mass meetings, torchlight processions and an elected Convention culminated in a monster petition to Parliament, with 1,200,000 signatures. It was contemptuously rejected by the House of Commons. The Convention dithered, first issuing a call for a 'National Holiday' (or General Strike), and then withdrawing it. A serious riot took place in Birmingham, and an abortive armed rising followed in Newport, on the edge of the South Wales coalfield. The only result was a nationwide wave of mass arrests. There was another Convention in 1842, and a petition with 3,250,000 signatures. Once again, it was contemptuously rejected.

The last act came in 1848, Europe's year of revolutions. On 10 April, a third Chartist petition, this time with around 2 million signatures (many of them forgeries), was presented to Parliament. A crowd of around 150,000 gathered on Kennington Common, but London was blanketed with special constables – among them, Louis Napoleon, later President and later still Emperor of France – as well as with armed police and troops. The petition was carried to the Palace of Westminster in cabs, but troops and police had secured the Thames bridges and the procession that was supposed to follow the cabs was not allowed across. Although the Chartists lingered on for another ten years, they were no longer a force to be reckoned with after

1848. For a brief but brilliant moment, they had rekindled the 'sacred flame' whose extinction the Sheffield reformers had once mourned. Now it seemed well and truly doused.

REFORM FROM ABOVE

Appearances were deceptive. After the 1848 fiasco there were no more serious threats to the social and economic order; henceforth, democratisation would owe more to top-down reform than to bottom-up defiance. Yet popular agitation still loomed in the background; and at key moments it became a crucial factor in elite calculations. The pace was slow. On the eve of the First World War, which the British Government later presented as a war for democracy, only 60 per cent of the adult male population had the right to vote in parliamentary elections. (In Imperial Germany – no democracy, it must be said – the Reichstag was elected by manhood suffrage.) British democratisation went slowly partly because the process was mired in confusion. Statistics were lacking and, in any case, unreliable. Members of Parliament were often uncertain of what they were doing, where they were going or even where they wanted to go.

All the same, two landmarks stand out – the second Reform Act passed in 1867, and the third passed in 1884. Between them, these Acts enfranchised nearly 3 million adult males, raising the proportion of the adult male population entitled to vote in parliamentary elections from around 14 per cent to nearly 60 per cent. Though some dual-member constituencies survived well into the twentieth century, the Redistribution Act that followed on the heels of the third Reform Act initiated the system of first-past-the-post elections in single-member seats that still prevails in elections to the Westminster Parliament.

The 1867 Act was the real watershed. It was made possible by far-reaching shifts of attitude and behaviour, due in part to the collapse of Chartism and in part to the economic upswing of the mid-nineteenth century. Working-class leaders made their peace with the state and stopped kicking against the pricks of an increasingly hegemonic capitalism. They abandoned Bronterre O'Brien's search for 'POWER' and concentrated on building up friendly societies, co-operatives and craft unions. These were schools for citizenship, but for citizenship of the existing polity, not of a radically different one. Elite leaders sought to detach the upper echelon of provident, self-denying, respectable skilled workers from the undeserving, improvident and allegedly corruptible, if not downright criminal, 'residuum', in the way that the Whigs had detached the hitherto unenfranchised sections of the middle class from the working class in 1832. By the late 1850s, suffrage reform had returned to the agenda of high politics.

In 1864, Gladstone, having achieved his apotheosis as a budgetary reformer, gave the question a further push. Every man 'who is not presumably incapacitated by some consideration of personal unfitness or of political danger', he declared, in a sonorous but delphic phrase, which eventually became one of the most celebrated of the century, 'is morally entitled to come within the pale of the constitution'. The test of capacity, he made clear in another speech, was 'self-command, self-control, respect for order, patience under suffering, confidence in the law, regard for superiors'.[36] Self-evidently, the feckless and irresponsible failed that test, while the self-disciplined and law-abiding passed. The scene was set for another instalment of moderate reform; and the hunt was on for patient, self-controlled workers capable of reaching Gladstone's standard of political probity.

The 1867 Act reached the statute book against that background. The story of its passage is one of the most astonishing in British parliamentary history. It was the product of a bizarre parliamentary ping-pong match between Gladstone and Disraeli, in which the latter's outrageous but captivating chutzpah easily prevailed over the former's stubborn but often boring rectitude. The details of the story are extraordinarily complex; its leading historian has aptly called it the 'Serbonian Bog' of nineteenth-century British history.[37] Fortunately, there is no need to wade through the bog here. What matters is that in 1866, a Liberal Government, headed by the 74-year-old Lord John Russell, flanked by Gladstone as Chancellor of the Exchequer, brought in a bill carefully designed to enfranchise the upper layer of the artisanate while ensuring that working-class voters remained a minority of the total electorate. Its centrepiece was a proposal to lower the £10 borough franchise qualification to £7, enfranchising around 400,000 adult males. Despite the care with which Gladstone had excluded the residuum, this was too much for a rebel group of moderate Liberals, nicknamed the 'Cave of Adullam' and led with barely controlled passion by the brilliant Wykhamist albino and future Liberal Chancellor of the Exchequer, Robert Lowe. Eventually, a combination of Adullamites and Conservatives defeated the Government's bill and brought the Government down.

A minority Conservative Government headed by Lord Derby, with Disraeli as Chancellor of the Exchequer, then took office. Thanks largely to Derby, who had come to believe that the issue of franchise reform could be settled only by a more far-reaching measure than the abortive Liberal one, it brought in a bill based on the emotive (and, at the time, highly radical) principle of 'household suffrage'. However, the principle was applied restrictively, and coupled with plural voting for the better-off. The net effect was to leave the existing class balance in the electorate unchanged. As the bill ploughed wearily through the Commons, however, the restrictions on household suffrage and the provisions for plural voting were swept away, largely by Liberal amendments that Disraeli dextrously accepted. The end result was household suffrage for the boroughs, unbalanced by extra votes for the propertied, and the extension of the suffrage to more than a million men.

Where the Liberal bill would have increased the electorate by about 40 per cent, the nominally Conservative Act increased it by more than 80 per cent. In the boroughs of England and Wales, working-class voters were in the majority – the very outcome that the Liberal bill had been deliberately designed to avert. With logic-defying bravura, Derby and Disraeli had first clambered into office on the backs of the Liberal right, and then retained it by clinging to the backs of the Liberal left. Against their original intentions, they created a new electoral and party system, which lasted for forty years. The 1884 Reform Act, which extended household suffrage from the boroughs to the counties, merely set the seal on their achievement.

The Conservatives' creation was new. It was not democratic, nor was it intended to lead to democracy in years to come. For most of the protagonists in the parliamentary saga, democracy was almost as great a bogey as it had been for the Whigs in 1832. The Liberal Adullamites saw Gladstone's bill as the first step on a democratic slippery slope and for that reason resisted it with occasional savagery. Conservative rebels, headed by Lord Cranborne, the future Marquess of Salisbury and eventual Prime Minister, fought with equal passion against Disraeli's bill, for the same reason. Reformers were scarcely more enamoured of democracy than were opponents of reform. John Stuart Mill, the most distinguished intellectual radical of the day, hoped to counterbalance the new working-class voters by giving extra votes to the educated. John Bright, the idolised tribune of the disfranchised masses, wished to exclude those trapped in 'poverty and dependence' on the grounds that their interests were opposed to those of 'intelligent and honest working men'.[38]

Gladstone fought hard against household suffrage, even after the Conservatives had brought in their bill – provoking a serious revolt among his own followers for his pains. Disraeli, presumptive tobogganist-in-chief down the democratic slope, differed from Gladstone over means, not ends. Where Gladstone wished to avert a lurch towards a democratic suffrage by separating the rational and virtuous working-class sheep from the excitable, unregenerate goats, Disraeli put his faith in non-rational, working-class

deference. After the 1867 Act reached the statute book he vigorously denied
that he had brought the country to the verge of democracy:

> [B]elieve me, the elements of democracy do not exist in England (cheers).
> ... We are warned of the example of America and against entering upon
> the course pursued by the United States. I say there is no similarity of
> position of the United Kingdom and the United States. ... They have
> settlements of democracy in America; they have unbounded possession of
> land, and they have no traditions. We, on the contrary, have a very limited
> portion of land, and a vast, numerous, artificial and complicated state of
> society, entirely governed and sustained by its traditionary influences.
> Therefore I have no fear of England.[39]

Disraeli was a master of oratorical legerdemain, but there is no reason to
doubt that on this occasion he meant what he said.

In a replay of 1831–2, popular radicals outside Parliament, most of them
enrolled in the National Reform League founded in 1865, brought pressure
on laggard ministers and MPs. In the summer and autumn of 1866, Lowe's
anti-working-class jibes, the defeat of Gladstone's bill and the fall of the
Liberal Government provoked mass meetings, inspiring marches and furious
editorials in the radical press. A throng of 150,000 people marched through
Leeds; 120,000 through pouring rain in Manchester; and 130,000 through
Glasgow. In July 1866, a foolish attempt to ban a massive demonstration in
Hyde Park led to a confused mêlée in Park Lane, in which the park railings
were broken down. But 1860s popular radicalism was a more cautious
creature than its Paineite and Chartist forerunners. Radical leaders like the
secularist campaigner and future MP, Charles Bradlaugh, and the shoemaker
secretary of the London Trades Council, George Odger, came from the
same emotional stable as the Levellers, the British Jacobins and the Chartists.
The League proclaimed a robust egalitarianism reminiscent of Lilburne,
Paine and Bronterre O'Brien. But its ostentatiously pacific marches and
demonstrations were a far cry from the clandestine conspiracies of the late
1790s and the Newport Rising of 1839.

The popular radicals' conception of democratic citizenship was full of
ambiguities. They called eloquently for manhood suffrage, but they wished
to enfranchise the robust, manly and independent-minded, not the weak
and dependent. For one radical journalist, the franchise was 'the manhood
right of every moral, educated and sane minded Englishman' – a richly
ambiguous formula that Gladstone could not have bettered. Another
wanted manhood suffrage, while also wanting to exclude the Dorsetshire or
Suffolk farm labourer who 'is to all intents and purposes as much the

bondslave of his employer as if he had been bought in a public market'. The radical *Newcastle Chronicle* thought it a disgrace that the suffrage was more restricted in Britain than in France or the United States, yet held the view that the sturdily independent farm workers of Northumberland and Durham were in a different moral and political category from their counterparts in the South, who lived in a 'state of abject slavery and poverty'.[40]

There were notable absentees from the reform debate. Unlike their Paineite and Chartist predecessors, the radicals of the 1860s offered no serious challenge to the existing economic order. The old Paineite argument that political inequality led to social injustice hardly surfaced in their rhetoric. Nor did the argument that political equality was a natural right. Popular radicals passionately asserted the rights of Englishmen; they said virtually nothing about the rights of man. They indignantly rebutted Lowe's charge that the working class was too ignorant, venal and drink-sodden to be enfranchised, but they agreed that ignorance, venality and drunkenness should be barriers to enfranchisement. For Gladstone, reform of the suffrage was part of a greater project of political moralisation that also included reform of the civil service, transparent public expenditure control, the secret ballot and legislation against electoral corruption. Yet this project had nothing to do with rights. Its purpose was to purify public life and cleanse the state of nepotism, corruption and waste.

For Liberals and radicals alike, what counted was desert, not rights. They wanted to open the political nation to those who possessed the economic and moral prerequisites of independent citizenship, while closing it to those who did not. Disraeli did not use the language of rights at all and said little about desert. For him, the case for widening the suffrage rested on a curious mixture of sociology and history: working-class householders could be trusted with votes because they could be relied on to respect tradition. By the same token, no one sought a comprehensive transformation of the political order, as the Levellers, Paineites and the Chartists had done. Conservatives and Liberals were determined to preserve the essentials of the existing order while widening the boundaries of the political nation. Radicals were determined to widen the boundaries of the political nation, but content to leave the essentials of the existing order in place. At the start of the twenty-first century, British politics still carried the marks of this unacknowledged confluence.

❦

The third Reform Act followed hard on the heels of the second. By late 1884, when it reached the statute book, household suffrage had been extended from the boroughs to the counties, and around 1,700,000 new voters had joined the political nation. For radical Liberals it was a glorious moment. The road from 'political slavery' lay behind, declared the *Leeds Mercury*, 'before us lies the future in which the nation will be master in its own house.'[41] The *Mercury's* rejoicing was premature. Far from speeding up, the pace of democratisation slowed down. The journey from the second Reform Act to the third had taken seventeen years; more than thirty would pass before manhood suffrage and partial female suffrage finally arrived in 1918.

One reason was that there was little popular pressure for more franchise reform. The 'sacred flame' had survived repression and failure, but partial success very nearly smothered it. The 'residuum' left behind by the 1867 and 1884 Acts lacked the leaders, and perhaps the will, to press for its own enfranchisement; among the elite appetites for constitutional change were sated by the long battle over Irish Home Rule that dominated British politics for a generation. However, that was not the only reason for the change of tempo. Equally important was a shift in the intellectual climate. No sooner was the ink dry on the 1867 Act than signs of a backlash appeared among the intelligentsia. The anguished prophet of heroic leadership, Thomas Carlyle, was particularly strident.[42] Thanks to Disraeli, the 'Hebrew conjuror', democracy was now inevitable. Its guiding principle would be '"the equality of men", any man equal to any other; Quashee Nigger to Socrates or Shakespeare; Judas Iscariot to Jesus Christ'. The only hope was an aristocratic revival, but it was a slender one. The aristocrat could not 'bridle the wild horse of a Plebs any longer: – for a generation past, he has not even tried to bridle it; but has run panting and trotting meanly by the side of it, patting its stupid neck'.

Carlyle was no liberal and his doom-laden savagery was peculiar to him, yet milder versions of his anxieties were common. In 1867, Walter Bagehot, the clever, cynical, cocksure editor of *The Economist*, published one of the most influential anatomies of British Government ever written, with the deceptively bland title *The English Constitution*. Bagehot stripped away the veil of sentiment and myth surrounding British government, so as to expose the hidden realities beneath. But his intentions were celebratory, not subversive. The British constitution, he argued, owed its success to a subtle combination of aristocratic show and bourgeois substance. The masses obeyed their real rulers, 'secreted in second-rate carriages', because they deferred to the 'apparent rulers' at the head of the social procession. No sooner was Bagehot's anatomy published, however, than the Reform Act appeared to undermine its central premise. The masses now had power. There was a serious danger that they would receive deference instead of giving it, with disastrous results. As Bagehot put it in the introduction to his second edition:

> In plain English, what I fear is that both our political parties will bid for the support of the working man; that both of them will promise to do as he likes if he will only tell them what it is. ... I can conceive of nothing more corrupting or worse for a set of poor ignorant people than that two combinations of well-taught and rich men should constantly offer to defer to their decision, and compete for the office of executing it. *Vox populi* will be *vox diaboli* if it is worked in that manner.[43]

Fears of *vox diaboli* were rife. In his *Culture and Anarchy*, Matthew Arnold, poet, essayist and champion of 'sweetness and light', divided the population into three groups – 'Barbarians' (the aristocracy), 'Philistines' (the middle class) and 'Populace' (the working class). He reserved his hottest fire for the crass and selfish Philistines, but the spectre of the proletarian 'rough' haunted his pages. The working class, he thought, had been infected with its own version of middle-class individualism. It was beginning to assert the 'Englishman's right to do what he likes; his right to march where he likes, enter where he likes, hoot as he likes, threaten as he likes, smash as he likes'.[44] George Eliot put similar anxieties into the mouth of Felix Holt, the watchmaker hero of her most overtly political novel, *Felix Holt, the Radical.* In any crowd, Eliot-Holt declared in an 'address to working men', published separately after the novel had appeared, there were 'Roughs, who have the worst vices of the worst rich – who are gamblers, sots, libertines, knaves, or else mere sensual simpletons and victims'.[45]

Arnold's and Eliot's misgivings centred on culture and morality. For the jurist and legal historian, Sir Henry Maine, writing nearly twenty years later, the 'Wire-puller' had replaced the 'Rough' as the villain of the democratic piece. The wire-puller's business was to fan the flame of party and the end result would be a 'mischievous form of Conservatism'. Universal suffrage, Maine insisted, would have 'proscribed the Roman Catholics with the mob which burned Lord Mansfield's house and library in 1780, and it would have proscribed the Dissenters with the mob which burned Dr Priestley's house and library in 1791'. For democracy and liberalism were incompatible. Reactionary populism was the dark side of popular government. At the start of the twenty-first century the warning seems uncannily prescient.

⚬⚬⚬

By the early twentieth century, the spectre of the 'Rough' which had tormented elite imaginations for so long had been joined by an even more disconcerting one – that of the unwomanly, possibly lesbian, probably hysterical and patently subversive campaigner for votes for women. Like the Levellers, the Chartists and the Paineites, the burgeoning women's movement was in revolt against subordination, indignity and exclusion. 'Why have women passion, intellect, moral activity . . .' asked the young Florence Nightingale in 1859, 'and a place in society where no one of the three can be exercised?'[46] Excluded women, like excluded men, demanded full citizenship rights, not primarily for instrumental reasons but because second-class citizenship was a badge of second-class humanity.

The indomitable Mary Wollstonecraft had 'vindicated' the 'rights of woman' as far back as 1792,[47] but the first significant blow against male domination of the polity came in 1867, when John Stuart Mill moved an amendment to the Reform Bill, substituting the word 'person' for 'man'. His amendment was lost by 194 to 73 votes – a severe defeat, but not a humiliating one. During the 1870s, bills to enfranchise women in parliamentary elections were repeatedly debated, and invariably defeated. However, women ratepayers won the right to vote in municipal elections in 1869; and over the next twenty-five years school boards, Poor Law boards, county councils and parish and district councils followed suit. Albeit more slowly, women also won the right to serve on a wide range of elected local bodies. By 1900, the total female membership of school and Poor Law boards and of rural and urban district councils was well over 1500.[48]

That fact was the weakest link in the anti-suffragist chain. The case against enfranchising women was, in many ways, a replay of the case against enfranchising poor men. True, women were not rough. Indeed, one frequent argument against enfranchising them was that they were not rough enough; that they were too delicate and refined to be trusted with votes. But though no one thought women were rough, many thought they shared the notorious irrationality of the male residuum of the 1860s. For one anti, they were 'more easily swayed by sentiment, less open to reason, less logical, keener in intuition, more sensitive than men'[49] – attributes that manifestly disqualified them from taking part in the hurly-burly of politics. Female excitability and lack of self-control, declared another anti, had been responsible for the decline of the Roman empire and the excesses of the French Revolution; even the great Queen Elizabeth had suffered from them, as evinced in her 'partiality for handsome scoundrels like Leicester'.[50]

To all these charges, the presence in local government of rational, unexcitable and self-controlled women, with no obvious partiality for handsome scoundrels, was a powerful counter-argument. So was the onward march of female enfranchisement in North America and Australasia. By the end of the nineteenth century, women had won the vote in New Zealand and four western American states; in 1902 Australia followed suit. If these hardy outposts of the English-speaking race had enfranchised women with no evil consequences, asked the pro-suffragists, why should Britain hang back?

Ironically, however, suffragist advances increasingly coincided with divisions in the ranks. The last third of the nineteenth century saw a steady growth in the number of suffragists, culminating in the formation of the National Union of Women's Suffrage Societies (NUWSS), led by the formidable Millicent Fawcett, wife of the Radical MP Henry Fawcett, and a future Dame. The NUWSS was pertinacious, adroit, respectable, eminently rational and just a little dull, rather like the moderate socialists in the Fabian Society. By the turn of the century, it was winning the argument where it counted. From the late 1890s onwards, suffragists regularly won Commons votes by substantial majorities. Political leaders as various as Sir Edward Grey, Foreign Secretary in the pre-1914 Liberal Government, and Arthur Balfour, Conservative Prime Minister from 1902 to 1905, became suffragist fellow travellers.

But in the heady climate of the early 1900s, ardent spirits in the suffragist ranks grew increasingly dissatisfied with the slow, dogged, salami tactics of the NUWSS leadership. The result was a breakaway movement called the Women's Social and Political Union (WSPU), whose members were nicknamed suffragettes. They were led by Emmeline Pankhurst, the widow of a leading member of the Independent Labour Party (ILP), and her charismatic, fervent, domineering and passionately eloquent daughter, Christabel. (Her second daughter, Sylvia, was equally charismatic and eloquent, but more independent-minded, and eventually she broke away from the senior Pankhursts' strategy.) Whatever else it was, the WSPU was not dull. Its leadership was autocratic. Heretics were often expelled, and sudden switches of line were common. If the NUWSS were the Fabians of early feminism, the WSPU were the Bolsheviks. In place of unexciting gradualism they offered militant protest, varying from window-smashing to arson to hunger strikes; in place of tedious respectability, they promised heroism, self-sacrifice, glory and even martyrdom. The most spectacular case of martyrdom came in 1913 when Emily Davidson threw herself under the king's horse in the Derby, and was killed. As the suffragist Ray (Rachel) Strachey put it:

Miss Davidson's funeral was the occasion of a great militant procession, and the crowds which silently watched it pass through the London streets knew not what to think. They knew this cause, to which they were growing friendly, and they knew militants at whom they were accustomed to jeer; and now they were faced with a martyr, at once reckless and tragic, and they were moved and distressed.[51]

Although suffragette militancy dramatised the cause and helped to push it further up the political agenda, it also alienated supporters in the political elite. Moderate suffragism gained ground; between 1908 and 1914, the membership of the NUWSS rose from around 8000 to nearly 55,000. Yet, on the eve of the war, the ultimate goal must have seemed depressingly elusive to suffragists of all stripes. Female enfranchisement was entangled with manhood suffrage, registration reform and constituency redistribution in a hideously complicated cat's cradle that no one seemed able to unpick. Traditionally, suffragists had demanded votes for women on the same terms as men, but that would have meant enfranchising a comparatively small number of well-to-do women, to the advantage of the Conservative Party and the disadvantage of the Liberals. In the fiercely partisan atmosphere of the time, with the Conservatives flirting with armed rebellion in Ulster and the Liberal Government making unprecedented inroads on property rights in the teeth of Conservative opposition, that was a risk that few Liberals or Labour people were willing to run.

Manhood suffrage without enfranchising any women was now unthinkable; that much the long campaign for female enfranchisement had accomplished. Since women lived longer than men even in those days, manhood suffrage coupled with universal female suffrage would have produced an electorate with a female majority – too rich a stew for tender male suffragist stomachs. Besides, the Irish Home Rule Party, on which the Liberal Government depended to stay in office, feared that manhood suffrage might endanger the hegemony it had achieved over most of Ireland. The result was parliamentary gridlock. In the summer of 1913, Willoughby Dickinson, a Liberal backbencher, introduced a Representation of the People Bill that would have enfranchised 5 or 6 million women, only to see it voted down by a majority largely composed of Conservatives and Irish Home Rulers.

From a radical or socialist perspective, the story had a disconcerting moral. In 1832, and to a lesser extent in 1867 and 1884, popular pressure had combined with elite manoeuvring to extend the suffrage. In the years before the First World War elite manoeuvres stultified franchise reform, with little popular opposition apart from the increasingly militant women's movement. Part of the explanation may lie in the unprecedented wave of industrial unrest that swept through Britain in the years before the First World War. Among class-conscious working men, the familiar vision of full political citizenship may have been eclipsed by a newer, more immediate vision of industrial citizenship. But another possible reason is that Disraeli's undemocratic 'traditionary influences' were still at work: that disfranchised men were content with their lot. Be that as it may, one thing is clear. In the arguments over franchise reform before 1914, they were the dog that did not bark in the night.

❦

In 1918 democracy of sorts came to Britain, but it did not come through a deliberate break in continuity on the lines once proposed by Lilburne, Rainborough and Paine, or through a crisis in which the ultimate questions were asked and answered. In J.G.A. Pocock's memorable phrase, it came through 'the medieval technique of expanding the king-in-parliament to include new categories of counsellors and representatives'.[52] By 1918 many of the building blocks of democratic government had been in place for some time – notably the rule of law, an independent judiciary and a society rich in intermediate bodies standing between the state and the citizen. But at the heart of British Government lay a long tradition of autonomous executive power, going back to the eighteenth century and perhaps even to royalist apologetics at the start of the English civil war. For most of the time, informal understandings and customary practices constrained the executive's freedom of action, but its formidable array of powers was always present in the background. The 1911 Official Secrets Act, prohibiting the unauthorised disclosure of any official information, however trivial, passed through all its stages in a single day. In 1920 no less than in 1820 or 1720, Britain's was a parliamentary *monarchy* and both words in that phrase counted equally.

The monarch's prerogative powers had passed to the king's ministers, not to Parliament or the people; and they were still essentially monarchical in character. War-making and treaty-making were prerogative acts. The honours system was controlled by the government of the day, by virtue of the royal prerogative. The Home Secretary's role as the ultimate keeper of the peace stemmed from the royal prerogative, as did the Foreign Secretary's role in the conduct of foreign policy and the Prime Minister's role in the appointment of ministers and the dispensing of patronage. Ministers were the king's ministers; civil servants were servants of the Crown. This formidable engine of power was sustained and legitimised by the doctrine of the absolute sovereignty of the Crown-in-Parliament, which went back to the sixteenth century, if not to medieval times.

The king was no ordinary king. Thanks to Disraeli's PR coup in making Queen Victoria Empress of India, he was a King-Emperor; thanks to the disappearance of the Hapsburg, Romanov, Hohenzollern and Ottoman

empires at the end of the First World War, he was the last emperor left in
Europe. His domains covered a quarter of the earth's surface, including the
Indian subcontinent, vast tracts of Africa, Canada, Australia and New
Zealand, as well as assorted bases and islands, stretching from the Pacific
to the Caribbean. Imperial splendour owed as much to modern stage-
management as to historic usage, but that did not make it any less splendid.
At George V's Coronation Durbar in Delhi in 1911, he and the Queen found
before them a canvas city, complete with pavilions, a reviewing ground and
an amphitheatre:

> [T]here they resided, among princes, governors, heralds, troops and
> escorts, and two hundred thousand visitors. They made their formal
> state entry in a five-mile-long procession, and they later appeared in full
> coronation finery to receive the homage of the princes. It was, the king
> recalled with rare effusiveness, 'the most beautiful and wonderful sight I
> ever saw'.[53]

Closely linked to the formal empire was an informal empire of capital
movements, trading relationships and political influence. Even after the
First World War, the British state was still a world-state, with a high level
of spending on a technology-hungry navy and air force, and with the
capacity to project power in every continent.[54] The 'hard power' of
the Royal Navy was linked to the 'soft power' of the City of London, the
gentlemanly ideal of the only partially modernised *ancien régime* and the
tradition of ordered freedom embodied in the Westminster Parliament.
The combination of 'hard' and 'soft' power had made Britain the pivot of
the first global political economy in history. It still gave the British governing
elite a certain urbane authority that none of its foreign counterparts could
match.

However, this mélange of stubborn medievalism, tough-minded modernism and often ersatz imperial pomp meant different things to different
people: sometimes it meant different things to the *same* people. No one
disputed that a succession of new groups had been incorporated into the
political nation during the nineteenth and early twentieth centuries, or that
executive authority had gradually been transferred from the Crown to the
leaders of the majority party in the House of Commons. Equally, everyone
could see that the rituals and iconography of the *ancien régime* had survived,
along with many of its institutions. Judges' robes, the Speaker's wig, the
Lord Chancellor's woolsack, Black Rod, the Ruritanian niceties of the
honours list and the state opening of Parliament all told the same story:
Britain's parliamentary monarchy was there because it was there, and

because it had always been there. Its title was founded on ancient custom, not on transient intellectual notions or the quicksands of popular goodwill. Its legitimacy was rooted in its history, and its history was beyond argument.

Parliament itself was one of the chief protagonists in that story. As the suffrage widened, new men, and after 1918 the occasional new woman, penetrated its portals. They changed it, of course, but they were also changed by it. In a sharp comment on the eve of the First World War, one observer painted a vivid picture of the impact of parliamentary fame on those who achieved it. In England, he wrote,

> The men who direct the great dominating interests, commerce, the law, finance, the press, are brought very close together. Even the brilliant platform rhetorician, who may have been lifted into power as the champion of the masses or the minor bourgeoisie, is apt to forget his clients and his past in this constant association with opulent and well-born persons, whose luxuries and tastes he shares.[55]

The House of Commons was as good at instilling old norms into new members as any public school, officers' mess or miners' lodge. 'A constitution which enables an engine-driver of yesterday to be a Secretary of State today,' rejoiced the railwaymen's leader J.H. Thomas in 1924, 'is a great constitution.'[56] In similar vein, the cotton workers' leader, J.R. Clynes, marvelled 'at the strange turn in Fortune's wheel' that had brought 'MacDonald the starveling clerk, Thomas the engine driver, Henderson the foundry labourer and Clynes the mill-hand' to receive the seals of office, amid the gold and crimson of Buckingham Palace.'[57] The titles that working-class leaders chose for their memoirs – *Workman's Cottage to Windsor Castle; From Workshop to War Cabinet* – exuded the same incredulous delight at having been incorporated into the political class. In a study of high politics in the 1880s, A.B. Cooke and John Vincent suggested that the Palace of Westminster was a 'highly specialised community', obsessed with its own affairs.[58] It had been recognisably the same community in the 1780s and was recognisably the same community in the 1980s. Like townees settling in a rural village, its new inhabitants gradually adopted the ways of the old ones; they had to if they were to flourish within it.

Yet the settlers did not all react in the same way. Aneurin Bevan, the lion of the Labour left for more than thirty years, is a telling witness. He was first elected to Parliament in 1929, a decade after the belated arrival of manhood suffrage. Later, he remembered that a new Member's first impression of the House of Commons was that he is in church. The vaulted roofs and stained-glass windows, the rows of statues of great statesmen of the past, the echoing halls, the soft-footed attendants and the whispered conversation, contrast depressingly with the crowded meetings and the clang and clash of hot opinions he has just left behind in his election campaign. Here he is, a tribune of the people, coming to make his voice heard in the seats of power. Instead, it seems he is expected to worship; and the most conservative of all religions – ancestor worship.[59]

Bevan's sardonic description of the 'ancestor worship' that he encountered when he entered the Commons was a vivid piece of reportage, but it was also a cry of protest. He became one of the greatest parliamentarians of his generation, as well as a successful minister, adept at the exercise of monarchical power. At the same time, he was an heir of the Paineites of the 1790s and the Chartists of the 1830s and 1840s. He was a democratic centralist, but also a wayward rebel; a practitioner of top-down reform who dreamed of bottom-up defiance. He was a thoroughgoing democrat, but he oscillated between two understandings of democracy. With part of his mind, he thought universal suffrage had brought democracy to Britain. With another, he saw the British version of democracy as a pale shadow of the real thing.

Bevan's oscillations were mirrored by other political leaders and followers. Britain's long march to democracy generated rival, sometimes overlapping, narratives and understandings; they in turn generated competing strategies for mobilising support and holding power. Like Bevan, most political actors lurched from one understanding to another, sometimes without realising what they were doing. These understandings, the narratives that supported them and the strategies that flowed from them are the stuff of the next chapter.

3

PRIMEVAL CONTRACT

✣

In youth one *believes* in democracy; later on, one has to *accept* it.
Ramsay MacDonald, diary entry, March 1919

I dread the mass mind.
Stanley Baldwin, April 1937

✣

WITH THE PEOPLE

Britain's long march to a more or less democratic suffrage ended in February 1918, when the Representation of the People Bill became law. In November, Germany capitulated. The first British general election fought under the new statute took place in December, when wartime emotions were running high. The Lloyd George coalition crushed its opponents, winning 478 seats out of 707. Most of the Asquithian Liberals who had stayed loyal to their old leader when Lloyd George supplanted him in 1916 were swept away. So were most of the small band of Liberal and Labour dissidents who had opposed the war and campaigned for a compromise peace.

One such was Ramsay MacDonald, the hero of the anti-war left, whose career epitomised the ambiguities of the growing Labour movement. He was born in 1866 in Lossiemouth, on the north-east coast of Scotland, the illegitimate son of a ploughman and a farm servant. He was educated as a pupil teacher in a nearby school and never went to university. At the age of twenty he made his way to London, and became an active socialist. While still in his early thirties, he played a leading part in the creation of the Labour Party and served as its first secretary. He was handsome, charismatic, prickly and a stirring platform speaker in the flowery style of the time. In 1906 he was elected to Parliament; in 1911 he became chairman of the parliamentary Labour Party. When his parliamentary colleagues voted for war credits in August 1914, he resigned from the chairmanship. Thereafter he was the chief standard-bearer of the anti-war forces. In the 1918 election he lost his seat by 20,510 votes to 6347. 'Here the reason of the anti-parliamentarian has it all its own way', he noted bitterly. 'One of these friends of mine remarked the other day, "This is the fetish you worship." "The very Gods go mad sometimes," I replied. But what respect can we pay to decisions which can be worked in this fashion?"[1]

MacDonald was not alone. John Maynard Keynes, wartime Treasury official and eventually one of the greatest economists of the age, described Lloyd George's final manifesto as a 'concoction of greed . . . prejudice and deception'.[2] For the Asquithian weekly, *The Nation*, the coalition's victorious election campaign was 'an orgy of sops and sophistry'.[3] It was as if democracy had turned traitor. The residuum had been enfranchised, and it had proceeded to justify the forebodings of liberal intellectuals like John Stuart Mill and public moralists like George Eliot.

The apprehensions of the intellectual left were soon echoed on the victorious right and centre. Like an avalanche crashing through an Alpine valley, the war had swept away old landmarks and transformed familiar vistas. The size and role of the state had grown out of all recognition. Trade-union membership had doubled, as had membership of the Labour Party. The Liberal Party had split; though it soon recovered a precarious unity, it never recovered its sense of direction. Thanks partly to a febrile post-war boom, industrial unrest reached unprecedented heights. After the boom broke in 1921, an acute trade depression gave new force to an increasingly resonant socialist critique of capitalism. The old struggle between dissent and the Church, which had once given the Liberal Party a cause and a constituency, faded away. A fiercer struggle between labour and capital came to the fore.

Most political leaders had reached maturity in the reign of Queen Victoria. Now they found themselves in a baffling and menacing new world. Its menaces were compounded by the effects of the Representation of the People Act. Despite the long years of struggle and debate before it arrived, democracy had, in the end, crept up on the political class like a thief in the night. The 1918 Act was a step change, for which no one was fully prepared. Politicians, commentators and officials had to pick their way through unfamiliar terrain, full of traps for the unwary. The Coalition Government was haunted by the spectre of class politics, behind which loomed the even more ominous spectres of a class war and even a Russian-style revolution. Opposition Liberals were still more alarmed by the seeming emergence of a polity divided on class lines, on which liberalism would have no purchase. Moderate Labour men like MacDonald, Arthur Henderson, the party secretary, and Philip Snowden, its chief financial spokesman, were equally alarmed by the prospect of a radicalised working class, egged on by a militant left, suspicious of and sometimes hostile to the norms of parliamentary government.

Questions crowded in. What did the coming of democracy mean? What story or stories explained its arrival and made sense of it now that it had arrived? How were political leaders and institutions to cope with it? What did it imply for identity – for the primordial political questions, 'Who are we?' and 'Who belongs to the political community?' What did it imply for the seemingly perennial conflicts between employers and employed? How was the tension between democracy and capitalism to be resolved? How was a polity divided along class lines to be managed and led? More generally, what did democracy imply for statecraft? How should the democratic state relate to the wider society? What strategies could (and should) be followed by those who sought to win, hold and exercise power in this baffling new system?

✺

The answers were multifarious, cacophonous, fluctuating, and tacit rather than explicit. They reflected shifting visions, overlapping understandings and sometimes ambiguous narratives, with multiple authors and contested meanings. Yet four grand stories or sets of stories emerge from the cacophony. Each distilled a tacit tradition of political understanding and statecraft, and each implied a particular solution to the democratic problem: the problem of how a political class formed in the pre-democratic era would cope with democracy. These traditions cannot be squeezed into the conventional categories of left and right, or the well-known language of conservative, liberal and socialist. They spill across these familiar boundaries like mercury slithering across a polished surface. In any case, they were not mutually exclusive. The frontiers between them were hazy and porous, and they often overlapped in practice.

The protagonists in the never-ending conversation of politics were men (and eventually women) of action, not of theory. They were less concerned with consistency than with what 'played', and they were apt to slide from one tradition to another – sometimes without realising it – as circumstances or audiences changed. Besides, the political conversation took place within the divided souls of those taking part in it as well as between them. Few belonged exclusively to one tradition; to take only two remarkable examples, Tony Blair straddled all of them while Winston Churchill straddled two, as later chapters will show. Yet the four traditions and the narratives encapsulating them illuminate aspects of twentieth- and twenty-first-century British history which a focus on party and ideology leaves in darkness.

I shall call them, respectively, 'whig imperialist', 'tory nationalist', 'democratic collectivist' and 'democratic republican'. ('Whig imperialist', 'tory nationalist' and 'democratic republican' are my own coinage; 'democratic collectivist' was invented by the pioneer of Fabian Socialism, Sidney Webb.) The whig imperialist story held the field for most of the time between 1918 and 1945, and again for most of the 1950s and early 1960s. It was a story of gradual progress, timely accommodation, responsive evolution and subtle statecraft. Most of all, it was a story of balance – between freedom and order, change and stability, rulers and ruled and, not least, central and local power. It came from the heart of the most relaxed and confident political elite in Europe. The storytellers were mostly men of *government*, used to the exercise of power. They saw themselves, above all, as practical men of the world, genially tolerant rather than self-righteously shrill. (That was what Roy Jenkins meant when he called his father, the miners' leader and trade-union MP, Arthur Jenkins, a 'natural whig'.[4]) They were repelled by dogmatic absolutes and believed that the subtleties of practice could not be captured in any theoretical formula or neatly packaged creed.

In Harold Nicolson's political novel, *Public Faces*, a pompous Foreign Office official called Arthur Peabody, and known to his staff as 'old Pea-bottle', likens foreign policy to 'a majestic river, flowing in a uniform direction, requiring only, at moments of crisis, a glib rectification of the banks'.[5] That was the whig imperialist story in a nutshell. The majestic river of evolutionary progress had flowed, virtually undisturbed, since the Glorious Revolution of 1688. Glib rectifications of the banks had been necessary from time to time, but they had been designed to aid the flow and they had succeeded in their aim. Their authors had been guided by intuition rather than doctrine, by shrewd horse sense rather than fixed principles. If the result was opaque and confusing, so much the better: the price of evolutionary success was a decent ambiguity.

The canonical whig imperialist was Edmund Burke – one of the most gifted, original and complex figures in British parliamentary history.[6] He was born in Dublin in 1729, at a time when Ireland was effectively a colony, whose native population – the Catholic Irish – was held down by force. He died in 1797. His father, Richard Burke, was an attorney in the Irish Court of Exchequer and therefore, of necessity, a Protestant. (In fact, he belonged to the established Church of Ireland.) However, he may have converted to Protestantism in order to pursue a legal career. In any case, Burke's mother was a Catholic, from an impoverished family of Catholic gentry in County Cork; and Burke's sister was brought up as a Catholic. Burke himself was baptised into the Anglican Church of Ireland, but he spent much of his childhood with his mother's Catholic relatives in County Cork; and he was always acutely aware of his Catholic connections.

They were not healthy connections in an age when a ferocious Protestantism was a crucial component of British patriotism, and when an anti-Catholic mob terrorised London during the so-called Gordon Riots. Burke was never fully at home in the British political elite. Beneath the carapace of measured Whig statesmanship lay a mercurial, tempestuous and prickly Celt – and a colonial, arriviste Celt to boot. Talent, determination and courage carried him into the governing class, but he held on to membership of it by his fingernails and never penetrated to its heart. He eulogised it extravagantly. The British House of Commons, he insisted implausibly, was 'filled with everything illustrious in rank, in descent, in hereditary and in acquired opulence, in cultivated talents, in civil, naval, and politic distinction that the country can afford'.[7] Dithyrambs like this reflected the marginality that helps to account for the depth and breadth of Burke's political imagination. He was always a dazzled, aspiring outsider looking in, not an insider looking out. The real insiders treated him accordingly. Despite long and devoted services to the cause of his own branch of the ramifying Whig political family, the so-called Rockingham Whigs, they never rewarded him with a Cabinet post.

After graduating from Trinity College, Dublin, Burke settled in London, where he hoped to pursue a literary career. He was elected to Parliament in 1765. By then he was secretary to the Marquess of Rockingham and soon became the main intellectual inspiration of the Rockingham Whigs. In debate, he was outstandingly eloquent and versatile as well as a formidable polemicist; rhetorically speaking, he shot to kill. His written style was marvellously rich and commanding, and his mastery of the pointed epigram equalled Tom Paine's. ('Kings will be tyrants from policy, when subjects are rebels from principle' is one example from his *Reflections on the Revolution in France.* 'When bad men combine, the good must associate' is another, from his earlier *Thoughts on the Present Discontent.*[8]) Before long he was a painful thorn in the flesh of George III and the so-called 'King's friends', He accused them of 'striking a palsy into every nerve' of the constitution by covertly extending the power of the Crown and undermining the role of the House of Commons as a check on executive power.[9]

As the troubles in the American colonies mounted in the 1760s and 1770s, he developed into one of the most eloquent and determined of the Americans' British champions. In the 1780s, he devoted the lion's share of his energies to a passionate campaign against the East India Company's misrule in Bengal, culminating in an ultimately unsuccessful attempt to impeach Warren Hastings, the Governor-General, whose misdeeds he exaggerated. Throughout, Burke tried to alleviate the wrongs of the native Irish. Then came the French Revolution and Burke's onslaught on the revolutionaries and their British sympathisers, *Reflections on the Revolution in France.*

At first sight, the anti-revolutionary Burke of the 1790s belongs to a different political universe from the Burke who excoriated Crown pretensions, championed the American colonists, savaged the East India Company and fought to mitigate the Protestant Ascendancy in Ireland. Yet there was a deeper consistency beneath the surface inconsistency. As an Irishman with close Catholic connections, Burke knew what it was like to be on the receiving end of arbitrary and abusive power; during the Gordon Riots he had discovered what it was like to be threatened by a bloodthirsty mob. The eruptions of passionate, sometimes anguished indignation that studded his career nearly all sprang from his fellow-feeling with victims of oppression and violence. For him, the revolutionaries in France were as guilty of the abuse of power as Warren Hastings or the authors of the Irish Penal Code.

Five grand themes sound through Burke's political career. Although the language and emphasis changed during his thirty-odd years in Parliament, the essentials were present throughout. The first concerned the nature of political authority and political communities. For most of his political life, Burke was a hero to extra-parliamentary radicals. Long after his death, Gladstone thought his writings 'a magazine of wisdom'.[10] Burke thought of himself as a reformer and declared that when the people were in dispute with their rulers, 'the presumption is at least upon a par in favour of the people'.[11] However, the notion that political authority stemmed from the people – and the associated notion that political communities were the products of human reason, embodied in freely made contracts between individuals – seemed to him wicked and dangerous. If the social fabric could be destroyed at will, as these notions implied, the bonds of tradition and inheritance that linked one generation to another, and made human beings human, would be sundered. 'Men would become little better than the flies of a summer.'[12]

In truth, individuals were born, willy-nilly, into communities that existed before their births, survived their deaths and sprang from much deeper roots than rational calculation. The fashionable Enlightenment concept of the 'social contract', common to thinkers as diverse as John Locke and Jean-Jacques Rousseau, was therefore spurious. The metaphor of a contract might have some value, Burke conceded, but only if it were reinterpreted to mean that the ties between generations were unbreakable, that political authority and political communities had a sacred quality about them, which could not be understood in rational terms. Society, he wrote in one of his most famous passages, 'is indeed a contract', but a contract of a special kind:

> Subordinate contracts for objects of mere occasional interest may be dis-solved at pleasure – but the state ought not to be considered nothing better than a partnership agreement in a trade of pepper and coffee, calico or tobacco ... It is a partnership in all science; a partnership in all art; a partnership in every virtue and in all perfection. As the ends of such a partnership cannot be obtained in many generations, it becomes a part-nership not only between those who are living, but between those who are living, those who are dead, and those who are to be born. Each contract of each particular state is but a clause in the great primeval contract of eternal society ... sanctioned by the inviolable oath which holds all physical and all moral natures, each in their appointed place.[13]

The second theme – of culture, identity and difference – was closely related to the first. Law, Burke repeatedly declared, mattered less than what he called 'manners' or 'temper', or what we would now call culture. 'The law touches us but here and there, and now and then,' he wrote. 'Manners are what vex or soothe, corrupt or purify, exalt or debase, barbarize or refine us.'[14] And different societies had different manners, which their rulers had to respect. Burke loathed the pettifogging legalism that he detected in the government's response to American disaffection, partly because it was inexpedient, but much more because it ran counter to his vision of culturally sensitive statecraft. The American colonists breathed 'a fierce spirit of lib-erty', reflecting the dissenting Protestantism of New England and the 'high and haughty' pride of Southern slaveholders.[15] Attempts to govern them in defiance of their culture were doomed to fail; insofar as they succeeded they would undermine freedom in Britain as well.

Burke's critique of British misrule in India sprang from the same emo-tional roots. The East India Company's apparent contempt for Indian culture shocked him almost as much as its rapacity. Britain's Indian subjects, he declared, in a passage of extraordinary empathy, had been 'cultivated by all the arts of polished life, whilst we were yet in the woods'. Among them were:

> an ancient and venerable priesthood, the depository of their laws, learning and history, the guides of the people whilst living and their consolation in death; a nobility of great antiquity and renown ... merchants and bankers, individual houses of whom have once vied in capital with the bank of

England ... [and] almost all the religions professed by men, the Brah-
minical, the Mussulman and the Eastern and Western Christian.[16]

Yet, under the East India Company, the members of this ancient culture
were governed by raw young men 'without sympathy with the natives. ...
Were we to be driven out of India this day, nothing would remain, to tell
that it had been possessed, during the inglorious period of our dominion,
by anything better than the ouran-outang or the tiger.'[17]

From all this sprang an imprecise but generous and pluralistic conception
of empire and Britain's imperial destiny (the third theme). Burke's conception eventually became a leitmotiv of British geopolitics, yet in his own
day it posed a radical challenge to prevailing assumptions. Burke was no
enemy to what later generations called imperialism. He fought for a change
in government policy towards the American colonies because he wanted to
keep them in the empire. One reason was that he saw the colonists as
Englishmen. On a deeper level, he believed that a great empire like Britain's
should be governed with a loose rein. Burke insisted that 'unity of spirit'
should go hand in hand with 'diversity of operations' – partly because the
alternative was either dissolution or despotism, but also because he relished
diversity for its own sake. For him an empire was 'the aggregate of many
states under one common head'. Only 'the dismal, cold, dead, uniformity
of servitude' could prevent its subordinate parts from acquiring local privileges and immunities. Inevitably, there would be disputes between the
common authority and the subordinate parts. These would have to be settled
by the 'barter and compromise' that lay at the heart of all government.[18] In
the twenty-first century, when the British empire is little more than a
memory, it is all too easy to miss the significance of Burke's vision of
pluralistic imperialism; nonetheless, it played a central role in shaping the
tradition that helped to make the peaceful liquidation of empire possible.

Interwoven with the first three themes was a fourth – the theme of
prudence, practice and a judicious combination of preservation and reform.
'Impracticable' virtue, Burke declared in a pregnant throwaway line in
Thoughts on the Present Discontents, was 'spurious'.[19] The mysteries of government were 'not to be taught *a priori*'.[20] In political life, experience easily
outweighed reason. The British, he boasted, were 'afraid to put men to live
and trade each on his own private stock of reason; because we suspect that
the stock in each man is small, and that the individuals would do better to
avail themselves of the general bank and capital of nations and of ages'.[21]

Revolutionary France was a terrible counter-example. The abstract rationalism of the *philosophes* had given birth to a 'barbarous philosophy, which
is the offspring of cold hearts and muddy understandings ... In the groves

of *their* academy, at the end of every visto, you see nothing but the gallows.'[22] One obvious implication was that reform – and even in his fiercest anti-revolutionary phase, Burke insisted that reform was sometimes essential – had to run with the grain of history and tradition. He could not conceive, he wrote, how anyone could be so presumptuous as 'to consider his country as nothing but *carte blanche*, upon which he may scribble whatever he pleases. . . . A disposition to preserve, and ability to improve, taken together, would be my standard of a statesman.'[23] And practice required practitioners. Statesmanship was a skill. It could not be taught; it could only be absorbed through the pores by a history-respecting, theory-eschewing governing class, seeking 'so to be patriots as not to forget we are gentlemen'.[24]

Burke's fifth theme was the simplest and in some ways the most portentous. It was the theme of balance, of judicious accommodation to changing circumstances, of knowing when the unforeseeable contingencies of politics made it necessary to tack. It was summarised with marvellous economy in the final paragraph of his *Reflections*. His opinions, he wrote, came from one 'who wishes to preserve consistency, but who would preserve consistency by varying his means to secure the unity of his end; and, when the equipoise of the vessel in which he sails may be endangered by overloading it upon one side, is desirous of carrying the small weight of his reasons to that which may preserve its equipoise'.[25]

∞

The half-century between the 1832 and 1884 Reform Acts was the golden age of whig imperialism. The political elite consisted overwhelmingly of Burkean 'gentlemen', albeit with a growing admixture of professionals. All three Reform Acts were framed in the Burkean spirit of equipoise. (When Gladstone told the House of Commons in 1884 that the Representation of the People Bill did not 'aim at ideal perfection ... ideal perfection is not the true basis of English legislation',[26] it might have been Burke speaking.) The same was true of the Liberals' reforms, designed to rid public administration and the electoral process of nepotism and corruption. Thus Britain's *ancien régime* was transformed but not destroyed. The frontiers of the political nation were widened beyond all expectation, whilst in a host of ways its 'manners' were unchanged.

For whig imperialists looking back from the vantage point of the 1920s, the moral was obvious. Thanks to a statecraft of judicious, tradition-respecting accommodation to changing times, the British political elite had turned a trick that none of its foreign counterparts had managed to turn. The result was a uniquely happy blend of old and new. As G.M. Trevelyan, the nation's favourite historian, boasted in 1937, the 1832 Reform Act had enabled Britain to escape 'the vicious circle of continental revolution and reaction', while retaining the 'Anglo-Saxon moorings' of her political life. This was no accident. 'Political self-government, central and local,' he declared in a later passage, 'was an English invention.'[27] (So much for ancient Athens and the city-states of Renaissance Italy.)

Shortly after the Second World War, the All Souls Fellow and combative Conservative statesman, Leo Amery, made essentially the same point, in a more provocative way. Nineteenth-century commentators, he argued, had misread the constitution that they purported to describe. Authority was not delegated by the electorate to Parliament, and then by Parliament to the government, as they imagined. Since Norman times, the essence of the constitution had lain in a dialogue or 'parley' between two co-equal elements – the Crown or government, which directed and energised, and the nation, which assented or acquiesced. That ancient tradition of responsive but autonomous executive power was the key to Britain's political good fortune, enabling her to escape the weak government and political instability which were the curse of less happy lands. Amery clinched his argument with a mischievous parody of Abraham Lincoln. The British system, he wrote, was 'one of democracy, but of democracy by consent ... of government of the people, for the people, with but not by the people'.[28]

A second moral loomed in the background. Keynes, an admirer of Burke since his schooldays, epitomised it in a celebrated essay, 'The End of Laissez-Faire'. The '*Agenda*' and '*Non-Agenda*' of government, he wrote, could not be determined on 'abstract grounds'. The question of what the state should do and what it should leave to private individuals could be answered only 'on its merits in detail' – a classic example of the whiggish fudge beloved of the British mandarinate. The agenda would change as circumstances changed. In fact, it was changing now. The time had come for the state to control credit and the currency, while following deliberate population policy.[29] New winds were blowing, and the state had to change tack accordingly. The flexible statecraft that had saved the parliamentary monarchy in the nineteenth century would save capitalism in the twentieth.

It was the same story with empire. Although Burke was ahead of his time when he put forward his vision of a pluralistic empire, he was vindicated after his death. The nineteenth-century British state was the heir of the ruthless imperial predator that had grown rich on the proceeds of the slave trade, and humbled the France of Louis XIV and later of Napoleon. Indeed, the empire's boundaries widened dramatically in the century after Waterloo. But it was not an empire in which the governments that fought the American colonists would have felt at home. The classically educated Burkean gentlemen who presided over it sometimes compared themselves to ancient

Romans, yet nothing could have been less Roman than the loose-knit collection of bases, trading posts, colonies of settlement, directly ruled territories and variegated dependencies that constituted the British empire at its zenith. The colonies of settlement, in particular, developed on Burkean lines. Not long after an abortive revolt in French Canada in 1837, the Canadian colonies were granted responsible government. Their Australian counterparts soon followed suit, as did New Zealand and (much later) South Africa. By the 1914-18 war, the so-called 'white dominions' were all effectively self-governing, as their presence at the post-war peace conference testified. More remarkably, India also sent a delegation to the conference, albeit one chosen by the British and headed by the British Secretary of State, Edwin Montagu.

As far back as 1833, Viscount Goderich, then colonial secretary, had declared that the aim of Britain's imperial policy was to embed 'the spirit of civil liberty' and British 'forms of social order' in 'distant regions'.[30] That was the essence of the whig imperialist vision of empire: blatantly condescending but emotionally satisfying. As the brutal repression of the Indian Mutiny made clear, the Raj was based ultimately on force,[31] while the notion that distant regions would benefit from British ways presupposed British superiority to other peoples. This, however, did not detract from its persuasive power. It was a myth with a capital 'M' – not only in the sense that it distorted reality, but in the deeper sense that it gave its votaries a vocation and an identity in which they could take pride. It was propagated at least as vigorously in the 1930s as it had been in the 1830s. It had two dimensions: it told the British not only that they were a uniquely freedom-loving people, but that they were also a uniquely imperial, maritime one, who had become a people when they decided to turn their backs on continental absolutism and to 'plant the flag of liberty beyond the ocean'.[32]

Thus, for Sir John Marriott, the evolution of the self-governing colonies into a 'self-governing Commonwealth' would for 'all time distinguish the Victorian era'.[33] For the half-American Winston Churchill, British history was only part of the history of the freedom-loving 'English-speaking peoples', which he wrote in four substantial volumes.[34] George V's speech on the occasion of the Royal Jubilee in 1935 (drafted by G.M. Trevelyan) belonged to the same genre. Britain's balanced constitution, he enthused, sprang from 'the impulse towards liberty, justice and social improvement inherent in our people down the ages'. His audience, he added, should give thanks that 'under our flag of freedom, so many millions eat their daily bread, in far distant lands and climates, with none to make them afraid'.[35] (What Irish Republicans and Indian nationalists made of that is not recorded.)

The whig imperialist vision of empire and identity helped to shape the mentalities of most of the political class, including those of many opponents of empire in the Liberal and Labour parties. Before the First World War, Ramsay MacDonald returned from a visit to India bitterly critical of 'bombastic imperialism', but convinced that Britain would have to remain the 'nurse of India' for the foreseeable future.[36] A generation later, whig imperialist assumptions would shape the foreign and colonial policies of the post-war Labour Government. Regimental battle honours from half-forgotten colonial wars, Rudyard Kipling's Indian tales, G.A. Henty's schoolboy adventure stories, the ties of ethnicity that bound the 'mother country' to the self-governing white Dominions, the ritual of Empire Day (another recent ersatz invention) and innumerable globes spattered with red all told the same story.

Its audience cut across the boundaries of class as well as of party: as Robert Roberts remembered them, the Salford slum-dwellers among whom he grew up before the First World War were 'staunchly patriotic. "They didn't know", it was said, "whether trade was good for the Empire or the Empire was good for trade, but they knew the Empire was theirs and they were going to support it."'[37] Roberts may have been untypical; Bernard Porter has argued forcefully that most working-class people were indifferent to the empire, while some were hostile to it.[38] But we should not make too much of that. The indifferent and hostile had no counter-Myth to tell the British who they were and what their national vocation was. A few anti-imperialists may have flirted with the notion that the ruling class had forced the British working class into imperial aggrandisement against their will. J.A. Hobson, the precursor of Keynesian economics, saw imperialism as the product of a search for markets on the part of profit-hungry capitalists. But it was hard to construct a counter-Myth out of such flimsy and uninspiring materials, and occasional attempts to do so were signally unsuccessful. (The Leninist theory of imperialism as the last stage of capitalism was derived, in part, from Hobson, but it had little influence in Britain.)

There were plenty of challenges to the whig imperialist vision of democracy and the democratic state, but outside the far left and the far right the whig imperialist understanding of Britain's identity and place in the world held the field for most (though not all) of the nineteenth century as well as the first half of the twentieth.

AGAINST THE PEOPLE?

The most outstanding feature of the whig imperialist tradition was its optimism. Tory nationalists were instinctive pessimists, for whom the world was an uncertain and threatening place, haunted by spectres of disruption and disorder. On one fundamental point, the two traditions overlapped. For both, the prime task of statesmanship was to defend and sustain authority, social and political, but they saw that task in profoundly different ways. Whig imperialists assumed that it could best be performed through adroit accommodation to changing times, carried out by a skilful and responsive governing class. Tory nationalists feared that accommodation would mutate into surrender, and responsiveness into defeatism. Whig imperialists tended to believe that evolutionary change, promoted by the right kind of leadership, was usually for the better. Sometimes, tory nationalists were willing to make changes too, even radical ones, but when they did so it was to restore a lost golden age of order, discipline and respect for tradition. Their default mode was suspicion of change. For whig imperialists, authority was rather like an elegant Palladian mansion, surrounded by peaceful gardens. For tory nationalists, it was more like a sombre fortress, holding down an unpredictable population that might, at any moment, lay siege to it.

In calm periods, when authority seemed secure, tory nationalist voices were rarely heard. In times of trouble, when it was under threat, they were clamant and even raucous. At such times, they often evoked widespread popular support – disconcerting followers of other traditions, who found it hard to believe that the tory nationalist emphasis on authority offered dignity and meaning to those at the bottom of the social scale as well as to those at the top. Over 300 years, targets, tactics and vocabulary changed, yet the twin themes of authority and danger were always present. The conflict-ridden, occasionally blood-soaked seventeenth century saw a number of early examples. Champions of the Divine Right of Kings insisted that the authority of the monarch came from heaven. Kings, as James I put it, were 'not only God's lieutenants on earth and sit upon God's throne, but even by God himself, they are called Gods'.[39] For the Kentish country gentleman Sir Robert Filmer, royal authority was part of an all-embracing structure of patriarchal authority, dating from the Creation.[40] However, the century's most resonant expressions of the tory nationalist sensibility were uninhibitedly secular. They came from the harsh, coruscating, intellectually ruthless pen of Thomas Hobbes, perhaps the greatest of all English political philosophers.

He was no ordinary tory nationalist, even in embryo: he was not an ordinary anything. He was too original, too unsettling, too shocking and too philosophically subversive for that. But the much quoted passage in his *Leviathan*, picturing a state of nature with no settled authority to subdue the self-destructive passions of men, distilled the primal anxieties at the

heart of the tory nationalist world-view more powerfully than anyone else
has ever done. In one of the most haunting passages penned by an English
philosopher he wrote that a state of nature of this sort would be a state of
permanent war, in which 'every man is enemy to every man':

> In such condition, there is no place for industry; because the fruit thereof
> is uncertain: and consequently no culture of the earth; no navigation, nor
> use of the commodities that may be imported by sea; no commodious
> building; no instruments of moving, and removing, such things as require
> much force; no knowledge of the face of the earth; no account of time; no
> arts; no letters; no society; and which is worst of all, continual fear, and
> danger of violent death; and the life of man, solitary, poor, nasty, brutish,
> and short.[41]

His conclusion is equally famous, but it too deserves repetition. Social peace
could be maintained only by an all-powerful sovereign (either an individual
or an assembly): a 'great LEVIATHAN' or 'mortal god'.[42]

The choice between Leviathan and anarchy seemed almost as stark to
much of the panicky governing elite in the aftermath of the French Revolution. An extreme but revealing example is the notorious Lord Eldon, author
of the Act extending the definition of high treason in the 1790s, chief
prosecutor during the treason trials, and unyielding enemy of reform in any
guise throughout his mammoth term as Lord Chancellor from 1801 to 1827.
(It was not for nothing that he was nicknamed 'Lord Endless'.) For Eldon,
as Rose Melikan nicely puts it: 'General measures were too sweeping.
Specific proposals encouraged inconsistency. Legislation of any sort was
unnecessary.' He opposed anti-slavery legislation because it would unfairly
damage property owners, measures to regulate mental asylums because they
would undermine the authority of the medical profession, and measures to
disfranchise corrupt boroughs because the franchise was a property right,
'sacred in the eyes of the law'.[43]

Eldon stood at the outer edge of the tory nationalist spectrum. The
greatest tory nationalist of the nineteenth century – perhaps of the last two
centuries – was Robert Gascoyne-Cecil, 3rd Marquess of Salisbury. He was
born in 1830, the third son of the second marquess (the second son had
died in infancy). When his elder brother died in 1865, he became the heir
to the marquessate; on the death of his father in 1868 he inherited a
substantial fortune; and entered the House of Lords as Lord Salisbury.
Anxiety was his lifelong companion. A frail, lonely and unhappy child, he
had been bullied so mercilessly at Eton that his father had taken him away
at the age of fifteen. At seventeen, he went up to Christ Church, Oxford,

where he suffered a breakdown after two years and had to leave the university with an honorary fourth-class degree. (He redeemed himself later by winning a Fellowship at All Souls.) In 1853, at the age of twenty-three, he entered Parliament as Conservative Member for Stamford, a pocket borough in the gift of his cousin, the Marquess of Exeter.

Salisbury cut a curious figure. He loathed small talk, detested balls and hated the country pursuits beloved of males of his class. He never fished, never shot, never hunted and was famous for being atrociously dressed. In high society, he was known as 'the Buffalo'. Although sustained by a profound Christian faith, he never spoke of its inner content. He was tall, thin, stooped, short-sighted, awkward, hyper-tense, highly intelligent and prone to periodical outbreaks of depression, which he called 'nerve storms'. At such times, his senses of touch and hearing became 'morbidly acute' and the 'slightest noise or the slightest physical contact became painful to him'.[44] In a love match opposed by his father, Salisbury married a judge's daughter, Georgina Alderson. Thereafter, the anxieties that haunted him gradually became less acute, but they never vanished. During the American civil war he passionately supported the South, despite detesting slavery. As the Northern victory approached, he became increasingly agitated and took to sleepwalking. Once his wife saw him standing at an open window, 'fast asleep but in a state of strong excitement and preparing to resist forcibly some dreamed-of intrusion of enemies – presumably Federal soldiers or revolutionary mob leaders'.[45]

These inner tensions gave a hard, crystalline, sometimes savage edge to his speeches and writings. As a younger son, Salisbury had to earn his living and did so through journalism, soon becoming an accomplished political commentator. He was not a systematic thinker, and never published a sustained work of political theory, but in a series of substantial essays on current events he set out a bleakly coherent approach to politics and statecraft, expressed with a brutal clarity reminiscent of Hobbes, and suffused with an emotional violence that still crackles across the page. It is hard to summarise his political vision in a phrase, but a good shorthand description would be 'Marxism through the looking-glass'. He and Marx were on opposite sides, but of the same war. Like Marx, Salisbury thought that class held the key to politics and saw the state as the instrument of the dominant class. For him, as much as for Marx, attempts to camouflage the brute reality of class conflict with high-sounding appeals to common citizenship or Christian fellowship were empty and contemptible cant.

Again like Marx, Salisbury thought the battle between property and socialism would be a 'death-struggle'.[46] And there was more than a touch of

Marx (and, indeed, of Hobbes) in his picture of the future. The 'primeval subject-matter of all human conflict' was moving to the centre of the stage, he wrote, and the rival classes would soon have 'to meet each other face to face'.[47] His self-appointed task was to stiffen the propertied for the fight, even though he was not at all sure that they would win. Incorrigibly prone to self-deception, they would 'always be ready to nibble at fine sentiments about confidence in the English people until they are caught and landed beyond escape'.[48] The Hobbesian spectre of 'disintegration', as he called it in one of his best-known essays, was ever-present.[49]

The door to disintegration was democracy, and the door to democracy was a wider franchise. When suffrage reform returned to the political agenda in the 1860s, Salisbury came into his own. He did not allow party loyalty to stand in his way. Disraeli, the Conservative leader in the Commons, was the 'Artless Dodger', who had to be unmasked.[50] The democratic enemy was now in sight; and it had to be crushed at all costs. 'Discontent, insurrection, civil war itself', Salisbury insisted in a wild flourish, would 'produce no worse dangers than absolute and unrestrained democracy. Such commotions can only end in a military government; and the despotism of a successful soldier is a lighter burden than the despotism of the multitude.'[51]

His fear of democracy was rooted in powerful emotions. Even when the suffrage was limited, he expressed a visceral loathing for 'the nauseous mire of a general election', with its

> days and weeks of screwed-up smiles and laboured courtesy, the mock geniality, the hearty shake of the filthy hand, the chuckling reply that must be made to the coarse joke, the loathsome, choking compliment that must be paid to the grimy wife and sluttish daughter, the indispensable flattery of the vilest religious prejudices, the wholesale deglutition of hypocritical pledges.[52]

But his adamantine opposition to the Reform Bills of the 1860s also stemmed from a fiercely held vision of the state and the political economy. The state had to be strong to defend its position in the Hobbesian world of international relations, as well as to maintain order and social discipline at home. To safeguard the market economy it also had to be limited. Democracy would produce an unlimited state, open to capture by a 'barbarous' proletariat, acting '*en masse* with a success which no class or order of men not bound together by religious ties has ever succeeded in attaining to before.'[53]

Above all, Salisbury fought to defend the whole structure of political authority, property rights and social hierarchy that gave him and his caste a moral *raison d'être*. It seemed to him that the approach of democracy threatened it at almost every point. In Denmark and the northern states of America, it had led the upper classes to abandon political life, leaving it to 'educated men who have lost their character, and ... ready-tongued adventurers'.[54] This could easily happen in Britain; in large constituencies it was starting to do so. The Anglican Church, a crucial bulwark of social and political authority, was also in the firing line. For dissent and democracy were natural allies; dissenting chapels were 'earthworks and blockhouses for the maintenance of an untiring political guerilla'.[55] Worst of all, democracy threatened property, the heart and soul of the established order. 'To give the suffrage to a poor man is to give him as large a part in determining that legislation which is mainly concerned with property as the banker whose name is known on every exchange in Europe. ... [T]wo day labourers shall outvote Baron Rothschild.'[56]

In 1867, however, the 'Artless Dodger' won and Salisbury lost. There was no point in fighting the battles of the 1860s all over again. Salisbury made peace with the loathed Disraeli, and between 1874 and 1880 served under him, first as Secretary of State for India and then as Foreign Secretary. When Gladstone's second government extended household suffrage to the counties in 1884, Salisbury, by now Conservative leader in the Lords, acquiesced. But that did not mean that he no longer saw democracy as a threat to the social order. As he saw it, his task now was to divert the democratic currents unleashed in 1867 into harmless channels: to 'discipline popular government'.[57] These became the central themes of his statecraft. They posed formidable political difficulties. Once the battle over a wider suffrage had been lost, overt opposition to the very notion of democracy would be dangerous, perhaps suicidal, politically. To resist disintegration effectively, Salisbury had to find new causes, new constituencies and a new language.

He was astonishingly successful. He formed his first government in 1885, and for most of the next twenty years his surprisingly supple tory nationalism dominated the political stage. The Liberals' 1886 split over Irish Home Rule – the last, doomed cause of Gladstone's political life – gave him his opportunity. The secession of the Liberal Unionists, whose ranks included distinguished Liberal intellectuals like the Oxford jurist, Albert Venn Dicey, whig magnates like Lord Hartington, the heir to the Duke of Devonshire, and the charismatic radical hero, Joseph Chamberlain, procured a party realignment whose effects could still be detected a century later.

The Liberals were toppled from their perch as the normal party of government. Their place seemed to have been taken by a new, Conservative-dominated social and political coalition, embracing business leaders and the so-called 'Villa Tories' of the suburbs as well as the landed interest.

Hand in hand with the party realignment went a deeper realignment of feeling and of perception. The Conservatives ceased to be the party of land, and became the party of property as such. Above all, they also became the party of empire and of nation. Under Salisbury, and in large part thanks to him, the British empire acquired 6 million square miles of territory, containing around 100 million people; more importantly he fended off the threat of Irish Home Rule.

The Home Rule battle went to the heart of the British state and Britain's identity. Gladstone hoped to reconstruct the state on pluralistic, Burkean lines. Ireland would remain in the United Kingdom and the British empire, but it would belong to a different kind of United Kingdom and therefore to a different kind of empire. Salisbury's adamantine opposition to this project stemmed, in part, from political calculation. He could see that Irish Home Rule stuck in the gullets of many moderate Liberals and correctly thought he could use it to break open the increasingly fissiparous Liberal coalition. But his reaction had deeper roots than that. The vision of nation and identity implicit in the Home Rule legislation was abhorrent to him. Three years before the Home Rule Bill was introduced, he warned:

> The highest interests of the Empire, as well as the most sacred obligations of honour, forbid us to solve [the Irish] question by conceding any species of independence to Ireland. ... It would be an act of political bankruptcy, an avowal that we were unable to satisfy even the most sacred obligations, and that all claims to protect or govern any one beyond our narrow island were at an end.[58]

In opposition to Gladstone's fuzzy, pluralistic vision of the British state and identity, Salisbury offered a bleak, clear, intransigent and non-negotiable vision of an English empire and an English identity. For twenty years, the politics of intransigent Englishness trumped the politics of pluralistic power-sharing within the United Kingdom. In a foretaste of Margaret Thatcher's similarly intransigent nationalism nearly 100 years later, they also trumped the politics of class.

The Salisbury coalition barely outlived its creator. Salisbury surrendered the seals of office in 1902, a year before his death. In 1903, Chamberlain launched a campaign for protective tariffs, provoking a deep split in the Unionist ranks. In 1906, the Liberals won a crushing election victory. The ensuing Liberal governments curbed the House of Lords, breathed new life into the dead duck of Irish Home Rule and encroached on property rights with an enthusiasm that made Salisbury's worst forebodings seem understated. Instead of protecting authority, order and nationhood, the state seemed bent on undermining them; the spectre of disintegration which Salisbury had held at bay for nearly twenty years now gibbered from the government front bench. Tory nationalist anxieties reached a peak not seen since the 1860s; tory nationalist voices acquired an edge of passion that often bordered on hysteria. In 1909, the House of Lords threw out Lloyd George's radical budget, defying the convention that the Commons were supreme in financial matters; Lord Milner, the austere, craggy former High Commissioner for South Africa and self-styled 'British race patriot', egged on his fellow peers with the notorious cry, 'Damn the consequences.'[59] In the battle over the 1911 Parliament Act abolishing the Lords' legislative veto, the government won the day by making it clear that it was prepared to swamp the built-in Unionist majority in the Lords with new Liberal creations. Even so, more than 100 tory nationalist irreconcilables defied their leaders and voted against the government. (They were known as 'ditchers' because they were willing to die in the last ditch for their privileges. 'Hedgers' voted with the government.)

In the ensuing battles over Irish Home Rule, a swelling tide of anxiety and bitterness led many tory nationalists to defy the authority of the state whose paramount defenders they claimed to be. Unionists denounced Asquith and his colleagues as traitors, engaged, as the Ulster Unionist leader, Edward Carson, put it, in 'the most nefarious conspiracy that has ever been launched against a free people'.[60] Andrew Bonar Law, the morose and self-effacing Unionist leader, declared that he would back Ulster's resistance to Home Rule, no matter what form it took – in effect, giving the paramilitaries in the Unionists' Ulster Volunteer Force a blank cheque. In Northern Ireland itself, Unionists flirted with mutiny, gun running and armed resistance. The crisis ended only with the outbreak of the First World War.

In the whig imperialists' halcyon years between the wars, tory nationalist voices were more quiescent, but they still emitted occasional rumbles. A leading rumbler was William Joynson Hicks (nicknamed 'Jix'), the Conservative Home Secretary from 1924 to 1929, who had once described the Labour leader, Keir Hardie, as 'a leprous traitor', and whose main aim at the Home Office was to 'stem the flood of filth coming across the Channel'.[61] In the 1930s, as the next chapter will show, much more formidable rumbles came from Conservatives fighting against dominion status for India – with Winston Churchill, for most of his career a thoroughgoing whig imperialist, in the van.

In the complacent and consensual Britain of the post-war years, tory nationalism slumbered, but those who expected it to slumber for ever were flying in the face of 300 years of British history.

FOR THE PEOPLE

The democratic collectivist tradition could boast no great figure comparable to Edmund Burke or even Lord Salisbury. Democratic collectivists shared Marx's determinism and, in some cases, his faith in the redemptive powers of the proletariat. But their politics were gradualist and ameliorative, not revolutionary. More importantly, they also drew on a long tradition of technocratic, state-centred, utilitarian radicalism that went back to the legal reformer, Jeremy Bentham, and his great disciple, Edwin Chadwick, the pioneer of public health legislation and part-author of the 1834 New Poor Law. Yet none of these could be credited with its paternity. It was the work of many hands, responding to shifting public preoccupations with different arguments. All the same, certain themes were common to nearly all its exponents. Where the whig imperialist story was one of skilful accommodation to changing circumstances and its tory nationalist equivalent one of looming danger, democratic collectivists told a story of ineluctable advance towards a new and better social order.

Like whig imperialists, democratic collectivists believed that leaders had a duty to lead and assumed that followers would follow if leaders fulfilled that duty. However, the democratic collectivist elites based their claim to authority on superior training, professionalism and expertise, not on the inborn wisdom of Burkean gentlemen. They also had their own distinctive view of the state. Like whig imperialists and tory nationalists, most democratic collectivists were content with the existing British state, but for them, it was the agent of social transformation, guided by science, reason and their own grasp of the dynamics of historical change – legitimate because it was the emanation of an overarching society that transcended the individuals who composed it. Whig imperialists and tory nationalists celebrated the legacy of the past. Democratic collectivists looked forward to a future of emancipation, justice and rationality.

A few examples must suffice. One of the most revealing occurs in a seminal collection of essays published in 1889 by the six-year-old Fabian Society, then a small group of obscure, London-based, socialist intellectuals, with high ideals but little influence. One of the contributors was the still-unknown Irish journalist and would-be novelist, George Bernard Shaw. In the early nineteenth century, Shaw wrote with characteristic impishness, state ownership had not been a practical alternative to private ownership; in those days, incompetence and corruption had been 'inherent state qualities, like the acidity of lemon'. The modern state was a quite different animal.

Make the passing of a sufficient examination an indispensable preliminary to entering the executive; make the executive responsible to the government and the government responsible to the people; and State departments will be provided with all the guarantees for integrity and efficiency that private money-hunting pretends to. Thus the old bugbear of State imbecility did not terrify the Socialist: it only made him a Democrat. But to call himself so simply, would have had the effect of classing him with the ordinary destructive politician who is a Democrat ... for the sake of formal Democracy. ... Consequently we have the distinctive term Social Democrat, indicating the man or woman who desires through Democracy to gather the whole people into the State, so that the State may be trusted with the rent of the country, and finally with the land, the capital, and the organization of the national industry.[62]

'Gathering the whole people into the state' was pitching it high, but, in one form or another, Shaw's confident *étatisme* was fundamental to the democratic collectivist tradition. Democratic collectivists were haunted by suffering, unemployment, poverty, disease, exploitation, greed and what they saw as gross and inexcusable social irrationality. They thought their overriding duty was to do all they could to replace the wasteful, unjust, cruel chaos of the market-place with communal control and planned co-ordination. They took it for granted that this could be done only through the democratically accountable, technocratic and rational state pictured in Shaw's essay. The anarchist dream of an emancipated humanity, living in harmony and justice, free of the coercive power of the state, seemed to them dangerous nonsense. So did the syndicalist vision of working-class self-emancipation through industrial action, followed by direct proletarian democracy at the workplace. Further reforms in the structure of the state were dangerous too. What mattered was to win control over the existing state and to use it to build a better society. Anything else was a frivolous diversion which could only give aid and comfort to the massed vested interests that stood in the way of a new and just social order.

By the early twentieth century, democratic collectivist *étatisme* had acquired a new twist, but it had lost none of its force. Society and the state ceased to be identical as they had been for Shaw. Instead, they became organically connected. In a polemic of 1909, J.A. Hobson, still a 'New' Liberal in politics, argued that a political community had 'conscious interests and ends of its own' and should therefore 'be regarded as "organic"'. The 'general will and wisdom of the Society', he added, were 'embodied in the State'.[63] The young Ramsay MacDonald also insisted that society was an organism, akin to a biological organism. The individual was to society what the cell was to the body. The state was society's 'organised political personality', which 'thinks and feels for the whole'.[64]

MacDonald and Hobson differed over the implications. For MacDonald, measures like the referendum or proportional representation or an elected second chamber sprang from an individualistic conception of democracy, which the organic conception of the state had superseded. Equally, the liberal notion of individual rights against the state was nonsensical. Rights against the state would be rights against society; and to say that individuals had rights against society was like saying that cells had rights against the body. Society's claims on the individual were paramount; the individual had no claims on society. The state did 'not concern itself primarily with man as the possessor of rights, but with man as the doer of duties. A right is the opportunity of fulfilling a duty.'[65]

Even the right to vote was illusory. The case for democracy did not rest on justice or natural rights. It was utilitarian. When the state reached a certain stage in its development, MacDonald argued, it could no longer carry out its functions properly unless it represented the 'experience of all ... rich and poor, propertied and propertyless, the possessor and the dispossessed'.[66] He was strongly in favour of female enfranchisement, but not, he emphasised, to do justice to women. Women should have votes solely because women's experiences differed from men's. Unlike MacDonald, Hobson favoured proportional representation, an elected second chamber and even the referendum, but the differences between them were less important than the similarities. Like MacDonald, Hobson saw the cry 'One man one vote' as 'undiluted individualism', which evolutionary sociology had discredited. The vote was not a right. Rather, it reflected the individual's *'duty* as a member of Society to contribute as best he can to the administration of the common property for the common good'.[67]

Étatisme and determinism went together. Democratic collectivists were for progress; for modernisation; for the future still buried in the womb of the present. They took it for granted that history moved in a fixed, knowable direction; that they knew what that direction was; that a just and rational society would inevitably come into being one day; and that, by virtue of their superior understanding of the dynamics of change, they were duty-bound to overcome the obstacles to its emergence. Ramsay MacDonald's determinism was founded, like his theory of the state, on Darwinian biology. Society evolved as biological organisms evolved. Higher social forms gradually emerged out of lower ones. The pace and direction of this process were determined by society's 'General Will' – an elastic concept borrowed from Rousseau, by way of the Hegelian idealist, Bernard Bosanquet. MacDonald interpreted it to mean society's 'inherited habits, modes of thought, axioms of conduct, traditions of both of thought and activity'.

Often, the General Will was slow to move, but it was now gearing itself up for a period of rapid advance. Industry was the 'nutritive process of Society'; and a whole series of developments, ranging from government inquiries into physical deterioration to the establishment of state old age pensions showed that the existing nutritive system was inadequate. The conclusion was inescapable. Ideas and experiments that would 'establish the rationality and practicability of socialism' were now inevitable. Indeed, socialism was best defined as 'that stage in social organisation when the State organises for Society an adequate nutritive system'. Thanks to democracy, it was now beginning to do so.[68]

More austere versions of the same themes ran through the writings of those quintessential democratic collectivists, Sidney and Beatrice Webb. They were an extraordinary couple. Their marriage was warm and loving, but private happiness came a poor second to the public good: they began their honeymoon with a visit to Dublin to examine the records of Irish trade societies. Sidney was an upwardly mobile *petit bourgeois*; Beatrice was rich. They treated her private income as a lifetime research grant. Thick, heavy books poured from their pens – learned, solid and mostly indigestible. Beatrice supplied the inspiration, Sidney the hard grind. Beatrice's diaries are a rich source for social and political historians; they are also wonderfully entertaining – catty, funny, insightful and occasionally moving. Sidney and Beatrice were not content to investigate. They were also indefatigable oilers of political and administrative wheels, a two-person think-tank, with an uncanny grasp of the possible and a shrewd eye for the up-and-coming. Whenever new ideas were wanted, they stood ready to supply them. Sidney was also an assiduous member of the London County Council and, perhaps because of him, municipalisation ranked higher than nationalisation in the Fabian scheme of things before the First World War.

Like Hobson and MacDonald, the Webbs saw society as an evolving organism, in which collectivist rationality was inexorably replacing individualistic chaos. The process was cumulative and irreversible. 'No nation having nationalized or municipalized any industry,' wrote Sidney Webb complacently, 'has ever retraced its steps or reversed its action.'[69] This was because the growth of collectivism was the product of practical imperatives, not of doctrines – of facts, not of values. 'The "practical man", oblivious or contemptuous of ... general principles of social organisation,' as Webb put it in a later passage in the same book, 'has been forced by the necessities of the time, into an ever deepening collectivist channel.'[70]

In that channel, rights had no place. In a portentous, not to say ominous, semantic conjuring trick, the Webbs redefined 'Liberty' and 'Freedom' to mean 'not any quantum of natural or inalienable rights, but such conditions of existence ... as do, in practice, result in the utmost possible development of faculty in the individual human being'.[71] But in the Webbs' ideal society, individuals would not decide for themselves how to develop their faculties. As Sidney warned sternly, individual development was not a matter of personal cultivation. Its purpose was to equip the individual to fulfil 'his humble function in the great social machine'.[72] Beatrice made the same point in more elevated language. She and her husband, she wrote, wished to 'constrain' the individual, through a better social environment, to become 'a healthier, nobler and more efficient being'.[73]

An obvious question arose. Who dug the collectivist channel in which the Webbs put their evolutionary faith? Here they diverged from Mac-Donald. For MacDonald, the parliamentarian and platform orator, political arguments played a crucial part in distilling and shaping the General Will that drove the evolutionary process. The arguments could, and probably would, come from a minority. In the early nineteenth century, the radicals who followed Jeremy Bentham had been few in number. However, 'the men who were responsible for the work of the legislative organ ... could not help accepting the common-sense of Benthamism,' which reflected the stage that the evolutionary process had then reached. The same thing was now happening with socialism. Few consciously accepted the 'philosophy and utopia of Socialism', but because society had now reached a stage where a socialist common sense corresponded with its needs, socialist principles gave the 'soul of the people' a will and a direction, and furnished it with 'an outlook and a path'.[74]

The Webbs, with their faith in the sovereignty of the fact, saw things slightly differently. For them, the drill sergeants on society's march to greater nobility and efficiency were dispassionate, objective, scientifically trained experts who knew what the facts were. For the facts were collectivist by definition. A trivial but revealing example of this mindset occurred in 1894. An eccentric solicitor, Henry Hutchinson, left £10,000 (around £760,000 at today's prices) to further the purposes of the Fabian Society 'and its Socialism'. Sidney Webb, the president of the charitable trust set up under Hutchinson's will, persuaded his fellow trustees to spend most of the money on setting up a School of Economics and Political Science. (It eventually became the London School of Economics.) This curious transaction caused the Webbs no qualms. On the face of it the LSE had nothing in common with Hutchinson's wishes. It was not intended to be a socialist institution, nor did it become one. But, for the Webbs, this was irrelevant. Its function was to develop the social sciences and train social scientists; and no matter what values individual social scientists might hold, the social sciences were bound to point in the direction that the Webbs thought society should take. The just and rational society of the future would be hewn from the rock of British empiricism, with no help from cloudy philosophical speculation.

The 1914–18 war brought changes of emphasis and vocabulary. The democratic collectivists of the pre-war years had assumed that the capitalist market economy was successful in its own terms, however gross the waste and injustice that disfigured it. Now it looked as if capitalism was failing and might be in crisis. The great question of the age was no longer how to use the surplus produced by a successful economy, but how to put a decrepit economy back on its feet. After sterling's forced departure from the gold standard in 1931 and the Labour Party's crushing defeat in the subsequent general election, talk of a capitalist crisis became almost de rigueur on the left. All this gave a new edge and urgency to democratic collectivist debates.

Yet the old determinism marched on. At the 1923 Labour Party conference, Sidney Webb complacently declared that socialism was coming 'with the inevitability of gradualness'.[75] Faced with the tumults of the 1930s, he and his wife changed their minds about gradualness, but not about inevitability. Gradualness, Beatrice Webb confessed in a diary entry early in 1931, might not be inevitable after all. However, she saw no reason to abandon her lifelong faith in ineluctable progress towards a collectivist future. Mendel, she remembered, had taught that biological evolution proceeded through 'sudden jumps', and the Communist experiment in Russia exemplified the 'Mendelian view'.[76]

After the 1931 crisis, this train of thought led the Webbs to undertake a voyage of sociological discovery to the Soviet Union, then in the throes of savage repression and devastating man-made famine, to which they were blind. But their reaction to their visit reveals more than simple credulity. They followed it with their last major work, *Socialist Communism, A New Civilisation?* (In the second edition, the question mark was deleted.) At the end of the book, they asked themselves whether 'this new civilisation, with its abandonment of the incentive of profit-making, its extinction of unemployment, its planned production for community consumption, and the consequent liquidation of the landlord and the capitalist' would spread to other countries. Their answer was a confident: '"Yes, it will".'[77] The reader can almost hear their sigh of relief at having found a new focus for the determinism that they had preached for forty years.

The Webbs were a special case and by the 1930s an uninfluential one. Although Marxist-Leninism made more strides in the 1930s than ever before, most democratic collectivists stuck to their belief in progress through the democratic state and spurned the light from the Soviet East. However, many thought the crisis of the times called for much faster progress, and a stronger state with fewer protections for minorities. Their most eloquent (and least likely) champion was Sir Stafford Cripps, a brilliant, eloquent, highly paid barrister of upper-class origins, who had served briefly as Solicitor-General in the second Labour Government, and went on to become an unusually dominant Chancellor of the Exchequer after the war. Cripps was haunted by the spectre of capitalist sabotage. To prevent it, he insisted that when Labour returned to office it would have to push through an Emergency Powers Act on its first day, to limit parliamentary debating time, to make more use of delegated legislation, to set up 'Socialist Regional Councils' and to abolish the House of Lords. Conceivably, capitalist resistance might take the form of a military dictatorship. If the Socialist Government thought that was a 'real danger', its best response would be to turn itself into a dictatorship, pending another election.[78]

Others were more optimistic. Hugh Dalton, a booming-voiced, intrigue-obsessed Old Etonian, who had become a central figure in Labour policy-making and would be the party's first post-war Chancellor, also wished to streamline parliamentary procedure, but saw no need to acquire emergency powers. After all, history was already moving towards socialism; Labour's task was to give history a further push. The laissez-faire of individualist theory 'belonged to a short and peculiar phase in our history which has already passed away'. A Labour Government committed to 'social planning' would be running with the grain of the times.[79] At the end of the decade, Evan Durbin, an Economics Lecturer at LSE, and later a Labour junior minister who died tragically at the age of forty-two in a bathing accident, published *The Politics of Democratic Socialism* – a much more ambitious attempt to restate the democratic collectivist vision in the idiom of the day.[80] In it, gradualness and inevitability both received a kiss of life.

Thanks to the coming of democracy and the rise of the trade unions, Durbin argued, the market economy had ceased to function properly. However, democracy and trade-union power were irreversible. Only economic planning offered a way out of the impasse. A planned economy would entail the creation of a Supreme Economic Authority in charge of an extensive nationalised sector. Only a strong state could do all this; but the existing British state was perfectly suited to the task. Like MacDonald thirty years before, Durbin had no truck with liberal reforms designed to give more weight to minority opinions. And he underpinned his political argument with an ethic of holistic social transcendence that would have warmed MacDonald's heart:

The interests of the whole are sovereign over the interests of the part. In society we are born; in society we must live. To the centralized control of a democratic Community our livelihood and our security must be submitted. It is the business of society to secure the welfare of all. To do so it must be able to set limits to the welfare of each one of us.[81]

BY THE PEOPLE

The democratic republican story is the most difficult to summarise. The storytellers were the awkward squad of British democracy – outsiders by temperament, not insiders. In the language of the economic historian R.H. Tawney, one of the most attractive of them, they were 'the salt in the heap, the leaven in the lump'.[82] They suffered repeated defeats, but after each defeat their tradition re-emerged from the ruins. Its boundaries were peculiarly fluid. Sometimes democratic republican themes were mixed up with a resentful populism, alien to the austere and testing conception of citizenship that its rhetoric implied. Many democratic republicans had a streak of democratic collectivism in their make-up; a few had a streak of whig imperialism. Some flirted with democratic collectivism at one stage in their lives, only to abandon it later. Some moved towards democratic collectivism as circumstances changed.

Democratic republicans shared the whig imperialists' localism and humanism, but they had no truck with Burkean gentlemen or the British tradition of autonomous executive power. Many of them shared the democratic collectivists' commitment to equality, but they interpreted that slippery term in a different way. They were for fellowship and dignity more than economic equality. They put their faith in the kinetic energy of ordinary citizens, and rejected the determinism that lay at the heart of the democratic collectivist tradition. And most democratic republicans abhorred *étatiste* social engineering. Tawney spoke for many when he asked how anyone would be willing to live in a Fabian 'paralytic paradise' and confessed that Beatrice Webb's talk of a regime of 'mental and moral hygiene' froze his blood.[83]

The democratic republican tradition went back to the Levellers in the seventeenth century and the Paineites in the eighteenth, yet it reached more widely than either. One of the first democratic republican storytellers was John Milton – scrivener's son, secretary for foreign tongues under the Commonwealth and the greatest English poet after Shakespeare. There are strong traces of democratic republicanism in John Stuart Mill, in the

middle-class municipal radicals of the nineteenth century, in the proletarian
syndicalists of the early twentieth, in the so-called 'Guild Socialism' of the
prolific and intellectually restless socialist thinker, G.D.H. Cole, and in the
writings of A.D. ('Sandy') Lindsay, the Labour-voting Master of Balliol
between the wars. However, the most resonant democratic republican utterances of the twentieth century came from Tawney himself – tough-minded
patriot, devoted Francophile, prophet of equal citizenship and master of a
rich, ironic, frequently ambiguous and sometimes almost biblical English
prose.

From Milton and the Levellers onwards, three overlapping themes
sounded through democratic republican rhetoric: republican self-respect
versus monarchical servility; civic activity versus slothful apathy; and, most
of all, government by vigorous discussion and mutual learning versus passive
deference to monarch, capitalist or state. Milton's thunderous treatment of
the first theme is as evocative today as it was 350 years ago. He wrote in the
tradition of 'neo-Roman' liberty for which dependence on another's will
was, in itself, a denial of freedom.[84] To say that the king had a hereditary
right to the crown, he declared in one of his great apologias for regicide,
was 'to make the subject no better than the king's slave, his chattel, or his
possession that may be sold at will'.[85] He returned to that theme on the eve
of the Restoration, when he made a last desperate attempt to hold back the
monarchical tide. To bring back the king, he wrote, would be to bring back
'the base necessity of court flatteries and prostrations'. It would be an
'ignominy' for a people which had won 'their liberty in the field ... basely
and besottedly to run their necks into the yoke which they have broken'.[86]
Although Milton's target was monarchy, the same case could be made against
other forms of hierarchy and in later generations it would be.

But Milton's denunciations of ignominy went unheard. The king
returned. The 'good old cause' was vanquished. For a while Milton went in
fear of his life. Republican liberty seemed an impossible dream. To understand what Milton meant by it, we should go back to the most exhilarating
of his prose writings, his immortal attack on censorship, *Areopagitica*. It was
published in 1644, the year of Cromwell's great victory at Marston Moor.
(It hardly needs saying that Milton's defence of free expression did not cover
Roman Catholics.) For Milton, the censors' central premise – that virtue
needed protection from vice – was not just false: it was the reverse of the
truth.

There was no merit in a 'fugitive and cloistered virtue unexercised and
unbreathed, that never sallies out and sees her adversary'; true virtue proved
itself in intellectual combat. The same applied to the extraordinary ferment
of ideas in revolutionary London. The city was the 'mansion house of

liberty'. It was full of 'heads ... sitting by their studious lamps, musing, searching, revolving new notions and ideas': the capital of a nation 'of a quick, ingenious and piercing spirit; acute to invent, subtle and sinewy to discourse'. Yet far from weakening the parliamentary cause, the clash of ideas was one of its chief assets. It was through 'disputing, reasoning, reading, inventing, discoursing' that the people acquired their 'gallant bravery and well-grounded contempt of their enemies'. (George Orwell said the same thing in different words when he called for a socialist war in 1940.)

Altogether, an extraordinary process of national regeneration was under way:

> Methinks I see in my mind a noble and puissant nation rousing herself like a strong man after sleep, and shaking her invincible locks; methinks I see her as an eagle mewing her mighty youth, and kindling her undazzled eyes at the full midday beam, purging and unscaling her long-abused sight at the fountain itself of heavenly radiance, while the whole noise of timorous and flocking birds, with those also that love the twilight, flutter about, amazed at what she means.[87]

These were astonishing claims. Milton was trying to subvert the age-old assumption that the wise and holy had a lien on the truth, and therefore a right and duty to impose their views on everyone else.[88] He was not a democrat any more than he was a Leveller, yet his challenge to that assumption was quintessentially democratic: poor as well as rich, unschooled as well as learned, could and did take part in the subtle and sinewy discoursing that he celebrated. But it was democratic in a special way. It did not point to a democracy of head-counting; it pointed to a democracy of vigorous and sustained collective deliberation.

Although Milton's effervescent mixture of republicanism and patriotism was unique, there was more than a touch of it in the civic radicalism of the mid- and late nineteenth century. Civic radicalism was first cousin to religious nonconformity. Joseph Chamberlain, the radical Lord Mayor of Birmingham before he entered Parliament, was a unitarian; Robert Dale, one of the most influential of the city's radical politicians, was a congregationalist minister as well as being part-founder of the intended power-house of dissenting theology, Mansfield College, Oxford. And the nonconformists of the nineteenth century were the spiritual descendants of the seventeenth-century puritans whose 'discoursing' Milton lauded. The iconography of the great Northern city halls told the same story. Some were Victorian Gothic; some mimicked Renaissance palazzi. All conveyed a message of civic regeneration reminiscent of Milton's message of national regeneration. It was epitomised in Robert Dale's description of the mood he saw spreading through Birmingham in the late 1860s. At ward meetings, he wrote, the protagonists spoke

> of making the town cleaner, sweeter and brighter; of providing gardens and parks and museums; they insisted that great monopolies like the gas and water supply should be in the hands of the corporation ... Sometimes an adventurous orator would excite his audience by dwelling on the glories of Florence, and of the other cities of Italy in the Middle Ages, and suggest that Birmingham too might become the home of a noble literature and art.[89]

Meanwhile, John Stuart Mill had added a new ingredient to Milton's case for a democracy of deliberation and mutual education. Like Milton, he had no time for cloistered virtue. Truth could be established only in open and continuous contest with error. But Mill, the well-known champion of individual liberty, was also Mill, the less familiar prophet of collective practice. He was for limited government and laissez-faire, but for moral rather than economic reasons: because he feared that an over-mighty state would choke the springs of personal growth and public spirit. If the state did too much, there would be no space where the public could learn the practices of active citizenship. The consequences would be disastrous. A people who lacked the habit of 'spontaneous action for a collective interest' would be governed like 'sheep by their shepherd'.[90]

In all this, Mill leaned heavily on the aristocratic French liberal, Alexis de Tocqueville, whose *Democracy in America* was one of the talking points of the age. Against his early misgivings de Tocqueville found that, thanks to municipal self-government and the vigorous political culture it fostered, American democracy went hand in hand with political freedom. Mill drew two conclusions. The first was that local self-government was a prerequisite for self-government on the national level. '[A]s we do not learn to read or write, to ride or swim, by merely being told how to do it, but by doing it,' he wrote in a pregnant passage, 'so it is only by practising popular government on a limited scale, that the people will ever learn how to exercise it on a larger.'[91] The second conclusion went further. Civic activism would widen horizons, strengthen communal bonds and ennoble the individual citizen, who would come to see not only that 'the common weal is his weal, but that it partly depends on his exertions.'[92] (The establishment of parish councils by Lord Rosebery's Liberal Government in 1894 testified to Mill's enduring influence in Liberal politics.) A century after Mill, 'Sandy' Lindsay reached the same destination by a different route. For Lindsay, democracy was not primarily about majority decision. What mattered was that everyone should have a chance to contribute to the debate before the decision was taken, and that could happen only in the smaller groups that made up the wider society.[93]

Lindsay and Mill viewed society, not perhaps from the top down but certainly from the middle down. The syndicalists who championed industrial against political democracy in the early years of the last century viewed it from the bottom up. Many of them started as parliamentary socialists. Their most famous leader, the prince of agitators, Tom Mann, stood for Parliament in 1895. Yet he and his followers were disillusioned by the agonising sluggishness of parliamentary Labour's march towards the promised land. They turned to syndicalism – an originally French doctrine, strongly tinged with anarchism, that proposed a strategy of unremitting class war through strike action at the point of production as an alternative to the compromising twists and turns of conventional politics. There was more to syndicalism than direct industrial action, however. It offered an alternative, essentially democratic republican vision of a socialist society. The most resonant syndicalist manifesto, *The Miners' Next Step*, published in the heart of the turbulent South Wales coalfield in 1912, distilled the vision in rhetoric reminiscent of the Levellers and Milton. A Central Production Board would 'ascertain the needs of the people', but it would be left 'to the men themselves to determine under what conditions and how the work should be done. This would be real democracy in real life, making for real manhood and womanhood. Any other form of democracy is a delusion and a snare.'[94] Democratic collectivists were appalled; Sidney Webb memorably scoffed that the cry of the land for the labourer and the mine for the miner might well be augmented by 'the sewer for the sewerman'.[95] But though full-blown syndicalism soon fizzled out, residues of it would pop up again and again in the course of the century, sometimes in ill-fitting *Marxisant* clothes that distracted attention from their real meaning.

The same fate befell G.D.H. Cole's 'Guild Socialism' – an attempt to find a middle way between state socialism and syndicalism that flourished around the time of the First World War. It inspired an elaborate scheme for economic and political reorganisation. Control of industry would be vested in 'National Guilds' of workers by hand and brain, balanced by consumer co-operatives and a minimal state. But Guild Socialist theories matter less than the mood and tone of the movement. Like syndicalism, Guild Socialism was a cry of revolt – against capitalism, of course, but also against bureaucracy, hierarchy, subordination and unaccountable power. Cole epitomised it in a phrase that could have come from Lilburne or Paine. When asked what was society's 'fundamental evil', he wrote, most people 'would answer POVERTY when they ought to answer SLAVERY'.[96] Guild Socialism got nowhere, but the dream of industrial citizenship flickered on.

Tawney joins the dramatis personae of democratic republicanism at this point. He was an extraordinary mixture – an amalgam of English gentleman, gradualist committee-man and Old Testament prophet, an insider who would have liked to be an outsider. By birth and formation he belonged to the confident, public-spirited, upper-middle-class salariat; and, as befitted his origins, there was a strong element of democratic collectivism in his thought. He was born in 1880 in Calcutta, where his father was principal of Presidency College. William Beveridge, the author of the wartime report on the social services that set the scene for the post-war welfare state, was his brother-in-law. Like Beveridge, Tawney was educated at Rugby and (inevitably) at Balliol. After Oxford he became what we would now call a social worker at Toynbee Hall, in London's East End. He taught briefly at Glasgow University and lectured for the Workers' Educational Association (WEA) in Lancashire and the Potteries; his classes, he insisted, taught him more than he taught them. He enlisted as a private in the Manchester Regiment during the First World War, refused a commission and rose to be a sergeant. He was grievously wounded in the first day of the Battle of the Somme and narrowly escaped death. A bricklayer who had been beside him in the battle, he remembered later, was the 'man whom of all others I would choose to have beside me at a pinch'.

After the war he spent virtually his entire working life at LSE, where he became Professor of Economic History. He published at least one masterpiece of cultural and economic history, *Religion and the Rise of Capitalism*, and two seminal social-democratic texts, *The Acquisitive Society* and *Equality*, as well as innumerable articles and several other books. He served as president of the WEA for fifteen years and stood unsuccessfully for Parliament on four occasions. He was heroically untidy. At gatherings of young socialists in the Tawneys' flat in Mecklenburgh Square, scraps of 'half eaten food sat among piles of books. Now and then a mouse would hop over the one to get at the other. But Tawney's imperious bearing was not shaken.' He died during the hard winter of 1962–3. At his memorial service, Hugh Gaitskell, then leader of the Labour Party, called him 'the best man I have ever known'.[97]

Tawney has been called a 'prophet of equality', an 'ethical socialist' and a 'Christian socialist', and in his own idiosyncratic fashion he was all of these things. He certainly thought of himself as a socialist. But he was formed intellectually in the years before the First World War, when democratic socialists had so much in common with 'advanced' liberals that it was sometimes hard to tell them apart, and strong traces of the pluralistic liberalism of those days shone through. In good Millian fashion, he believed in the dispersion of power, and looked forward to the day when Birmingham, Manchester and Leeds would be 'little republics'.[98] Religion was a more straightforward influence. Although Tawney was an unostentatious and not particularly observant Christian, his faith lay at the core of his politics. 'The Christian tradition does not deny man's animal nature ...' he wrote. 'But it holds that the most important fact about human beings is not the nature they share with other animals, but their humanity, which, in virtue of the Incarnation, they share with God.'[99] Yet no one could have been less sentimental about those clamant abstractions, the 'working class', the 'masses' and the 'people'; the trenches had inoculated him against sentimentality.

His name for the average, down-to-earth ordinary citizen was 'Henry Dubb'; and, as he put it in a characteristic phrase, 'In the interminable case of *Dubb v. Superior Persons and Co.*, whether Christians, Capitalists or Communists, I am an unrepentant Dubbite.'[100] He was also an unillusioned Dubbite, however. He knew that there could be no democratic culture without Dubb, and he hoped against hope that Dubb would one day help to build it. But he did not allow his hopes to become dupes. 'I have not yet despaired of Henry,' he wrote. 'I consider it not impossible that he may one day wake up; make an angry noise like a man, instead of bleating like a sheep; and in England, at any rate ... win economic freedom.'[101] The 'not yet' and 'not impossible' were distinctly double-edged – more so, perhaps, than Tawney realised himself.

The problem was that Dubb was caught in a vicious circle. Democracy without a democratic culture was a contradiction in terms. But Dubb and his fellow citizens had been shaped by a profoundly undemocratic one. In her transition to political democracy, Tawney wrote in a resonant passage that contains the gist of his vision of democratic citizenship, Britain had undergone 'no inner conversion':

> She accepted it as a convenience, like an improved system of telephones; she did not dedicate herself to it as the expression of a moral ideal of comradeship and equality, the avowal of which would leave nothing the same. She changed her political garments, but not her heart. She carried into the democratic era, not only the institutions, but the social habits and mentality of the oldest and toughest plutocracy in the world ... She went to the ballot box touching her hat.[102]

The great question was how to bring the heart into line with the garments; and this was a cultural and moral question far more than an economic or even a political one. Like most socialists of his generation, Tawney advocated extensive nationalisation as well as increases in social spending. *The Acquisitive Society* is a mordant critique of the functionless property of the *rentier; Equality* focuses, among other things, on the growth of irresponsible corporate power and the need to master it.

But for Tawney, there was a prior question. What mattered was not 'merely whether the State owns and controls the means of production. It is also who owns and controls the State.'[103] Until the people owned and controlled it, as they could not do in the strangulated British version of democracy, the 'religion of inequality' and its 'great god Mumbo-Jumbo' would continue to hold sway. Tawney loathed the servile preoccupation with rank and wealth that he saw all around him, but that was not the only reason why he directed some of his heaviest fire against it. His rhetorical strategy was reminiscent of Paine's 140 years before. He sought to cut through the vicious circle of subordination and submissiveness in which Dubb and his fellows were trapped, and to do that he had to strip away the mystique of hierarchy.

He dreamed of a democracy of free and equal citizens, bowing their knees to no one. He did not know how to achieve it, but he was sure of one thing: that one of the chief obstacles to it was the pre-democratic culture of the British state, with its petty snobberies and pervasive flunkeyism. It followed that institutional change would get nowhere without a change of mentality and feeling; and in his most powerful passages he was more anxious to arouse feelings than to refine arguments.

One example stands for many. In a letter to the *New Statesman*, protesting against the Labour chief whip's acceptance of a knighthood, Tawney asked whether Labour had jettisoned its belief in social equality:

> Or does it suppose that it will convert the public to a belief in Equality if it does not, in its heart, believe in it itself? And does it expect to persuade them of the genuineness of its convictions, if prominent members of the Party sit up, like poodles in a drawing-room, wag their tails when patted, and lick their lips at the social sugar-plums tossed them by their masters? ... It has declared that it is committed to an uncompromising struggle with the plutocracy and all its works. Then why stick in its hair the very feathers which the plutocracy, in its more imbecile moments, loves to wear in its own? ... The truth is, that the whole business of political honours stinks – stinks of snobbery, of the money for which, unless rumour is wholly misleading, a good many of them are sold, of the servile respect for wealth and social position which remains even today the characteristic and contemptible vice of large numbers of our fellow-countrymen.[104]

Milton and Paine would have cheered. But they might have wondered why poodles were still so prevalent.

◐

There were gaps in all these stories, and the storytellers were prone to baffling bouts of cross-dressing. As I implied a moment ago, none of the other traditions had inspired a national Myth to challenge the whig imperialist Myth of Britain and the British. As we shall see in the next few chapters, evolutionary whiggism often overlapped in practice with democratic collectivist determinism. Less obviously, it also overlapped with democratic republicanism. Respect for local traditions and even for local self-government was a favourite trope of whig imperialist rhetoric, and a central theme of the democratic republican world-view. In some ways, democratic republicanism even had something in common with tory nationalism: both drew sustenance from a myth of robust and patriotic ordinary people scorning an effete establishment. Though democratic republicans rejected the British tradition of autonomous executive power and the rituals and practices of the parliamentary monarchy, all the other traditions accepted them with varying degrees of enthusiasm. For whig imperialists and tory nationalists, they were sanctified by history; for democratic collectivists, they were good enough to be going on with.

Still, one point shines through the confusion. In Britain, as elsewhere, democracy was less a sanctuary than an arena. There was no single, monolithic, universally accepted vision of democratic politics and the democratic state. The four traditions I have tried to describe in this chapter were all in constant flux. None of them ever enjoyed a total hegemony; none disappeared irrevocably from the political stage. All of them, in modern times even the tory nationalist tradition, could lay claim to a democratic mantle. Democratic politics in Britain have been the politics of rival *democracies*, not of one, all-embracing democracy. Those politics provide the stuff of my remaining chapters.

PART II
TAMING CAPITALISM

4

GOLDEN CIRCLE

It is a spiritual inheritance which we hold in trust not only for its members, but for all the nations that surround it.

Stanley Baldwin on the British empire, 1927

I have not become the King's First Minister in order to preside over the liquidation of the British Empire.

Winston Churchill, House of Commons, November 1942

This is something you ought to know: each time we have to choose between Europe and the open sea, we shall always choose the open sea. Each time I have to choose between you and Roosevelt, I shall always choose Roosevelt.

Winston Churchill to Charles de Gaulle on the eve of the Normandy invasion, 1944

THE AGE OF BALDWIN

If the nineteenth century was the golden age of whig imperialism, the silver age ran from the early 1920s to the closing years of the Second World War. Its origins were inauspicious. It was built on the ruins of the coalition which Lloyd George had led to a crushing victory in December 1918. There was no obvious explanation for the coalition's collapse. Lloyd George was as magnetic and resourceful as ever. He towered over his Cabinet colleagues and, on the rare occasions when he addressed it, over the House of Commons. By 1922 the government had lost its early bloom, but it had substantial achievements to its credit. It had extended the scope of unemployment insurance, increased old-age pensions, raised the school-leaving age, and launched an ambitious (though only partially successful) programme of slum clearance and house building. Yet its fall was total. Less than four years after his 1918 victory Lloyd George was out of office, never to return.[1]

His fall had little to do with policy. The Cabinet's policy differences did not go deep. It was split over Lloyd George's bellicose approach to the Chanak crisis of October 1922, when his philhellenic enthusiasms seemed likely to drag the country into a pointless war with Turkey, but a majority of the Cabinet was against him, and he soon retreated. Despite Chanak, most Conservative Cabinet ministers wanted the coalition to continue. It was brought down at a famous Carlton Club meeting of Conservative MPs on 19 October 1922, when disgruntled backbenchers and junior ministers successfully revolted against their own leaders' wish to fight an early election under the coalition banner. No great changes of direction followed.

Lloyd George's critics made much of his flagrant sale of honours, but this was a side issue – albeit a revealing one. His real offence lay in his wayward disdain for consistency and, still more, in the unprincipled approach to government that that implied. Keynes caught the central point when he wrote that Lloyd George was 'rooted in nothing; he is void and without content; he lives and feeds on his immediate surroundings; he is an instrument and a player at the same time which plays on the company and is played on by them'.[2] The struggle between the Conservative rebels and Lloyd George was a struggle between two responses to the coming of democracy. Lloyd George's conception of democratic politics was populist, not parliamentary; and he saw himself both as the shaper and as the medium of the popular will from which his authority came. As Kenneth Morgan, the historian of the coalition, puts it, he wished to 'vault over parties, pressure-groups, and parliament to communicate with the mass electorate',[3] and he had a chameleon-like ability to switch from one political identity to another, as circumstances changed.

His Conservative critics found all this abhorrent. During the war, he had vaulted over the Liberal Party, destroying it in the process. The Asquithian Liberals had become a marginalised sect. The Coalition Liberals were little more than the praetorian guard of an unaccountable and unpredictable elective dictator. Conservatives feared that if Lloyd George had his way, the same fate would overtake them. Behind that fear lay a greater one. The whig imperialist and tory nationalist traditions which were the warp and woof of the Conservative Party were suffused with the history and culture of Britain's parliamentary monarchy. For Conservatives of almost all stripes, the great challenge of the time was to ensure that the established institutions and norms of the British state, and the interlocking elites associated with them, retained their old authority in the bewildering new world of mass democracy. In their eyes, the Crown, the Church, the Cabinet, the Bank of England, Parliament, party, the armed forces and the senior civil service were part of a wider structure of leadership and consent which they were duty-bound to defend.

The anti-coalitionist Conservatives saw Lloyd George's populism as a threat to the stability on which all established authority depended. They were right to do so. Lloyd George viewed the institutions, norms and elites that his Conservative opponents fought to preserve with indifference bordering on contempt. They shackled his freedom of action and clogged up the channels through which he communicated with the people. He had escaped from them in 1916 and the last thing he wanted was to return to them. Before the war, J.A. Hobson had warned that, in the absence of effective checks and balances, Britain might lurch into 'Caesarism'.[4] Lloyd George's inconstant populism underlined the point, but his fall showed that the time for a British Caesar had not yet come.

⚜

Lloyd George's Brutus was the unlikely, unglamorous, almost unknown figure of Stanley Baldwin, the 55-year-old President of the Board of Trade. To everyone's surprise, it turned out that he had mastered the arts of popular politics as successfully as had Lloyd George himself. He had served in the Cabinet for only eighteen months. Before that he had been an inconspicuous junior minister for four years, and an obscure, virtually silent, backbencher for nine. Yet his attack on Lloyd George at the Conservatives' Carlton Club meeting in October 1922 was a masterpiece of carefully modulated rhetoric. He conceded that Lloyd George's ally, the Conservative Lord Chancellor, Lord Birkenhead, was right in saying that the Prime Minister was 'a dynamic force'. Then he added, in one of the most deadly political phrases of the century: 'A dynamic force is a very terrible thing; it may crush you, but it is not necessarily right.'[5] After that, the coalition was dead.

In the Conservative Government that followed its break-up, Baldwin became Chancellor of the Exchequer. When the Prime Minister, Andrew Bonar Law, resigned on health grounds in May 1923, Baldwin shot to the top of the greasy pole as Prime Minister. In December 1923, he called an unexpected general election to obtain a mandate for protective tariffs. It produced a hung Parliament in which the Conservatives were the largest party but lacked an overall majority. Baldwin resigned and Ramsay Mac-Donald became Prime Minister, at the head of Britain's first Labour Government. After nine months, the government fell; and in the general election of October 1924 the Conservatives won a crushing victory, with Baldwin at their head. He was the leading figure in three out of the four British governments that held office between 1924 and his retirement in 1937. He was also the chief architect of the Whig imperialist ascendancy that lasted, in one form or another, until the end of the Second World War and it was stamped through and through with his complex impress.

His public persona was far from complex. It was disarmingly straightforward, even simple. Baldwin presented himself as an ordinary man, who merely happened to be Prime Minister. In his first, brilliantly successful election broadcast he apologised to the listeners for interrupting the regular programme and insisted that, unlike Ramsay MacDonald, who had preceded him, he was 'no orator'.[6] Sometimes he seemed to suggest that he was not even a politician: had he not been leader of the Conservative Party, he declared in another broadcast, 'I should like to be leader of the people who do not belong to any party.'[7] Not only did he stress his ordinariness; when photographers were present (as they frequently were) he presented himself as, above all, an ordinary countryman – pipe-smoking, clad in a baggy tweed suit, striding along leafy lanes with a dog and a stick, and redolent of the timeless verities of the English shires. His rhetoric was designed to underscore his image as the embodiment of rural serenity in the age of the hard-faced city slicker and the bitter, clamorous class warrior. He was more at home, he contrived to suggest, with 'the tinkle of the hammer on the anvil in the country smithy, the corncrake on a dewy morning, the sound of the scythe against the whetstone, and the sight of a plough team coming up over the brow of a hill'[8] than with the hustle and bustle of Westminster and the public platform. It was the politics of anti-politics – or the populism of the anti-populist.

All this was a product of the art that conceals art. Baldwin spoke to and for an England of the imagination with which his own biography – to say nothing of the biographies of most English people – was at odds. He loved the Worcestershire countryside where he grew up, but he was not a countryman in any normal sense of the term. His father was an innovative and successful iron-master, who transformed the family firm, through judicious amalgamations, into a big, multi-divisional public company, with more than 4000 employees and large overseas sales. Until his appointment as a junior Treasury minister in 1917, Baldwin himself was a senior manager in this company – a classic exemplar of the British version of emerging corporate capitalism. His self-proclaimed lack of oratorical skill was equally misleading. In truth, he was a master of evocative, beautifully phrased but economical rhetoric, skilfully tailored to his audiences. And he was not in the least ordinary. (No Prime Ministers are.) His phlegmatic, easygoing, pipe-smoking exterior was belied by a host of nervous mannerisms – twitchings of the eye, snappings of the thumbs and fingers, flickings of the tongue before making speeches, staccato grunts, curious humming noises, and a strange habit of sniffing objects of all kinds, particularly books.[9] Despite, or perhaps thanks to, the nervous tension that these mannerisms revealed, he was a highly effective and occasionally ruthless political operator.

It was not for nothing that Winston Churchill called him 'the most formidable politician' he had come across in his public life.[10]

Two great questions preoccupied him: how to respond to the challenge of democracy and the rise of Labour; and how to reconcile Britain's imperial role and identity with overstretched resources and emerging nationalist movements. Baldwin viewed both through a whig imperialist prism. Like the Whigs in 1831–2, he thought the political and social order was under threat, partly from the deterioration in public standards caused by Lloyd George and his 'thieves' kitchen',[11] but much more from the unanticipated consequences of a wider suffrage. There were 'millions of untrained and inexperienced voters' who might be seduced by 'specious appeals';[12] thanks to the rise of Labour, a new and dangerous class politics put the capitalist system at risk. Democracy was on trial and there was no telling what the verdict would be. Given that Athenian democracy had lasted for only a century, there could be no certainty that British democracy would do better.[13] For destructive passions were forcing their way to the surface of politics. In a vivid passage in 1925 Baldwin warned:

[C]ivilisation is but the ice formed in process of ages on the turbulent stream of unbridled human passions, and while this ice seemed to our fathers secure and permanent, it has [now] rotted and cracked ... and in places the submerged torrent has broken through, leaving fragments in constant collision threatening by their attrition to diminish and ultimately disappear.[14]

Also like the Whigs, he believed that the answer was inclusion. His aim was to take the edge off class conflict, and to avert the constitutional and economic threat that class politics seemed likely to bring in its train. That entailed integrating Labour into the political order, much as the £10 householders had been integrated in 1832; and integration had to do with emotion and mentality even more than with interest. He sought, he explained, 'to get at the soul of working people'.[15] His favourite weapon was rhetoric, directed to his own followers as well as to Labour. He insisted that he was a 'healer'; that trade unions were 'indispensable'; that 'industrial absolutism' was out of date; even that there was a good, altruistic, idealistic side to the Labour Party's socialism, as well as a misguided one.

His stance was epitomised in his greatest Commons speech, delivered a few months after his crushing 1924 victory. He made it in opposition to a widely supported Conservative private members' bill changing the law on the trade-union political levy. Union members would have to 'contract in' if they wished to pay the levy, instead of 'contracting out' if they did not.

Whilst this would remove a long-standing Conservative grievance, it would also endanger the Labour Party's finances. Baldwin dwelt lovingly on the paternalistic harmony of his family's firm where he 'had known from childhood every man on the ground'. Then he turned to the changes that were squeezing out small firms and giving birth to great amalgamations on both sides of industry, and insisted that, sooner or later, there would have to be a 'pretty close partnership' between them. His peroration epitomised his domestic statecraft:

> We stand for peace. We stand for the removal of suspicion in the country. We want to create an atmosphere, a new atmosphere in a new Parliament for a new age, in which people can come together. . . .
>
> Although I know that there are those who work for different ends from most of us in this House, yet there are many in all ranks and all parties who will re-echo my prayer: 'Give peace in our time, O Lord.'[16]

After he sat down at least one Labour MP was seen with tears running down his cheeks. It was a Burkean moment.

✑

Words matter; and Baldwin's words helped to shape the history of the British political economy. When it came to deeds, things were more complicated. The inclusion strategy met with little opposition from the political Labour Party. Labour's leaders wanted nothing better than to be included. As befitted good democratic collectivists, they had no quarrel with the assumptions and practices of the existing British state. They too wanted to banish the spectre of Lloyd Georgian populism; they too looked forward to a stable Conservative versus Labour party system in place of the old Conservative versus Liberal one. The minority Labour Governments of 1924 and 1929–31 testified vividly to this shared interest. Before the 1924 government took office, political circles resounded with talk of a Conservative–Liberal alliance to keep Labour out, but Baldwin made it clear that he would have no truck with anything of the sort.

His reward was a huge step towards the Conservative versus Labour party system that he wanted to see. 'The Liberals get meaner and meaner,' MacDonald noted in a revealing diary entry in March 1924, 'and we respect the Conservatives more and more.'[17] Labour's private respect for the Conservatives went hand in hand with public respect for tradition. Pre-war talk of a radical change in the role and structure of the Cabinet was forgotten. The only departure from established custom was that ministers were allowed to smoke during meetings. When the Transport and General Workers'

Union threatened to bring London's transport to a halt, the government proclaimed a state of emergency under the Coalition Government's Emergency Powers Act. Thanks to insistent pressure from King George V, some ministers even wore Court dress to attend levees at Buckingham Palace, MacDonald chief among them. More generally, the government was spectacularly successful in foreign affairs and boringly competent at home – the perfect combination for a party whose chief priority was to prove that it could govern successfully by the established rules. The aftermath of its fall in October 1924 was a further bonus. Not only did the Conservatives win a big Commons majority, but Labour increased its vote by 1 million, despite losing forty seats. The Liberals were slaughtered, losing 118 seats and more than a million votes.

The second Labour Government followed a very different path, but the eventual outcome was much the same. Though still in a minority, Labour was the largest party. MacDonald returned to office with the wind set fair for a majority Labour Government in the not-too-distant future. But, within a few months of taking office, the government was overwhelmed by the deepest depression in the history of capitalism. Unemployment rose inexorably to unprecedented levels. Ministers twisted hither and thither in search of a solution, but they were deadlocked over all the proposals on offer. Protection was ruled out by Labour's traditional free-trade faith and the adamantine intransigence of the chief keeper of the flame, the Chancellor of the Exchequer, Philip Snowden. The Treasury and the Ministry of Transport shot down the much-touted nostrum of loan-financed public works, favoured by economic radicals such as Keynes, Lloyd George and the future leader of British Fascism, Oswald Mosley. Harsh deflation was blocked by Labour's primordial commitment to defend the living standards of the working class.

In August 1931, the government ignominiously imploded when a sizeable Cabinet minority, led by the Foreign Secretary, Arthur Henderson, followed the TUC in refusing to accept a package of spending cuts to halt an accelerating sterling crisis. In response to the king's gruff appeal to his patriotism and sense of duty, and against his original inclinations, MacDonald then formed an allegedly non-party National Government. It went on to win a landslide victory in the general election of October 1931, but MacDonald was the prisoner of an overwhelmingly Conservative majority. Though he hung on as Prime Minister for four years of failing health and growing misery, everyone knew that Baldwin was the pivot around which the government turned. Labour suffered the worst defeat in its history and emerged with fewer seats than in 1918. But inclusion still beckoned. After a sharp but short swing to the left, it returned to a refurbished version of the moderate, constitutional statecraft of the 1920s. In 1935, MacDonald at last resigned and Baldwin took his place. In the general election that followed a few months later, the now obviously Conservative-dominated National Government won another three-figure majority.

Yet Labour had a higher share of the vote than ever before. The Liberals were crushed, winning only twenty seats. A stable new two-party system had finally come into existence. The Liberals were no longer serious contenders for power, and Labour was unmistakably the kind of party that MacDonald and Baldwin had both wanted it to be. Clement Attlee, the party leader, was a spare, trim, laconic Old Haileyburian, who was always referred to as 'Major Attlee'. Herbert Morrison, his only serious rival for the leadership, was the son of a policeman, a staunch MacDonaldite before 1931, the chief architect of the London Labour Party that controlled the LCC for a generation, and an assiduous courtier of the so-called 'black-coated worker'. Both exuded caution, moderation and constitutional propriety.

Better still from Baldwin's point of view, the Conservative Party was unquestionably the senior partner in this new system. The old Salisbury social coalition, which had come to grief at the beginning of the century, had been replaced by a broader Baldwin coalition, that embraced barnacled diehards like Churchill's boon companion, Lord Birkenhead, and social and economic radicals like the young Harold Macmillan. It covered virtually the entire nation, geographically, sociologically and culturally. Labour was the party of the old industrial regions and the unionised, blue-collar working class. These gave it a solid base, on which its grip was virtually unshakeable, but beyond its base it was in a hopeless minority. All the omens suggested that the Conservatives' victory in 1935 would be followed by another victory in the following election. In the sphere of party politics, Baldwinian Whiggery had worked.

❧

One reason was that Baldwin did not confine himself to political inclusion. He groped for two more problematic forms of inclusion as well – social and industrial. Under the 1924 Conservative Government, and again under the National Governments of the 1930s, the confused medley of welfare services bequeathed by the pre-war Liberal Government and the post-war coalition became more coherent and more generous. Three examples stand out. Thanks largely to the restless reforming zeal and administrative drive of the shy, angular, superficially cold Minister of Health, Neville Chamberlain, the 1924 Government introduced contributory old-age pensions at sixty-five, and carried through a far-reaching reconstruction of local government, presaging the break-up of the Poor Law. The 1931 National Government went much further. The 1934 Unemployment Act put unemployment insurance on a sound financial footing for the first time since the early 1920s. A statutory commission was set up to administer it. An Unemployment Assistance Board took over responsibility for other forms of unemployment relief; the levels of these were to be determined by national measurements of need. The Board's initial scales produced a cut in payment levels in many places and provoked a furious outcry, but the new system settled down after the government made it more flexible. The important thing was that the ghost of the hated 1834 Poor Law had at last been laid to rest: that, in this crucial sphere, the ethic of the market-place had been trumped by an ethic of common citizenship. The historian Bentley Gilbert's verdict stands. The British state 'had committed itself to the maintenance of all its citizens according to need as a matter of right. ... Britain had attained a de facto national minimum.'[18]

Deep class divisions remained. The working class and middle class viewed each other across a chasm of ignorance, incomprehension and suspicion. They had different accents, different ways of life, different moral codes, different life chances, different work experiences and, in some (though far from all) cases, different political values and allegiances. Notoriously, the maverick Old Etonian socialist, George Orwell, remembered that, as a child, he was taught 'four frightful words. ... *The lower classes smell.*'[19] The fictional middle-class suburb of 'Richford', depicted by the Liberal politician and commentator, Charles Masterman, hated and despised the working classes 'partly because it has contempt for them and partly because it has fear of them'.[20] A notorious real-life example of Richfordian anxiety was the 'Cutteslowe wall', built to make sure that council tenants on an estate in north Oxford were kept out of an adjacent private estate.[21]

Class differences did not depend on physical barriers. Richard Hoggart's evocation of the 'us' and 'them' culture of working-class Hunslet is deservedly famous. 'They' were the wielders of authority – capricious, condescending and never to be trusted. They 'talk posh', were 'all twisters really', would 'do y' down if they can', were apt to 'clap yer in clink', were 'all in a click [clique] together' and 'treat you like muck'.[22] Bryan Magee, the writer and philosopher, paints a similar picture of his upbringing on the borders of London's East End – though people who talked posh appear not to have figured in it. (The only person who did was an unfortunate curate just down from Oxford, who seemed ludicrous rather than oppressive.) Magee spent his early childhood in Hoxton, where his parents kept a shop. As he remembered it later, 1930s Hoxton was a working-class urban village, a social world away from middle-class neighbourhoods in other parts of London.

Life centred on the street; and the street was a place of colour, drama, frequent drunkenness and occasional violence. Most men gambled obsessively, chiefly on horses; since off-course cash betting was illegal, this meant that minor law-breaking was almost universal. The police turned a blind eye, not least because they could not function without close, venal relationships with the criminal community and were often corrupted by them. However, working-class Hoxton was not homogeneous. As in the debates over parliamentary reform in the nineteenth century, an invisible but universally recognised dividing line separated the 'rough' from the 'respectable'. It ran between

> those who strove to get and keep work, staying out of debt and above all out of prison, not committing crimes, bringing up their sons honestly and their daughters chastely, and generally maintaining their self-respect, and those who tried to live without working, always on the lookout for tricks and fiddles, anything for a few bob, but usually broke; pawning clothes, bedding or furniture when desperate, sending children to school without shoes or breakfast, doing moonlight flits when they could not pay the rent, in and out of petty crime and in and out of prison. . . .
>
> For individuals of spirit and intelligence there might seem at least as much to be said for being rough as for being respectable, and so a high proportion of the ablest in Hoxton ended up on the wrong side of the law. The life of the respectable poor was essentially a life of repression, a great deal of it self-repression and was no life for anyone with drive and ambition unless he were dedicatedly self disciplined.[23]

The middle class was riven too, but in a much more complicated way. Public-school men looked down on grammar-school ones; established professionals on vulgar nouveaux riches; inhabitants of the stockbroker belt on those living in estates of suburban 'semis'; speakers of the strangulated 'received' English of the BBC on those with authentic provincial accents. George Orwell, an obsessive topographer of the gradations of the British class system as well as an Old Etonian, described himself as 'lower-upper-middle class'.[24] Few were as honest, but many were as fascinated by their position in the pecking order. Sometimes fascination mingled with self-disgust, a combination that Orwell caught beautifully in an interior monologue by George Bowling, the lower-middle-class hero of his novel, *Coming Up For Air*. The street he lives in, Bowling tells himself, is typical of streets that 'fester' all over the suburbs:

Always the same. Long, long roads of little semi-detached houses – the numbers in Ellesmere Road run to 212 and ours is 191 – as much alike as council houses and generally uglier. The stucco front, the creosoted gate, the privet hedge, the green front door. The Laurels, the Myrtles, the Hawthornes, Mon Abri, Mon Repos, Belle Vue. At perhaps one house in fifty some anti-social type who'll probably end in the workhouse has painted his front door blue instead of green.[25]

From a whig imperialist standpoint, these divisions hardly mattered. The last thing Baldwin wanted was to turn Britain into a classless society. He wanted to damp down the fires of class conflict and to save the existing economic and social order. Under his aegis, this is broadly what happened. One reason was that a regional divide mitigated the class divide. Except in the depths of the depression, long-term unemployment was concentrated in the old staple industries north and west of the Severn–Humber line – above all, coal, textiles, shipbuilding and steel. That was where Hoggart's 'Us and Them' culture was most deeply rooted; where the Labour movement was born and most of its seats were concentrated; where trade-union density was at its highest; where privation, indignity and despair were commonplace; and from where the Hunger Marchers of the 1930s set off.

The experience of the Midlands and the South-East was strikingly different. Thanks to low interest rates, better terms of trade and the housing boom that these helped to generate, they weathered the depression much more successfully than the old industrial regions and recovered more quickly. Between 1932 and 1937 unemployment in London and the South-East averaged 9.3 per cent as against 20.5 per cent in Scotland and 30.9 per cent in Wales. Britain as a whole was swifter to emerge from the depression than its foreign competitors, suffered less and enjoyed a higher rate of growth. And, everywhere, those in work saw their real earnings increase, since money wages declined more slowly than prices. For all except the long-term unemployed (admittedly a harsh and flagrant exception), the Baldwin Age was one of rising living standards and widening horizons.

Thanks to technological advances and falling prices, radio and car ownership soared. (The Magee family owned a radio throughout the 1930s and bought a car later in the decade, paid for with gambling winnings.) Higher individual consumption went hand in hand with an expanding public domain and more generous social policies. Between 1923 and 1939 the coverage of unemployment insurance increased from a little more than 11 million to nearly 14 million. From 1920 to 1938 the percentage of GDP going to state spending on social services increased by more than 50 per cent.[26] Meanwhile, electricity generation was nationalised and the BBC was brought under public control. Baldwin and Chamberlain used to get a poor press from left-inclined historians, but now that the dust of old battles has settled, it is clear that they stand as high in the pantheon of reforming ministers as Asquith and Lloyd George. They did not achieve full social citizenship, but by the eve of the Second World War the road towards it was open.

༚

Industrial inclusion was a harder trick to turn. Baldwin sought to coax employers and trade unions into a form of collaborative capitalism, fore-shadowing the collaborative capitalisms of central Europe after 1945. Unions and employers would co-operate to promote industrial rationalisation and enhance international competitiveness. Industrial inclusion for the unions would complement political inclusion for the Labour Party; the shibboleths of socialism and laissez-faire economics would fade away. Industrial inclu-sion on these lines, Baldwin insisted, would run with the grain of the times. A new industrial revolution was squeezing out small firms, impelling workers to respond in kind, and so giving birth to 'great consolidations' of capital and labour.[27] The free market depicted in the classical economic texts no longer existed in the real world; laissez-faire was as dead as the 'slave trade'.[28] In this new economy, collaboration was the only alternative to anarchy.

The premise was widely accepted. Obsequies for the self-regulating market of laissez-faire theory came from figures as varied as Keynes, the political Whig and economic radical; Robert Boothby, the maverick Con-servative; Hilary Marquand, the young applied economist and future Labour minister; Lord Weir, the industrial magnate and wartime government adviser; Sir Arthur Steel-Maitland, Baldwin's Minister of Labour; and Ernest Bevin, the truculent, massively built, power-retentive and marvellously creative architect and boss of the huge, octopoid, trade-union amal-gamation, the Transport and General Workers' Union.

Yet Baldwin had a long and rocky road to tread. For most of the 1920s, his vision of collaborative capitalism found few takers. After the collapse of the post-war boom, the export-dependent old staples faced stiff competition from lower-cost foreign producers. Employers had to cut costs. Typically, they tried to do so by cutting wages. The unions were bound to resist. Haunting the collective imagination of the trade-union movement, more-over, was the hazy but intoxicating syndicalist dream of industrial 'Direct Action' to bring the economy to a standstill and the capitalist system to its knees. For the best part of a decade, the still, small voice of industrial inclusion was drowned out in the clash of these opposing forces.

They were not the only rocks in Baldwin's path. His industrial logic pulled against the financial and imperial logic to which the City of London, the Bank of England and the Treasury clung with iron conviction, and which he half accepted himself. Before 1914, London had been the financial capital of the world, as crucial an element in British power as the Royal Navy. Its global supremacy had rested on the celebrated tripod of balanced budgets, free trade and the gold standard. During the war the tripod had been knocked sideways. If London were to return to its old position in the global economy – and, almost without exception, the political class took it for granted that its return was a vital national interest – the tripod would have to be put back. The balanced budget had been restored in the closing years of the Lloyd George coalition. Despite some loopholes, the same was broadly true of free trade. Though Baldwin had fought the 1923 election on a protectionist platform, it seemed clear (not least, to him) that his defeat had entrenched the principle of free trade for years to come. That left the gold standard. It had been in abeyance during the war and was formally suspended in 1919. The Treasury, the Bank of England and the vast majority of financial opinion-leaders took it for granted that it had to be restored as well.

The outcome threw a vivid light on a persistent tension between global and national imperatives that dogged whig imperialist statecraft for most of the next fifty years. After much cogitation, Winston Churchill – now Baldwin's improbable, impulsive, irrepressible and fiscally unsound Chancellor of the Exchequer – bowed to the conventional wisdom of the financial community. In April 1925, Britain returned to gold at the pre-war parity of $4.86 to the pound. Few now doubt that the pound was overvalued as a result, though by how much is uncertain. Renewed pressure for wage cuts to reduce costs seemed inevitable. The prime candidate for such pressures was the undercapitalised and often hopelessly inefficient mining industry. British coal had been hard put to withstand foreign competition even before the return to gold. Now the coal owners announced their decision to abrogate their existing agreement with the union, and insisted on lower wages and longer hours. The miners responded with the celebrated negation: 'Not a penny off the pay, not a minute on the day.'

Partly because the mining industry was the biggest in the country, partly because the miners had a legendary status in the Labour Movement, other unions saw the Miners' Federation as the first line of defence for the working class as a whole. They felt bound to back it against the employers and, if need be, against the government. These conflicting pressures led to the General Strike of May 1926, to the humiliating but inevitable unconditional surrender of the TUC on its ninth day, and to the seven-month-long agony of the subsequent mining lock-out, which ended in total victory for the coal owners. In the summer of 1925, in a slashing attack on the return to gold, brilliantly entitled *The Economic Consequences of Mr Churchill*, Keynes had warned that the miners would be the victims of 'the economic juggernaut'. They would be 'offered the choice between starvation and submission, the fruits of their submission to accrue to the benefit of other classes'.[29] In fact the miners starved and submitted. It was a catastrophic defeat, not just for them but for the British trade-union movement as a whole.

It was also a defeat for Baldwinian industrial inclusion. For a fleeting moment in the summer of 1926, the government had a chance to settle the mining dispute on comparatively fair terms. But it would have had to coerce the owners or at least to threaten to do so; and the Cabinet shrank from the prospect of their wrath. Once the miners had been forced back to work on the owners' terms, Conservative pressure for anti-union legislation became irresistible. In 1927, the government put through a Trade Disputes and Trade Unions Act, making sympathetic strikes designed to coerce the government illegal. By a terrible irony, it included a provision substituting contracting in for contracting out in respect of the political levy – the very measure that Baldwin had smothered with his 'peace in our time' speech only two years earlier.

Although the Act made little difference to trade-union behaviour, it was a symbol of humiliation. Equally significant was the fate of the decade's most ambitious step towards collaborative capitalism, the much applauded Mond–Turner talks that started in 1928.[30] The protagonists were a subcommittee of the TUC, in which Bevin played a leading part, and an ad hoc group of big businessmen, assembled by Sir Alfred Mond, Conservative MP, industrial tycoon, creator of ICI and former minister in the Lloyd George coalition. The aim was to hammer out an agreed strategy for industrial rationalisation, higher real wages and continuous consultation between unions and employers. The government kept out of the limelight, but Baldwin and Steel-Maitland helped to launch the idea from behind the scenes. Yet, despite honeyed words at the start, it soon became clear that Mond and his fellow industrialists did not speak for employers in general. Despite savage opposition from the miners' leader, A.J. Cook, most of the leading figures in the now-chastened TUC were eager for collaboration. However, the National Council of Employers' Organisations (NCEO), whose members had their tails up, was in no mood for concessions. The talks limped on into the early 1930s, but with scant achievements to their credit.

By then, the story had already started to take a new turn. In August 1931, the National Government was formed to save the pound. In September, another confidence crisis forced it to leave the gold standard after all. (Sidney Webb, Colonial Secretary in the outgoing Labour Government, is supposed to have complained, 'No one told *us* we could do that.') The pound rapidly floated down to a dollar parity of $3.23. It rose again when the Roosevelt Administration in the United States substantially increased the dollar price of gold (in effect, devaluing the dollar), but the exchange-rate constraint on domestic policy-making had gone. Early in 1932 protective tariffs were introduced; following an acrimonious Imperial Conference in Ottawa during the summer, an elaborate scheme of imperial preference followed suit. Eventually, most empire countries also joined a sterling block (known as the sterling area), whose members held their reserves in sterling and stabilised their currencies in terms of sterling. For the first time since the repeal of the Corn Laws in 1846, a British Government had consciously and deliberately abandoned the laissez-faire vision of a global free market in favour of a form of economic nationalism.

Economic nationalism had two faces, not one. Behind the defensive wall of import duties, the government tried to shore up ailing industries, often with subsidies, while cajoling and sometimes prodding them to become more efficient. The details varied from case to case, but the broad thrust was the same in all the industries concerned. Everywhere, the visible hands of price-fixing oligopolists and an interventionist state replaced the invisible hand of the market. In a range of industries, including steel, shipbuilding, coal-mining, agriculture, road transport, shipping and cotton textiles, state-sponsored cartels restricted output, fixed prices and (in theory, if not in practice) promoted rationalisation. It was a form of quasi-corporatism or, as Hilary Marquand called it, of 'capitalism-on-the-dole'.[31]

By this roundabout route, a pallid version of Baldwinian industrial inclusion at last arrived on the scene. Unprecedented industrial peace prevailed. In some cases, capitalism-on-the-dole positively fostered orderly collective bargaining. In almost all, it brought benefits to labour as well as to capital – sometimes higher wages, sometimes consultation, sometimes both. Above all, wage bargaining was no longer held in the vice of an unrealistic exchange rate. The trade unions still had much less weight than the employers. Their total membership was a little more than half what it had been in the turbulent days following the war and they were stronger in declining industries than in rising ones. Still, they had a foot in the Whitehall door: they were junior partners in the management of industrial obsolescence. The award of a knighthood to Walter Citrine, the lucid, incisive and supremely competent General Secretary of the TUC, was a symbol of acceptance for both recipient and donor. Except in rhetorical flourishes on high days and holidays, the trade-union movement no longer challenged the fundamentals of the capitalist order. But the partially tamed capitalism that it accepted bore little resemblance to the free-market capitalism of the past. Here too Baldwin's Whiggery had worked, if not quite in the way its author had intended.

⊛

Over imperial policy Baldwin's path was harder still. Britain emerged from the war with her imperial appetites unsated. The peace settlement gave her paramountcy in the Middle East, buttressed by League of Nations mandates in Mesopotamia (now Iraq) and Palestine. The former German colony of Tanganyika became a British mandate, and South-West Africa a South African one. Australia and New Zealand were awarded mandates over a clutch of former German colonies in the Pacific. However, these acquisitions were like the final curtain call of an ageing diva – echoes of a glorious past, not pointers to the future. Signs of strain were unmistakable. British governments, trying to finance social inclusion while sticking to fiscal orthodoxy, had to run the empire on the cheap.

An emblematic moment came in 1922 when Britain signed the Washington Treaty, giving the United States parity with her in capital ships. In practice she had ceased to be supreme at sea at the end of the nineteenth century, but it was one thing to abandon supremacy in practice, another to sign a treaty announcing that she had done so. Meanwhile, spending on the army was heavily cut.[32] In most places strain was not obvious. Where it was, painful change was unavoidable. One such place was Ireland. In the years after the First World War, a handful of republican guerrillas successfully defied the might of a recently triumphant Britain, and forced the Lloyd George Government to concede virtual independence to the twenty-six counties in the south of the island. A second, far more complex, example was India. Instinctively, Baldwin approached the Indian quagmire in the spirit of evolutionary whiggism that governed his approach to domestic politics. The empire, he insisted, was 'organic and alive, in a constant process of evolution'; and India was evolving too.[33] But he had to stake his leadership on the proposition.

India was more than a patch of red on the map; it was the mainspring of Britain's imperial vocation. 'As long as we rule in India we are the greatest power in the world,' declared the future Viceroy, Lord Curzon, in 1901. 'If we lose it we shall drop straight away to a third rate power.'[34] Curzon's hysteria was as significant as his hubris. Yet Britain could not hold India down by force. Despite the intoxicating grandeur of the Raj, her control over India depended on the collaboration of Indian elites. The result was an increasingly cruel dilemma. To keep her collaborators happy, Britain had to make concessions to the growing Indian wish for self-government. In doing so, she risked undermining the foundations of British rule. Yet the alternative to concession was repression. That might put an end to collaboration, and was in any case unfeasible over the long term. One solution was to treat India as the Whigs had treated Canada in the 1830s: to make India a dominion on a par with the white dominions. The Burkean vision of loose-knit, decentralized, imperial pluralism would cover millions of non-European, brown-skinned people, as well as kith and kin of British (or at least European) stock. The alternative was Salisbury-style resistance.

The struggle between these two solutions provides one of the central themes of the Baldwin Age.[35] It was, above all, a struggle over identity: over India's identity (or identities) and also over Britain's. The story begins in 1917, when Edwin Montagu, the Liberal Secretary of State for India, announced that the government looked forward to the 'progressive realisation of responsible government in India'. Two years later, continuing viceregal control at the centre was coupled with modest devolution of power to elected representatives in the provinces. This did not mollify the growing nationalist movement in India or its saintly, charismatic and often devious spokesman, Mahatma Gandhi, the dominant force in the Indian National Congress.

By the late 1920s moderates on both sides of the House of Commons were searching for something more. In October 1929 the 'something' was supplied by another viceroy – Baldwin's much loved friend, Lord Irwin, later Viscount Halifax and later still Earl of Halifax – working in close co-operation with the new Labour Government. In theory, what came to be known as the Irwin Declaration merely amplified Montagu's 1917 declaration. In practice, it went much further. The 'natural issue of India's constitutional progress', Irwin announced, was dominion status. As everyone knew, dominion status now meant more than responsible government: in 1926 it had been defined to mean legal and constitutional equality with Britain. Irwin said nothing about the route or the timing, but what he said about the destination was explosive. At some stage, presumably far into the future, India would be, in effect, a sovereign state. She would still be part of the empire, but thanks to her new status it would be a radically different empire. An inescapable corollary was that Britain, at the heart of empire, would have to be a different country – no longer the ruler of the vast Indian subcontinent, but the partner of an Indian Government responsible to the Indian people.

The Irwin Declaration was the prelude to a long, fiendishly complicated and often bitter battle for the future of India and the soul of the Conservative Party. It was a battle between Indians and Indians, and Conservatives and

Conservatives. In India, moderates were ranged against radicals and Muslims against Hindus. In Britain, Baldwinian whig imperialists struggled for supremacy against a coalition of Salisburyesque diehards and assorted press lords, led by Winston Churchill. Churchill was a natural whig imperialist, whose career was a textbook example of Burke's equipoise. Before 1914 he had been one of the leading radicals in Asquith's government. As Chancellor of the Exchequer he had strongly supported Neville Chamberlain's pursuit of social reform. But he was also prone to spasms of catastrophically bad judgement, subject to mood swings that varied from roguish ebullience to a depressive state that he called his 'black dog', fixated on misleading memories of the India that he had known as a subaltern in the 1890s and obsessed by forebodings of national decline. He now became the spokesman of a peculiarly intransigent tory nationalism, reminiscent of Lord Salisbury in the struggle over suffrage reform in the 1860s, and not a million miles from Lord Eldon.

In the Commons debate following the Irwin Declaration, Baldwin quelled most of the doubts in his own party with a beautifully crafted speech, invoking the alleged common descent of the British and the Indians from the 'great Aryan race' and warning that if his party had no room for Irwin 'then I have finished with my party'.[36] Churchill replied with an article in the *Daily Mail*, describing the Irwin Declaration as 'fantastic in itself' and 'criminally mischievous in its effects'.[37] The battle ebbed and flowed over a period of six years. Three Round Table conferences took place in London, at which Indian leaders and British politicians tried unavailingly to reconcile the principle of Indian unity with the growing gulf between Muslims and Hindus on the one hand and with the interests of the semi-autonomous, princely states on the other.

In the end the government imposed a solution – an All-India federation, embracing the princely states as well as British India, with elected legislatures in the provinces and at the centre, and safeguards in the form of reserved powers for the Viceroy (or Governor-General). This was a long way short of dominion status as understood in the white dominions, but Churchill and his diehard allies fought it every inch of the way. In March 1931, when Irwin had the temerity to negotiate directly with Gandhi, Churchill famously declared that he found it

> alarming and almost nauseating to see Mr Gandhi, a seditious Middle Temple lawyer, now posing as a fakir of a type well-known in the East, striding half-naked up the steps of the Vice-regal palace, while he is still organising and conducting a defiant campaign of civil disobedience, to parley on equal terms with the representative of the King-Emperor.[38]

Despite incessant, sometimes almost blood-curdling, and politically self-destructive Churchillian rhetoric, alarmingly close votes at Conservative Party conferences, interminable committee sessions in the Commons, and a doomed appeal by Churchill to the Commons Committee of Privileges, Baldwin won the battle for the soul of the Conservative Party. In July 1935, the Government of India Bill reached the statute book. Except to hardline tory nationalist frondeurs, Churchill seemed a backward-looking and slightly ridiculous spent force. The battle for the future of India was another matter. The Government of India Act did not satisfy Congress, and the Second World War made it a dead letter. Yet it is conceivable that a few more years of peace would have enabled it to take root. In any case, what counted in the long run was Baldwin's contribution to the evolving British vision of empire and to the slow reconstruction of Britain's identity in the second half of the twentieth century.

He and Churchill both wanted to save the empire and maintain Britain's role in the world, but their conceptions of empire and of Britain's role differed profoundly. Churchill dreamed of an empire of power and glory; Baldwin sought an empire of collaboration. For Churchill, Britain had saved the Indians from 'ages of barbarism, intestine war and tyranny', which might return if they were left to their own devices.[39] For Baldwin, the British had taught India the lesson of 'English institutions and democracy' and now had to adapt to the consequences. For Churchill, what mattered was 'hard' power. If India gained power through self-government, Britain would be bound to lose it. Baldwin was groping for a notion of 'soft' power. For him, India's inclusion in a Commonwealth of self-governing nations would enhance British influence in the world. To a modern ear, his language sounds patronising, but when he said that there was a 'wind of nationalism and freedom blowing round the world', he unknowingly foreshadowed the liquidation of empire after 1945 and the post-imperial Britain of today.[40] Imperial whiggery may or may not have worked at the time, but it did so after his death.

THE IRONIES OF CHURCHILL

Baldwin resigned as Prime Minister in May 1937, enveloped in clouds of glory. He had seen off Lloyd George in the 1920s and Churchill in the 1930s. He had squashed a challenge to his leadership from the press magnates Lords Rothermere and Beaverbrook, whom he accused of seeking 'power without responsibility – the prerogative of the harlot through the ages'. In the abdication crisis of 1936 he had done more than anyone else to end the reign of the louche, self-indulgent, Germanophile Edward VIII. He had watched the coronation of George VI and presided over a recovering economy. His place in history seemed secure.

His successor was Neville Chamberlain, the best Chancellor of the Exchequer between the wars. (Not, it has to be said, a role for which there was much competition.) At sixty-eight, Chamberlain had lost none of his grasp or drive. He seemed ideally fitted to be a great reforming Prime Minister. Unfortunately, no such office was on offer. By 1937 the social problems he would have liked to tackle were small beer in comparison with the alarming growth in the appetite and power of Hitler's Germany. As everyone knows, his response was 'appeasement' – the pursuit of agreements designed to remove alleged German grievances. At first, Germany seemed to have no grievances to appease. By the time Chamberlain became Prime Minister, Hitler had substantially shifted the European balance in Germany's favour. He had introduced conscription, hugely expanded the armed forces, occupied the demilitarised Rhineland and forged ahead with a vigorous rearmament programme. But it was hard to argue that any of this provided grounds for some extraordinary new initiative; in any case it was water under the bridge.

Then the skies fell in. In the Anschluss of March 1938, Austria was incorporated into the Nazi Reich. In September 1938 came Hitler's demand that Czechoslovakia should cede the German-speaking Sudetenland to Germany, and the Munich agreement that forced the Czechs to do so – the most spectacular example of Chamberlainite appeasement. In November 1938, Munich was followed by the Kristallnacht – a vicious, nationwide anti-Jewish pogrom that showed everyone with eyes to see that Nazi Germany was not a normal country, seeking pragmatically to pursue its interests, but a revolutionary state, driven by an ideological dynamic at least as powerful as that of Stalin's Russia. Most British politicians were ill-equipped to see anything of the sort. The appeasement tide did not turn until March 1939 when Germany occupied the non-German parts of Bohemia.

At that point Chamberlain and his ministers decided that enough was enough. The result was a guarantee to Poland, and a desultory, unconvincing search for an agreement with the Soviet Union. But Hitler easily overtook the British in the race for Stalin's favour. In August 1939, Nazi Germany and Soviet Russia concluded the Molotov–Ribbentrop Pact. War followed on 3 September, when Germany refused to desist from the invasion of Poland, which she had launched two days before. Winston Churchill, the leading diehard of the Indian battle and the most formidable anti-appeaser, was appointed First Lord of the Admiralty with a seat in the War Cabinet.

Nine months later he was Prime Minister. He would preside over a dramatic shift in public language and the public mood, a revolution in the political economy, the tentative birth of a new version of Britain's imperial identity and the slow collapse of the whig imperialist ascendancy that Baldwin had painstakingly created. Although Churchill did not seek any of these changes except, to some extent, the first, he was the unwitting author of them all. No British Prime Minister has had a bleaker inheritance. Chamberlain was brought down by a revolt of Conservative MPs after an angry Commons debate on the disastrous Norwegian campaign of April–May 1940. By general agreement, the combination of the Norwegian fiasco and the Conservative revolt showed that a coalition government was now essential. Labour refused to take part unless Chamberlain resigned as Prime Minister. The choice of successor lay between Halifax, Churchill's bête noire during the struggle over India and now Foreign Secretary, and Churchill himself. Halifax excluded himself on the grounds that he was a peer. At 6 p.m. on 10 May, Churchill went to the Palace and kissed hands as Prime Minister. By now, the German blitzkrieg against Holland and Belgium was under way.

In a brilliant feat of arms, the German panzers then broke through the French defences at Sedan, having advanced surreptitiously through the supposedly impassable Ardennes. Instead of turning south-west towards Paris, as the Allies expected them to do, they raced for the Channel By 24 May they had taken Boulogne and started to besiege Calais. Between 27 May and 4 June the bulk of the battered British Expeditionary Force, together with over 100,000 French and Allied troops, was evacuated from Dunkirk, leaving most of its equipment behind. In a passage that still brings a lump to the throat, Churchill told the House of Commons:

> We shall go on to the end, we shall fight in France, we shall fight on the seas and the oceans, we shall fight with growing confidence and strength in the air, we shall defend our island, whatever the cost may be, we shall fight on the beaches, we shall fight on the landing grounds, we shall fight in the fields and in the streets, we shall fight in the hills; we shall never surrender, and even if, which I do not for a moment believe, this island or a large part of it were subjugated and starving, then our Empire beyond the seas, armed and guarded by the British Fleet, would carry on the struggle, until, in God's good time, the new world, with all its power and might, step forth to the rescue and liberation of the old.[41]

On 17 June, France sued for peace, under a new government, headed by the aged First World War hero, Marshal Pétain. Britain fought on.

That was the headline story – true, but not the whole truth. Churchill's appointment was greeted with dismay by much of Whitehall and by large sections of the Conservative Party. Lord Hankey, the bureaucrat's bureaucrat, who had served as Cabinet Secretary for twenty-two years, feared that 'the wise old elephants' would never 'be able to hold the Rogue Elephant'. R.A. Butler, Parliamentary Under Secretary at the Foreign Office, spoke privately of 'the sudden coup of Winston and his rabble'. 'Chips' (Henry) Channon, MP for Southend, inveterate gossip and egregious snob, feared that Churchill and his associates would 'oust all the gentlemen of England'.[42]

Much more serious than such bitter murmurs was a potentially fatal challenge to the centrepiece of Churchill's policy. In the final days of May 1940, with the French army beginning to collapse and the fate of the BEF hanging in the balance, Lord Halifax, still Foreign Secretary, raised the deadly question: should Britain seek a compromise peace? Halifax made it clear that he thought so. Churchill declared that negotiations would be a slippery slope from which it would be impossible to climb back. They would erode Britain's will to resist, and no one would be able to revive it later. Besides, 'nations which went down fighting rose again, but those which surrendered tamely were finished.'[43]

Halifax persisted. At one point he made a veiled threat of resignation. Conscious of his weakness in a still-Chamberlainite Conservative Party, Churchill was careful not to rule out the possibility of negotiations at some future stage, when the balance of forces had shifted in Britain's favour.[44] But he insisted repeatedly that that stage had not yet come and outmanoeuvred Halifax by taking the argument from the five-man War Cabinet to the wider Cabinet, which enthusiastically supported him. His Commons promise to 'go on to the end' was, among other things, an affirmation of his victory, closing off further discussion. It also had a wider significance. Though this was not clear at the time, Churchill's victory over Halifax was one of the most decisive episodes in the history of the twentieth century. Had Britain opened negotiations with Hitler, Churchill's fears would almost certainly have come true; Britain would have gone the way of France, and Hitler would have had a free hand to deal with the Soviet Union as he wished. Churchill had not won the war by defeating Halifax, but he had ensured that Hitler would not win it.

Churchill's wartime rhetoric served a dual purpose. It gave heart to a nation fighting for its life against fearful odds. It also told the nation what it stood for, and what kind of nation it was. The archaic language, the rolling periods, the alternation of hard, terse, simple words with complex Latinate constructions and, above all, the message of intransigent, sea-girt defiance evoked a vision of Britain and British history in which Churchill passionately believed and which he managed to impose on his audiences. It was an old vision, with deep roots; not the least of Churchill's achievements was to give it a new lease of life, which lasted for more than a generation. There was a strong whig imperialist element in it. The references to the empire beyond the seas, and to the mighty new world rescuing the old, in the passage quoted above, are evidence of that. But Churchill also mined deeper seams. There was a touch of Shakespeare's 'precious stone set in the silver sea' in his vision, and more than a touch of Milton's boast that London was the 'mansion house of liberty'. It was a vision of the British as a providential people, summoned by a higher power to fight for freedom against slavery, and for good against evil. It evoked memories of Britain saving Europe from the Corsican tyrant, and of Drake harrying the Armada as it sailed up the Channel to its doom. Churchill himself stood in a long line of heroic wartime leaders, from Lloyd George through the younger Pitt to Chatham and even Queen Elizabeth I.

Churchill was not alone in holding up a mirror to a Britain of the mind. Inchoate visions of a better future challenged his vision of a heroic past. Most challengers thought of themselves as socialists, but they stood aloof from the official Labour Party and did not appeal to the traditional Labour constituency. They drew on the democratic collectivist tradition, but democratic republican blood ran in their veins. Their rhetoric was as patriotic as Churchill's, but it was also classless, altruistic, meritocratic and at the same time egalitarian. George Orwell's passionate, limpid, occasionally curmudgeonly polemic, *The Lion and the Unicorn*, is the most resonant example I know.[45]

In a haunting few pages at the beginning Orwell pictured an idealised England (not 'Britain', it should be noted) that owed as much to his imagination as Churchill's dauntless islanders owed to his. Orwell's England was a unique and special place, quite unlike continental Europe. The English were gentler than other peoples; their grass was greener and their coins heavier; they had 'mild knobby' faces; and their culture was shaped by 'solid breakfasts and gloomy Sundays'. England was, in fact, a family, 'a rather stuffy Victorian family ... with all its cupboards bursting with skeletons'. Like all families, it closed ranks at the approach of an enemy. Famously, however, it was a 'family with the wrong members in control'. Its ruling class were 'simply parasites, less useful to society than his fleas are to a dog'. Although not treacherous, as were many continental ruling classes, they were stupid and reactionary. They had to be: if they had acknowledged that the world was changing, they would not have been able to justify their privileges to themselves. Victory was impossible until their grip had been broken. England could not 'win the war without introducing Socialism, nor establish Socialism without winning the war'. Only when productive goods had become state property would ordinary people feel that 'the State is themselves', and be willing to make sacrifices for it on the necessary scale.

Like Milton, Orwell put his faith in a war of ideas: a revolutionary war between the new and the old, 'the living and the dead'. His approach to the sociology and mentality of the revolution that he called for was characteristically individual. It would not be a proletarian revolution, he insisted; working-class support would be essential, but the working class was not equipped to lead it. The same was true of the Labour Party, and doubly true of his *bête noire*, the intellectuals of the left: the 'Bloomsbury highbrow, with his mechanical snigger, is as out of date as the cavalry colonel'. The revolution would be led by 'the new indeterminate class of skilled workers, technical experts, airmen, scientists, architects and journalists, the people who feel at home in the radio and ferro-concrete age'. But – a crucial 'but' for Orwell – it would be a quintessentially *English* revolution:

> It will not be doctrinaire, nor even logical. It will abolish the House of Lords, but quite probably will not abolish the monarchy. It will leave anachronisms and loose ends everywhere, the judge in his ridiculous horse-hair wig and the lion and the unicorn on the soldier's cap buttons. ... [I]t will never lose touch with the tradition of compromise and the belief in a law that is above the State. It will shoot traitors, but it will give them a solemn trial beforehand and occasionally it will acquit them. ... It will show a power of assimilating the past which will shock foreign observers and sometimes make them doubt whether any revolution has happened.
>
> But all the same it will have done the essential thing. It will have nationalized industry, scaled down incomes, set up a classless education system. Its real nature will be apparent from the hatred which the surviving rich men of the world will feel for it.[46]

There was only one Orwell, but others echoed some of his themes. A notable example was the maverick, originally Liberal baronet, Sir Richard Acland, who became the prime mover in a new party, founded in 1942, with the evocative name of Common Wealth. It stood for common ownership, 'vital democracy' and morality in politics. It was Orwell's indeterminate class made flesh. For a brief moment, Stafford Cripps – who had been expelled from the Labour Party before the war for advocating a popular front and had been despatched as Ambassador to Moscow in 1940 – swam in the same waters. In a bad moment in the war in early 1942, many saw him as a messiah of hair-shirted, patriotic and, above all, competent self-sacrifice – even as an alternative to Churchill. But despite vigorous proselytising by a group of disciples known as the 'Crippery', the Cripps boom soon evaporated.[47] After a few dizzy months as Leader of the House of Commons and member of the War Cabinet, he subsided into the more congenial post of Minister of Aircraft Production in November 1942. But the dream behind the boom lived on.

༺༄༻

Churchill's decision to fight on sprang from his deepest instincts and beliefs: about his country and also about himself. Like Martin Luther, he could do no other. But he did not – could not – foresee the consequences; and as time went on they were tinged increasingly with unadmitted ironies. The most obvious domestic consequence was war socialism – a command economy, run on egalitarian lines. 'Going on to the end' entailed total war; and total war entailed an enormous growth in the size and scope of the state as well as tight limits on the play of market forces. Under the Emergency Powers Acts of 1939 and 1940, the government had complete control over private property and persons. This made possible an extraordinary concentration of effort on military purposes. At the time of the Normandy landings in June 1944, the armed forces and munitions industries absorbed 55 per cent of the labour force, compared to the American figure of 40 per cent. Government spending soared. Fiscal prudence was thrown to the winds. The pursuit of victory at all costs took precedence over all else. By 1943 public expenditure accounted for 54 per cent of GDP as against 24 per cent in 1938. (The comparable figure for 1917, the third year of the First World War, was 37 per cent.)[48] The means of production were still privately owned, but in the key sections of the economy, the government, not the owners, decided what should be produced and what to charge for it.

Ministers and officials in Whitehall could and did allocate raw materials, ration most items of consumer expenditure, control prices, fix profit margins, subsidise food, conscript women and evacuate children. In his memoirs Douglas Jay, a wartime civil servant in the Ministry of Supply and later a Labour Cabinet minister, painted a telling picture of how the state distributed manpower, the key wartime resource. From the summer of 1941 until nearly the end of the war a committee of four relatively low-level officials, known as the Preference Committee, met at 9.30 a.m. once a fortnight to decide which demands for labour should have priority. The committee issued a secret list of preference vacancies teleprinted an hour after its conclusions to every Ministry of Labour office in the land. It became known as PAL or 'Preference in the Allocation of Labour'. It normally took four hours to complete the fortnightly business. ... We scarcely ever failed to reach agreement on each demand by the time limit of 1.30 p.m.[49]

Meanwhile, new ministries proliferated – Food, Shipping, Information, Aircraft Production, Economic Warfare. The result of all this was a level of mobilisation unsurpassed by any other belligerent. It would have been hard to devise a more persuasive advertisement for the dirigiste state dreamed of by democratic collectivists and, for most of his career, abhorred by Churchill.

That was only the beginning. The mood of wartime was, and is, elusive, but the available evidence does not suggest that the British were fighting for an ideology, as liberals and socialists imagined. They hoped for a better world after the war, but their expectations were much more modest than their hopes.[50] Few shared Orwell's dream of a revolutionary war. All the same, the coalition's war socialism amounted to a revolution of sorts. In comparison with their pre-war standards the rich suffered far more than the poor from the inevitable cut in private consumption. The standard rate of income tax reached 50 per cent, and the top rate of surtax 48 per cent. Revenue from direct taxation on incomes rose twice as fast as from indirect taxation on consumption. Private motoring was suspended. Prices of restaurant meals were limited to five shillings (£6.17 in today's money). Thanks to food subsidies, rationing and the virtual disappearance of unemployment, real earnings rose much faster than prices. Free school meals, cheap milk for children and expectant mothers, and free cod liver oil benefited the working class more than the middle class. In real terms, wage incomes rose by 22 per cent from 1938 to 1949 and 'social incomes' by 57 per cent. Salary incomes fell by 22 per cent and incomes from property by 15 per cent.[51]

Meanwhile, the half-hearted industrial inclusion of the Baldwin Age became much more extensive, complementing war socialism with an informal war corporatism. Its extension was due, in part, to the unprecedented increase in trade-union power that total war and full employment brought in their train, but it was also due to Churchill's inspired decision to appoint Ernest Bevin as his Minister of Labour when the coalition was formed. Bevin gave full vent to his power-retentive instincts and his vaulting ambition for his people. He turned the Ministry of Labour not only into the powerhouse of the wartime economy, overshadowing the Treasury in fact even if not in appearance, but also into the spearhead of the loose, voluntaristic British version of the collaborative capitalism of the post-war period.

Tripartite consultation between government, employers and unions became a central feature of the wartime political economy, on the national level via a Joint Consultative Committee, and in a range of particular industries via advisory panels of one sort and another. But this was evolution, not revolution: a milestone on an old road, not the first step on a new one. Bevin, the wartime Minister of Labour, was the child of Bevin, the arch-practitioner of Mond-Turnerism – and, for that matter, of Baldwin, who had dreamed unavailingly of class collaboration in the 1920s.

Wartime Britain was an increasingly dingy and dilapidated country. *Luftwaffe* bombing of British cities was a pinprick compared to the devastation that the Allies inflicted on German ones, but even so around 750,000 houses were destroyed or severely damaged by enemy action. The capital stock was allowed to run down. The blackout was ubiquitous. The civilian population was overworked, tired, stressed and sometimes frightened. Nevertheless, the economic pie was divided more equally than ever before or since. The middle class was worse off than in 1939, but despite the strains of war the working class was healthier, better fed and better paid than it had ever been. This revolution was the work of patriotic, middle-class public servants who, as individuals, stood to lose from it. Here too the democratic collectivist vision of the just and rational state seemed triumphantly vindicated.

As Jay's description of the Preference Committee implied, the culture of government was transformed as well as its capacity. Staid administrators discovered reserves of energy and inventiveness that they had not known they possessed. Innovative outsiders swept into the sanctums of Whitehall. Keynes was given a roving commission as an unpaid adviser in the Treasury, where he became a cross between Olympian sage and 'creative imp'.[52] Beveridge, who had been a congenitally discontented civil servant during the First World War before moving to the LSE, found an unsatisfactory berth in the Ministry of Labour in September 1940. Buttressing these grandees was a glittering phalanx of lower-level newcomers. The roster of these wartime temporaries reads like an *Almanach de Gotha* of the post-war British establishment. Economists were specially favoured. At the age of thirty-three, James Meade, a devoted Keynesian and future Nobel Prize winner, joined the newly formed Economic Section of the Cabinet Office. Serving alongside him was Alec Cairncross, only twenty-nine, later 'Sir' Alec and head of the Government Economic Service. Donald MacDougall, three years his junior, another future head of the Economic Service and future knight, was plucked from an Assistant Lecturership at Leeds to join the Prime Minister's Statistical Branch at the heart of the wartime state. It was headed by the 'Prof', the Oxford physicist Professor Lindemann, a long-standing and devoted Churchill adviser who later became Lord Cherwell.

In 1940, Hugh Gaitskell, then thirty-two, already a budding Labour politician as well as Reader in Economics at University College, London, joined the Ministry of Economic Warfare, headed by Hugh Dalton. Harold Wilson was just twenty-four when he joined the Economic Section in 1940. He ended his civil service career in the Department of Mines, where he was credited with 'revolutionizing the statistics'.[53] At least one non-economist did even better. Oliver Franks, Professor of Moral Philosophy at Glasgow University, later ambassador to the United States and later still Vice-Chancellor of Oxford University, joined the Ministry of Supply as an assistant principal in 1939 at the age of thirty-four; by the end of the war he had become a Permanent Secretary. Young men (and the occasional young woman) like these may not have been philosopher kings, but they were certainly philosopher princes – exemplars of a heady amalgam of brains, youth and power that helped to give the wartime state its extraordinary reach, self-confidence and effectiveness. And its impact on them was as important as theirs on it. They were not all democratic collectivists, by any means, but they all imbibed an essentially democratic collectivist moral: given the right mixture of rationality, intelligence and public spirit in its managers, there was hardly anything the state could not do.

૭ૐ૭

The exhilarating ferment of wartime government inevitably spilled over into planning for the peace. With a variety of dramatic flourishes, the plans defined the outlines of the post-war settlement, but they looked back to the Age of Baldwin as well as forward to the Age of Attlee and Macmillan. The war was like a pressure cooker, speeding up developments that were already under way. Two great examples stand out – the Beveridge Report on social welfare reform and the government's white paper on employment policy. In form, Beveridge's report was the work of an interdepartmental committee of officials, of which he was chairman. In fact, it was the fruit of his own extraordinary combination of messianic idealism, mastery of detail and relentless self-promotion. Beveridge was a remote, autocratic and frequently rebarbative figure, but he had a genius for publicity.

His report, soberly entitled *Social Insurance and Allied Services – Report by Sir William Beveridge*, was published in December 1942. Easily the most popular of the post-war plans produced under the aegis of the Churchill coalition, it proposed a co-ordinated attack on the 'five giants' of Want, Ignorance, Squalor, Idleness and Disease. (A conference of free churchmen regretted its failure to mention the giant Sin.)[54] A single, comprehensive system of compulsory social insurance, buttressed by family allowances, a free and universal health service and full employment would replace the patchwork quilt of pre-war days. There would be an end to poverty and also to the indignity of the Means Test. Flat-rate benefits, sufficient to keep the beneficiaries above the poverty line, would be earned by flat-rate contributions. They would be entitlements, not 'doles': social-citizenship rights, not discretionary state charity. A peculiarly British form of social democracy would complement the peculiarly British version of political democracy.

The public impact was sensational. The combined sales of the report and a brief official summary totalled more than 600,000. Beveridge became an unlikely popular hero. 'A revolutionary moment in the world's history,' he proclaimed, 'is a time for revolutions, not for patching.'[55] That was hype, not history. In reality, Beveridge followed where Lloyd George and Neville Chamberlain had led. Like Bevin's experiments in corporatist collaboration, his plan was evolutionary, not revolutionary. It sought to consolidate and synthesise the partial systems that had grown up over the previous half-century. It did not propose a completely new system, derived from first principles. Its gradualism reflected a consensus that already existed among those working in the field.

However, that did not mean that all was over bar the shouting. At first, there was no consensus among ministers or officials. Alarm bells rang in the Treasury where well-founded fears of post-war national bankruptcy were widespread. They were echoed in sections of the Conservative Party. Yet at a time when the government was pouring resources into the war effort, without counting the cost, and when the public yearned for better and fairer social provision, Treasury caution on the peace sounded crabbed and mean-spirited. At first, Churchill prevaricated. But overwhelming support for Beveridge in the Labour and Liberal parties; minority support in the Conservative Party; a serious anti-government revolt in the division lobbies'; the patent enthusiasm of the general public; and high by-election votes for candidates standing on a Beveridgean ticket wore the resistance down. By the end of the war, the coalition had published a white paper accepting the gist of Beveridge's insurance proposals as well as a more guarded one committing it to the principle of a free and comprehensive health service. For good measure, it also passed an Act bringing in family allowances.

Employment policy had a more complex history, but here too evolutionary gradualism prevailed.[56] The white paper emerged from an arcane struggle between the Keynesian Young Turks of the Cabinet Office Economic Section, led by James Meade, and the old hands of the Treasury, led by the Permanent Secretary, the redoubtable Sir Richard Hopkins, a shy and diminutive figure who looked like 'an extremely intelligent monkey'[57] and was known as 'Hoppy'. Keynes loomed in the background, administering occasional Olympian rebukes to the Treasury protagonists. Politicians played supporting roles, but little more. Party loyalties were irrelevant. Some of the young economists who had formed a Keynesian praetorian guard in debates within the economics profession in the 1930s were Labour in politics. Some Labour intellectuals who were at first suspicious of Keynes's teaching were converted to it in the course of the decade, notably Hugh Dalton.

Outside these exalted circles, however, the bulk of the Labour movement was sceptical or indifferent. (When the House of Commons debated the employment white paper, Aneurin Bevan savagely attacked it on the grounds that if its underlying assumptions were sound the Labour Party would have no justification for existing.) By the same token, Conservatives were not, as such, hostile to Keynes. Told that the essence of the new theory was that governments should launch into extra spending when times were bad, Churchill commented benignly that, at such times, it might perhaps be helpful to have 'a series of Cabinet banquets, a sort of Salute the Stomach week'[58] – scarcely a sign of root-and-branch opposition.

The real battle took place among officials. The chief combatants were the largely Keynesian Cabinet Office Economic Section and a Treasury leadership determined to cling to what remained of the implicit fiscal constitution of the nineteenth century. As we have seen, that constitution had contained three guiding principles – free trade, the gold standard and the balanced budget – the first two of which had gone. Even budgets had been balanced only by massaging the figures. But it was one thing to relax the practice; another to jettison the principle. In the Treasury's eyes, the doctrine of the balanced budget was the last surviving bulwark against the inherent irresponsibility of elected persons. It was not willing to let that go as well. It was 'useless to hope that Chancellors would propose taxation to secure in good times Budget surpluses corresponding to Budget deficits in bad times', warned Hoppy;[59] only firm rules could keep governments on the path of fiscal virtue. But the quarrel went deeper than that. The Treasury was fighting for its traditional role as the guardian of the public purse. The Economic Section's whole analysis implied that the traditional conception of the public purse had become redundant.

Keynes did his elegant best to devise a compromise between the two sides, with an ingenious scheme for separate capital budgets, so that investment could be increased during a depression without unbalancing the ordinary budget. Perhaps inevitably, the 1944 white paper on employment policy that emerged from the bargaining was full of fudge and weasel words.[60] Keynesians and quasi-Keynesians could draw comfort from the trumpet blast at the beginning: 'The Government accept as one of their primary aims and responsibilities the maintenance of a high and stable level of employment after the war.' Treasury sceptics and anti-Keynesians could console themselves with the qualification that there would be no 'deliberate planning for a deficit in the National Budget in years of sub-normal trade activity'. A lucid exposition of the case for demand management was balanced by the well-founded caveat that two critically important components of demand – private investment and the foreign balance – were not under the government's control.

But the significance of the 1944 white paper does not lie in its caveats. The important point is that, for the first time in history, a British government had acknowledged a responsibility to maintain employment and had undertaken to manage demand in order to do so – not in a socialised or planned economy, but in a capitalist society where the means of production were largely in private hands, and resources were largely allocated by the market. Keynes's purpose had been to show, in the teeth of socialists and traditional economic liberals, that it was possible and necessary to do just that: that capitalism could be saved by a Burkean combination of improvement and preservation, just as the parliamentary monarchy had been saved in the nineteenth century. Now the heart of his message had been included in a state paper. It was a triumph for the wing imperialist tradition as well as for Keynes himself.

✾

Keynes and Beveridge were both liberals, not socialists. Their evolutionary gradualism was perfectly compatible with Churchill's view of the world. His caution over the Beveridge Report stemmed from understandable fears about its costs, not from principle; and, as discussed above, he accepted the gist of Keynes's economics without serious demur. Even war socialism did not challenge him directly. The mighty wartime state was, by definition, a product of war; the real question was what would follow it when the fighting stopped. But politics have more to do with mood than with logic; and the political reality was that war socialism chimed with the mood of the time. No one could deny that the command economy delivered the goods – not just an extraordinary level of mobilisation, but full employment and fair shares as well.

Given the government's commitment to victory at all costs, it was a wartime necessity. Increasingly it also became a template for peace. Democratic collectivist dirigistes discovered a seemingly unanswerable argument. As the Labour Party put it smugly in 1942, 'We have learned during the war that that the anarchy of private competition must give way to ordered planning.'[61] In reality, Keynes and Beveridge had learned no such thing. Each offered a middle way between laissez-faire and state direction. But, as victory approached and debate began to focus on the shape of the post-war political economy, the distinctions between their evolutionary liberal collectivism and the determinist *étatisme* of would-be Labour planners were ignored. As the next chapter will show, Labour dirigistes offered a potent cocktail, in which Keynesian economics, Beveridgean welfare policy and a planned economy were shaken up together. In the climate created by five years of war socialism it was irresistible.

That was only one of the ironies in Churchill's pursuit of victory at all costs. A greater one was that Britain became increasingly dependent on the United States. On one level Churchill had expected this, even hoped for it. That was the meaning of his evocation of the new world in his 'fight on the beaches' speech. However, his picture of the United States owed more to the passionate intensity of his war-boosted capacity for wishful thinking than to a sober assessment of the traditions that shaped American policy. For him, the United States was not an ordinary foreign power. She was as much a part of the global community of the English-speaking peoples as was Britain herself. As such, she had a duty to range herself alongside Britain in her hour of need. The fact that millions of Americans were not of British descent, were often instinctively hostile to Britain and, in any case, felt no special kinship with her, eluded him. So did the deep, instinctive anti-imperialism that was fundamental to the Americans' understanding of themselves. In October 1942, *Life* magazine published a notorious 'Open Letter' to the people of England that epitomised the American view of the British empire:

> One thing we are sure we are *not* fighting for is to hold the British Empire together. We don't like to put the matter so bluntly, but we don't want you to have any illusions. If your strategists are planning a war to hold the British Empire together they will sooner or later find themselves strategising alone.[62]

That was an understatement. Not only was the United States not fighting to hold the British empire together, but American policy-makers sought, with unremitting zeal, to undermine Britain's imperial role, economic as well as political. At some level, Churchill must have realised this, yet he could not understand how deep American anti-imperialism went. For him, the British empire was a force for good. He could not bring himself to see that for most Americans it was a force for bad.

He bent over backwards to charm the American President, Franklin Roosevelt, and the two established a close, and unusually frank, working relationship. But he never fully plumbed the baffling mixture of idealism, guile, opportunism, vacillation and ruthlessness that characterised Roosevelt's politics. (Nor did most Americans.) Churchill knew, of course, that there was a huge disparity between American and British power. That knowledge was implicit in his policy from Dunkirk on. Yet he found it hard to accept that, as American power waxed, British power was bound, in relative terms, to wane. In a neat one-liner in 1942 he told the king that Britain and the United States were no longer 'walking out' but 'married'.[63] He failed to add that the United States was an increasingly domineering spouse, with a tight hand on the housekeeping money. Above all, he found it hard to accept that American interests and the American vision of the post-war world order differed quite radically from Britain's.

Fate gave him ample opportunities to learn. In the terrible, glorious summer of 1940, when the RAF narrowly won the Battle of Britain and warded off the threat of a German invasion, the United States was neutral. For another year Britain stood alone, glowering impotently at a German-dominated continent. German submarines in the North Atlantic took a fearful toll of her shipping. Italian forces threatened her control of Egypt. She also had to cope with a menacing financial haemorrhage. The United States was by far the most important source of the supplies she needed to carry on fighting; and these had to be paid for. By the end of the year her gold and dollar reserves had fallen to a dangerously low level.

The promise of salvation came in the early months of 1941 with the introduction of Lend-Lease – the first really critical American intervention on Britain's behalf. Supplies for the British war effort would be purchased in the United States, by American agencies, and transferred to Britain without payment. In a now legendary phrase, Churchill called Lend-Lease 'the most unsordid act in the history of any nation' and thought it presaged an early American entry into the war. As so often, he was disappointed. The United States was now waging war against Germany by proxy, a state of affairs with which Roosevelt was understandably content. It was not until June 1941, when Hitler invaded the Soviet Union, that Britain acquired a great-power ally, but it was a totalitarian state whose rulers were as murderous as those of Nazi Germany. American neutrality lasted until December 1941 when the Japanese attacked Pearl Harbor and Hitler obligingly declared war on the United States in support of his Japanese ally.

The day after Pearl Harbor, Churchill told the chief of the General Staff, Sir Alan Brooke, with 'a wicked leer' that it was no longer necessary to court the United States since she was now 'in the harem'.[64] In truth, she was more difficult to deal with in the harem than she had been outside it. Inevitably, American leaders, military and civilian, had their own ideas about how the war should be fought and the peace secured; and the huge build-up of American power gave them ever more muscle to make their will prevail Like Stalin, the American military wanted to open an early second front, by way of an amphibious cross-Channel invasion of France. Fearing heavy losses, Churchill demurred, but he did not dare to oppose the Americans head-on. Instead he temporised – with some difficulty persuading the Americans to agree to an early invasion of Italy as a mini-second front, and toying with plans for an invasion of Norway.

But, in spite of his lack of enthusiasm (concealed from the public, but well known both to the Americans and to Stalin), a cross-Channel, Anglo-American invasion of France finally took place in June 1944. Under duress, Churchill also agreed to the so-called 'Morgenthau Plan' – a crackpot project, fathered by the US Secretary of the Treasury, Henry Morgenthau, for forcibly de-industrialising Germany and turning her into a pastoral nation. (Needless to say, the Plan was never implemented.) Dwarfing these strategic difference was a profound difference of attitude over the shape of the post-war world. Churchill sought an enduring Anglo-American axis in which, as a Foreign Office official put it, Britain would 'steer this great unwieldy barge, the United States, into the right harbour'.[65] Roosevelt had no intention of allowing his barge to be steered by Britain. He sought a world of harmonious international co-operation, with no power blocs and no empires, in which American values would prevail universally; and he thought he could charm Stalin into it. Churchill did not believe in Roosevelt's world, and as the Red Army raced west after its great victory at Stalingrad he became increasingly jittery about Stalin's intentions. But Roosevelt's messianic self-deception remained undented.

⚜

The most damaging displays of American muscle concerned currency and trade.[66] The American economy was by far the strongest in the world; in glaring contrast to the economies of the other main belligerents, it received an immense boost from the war. Like their British equivalents in the nineteenth century, American policy-makers were determined to create a global economic order reflecting their values and shaped by their priorities. They were not imperialists in the classic sense. They had no desire to acquire territory or to rule other peoples. Their ambitions were more grandiose and, in their own eyes, more moral. They wanted to use the vast arsenal of soft power that the strength of the American economy had given them to build a better world; and, for them, it went without saying that a better world would be run on American lines.

They wanted currencies to be freely convertible as they had been in the heyday of the gold standard. They also wanted global free trade, based on the principle of non-discrimination. They thought that the chief obstacle to their new order was the wall of preferential trade agreements and currency controls that had grown up in and around the British empire in the 1930s, shielding the British economy from the deflationary external pressures which had damaged it so grievously in the 1920s. For true believers in the free-trade messianism that prevailed in Washington, the British combination of imperial preference and the sterling area was trebly offensive. It was designedly discriminatory; it hindered American trade; and it was morally reprehensible.

It smacked of the autarchic economics of Hitler's notorious Finance Minister, Hjalmar Schacht. It stood in the way of the open global market whose coming was a prerequisite for a peaceful, prosperous, democratic and American-centred world. The conclusion was obvious. Britain would have to be coaxed, cajoled and, if necessary, forced to change her ways. Her desperate need for American aid was a perfect lever for prising her out of her discriminatory shell.

The Americans achieved only a partial success. Britain ended the war with imperial preference intact. Sterling did not become fully convertible until 1958. Yet in the course of its campaign to impel Britain into the American-centred new order, the Roosevelt Administration did great damage to Britain's post-war economic prospects. The 'most unsordid act' of Lend-Lease had a sting in the tail. Britain had to provide a reciprocal benefit to the United States, known as a 'consideration'. The US State Department demanded a British commitment to non-discrimination in trade, implying an end to imperial preference and presumably to the sterling area as well. After furious expostulations from Keynes, the leading British negotiator, and bitter complaints in the British Cabinet, the Americans climbed part of the way down. Britain escaped with a commitment to unspecified 'agreed action' to eliminate trade discrimination at an unspecified stage in the future.

But the US Administration also used cruder instruments for keeping Britain in line. It insisted that Britain should be debarred from exporting goods incorporating Lend-Lease materials; goods similar to those supplied under Lend-Lease; and goods that contained materials in short supply in the US. In addition, the US Treasury manipulated the Lend-Lease system so as to ensure that Britain's reserves were kept below whatever figure the relevant American agencies laid down. The end result was that she was locked into a dangerously lopsided economic posture. She was able – almost compelled – to go on fighting, at a level of intensity far higher than that of the United States. At the same time she was prevented from building up her grievously depleted reserves; and she had to run down her exports to a point far below the cost of the goods that she would have to import when the fighting stopped. (By the end of the war the volume of her exports was less than one-third of the pre-war figure, while the proportion of the labour force engaged on exports had fallen from 9.5 per cent to less than 2 per cent.)[67] The implications were startling. Britain had bartered economic independence for the wherewithal to fight what had become an American-run war. It is not difficult to see why. In British eyes, the war was *their* war; the Americans were latecomers – stronger and richer than they, no doubt, but less deserving morally. Britain had been in at the start and would stay in until the end, no matter how much it cost. Few foresaw how high the price would be.

American muscle was equally apparent in the complex negotiations over the future shape of the global monetary system that dragged on from 1943 to 1945. The questions at issue went to the heart of Britain's post-war aspirations. Should governments be free to alter the exchange rate to protect employment against external deflationary pressures? Would the system combat such pressures? Would the weak alone be expected to correct their balance of payments deficits, as under the gold standard, or would the burden fall on the strong as well? The British and Americans gave radically different answers to all these questions. Keynes, the chief British negotiator, sought a form of managed global liberalism, embodying the essence of the economic vision that he had preached since the 1920s. The pre-war conflict between domestic needs and international pressures would come to an end. The weak would no longer be disciplined by the strong. No one would be tempted to erect autarchic barriers against deflationary pressures from the outside world because there would be no such pressures; the world economy would be run on Keynesian lines.

The Americans proposed a new, more flexible version of nineteenth-century orthodoxy. They too wanted a managed global system, but one in which strong currencies and strong economies called the tune, as under the gold standard of old days. The final settlement – reached at what then seemed a historic international conference in Bretton Woods in New Hampshire in the summer of 1944 – included a little balm for the British. A 'scarce currency' clause was supposed to ensure that countries in massive and persistent surplus could not impose deflation on the rest of the world. Nevertheless, in essentials, the Bretton Woods agreement embodied the American vision. The International Monetary Fund (IMF) that it established was effectively under American control, while its operating principles were tailored in Washington and New York. It was less a powerhouse of global Keynesianism than the guardian of a monetary *pax Americana*.

In one sense, Keynes's defeat hardly mattered. The Bretton Woods agreement did not come into operation until well after the war, in a very different world. But though the practical significance of the negotiations was small, their moral and psychological significance was vast. Once again, the British made the unsurprising discovery that the Americans would use their muscle to impose their vision of the post-war world order on their allies. Once again, the whig imperialist British elite, of which Keynes was almost as glittering an ornament as Churchill, could not bring itself to admit that the American vision differed radically from its own. What went through Keynes's mind during the years of negotiation that culminated at Bretton Woods will never be known. The subtleties of that mind have eluded his biographers as thoroughly as they eluded contemporaries. Nonetheless, there is no doubt that the eventual agreement was a defeat for him, albeit with consolatory sweeteners.

Equally, there is no doubt that he settled for it, and did his Merlin-like best to bewitch the rest of the political elite into doing so too. One reason was that he thought it was the most he could get. It might be half a loaf, but that was better than no bread. That was not the only reason, however. Glinting between the lines of his advocacy was the dream of a generous, whiggish Anglo-American condominium, in which a youthful America would march alongside a wise Britain. The 'world's best hope', he told the House of Lords, was 'an Anglo-American understanding which brings us and others together in international institutions which may be in the long run the first step towards something more comprehensive'.[68] The dream had elements of nobility about it; it was certainly a comforting one for much of the British political class. It was a new version of the classic whig imperialist vision of Britain and Britishness, designed for the new age of American primacy. The Americans would be honorary Britons and the British honorary Americans. The only problem was that the Americans had no wish to be anything of the sort, though it took a long time for that to sink in – if, indeed, it ever did.

The old vision still had some life in it. Nine months after Bretton Woods, Germany surrendered unconditionally. The two strands of the whig imperialist tradition – evolutionary constitutionalism and freedom-loving globalism – came together in a vintage Commons speech by Winston Churchill, to whom it fell to congratulate the king on the victorious conclusion of the war in Europe. The victory, Churchill insisted, was not due to British arms alone. British institutions, British traditions and the genius that had carried them across the globe had triumphed as well:

> It is the golden circle of the Crown which alone embraces the loyalties of
> so many States and races all over the world . . .
>
> The wisdom of our ancestors has led us to an envied and enviable
> situation. We have the strongest Parliament in the world. We have the
> oldest, the most famous, the most secure and the most serviceable monarchy
> in the world. King and Parliament both rest safely and solidly upon the
> will of the people expressed by free and fair election on the basis of universal
> suffrage. Thus this system has long worked harmoniously both in peace
> and war.[69]

It was Churchill's apotheosis. It was also an elegy for the imperial Britain
that he had incarnated for five years.

The coalition ended three weeks later; and on 5 July a general election
took place. For Labour people, in particular, the 1945 election has been
covered by a haze of nostalgia. In his memoirs, Lord Elwyn-Jones, Labour
Lord Chancellor in the 1970s, recalled a 'packed eve-of-poll meeting' in
Canning Town, with 'rows of intent, uplifted faces – dockers in their caps
and white mufflers, the wives and children and old men and women
who had been through so much'. Barbara Castle remembered 'a sort of
unbelievable buoyancy in the atmosphere' at her eve-of-poll meeting in
Blackburn. It was as if people who had been through the hardships of the
depression and the war 'suddenly thought, "My heavens, we can win the
peace for people like us."' Contemporary accounts were more downbeat.
The social research organisation Mass-Observation found more scepticism
than enthusiasm among ordinary voters; in a search for popular reactions
to the campaign, George Orwell heard no spontaneous election talk and
saw no one looking at an election poster.[70]

Later Labour nostalgia was understandable. When the votes were
counted, the Labour Party emerged with nearly 48 per cent of the popular
vote and a Commons majority of 146 over all parties. The coalition's war
socialism was the chief author of Labour's victory, but the indeterminate
new class that Orwell had eulogised, and that Acland and Cripps had tried
to mobilise, was a crucial ingredient. Not the least of the questions facing
the new government was whether it would manage to construct a lasting
social coalition embracing Orwell's people as well as the core Labour
constituency.

5

PALEST PINK

❖

We are the masters at the moment – and not only for the moment, but for a
very long time to come.

Sir Hartley Shawcross, Attorney-General, House of Commons, April 1946

[A] mixed economy is what most people of the West would prefer. The victory
of Socialism need not be universal to be decisive. ... It is neither prudent, nor
does it accord with our conception of the future, that all forms of private property
should live under perpetual threat. In almost all types of human society different
forms of property have lived side by side. ... But it is a requisite of social stability
that one type of property ownership should dominate. In the society of the future
it should be public property.

Aneurin Bevan, *In Place of Fear*, 1952

The people's flag is palest pink,
It's not as red as you might think.

Old song

❖

BEVIN'S BASTION

The 1945 election put democratic-collectivist *étatisme* into the saddle for
the first time. The next two years would show that its seat was far from
secure, but for the moment an exuberant triumphalism swept through the
Labour movement. The leftist political theorist, Harold Laski, told a rally
in the Central Hall, Westminster, that Labour's victory would 'bring a
message of hope to every democracy all over the world'; even the normally
reticent Clement Attlee declared, 'We are on the eve of a great advance in
the human race.'[1] In all the excitement, the democratic republican strand
in the party's heritage, with its participatory values and its disdain for the
time-worn traditions and reflexes of the British parliamentary monarchy,
was almost forgotten. It was enough that Labour at last had its hands on
the levers of power. It would have seemed frivolous to ask whether they

were the right kind of levers for a professedly democratic party.

In his memoirs, Hugh Dalton, Attlee's first Chancellor of the Exchequer, looked back at the mood of the incoming Labour ministers with misty-eyed nostalgia. 'Our first sensation,' he wrote, 'tingling and triumphant, was of a new society to be built; and we had power to build it. There was exhilaration among us, joy and hope, determination and confidence. We felt exalted, dedicated, walking on air, walking with destiny.'[2] That was the democratic collectivist vision *in excelsis*. The people had spoken through the ballot box. Their task now was to give 'personal support' to the government they had elected.[3] Meanwhile, the omnicompetent central state would use its powers to make society more rational and more just, and to ensure that history marched forward along its predestined path.

Labour's leaders thought they knew where their walk with destiny would take them. The party's ultimate purpose, they declared defiantly in their election manifesto, *Let Us Face the Future*,[4] was to establish 'the Socialist Commonwealth of Great Britain – free, democratic, efficient, progressive, public-spirited'. That was for later, however; socialism could not come overnight in a 'weekend revolution'. Here and now, Labour's programme had two main prongs. The first – a free health service, comprehensive social insurance and 'jobs for all' – spoke powerfully to the war-weary and depression-haunted British public, but it was essentially a mélange of Keynes and Beveridge. Though Labour people, then and since, have been loath to acknowledge the fact, it found an equally prominent place in the Conservative programme. Labour's second prong was more distinctive. The Conservatives might say the right things, it conceded, but they could not be trusted to do them. The reason was that Labour alone knew how to master economic forces for public ends.

Its secret was planning. As *Let Us Face the Future* put it, a Labour Government would 'plan from the ground up'. Private investment and development would conform to government purposes, instead of the other way around. To ensure that the government's will prevailed, basic industries ranging from fuel and power to inland transport would be brought into public ownership. Industries 'not yet ripe' for it would be subject to 'constructive supervision'. This would ensure that progress and efficiency – the lodestars of the democratic collectivist tradition – went together. Foreign policy hardly figured in the manifesto; beyond a warning growl against obstruction by the House of Lords, the constitution did not figure at all.

꿍

Alas for destiny. There was a leathery toughness about the 1945 government that ranked it with the great reforming governments of Gladstone and

Asquith, but it needed all the toughness it could find. The so-called 'Big Five' of the new Cabinet – Attlee; Dalton; Bevin, the Foreign Secretary; Morrison, the Leader of the Commons and Lord President of the Council; and Cripps, the President of the Board of Trade – were all seasoned by wartime office. This, however, was a mixed blessing. The strain showed. Morrison was out of action with thrombosis for four critical months in 1947; Dalton kept going with benzedrine and sleeping pills; Cripps would retire, worn out, at sixty-one and die two years later; the litany of Bevin's ills ran from insomnia, sinusitis, an enlarged liver and damaged kidneys to constant trouble from the 'old ticker'. Only Attlee's spare frame seemed impervious; and by the end of the government's term of office, even he would find himself in hospital at a moment of grave political crisis. If we are to understand the course of high politics under Attlee's government, the effects of constant wear and tear on ageing and often sickly bodies must never be forgotten.

That said, the 'Big Five' would have stood out in any Cabinet. Attlee was a competent staff officer by temperament, not a visionary commander-in-chief, but, with only occasional exceptions, he managed his more ebullient colleagues with extraordinary skill. His clipped, laconic style, modest demeanour, penchant for understatement and public-school education symbolised his party's determined respectability; his long years of service to the movement reassured those in its own ranks who thought it might become too respectable for its own good. He seemed, and to a large extent was, a perfect embodiment of the professional service class whose ethos and values had always been central to the democratic collectivist world-view. Rebutting the notion that Attlee was an enigmatic figure whom no one could fully understand, Douglas Jay, who worked in his private office in Number Ten before entering the House of Commons himself, wrote that the truth was simple: 'Attlee was a straightforward Victorian Christian, who believed one should do one's job and one's duty, whether as an Army officer, or Member of Parliament or Prime Minister.' It should not be supposed, he added, 'that because this type may now be extinct, it therefore never existed'.[5] It certainly existed in the still partially Victorian society of 1940s Britain, and the fact that Attlee exemplified it so well was one of his government's most potent assets.

Morrison ranked second in the formal hierarchy, though not in political weight. As Lord President he was, in theory, the home front supremo and planning overlord, but his energies were fully occupied in managing the parliamentary party, overseeing the legislative programme and preparing the nationalisation bills. He was no intellectual, but he was a formidable fixer, a persuasive debater and what would now be called a spin doctor. He was surprisingly open-minded and had a better nose for middle opinion than any of his colleagues. His background was respectably lower-middle class. His parental home was a double-fronted, detached house; his father was a policeman and a strong Tory. Perhaps because of this, Morrison had an unrivalled feel for what he called the 'useful people' – in effect, Orwell's intermediate class. More clearly than any of his senior Cabinet colleagues, he realised that Labour needed them, as well as the blue-collar manual workers, in its fortress seats, and did his best to enroll them in a Labour social coalition comparable to the Baldwin coalition of the interwar years. He has gone down in history as the inventor of the centralised, bureaucratic model of public ownership that prevailed during the Attlee years, and he saw the role and purpose of nationalised industries in uncompromisingly technocratic terms. 'Socialisation,' he told the House of Commons, was 'not an end in itself. The object is to make possible organisation of a more efficient industry, rendering more public service.'[6] But there was more to him than that. He had risen to the top of Labour politics through local government. In the 1930s he had been one of the most formidable leaders in the history of the London County Council (LCC) and Morrison, the centralising nationaliser, ran alongside a decentralist Morrison who would have liked to temper the wind of Labour's dirigisme to the shorn lamb of local democracy.

Dalton – Etonian, Kingsman, son of the Dean of Windsor and an 'upper-class renegade'[7] who loved tormenting the class he had left – was the least of the five. He had charge of the Treasury and should have been a power in the Cabinet, but his zest for intrigue, his wide circle of bright (and, if possible, handsome) young protégés and his bullying habits concealed a curious lack of inner confidence. On the crucial financial issues that haunted the government, he failed to get his way. Two years after the government was formed, he would become its most conspicuous casualty. Well before the end of the government's life, however, the rise of two brilliant younger men, Aneurin Bevan and Hugh Gaitskell, had amply compensated for Dalton's decline.

The twin peaks of the government were Bevin and Cripps. They could hardly have been more different. Bevin was the illegitimate son of a poverty-stricken Somerset woman who had died when he was eight.[8] After leaving school at eleven, he had clawed his way to the top of Labour politics in bitter battles with employers, trade-union rivals and rebels in his own ranks. Thanks to a glandular illness as a young man, he was grossly overweight. He was also frequently drunk, massively confident, infuriatingly garrulous, often brutal in debate, vindictive in enmity but rocklike in loyalty, and capable of soaring flights of political imagination and passion. He was a mine of stories, mostly about his own extraordinary career, and loved regaling his staff with them.

His politics defied classification. He relied on instinct, not theory; on people, not books. Like Orwell and Tawney, he was a tough-minded social patriot, but unlike them he viewed Britain's role in the outside world through whig-imperialist spectacles, fashioned in the days of Queen Victoria and not very different from Churchill's. He was a planner of sorts, but only of sorts. He did not share the Fabian faith in the expert. In Labour Party debates in the 1930s he had fought unsuccessfully for workers' representation on the boards of future nationalised industries, and traces of the old syndicalist dream of working-class self-emancipation still lingered in his approach to political economy. Above all, he was proud of his class. 'We are imbued with the idea that we are the last great class to march onward, to rise to power and equity,' he told his union conference in the bitter aftermath of the General Strike. 'We believe that we shall rise to the occasion.'9 With good reason he thought that the war had vindicated that belief; and it ran through his frequent interventions in economic policy-making in the post-war years. The working class could be led (preferably by him), but woe betide anyone who tried to dragoon it.

Cripps was born into a wealthy family with impeccable establishment credentials. He was a scholar at Winchester and after taking a science degree became one of the best-paid barristers in the country. By the time Labour took office in 1945, his lifestyle had become self-laceratingly ascetic. Chronic ill health had led him to become a vegetarian and a teetotaller. He rose at 4 a.m., worked for three hours before a short walk with his wife, followed by a cold bath and a light breakfast. His working day usually lasted from sixteen to eighteen hours. Throughout his life, he was sustained by a profound, unquestioning Christian faith. It was coupled with the most formidable intellect in the government. He once told his protégé, Edwin Plowden, that if he were given the papers of any case he had fought in the last twenty years for an hour, he could go into court and fight it again. Then he had corrected himself: 'No, I would not need the papers.'10

Unlike Bevin, he was a whole-hearted planner. At the start of the new government's term of office, James Meade cast him (wrongly) as a dangerous advocate of a Soviet-style 'Gosplan', which would entail 'socialising all or most industries'.11 In fact, he had abandoned the *Marxisant* sympathies he had trumpeted in the 1930s. He was a democratic planner, he insisted; a planner-by-consent. As we shall see, it was not at all clear what he meant by that; in practice he behaved like an odd mixture of national management consultant and public moralist. Although he and Bevin had clashed bitterly before the war, they had more in common than met the eye. Both were men of towering force and will. Both were sublimely confident in their own judgement; and both had a lordly contempt for the small change of parliamentary manoeuvre. After Cripps's ascent to the chancellorship they formed an axis of power around which the entire government revolved.

Few governments have left a deeper footprint on their times; partly because of this, no other government has won a comparable place in the mythology of the Labour movement. (Even New Labour ministers have been known, at a pinch, to clothe themselves in Attlee's mantle.)[12] But the myth is delusive, for the footprint was not what it seemed. The transition from total war to uneasy peace created a host of problems that the government had not foreseen. So did the precipitous decline in British power and wealth that the war had brought in its train and, less obviously, the after-effects of five years of physical destruction and nervous strain. Many cities were pock-marked with bomb damage, and some city centres had been flattened by it. Ports like Liverpool, Hull, Plymouth, Swansea and Belfast had been particularly hard hit, but London had suffered most. The area around St Paul's Cathedral had become a 'golden and green and purple wilderness', wrote the novelist Rose Macaulay, where 'shells of flats soared skyward on twisting stairs, staring empty-eyed at desolation'.

> Poor merchants, poor manufacturers, poor agents, poor warehousemen, where are they all now? Blown sky high, burnt up by that horrid, malicious bloody flame, many have seeded themselves again elsewhere, struggling valiantly against extinction. Others have vanished, destroyed utterly and commerce knows them no more. In any case, they no longer flourish in Cripplegate, Aldermanbury and Basinghall; Monkwell and Addle Street ramble oblivious through stony deserts, and the pavements they so lately, so venally trod are craters where the rose-bay and the chickweed sprawl.[13]

Food was adequate, but dismal; queues were ubiquitous; black markets flourished. 'Spivs', sporting wide-lapelled coats with padded-out shoulders, pencil moustaches and florid ties, were 'grudgingly admired, simultaneously disliked'.[14] The cruellest shortage was of housing. Organised 'squatting' in empty accommodation was frequent; a total of 40,000 people occupied disused service camps. Even in comfortable suburbs, conditions in requisitioned housing were sometimes appalling. In 'a large, dilapidated room without light, water and (yesterday at least) without fuel for a fire', recorded a Stanmore rehousing officer, were a 'bus conductor, two women, and three schoolchildren, desperate for somewhere to live'. 750,000 new homes were built in the government's first three years, but when it left office an immense pool of uncleared slums and unsatisfied demand remained.[15]

As well as bomb-damaged cities and a run-down infrastructure, Attlee and his colleagues inherited a near-bankrupt economy and grossly overstretched resources. The net result was a seemingly endless series of economic crises and forced changes of direction. Like Columbus disembarking in America after setting sail for the Indies, the government discovered a New World, but not the one it had hoped to reach. Under its leadership the British state groped its way towards the geopolitical niche that it still occupies, with some variations, at the start of the twenty-first century. It also acted as the midwife of the British version of the tamed welfare capitalism that underpinned the longest period of economic growth and social peace in European history. But these achievements owed more to the whig imperialist tradition of evolutionary adaptation than to the democratic collectivist vision of purposive social reconstruction.

☙

Three interwoven themes dominated the new government's life: a long-drawn-out, occasionally lackadaisical, but more often desperate search for national solvency; a hard-fought rearguard action in defence of Britain's bedraggled great-power status; and a heroic attempt to turn the democratic collectivist vision of a just and rationally organised society into reality. The search for solvency began within days of the government's entry into office, when the new ministers found themselves face to face with a yawning abyss of bankruptcy and humiliation. During the war, Britain and her colonies had lost between a quarter and a third of their merchant shipping fleet. Almost half her gold and dollar reserves had gone. Around half her overseas investments had been sold, often at knock-down prices. Foreign debt had almost quintupled, rising from £700 million to £3.3 billion, most of it owed to sterling area countries in the form of sterling balances.[16] As we saw in the last chapter, her exports had plummeted. In 1938, Britain had been the world's largest creditor country. Now she was its largest debtor.

The first and most alarming of the crises that drove the government off its course was immanent in these figures. During the war, Lend-Lease had kept Britain afloat, disguising her economic weakness from the general public and even from much of the political elite. (That was why Treasury fears that Beveridge's proposals were unaffordable had been so easily brushed aside.) When Japan surrendered on 14 August 1945 the war came to a sudden end. Lend-Lease ended with it. Labour's forward march to rationality and justice seemed likely to be halted before it had begun. In one of the most portentous official memoranda of the entire post-war period, Keynes warned that, without intense concentration on the expansion of exports, drastic economies in overseas expenditure and substantial aid from the United States, there would be no hope of escaping 'a financial Dunkirk'. Britain would become a 'second-class Power' on a par with France; austerity would be harsher than at any time during the war. And 'the best hopes of the new Government' would have to be indefinitely postponed.[17] Why the Americans would wish to give substantial aid to help a professedly socialist government to realise its hopes, he did not explain.

Attlee and his colleagues spent nearly six months trying to stave off the threatened Dunkirk, with consequences that would haunt the rest of their term of office. Whitehall was already half committed to an extraordinary gamble that Keynes had proposed before the general election.[18] He had forecast a cumulative balance of payments deficit of £2 billion over the reconstruction period. There were three possible solutions: 'Starvation Corner', which meant Soviet-style autarchy and intolerable austerity; 'Temptation', which meant an interest-bearing American loan and substantial concessions to the American position on international trade; and 'Justice', which meant a massive $8 billion of American aid, de facto sterling convertibility within a year of the end of the war and a negotiated settlement of the sterling balances. 'Justice' was the only satisfactory option. Since it was in the Americans' interests as well as in Britain's, Keynes insisted, it was also a realistic one.

In the summer of 1945 two Treasury officials – Sir Wilfred Eady and the formidable Richard ('Otto') Clarke – worked out a fall-back plan for a multilateral grouping based on the sterling area together with France, Belgium, the Netherlands and Scandinavia. But Keynes had set his heart on 'Justice'. He wished to save his country and the world for the vision of reformed capitalism which it had been his life's work to define. The point of 'Justice' was not only to give Britain a fair deal; it was to make it possible for the British to become 'partners and coadjutors' of the Americans in setting up the new, enlightened economic order in which he passionately believed. He had no interest in fall-backs. He rubbished the Eady–Clarke alternative, which sank without trace.[19]

In late August 1945, a panic-stricken group of senior ministers and officials adopted a watered-down version of Keynes's strategy. Britain would seek an American grant in aid of $5 billion and, by implication, accept the corollary of early convertibility and non-discrimination. Keynes was despatched to Washington to negotiate on these lines. The negotiations were a disaster.[20] Keynes was a sick man, desperate to reach an agreement. (He died in April 1946.) Thanks to his disdain for the Eady–Clarke fall-back plan he had nothing to negotiate with. His cutting witticisms, delivered in the exquisite tones of Eton and King's, did not endear him to the American negotiators.

Nor did his long and brilliant exposition of the contribution that Britain had made to the common cause. At one point, he burst out, 'You cannot treat a great nation as if it were a bankrupt company.'[21] but now that the fighting was over and the common cause a memory, bankruptcy was Britain's most obvious attribute in the Americans' eyes, and they had no compunction about exploiting it. The end result was a humiliating failure – in an understandably bitter phrase of Hugh Dalton's, 'a long agonising slide', leading to 'strings so tight that they might strangle our trade and, indeed, our whole economic life'.[22]

Britain had to settle for a loan of $3.75 billion, together with $650 million to cover Lend-Lease supplies in the pipeline. Not only was the loan more niggardly than the government had expected, but the conditions were far more onerous. Britain had to promise to make all sterling earned in current transactions convertible into other currencies a year after the agreement came into force. Discrimination against American imports would cease at the end of 1946. Britain would ratify the Bretton Woods agreement, which Keynes had accepted seventeen months before. This was not 'Starvation Corner', but only besotted Keynesians could see it as 'Justice'. Keynes had hoped that American generosity would bind Britain into a multilateral global order. The Americans had preferred to bludgeon her into one.

In a brilliant and passionate speech in the Commons debate on the loan agreement, the maverick Conservative MP, Robert Boothby, denounced it as Britain's 'economic Munich', attacked Keynes as a 'siren, beckoning us to our doom from the depths of Bretton Woods', and accused the government of selling 'the British Empire for a packet of cigarettes'.[23] The government's only answer was that it had no alternative, but this was at most a quarter-truth. There is no way of telling whether the Eady–Clarke fall-back plan would have worked, but it could hardly have been less successful than the course Keynes actually followed, and it would at least have strengthened his negotiating hand. But by the time the Commons debated the agreement it was too late; the deed was done. Once again, Keynes's messianic belief in an Anglo-American partnership of economic enlightenment had carried all before it.

❧

Munich or not, the loan agreement had bought Britain time. Now ministers had to decide how to use it. The second dominating theme of the period – the struggle for continued great-power status – comes into the story at this point. To understand it, we must make a leap of historical imagination. At the start of the twenty-first century, it seems self-evident that Britain's days as a great power were numbered, if not over. It was far from self-evident in 1945. Policy-makers knew that Britain was the weakest of the 'Big Three'. As Sir Orme Sargent, soon to be Permanent Secretary at the Foreign Office, put it in 1945, she was 'Lepidus in the triumvirate with Mark Antony and Augustus'.[24]

But Labour's leaders would have been as outraged as their Conservative opposite numbers if they had been told that she did not belong in the Big Three at all. So would the British public. They held their heads high at the end of the war, and with good reason. Alone among the victor nations, Britain and her Commonwealth had fought Nazi Germany from start to finish. Unlike the United States and the Soviet Union, she had not waited to be attacked. Though she could not claim to have won the war all by herself, her solitary stand in 1940 had ensured that Hitler would not win it. Economically as well as militarily, she was easily the most powerful country in Europe west of the Soviet bloc. More than 450 million people, spread over huge areas of Africa and Asia, were ruled from London. The ties of sentiment and memory that bound the self-governing dominions to the 'mother country' were still intact. The sterling area that helped to hold the Commonwealth together was the world's largest currency and trading bloc. Ministers and officials knew that Britain's wartime sacrifices had bankrupted her, but they would have thought it shameful to accept relegation to second-class status on that account. Her economic difficulties seemed temporary; her global mission permanent.

Bevin, at this stage the most powerful member of the Cabinet after Attlee, gave that mission his own special gloss. In his days as a union leader, he had fought to win power for the working class; as Foreign Secretary he was determined to hang on to every scrap of power Britain still possessed, and tireless in searching for new ways to sustain it. In an early Cabinet paper, he justified his search on the revealing grounds that Britain was 'the last bastion of social democracy', the only alternative to 'the red tooth and claw of American capitalism and the Communist dictatorship of Soviet Russia'.[25] In a Churchillian moment in a speech to the TUC in 1947, he rebutted the charge that he was tying Britain to the United States:

> My God! I am here this morning to appeal to you to fight for our independence in the workshop, in the mine, in the field. It is a very ignoble thing for any Foreign Secretary to have to deal with anybody upon whom you are dependent. Who wants that position? Who wants it with a trade-union training such as I have had, who built a great union on purpose so that I could stand up equal to anyone in the world? ... I want Britain to stand self-reliant, and to come back.[26]

He knew that Britain could not 'come back' to the position she had held in the days of Lord Salisbury, or even of Lord Curzon. But, as the historian Michael Hogan has shown, he dreamed of a 'middle kingdom', led by Britain, and embracing the Commonwealth and non-Communist Western Europe, strong enough to follow its own course independently of the superpowers.[27] Mere pounds, shillings and pence could not be allowed to trump that dream.

Not everyone agreed with the conclusions Bevin drew from it. To the Foreign Office's dismay, Attlee wanted to abandon the Middle East. Dalton fought feebly and unavailingly to overcome 'mulish' Foreign Office resistance to defence cuts.[28] Before his death, Keynes would fire a characteristically elegant shot across the defence spenders' bows. Yet no one disputed that Britain was, and must remain, a world power. Attlee's alternative to Britain's role in the Middle East was a defensive line across Africa 'from Lagos to Kenya', with British troops concentrated in the latter.[29] As we have just seen, Keynes believed as passionately as any general or diplomat that it was unthinkable to allow Britain to become a second-class power. Morrison, whose enthusiasm for the 'jolly old empire' shocked his party,[30] Dalton, who thought the colonies a nest of 'pullulating, poverty stricken, diseased nigger communities',[31] and Cripps, who spent long hours trying to persuade the Indian Congress leaders to moderate their demands, held equally firmly to the whig-imperialist assumptions which had been part of the mental furniture of the entire political class, irrespective of party, since the nineteenth century. In any case, Britain *was* a world power, whether she liked it or not. She, not the United States, held the line against Soviet incursions in Iran; her troops held off the apparent threat of a Communist takeover in Greece; for better or worse (and few can now doubt that it was for worse, so far as British national interests were concerned) she was the mandatory power in Palestine.

In a sardonic note in February 1946, Keynes warned that, on existing policies, overseas political and military expenditure would be at least £1 billion and perhaps as much as £1.5 billion in the three years 1945–8. It would, he added tartly,

considerably upset the hard-pressed British public if they were to become aware that ... not a single bean of sustenance for themselves or of capital equipment for British manufacturers is likely to be left over from the American credit; and that we shall require, on balance, the whole of it, and unless we change our ways, much more ... to cut a dash in the world considerably above our means.[32]

Undeterred, ministers dashed on. For Attlee and most of his colleagues, defence spending was not an optional extra. It was the price of national independence. They would have wanted to cut a dash in the world even if the Americans had been willing to treat Britain as a partner, in the spirit of Keynes's 'Justice'. American unwillingness made them even more determined. Scarce resources, particularly of scientific and engineering manpower, were poured into the development of nuclear energy. Most of those involved assumed that this would cover military as well as civil purposes, but it was only in January 1947 that a highly secret Cabinet Committee formally decided that Britain would build her own atomic bomb. In a pithy phrase, Bevin spelled out the rationale: 'We could not afford to acquiesce in an American monopoly of this new development.'[33] (Legend has it that he said he wanted a bomb with a 'bloody great union jack on it'. The legend may be true.) In this field, at least, the bastion held firm. The cost averaged out at around £20 million a year: money well spent in the eyes of those who took the decision.

The pursuit of nuclear independence was only part of the price of globalism. As late as December 1946, Britain's armed forces still totalled more than 1,400,000.[34] In 1946, defence spending came to £1.5 billion, more than one-third of total government expenditure. In 1947, the figure was still £930 million, or more than one-quarter.[35] British troops did not withdraw from Greece until February 1947. The running sore of the Palestine mandate lasted longer and brought more grief. Britain was caught in the crossfire between two nationalisms, each with a claim to the same territory. An intransigent Zionism, fuelled by the still-recent horrors of the Holocaust and the plight of helpless and often traumatised Jewish survivors, confronted an equally intransigent Arab nationalism, determined to prevent the emergence of a Jewish state in what had been Arab land. The result was a long, dragging conflict with both communities, which Britain did not have the resources to win, as well as a bitter quarrel with the passionately pro-Zionist United States. The decision to withdraw was not taken until September 1947, after two years of odium and acrimony.

In India, the government fought a long, doomed battle for a federal solution to the conflict between Muslims and Hindus. A federal but united India, the chiefs of staff hoped, would be a base for operations against Siberia in the event of war. It was clear by the summer of 1946 that these hopes were vain, but it was not until February 1947 that the government announced its decision to withdraw unconditionally from the subcontinent in mid-1948. (The date was later moved forward to August 1947.) The end result was the creation of the two self-governing dominions of India and Pakistan. Over time, this would lead to a profound change in the nature of the British Commonwealth and the self-understanding of the British state and people, along the Burkean lines foreshadowed by Baldwin in the 1930s. In the perspective of the 250-year-long history of the British state, this was the Attlee Government's greatest achievement, but it departed radically from the Cabinet's original intentions.

✌

The third overarching theme of the Attlee years – the government's attempt to make a reality of the democratic collectivist vision of a new society – bulked largest in the minds of Labour people at the time, and still accounts for its legendary status in Labour memories. The attempt had three main prongs: the pursuit of welfare policies on the lines that Beveridge had set out during the war; an extensive programme of nationalisation; and a puzzled search for the 'nebulous but exalted' holy grail of a planned economy.[36] Once in power, ministers lost no time in translating Beveridge's proposals into law. By early December 1945, James Griffiths, the emollient but inspirational South Wales miner whom Attlee had appointed Minister of National Insurance, had prepared a scheme of universal and compulsory social insurance, based on the Beveridgean principle of entitlement, through flat-rate contributions, to flat-rate benefits. The legislation received the royal assent on 1 August 1946.

Universal social insurance was the first great pillar of the Beveridgean system. A free and comprehensive health service was the second. The coalition government's health white paper had proposed a comprehensive service, but had left the structure vague. Responsibility, for translating its generalities into statute went to Griffiths' equally inspirational though less emollient fellow miner and fellow countryman, Aneurin Bevan, Attlee's untried Minister of Health. There was a magic about Bevan, which none of his ministerial colleagues could equal. He was the Charles James Fox of twentieth-century British politics, loved by his followers, hated by his enemies and possessed of a devastating wit, coupled with a Bohemian lifestyle and an aristocratic disdain for bureaucratic plodders. ('Poor man,' he once said of Walter Citrine, 'he suffers from files.') For many on the Labour right, he was the Lucifer of the movement – a fallen angel, blessed with a mellifluous tongue, but cursed with overweening ambition and flagrant irresponsibility. To increasing numbers on the left, he was the sea-green incorruptible of socialist purity. Few gave due weight to the extraordinary mixture of charm, toughness, imagination and executive ability that made him one of the greatest leaders Labour never had.

In his days as Minister of Health these attributes were tested to the limit. He had to realise the Beveridge vision, while winning the acquiescence of a notoriously prickly profession, suspicious of anything that smacked of lay encroachment. The result was an exercise in political legerdemain which has confused later generations as much at it confused contemporaries. Bevan was a quintessential democratic collectivist in democratic republican clothing. He was a master of the millenarian *hwyl* beloved of the Welsh valleys; his policy was shaped by a technocratic centralism that would have delighted the Webbs.

His biggest problem was the split between voluntary and municipal hospitals. Reformers agreed that the dual system had to go, but they could not agree about how to end it.[37] His solution was to nationalise the entire hospital service. There was 'an overwhelming case' for putting the voluntary hospitals under public control, he told the Cabinet in October 1945, but local-government areas were too small for this to be done by the local authorities. The only answer was a new National Hospital Service to take over both the voluntary and the local-authority sectors.[38] A fierce Cabinet battle followed. Herbert Morrison, Labour's party manager in chief, resisted nationalisation in the name of local democracy and civic engagement. Bevan, the wayward rebel of the 1930s, insisted on it in the name of rationality and uniformity. Local democracy, Morrison replied, should trump 'administrative convenience and technical efficiency'. Public utilities, many of them owned by local government, were due to be nationalised; if the local authorities also lost hospital services, 'the fabric of local government might be dangerously weakened'. The 'only way to make the hospital services efficient', Bevan replied uncompromisingly, 'was to centralise responsibility for them'.[39] Bevan won. But he coupled toughness towards local councillors with tenderness towards doctors. He dropped the Labour Party's commitment to a salaried service and, in one of his best-known phrases, stuffed the consultants' mouths with gold by allowing them to keep their pay beds. Medical control over the hospitals was reinforced; the BMA was given the right to be consulted before the minister promulgated regulations; doctors served on the new health authorities alongside elected representatives and in practice had a louder voice.

The National Health Service was the most impressive and enduring of the Attlee Government's domestic legacies. For the vast majority of British citizens, health care was no longer a commodity, to be purchased in the market-place, but part of the public domain where market power was subordinate to citizenship rights. It was soon immensely popular – 'almost a part of the Constitution', as the Harvard political scientist, Harry Eckstein, put it – approved by almost 90 per cent of the population.[40] There was a sting in the tail, however. The NHS was a monument to Beveridge's evolutionary whiggism, but it was also the child of a marriage between democratic collectivist statecraft and professional expertise. Not only did the state suppress the unfairness of the market; central control suppressed the untidiness of local democracy and civic engagement. Ministers and officials in remote Whitehall gained power; local communities lost it. The service was run, in practice, by humane and qualified professionals, recruited on merit and pursuing the public interest. No one had to fear a doctor's bill; the poorest in the land had access to the best health care available. But though social citizenship made one of the greatest advances of the century, political citizenship fell back.

☙

The government's nationalisation programme was equally centralist in conception, but the centralism was curiously strangulated in practice. Between 1945 and 1948 the government nationalised the Bank of England, Cable and Wireless, civil aviation, electricity and gas supply, coal mining, the railways and long-distance road haulage. Steel followed in 1949, after a bitter battle within the Cabinet, where Morrison and John Wilmot, the departmental minister concerned, argued unsuccessfully for government control without nationalisation. The nationalisation programme was an immense legislative and administrative achievement, absorbing huge quantities of time, energy, political capital and cash.[41] A total of £2.6 billion was paid out in compensation; more than two million workers were transferred from the private to the public sector. The measures concerned carried a heavy symbolic charge. Nationalisation, as Attlee once put it, was the 'distinctive side' of the government's programme:[42] the side that justified Labour's claim to stand for social transformation rather than mere social reform. Yet the logic of the nationalisation statutes was far from clear. Labour had campaigned on the proposition that public ownership was a means towards the end of economic planning. It was supposed to put the levers of economic power – the 'commanding heights of the economy' as Aneurin Bevan liked to call them in an echo of Lenin – into the hands of the state, while the state was supposed to use the power thus gained to channel economic forces in the direction that the public interest required.

The outcome did not come up to expectations. Nationalisation had immense moral significance. It carried the message that private property rights were not sacrosanct; that private owners had public obligations, and might be expropriated if they failed to fulfil them. It also had important practical consequences. The nationalisation statutes gave a powerful boost to the state's role as a purchaser, often a monopoly one, enabling it to support domestic suppliers of a wide range of products including rolling stock, locomotives, telephone equipment and aeroplanes, among others.[43]

But they did not procure a planned economy. For one thing they were based on a curious misreading of the realities of economic power. Financial services – the true 'commanding heights' of any modern capitalist economy, and a decisive influence on British statecraft since the eighteenth century – were left untouched.

Besides, the nationalisation statutes came straight out of the repertoire of indirect rule to which British officials turned instinctively when new instruments of governance were in demand. Each statute set up a public corporation at arm's length from government, virtually unaccountable to Parliament, and with a duty to manage its industry as it thought fit. These corporations were vulnerable to informal ministerial arm-twisting on particular questions; in theory, ministers could also issue general directives to them. However, general directives turned out to be ineffective, while ministerial arm-twisting focused on short-term political imperatives rather than on long-term strategy. Ministerial intervention helped to keep the price of coal lower than the market would have borne, but when Morrison tried to set up a national efficiency unit to scrutinise the entire publicly owned sector, he was rebuffed. As the Attorney General pointed out in 1949, the statutes did not allow the nationalised industries 'to be used as instruments for promoting economic results outside their own economic field'.[44] Although they could be bullied, cajoled or bribed into following Government policy, so could their privately owned counterparts. Their relationship to government was that of feudal baron to harassed king, not that of army corps to high command. They were not so much the panzers of the planned economy as an unmanoeuvrable wagon train.

✿

One reason was that the high command did not know what it wanted. The dream of a socially controlled economy, in which economic agents took their cues from a coherent plan rather than from incoherent market forces, lay at the heart of the democratic collectivist project.[45] Unfortunately, planning was a humpty-dumpty word; it meant whatever its users wanted it to mean, and all too often they did not know. Generous ambiguity, not semantic precision, was the hallmark of Labour's economic vision. In good democratic-collectivist fashion, it was for administrative direction in place of market forces; for public control instead of private greed. For most Labour people, competitive markets were sites of exploitation, insecurity and waste; even Dalton, the former economics don, once shocked Meade by telling him that moderate inflation was positively desirable because it interfered with the price mechanism and encouraged state control.[46] Bevan was more uplifting.

'The language of priorities,' he declared, in one of the gnomic epigrams in which he delighted, 'is the religion of socialism.'[47]

But the religion covered three fundamental questions with a thick coating of fudge. It did not explain what planning was *for*. To modernise the industrial structure or to sustain it in its existing form? To pave the way for socialism, as Bevan thought, or to tide over a capitalist economy in a temporary time of trouble, as most of Whitehall believed? Nor did it explain who would draw up the plans. Whitehall officials working to partisan and inevitably short-termist ministers accountable to Parliament? Or expert technocrats capable of taking a long view and working outside government? Finally, it fudged the more immediate questions: should the planners intervene in the labour market as well as in other markets? If they did intervene, what would happen to collective bargaining and the trade unions? If they did not, what would happen to planning? The story of the Attlee Government's democratic collectivist experiment is, in large part, the story of how the fudge dissolved.

In appearance, planning was on a rising curve throughout the government's first two years. Ministers speedily renewed the economic controls exercised by the wartime coalition. Sir Edward Bridges, the Permanent Secretary of the Treasury, created an elaborate committee structure to 're-group' departmental policies 'into a coherent whole'.[48] By December 1945, the Economic Section had prepared a draft economic survey for 1946. It never saw the light of day, but in February 1947 the survey for that year was published as a government white paper. Morrison was gravely ill; Cripps took over responsibility for it, to the extent of writing the introduction himself. In the limpid prose of a great advocate, this set out the philosophy by which the planners thought they were guided. Where totalitarian planning subordinated 'all individual desires and preferences to the demands of the state', democratic planning preserved the 'maximum possible freedom of choice'. Government had to lay down the nation's 'economic tasks' and 'to use its powers of economic control to influence the course of development in the desired direction'. But that was all it could do.

> [T]he task of directing by democratic methods an economic system as large and complex as ours is far beyond the power of any Governmental machine working by itself. . . . Events can be directed in the way that is desired in the national interest only if the Government, both sides of industry and the people accept the objectives and work together to achieve the end.[49]

In March 1947, Sir Edwin Plowden was appointed Chief Planning Officer at the head of a Central Economic Planning Staff (CEPS). In July, this was buttressed by an Economic Planning Board, representing both sides of industry.

Sadly, there were gaping holes at the heart of Cripps's conception of democratic planning. There was (and could be) no mechanism for ensuring that individual 'people' accepted the plan's objectives or for telling them what they were supposed to do to achieve them.[50] The inherent tension between the British conception of ministerial responsibility to Parliament and a corporatist Planning Board, operating at arm's length from government, was not acknowledged, much less resolved. Above all, Cripps's fundamental assumption – that government knew what the nation's economic tasks should be – turned out to be false. On the two most pressing problems of the moment, the Cabinet was deadlocked, while the planning machine ground empty air.

The first was manpower policy. As the swollen armies and munitions industries of wartime ran down, labour flooded back into civilian occupations. But too little flooded into the export industries which held the key to Britain's economic survival. Wartime direction of labour was effectively abolished and a return to it ruled out. That meant that the only way to shift manpower into priority industries was to change relative wages. However, a change in relative wages was exactly what the well-tried British system of free collective bargaining could not produce. The logic pointed inexorably to a formal wages policy. But a formal wages policy was anathema, both to the Ministry of Labour and to that ever-vigilant champion of industrial voluntarism, Ernest Bevin. Would-be wage planners repeatedly pointed to the danger of wage inflation and the manpower needs of priority industries. They were invariably overwhelmed by dire warnings of the political dangers involved in a break with the past. If a central authority attempted to discuss the wages and conditions of union members, Bevin told the Cabinet in March 1946, 'conflict will arise immediately'.[51] The existing system of free negotiation had been supported by all governments since 1919, George Isaacs, the Minister of Labour and Bevin apostle, argued six months later. Abandoning it would 'destroy the general harmony of industrial relations' and make government the target for strikes.[52] The dialogue of the deaf rumbled on into the summer of 1947, but without a discernible result.

Still more intractable was the fundamental problem of how to marry claims to resources. The case for planning rested on the assumption that priorities were better determined by planners than by the price mechanism – that if they were determined by 'chance', as Cripps put it in the 1947 survey, 'vital requirements' would be squeezed out by non-vital ones. But that assumption depended on the further assumption that the planners could decide which requirements were vital and which were not. That decision was beyond them. Geopolitical power, working-class living standards, welfare programmes and capital investment all competed for desperately scarce resources with the imperatives of increased exports and national solvency. Each set of claims had powerful champions, backed by insistent pressures, while ministers lacked the collective political will to bring them into balance. Defence cuts were slow and small; import cuts were violently resisted; the Cabinet did not even consider cutting food subsidies or welfare expenditure. Though exports, investment and industrial production all grew impressively, the result was an economy mired in suppressed inflation. The pent-up demand created by increased wages, full employment, redistributive tax-ation, rationing and subsidies could neither be satisfied nor squeezed out; the price mechanism was jammed while planning was stultified. Another crisis was waiting to happen.

cℜ

It approached with the inexorable menace of a bad dream.[53] 1946 saw a dramatic rise in British exports, but too few of them went to the United States. In the second half of the year Britain's trade deficit with the dollar world widened, while a huge flow of investment capital went to sterling area countries. In January–March 1947 the worst winter of the century imposed an insupportable extra burden on coal supplies that a distracted, Micawber-like Cabinet – advised by the even more Micawber-like Fuel Minister, Emanuel Shinwell – had allowed to fall to a dangerously low level. In the fuel crisis that followed, industrial output fell steeply. Two million people were thrown temporarily out of work and the country suffered a £200 million loss of export income. The death rate among the elderly soared. Many schools were forced to close. The opening hours of dance halls, cinemas, theatres and music halls were restricted. Greyhound racing was banned. There was a lengthening queue of would-be migrants to Australia – most of whom were prevented from going because of a shortage of shipping.[54]

In mid-March 1947, Dalton warned the Cabinet that the American credit was disappearing at 'ever-accelerating speed'.[55] By early May, the Treasury was forecasting that it would be used up by mid-1948. But the fatal com-bination of procrastination and wishful thinking that had caused the fuel crisis still had ministers in its grip. In a savage diary entry in April, 'Otto' Clarke had noted, 'For fifty years and more the best of the working class have fought and suffered and struggled so that Labour should rule ... now the chosen leadership of the workers was sitting there, not only baffled by the problems but apparently disinterested [sic], not seeming to appreciate that there was a crisis at all.'[56] June 1947 was dominated by a long, dragging

Cabinet battle over cuts in the hard-currency import programme, in which the Treasury's request for a £150 million cut in food imports was beaten down to £50 million. On 15 July the convertibility clauses of the American loan agreement came into effect. Sterling holders switched into dollars. The markets soon concluded that convertibility would not last. As so often, market sentiment was self-reinforcing. Speculative pressures mounted;[57] the drain of sterling became a flood; and on 20 August convertibility was suspended. The North American credits, negotiated with so much pain less than two years before, were almost exhausted.

The convertibility crisis was a climacteric, forcing a change of mood, tempo, direction and machinery that helped to give the government's last four years in office a radically different flavour from that of its first two. Before the fatal summer of 1947, external solvency had been one aim among many. (That was why the Cabinet had been deadlocked.) Now it became the dominating priority. Within weeks of the suspension of convertibility, imports, investment, consumption and even defence spending were all cut by previously unthinkable amounts. Particularly unkind was a cut in food imports, which was expected to reduce the average calorie intake per person to a lower level than in the final year of the war.[58] The swollen subsidies that kept food prices down were capped – though not abolished, as Keynesians in the Economic Section as well as traditionalists in the Treasury would have preferred.

In early November 1947, Dalton introduced a harsh emergency budget, explicitly designed to ward off inflation. Taxes were increased by £200 million, not to balance the government's books, but to generate a surplus to 'mop up' purchasing power.[59] Though the language was Keynesian, Keynesian theory had not yet become the centrepiece of Treasury doctrine. The real point about Dalton's 1947 budget is that it marked the end of the economic insouciance of the first two years, not that it was Keynesian. In two crucial respects, moreover, policy did not change. Far from abandoning the dream of a planned economy, ministers redoubled their planning efforts, while Bevin's search for a middle kingdom continued apace.

The change in tempo that followed the convertibility crisis owed much to a change in personnel. A clumsy September plot, concocted by Cripps and Dalton, and aimed at making Bevin prime minister in place of Attlee, ended with Cripps becoming Minister of Economic Affairs and taking over the planning powers previously exercised by Herbert Morrison. Another turning point followed soon afterwards. A trivial indiscretion by Dalton on his way to make his budget statement led to his resignation the following day. Cripps became Chancellor of the Exchequer in his place, still retaining his post as Minister of Economic Affairs and the planning powers that went with it. The Treasury was back in the Whitehall driving seat, with the strongest Chancellor since Gladstone at its head. The government's heroic phase was over.

CRIPPS'S REQUIEM

For the next three years, Cripps dominated the domestic scene. One reason was that, unlike the hapless Dalton, he had unchallenged control both over the Treasury and over the planning machinery. There was more to it than that, however. Like Gladstone's, his extraordinary authority was personal as much as institutional. Religious faith, driving will and intellectual power were coupled with transparent honesty and an almost masochistic relish for facing unpleasant facts. When he declared that he hoped to infuse industrial life with 'those basic principles of honesty and honour which we have so long declared to be the foundation of our spiritual life',[60] he patently meant what he said. In one of the most frequently quoted phrases of the period Churchill jibed: 'There but for the grace of God, goes God.' More revealing was a comment by Hugh Gaitskell: 'You feel with Cripps that almost nothing is politically impossible. He sails on simply concerned with what is the best solution from every other point of view and ignoring all the rocks which lie ahead.'[61]

The rocks were even more menacing than they looked at first sight. The fuel and convertibility crises had taken the sheen off the government and smirched the vision of rationality and justice it had offered in 1945. In 1947, the polls showed Labour trailing behind the Conservatives for the first time since the middle of the war. Though no parliamentary seats changed hands, by-elections also recorded significant swings to the Conservatives. In the local elections in November 1947, Labour lost 652 seats. Behind all this lay a deeper change in the public mood and the intellectual climate. In 1945, as we saw in the last chapter, Labour had seemed poised to create a new social coalition – the interwar Baldwin coalition in reverse. It had broken out of its working-class ghettoes in the old industrial regions and into the déclassé new England of the technicians and industrial chemists celebrated in *The Lion and the Unicorn*.

Its working-class constituency was unshakeably loyal (understandably, since it was a better friend to blue-collar workers than any other peacetime government in British history), but Orwell's indeterminate class was more restive socially and more volatile politically than most leading Labour politicians realised. Much of it had been attracted by the altruistic radicalism and classless managerialism tapped by the Cripps boom of 1942 and by

Common Wealth in 1943 and 1944. In 1945, these yearnings had carried it into the Labour camp. But it had not found secure new political moorings to replace the ones it had left during the war. Though Orwell's people could be moved by an appeal for self-sacrifice, they also expected competence and professionalism. After the mismanagement and self-deception of 1947, it was hard to argue that Labour had a lien on these.

Besides, appeals for self-sacrifice were beginning to wear thin. Wartime austerity had been irksome enough, but its objective had been self-evident and had been supported by a vast majority of the population. Peacetime austerity was a different matter. There was no consensus for it; the reviving Conservative opposition attacked it with unremitting persistence and impressive rhetorical skill.[62] The objective was no longer victory over a tangible and deadly enemy, but the thin and bloodless abstractions of more exports, fewer imports, higher production and higher investment. The government promised jam tomorrow, but tomorrow never seemed to come. For children who grew up under the Attlee Government and could not remember the 1930s, the late 1940s were a time of expanding horizons and new delights: bananas, ice-cream, pineapples. For adults, it was a different story. All too often, the ration books, drab clothes, dreary diet, shortages and queues that were part of the texture of post-war life seemed pointless exercises in national self-flagellation, imposed by ministers who believed in controls for their own sake.

Austerity bore most heavily on women; and Labour politicians, imprisoned in the 'masculinist' assumptions that the Labour movement had always taken for granted, signally failed to match the Conservatives' attempts to woo women voters.[63] A notorious comment by Douglas Jay, by now a junior minister, goes a long way to explain why Labour was outclassed in this competition:

> Housewives as a whole cannot be trusted to buy all the right things, where nutrition and health are concerned. This is really no more than an extension of the principle according to which the housewife herself would not trust a child of four to elect the week's purchases. For in the case of nutrition and health, just as in the case of education, the gentleman from Whitehall really does know better what is good for people than the people know themselves.[64]

As well as the women's backlash, Cripps and his colleagues had to contend with an often ferocious middle-class backlash. Ironically, this was a child of the wartime coalition. As we saw in the last chapter, war socialism had raised working-class living standards, but middle-class ones had fallen, certainly relatively and in many cases absolutely. Before the war, the middle-class calorie intake had been 123 per cent of the working-class figure. By 1945, the gap between them had almost disappeared, and it remained negligible throughout the Attlee Government's term of office.[65] Middle-class people who had expected to return to their old position in the pecking order when the war was over were cruelly disappointed; inevitably, the government in power was a target for their wrath.

As a Treasury note to ministers pointed out in early 1947, the working classes were 'eating more meat and drinking more milk (and more beer, notwithstanding the dilution) than they did before the war', whereas 'the average black-coated worker is conscious of nothing but acute shortage.'[66] In the home counties, reported the opinion researchers of Mass-Observation in 1948, the middle classes had been reduced from their pre-war position to 'little more than living'.[67] The proletarianism that was second nature to many Labour politicians added insult to injury. When Emanuel Shinwell boasted that Labour had the support of the organised workers and that the rest did not matter a tinker's cuss, or when Aneurin Bevan said that the Tories were lower than vermin, they not only made a mockery of Labour talk of community and classlessness; they poured petrol on the flames of middle-class anger.

Not all middle-class people reacted as savagely as the Oxford don in one of Angela Thirkell's best-selling novels who complained, 'we are living under a Government as bad as any in history in its combination of bullying and weakness, its bid for the mob's suffrages ... its efforts to crush all personal freedom.'[68] Nonetheless, softer versions of that theme resounded through the suburbs where Labour had made its most unexpected gains in 1945, and helped to drive it out of the middle ground. There, the politics of production which had always been part and parcel of the democratic collectivist trad-ition were losing out to the politics of consumption. When Cripps announced, with his usual uncompromising honesty, that in the gov-ernment's list of priorities, 'the comforts and amenities of the family' came third after exports and investment,[69] he gave the process a further push.

❦

Nothing daunted, Cripps forged ahead with a programme of autarchic austerity reminiscent of the 'Starvation Corner' with which Keynes had made Whitehall's flesh creep in 1945. A battery of controls and bilateral trade agreements kept dollar imports down and steered resources into exports and investment in priority industries.[70] Personal consumption was squeezed even harder; rations were cut. Strange and mostly unpleasant meat substitutes appeared in the shops – notably, whalemeat, reindeer and the

notorious tinned snoek, a much loathed fish, which even the Minister of
Food confessed to finding 'dull'.[71] Meanwhile, Cripps maintained the rigour
of Dalton's final budget. The budget surplus for 1947–8 was an astonishing
£636 million (against a deficit of £586 million in 1946–7). There was an
even bigger surplus the following year and an only slightly smaller one in
1949–50. The government even found the courage to negotiate a wages
policy with the unions. In March 1948, after much perturbation, a conference of union executives voted in favour of a voluntary wage freeze.
Sweeteners included an FBI agreement to freeze dividends and a once-for-
all capital levy.

A streamlined government machine helped to drive Cripps's programme
forward. Its key components were a Cabinet Economic Policy Committee,
chaired by Attlee, and a Production Committee, chaired by Cripps. CEPS
under Plowden and the Economic Section under Robert Hall, a Keynesian
Oxford economist, were both brought into the Treasury.[72] At first sight, all
this seemed to herald a new planning dawn – the more so because the first
long-term economic plan in British history, *The Long-Term Programme of
the United Kingdom*,[73] was published in December 1948. The reality was
more complex. Cripps was the Churchill of the battle for national solvency.
He was a convinced planner, but for him the chief motors of the planned
economy were moral leadership and patriotic duty rather than institutions.
The new planning instruments invented in 1947 did not live up to their
billing. The Economic Planning Board was little more than a talking shop
and soon faded away. At CEPS, Plowden saw planning as a short-term
expedient, not as a long-term necessity. As for the *Long-Term Programme*,
this was not so much a plan as a statement of intent – in effect, a sophisticated
wish list. Its authors tacitly acknowledged that nothing more was possible
in an open economy, dependent on the ups and downs of foreign trade that
no British Government could control.

Crucially, the government made no attempt to set up a British equivalent
of the powerful, technocratic Planning Commission that spearheaded the
modernisation of the French economy under the Fourth and Fifth Republics. Such a Commission would have challenged the primacy of Whitehall
in policy-making and undermined the doctrine of ministerial accountability
to Parliament; in doing so, it would also have cast doubt on the fundamental
democratic collectivist assumption that the new wine of rationality and
justice could perfectly well be stored in the old bottles of the parliamentary
monarchy. For Cripps and his colleagues, such an innovation was literally
unthinkable.

Ministers and officials thought they were running a planned economy;
in fact, they ran a controlled economy. But controls were losing their bite.

They were hangovers from the war; government used them to stop scarce resources from going to activities with a low priority. As resources became more plentiful, they ceased to work.[74] On Guy Fawkes Day of 1948, Harold Wilson, Cripps's successor as President of the Board of Trade, lit his notorious 'bonfire of controls', in which restrictions involving around 200,000 licences and permits per annum were abolished. Though some controls escaped the flames (exchange controls lasted until 1979) decontrol thereafter loomed larger in government policy than control. Under Cripps, the government's leading dirigiste, the state's capacities for economic direction steadily shrank.

Yet his mixture of public moralism, economic nationalism and heroic belt-tightening worked. The voluntary wage freeze was a far cry from the wages policy that would-be planners had dreamed of before the convertibility crisis. It was a fishing net, not a harpoon. It was supposed to contain wage inflation across the entire economy, not to attract labour to priority industries. In its own terms, however, it was an astonishing success. Following the freeze, the annual rise in hourly wage rates fell from nearly nine per cent to less than three per cent. Exports soared; in the second half of 1948 the balance of payments deficit, which had reached £380 million in 1947, was wiped out. Even the dollar deficit was halved. Investment, labour productivity and the growth rate of GDP per head all rose vigorously. With all its pains, the age of austerity was also an age of exuberant economic dynamism. Substantial flows of American Marshall aid, which began in 1948, deserved much of the credit, but for the still-bruised Cabinet the source of the exuberance of 1948 hardly mattered. What did matter was that by the spring of 1949 the economic weather seemed set fair.

⚭

Not for long, however. The third of the crises that racked the Attlee Government broke within weeks of Cripps's 1949 budget. Its underlying origins were debated gloomily and at length in the Treasury and Bank of England, but the proximate cause was clear enough.[75] By the summer of 1949 an American recession was cutting heavily into Britain's exports to the United States, with disastrous consequences for her dollar earnings and reserves. In the first quarter of 1949 the dollar deficit was £60 million lower than it had been twelve months earlier. By the second quarter it had reached £157 million, and the hard-won gains of the previous eighteen months had been wiped out. The strain on the reserves mounted, exacerbated by the usual speculative pressures – this time fortified by the increasingly well-known American view that sterling ought to be devalued. By the summer of 1949, Cripps was a sick man, exhausted by overwork and almost crippled by insomnia. On 18 July, he left for a sanatorium in Switzerland. In his absence, and after long and anguished debate as the reserves continued to plummet, his colleagues decided that devaluation was indeed the only solution. When he returned from Switzerland in August, Cripps reluctantly agreed. In early September, he and Bevin, both physically worn out, sailed for Washington to confer with top American and Canadian officials. On 19 September, sterling was devalued by a swingeing 30 per cent, cutting the exchange rate to $2.80 to the pound.

The 1949 crisis struck at the heart of the democratic collectivist vision. For Keynesians like Robert Hall, 'Otto' Clarke and Cripps's young ministerial colleagues, Hugh Gaitskell and Douglas Jay, devaluation held no terrors. It was a neat market mechanism to correct a familiar market distortion. Their aplomb was amply justified. In the nine months after devaluation, the reserves rose by 70 per cent; in the course of 1950, the trade balance with the United States improved by £200 million. But for Cripps, the instinctive dirigiste and self-styled planner, market mechanisms had always been suspect. That was why he was a planner; that was what he meant when he said that economic priorities should not be determined by 'chance'. He had no alternative to devaluation. At first he hoped to ride out the crisis with more cuts in dollar imports and tighter curbs on public spending, but no one could seriously believe that a further dose of autarchy could overcome the underlying imbalance between the sterling and dollar worlds.

Yet, though he allowed his colleagues to talk him into devaluation, he did so against his instincts and after prolonged resistance. One reason for his reluctance was that, like all finance ministers faced with a confidence crisis, he had had to declare publicly and repeatedly that the parity would be held. But it is hard to believe that that is the whole story. He was no economist and was not given to theoretical speculation, but at some level he must have known that devaluation was a defeat for the democratic collectivist vision of a socially controlled economy, governed by a rational, justice-seeking state rather than by the vagaries of the market-place. The fact that devaluation succeeded only made the defeat more obvious. Thirteen months after the change of parity he left office for ever, to die nineteen months later. Hugh Gaitskell became Chancellor in his stead.

Cripps's final year at the Treasury had a tragic quality about it. His health was broken; he was still ravaged by insomnia; and he looked increasingly haggard and gaunt. The economic approach which he had made his own and which encapsulated his vision of the moral economy had been effectively superseded. By April 1950, when he presented his third budget, he had become a Keynesian in all but name. He used the language of planning with all his old conviction, but he had now redefined it to mean demand management. In a contorted passage in his budget speech, he began by reaffirming his 1947 faith in what he still called 'democratic planning'. The objective, he declared, was to 'combine a free democracy with a planned economy' in which all would 'share in the democratic control of their country's economy'. But when it came to specifics, these abstractions dissolved into a series of negations. There would be no 'violent compulsions', no attempts by the centre to determine 'the details of production and distribution' and no 'rigid targets'. That left the budget as 'the most important control and as the most powerful instrument for influencing economic policy which is available to the Government'.[76]

It is hard to quarrel with Sir Alec Cairncross's verdict: in that speech, Cripps 'pronounced a requiem on economic planning as he had once conceived it'.[77] It was a personal requiem as well. Keynes's evolutionary whiggism had beaten democratic collectivist *étatisme*. As anything more than a rhetorical flourish, the vision of a just and rational economic system, in which public purpose took precedence over market forces, had receded beyond the horizon. Just as Churchill, the aristocratic whig imperialist, had presided over the most dirigiste regime in British history, Cripps, the moralistic planner, had become the unwilling and perhaps unwitting midwife of a whig imperialist rebirth.

⟡

By the time Cripps left office, Bevin's middle-kingdom aspirations had also come to a sad end. For more than two years they had provided the central theme of British foreign policy. With extraordinary panache, Bevin had orchestrated the European response to the American offer of Marshall aid in a way designed to protect Britain's global role from American interference. The Americans wanted to remake Europe in their own image and thought that only strong supranational institutions could bring the Europe they wanted into being. To the Foreign Office's alarm, they saw Britain as 'just another European country', not as a global power.[78] Bevin's agenda was radically different. He too wanted a united non-Communist Europe, but one led by Britain and buttressed by the Commonwealth, which would also be led by Britain.[79] An Anglo-European union of this sort, wrote Gladwyn Jebb, one of Bevin's favourite Foreign Office advisers, could procure a new balance of global power and countervail the 'two semi-barbarian states on the cultural periphery.'[80]

To Bevin and the Foreign Office, it seemed self-evident that a union strong enough to do this would have to be a coalition of states, in which Britain would continue to play her familiar imperial and sterling area roles, not a supranational entity on the American model. By dint of a dazzling mixture of obduracy, pathos, fast footwork and negotiating skill, Bevin ensured that the ERP (the official name for the Marshall Plan) conformed to British specifications. The spectre of a tightly integrated, supranational Europe was kept at bay. Intergovernmentalism prevailed, while American aid cascaded forth. Not content with obstructing the Americans, Bevin also flirted with a positive intergovernmental alternative to the supranational Europe they hankered for. He called it 'Western Union'. It was to be a British-led, Commonwealth-buttressed union of western European states and their colonies forming 'a *bloc* which, both in population and productive capacity, could stand on an equality with the Western hemisphere and Soviet *Bloc*'.[81]

The alarming combination of a Communist coup in Czechoslovakia in February 1948 and the beginning of the year-long Soviet blockade of West Berlin in June called a brutal halt to such imaginings. The notion that Stalin's Soviet Union was a sated power, with no wish to extend the existing frontiers of the Communist *bloc*, lost what credibility it had once had. As the Cold War grew more intense and the danger of a hot war seemed to mount, memories of 1940, when Britain's European allies had collapsed before the German onslaught while the United States stood on the sidelines, stirred in British breasts. The nightmare thought of being left alone in Europe, while the Red Army drove to the Channel, wiped out the dream of a middle kingdom. Bevin's chief aim now was to bring the American 'barbarians' further into Europe in order to keep the infinitely more bar-barous Soviet ones out – a project consummated in April 1949, when the North Atlantic Treaty (establishing NATO) was signed in Washington.

By now, Bevin too was a seriously sick man. (He would die in April 1951, only a little more than two years after NATO was born.) He suffered recurrent bouts of disabling angina, and strong medication caused him to fall asleep in meetings. In 1950, he had two operations; by May of that year, Kenneth Younger, the Foreign Office Minister of State, thought him 'a shadow of his real self'.[82] Although he fought indomitably against his physical decline, it was a losing battle. On good days, he was as impressive as ever, but his old inventiveness and zest were fading. He was in no condition for new departures and, for the rest of his term, foreign policy marked time. He and his colleagues consoled themselves for the death of his middle-kingdom dreams with the thought that, as the rising Foreign Office star, Roger Makins, put it, Britain was the 'nodal point of three systems, the Commonwealth, Western Europe and the Atlantic Com-munity'.[83] This, however, was not a policy; it was a brave façade concealing a policy vacuum. The Atlantic Community was a chimera. The Americans, without whom no such community was possible, persisted in seeing Britain

ANCESTRAL VOICES

CLOCKWISE FROM TOP LEFT
Edmund Burke looking statesmanlike, 1780.
Lord Salisbury looking prime ministerial, 1890.
Sidney and Beatrice Webb (Lord and Lady
  Passfield) looking quizzical, 1929.
R.H. Tawney looking biblical, 1960.

POPULISTS IN SPATE

David Lloyd George orating at Buckie, Banffshire, 1925; Enoch Powell at the Safeguard Britain Campaign, June 1976; Margaret Thatcher rejoicing on election night at Finchley, 1987; Tony Blair charming a Labour Student Conference, February 2007.

WOMEN ON THE MARCH

CLOCKWISE FROM TOP LEFT
Florence Nightingale in 1845.
Lady Astor (the first woman MP)
    electioneering in Plymouth, 1923.
The irresistible force meets the
    immovable object: Barbara Castle at
    an AEU conference at Eastbourne,
    1968.
'Brash, bawdy and glamorous':
    Germaine Greer in 1971.

THE RISE OF THE GRAMMAR SCHOOL BOYS

CLOCKWISE FROM TOP LEFT
Michael Frayn in 1979. Not yet a national treasure, a downbeat Alan Bennett campaigning for London's theatres, 1973. An upbeat Brian Walden on Westminster Bridge, 1980. Dennis Potter as editor of the student magazine *Isis*, Oxford, 1958.

TOP: Armoured cars in front of the Hyde Park gates during the General Strike, May 1926.
ABOVE: Hunger Marchers passing through Lavendon, near Bedford, October 1936.

'Impulsive, irrepressible and unsound': Winston Churchill returning to Britain after a nearly fatal accident in New York, 1932.

BELOW: Postwar austerity: collecting coke rations from a depot at Vauxhall during the fuel crisis of 1947.

LEFT: 'Grossly overweight, frequently drunk, and rock-like in loyalty': Ernest Bevin arriving at Number Ten for a Cabinet meeting, 1947.

RIGHT: Stafford Cripps taking an unlikely break from austerity, August 1947.

TOP: Anti-Suez demonstration in Trafalgar Square, November 1956.
ABOVE: The 'last imperialists'? CND march from Trafalgar Square to Aldermaston, April 1958.

as a European power, distracted from her proper vocation by vain global ambitions.

After sterling's devaluation a new chimera appeared on the scene.[84] The British had now done what the Americans had always wanted them to do: instead of sheltering behind a thicket of autarchic barriers, they had taken the market route to solvency. The Americans no longer needed to lever them into an integrated European market; the spectre of a protectionist sterling area disputing the hegemony of the dollar had vanished. Though American policy-makers still did all they could to bring a supranational and integrated Western Europe into being, they now accepted British non-participation as a fact of life. With the forlorn persistence of a much rejected but ever-hopeful suitor, Bevin and his colleagues convinced themselves that the great days of the wartime Anglo-American alliance were about to return. After devaluation, the ubiquitous Sir Oliver Franks, now British Ambassador in Washington, wrote gleefully that the Americans had 'decided to regard us once more as their principal partner in world affairs and not just as a member of the European queue'.[85]

British policy-makers saw this as a pearl beyond price, but the pearl was made of paste. The Americans had acknowledged British exceptionalism, but that was all. They had no intention of recreating the wartime partnership. The British thought they had a special relationship with the United States, and in a sense they were right. However, as Dean Acheson, Marshall's Anglophile successor as US Secretary of State, would put it in his memoirs, 'Of course a unique relationship existed between Britain and America. ... But unique did not mean affectionate.'[86] In truth, a huge chasm of misunderstanding and self-deception lay between the British view of the United States and the Americans' view of Britain. On serious matters, the Americans viewed Britain with a cool, neo-Machiavellian pragmatism. Their alliance with her was a tool of policy, useful in some spheres but not in others. In his middle-kingdom days, Bevin had viewed the United States equally coolly, but after the Washington talks over devaluation he and the rest of the government relapsed into Churchillian romanticism.

In late October 1949 he told the Cabinet that Britain was now forging 'a new relationship' with the United States and the Commonwealth, which set a limit to the part she could play in a European Union.[87] Albeit with occasional departures from the script, successive British governments would stick thereafter to an essentially Churchillian view of Anglo-American relations, spurning the real European Community on their doorstep and chasing after an imagined Anglo-American community, based on a fatal misreading of American history and culture.

❧

The first critical manifestation of the government's conversion to Churchillian romanticism came in May 1950, when the French Foreign Minister, Robert Schuman, put forward a brilliantly conceived project for placing the coal and steel industries of Western Europe under the control of a supranational High Authority. Britain was invited to take part, but only on condition that she accepted the principle of supranational control – the heart and soul of the scheme. For the best part of three years, one of the central objects of Britain's foreign policy had been to have her European cake and eat it: to play a leading part in an intergovernmental Europe, while putting every obstacle she could think of in the path of would-be supranationalists. Now she had to choose between supranationalism and self-exclusion from a crucial European development. The government chose the latter. Not surprisingly, its choice has been the subject of endless post-mortems. In rejecting the Schuman Plan, Britain ended a four-year-long attempt to play a leading role in European politics, ensuring that the future shape of the western half of the continent would be settled by others. Yet much of the debate on the Cabinet's decision has been beside the point. After devaluation, any other decision would have been astonishing. If Britain had chosen the supranational option, she would have gone back into the 'European queue' from which she thought Washington had rescued her. When the Cabinet rejected the Schuman Plan in June 1950, the real moment of truth had already come and gone.

By June 1950, the whig imperialist rebirth was well under way. Labour had won an astonishingly ill-timed election in February, but only with a paper-thin majority of five seats. It had held on to its core vote in the unionised manual working class, but large sections of Orwell's new class had deserted it. On a deeper and more important level, it had failed to construct a new project to follow the democratic-collectivist experiment it had launched in 1945. The planning ideal of old days was broken-backed. Controls no longer seemed a precondition of fair shares. In any case they were on the way out. Nationalisation was unpopular, and no one could think of a convincing rationale for further instalments. Labour boasted that it had delivered full employment, but in truth the tight labour market owed more to the pressure of pent-up demand accumulated during the war than to government policy. The central economic problem of the day was inflation, not deflation.

Besides, the Conservatives were as committed to full employment as Labour and, as events would show, they too had been converted to Keynesian demand management. The same applied to the welfare state. The real domestic legacy of the Attlee Government was managed welfare capitalism – the mix of Beveridgean social policy, Keynesian economics and quasi-corporatist relations between the state, the unions and the employers that had been foreshadowed under the wartime coalition and, before that, under the National Government of the 1930s. The parties differed over the details of this mix, but the broad outlines were no longer controversial, if they ever had been.

Among Labour intellectuals, there were occasional signs of a democratic republican revival. G.D.H. Cole, a fervent planner in the 1930s, reverted to his Guild Socialist youth. He denounced the government's model of nationalisation as a 'bad cross between bureaucracy and big business' and declared that it had succumbed to 'the tendency to centralisation and authoritarian control which it should have been its mission to fight'.[88] Within the Cabinet, Harold Wilson, Cripps's successor as President of the Board of Trade and still only thirty-four, put forward an innovative scheme to deal with unaccountable economic power by putting government directors on the boards of the biggest private companies.[89] But these were intimations of a possible new direction at some stage in the future. They did not add up to a project for government. Labour was still the repository of the hopes of the oldest working class in the world. It could still tap a reservoir of millenarian idealism. But its strengths were negative, not positive; defensive, not offensive. For a brilliant moment during and immediately after the war it had been the party of the future. Now it was stuck in a rut pointing to the past.

Its last sixteen months in office were a cruel diminuendo. Following Communist North Korea's attack on South Korea in June 1950, Britain joined the United States in intervening on the South Korean side. Under strong American pressure, the Cabinet then approved a greatly enhanced defence programme of £3.4 billion over the period 1950–54. In October, Communist China intervened in Korea in response to a wild American drive to the Yalu river. In an unconsidered answer to a question at a press conference in late November, President Truman used a form of words that could be interpreted as meaning that the US intended to use the atomic bomb against the Chinese. Attlee proceeded to fly to Washington, supposedly to hold Truman back. He returned with the news that Truman would not use the bomb (something he had never intended to do in any case), and that a further enlargement of the rearmament programme had become unavoidable, since Britain had to give a lead to the other American allies. In late January 1951, the Cabinet approved a new total of £4.7 billion – 40 per cent up on the total agreed in the summer.

From then on, the government slithered slowly to its demise. In promoting Gaitskell to the chancellorship when the dying Cripps retired, Attlee had followed the dictates of what he had assumed to be common sense. Gaitskell had, after all, been a highly competent, middle-rank minister and was a trained economist to boot. Unfortunately, common sense turned out to be less sensible than it had seemed at first sight. Attlee had failed to foresee the impact of Gaitskell's promotion on the personal and political dynamics of his own Cabinet, and had set the scene for a bitter struggle for party power which would last for more than a decade. Aneurin Bevan, creator of the National Health Service and darling of ordinary party members, had also been a highly competent middle-rank minister as well as an orator of genius. He was ten years older than Gaitskell and had first been elected to Parliament when Gaitskell was only two years down from Oxford. No one will ever know whether Bevan would have been a successful Chancellor, but in terms of party service and public prominence his claim to the post was at least as good as Gaitskell's. His sideways move to be Minister of Labour did nothing to console him. Quite apart from personal factors, he did not share Gaitskell's Atlanticism and thought (as it turned out, with good reason) that the rearmament programme was excessive. For Bevan, Gaitskell's promotion was both a personal slap in the face and a sign that the party was drifting too far from its roots.

The worst Labour split since 1931 took place against that background. Gaitskell's emotional warmth, stubborn courage and passionate egalitarianism went hand in hand with an often priggish inflexibility and a keen nose for power; he was also a fervent Atlanticist. To fund the new arms programme he had to make cuts elsewhere. The rising health budget was an obvious target, partly because of long-standing Treasury suspicions that it was out of control, and partly perhaps because Gaitskell wanted to prove, as dramatically as possible, that he would allow nothing to stand in the way of his cost-cutting zeal. Hilary Marquand, now Minister of Health, agreed to a cap on health spending, entailing a charge for teeth and spectacles. In early March 1951, in another display of political insensitivity, Attlee exacerbated Bevan's sense of grievance by making Herbert Morrison Foreign Secretary in place of the mortally sick Bevin. Bevan threatened publicly to resign rather than accept NHS charges. Gaitskell refused to give way in what had now become an open battle for dominance between the two emerging chieftains of the post-Attlee generation. In April 1951, Gaitskell introduced his budget, with health charges included. After much anguish, Bevan then resigned, accompanied by Harold Wilson.

The ostensible issue – modest charges to save £30 million in a full year – was trivial and left ample room for compromise. However, the real issues – the scale and scope of the rearmament programme, the international role of a social-democratic Britain as the Cold War intensified, and the inviolability or otherwise of a free health service – went to the heart of Labour's foreign policy, approach to social welfare and self-understanding. When a general election came in October 1951, in the middle of yet another balance of payments crisis, the narrow Conservative victory seemed to have been set in the stars. For more than a decade, Labour's energies would be consumed in a savage party civil war.

The Attlee Government did more good to more people than any previous or subsequent British Government, but it did it by following the evolutionary signposts erected by Beveridge and Keynes; Dalton's dream of a new society built by a justice-seeking central state remained a dream. Whig imperialism was in the ascendant once again.

6

LONG RECESSIONAL

✣

Far-call'd our navies melt away —
    On dune and headland sinks the fire —
Lo, all our pomp of yesterday
    Is one with Nineveh and Tyre!
Judge of the Nations, spare us yet,
Lest we forget, lest we forget!

                                    Rudyard Kipling, 1897

Don't clap too hard. It's a very old building.

                    Archie Rice in *The Entertainer*, John Osborne, 1957

✣

SECOND COMING

Inevitable or not, the Conservatives' victory in the 1951 election was a close-run thing. They won fewer votes than Labour and had an overall Commons majority of only seventeen. The electorate was divided into two great armies of approximately equal size, with a forlorn Liberal battalion lost in no-man's land. The new government had no mandate for radical departures; Churchill, the new Prime Minister, had lost the impish zest for battle that had been one of his most endearing (and infuriating) traits for most of his political life. At a few weeks short of seventy-seven he was an old man and seemed older than had Gladstone or Palmerston at the same age, or than Konrad Adenauer seemed among his contemporaries. He still loved the trappings of power, but he had no stomach for the risk-taking that he had relished as a younger man. Like Charles II after the Restoration, he was chiefly anxious not to go on his travels again.

He felt passionately about the danger of nuclear war and dreamed, with a kind of wistful nobility, of averting it through some spectacular exercise of summit diplomacy. After Stalin's death in 1953 he told his doctor hopefully that he was 'playing a big hand – the easement of the world, perhaps peace over the world'.[1] But in home affairs his only real ambition was to maintain social and industrial harmony. The hallmarks of his government were strangely reminiscent of the interwar years – whiggish inclusion, statesmanlike adaptation and rule by a responsive and authoritative governing elite. He had become the Baldwin of the 1950s.

An emblematic moment came in the early months of 1952. The government entered office in the middle of the third sterling crisis in five years, to discover that Labour had bequeathed it a balance of payments deficit running at more than £100 million a month.[2] The new Chancellor of the Exchequer was R.A. Butler. Though an habitué of the corridors of Whitehall, he had no previous experience of the Treasury and had held none of the great offices of state. He had been a zealous appeaser as a junior Foreign Office minister in the 1930s, Education Minister during the war and the chief architect of the Conservative renewal after the defeat of 1945. He came from a long line of Cambridge dons; he was born in India where his father was a functionary in the ICS. Butler was a whig imperialist to his fingertips. For him, politics was 'the art of the possible'. The tradition that had shaped him, he wrote, was

> not a collection of causes for which we were obliged to die in the last ditch, nor a set of premises by whose consistent application we might infallibly regulate our conduct, but a mature tradition of political thought and behaviour which is neither fixed nor finished. This tradition at its best is responsive to the demands of each new age, empirical as to method, resourceful in expressing itself in popular idiom.[3]

He would become a master of the sly innuendo, the darling of up-market political commentators and the intelligentsia's favourite Conservative. But all that came later. His Treasury baptism could hardly have been less propitious. On the day of his appointment he lunched with his private secretary, the future head of the civil service, William Armstrong, and Sir Edward Bridges, head of the Treasury. They told him a horror story 'of blood draining from the system and a collapse greater than had been foretold in 1931'.[4] In November 1951, Butler responded with a deflationary package, including a swingeing £360 million worth of import cuts. Further cuts followed in January 1952.

Under Dalton and Cripps such measures had become only too familiar, but in the Bank of England and the Overseas Finance division of the Treasury, where successive sterling crises had created a mood of mingled messianism and despair, the hunt was on for a thoroughgoing break with post-war practice. The hunters produced a revolutionary plan, code-named

ROBOT, probably after the initials of its three authors – Sir Leslie **Ro**wan, of the Treasury; Sir George **Bo**lton of the Bank; and '**Ot**to' Clarke, also of the Treasury. ROBOT had three prongs – a floating pound; convertibility of 'non-resident' sterling (that is, of sterling held outside the sterling area); and the blocking or funding of 80–90 per cent of the sterling balances. In a phrase that became their mantra, the robotniks explained that the object of the exercise was to take the strain of balance of payments deficits 'off the reserves' and to put it on the exchange rate.

ROBOT provoked one of the most passionately fought and politically charged Whitehall battles of the post-war period. Personal relationships were strained; there were dark allegations of disloyalty and inconstancy. The battle ranged widely.[5] Robotniks insisted that, on existing policies, the reserves would probably drain away until their exhaustion forced a second devaluation; that convertibility was essential to sustain the sterling area and Britain's position as a great power; and that floating was essential for convertibility. But blocking the sterling balances was essential too: if balance holders were free to convert them into dollars at will, sterling would collapse. Like the Holy Trinity, in fact, the three elements of the plan were interdependent. Anti-robotniks retorted that floating was incompatible with the rules of the IMF and might destroy the only recently formed European Payments Union. Blocking the balances would be dishonourable; and convertibility could not 'make a weak currency strong'.[6]

Behind the economics lay the politics – the real battleground. Treasury robotniks wanted to break out of the straitjacket of rigidity and illusion that they had come to see as the root cause of Britain's balance of payments weakness. Floating, they claimed, would automatically generate 'equilibrating pressures' in the economy. These would force consumers, workers and employers to adjust to the realities that a fixed rate allowed them to evade until it was too late. Had the rate been allowed to float during the past few months, Clarke wrote, food and raw material prices would have gone up by 25 per cent, and consumption would have fallen. 'We should now have been in great pain, but adjustment would have been going on. But we can lose $1,500 million of gold without anybody noticing.'[7] For once, Butler, the supple whig imperialist, threw his instinctive caution to the winds and backed the plan. Robot, he wrote, would entail rethinking the economic policies that had been supported by all parties during the last few years. Stable prices and wages as well as full employment would all have to be sacrificed. The pressure of 'change and readjustment' would be continuous, unpleasant and inescapable.[8]

The anti-robotnik counter-argument was as deadly as it was simple. Churchill's wartime familiar, the 'Prof' (now Lord Cherwell and a member of the Cabinet), phrased it with brutal clarity. ROBOT, he conceded, might put an end to dollar crises:

> But whether the electorate, or Members of Parliament for industrial constituencies (even Conservatives) would swallow such a programme, however strongly recommended by the Bank, is another matter. . . .
>
> To rely frankly on high prices and unemployment to reduce imports would put the Conservative Party out for a generation.[9]

The battle dragged on for several months, but the crux came at the end of February 1952 when the Cabinet decided that although action on ROBOT lines might be taken later, it should not be introduced immediately, as the robotniks had urged. A mildly deflationary budget followed in early March. Then, as if by a miracle, the balance of payments and the reserves rapidly improved. (In reality, the improvement was not the product of supernatural intervention; it was largely due to the unwinding of the stockpiling boom generated by the Korean war.) By the end of the year, the reserves stood at $1.85 billion, as against a Treasury forecast of $0.6 billion to $1.25 billion. ROBOT was dead, never to be exhumed.

◦❧◦

What would ROBOT have meant, and what did its rejection mean? The debate had a curiously manic quality. Both sides exaggerated wildly. Robotniks warned of financial nemesis; anti-robotniks of political catastrophe. Yet two rocks of comparative certainty loom through the fog of charge and countercharge. The first is that, although the battle was fought on economic terrain, its inner meaning was political. There is no way of telling what would have happened to the economy if ROBOT had been adopted; events might well have belied both the robotniks' hopes and the anti-robotniks' fears. (They did not come true when the pound was floated, albeit in very different circumstances, in the 1970s.) But that is not the crucial point. What matters is that the consequences that the robotniks expected and wanted patently implied a revolutionary change in statecraft.

The object of the exercise was to force employers, workers and consumers to adjust more quickly to the pressures of the global market-place, and to punish them if they did not. For that to happen, the slow changes of attitude and behaviour that had reshaped the moral and political economies over the previous thirty years would have had to be reversed. The obstacles to market adjustment would have had to be swept aside. The old Adam of untamed capitalism would have had to emerge from his cage. It would have been necessary to topple Keynes and Beveridge from their perches, and to curb the power of organised labour. And here we come to the second rock. It is that the politics of Whig accommodation, as practised by Baldwin, Chamberlain and Churchill, and the politics of rationalistic étatisme, fitfully attempted under Labour, would have had to give way to a harder, sharper, more aggressive politics from the same emotional and rhetorical stable as Lord Salisbury's tory nationalism.

These politics would have had an international as well as a domestic dimension. The robotniks were not full-blooded tory nationalists in the Salisbury or Milner mould, but they were certainly economic nationalists, albeit in laissez-faire clothing They viewed the emerging global economic order, whose foundations Keynes had helped to lay, with distaste bordering on contempt. They were positively hostile to the EPU and hoped that it would collapse. Between the lines of their memoranda lay the wounded pride of a great power and a great financial centre which had come down in the world. It was time, they felt, to stop the rot and put British interests first. The international system could go hang. Given all this, the surprising thing is not that they lost, but that for a while it looked as if they would win. And that, in turn, implied that the changes that had taken place in the moral and political economies during the past thirty years were not as deeply embedded as they appeared at first sight. ROBOT's defeat was a victory for the status quo bequeathed by the wartime coalition and the Attlee governments. But it was not a total victory.

With ROBOT out of the way, Churchill and his colleagues sank back into the comfortable neo-Baldwinism which would be the hallmark of British political economy for the rest of the decade. The Conservative versus Labour two-party system, which Baldwin had helped to create, was as stable as it had been in the 1930s. At the beginning of the decade Labour had a fraction more than a million individual members; though precise figures were lacking, Conservative Party membership probably stood at around 2,800,000. Labour's share of the vote declined at successive elections, while the Conservative share rose. But at the end of the decade the two big parties won more than 90 per cent of the popular vote between them; and though the Liberal share had doubled it was still under six per cent.

In spite of six years of war followed by six years of Labour rule, the pre-war structure of authority and consent was virtually intact. The landed class lauded by Burke had lost much (though by no means all) of its power and status, but there were plenty of its scions in the governing elite – Churchill, of course, pre-eminent among them. In any case, the professional service class of the English home counties, which now supplied most of the elite, had generally been formed in public schools and ancient universities suffused with a quasi-aristocratic ethos.[10] Whether professional or aristocratic in origin, members of the elite spoke with a distinctive, upper-class drawl that is virtually extinct today and seems comically antediluvian in old films or newsreels.[11] They also had distinctive clothes, distinctive linguistic conventions, distinctive manners and (at least to some extent) distinctive leisure pursuits. The ancient ritual of Queen Elizabeth's coronation – a 'phoenix time'[12] watched by more than 20 million television viewers – was a prolonged hymn to the whig constitution, an assertion of national pride and unity and, as Edward Shils and Michael Young put it, the celebration of a national 'communion with the sacred'.[13]

The main intellectual currents of the time ran in the same direction. 'The originators, the exuberant men, are extinct', wrote Evelyn Waugh of the novelists of the period, 'and in their place subsists and modestly flourishes a generation notable for elegance and variety of contrivance.'[14] Much the same could have been said of the philosophers, historians and social theorists. The passionate enthusiasms and conflicts of the 1930s had faded. Challenges to the established order were rare. Audacious system-building was suspect. Influences from continental Europe were held at bay. A mixture of knowing realism, self-congratulatory historicism and cosy insularity prevailed. In philosophy, the brash radicalism of logical positivism gave way to the ingenious, quintessentially conservative and ultimately barren navel-gazing of linguistic analysis. Among historians the mood of the time was epitomised by the Manchester professor, Lewis (soon to be Sir Lewis) Namier, and his aggressive disciples. Namier was an upper-class Galician Jew by extraction, a Catholic by upbringing, a fervent British patriot by adoption and a combative Zionist by conviction. He debunked the role of ideas (and especially of radical ideas) in history, dwelt with loving erudition on the struggles of individuals for place and patronage, and venerated the Westminster Parliament as a unique, because 'organically generated', microcosm of the nation.[15]

His veneration found plenty of echoes outside the historical profession. In a characteristic passage, the Cambridge jurist, Ivor Jennings, declared confidently that 'In the process of constitutional development England first and Great Britain afterwards have led the way . . . the nations who dare to call themselves free have built largely on British experience.'[16] American observers were particularly enthusiastic about the British system and their enthusiasm fed back into Britain. For the Harvard political scientist, Harry Eckstein, British government owed its 'unique' effectiveness to the survival into modern times of 'the medieval sanctification of authority and the absolutist realization of autonomous power'.[17] In a well-known study, Gabriel Almond and Sidney Verba concluded that, of the five countries they looked at, Britain approximated most closely to the model of a 'civic culture', capable of sustaining a modern pluralist democracy. She did so, they thought, because the 'notion of the independent authority of government under law has continued to exist side by side with the notion of the political power of the people'.[18]

However, the most striking manifestation of the intellectual mentality of the time came in 1951, when the Cambridge philosopher, Michael Oakeshott, succeeded the renowned (if incorrigibly inconstant) left-Labour intellectual, Harold Laski, as Professor of Political Science at the London School of Economics. Like Namier, Oakeshott deprecated ideas and venerated tradition. In a soon-to-be-notorious inaugural lecture, he declared that politics was an activity rather like cooking – a 'conversation, not an argument'. What mattered were 'intimations', not ideologies. In political life, as he put it in one of his most audacious passages,

> men sail a boundless and bottomless sea; there is neither harbour for shelter nor floor for anchorage, neither starting-pace nor appointed destination. The enterprise is to keep afloat on an even keel; the sea is both friend and enemy; and the seamanship consists in using the resources of a traditional manner of behaviour in order to make a friend of every hostile occasion.[19]

It was an illusion to think there could be 'a destination to be reached or even a detectable strand of progress. "The world is the best of all possible worlds, and *everything* in it is a necessary evil." '[20] Oakeshott was a 'deviant',[21] but his belligerent quietism reflected an important strand in the mood of the early 1950s – albeit in a distorting mirror.

⚬⚬⚬

Quietism in the academy was bolstered by quietism in the economy. The succession of painful and disorientating crises that had haunted the Attlee governments was forgotten. Suggestions that there might be something seriously wrong with Britain's economic performance, or that government might have to make hard economic choices, were conspicuous by their absence. The British economy was more sluggish than those of continental Europe, but it too was buoyed up by the long post-war boom that was now getting into its stride, and in any case it was still the most productive of the big economies of non-Communist Europe.[22] In the European economic convoy, Britain chugged along at a stately pace, but the faster vessels were so far behind her that her captain and crew saw no reason for alarm. By historic British standards, the growth rate was remarkably high – higher than it had been in the glory years of Britain's nineteenth-century industrial supremacy. The return to the bad old days with which Labour had tried to make the electorate's flesh creep in the elections of 1950 and 1951 obstinately failed to materialise. Unemployment oscillated between a high of 2.1 per cent and a low of 1.2 per cent – figures that Keynes and his wartime associates would have thought inconceivably low.

Living standards rose; rationing became a memory. Restaurant meals were still dire; British travellers to North America were astonished by the taste of real hamburgers and ice-cream, the generosity of American steaks and the profusion of American salads. However, *The Good Food Guide*, edited by the maverick socialist Raymond Postgate, shone like a candle in a naughty world, while Elizabeth David's *Mediterranean Food* became the culinary bible of the more adventurous members of the salariat. Cuts in income tax benefited the middle class more than the working class, but earnings went up faster than prices, so that real wages increased. The frontiers of social citizenship and the public domain were as wide as they had been under Labour. Of the Attlee Government's nationalisations, only steel and road haulage were reversed. Social spending increased absolutely and held its existing share of GDP; the net effect of the tax and welfare system was to make household incomes somewhat less unequal. On house building, the government's record far surpassed Labour's. Its target of 300,000 houses a year was reached in December 1953 – establishing Harold Macmillan, the minister in charge of the housing drive, as a politician of the first rank. Paid holidays, motor cars, radios, television sets and electric and gas appliances spread ever more widely among manual workers and their families. The prospect ahead seemed equally rosy. In a speech that epitomised the temper of the times, Butler looked forward to a doubling of the standard of living in twenty-five years. Not to be outdone, the glamorous young Labour politician, social-democratic thinker and erstwhile Oxford economist, Anthony Crosland, added that on present trends output would increase fourfold in sixty-two years.[23]

Budgetary policy was conducted in the same genial spirit. The anti-robotnik argument that unemployment would spell political death was seared into the Cabinet's soul. Henceforth, Butler took care to eschew further adventures. His unspoken motto was Talleyrand's: 'Surtout, Messieurs, point de zèle.' With the help of a vulgarised Keynesianism, he trod a tightrope between economic overload and political trouble: between too much demand to keep the balance of payments in the black, and too little to maintain full employment. The result would become notorious as 'Stop-Go' – a series of zig-zags from budgetary expansion to contraction and back again – but charges that this destabilised the economy and inhibited investment would not become current until later.

The first warning sign came in 1955, when Butler fell off the tightrope.

In March of that year, Churchill at last resigned as Prime Minister. He was succeeded by his impatient and far from healthy crown prince, the charming, debonair, but chronically tense, often testy and sometimes foul-tempered Anthony Eden, his Foreign Secretary. In April, with the economy booming, Butler brought in an expansionist budget, including a cut in income tax of sixpence in the pound. In May, the Conservatives won a general election with a greatly increased majority. In July, pressure on the reserves forced Butler to restrict credit and cut investment. In October, he had to increase taxes by almost as much as he had cut them in April. But the warning was easily ignored. Butler's reputation was damaged, but far from fatally. He left the Treasury to become Leader of the House of Commons and Lord Privy Seal in December 1955. Though he would never become Prime Minister, he would hold two more of the great offices of state – the Home Office and the Foreign Office – and stay at the top of Conservative politics until his departure from the House of Commons in 1966.

Vulgar Keynesianism helped to sustain a genteel quasi-corporatism. This had a superficial resemblance to the more full-blooded corporatist systems that took root in Scandinavia and central Europe, but the differences were more important than the similarities. British-style quasi-corporatism was fluid, shifting, ambiguous and unacknowledged.[24] Like the parliamentary monarchy, it depended on tacit understandings that were not always understood, and unwritten conventions that were inherently contestable. However, there were few contests in the halcyon days of Churchill's neo-Baldwinism. Like Members of Parliament, the leaders of the interests enmeshed in the quasi-corporatist system had more in common with each other than they had with their respective constituents. Professional civil servants dealt with professional managers; both dealt with professional trade-union bureaucrats. Besides, economic growth blunted the edge of distributional conflicts. Organised labour, organised capital and the state could all enjoy a growth dividend; the only question was how large their respective dividends would be. The result was an atmosphere of cosy, somnolent contentment, quite different from the atmosphere of crisis that had prevailed during and after the war, when quasi-corporatism had grown to maturity.

Most of the direct controls on private industry which had survived Harold Wilson's bonfire were abolished, but government still influenced private companies in a host of ways, including subsidies, loans, defence procurements, tax breaks and what the economist, D.H. Robertson, happily called 'ear stroking' – the use of 'encouragements which are not quite promises, frowns which are not quite prohibitions, understandings which are not quite agreements'.[25] And while government stroked industry's ears, industry stroked government's. Both stroked organised labour's.

To general surprise, Churchill appointed the elegant and distinguished KC, Walter Monckton, as Minister of Labour. Monckton was a nominal Conservative, but not much more. He was not even a Member of Parliament until February 1951, by which time he was aged sixty. He had been a close friend of Stafford Cripps, whose Anglican faith he shared. He had once advised Edward VIII and later did the same for the Nizam of Hyderabad. Faced with a conflict, his instinct was to search for a compromise. His brief was to avoid strikes and to prove that the Conservatives could be as friendly to the unions as could the Labour Party. He succeeded brilliantly. If anything he had a better rapport with the union leaders than Labour ministers had had. In a 1953 speech, Arthur Deakin, Bevin's belligerent successor as General Secretary of the TGWU, confessed that, under Monckton, 'we have been able to do things that were difficult under our own people'.[26] An anecdote of R.A. Butler's illuminates the inner meaning of Deakin's accolade. Churchill phoned Butler in the middle of the night to tell him that he and Monckton had settled a railway dispute which had seemed likely to disrupt the Christmas holiday. On what terms, Butler asked. 'Theirs, old cock,' replied Churchill.[27] It could serve as the epitaph of the responsive whiggery of the time.

⚘

Responsive whiggery could accommodate the growth of trade-union power without much pain. The rising tide of colonial nationalism was another matter. By October 1951, when Churchill formed his last government, India, Pakistan, Ceylon and Burma had all become independent. British troops had left Greece; British rule in Palestine had ended. Yet Britain's global role, and the associated whig imperialist vision of her history and identity, still had plenty of life in them. Britain was still the predominant power in the Middle East; her colonies still sprawled across sub-Saharan Africa; half the world's trade was still denominated in her currency; she was winning the war against Communist guerrillas in Malaya; and thanks to the Attlee Government's staunchly whig imperialist reflexes she was also a nuclear power. The British lion might be a little mangy, but it was still a lion. Two great questions haunted the whig imperialist rulers of mid-century Britain. Could they hold that position? If not, how should they respond to its loss?

These questions were posed with special force in Egypt – a British dependency (though not a colony) since 1882. For sixty years Suez had been the nodal point linking the British-dominated Indian Ocean to the shipping lanes of the Mediterranean. The Suez base was still thought to hold the key to British predominance in the Middle East and East Africa, and to the flow of oil on which Britain depended; for Lord Hankey, now one of the British directors of the Suez Canal Company, the canal was the 'jugular vein of World and Empire shipping'.[28] Above all, Suez was a symbol of global power and glory. It evoked memories of the white man's burden in distant climes; it conveyed the message that, in spite of everything, Britain was still the country she had always been.

Unfortunately, Britain's presence there rested on precarious foundations. In 1936, Britain and Egypt had concluded a treaty, acknowledging Egypt's formal independence and giving Britain the right to defend the canal zone for a twenty-year period, to be reviewed when the time limit was reached. Well before then, however, gales of Egyptian resentment of the humiliations suffered at Britain's hands were beginning to call the future of the zone into question. In 1951 the Egyptian Government unilaterally abrogated the treaty. In 1952 a revolutionary coup by a group of junior officers drove the Egyptian king from the throne. The Suez base was subject to repeated terrorist attacks, and British ministers slowly came to the conclusion that the costs of staying there outweighed the benefits. In 1954, the Churchill Government, with Eden, still Foreign Secretary, in the lead, decided to cut its losses. Britain and Egypt agreed on a staged withdrawal of British troops from Egypt, to be completed by June 1956.

1954 also saw the charismatic nationalist, Colonel Gamal Nasser, emerge as the real leader of the Egyptian revolution. Nasser's ostentatious neutralism and violent anti-Western propaganda soon made him a suspect figure in Washington and London. An arms deal between Egypt and Czechoslovakia, for all practical purposes a proxy for the Soviet Union, gave their suspicions an edge of paranoia. Eden thought the Soviet Union had shown that it planned to 'open a third front in the Cold War, this time in the Middle East'.[29] The American Secretary of State, the morose and devious cold warrior, John Foster Dulles, feared that the USSR might become 'the guardian of the Suez Canal'.[30] The countdown to crisis began on 19 July 1956. To punish Nasser, the United States, with Britain lagging in her wake, withdrew an offer of aid to build a high dam at Aswan on the Nile. The Egyptian response was swift and brilliantly aimed. On 26 July, Nasser (now President of Egypt) told a vast and exalted Alexandria crowd that the Suez Canal had just been nationalised.[31]

Eden had been Prime Minister for fifteen generally placid months. Now he faced the supreme test of his prime ministership and ultimately of his career. His response was swift. Within hours of the nationalisation announcement, he told a meeting of ministers and service chiefs at no. 10 Downing Street that Nasser must not be allowed to 'have his hand on our windpipe'.[32] There followed a long and desperate search for a way to loosen Nasser's grip and if possible to destroy his regime. As early as 27 July, the Cabinet agreed that, if necessary, Britain should use force to restore international control over the canal – if need be, alone. It soon became clear that France would act with her: the French Government, headed by the socialist Guy Mollet, was embroiled in a savage struggle to keep Algeria French and saw Nasser as the evil genius of Algerian nationalism. But the American President, Dwight Eisenhower, was adamantly opposed to the use of force – either by the United States or by anyone else. (Dulles's 'maddening twists and turns'[33] sometimes gave a different impression of American policy.) After much fruitless coming and going between the British, the French, the Americans and the maritime powers, the French thought up a wheeze, on which Eden seized with foolish relief. Israel would invade Egypt and make for the Suez Canal. France and Britain would call on Israel and Egypt to withdraw their forces from the canal. If Egypt accepted, it would be the end of Nasser. If she did not, the French and British would intervene to ensure the canal's safety. They would not be aggressors, invading someone else's territory. They would be policemen suppressing a breach of the peace.

At first, all went according to plan. On 22 October, the British Foreign Secretary, Selwyn Lloyd; the Israeli Prime Minister, David Ben Gurion; the French Prime Minister, Guy Mollet; and assorted aides all met secretly in an old Resistance safe house in Sèvres and agreed to the French plan. (Selwyn Lloyd had travelled incognito, wearing an old mackintosh.) On 29 October, Israeli forces duly invaded Egypt. Next day, Britain and France issued ultimatums to Egypt and Israel on the agreed lines. Nasser refused to comply; on 31 October the RAF bombed Cairo. On 6 November, British and French seaborne troops landed at Port Said.

But by now the wheeze was coming apart. Liberal opinion in Britain was outraged as it had not been since Munich. There were furious scenes in the House of Commons and a mass demonstration in Trafalgar Square, which ended with mounted police charging a crowd surging down Whitehall. Much more serious than opposition at home were the indignation of President Eisenhower, who justly thought he had been double-crossed, and the reaction of the United Nations, where Britain and France were outvoted by 64 to 5. Most serious of all was an accelerating fall in Britain's gold and dollar reserves, encouraged by the US Treasury. The run had started when the canal was nationalised, but at first it had been fairly restrained. However, it accelerated ominously when British troops were engaged. The American Treasury Secretary made it clear that Britain would have no hope of obtaining IMF credits to support sterling unless there were an immediate ceasefire. At the start of the crisis Harold Macmillan, now Chancellor of the Exchequer, had been one of the Cabinet's leading hawks. American financial blackmail turned him into its most persuasive dove. When the Cabinet met on the morning of 6 November, he 'put the fear of God into the Cabinet on finances'.[34] At 6 p.m. on the same day Eden told the House of Commons that the Franco-British force would cease its operations at midnight. It was a consummation worthy of the Grand Old Duke of York.

The sequel was cruelly ironic. Instead of toppling Nasser, Eden was toppled himself – not by his colleagues or opponents, and still less by the Egyptians, but by his own body. At periodic intervals during the crisis he had suffered exhausting shivering fits and high fevers, the after-effects of a 1953 operation on his gall bladder that had gone wrong. Two weeks after the ceasefire, his doctors told him to take a complete rest in a warm climate. On 23 November, he flew to Jamaica. He returned bronzed and apparently fit, but badly damaged politically. In the New Year, his fevers and sleepless nights returned. On 9 January 1957, he resigned on health grounds. Most of the political world assumed that Butler would succeed him, but the Cabinet was overwhelmingly for Macmillan and only the Cabinet had a voice. On 10 January, Harold Macmillan duly kissed hands as Prime Minister.

OYSTERS AND CHAMPAGNE

The new regime began with an engaging display of panache. 'Where is the Chief Whip?' called Macmillan, on the evening following his appointment. 'We're off to the Turf to celebrate.' He and the chief whip, Edward Heath, then disappeared for a supper of oysters and champagne.[35] However, Macmillan needed more than panache to staunch the wounds left by the Suez affair. True, the electorate was behind it. So far from winning votes by opposing it, Labour lost support, not least in its working-class constituency. But in almost every other way Suez was a disaster. The Sèvres plot with Israel and France was both shabby and farcical. Though the details would not be known for years to come it was painfully obvious that Britain, France and Israel must have colluded in some way. As a result the plotters gained nothing from their attempted deception; they only made themselves look furtive as well as chauvinistic, reactionary and incompetent.

The political and economic judgements on which government policy was based were manifestly flawed. Nasser was not a second Mussolini and still less a second Hitler, as the British and French believed, and Arab nationalism was far more than an evanescent emanation of his will. Had he been deposed, it would have been at least as big a thorn in French and British sides as it had been before. Eden and his colleagues failed to understand how deep American anti-colonialism went or how passionately Eisenhower shared it; even more culpably they failed to give proper heed to sterling's endemic weakness. At the United Nations, in Washington, throughout the Arab world, in most Commonwealth capitals, and even in Paris and Jerusalem, Britain cut a sorry, and at the same time risible, figure. British ministers were exposed, not just as liars, but as bungling and unconvincing liars. The lilting cadences of Bevan's invective at the anti-Suez demonstration in Trafalgar Square said it all: 'If Sir Anthony is sincere in what he says – and he may be – then he is too *stupid* to be Prime Minister.'[36] Above all, the Cabinet were exposed as hypocrites. They were willing to wound, but afraid to strike – or at least to be seen to strike. Altogether, Suez was the most humiliating episode in twentieth-century British history.

The humiliation did not last, but the after-effects smouldered on like a slow-burning fuse. The gentlemanly elite, whose authority and skill had sustained the whig imperialist tradition for more than a century, had been humiliated along with the country it led. It remained in place. There were no tumbrils in Westminster, Whitehall or the City. Macmillan's Cabinet contained one fewer former public-schoolboy than Eden's (seventeen out of eighteen as against eighteen out of eighteen), and two fewer Etonians (eight as against ten). However, fifteen of its members were Oxbridge graduates as against fourteen under Eden. Grammar-school products were beginning to climb the commanding heights of the state. (Sir Norman Brook, the suave, discreet and immaculately tailored Cabinet Secretary, was one of them.) But public-school-educated offspring of the professional service class, leavened by a small admixture from the landed class of earlier days, still predominated in the judiciary, the episcopate and the directorate of the Bank of England, and although the top ranks of the civil service were more open to grammar-school talent, they were still dominated by Oxbridge graduates.

In 1962, Anthony Sampson, the pertinacious anatomist of Britain's ruling elite, found that of the forty-two judges who listed their education in *Who's Who* seven came from Christ Church, Oxford, and six from Trinity College, Cambridge. Eleven came from grammar schools, but only one from a red-brick university. Three-quarters of the bishops had been to public schools, and the vast majority to Oxford or Cambridge.[37] Geoffrey Fisher, Archbishop of Canterbury from 1939 to 1961, was educated at Marlborough and Oxford; his liberal successor, Michael Ramsey, was a product of Repton and Cambridge. Lord Cromer, the Governor of the Bank of England, was a product of Eton and Trinity College, Cambridge, as was his predecessor, Lord Cobbold. In 1958, fifty of the 166 directors of the Bank of England and the 'big five' clearing banks were Etonians, while Harrow, Winchester, Rugby and Marlborough accounted for another thirty-three.[38]

Yet some of the sheen had gone. The elite's claim to rule rested, among other things, on its long training in statecraft: on its supposed mastery of R.A. Butler's 'art of the possible'. At Suez, it had insisted on banging its head against a wall of impossibility; its statecraft had been considerably less impressive than Nasser's. Imperceptibly, the structure of authority and deference that had protected it began to crack. Little by little, it started to look ridiculous rather than formidable. As early as 1955, Nigel Dennis's satire, *Cards of Identity*, held up the pompous mystifications of the elite to ironic scorn. A snatch of dialogue gives the flavour. A 'co-warden of the badgeries' is being inducted into his duties:

'There is a token badger, but according to tradition it is maintained by the yeomen of Hertford Forest. It is a stuffed one, of course.'

'I suppose they let us take it on ceremonial occasions.'

'Not the actual, token badger, except on the death of the Lord Royal. Normally you get a clip of the artificial fur set in an osier staff. This is an emblem of the token. Thus you retain your technical right to the token badger, and, thereby, to all living badgers in the country. . . .'

'In short', said Vinson, 'what is not symbolic is emblematic?'

'Except where it is token', agreed Channing. 'Then it is stuffed.'[39]

Scorn gradually became more outspoken. At Oxford and Cambridge, irreverent grammar-school arrivistes like Michael Frayn, the future dramatist and novelist; Brian Walden, the future MP and television interviewer; Bernard Donoughue, the future head of Harold Wilson's Policy Unit; Dennis Potter, the future television maestro; and Alan Bennett, the future national treasure, disputed the predominance of their public-school contemporaries. Meanwhile, new, disrespectful, sometimes uncouth voices began to make themselves heard beyond the university walls. One of the loudest belonged to Kingsley Amis, whose comic novel of the lower reaches of academic life, *Lucky Jim*, had appeared at the beginning of the decade. However, Amis's jokes left few scars. He was content to blow uproarious, but in essence gentle, raspberries at the conventional, self-satisfied and established.

In 1956, the year of Suez, a more abrasive voice joined the chorus. Its owner was the jobbing actor John Osborne, just twenty-seven, whose first successful play, *Look Back in Anger*, opened in London in May of that year and broke the mould of British drama. Over the next half-century Osborne's reputation declined, but in the mid-fifties he spoke to and for the bolshie irreverence of the post-war generation with an explosive force that none of his contemporaries equalled. (Young males, for whom two years' compulsory military service was a nursery of bolshieness, may have been more impressed than their female counterparts.) In an enthusiastic review in the *Observer*, the rising critic Kenneth Tynan, then twenty-nine, praised its picture of post-war youth. 'All the qualities are there . . .' he wrote, 'the drift towards anarchy, the instinctive leftishness, the automatic rejection of "official" attitudes.'[40] There was truth in that, but *Look Back in Anger* was not mere reportage. The hero, Jimmy Porter, the rootless, self-hating graduate of a 'white-tiled' university, was the vehicle for a cry of mingled rage and pain. Its most obvious target was the traditional governing elite, represented by Porter's brother-in-law, Nigel, a 'Platitude from Outer Pace', clearly destined to end up in the Cabinet:

> But somewhere at the back of that mind is the vague knowledge that he and his pals have been plundering and fooling everybody for generations. . . . But it wouldn't do for him to be troubled by any stabs of conscience, however vague. Besides, he's a patriot and an Englishman, and he doesn't like the idea that he may have been selling out his countrymen all these years, so what does he do? The only thing he can do – seek sanctuary in his own stupidity.[41]

The pain went wider than that. 'There aren't any good, brave causes left,' Porter complained in his most famous tirade. 'If the big bang does come, and we all get killed off, it won't be in aid of the old-fashioned grand design. It'll just be for the Brave New-nothing-very-much-thank-you.'[42] And though he railed against his wife's father, Colonel Redford, once the commander of an Indian maharajah's army, a tell-tale gleam of sympathy shone through:

> The old Edwardian brigade do make their brief little world look pretty tempting. . . . Always the same picture: high summer, the long days in the sun, slim volumes of verse, crisp linen, the smell of starch. What a romantic picture. Phoney too, of course. It must have rained sometimes. Still, even I regret it somehow, phoney or not. If you've no world of your own, it's rather pleasant to regret the passing of someone else's. I must be getting sentimental. But I must say it's pretty dreary living in the American age – unless you're an American of course.[43]

Mixed with the rage was a lament for lost glory and lost identity. The Edwardian brigade had had its day, and that was just as well, but the gimcrack American Age was a sorry substitute for the old certainties. The charge against the ruling elite was not just that it had plundered the ruled for generations, but that it had capitulated to the 'Brave New-nothing-very-much-thank-you': that it had betrayed its trust. The political elite spoke the 'thieves' language of Westminster'; the Church was a 'smooth confidence trick'; royalty was 'the gold filling in a mouthful of decay'.[44]

Few emulated Osborne's verbal violence, but the mood behind it was widely shared. The gentlemanly elite had been an imperial elite. It had been trained to rule over vast territories in Africa and Asia and to sustain the global roles of sterling and the City, as well as to lead at home. A nimbus of imperial glory had given it a special kind of authority, unequalled by any other European elite. The nimbus had started to dissolve before Suez and after the Cabinet's capitulation to the US Treasury's financial blackmail it rapidly disappeared. Ever since Bevin's middle-kingdom dreams had evaporated in the late 1940s, it had been obvious that no amount of diplomatic ingenuity could enable Britain to rival the superpowers. Now it seemed that, without the acquiescence of her superpower protector, she could not even pursue her own interests in her own way. Not only was she no longer a great power; in an important sense she was no longer an independent one. Suez, Oliver Franks remembered in 1990, was 'like a flash of lightning on a dark night', revealing a landscape in which 'everything was different'.[45]

Hard questions followed. Given that Britain's remaining imperial possessions had availed her nothing during the Suez crisis, and that the self-governing dominions had mostly opposed her, was she still, in any meaningful sense, an imperial power? If not, what was she? And what was the point of the once-imperial elite and of the myths and rituals that sustained it? These questions were not posed overtly in the painful aftermath of Suez, but they hung in the air like birds of prey.

☙❧

Macmillan became Prime Minister against this background. He approached his task with a characteristic mixture of agility and ambiguity. Indeed, ambiguity was his trademark. He had been brought up as a 'gown man', he wrote in his memoirs, but the First World War had turned him into 'a "sword man". Action – harsh, brutal, compelling – ousted learning.' Ever since, he had been conscious of a duality in his nature.[46] With his studied wit, patrician manner, military moustache, carefully cultivated 'unflappability' and well-publicised fondness for Trollope, he seemed, on the surface, a throwback to the lost glories of the Edwardian age: an infinitely grander version of Osborne's Colonel Redford in *Look Back in Anger*.

In some ways, that is what he was. He was the last Prime Minister to have been born in the reign of Queen Victoria; his time at university had ended in the summer of 1914, leaving an indelible impress. He had been unhappy as a scholar at Eton, but had blossomed after going up to Oxford in 1912, with an Exhibition at Balliol. He had forced himself to become an accomplished Union debater, joined the intense Anglo-Catholic circle around the future Roman Catholic Monsignor, Ronald Knox, and won a First in 'Mods'. He never forgot the golden summer of 1914, with its 'cloudless atmosphere' and 'voluptuous breezes'. In old age, as Oxford's devoted Chancellor, he loved to echo Talleyrand's phrase about the *ancien régime:* those who had not known the university before 1914, he insisted, had never known '*le plaisir de vivre*'.[47]

But Macmillan the nostalgic patrician was only one of several Macmillans. His wife, Lady Dorothy, the daughter of the Duke of Devonshire, belonged to one of the greatest Whig families in the land; her relatives looked down their noses at him and found him boring. In truth, Macmillan was a hereditary businessman. The Macmillans were highly successful publishers, with Thomas Hardy, Henry James and Kipling on their list, but they were still 'in trade'. More important than Macmillan the patrician, in fact, was Macmillan the manager, talent-spotter and entrepreneur. More important than either was Macmillan, the wartime captain in the Grenadier Guards. He fought at Loos and the Somme, displayed conspicuous courage and was wounded several times – the last time so badly that he almost died from the after-effects. Like many privileged young men who served as subalterns in the killing fields of Flanders and north-east France, he never forgot the 'big hearts' of the working-class youths under his command, and never quite expunged a sense of guilt at having survived. Of the eight Balliol scholars and exhibitioners who had come up with him in 1912, only two were still alive in 1918. After the war, Oxford seemed to him 'a city of ghosts'.

Hidden by these three Macmillans was a fourth – insecure, vulnerable, prone to well-concealed 'agonies of nervous apprehension'[48] and subject to bouts of depression which, like Churchill, he called 'Black Dog'. Between the wars, 'Black Dog' was particularly active. Lady Dorothy was the only woman in Macmillan's life, but after nine years of marriage she fell in love with the then dashing, handsome and alluring Robert Boothby, who was widely (and wrongly) believed to be one of the most promising Conservative politicians of his generation. Her marriage to Macmillan survived, but her relationship with Boothby lasted until her death in 1966, and it brought her husband abiding pain.

The pain, like the trenches, toughened him. By the time he kissed hands as Prime Minister in 1957, a fifth Macmillan – a canny, ruthless, courageous and, above all, iconoclastic professional politician – overshadowed the others. His courage had been unrewarded for a decade and a half. He was elected MP for Stockton in 1924 and, after a spell out of Parliament following the 1929 election, regained his seat in 1931 and held it until 1945. The experience of representing a working-class northern constituency with an unemployment rate of more than twenty per cent marked him as deeply as the trenches had done and made him an increasingly audacious rebel against his party's leaders. In the 1930s, he was a disciple of Keynes, whose books he published; he played a leading role in the cross-party 'Next Five Years Group', which campaigned for a British version of the New Deal with which Roosevelt saved American capitalism from itself; he seriously contemplated joining the Labour Party;[49] and he wrote a number of pamphlets and books, culminating in an ambitious call for national and sectoral planning, disloyally entitled *The Middle Way*.

At the end of the decade appeasement replaced unemployment as the chief focus for his rebellions, but he was an even more troublesome thorn in his party's flesh than he had been before. After Churchill took over from Chamberlain, junior office at last came his way. In 1942, he was given a plum job as Minister Resident in Algeria where he negotiated with the prickly de Gaulle, leader of the Free French, and liaised with Eisenhower, the Allied commander-in-chief. His private picture of Anglo-American co-operation would not have pleased the Americans. In a much-quoted conversation, he told Richard Crossman, later a maverick Labour MP but then the Algiers Director of Psychological Warfare:

> [Y]ou will always permit your American colleague not only to have a superior rank to yourself and much higher pay, but also the feeling that he is running the show. This will enable you to run it yourself.
>
> We, my dear Crossman, are the Greeks in this American empire. You will find the Americans much as the Greeks found the Romans – great big, vulgar, bustling people, more vigorous than we are and also more idle, with more unspoilt virtues but also more corrupt. We must run A.F.H.Q. [Allied Forces Headquarters] as the Greek slaves ran the operations of the emperor Claudius.[50]

From then on he rose steadily in the Conservative hierarchy until he replaced Eden as Prime Minister. His ascent to 10 Downing Street was not quite what it seemed, however. He had won as a strong man, in contrast to the fey and vacillating Butler, but he was a strong man with a difference. The earnest, bespectacled, uncharismatic, yet defiantly unbiddable 1930s Keynesian rebel had not disappeared; he had only taken cover.[51] The lessons of the trenches and of Stockton – that officers have a duty to look after their men, and a governing class a duty to look after the governed – had not been forgotten. Nor had the indifference to party and the disdain for economic orthodoxy that they bred. Macmillan was a whig imperialist to his fingertips. In an echo of Burke's contempt for the *philosophes* on the other side of the Channel, he insisted that Conservatives should combat 'the pretensions of those who believed – or at least said they believed – that their particular brand of doctrinaire politics at any particular time could solve every problem'.[52] But (like the young Burke) he was a whig imperialist with a radical disposition as well as a generous heart. Younger people, he conceded, could not remember the deflation of the interwar years.

> But the old ones have not forgotten. I was a Member of Parliament in those days on Tees-side. As long as I live I can never forget the impoverishment and demoralisation which all this brought with it. I am determined, so far as it lies within human power, never to allow this shadow to fall again upon our country.[53]

At the start of the twenty-first century, when interwar unemployment and Keynesian economic radicalism are both ancient history, it is all too easy to miss the full significance of this cry from the heart. It was Macmillan's political compass and, as we shall see, it was to lead him and his party into uncharted and perilous waters.

⚬⚬⚬

There were limits to Macmillan's radicalism. Like Churchill, he was half American; and, as his wartime conversation with Crossman implied, he viewed transatlantic relations through a sub-Churchillian prism. Over Suez, Eisenhower had behaved towards France and Britain like a peppery headmaster chastising badly behaved schoolboys. But there was an extraordinary contrast between French and British reactions. Both in the dying days of the Fourth Republic and under the Gaullist Fifth Republic which came into being shortly after the Suez debacle, French elites concluded, with their usual unsentimental realism, that the 'Anglo-Saxons' were not to be trusted, and that France would have to rely on her own right arm and a special relationship with Germany to prosecute her national interests.

British elites reacted in precisely the opposite way. For them, the moral of Suez was that Britain must never again risk Washington's wrath, and that if the price of returning to America's good books was a little self-abasement, it was a price worth paying. On the central question of Britain's global role that became the leitmotiv of Macmillan's prime ministership. Inevitably, his first task as Prime Minister was to restore his party's battered morale, but, as he saw it, his second – only one degree less urgent – was to repair the rift with Washington. Within months, it looked as if he had succeeded in both. Defeatist talk about Britain being a second-class power was 'nonsense!' he declared in his first television broadcast as Prime Minister. 'This is a great country ... there is no reason to quiver before temporary difficulties.' As for the United States, 'We don't intend to part from the Americans, and we don't intend to be satellites.'[54] An amicable meeting in Bermuda with Eisenhower in March 1957 convinced him that Anglo-American relations had returned to their old footing. (Whether he still thought he was a clever Greek slave to Eisenhower's coarse-grained Emperor Claudius is not known.) Two months later, a rousing reception after a debating triumph in the House of Commons seemed to show that Conservative morale had recovered too.

In other areas, Macmillan gave free rein to his radical instincts. Four long-term issues, each posing hard questions for whig imperialist statecraft, clamoured for his attention. First in this queue was defence policy. Britain still maintained a large conscript army and also spent a significantly higher proportion of GDP on defence than any other European member of NATO. Yet her military deployment during the Suez crisis had been slow, cumbersome and over-elaborate when the need was for speed and mobility. Would she do better with a leaner, meaner and, above all, cheaper defence establishment? Second, how should the Commonwealth in general, and the remaining colonies in particular, evolve in the post-Suez world? Since the late 1940s, Britain's policy-makers had assumed that her position at the point of intersection between the 'three circles' of Europe, the Commonwealth and the United States gave her a unique kind of global influence. But Suez had shown that the Commonwealth circle counted for little in the hard terms of *realpolitik*. How should it be viewed in future?

Third, where did the European circle now fit in? 1956 – the year of Suez – was also the year when the six member-states of the Coal and Steel Community put the finishing touches to what became the 1957 Rome Treaty, setting up the European Economic Community. In a pregnant comment, gnarled old Konrad Adenauer, the West German Chancellor and another unsentimental realist, told Guy Mollet that Europe should be France's 'revenge' for American treachery over Suez.[55] The British shrank from such thoughts. Yet, though Whitehall did its best to dodge it, the question of how Britain should relate to this new bloc would become one of the dominant themes of Macmillan's prime ministership. Finally, Suez had shone a peculiarly hurtful light on the enduring weakness and vul-nerability of the British economy. That would be a dominating pre-occupation – not just for Macmillan's term in office, but for the next forty years.

Defence was the first target for Macmillan's iconoclasm. His chosen Minister of Defence was Churchill's son-in-law, the ruthless, tireless and – to use a favourite Macmillan term – '*cassant*' Duncan Sandys. (Using French was a typical Macmillan affectation. The Harraps French–English dictionary lists three relevant translations for *cassant*: 'curt', 'abrupt' and 'imperious'.) With Macmillan's backing, and against strong opposition from the service chiefs and many Conservative MPs, Sandys forced through a white paper promising a revolution in Britain's defence posture. Conscription would end and the armed services would be cut. The 1957 total of 695,000 would fall to around 375,000 in 1962, when the abolition of conscription had worked itself through the system. There would be drastic cuts in British forces in Germany and the navy would lose its remaining battleships. Britain would still have bases in the Middle East and South-East Asia, but she would no longer be able to fight a large-scale conventional war. Slimmed-down, mobile, professional conventional forces would enable her to intervene on a small scale in distant trouble spots, but for protection against a serious enemy she would depend on a nuclear – and, after the successful test of a British H-bomb in May 1957, on a thermonuclear – deterrent.

It was a policy of 'big bangs and small forces',[56] with nothing in between, which presaged a geopolitical and, less obviously, a cultural revolution, as well as a revolution in defence policy per se. For nearly twenty years Britain had maintained a large conscript army on the pattern of continental Europe; compulsory national service had been part of the texture of life for a generation of young men. In each year between the end of the Second World War and the end of national service, some British conscripts had been in action somewhere. In effect, Britain had had a citizen army, albeit confined to men. Now all this was swept away. Britain no longer had a serious role in the defence of her continental neighbours, beyond the capacity to threaten mutual suicide in a thermonuclear exchange. And two years' military service was no longer a badge of common citizenship.

Small forces posed few problems; big bangs were a different matter. Although Britain could afford a thermonuclear bomb, the aircraft to deliver it soon became obsolete, and the costs of developing missiles to put in their place were beyond her. For these she had to turn to the United States. In April 1960, the government decided to cancel the vulnerable and expensive British Blue Streak missile, and the Americans undertook to let Britain purchase Skybolt missiles, then under development in the United States, instead. Unfortunately, the Americans were more inconstant than the rhetoric of the special relationship presupposed. After John Kennedy's election as President in November 1960, American enthusiasm for Skybolt in Washington cooled, and by December 1962 it was clear that it would be cancelled in its turn.

For Macmillan this was a potentially deadly blow. To the Americans, Skybolt was a weapons system; to the British it was a surrogate for the thin red line of empire.[57] Macmillan had repeatedly insisted that Britain was still a great power because she was a nuclear power; Skybolt had been his entrance card to the nuclear club. Now he was left high and dry, beached on the dunes of Washington bureaucracy. At a fraught conference in Nassau in December 1962, at which Macmillan deployed all his resources of eloquence, pathos and wit, he and Kennedy hammered out a formula designed to save British face while achieving American purposes. Britain would obtain Polaris submarine-borne missiles from the United States; she would build her own submarines and her own warheads; and she would 'assign' her Polaris submarine fleet to NATO, except when 'supreme national interests' were at stake. In its own terms, it was a good deal for Britain. She still had a bomb and, with the help of a little casuistry, she could claim that it was still under her own control.

But the real significance of the episode lay elsewhere. The whig imperialist vision of Britain's identity and place in the world still framed the thinking of the British political class, but the Skybolt affair showed that it was out of joint with the brute realities of the nuclear age. In the life-and-death sphere of national defence, Britain was no longer truly independent. Without fully realising the implications, she had become a nuclear client of the United States – albeit a client with pretensions.

❧

Pretension was Macmillan's forte. He strode the international stage with a panache not seen since the days of Ernest Bevin. He spent six weeks in early 1958 on a tour of the Commonwealth, from India to New Zealand. In New Delhi he had long talks with Nehru, whom he found 'full of charm, cultivated, and ruthless – all great qualities in a leader'. In Canberra he renewed his wartime association with Robert Menzies, the Liberal (that is, conservative) Australian Prime Minister.[58] In January 1959, he spent ten days in Moscow, where he sported a magnificent white fur hat dating from the Soviet-Finnish war of 1940, and addressed the Russian people on television. In January 1960, he began a six-week tour of the African Commonwealth countries, culminating in a celebrated speech to the South African Parliament, in which he cribbed a phrase of Baldwin's and declared that a 'wind of change' was blowing through the continent. In October he addressed the UN General Assembly, where he squashed Khrushchev's heckling with a patrician nonchalance that earned him abiding American admiration. He was the first Western leader to visit de Gaulle when the latter became Prime Minister of France in the summer of 1958; later he stage-managed a lavish state visit by de Gaulle to London. He bent over backwards to show that he was on close terms with Eisenhower, and later with John Kennedy, Eisenhower's successor.

However, this luxuriant icing concealed a meagre cake. True, there were one or two currants. Macmillan was an early and persistent advocate of a ban on nuclear tests, and deserved some of the credit for the 1963 test-ban treaty. In a different sphere, 1958 saw Britain despatch a paratroop force to help King Hussein of Jordan fend off alleged threats to his regime, proving that she still had the wherewithal to intervene in the Middle East. But since she felt obliged to get American approval first, the true lesson of the episode was that her old role as paramount power in the region had now been taken over by the United States. In the great international crises that punctuated Macmillan's prime ministership – over Berlin in 1958–61 and over Cuba in 1962 – the two superpowers dominated the action and determined the outcome. Over Berlin, Britain was, at most, a somewhat restive member of a chorus of second-class powers, with little influence on events; over Cuba she could only keep her head down and pray. And, as we shall see, Macmillan's eloquent wooing of de Gaulle failed to soften that sternly Cartesian heart.

Yet there was more to Macmillan's international appearances than stylish play-acting. He was trying to prove – to himself as well as to others – that clever British Greeks could hold their own alongside vulgar American Romans; that there was a role for the 'soft' power of convincing argument, in which the British thought they were pre-eminent, as well as for the 'hard' power of bombs and bases. At the same time, his incessant globe-trotting was the political equivalent of a conjuror's patter, helping the hand to deceive the eye. He and his colleagues accompanied their defence revolution with the equally revolutionary liquidation of what was left of Britain's colonial empire. For some of their followers this was treachery; for more it was defeatism. At an early stage in the process, Lord 'Bobbety' Salisbury – grandson of Queen Victoria's Prime Minister, Lord President of the Council and the bellwether of Conservative traditionalists – resigned from the government in protest. Lord Lambton, a backbench MP and another aristocrat of ancient lineage, was also a potential focus for rebellion. But for Macmillan's insistence on acting the part of an international statesman in season and out, the Cabinet might have found it even harder to quell the doubts on their own back benches, and perhaps in the inner recesses of their own souls as well.

Macmillan and his ministers moved with astonishing speed.[59] Britain had

had twenty years to get used to the idea of Indian independence; the liquidation of the colonial empire in Africa had seemed inconceivable until the eve of its accomplishment. Sudan became an independent member-state of the Commonwealth in 1956. Malaya and the Gold Coast (renamed Ghana) followed in 1957. Then came the 1959 election, in which Macmillan led his party to a third term with a 100-seat majority. He promptly appointed Iain Macleod – the toughest and most adroit of the brilliant Conservative intake of 1950 – as Colonial Secretary. Macleod turned out to be an even more determined liquidator of colonies than Macmillan himself. In 1960, Nigeria became independent in its turn. So did Cyprus, previously the scene of a bitter guerrilla campaign for *enosis*, or union with Greece. The Cypriot leader, Archbishop Makarios, joined his Ghanaian counterpart, Kwame Nkrumah (and, for that matter, his Indian counterpart, Pandit Nehru), in graduating from a British gaol to international respectability.

It was the same story in East Africa. Even in the late 1950s, early independence for the colonies of Kenya, Tanganyika, Zanzibar and Uganda would have seemed wildly unlikely. Yet in 1961 Tanganyika, together with Zanzibar, became the independent Commonwealth state of Tanzania. In 1962, Uganda followed suit. In Kenya, where the Mau Mau guerrilla rising had been brutally suppressed during the 1950s, a small but vociferous settler community stood in the way of progress towards black rule. Macmillan feared that Kenyan independence would provoke Salisbury and Lambton to 'rally a settler lobby' and split the party,[60] but it came in 1963 with no such consequences.

The central African story was more tangled, but the central theme was not very different. In 1953, the Churchill Government set up a Central African Federation, consisting of Nyasaland and Northern and Southern Rhodesia. The white settlers in the two Rhodesias hankered for dominion status so as to consolidate their supremacy, but the African nationalists were violently hostile to the idea, and did their best to bring the Federation to an end. At first the Macmillan Government tried to breathe life into it, but in 1963, after some adroit diplomacy by the government's maid-of-all-work, R.A. Butler, it was wound up. Northern Rhodesia and Nyasaland both became independent sovereign states within the Commonwealth, with majority rule; Southern Rhodesia went its own unhappy, and ultimately tragic, way as a white supremacist bastion.

An undertone of bitterness ran through the saga. At one point the government made preparations to counter an 'open rebellion' by the Rhodesian settlers;[61] at another a furious Lord Salisbury accused Macleod, in a phrase that spoke volumes about the values of the traditional elite, of being 'too clever by half'.[62] But, in comparison with the trauma that de Gaulle's withdrawal from Algeria brought to France, this was small beer. By the end of Macmillan's prime ministership, Britain's colonial empire in Africa had almost vanished, with scarcely a ripple of opposition in what had once been called the 'mother country'. The governing elite, which had once prided itself on its management of the empire, could now congratulate itself on winding it up so elegantly and so speedily that its disappearance went almost unnoticed. In a way, this was a triumph for the whig imperialist tradition: another example of responsive adaptation through pluralistic inclusion. However, the triumph left a void – not so much of policy as of sentiment, rhetoric and identity.

DUST AND ASHES

Rapid-fire radicalism over Africa was accompanied by a nervous shuffle towards radicalism over Europe. Here Macmillan had form. In opposition, he had served in the Council of Europe Assembly at Strasbourg, where he had extolled the Schuman Plan as 'a revolutionary and almost mystical conception'.[63] In government, however, his enthusiasm for such revolutionary mysticism was distinctly muted. The Rome Treaty, setting up the six-member European Economic Community, was signed in March 1957 and came into force on New Year's Day 1958. Britain had stood aside from the bargaining that had preceded it, but from an early stage British ministers had seen that the creation of a powerful economic and political bloc on the European mainland would have profound implications for the British state and economy.

It was not so clear what the implications would be or how to cope with them. While the negotiations that led to the Rome Treaty were still going on, Macmillan, as Chancellor of the Exchequer, and Peter Thorneycroft, as President of the Board of Trade, had persuaded the Cabinet to back a 'Plan G', emanating from the inner recesses of Whitehall, and designed to give Britain the palm of industrial free trade, without the dust of irksome conditions. There would be a European Free Trade Area, of which the new EEC would be a member, alongside Britain and any other European countries that wished to join. It would not cover agriculture; it would have no supranational institutions; and it would not affect Commonwealth preferences.[64]

Plan G reflected an ominous failure of imagination. Membership of a wider industrial free trade area attracted some (though not all) Germans, whose industries could expect to benefit from it. It was anathema to the French, who would gain nothing and might lose much. It would have meant unpicking the hard-won Franco-German bargain which lay at the heart of the European project, abandoning the precious synthesis of the supra-national and the national that was of its essence, and undermining the solidarity of the Six on which its future depended. For Macmillan that was part of the point. Britain, he told Thorneycroft, 'must take the lead, either in widening their project, or, if they will not co-operate with us, in opposing it'.[65] He did not broadcast these intentions, but it was not difficult to infer them from his actions. They were hardly calculated to win friends in Paris.

Yet, with a doomed and curiously self-righteous persistence, his government continued to chase the chimera of a 'wider' project until long after the Rome Treaty was signed. It gave up only in November 1958 when the French Government (now headed by de Gaulle) made it clear that France was not prepared to join a free-trade area tailored to British specifications.

During his visit to Paris immediately after de Gaulle's return to power, Macmillan had warned him that unless he abandoned the EEC, 'we shall be embarking on a war which will doubtless be economic at first but which runs the risk of gradually spreading into other fields.'[66] In a clumsy attempt to give point to that threat, Britain took the lead in setting up a mini-free-trade area of the so-called 'Outer Seven' – Sweden, Norway, Denmark, Austria, Switzerland, Portugal and Britain herself – in the summer of 1959. A long period of silence followed, while Macmillan brooded gloomily on the outrageousness of de Gaulle, the iniquities of supranationalism and the threat that the EEC posed to Western unity. De Gaulle, he wrote, was a 'Rip Van Winkle', who was 'determined to break up NATO'. Three groups sought a supranational Europe, 'the Jews, the Planners and the old cosmopolitan elite'. Would Britain, he wondered morosely, be caught 'between a hostile (or at least less and less friendly) America and a boastful, powerful "Empire of Charlemagne" ...?'[67]

In the end, that last question trumped his misgivings. In the summer of 1960 a Cabinet reshuffle gave him the opportunity to prepare the ground for a change of European policy. Three 'Europeans' were slotted into key positions. Edward Heath became number two at the Foreign Office; Christopher Soames, a future European Commissioner, went to the Ministry of Agriculture; and Duncan Sandys became Commonwealth Secretary. The Whitehall tide began to run in the same direction, and there was growing evidence that the Community was progressing faster than its founders had expected. By the summer of 1961 no one could seriously pretend that the Outer Seven were a counterweight to the Six, or deny that the 'empire of Charlemagne' was rapidly taking shape. In late July 1961 the Macmillan Cabinet finally stopped dithering and decided to open negotiations for full membership of the Community. But the decision was taken in a curiously lacklustre way. In his summing up at the end of the Cabinet meeting that took it, Macmillan emphasised that the government's purpose was merely 'to find out on what terms they [the Community] would agree to our joining'; and, for good measure, he added: 'A decision to negotiate was a very different matter from the later and much more critical decision to join.'[68] It was not a good start.

Negotiations over Britain's entry application started in October 1961 and dragged on for the best part of fifteen months, while de Gaulle glowered, with enigmatic menace, in the background. Much progress was made on the economic issues, but there was a fatal flaw in the government's approach to the politics.[69] It was forever looking over its shoulder at opponents in the Commonwealth and potential opponents in Britain; Macmillan, in particular, was obsessed by fears of an anti-EEC revolt in the Conservative Party, led by Butler. He and his colleagues forgot that Britain, not the Six, was the *demandeur*: that it was for Britain to adapt her policies to those of the Six, not the other way around: and that Britain was not doing the Six a favour in seeking membership, but asking them to do her a favour. The fundamental premise on which the Community was built was that its members had more in common with each other than any of them had with any outsider. The British did not share that premise and could not grasp it. Having failed to beat the Six, they had decided to join them, but they still saw themselves as a uniquely global people, with a global vocation qualitatively different from those of their prospective continental partners.

The denouement is well known. In December 1962, just before the Nassau conference over Skybolt, Macmillan and de Gaulle met at Rambouillet – de Gaulle's domestic political position having been enormously strengthened by decisive victories in a referendum and a general election. Macmillan used all his wiles, ranging from tears[70] to temper, to persuade his host that Britain was prepared to become more European. De Gaulle made it plain that he was not convinced. They had an elliptical discussion about nuclear weapons. Macmillan seems to have said that he was determined to get American agreement to sell Polaris missiles to Britain, but that she would build her own missiles independently if the Americans refused. De Gaulle may or may not have thought Macmillan had offered nuclear co-operation between France and Britain in that event.

Then came the Macmillan–Kennedy nuclear deal at Nassau. On 14 January 1963, de Gaulle effectively vetoed British entry into the Community in an oracular pronouncement at a press conference. His motives have been endlessly debated. One theory is that he was afraid that France would lose her hegemony over the Community if Britain joined. Another is that Nassau proved to him, once and for all, that Britain would always put the

Anglo-American relationship ahead of her ties with Europe. A third is that he had always wanted to veto British entry, but had waited until his referendum and election victories made him politically unassailable. In the end, however, these speculations are beside the point. What de Gaulle actually said at his press conference was that, while none of the Six was 'linked to the outside by any bilateral political or military agreement', Britain 'received privileged assistance from the Americans'. Notoriously, he also said:

> England is, indeed, insular and maritime, linked by her trade, her markets and her food supplies to diverse and often far-flung countries. . . . She has, in all her patterns of work, habits and traditions which are highly distinctive and original.
>
> How then could England, as she lives, as she produces, as she trades, be incorporated into the Common Market as it was conceived and as it works?[71]

In the light of British policy before and during the negotiations – and of Britain's role in European politics for the next forty years – it is hard to argue that he was wrong. But the implications for Britain in general, and for the whig imperialist tradition in particular, were cruelly perverse. Macmillan's belated turn towards Community membership had opened up the prospect of a new, post-imperial 'European' vocation and identity. De Gaulle's veto put paid to that, and shackled the country even more firmly to its past. On a more mundane level, it also inflicted irreparable political damage on Macmillan and his Cabinet.

⚜

Economic policy tested Macmillan's radicalism to destruction. By the late 1950s the vulgar Keynesianism of the beginning of the decade was falling into disarray. Britain's growth-rate was still high by historic British standards, but low by those of continental Western Europe; and, as the once-yawning gap between her GDP per head and those of her continental neighbours narrowed, the yardstick of past experience ceased to count. From 1951 to 1958, Britain's annual growth rate was less than a third of Germany's and less than half that of France. In 1950, Britain's GDP per head was far higher than Germany's; by 1960, Germany had almost caught up with her. It was scant consolation to know that the economy had grown more slowly under Queen Victoria.

Feverish short-term fluctuations loomed as large as depressing long-term trends. Nineteen-fifty-five saw a boom and a current-account balance of payments deficit. This was followed in 1956 by a downturn and a surplus. In 1957, Peter Thorneycroft succeeded Macmillan at the Treasury. Tax cuts were followed by a run on the pound and a crisis bank rate of 7 per cent. In 1958 the Cabinet split, in a fashion reminiscent of the ROBOT battle. Thorneycroft and his junior ministers – Nigel Birch, one of the most acerbic phrase-makers in the House of Commons, and Enoch Powell, the St John the Baptist of the eventual Thatcher counter-revolution – insisted that only tight control of the money supply and a ceiling on public expenditure could cure Britain's economic ills. This entailed a spending cut of £150 million. The Cabinet agreed to cuts of £100 million, but jibbed at the rest. Thorneycroft, Birch and Powell promptly resigned – overridden, not just by the political imperatives of full employment and industrial peace, as the robotniks had been, but by Macmillan's revulsion from the human consequences of deflation.[72]

The poisoned chalice of the chancellorship then passed to Derick Heathcoat Amory, a shy and frugal Devon bachelor. Despite rising unemployment, his 1958 budget left the level of demand unchanged. His reward was a handsome balance of payments surplus. His 1959 budget, introduced six months before the general election, was a horse of a different colour. It made drastic cuts in taxation, including a cut in the standard rate of income tax of 9d (3.75p) in the pound. The now familiar reckoning followed in 1960, in the shape of the biggest payments deficit in a decade. In 1961 this was followed by yet another sterling crisis.

Enough was clearly enough. Keynesian demand management was supposed to smooth out the fluctuations of the economic cycle; instead it seemed to be making them more extreme. Besides, there was growing evidence that demand management alone could not overcome the forces that held back Britain's growth rate and export performance. Keynesians had assumed that, if government increased consumer demand by the right amount, investment would follow. Governments *had* procured high levels of demand, but British investment levels obstinately lagged behind those on the European continent. Compounding these failures were the industrial and technological conservatism fostered by Britain's genteel quasi-corporatism, and the cost pressures generated by the hoary tradition of free collective bargaining. One solution – that of the robotniks in 1951–2, and of Thorneycroft and his junior ministers in 1958 – was to restore the disciplines of the age before Keynes. But that was incompatible with the accommodating whig imperialist statecraft that most Conservatives still took for granted; and, as we have seen, it was emotionally abhorrent and morally repugnant to Macmillan personally. An anecdote of Amory's captures the essence of his economic approach at this time. Asked whether he was thinking of his constituency in the 1930s, Macmillan exclaimed, 'I am thinking of the under-use of resources – let's over-use them!'[73]

With Stop-Go discredited, and pre-war orthodoxies ruled out, the government would have been condemned to look for a new approach in any case. Macmillan, the veteran expansionist and 1930s planner, infused the search with an inventive zeal it would have otherwise have lacked. Little by little the government felt its way towards a more explicit corporatism, designed to tame the jungle of wage bargaining and to overcome the obstacles to steady growth. In July 1960, Amory resigned as Chancellor, and Selwyn Lloyd took his place. Lloyd's chancellorship saw two far-reaching innovations and the bitterly contested gestation of a third. The first, launched in 1961, was a new system of public expenditure planning. The second came later in the same year, when a divided Cabinet agreed to set up a tripartite National Economic Development Council (NEDC or 'Neddy'), representing government, organised employers and organised labour, to hammer out a consensual strategy for faster growth. The employers gave it a fair wind from the start, but a grudging and suspicious TUC agreed to take part only after long negotiations. Its first meeting did not take place until March 1962. However, it soon spawned a range of 'little Neddies' to foster growth in particular industries, and published a report looking forward, with blithe optimism, to an average growth rate of 4 per cent a year over the period 1961–6 – 1.3 per cent a year more than the existing trend.

The third and most disputed innovation was 'Nicky' – the National Incomes Commission or NIC. Its ancestry was unfortunate and its birth traumatic. In the summer of 1961, Selwyn Lloyd imposed a fiercely resisted 'pay pause' on the public sector. Nicky was supposed to operate a long-term successor. Its task was to monitor wage increases against the yardstick of productivity growth, and to bring the force of public opinion to bear against excessive ones. It first saw the light of day in July 1962, after a long struggle between Macmillan and a lethargic Treasury, culminating in a brutal Cabinet purge universally known as the 'Night of the Long Knives'. Selwyn Lloyd and six other ministers lost their jobs; in the best phrase of his life, the young Liberal MP Jeremy Thorpe commented that Macmillan had laid down his friends for his life. The permanent incomes policy to which Macmillan proceeded to nail his party's colours could hardly have had a more painful birth.

Yet his government had pointed the way towards a revolution in British political economy as profound as the parallel revolutions in imperial and defence policy. In an astonishing role-reversal, reminiscent of the Derby Government's outbidding of Gladstone over suffrage reform in the 1860s, the Conservatives had become the party of planning. To be sure, theirs was a special kind of planning – indicative rather than directive, and consensual rather than dirigiste. One of its inspirations was the French *économie concertée*, but the Conservatives' Neddy stood at arm's length from the state, whereas the French Commissariat Général du Plan was embedded in the state machine. Neddy also drew on the thinking behind the Mond–Turner talks in the late 1920s, and on the centrist would-be planners of the 1930s, not least on Macmillan's own *Middle Way*. Nicky was an indispensable counterpart to Neddy. Its reports, the government hoped, would teach wage bargainers to trade short-term wage restraint for long-term income growth.

Echoes from the British past and the French present did not detract from the audacity of the Conservatives' turn to planning. The most revealing comparison is with the late 1940s, when Cripps was Attlee's planner extraordinary. Macmillan and his sometimes queasy ministers were a good deal more innovative than their Labour predecessors had been. Cripps's mixture of autarchic controls and moral exhortation was essentially a short-term expedient, designed to stave off the immediate threat of national bankruptcy; Macmillanesque planning was designed to procure a permanent transformation in the economic role of the state, and in the triangular relationship between it and the great power blocs of organised labour and capital. In the time-honoured, whig imperialist spirit of inclusion, Macmillan and his colleagues had drawn up the blueprint for a social-market economy on continental lines. The great question was whether the machine would conform to specifications.

༺❀༻

It was not to be. Planning could not succeed without the trade unions, and the unions held back. Despite their original suspicions, they had no quarrel with Neddy, the genial face of Macmillan's new structure. They viewed Nicky, the austere face, with a mixture of alarm and anger. The halcyon days of Deakin and Monckton were gone. Among rank-and-file trade unionists, a new militancy was abroad. It was voiced most powerfully by Frank Cousins, a lumbering, abrasive and prickly figure who had unexpectedly inherited the leadership of the TGWU in 1956, and with it the voting power once deployed by Ernest Bevin. In 'a period of freedom for all', Cousins declared menacingly, if opaquely, after his elevation, 'we are part of the all'.[74] The Labour Government had found it hard enough to win union support for wage restraint in the crisis years of 1948–9; in the climate that Cousins epitomised, union leaders could not have given it to a Conservative Government even if they had wished to do so. The TUC boycotted Nicky; even the government virtually ignored it. Neddy continued on its amiable way, but there was a hole where an incomes policy ought to have been.

Trade-union militancy reflected deeper shifts of attitude, born of full employment and rising living standards. Arthur Seaton, the boozy, promiscuous and nihilistic hero of Alan Sillitoe's novel of late-1950s engineering workers, *Saturday Night and Sunday Morning*, epitomised one element in it. The thousands who worked with him, he reflected, earned good wages:

> No more short time like before the war, or getting the sack if you stood ten minutes in the lavatory reading your *Football Post* – if the gaffer got on to you now you could always tell him where to put the job and go somewhere else. And no more running out at dinner time for a penny bag of chips to eat with your bread. Now, and about time too, you got fair wages if you worked your backbone to a string of conkers on piecework, and there was a big canteen where you could get a hot dinner for two-bob. With the wages you got you could save up for a motor bike or even an old car, or you could go on a ten-day binge and get rid of all you'd saved.

But Seaton's nihilistic hedonism was tinged with resentful rage. On the rifle range during his National Service reserve training, he mused, he knew whose faces he had in his sights:

> The bastards that put the gun into my hands. I make up a quick picture of their stupid four-eyed faces that blink as they read big books and papers on how to get blokes into khaki and fight battles in a war that they'll never be in – and then I left fly at them. Crack-crack-crack-crack-crack-crack. Other faces as well: the snot-gobbling get [*sic*] that teks my income tax, the swivel-eyed swine that collects our rent, the big-headed bastard that gets my goat when he asks me to go to union meetings or sign a paper against what's happening in Kenya. As if I cared![75]

There were plenty of Seatons in early-1960s Britain. Macmillan's whiggish generosity of spirit had turned traitor. A society that had it good was determined to have it better. In a seminal study of Luton car workers, a team of Cambridge sociologists found that affluence was Janus-faced. Affluent workers did not embrace middle-class lifestyles or middle-class attitudes to politics or the workplace. They still thought in terms of collective action, not of individual self-improvement, and remained more likely to vote Labour than Conservative. But their approach to collective action – political or industrial – had become instrumental instead of solidaristic. They joined trade unions to improve their living standards, not out of class loyalty; they voted Labour, when they did, because they thought they would be better off under a Labour Government than under a Conservative one.[76] They were collectivists, but for themselves, not for the collectivity; and their individualistic collectivism was impervious to the whig strategy of inclusion with which the Macmillan Government hoped to draw its teeth.

The whig imperialist tradition faced more insidious challenges as well. The cracks which had begun to appear in the structure of authority and leadership after Suez grew wider. The mood of the time was impatient, indignant and, above all, irreverent. At point after point, traditional institutions and conventions were mocked, defied or simply ignored. Sexual hypocrisy, literary censorship, nuclear weapons, social inequality, managerial incompetence, trade-union obscurantism and insular smugness all felt the lash. So, most of all, did the traditional elite. The irreverent came in many shapes and sizes. Teenage Mods and Rockers battled on south-coast beaches. The Beatles shot to fame with their haunting 'mixture of sexual invitation and adolescent pathos',[77] making Liverpool the world capital of pop music. The coruscating satirical revue, *Beyond the Fringe*, included a hilarious, but deadly sketch of Harold Macmillan as a doddery old man who had 'recently been travelling round the world – on your behalf and at your expense'. In America,

> I had talks with the young, vigorous President of that great country … We talked of many things, including Great Britain's position in the world as some kind of honest broker. I agreed with him, when he said that no nation could be more honest; and he agreed with me, when I chaffed him and said that no nation could be broker.[78]

Emboldened by the success of *Beyond the Fringe*, BBC Television ran a weekly satirical programme, *That Was the Week That Was*, lampooning, among others, the Roman Catholic Church, the nuclear deterrent, the trade unions and the police, as well as the inevitable Macmillan. *Private Eye*, founded at about the same time, and with similar parentage, combined pointed, sometimes savage, jokes with muck-raking journalism.

Sometimes, real life outdid satire. In 1959, Roy Jenkins, then a 39-year-old backbench Labour MP, steered a reform of the obscenity laws through Parliament, making literary merit admissible as a defence. The first test of the new Act came a year later, when Penguin Books were prosecuted for publishing an unexpurgated edition of D.H. Lawrence's *Lady Chatterley's Lover*. Thirty-five notables – ranging from the Bishop of Woolwich to E.M. Forster, and from the redoubtable Oxford literature don, Helen Gardner, to the historian C.V. Wedgwood – testified for the accused. In his opening address, the prosecuting counsel, Mervyn Griffith-Jones, made himself a laughing stock by asking the jury whether this was a book they would 'wish your wife or your servants to read'. For his part, the Bishop of Woolwich opined that Lawrence's purpose was to depict the sexual relationship as 'essentially sacred', and that the book was one that Christians ought to read. The jury found for the defence.[79]

Satire was negative, if sometimes deadly. The indignant impatience of the time also took more positive forms. One was the 'New Left' – an intellectually fertile, but inchoate and short-lived coalition of former Communists who left the Party after the Soviet invasion of Hungary in 1956 and of non-Communist socialists, radicalised by Suez.[80] Its values were humanistic, decentralist and participative. It focused on the 'whole culture as a way of life'[81] rather than on economics. E.P. Thompson, the future best-selling historian of the making of the working class, distilled the essence of its world-view in a contribution to a collection of essays, resonantly entitled *Out of Apathy*. Human nature, he wrote, was 'in essence, *potential*'; it was also 'potentially *revolutionary*'. Socialists could not be guided by 'absolute historicist laws' or 'biblical texts'. They should not aim 'to create a socialist State, towering above man'. Socialism could come only by building on 'real human needs and possibilities, disclosed in open, never-ceasing intellectual and moral debate'.[82] Beneath the *Marxisant* clothing, a strong streak of home-grown democratic republicanism shone through.

The New Left overlapped at several points with the Campaign for Nuclear Disarmament – an equally inchoate coalition against the British deterrent. It was led by such non-political figures as the novelist and playwright J.B. Priestley, the Methodist minister Donald Soper, the philosopher Bertrand Russell and the Oxford historian A.J.P. Taylor. In a narrow party sense it did more damage to the Labour Party than to the Conservatives. The Conservatives were solidly in favour of the British bomb. Labour was split, and in 1961 the party conference narrowly carried a unilateralist resolution, against the leadership. But the damage did not last. What stayed in the public mind was the memory of Hugh Gaitskell, the party leader, vowing passionately to 'fight, fight and fight again' to reverse the decision; and when the 1962 conference duly repudiated unilateralism Labour emerged from the split stronger than it had been at the start. In any case, CND was not a party affair. Its annual Easter marches to London from Aldermarston, home of the Atomic Weapons Research Establishment, some of them 100,000 strong, were collective affirmations of an ideal that transcended conventional politics and challenged the entire political class.

The marchers, wrote the journalist Alan Brien, were 'the sort of people who would normally spend Easter listening to a Beethoven concert on the

Home Service, pouring dry sherry from a decanter for their neighbours, painting Picasso designs on hardboiled eggs, attempting the literary competitions in the weekly papers, or going to church with their children. ... They were behaving entirely against the normal tradition of their class, their neighbourhood, and their upbringing.'[83] No clear ideology held the campaign together, but it too drew on the subterranean democratic republican strand in the political culture. It was inspired by an alternative, dissenting vision of Britain and Britishness – of Britain as a moral exemplar to the world – that went back to Bright, Blake and Milton, and ranged a patriotism of morality against the patriotism of power. As A.J.P. Taylor put it in a characteristically impish comment years later, CND-ers were 'the last Imperialists'.[84]

The New Left and CND helped to disrupt the quietism of the early 1950s and, in doing so, to reshape the mentality of the time. But they attacked the status quo from the outer edges of the political nation; and, in the short run, it was easy enough for its defenders to deflect or ignore them. The attacks that hurt most came from further in. Almost invariably, their target was the 'establishment'. The term was invented in 1955 by the brilliant, wayward *Spectator* journalist, Henry Fairlie, for whom it meant the 'whole matrix of official and social relations within which power is exercised'.[85] In a collection of essays devoted to the subject a few years later, Hugh Thomas, the former Foreign Office official and future historian of the Spanish civil war, produced a sharper definition. For him, the establishment was 'the English constitution, and the group of institutions and outlying agencies built round it to assist in its protection; it naturally also includes all those who stand like commissionaires before these protective institutions to protect *them*. (Italics in the original.) As such, it was an 'institutional museum of Britain's past greatness.' Britain could not exploit her 'resources and talents' to the full until 'the fusty Establishment, with its Victorian views and standards of judgement', was destroyed.[86]

'Fusty', 'museum', 'past greatness' and 'Victorian' were key words in a lengthening charge sheet. So were 'amateur' and 'decline'. The Hungarian-born Balliol economist and Fabian luminary, Thomas Balogh, denounced the professional civil service of Whitehall as 'the apotheosis of the dilettante'. Civil servants were untrained, ignorant of social science and possessed of 'the cross-word puzzle mind reared on Mathematics at Cambridge or Greats at Oxford'. Small wonder that British power had declined 'at a rate unparalleled since the crash of the Spanish Empire'.[87] He was echoed by the Manchester Professor of Government, Brian Chapman, who described the civil service as 'an over-specialized, parochial closed corporation'. The future Labour peer, Vivien Bowden, Principal of Manchester College of Technology, diagnosed a 'national neurosis which makes us accept our relative penury without being conscious of it; we seem to believe that if we are doing better than we were then no more should be expected of us'. Arthur Koestler edited a book of essays with the revealing title, *Suicide of a Nation*, in which he denounced the 'cult of amateurishness and the contempt in which proficiency and expertise are held'. Britain, he concluded, was ruled by a 'mediocracy'. Timothy Raison, a future Conservative minister, bemoaned the disappearance of 'the imagination to see that great things can be achieved by individuals or groups of individuals, which marked our history but which is today more conspicuous in the United States'.[88]

In this swelling indictment, two linked evils had pride of place: the class system and the public schools. In 1961, the *Financial Times* journalist, Michael Shanks, published a Penguin Special, brilliantly entitled *The Stagnant Society*, which sold 60,000 copies. The question, he declared, was:

> What sort of an island do we want to be? A lotus island of easy, tolerant ways, bathed in the golden glow of an imperial sunset, shielded from discontent by a threadbare welfare state and an acceptance of genteel poverty? Or the tough, dynamic race we have been in the past, striving always to better ourselves, seeking new worlds to conquer in place of those we have lost, ready to accept growing pains as the price of growth?[89]

His rhetoric was sugar-coating for a more pointed message. Equality of opportunity was the key to economic dynamism; society should offer 'rich prizes' but award them 'solely on merit'. Britain was sinking into lotus-eating sloth because that ideal was blatantly flouted; socially exclusive public schools were one of the chief causes of its flouting. Shanks had no complaints about the education they provided; he thought they were the best schools in the country. The charge against them was that they were closed to unmoneyed talent. The Oxford economist and future Conservative peer, John Vaizey, cut closer to the bone. For him, public schools were far from being the best in the country; rather they were breeding grounds of conformism, smugness and a sense of 'calm superiority' or 'uncalm snobbery'. They crushed spontaneity and inculcated a 'hierarchical model of society' appropriate to a ruling class for which there was no place in the modern world.[90] For Anthony Sampson, the real villains of the piece were the top schools, Eton in particular. Etonians ran the Foreign Office, BOAC, the Conservative Party, the Bank of England, Associated Television and a large part of the City. It was 'inherently absurd' that a large part of an industrial country should be 'run by this stage army of men, awarding each other GCMGs, and dressing up for ceremonies in fancy dress as if they were still in the school play'.[91]

᪥

Like an angry sea gouging out the bottom of a cliff, this flood of disaffection and denigration struck at the foundations of the whig imperialist tradition. A charge of elitism could have been shrugged off; the tradition's custodians were elitist by definition; and never pretended to be anything else. But the critics did not fight on that ground. Their charge against the establishment was that it was the wrong sort of elite: out of date, fuddy-duddy, hamstrung by obsolete conventions and values, and unable, by its very nature, to understand the modern world or to provide the kind of leadership that a modern country needed. That charge was deadly; it was also unanswerable. Whig imperialists prided themselves above all on their capacity for responsive leadership and evolutionary adaptation. They took it for granted that they *did* understand the modern world and knew how to change when change was needed. The Macmillan Government could fairly claim to have done just that. Despite his air of patrician nonchalance, Macmillan himself was one of the most radical prime ministers of the century. (He was certainly more radical than any of its Labour ones.) However, mere argument could not counter the impatient irreverence sweeping through the public culture. The battle was over manners, style and instincts, not policies; and arguments had no place in it. To the critics, the very idea of a governing class with an inherited vocation for leadership was a symptom of ossification and decline. Burkean gentlemen had become surplus to requirements – not because of what they did, but because of what they were.

More ominously still, the Macmillan Government's radicalism had itself called crucial elements of the whig imperialist tradition into question. Churchill's effulgent picture of the 'golden circle' of the Crown holding together a far-flung empire was an anachronism even in 1945, but the vision of British identity that lay behind it still shaped the thinking of the Attlee Government. It even survived the end of the Raj. Without undue violence to the facts, the Labour Government's decision to withdraw from India could be seen as a replay of earlier decisions to grant self-government to the so-called white dominions, and the Commonwealth of 1950 as the child of the empire of 1939.

It was far more difficult to view the Macmillan Government's helter-skelter decolonisation in Africa through that comforting prism. The Commonwealth retained a certain mystique. The Queen carried out her duties as its head with exemplary diligence and apparent enthusiasm; opponents of EEC entry dwelt lovingly on its role as a unique multiracial bridge between the First and the Third Worlds. But the mystique was fading and the identity it implied became increasingly threadbare. Had the government succeeded in its European venture, a new vision of Britain and Britishness might have taken the place of the old one, but de Gaulle's veto had put paid to any such hopes. Like Suez, the veto also undermined the elite's claim to possess a special, inborn talent for statecraft. With the old, globe-girdling empire a shadow of its former self, and Europe's shutters down, two centuries of whig imperialist rhetoric were petering out in disappointment, recrimination and self-doubt.

That was how matters stood in the immediate aftermath of de Gaulle's veto. Less than six months later, Macmillan, his government, the Conservative Party and the traditional elite were engulfed in one of the strangest (and ripest) scandals in British political history.[92] The chief protagonists were John Profumo, the rich, smart, louche Harrovian Secretary of State for War and high-living socialite; and Christine Keeler, an attractive, nineteen-year-old call-girl, with whom he had a short-lived affair in the summer of 1961. Even in early-1960s Britain, that was scarcely a hanging offence. What gave the scandal its bite was Keeler's claim that she had, at the same time, been sleeping with the Soviet Naval Attaché, Yevgeny Ivanov.

Extra bite was supplied by a rich array of lesser characters. One was Stephen Ward, who introduced Keeler to Profumo. Ward was an osteopath and amateur procurer to the rich and famous; he was also suspected of having links with Soviet intelligence. Another was Lord 'Bill' Astor, whose Cliveden estate was the scene of Profumo's first meeting with Keeler. Flanking these were two Jamaican lovers of Keeler, 'Lucky' Gordon and the marijuana pusher, 'Johnny' Edgecombe. Later, the cast list widened to include such shadowy characters as the 'headless man', erotic photographs of whom had figured in the Duchess of Argyll's divorce case; the 'man in the mask', who was supposed to have waited at luxuriously furnished tables in the nude; and eight anonymous High Court judges who were alleged to have taken part in illicit orgies.

The scandal was slow to develop, but by the summer of 1962 rumours of the Profumo, Keeler and Ivanov triangle were circulating in clubland, Fleet Street and Westminster. In March 1963, Profumo made a personal statement in the Commons, carefully vetted by a group of senior ministers. He acknowledged that he had been acquainted with Keeler but denied that there had been any impropriety in their relationship. However, the rumour mill ground on. In June 1963 Profumo confessed to his wife, the actress Valerie Hobson, resigned from the government and the House of Commons, and apologised to both for his deception. A mighty explosion of righteous indignation followed, vigorously stoked by *The Times*. In a notorious first leader, entitled 'It *Is* A Moral Issue', it declared: 'Eleven years of Conservative rule have brought the nation psychologically and spiritually to a low ebb.'[93]

Conservative MPs were in turmoil, and many thought that Macmillan might be deposed, among them his Press Secretary, Harold Evans. In the inevitable Commons debate on 17 June, Macmillan cut a dignified, if diminished and slightly pathetic figure. He did not, he confessed, 'live among young people fairly widely'.[94] In a savage attack on him, Nigel Birch built a devastating peroration around Browning's line, 'Never glad confident morning again.' The government won the vote with ease, but its majority was cut by twenty-eight. Macmillan's poll rating was lower than any prime minister's since Neville Chamberlain.[95] Tempers cooled a little when Macmillan announced that the Master of the Rolls, Lord Denning, would inquire into the affair. His report was published in September; though Macmillan and his colleagues were criticised for failing to deal adequately with the affair, they were exonerated of wrong-doing. Meanwhile, a massive police operation had been mounted against Ward, who had then committed suicide after being tried at the Old Bailey for living on immoral earnings. From a narrowly political point of view, that was the end of the story.

It was harder to dispose of the wider repercussions. The Profumo affair might have been designed to prove that the charges brought against the traditional elite were well founded. Macmillan and his closest colleagues had been exposed as credulous and out of touch. Profumo himself was everything an up-and-coming member of the elite ought to have been. He was rich, smart, suitably educated; and he had an excellent war record. Yet he had broken two sacred rules. He had lied to the House of Commons, and he had been found out. The set around 'Bill' Astor was self-indulgent, empty-headed and tawdry; the treatment meted out to Ward was vindictive and cruel. To many it seemed that the establishment itself, as well as Profumo, had been caught with its pants down. The *Guardian* columnist, Wayland Young, drew a widely perceived moral:

> In the Profumo Affair the political frivolity, the moral myopia, and the herd credulity of latter-day Toryism led to convulsion and the sacrifice of one life, one career, and several reputations. What happened was horrible; it is over, and there is not likely to be more. But we were heading for it; it could hardly not have happened, whether like that or in some similar form. It was the natural fruit of a period of government when convenience was set above justice, loyalty above truth, and appearance above reality.[96]

The government's travails were not yet over. On 7 October, after much dithering, Macmillan decided to lead the party into the next election; the following day he had to go into hospital with an inflamed prostate. The prospect of an emergency operation led him to change his mind and resign forthwith. His decision was announced on 10 October, during the Conservative Party conference at Blackpool. Furious caballing for the succession ensued, but no clear front runner emerged. Macmillan was determined to stop Butler, the Deputy Prime Minister and heir apparent, at any price. While in hospital he persuaded Lord Home, the Foreign Secretary, to make himself available. (A recent change in the law had made it possible for peerages to be renounced.) He also drew up an elaborate plan for a variety of Conservative dignitaries to sound out different sections of party opinion. The party rank and file were for Butler, as were the rising younger ministers, Enoch Powell and Iain Macleod.[97] Yet Home emerged as the winner from a patently flawed consultation. He was the 14th Earl and a quintessential Etonian – a 'votary of the esoteric Eton religion', as the literary critic Cyril Connolly once put it.[98] He was also rich, a former appeaser, an ardent cricketer and a passionate fisherman. He was dignified, honourable, charming, utterly conventional and utterly unintellectual. Macmillan thought he represented 'the old governing class at its best;'[99] and in many ways he did. Home's emergence was the last hurrah of the old patrician elite: a snook cocked at a world it found alien and distasteful.

The world soon hit back. In a biting article in the *Spectator*, Iain Macleod – who had refused to serve in Home's Cabinet – savaged the consultation process that Macmillan had devised.[100] Party opinion had been canvassed by five people, he wrote, four of whom were Etonians. The other central figures in the story were Home, Lord Hailsham and Macmillan himself. All of these had also been educated at Eton. The only non-Etonian out of this group of eight was the chief whip, Martin Redmayne, a Home partisan. The Tory Party, Macleod added, was now being led 'from the right of centre' for the first time since Bonar Law; it had once more rejected Butler, 'incomparably the best qualified of the contenders' for the premiership; worse still, it had confessed that it could not 'find a Prime Minister in the House of Commons'.

Much more damning than any of this, however, was a throwaway phrase in which Macleod attributed Home's emergence to a tightly knit 'magic circle'. The implications were more uncomfortable for the Conservative Party than Macleod himself may have realised. With astonishing success for the first six years of his premiership, Macmillan had combined radical deeds with a patrician style. Now one of the leading representatives of a new, professional, even technocratic Conservatism had served a notice to quit on the traditional patrician elite, and called Macmillan's deft blend of old and new into question. It was a portent of a profound change in the political culture, which would discomfit technocrats and patricians alike.

Home's Government was little more than a footnote to Macmillan's. Inevitably, it was dominated by the approach of the next general election, which was due, at the latest, in October 1964. Judged solely by electoral criteria it was more successful – or perhaps less unsuccessful – than seemed likely when it was formed. In October 1963, when Home became Prime Minister, Labour had a Gallup poll lead of 12 per cent. Little by little, the Conservatives ground it down. By June 1964 it had fallen to 9 per cent; by August it was 6 per cent.

But this improvement was purchased at a high economic price. Stop-Go was in business again and in a more virulent form than ever before. In 1962, Stop was in the ascendant. The balance of payments was in surplus, industrial production fell and unemployment rose. In 1963, it was the turn of Go. In the early months of the year, unemployment reached 3.5 per cent – a very high figure by post-war standards. Reginald Maudling, Lloyd's successor as Chancellor, had already brought in some modest reflationary measures. In his April 1963 budget, he made a soon-to-be-notorious 'dash for growth'. Around £300 million of purchasing power was pumped into the economy through tax cuts and spending increases. If expansion led to temporary balance of payments difficulties as stocks built up, Maudling promised, he would run down the reserves or borrow from the IMF rather than deflate. Go still dominated in 1964. Unemployment fell; demand soared; imports increased; and the balance of payments moved into the red. Maudling raised taxes by around £100 million in his 1964 budget, but this was not enough to curb the boom. When the election finally came in October 1964, the Conservatives were only 2 per cent behind in the Gallup poll, but the balance of payments was in heavy deficit.

Polling day was on 15 October. Labour won by a whisker – an overall Commons majority of four and a fraction more than 44 per cent of the popular vote against the Conservatives' 43.4 per cent. Harold Wilson, Gaitskell's cocky successor as party leader, became Prime Minister; and the Conservatives went into opposition. The following year the Conservative Party adopted new rules for the election of future leaders. Home resigned the leadership, to be succeeded by the Broadstairs grammar-school boy, Edward Heath. The old whig imperialist elite had had a longer and more successful innings than any other governing class in Europe, but its day seemed done.

7

SECOND CHANCE

*

Devaluation does *not* mean that the value of the pound in the hands of the British consumer, the British housewife at her shopping, is cut correspondingly. It does not mean that the pound in the pocket is worth 14 per cent less to us now than it was.
  Harold Wilson, television broadcast following devaluation in November 1967

I will never consent to preside over a Government which is not allowed to govern. ... I have no intention of being a MacDonald. Nor do I intend to be another Dubcek. Get your tanks off my lawn, Hughie!
  Harold Wilson to Hugh Scanlon during negotiations over the government's industrial relations proposals, June 1969

Don't just stand there – wank.
  Student graffito at Essex University, early 1969

*

WILSON'S POUND

Labour had left office in 1951 exhausted and divided, with the confident *étatisme* of 1945 in disarray. Now both had a second chance. The Britain of 1964 seemed made for Harold Wilson, the chipper 48-year-old ex-grammar-school boy from the North. She was more open to new talent and less deferential than she had been in 1951. The old industrial regions had lost population; the Midlands and still more the South-East had gained. Upward social mobility had increased, bringing with it a new self-confidence, but also new resentments of remaining barriers. There were more professionals, engineers, managers, foremen and technicians, but fewer manual workers, more of whom were skilled.

Britain was also more diverse, ethnically and culturally. Immigration on a significant scale from Third World colonies had started in the 1940s, but the 1951 census had recorded a combined Caribbean and South Asian population of less than 80,000. By 1961 the figure had reached 500,000 or around one per cent of the total population.[1] In 1951, Britain was still, in many ways, a Victorian society. Even in 1964, Victorian legacies were easy to find: slum housing, tight-knit mining villages, smoke-blackened buildings in Northern towns, Savile Row suits, upper-class drawls and St James's clubs, as well as sterling's role as a reserve currency and a chain of British bases east of Suez. But they were manifestly in retreat.

There were signs that the shifts of mood and mentality discussed in the last chapter had fostered new attitudes in the country's governing institutions. In his second voyage of discovery around the power centres of Britain, whose results were published in 1965, Anthony Sampson, the scourge of Eton, was struck by 'quite spectacular' changes since the 1950s. 'In politics, in the board rooms, the senior common rooms, the Inns of Court and even in the BBC,' he wrote, 'the familiar chorus of "Old Freddies" – of peers, soldiers or courtiers – has begun to troop off stage.' In their place was a new, thrusting, entrepreneurial generation, imbued with 'a new competitiveness'. Confronting the familiar 'Old Boy Net' was a 'New Boy Net'. Its epitome was the new Prime Minister, Harold Wilson – 'a man of determined isolation and professionalism, different from any previous inhabitant of Downing Street'.[2]

Sampson's impression of the new government and its head was widely shared. Labour's election slogan – 'Let's Go with Labour' – had said it all. Wilson and his colleagues had fought the election as the champions of the 'New Boys' held back by effete and snobbish 'Old Boys'. They were for change, dynamism, science, skill, professionalism and upward mobility. Most of all, they were for 'purpose', the 'purposive' and the 'purposeful'. Socialism, Wilson wrote in a 1964 collection of speeches, 'meant applying a sense of purpose to our national life: economic purpose, social purpose, moral purpose'. His definition of purpose was generous, to say the least. It meant 'technical skill – be it the skill of a manager, a designer, a craftsman, an architect, an engineer, a nuclear physicist, or a doctor, a nurse, a social worker'.[3]

The party manifesto promised a new Ministry of Economic Affairs to prepare a national plan and a Ministry of Technology to speed industrial modernisation. The unfortunate Home (an 'elegant anachronism', in Wilson's withering phrase) was subjected to ruthless and relentless mockery for his aristocratic lineage and pursuits, and his attractive habit of working out economic problems with the help of matchsticks. His quiet decency was no match for this barrage of resentful populism. On one occasion he made a suitably elegant retort. Tired of the taunt that he was the '14th Earl', he pointed out that Wilson was 'the fourteenth Mr Wilson'. But that was the only blow he managed to land.

Wilson launched Labour's campaign at a giant rally at Wembley's Empire Pool. With exhilarating panache he rode the waves of impatient irreverence that were sweeping through the public culture:

Those who are satisfied should stay with the Tories. We need men with fire in their bellies and humanity in their hearts. The choice we offer, starting today, is between standing still, clinging to the tired philosophy of a day that is gone, or moving forward in partnership and unity to a just society, to a dynamic, expanding, confident and, above all, purposive new Britain.[4]

Purposive new Britain heard the call. Although Labour's strength was still heavily concentrated in its core working-class constituency, its support rose in the top two census classes and fell in the bottom two.[5] The conclusion seemed clear. The New Boys were for Labour, and both were on the march.

✢

It was far from clear where they were marching to. Wilson's modernising rhetoric revealed more about Labour's past than about its future. The designers, craftsmen, physicists and engineers at whom he set his cap were the lineal descendants of the intermediate class once wooed by Herbert Morrison and of the 'practical men and women' whom Ramsay MacDonald had courted in the general election of 1929. Faith in the inexorable advance of science and technology had always been one of the hallmarks of the democratic collectivist tradition. Wilson's insistence on purpose and the purposive was equally venerable. It echoed the dream of an economy planned 'from the ground up' on which Labour had fought the 1945 election, and Cripps's 1947 assertion that resources should be allocated through democratic planning rather than by 'chance'. Wilson's bottles were new, but the wine he poured into them was reassuringly familiar.

Advisedly so. For most of the thirteen years of Conservative rule, Labour had been consumed by a bitter party civil war, reflecting profound differences over party purpose and belief. Everyone accepted that Britain now had a mixed economy, in which state ownership co-existed with a predominant private sector. But there were fierce disagreements about its historical significance. Was it a temporary resting place on the way to a fully socialised economy? Or was it an end state to which no further changes were needed? If the former, how could Labour mobilise support for further advances towards full socialism? If the latter, what were the implications for the democratic collectivist world-view and for Labour's political vocation?

Debate was passionate and wide-ranging, and no two protagonists gave exactly the same answers, yet two broad schools of thought emerge through the cacophony. Self-styled 'revisionists', whose leading seer was Anthony Crosland – Hugh Gaitskell's dashing, handsome and intellectually arrogant 'Ganymede' – thought that capitalism had changed so fundamentally that it barely deserved the name any longer.[6] The historic battle to subject private economic power to public purposes had been won for good. Thanks to Keynes, mass unemployment was a thing of the past and would never return. Socialism was no longer about ownership. It was about equality – of status and esteem as well as of condition. In the struggle for equality, further nationalisations had no place. What was needed were steady, incremental increases in social spending, financed by progressive taxation, supplemented by comprehensive education and sustained by economic growth.

Traditionalists, led by Aneurin Bevan and his followers, stuck to the classic themes of old days. (For their pains the revisionists nicknamed them 'fundamentalists'.) Capitalism, they insisted, had changed only in form, not in substance. The charge against it was what it had always been: that, as Bevan put it, it converted 'men and women into means instead of ends.'[7] In any case, socialism was not 'just about equality'; it was, first and foremost, about power.[8] The revisionists' disdain for further public ownership was short-sighted, even treacherous. The affluent society was 'meretricious' and working-class voters would soon see through its essential vulgarity. Whatever might be true of surface eddies, the deeper 'tides of history' were running towards socialism, not away from it.[9]

At the time, a vast gulf seemed to divide the two camps. What stand out in retrospect are the assumptions they had in common. Richard Crossman – the voluble, coruscating, occasionally infuriating and always mischievous Bevanite gadfly – hankered for a participatory 'social democracy' in which ordinary people 'lost their sense of helplessness and shared in the task of taking decisions'.[10] But he was almost alone. In a revealing diary entry two years after the government was formed, he noted ruefully that 'very few' of his colleagues shared the belief in participation he had learned from Tawney and Lindsay. For him, he wrote,

social democracy consists of giving people a chance to decide for themselves. ... This philosophy is extremely unpopular, I find, with most members of the Cabinet. They believe in getting power, making decisions and getting people to agree with the decisions after they've been made. They have the routine politician's attitude to public opinion that the politician must take the decisions and then get the public to acquiesce. The notion of creating the extra burden of a live and articulate public opinion able to criticise actively and make its own choices is something which most socialist politicians keenly resent.[11]

'Routine politicians' dominated both sides of the debate. Most revisionists and most fundamentalists belonged unmistakably to the same democratic collectivist family. Both camps took it for granted that history was moving ineluctably in the direction they favoured, and both saw the central state as the only effective instrument of social progress. Neither questioned the governing assumptions of the British parliamentary monarchy or the essentials of the whig imperialist conception of British identity that democratic collectivists had absorbed with the political equivalent of their mothers' milk. And, as Crossman saw, both shrank from the democratic republican dream of active self-rule and collective self-emancipation from below.

The fundamentalists' *étatisme* was blatant and unapologetic. They sought state control of the commanding heights of the economy, procured by the tried and trusted mechanism of 1940s-style nationalisation. The revisionists were more modest on the surface, but far more ambitious below it. Though they saw no need for more state ownership, they had a touching faith in the state's capacity for economic management. Their egalitarianism was based on the assumptions that Keynesian economics held the key to rapid and sustained economic growth, that governments could easily turn that key if they chose and, above all, that the state could engineer far-reaching changes in class relationships and social norms through the deft use of public spending, combined with appropriate changes in welfare and education policy.

However, family quarrels are often bitter, and this one was no exception. It was a quarrel of factions more than of ideas. Bevanites saw Gaitskellites as cliquish, self-righteous and intolerant; Gaitskellites saw Bevanites as cliquish, disloyal and disruptive. Between Gaitskell's election as leader in 1955 and the Conservative election victory in 1959, the quarrel smouldered in the background, but immediately after the Conservatives had won Gaitskell suddenly lifted it from the dry and abstract plane of doctrine to the fiery and dangerous one of symbol and myth. At the party conference after the election, he launched an attack on the commitment to wholesale common ownership enshrined in the notorious Clause Four of the party constitution. A bitter battle ensued, in which Gaitskell was defeated. Clause Four remained, but a vacuous new clause was added to clarify it.

Wilson had been a Bevanite of sorts, and he had opposed Gaitskell's attack on Clause Four. However, his own attitude to it could hardly have been less reverential: in a characteristic phrase he once compared it to 'the detailed architectural passages in the Book of Revelations'.[12] He had no taste for doctrinal disputation – or, for that matter, for doctrine. As an Oxford undergraduate in the turbulent 1930s he had steered clear of the passionate ideological debates that convulsed the student body; later he wrote contemptuously that he 'could not stomach all those Marxist public school products rambling on about the exploited workers'.[13] He was a statistician, a number cruncher, not a theorist – fascinated by the trees but wary of the wood. (One of his favourite topics of conversation was railway timetables, a taste he shared, rather improbably, with the staunch and urbane Gaitskellite, Roy Jenkins.)[14] When Wilson succeeded to the party leadership after Gaitskell's death in January 1963, his top priority was to close off the debate on party doctrine and purpose, to assure old Gaitskellites that he had no intention of pursuing a vendetta against them while assuring old Bevanites that he had not deserted them and, above all, to divert party energies into harmless new channels with which both sides would be content.

The hoary theme of scientific progress and technological modernisation gave him a perfect lever. In a dazzling tour de force at the 1963 Labour Party conference he managed to combine the determinist *étatisme* of his predecessors with the meritocratic modernism of the age. Technological progress, he insisted, 'put the whole argument about industry, economics and Socialism in a new perspective'. For such progress was ineluctable and inescapable; willy-nilly a new Britain was being forged in the 'white heat' of the scientific revolution. The 'easy-going world we are living in today' could not last. The choice was between

the blind imposition of technological advance, with all that that means in terms of unemployment, and the conscious, planned, purposive use of scientific progress to provide undreamed of living standards and the possibility of leisure, ultimately on an unbelievable scale. . . .

For the commanding heights of British industry to be controlled today by men whose only claim is their aristocratic connections or the power of inherited wealth or speculative finance is as irrelevant to the twentieth century as would be the continued purchase of commissions in the armed forces by lordly amateurs. At the very time that even the MCC has abolished the distinction between amateurs and professionals we are content to remain a nation of Gentlemen in a world of players.[15]

The mix was irresistible. Revisionists liked the fizzy new interpretation of old ideas; fundamentalists liked the old ideas. Even the New Left, which had reserved its most biting scorn for Wilson during the battle over unilateral nuclear disarmament, gave him a slightly patronising pat on the back. Perry Anderson, the editor of *New Left Review*, praised his 'trenchant criticisms of English capitalism' and, in one of the strangest misjudgements of an age rich in strange misjudgements, detected a 'quasi-Marxist flavour' in them.[16]

Few noticed that, instead of resolving the differences between revisionists and fundamentalists, Wilson had brushed them under a capacious rhetorical carpet. Fewer still saw that, with all his talk of purposiveness, Labour's purposes were as ambiguous as they had been since the dying days of the Attlee Government. Virtually no one guessed that the differences he had fudged would reappear later, in a more acute form.

෴

For the moment, Wilson was the man of the hour. He towered above his Cabinet in a way that had never been true of Ramsay MacDonald or Attlee, his only Labour predecessors. He and the new Foreign Secretary, Patrick Gordon Walker, were the only two ministers who had served in a Cabinet before, and Gordon Walker had lost his Black Country seat to a racist Conservative candidate – a blow from which he never fully recovered. The only ministers who could approach Wilson in political weight were his two defeated rivals in the 1963 leadership election: George Brown, the Deputy Leader and head of the new Department of Economic Affairs, and James Callaghan, the new Chancellor of the Exchequer. Both were formidable politicians. Neither had been to university, and both were painfully conscious of the lack, but the resemblance between them ended there.

Brown had started his career as a fur salesman, and came into Labour politics from the Transport and General Workers' Union. He was sentimental, self-indulgent, frequently drunk and given to blazing rows with all and sundry, but he had a marvellous capacity to cut to the heart of a complex problem and, on his day, he could carry a Labour audience to heights that none of his contemporaries could match. Callaghan was everything Brown was not. He too had been a trade-unionist before entering Parliament and had served in the Royal Navy during the war. He was a complete politician, deft, canny and possessed of an unrivalled feel for the contours of Labour power and the moods of working-class voters. But with all their strengths, neither man could hold a candle to the twin giants of the 1945 government, Bevin and Cripps, or outgun Wilson in argument. Had they joined forces against him, they might have prevailed. As it was, neither was willing to kill Wilson to make the other king.

Brown and Callaghan were both veterans of the 1945 Parliament, and both had held junior office in the Attlee Government. The most formidable Cabinet newcomer without previous ministerial experience was Denis Healey, who became Defence Secretary at the age of forty-eight.[17] Healey belonged to the glittering pre-war Oxford generation that also included Edward Heath, Roy Jenkins and Anthony Crosland. He *could* outgun Wilson in argument, and after three years in office he became a painful thorn in Wilson's side. He had won a classics Exhibition to Balliol from Bradford Grammar School, and followed it with Firsts in both parts of his four-year degree course. As a young man he was ruggedly handsome and a favourite with the girls; he was also self-confident to the point of arrogance, with a strong streak of intellectual ruthlessness about him. Like many of the brightest and best of his student generation (though unlike the indecisive Crosland and the lifelong moderate, Roy Jenkins), he joined the Communist Party in his first year. He sported a belted mackintosh, which made him look like a Soviet commissar, and impressed the future novelist and philosopher Iris Murdoch with the shameless deviousness of his approach to current politics. But, in spite of his burly physique he was, in some ways, an unlikely throwback to the aesthetes of the previous decade; even as a Communist, poetry, painting and philosophy mattered more to him than politics.

After a good war, in which he saw action in Italy and was mentioned in despatches, Healey became International Secretary of the Labour Party. He was close to Bevin, who became one of his heroes, and got to know a wide range of continental Social Democrats, many of them from Eastern Europe, where the Stalinist night was falling fast. He was elected to Parliament at a by-election in 1952. He specialised in foreign affairs and defence and became a noted figure on the international conference circuit. He backed Gaitskell in the vicious Labour battles over Clause Four and unilateral disarmament, but he was not a joiner by nature and he stood aloof from the Gaitskellite inner circle.

He adored his wife, Edna, and fought hard to preserve his 'hinterland' of family, literature, art and music from the pressures of political life. He had the most powerful intellect in the Cabinet, but there was a blind spot in his make-up, which would have fatal consequences for him and his party in years to come. Healey was a textbook example of the inadequacies of rationalism in politics. Supremely rational himself, he assumed that others were rational too. Despite his private warmth, he was curiously uninterested in people and remarkably bad at judging their motives. His parliamentary colleagues admired his wit, intelligence and forensic power, yet he had no base of personal support and loyalty. He was often compared to a tank – partly because of his pulverising power in argument, but even more because he had an alarming propensity to make sudden 180-degree turns of policy without regard for those affected by them. He was a democratic collectivist through and through, but a strangely incurious one. It was as if his appetite for doctrine had been sated by his youthful flirtation with Communism. He was a supremely competent pragmatist, fated to live in an age when pragmatism was ceasing to be enough.

Wilson's pre-eminence rested on firmer foundations than his senior lieutenants' unwillingness to combine. He too was a complete politician – endlessly fascinated by the twists and turns of the political game, and with virtually no interests outside politics apart from Gilbert and Sullivan, a holiday home in the Scillies and the occasional game of golf. His public persona was as misleading as Macmillan's. Where Macmillan, the successful publisher, played the part of a patrician grandee, Wilson – the striving middle-class professional, whose entire working life had been spent in the South-East – chose the role of solid, down-to-earth, pipe-smoking Northerner, uncorrupted by the high-living, precious, Southern establishment. He preferred tinned salmon to smoked and beer to champagne, he insisted, adding defiantly that his favourite meal was a North Country high tea.[18] The truth was more complicated. He may conceivably have preferred beer to champagne, but there is not much doubt that he preferred brandy to both. He was proud of his Northern roots, but he had taken the road to the South at an early age and had never looked back.

After a scholarship to Oxford from Wirral Grammar School, a brilliant First, a spell as statistical assistant to William Beveridge and five years as a wartime civil servant, Wilson had been elected to Parliament at the age of twenty-nine. Two years later he was promoted to the Cabinet. He seemed firmly placed on the escalator of preferment, but in 1951 he resigned with Aneurin Bevan, in protest against the scale of the rearmament programme, which he rightly thought unfeasible. His resignation was a turning point in his career. Hitherto he had seemed a supremely competent, calculating technocrat, a civil servant manqué rather than a potential leader. By resigning, he revealed a streak of rash courage in his make-up, which belied his prosaic exterior and made him seem both more human and more formidable.

The episode had a deeper significance as well. Wilson *was* a competent and calculating technocrat, and he had a deep respect for the Whitehall mandarinate. But he was also a gambler, a risk taker, buoyed up by incorrigible optimism and an india-rubber-like ability to bounce back after defeats. He had gambled again in 1960, at the height of Labour's civil war over unilateral disarmament, when he stood against Gaitskell for the leadership – not because he was himself a unilateralist, but to consolidate his hold on the Bevanite rump, which had been left leaderless when Bevan died in July 1960. At more than one key moment in his prime ministership, the gambling streak would loom larger than the calculating one.

Not only was Wilson's modernising rhetoric surprisingly venerable, but the change of course that it had presaged turned out to be surprisingly modest. The great political innovator of the age was Harold Macmillan; Wilson rarely diverged from the trail which that wily whig had blazed. The dominant questions facing his governments – how to overcome the constraints of a weak balance of payments and a fragile currency; how to deal with the big battalions of organised labour and capital; how to manage the retreat from empire and the 'special relationship' with the United States; and how to adapt to the growing cohesion and economic power of the Europe of the Six – had also faced Macmillan's. In some areas the Wilson governments diverged from their Conservative predecessors. The steel industry, which the Conservatives had privatised after Labour lost office in 1951, was renationalised. Successive Education Secretaries, Crosland most notable among them, made strenuous, and largely successful, efforts to push ahead with comprehensive education, the Ark of the revisionist covenant. But, on the great questions of the time, the similarities between the Wilson and Macmillan governments were more marked than the differences.

The economic questions were the most pressing.[19] Labour's strongest card in the election had been Wilson's claim to superior economic competence. It was put to the test sooner than anyone had expected. The new government found itself face to face with a mammoth balance of payments deficit of £800 million. (The figure was an aggregate of the deficits on capital and current account, and was later revised downwards to £759 million.) Despite warning signs of balance of payments trouble, Labour had made no contingency plans for dealing with a possible crisis. Now it had to act. There were two obvious options: devaluation, necessarily accompanied by deflation; and deflation without devaluation. The first was ruled out, and the second was not seriously considered.

Two days after the election, Wilson, Brown and Callaghan – flanked by Sir William Armstrong, Permanent Secretary of the Treasury, Sir Eric Roll, the designated Permanent Secretary of the new Department of Economic Affairs, and Sir Donald MacDougall, its designated Director-General – met at No. 10 to discuss the economic situation. Only MacDougall favoured devaluation; in any case the three ministers had already decided against it. Instead of devaluing, the new government imposed a 15 per cent surcharge on imports of manufactured goods, breaking EFTA rules, infuriating its partners and gaining only marginal benefits to compensate. As for deflation, Callaghan had discovered in opposition that convincing his colleagues of the need for fiscal prudence was 'as difficult as convincing a dipsomaniac of the virtues of barley water',[20] and he had no wish to repeat the experience. In the first Cabinet meeting after the election, he assured the assembled ministers that the deficit could be financed by recourse to central banks and the IMF.[21] On 11 November, he brought in a mildly deflationary mini-budget, combining modest tax increases with increases in old-age pensions and national insurance benefits, and a commitment to the early abolition of health charges. His reward was a heavy outflow of sterling, halted only by a bank rate rise from 5 per cent to 7 per cent and £3 billion worth of central bank support for sterling.

There is no mystery about the government's refusal to deflate. Labour had fought the election on the ticket of sustained growth and an end to Stop-Go. Its claim to power rested on the proposition that it was uniquely qualified to discover this holy grail of post-war British economic policy. For it to impose yet another Stop within days of its entry into office would have been to acknowledge that that proposition was false. Given its tiny majority, such an admission might have forced it out of office; it would certainly have inflicted unbearable pain on party members and supporters. The refusal to devalue is another story. Of course, devaluation would have had to be coupled with deflation, but the combination could fairly have been blamed on the outgoing government and hailed as a break with the Stop-Go years. The Bank of England and, to a lesser extent, the Treasury were against devaluation; so were Callaghan and Brown, but they were bit players in a drama whose author and hero was Wilson. If Wilson, at the plenitude of his power as the first Labour Prime Minister for thirteen years, had wished to devalue, he could have done so. His lieutenants would have followed him, and the machine would have swung into line. The decision, or non-decision, was his.[22]

His reasons have been endlessly discussed. He may have been influenced by Thomas ('Tommy') Balogh, the Hungarian-born Balliol economist and former Bevanite guru whom he had brought into Downing Street as his economic adviser. He can hardly fail to have been influenced by the knowledge that he and Callaghan had promised the American Federal Reserve before the election that Labour would not devalue if support for sterling were forthcoming.[23] According to his memoirs, he was afraid that if the 1949 devaluation were followed by another in 1964, Labour would be branded as the party of devaluation, with disastrous effects on foreign confidence in the longer term.[24] He may also have feared the political consequences of a second Labour devaluation at a time when the government's majority was paper-thin and another general election loomed.

Yet it is hard to believe that this is the whole story. At least as important were the cast of Wilson's mind and the nature of his intellectual formation. His preference for trees over woods, his disdain for theory, his slightly awed respect for scientists and technologists, his early years as an official and minister in the mighty wartime and post-war state and a certain puritanical distaste for the manipulation of money as opposed to the manufacture of things, all inclined him to a 'productivist' approach to economics. What mattered was the 'real' economy where goods were produced and people employed, not the paper economy of bankers and foreign exchange dealers. Britain's balance of payments weakness merely reflected deeper, structural weaknesses in this 'real' economy, which could be corrected only by 'real' solutions. Such solutions entailed detailed state intervention in specific industries and even specific firms.[25]

It was not enough to rely on market forces. In true democratic collectivist fashion Wilson was instinctively suspicious of markets and, above all, of financial markets. In a give-away phrase he once said that devaluation would 'water the weeds as well as the flowers';[26] the state had to be an a discriminating micro-economic gardener, armed with a well-directed watering can. That was what he meant when he said that devaluation was a soft option. It was too easy, too glib, too general; as such, it was a diversion from the hard graft of changing the real world. And so the die was cast. Labour would eschew the primrose path of devaluation and battle its way to solvency with selective intervention, economic planning and an incomes policy. The deficit would be finessed with foreign credits, temporary expedients and bullish speeches until the defects in the real economy had been put right, and the balance of payments with them. It was perhaps the greatest gamble of Wilson's career.

∽∾

Intertwined with the question of how to cope with a fragile currency and balance of payments was the question of how to relate to the United States. Like virtually all Prime Ministers since Suez, Wilson was an Atlanticist by instinct, and also by assumed necessity. He valued Anglo-American relations more than any other foreign relationships, and he luxuriated in the warm bath of welcoming rhetoric with which the American President, Lyndon Johnson, used to greet him on his visits to Washington. Like Macmillan, he needed American goodwill to maintain Britain's nuclear deterrent. Once devaluation had been ruled out, he also needed American help to defend the sterling parity. It was in the Americans' own interests to assist him; they believed that if sterling were devalued, the dollar might be the next in line. Yet, though they had their own selfish reasons for propping up the pound, their props came with a price tag. Their chief foreign-policy priority was to defeat the Communist insurgency in South Vietnam, and the months following the change of government in Britain saw them slide ever more deeply into a quagmire of military intervention against an astonishingly skilful and resolute enemy. In an ideal world, they would have liked Britain to fight alongside them as she had in Korea, but they knew that that was politically impossible. From time to time they urged Wilson to make a token military commitment; even a few Black Watch pipers, Johnson told him, would be better than nothing.[27] But these urgings were not very convinced; and Wilson easily fended them off.

However, the Americans were utterly convinced on two points. They were adamant that Britain's overseas military presence – above all, east of Suez – should continue; and they did not need to say out loud that they wanted Britain's moral support for their increasingly costly and brutal Vietnam involvement. The end result was cruelly ironic. Albeit with occasional wobblings, Wilson did give moral support to the Americans' Vietnam policy, to the disgust of a growing section of Labour opinion, by no means confined to the old Bevanite left, whose support he needed when the government's economic policies came under fire. Much more damagingly, he also stuck resolutely to the east of Suez policy, which contributed significantly to the balance of payments weakness that American credits were intended to offset Like a junkie hooked on heroin, he became ever more dependent on a supplier whose services made his condition worse.[28]

At first, all seemed to go well. The machinery of Wilson's gardening state was assembled with impressive speed. At its heart was George Brown's Department of Economic Affairs (DEA), at this stage buzzing with enthusiasm and hope.[29] A much fought-over 'concordat' between Brown and Callaghan assigned it responsibility for planning and incomes policy, the twin keys to Labour's New Jerusalem, while the Treasury kept control of taxation, public spending, monetary policy and overseas finance. (This was a recipe for turf wars, which duly took place.) The NEDC remained in being, but as a sounding board and forum for discussion: plans would now be a matter for government. Flanking the DEA was a new Ministry of Technology (Mintech), incongruously headed by Frank Cousins, who was inserted, with some difficulty, into a Commons seat.

Brown threw himself into his double role as planner extraordinary and incomes policy supremo with seemingly boundless energy. In a grandiose ceremony in Lancaster House in December 1964, trade-union and employer representatives signed a 'Statement of Intent', committing them to work with the government to raise productivity and to keep 'increases in wages, salaries and other forms of incomes' in line with increases in output.[30] March 1965 saw the creation of a tripartite National Board for Prices and Incomes (NBPI), whose role was to decide whether wage or price increases referred to it by the government were in the national interest. At the beginning of April, the government laid down a 'norm' of 3–3.5% per cent for wage and price increases. At the end of the month, a conference of union executives approved the developing incomes policy by 4,800,000 to 1,800,000, after a passionate speech by George Brown asking for their help in making 'a great, an enormous breakthrough in the achievement of the age-old and historic aim of our movement'.[31] In September, the government published a National Plan, laying down a growth target of 25 per cent over the six-year period 1964 to 1970 – an annual rate of 3.8 per cent – and setting out the ways and means of achieving it, sector by sector.[32]

Half hidden by the rush and bustle, the hallmarks of the exercise were gradualism, partnership and consensus-building. The incomes policy was voluntary; the NPBI was a cross between a management consultant and a psychotherapist, operating through factual inquiry and mutual learning. It was designed to foster long-term changes of attitude, leading wage bargainers to take account of the general interest as well as of their own sectional interests, not to compel short-term changes of behaviour. Much the same applied to the National Plan. The government could not force private companies to do what the plan said they should do. But since the plan's checklists for action sprang from elaborate consultations with the interests involved, the planners assumed that there would be no need for compulsion. The purpose was to remove the uncertainty which had held back private-sector investment in the past and, in doing so, to create a virtuous circle of raised expectations.[33] Private companies would act in accordance with the plan because they would know that everyone else was doing so. Like the Macmillan Government before it, Labour hoped to engender a more collaborative economic culture through step-by-step evolution, encouraged, but not dictated, by the state. This too was bound to be a slow process. And, if anyone faltered, all would falter.

The first to falter was the government. There was a fatal disjunction between the timescale of indicative planning and voluntary incomes restraint and that of impatient currency markets, where optimistic phrases about changes in attitudes cut no ice. The markets wanted early and tangible evidence of an improved balance of payments and a stronger currency. No such evidence appeared. In June 1965 there was another sterling crisis, followed by another deflationary package and more help from the American Federal Reserve and the IMF. Under American pressure, the government decided to take powers to require early warning of wage claims and to delay settlements – watering down the voluntary principle which had been a cornerstone of the incomes policy agreed with the TUC. (As a sop to the unions it agreed to hold the powers in reserve until wage-vetting by the TUC had been given a chance to work, and the legislation was not passed until the summer of 1966.) For a while, it looked as if this combination of deflationary nibbles and wage-policy muscle-flexing had done the trick. At the end of March 1966, Labour won a second general election with a majority of ninety-seven, after a campaign fought on the hubristic slogan, 'You know Labour Government works.'

Nemesis was swift. Callaghan's May budget contained another deflationary nibble, in the form of a Selective Employment Tax of Heath Robinsonian ingenuity. In an interview with David Butler, Callaghan's Permanent Secretary, William Armstrong later called it 'a far-fetched, academic, nonsensical, dream tax', but to the markets it was less a dream than a nightmare. Its effect on demand was unknowable and in any case would not be felt for several months. Faint stirrings of another confidence crisis were magnified by a seven-week-long seamen's strike starting in mid-May. By early July 1966, sterling was once again under heavy pressure. By 12 July, Callaghan was warning the Cabinet that the growth of the economy would be 'substantially below' the 25 per cent figure set out in the National Plan, that public expenditure was growing 'at a faster rate than was consistent with the economic health of the country' and that there could be no guarantee that existing policies 'would suffice to deal with the situation'.[34] Wilsonian productivism was falling apart under the pressure of incompatible expectations.

For twenty months, the government had been trying to dodge the choice between devaluation and deflation. Now the moment of truth had arrived. Brown's advisers had already converted him to devaluation;[35] for a brief but delusive moment it looked as if Callaghan might be converted too. In an atmosphere rife with rumours of anti-Wilson plots, and with tempers frayed by late-night sittings and the sticky heat of Westminster in July, a group of devaluationist ministers took shape and managed to force a Cabinet debate. Wilson, however, stayed firm in his anti-devaluation faith; and by nineteen to six, the decision went in favour of holding the parity.[36] At first, noted the staunch devaluationist Barbara Castle, 'it looked as though we were winning. ... But then the "do nothing yet" brigade mowed us down.'[37]

Not for the first time, Brown resigned and was promptly persuaded to withdraw his resignation. On 20 July, Wilson announced a deflationary package designed to cut demand by £500 million, buttressed by a wage freeze of six months, to be followed by a further six months of 'severe restraint'. *The Economist* commented that it was 'the biggest deflationary package that any advanced industrial nation has imposed on itself since Keynesian economics began'.[38] The National Plan had been eviscerated; its growth targets had become museum pieces. The very notion of voluntary incomes restraint was fatally wounded. The DEA survived, but it had lost its role; after George Brown's translation to the Foreign Office in August it faded away.

It was all for nothing. At first the July cuts seemed to have served their purpose. Unemployment rose as intended; the current balance of payments swung into surplus; funds flowed back to London. By March 1967, Callaghan felt able to cut bank rate from 7 per cent to 6 per cent. In April, he brought in a standstill budget, famously boasting, 'All seamen know the word of command – steady as she goes.'[39] It turned out to be one of the most unfortunate metaphors in recent British history. In June, the Six-Day war between Israel and her Arab neighbours led to the closure of the Suez Canal and an embargo on oil exports to Britain from Iraq and Kuwait. A drain on the reserves had already started, in response to poor trade figures for the first quarter of the year. During the summer it accelerated; by the third quarter it had reached £500 million. September 1967 saw the start of a prolonged dock strike, which further damaged British exports; the Treasury forecast a £300 million trade deficit for the year.

On 18 September, Sir Alec Cairncross, Head of the Economic Section, and until then an opponent of devaluation, noted grimly that Britain had 'lost share in our own market and in foreign markets in conditions calculated to help us to be *more* competitive'; the government, he thought, would either have to devalue or to impose import quotas within the next few months. On 4 November he told Callaghan that, in the light of the forecasts, he thought devaluation was now unavoidable.[40] Last-minute attempts to put together another package of support for the parity got nowhere. On 16 November, Callaghan told the Cabinet that he had decided that the pound must be devalued; this, he added, was 'the unhappiest day in my life'.[41] On 18 November, sterling was devalued from $2.80 to the pound to $2.40. Like Cripps before them, Wilson and Callaghan had discovered that the rational, far-seeing state of democratic collectivist imagining could not indefinitely defy the markets. It was a painful discovery for them and a disastrous one for the *étatisme* that they and virtually all their colleagues took for granted.

❧

Devaluation was Labour's retreat from Suez. In purely economic terms it was a success, just as the withdrawal from Suez had been a success in military terms. Callaghan and Jenkins swapped offices – Callaghan becoming Home Secretary and Jenkins Chancellor of the Exchequer. At forty-seven Jenkins was by now the Cabinet's most glittering star. Unlike his Oxford contemporary, Healey, he cultivated support on the back benches and turned himself into the most formidable parliamentary gladiator in the government. He had been born into the Labour Party's purple. His father,

Arthur Jenkins, had gone down the pit at the age of twelve and had risen to become Vice-President of the South Wales Miners, a Labour MP and Attlee's PPS. Jenkins himself had made his way to Balliol College, Oxford, from Abersychan Secondary School. After a First in PPE and war service as a Bletchley code-breaker, he had been elected to Parliament at twenty-seven. He had been a leading Gaitskellite, and also a leading Labour champion of Common Market entry. He had written several books, including an acclaimed biography of Asquith.

After a spell as Minister of Aviation, he was appointed Home Secretary in 1965, at the age of forty-five; he was the youngest holder of the office since Winston Churchill in 1910. With a dazzling mixture of toughness and diplomacy, he imposed his own reforming liberalism on a sometimes recalcitrant Home Office. To young Labour backbenchers, watching the government trudge from one economic false dawn to another, Jenkins' Home Office seemed a beacon of hope.

He was one of the most complex figures in post-war British politics. He was gregarious, but shy; working-class by origin, but Balliol and Brooks's Club by adoption. He could command an unruly Commons Chamber and enthuse the Labour benches more successfully than any other minister, but outside the Chamber, and beyond his own circle, he seemed aloof, even intimidating. Yet beneath the grand manner and posh accent that led *Private Eye* to call him 'Smoothiechops', he was a passionate and mercurial Celt, closer in temperament, as Richard Crossman once pointed out, to Aneurin Bevan than to Gaitskell.[42] His political attitudes were (and are) hard to read. As a young MP in the 1950s he had been an identikit democratic collectivist, albeit on Labour's revisionist wing, but by the time he reached the Cabinet he had moved on. He cared more for freedom than for equality; he sought to loosen the state's grip on personal conduct, and he was suspicious of intrusive social engineering. He was passionately committed to what he called the 'civilised society'; it was largely due to him that homosexuality and abortion were decriminalised and the flogging of prisoners abolished. But he showed no interest in comprehensive education, the talisman of revisionist egalitarianism. A streak of *étatisme* remained; as we shall see, he did not object to the use of state power to tame what he saw as overmighty groups. Yet, in general, his attitude to political change now had more in common with Burke's than with Sidney Webb's, or even Anthony Crosland's.

To the Treasury he brought steely resolve, vaulting ambition and an unusual ability to grasp what he liked to call the 'grandes lignes' of policy. He had not sat on the Cabinet economic committee before devaluation, but if anything that was an advantage. It meant that he came to the Treasury with clean hands. For a while, his touch was uncertain, but he learned on the job and he learned fast. His task was both very simple and very difficult. Above all, he had to hold the new parity. A second devaluation would probably have destroyed the government and might have provoked a 'free fall' of sterling, a default on foreign debts and a 'crash' in real incomes.[43] Jenkins also had to make a drastic cut in home demand to shift resources into exports and turn the balance of payments round. There was no need for economic sophistication or intellectual ingenuity; what was wanted was heavy deflation, backed by an iron will.

That was the simple part; the difficult part was to drive such policies through Cabinet, and to win consent for them in the parliamentary Labour Party, the wider Labour movement and the country at large. There were plenty of upsets. The 1967 devaluation was the first premonitory shudder of the wild currency upheavals that would end the era of fixed exchange rates in the following decade, and currency markets were already becoming increasingly febrile. Twice in 1968 sterling was heavily buffeted by the backwash of global confidence crises – one in March, caused by the prospect of a rise in the dollar price of gold, and one in November, provoked by rumours of an upward revaluation of the deutschmark.

Meanwhile, the balance of payments turnaround was agonisingly slow to appear. Cuts followed cuts with remorseless regularity. Minor spending cuts immediately after devaluation were followed by bigger ones in January 1968. They included the cancellation of an order for fifty American F-IIIA strike aircraft, effectively ending the east of Suez policy. The decision was taken only in the teeth of violent American objections and after a long, dragging battle at the top of the government, in which Jenkins had to beat down formidable opposition from Healey and the Defence Department.[44] The cuts for 1968/9 came to more than £500 million. In March 1968 the budget increased taxation by £923 million, the biggest rise since the war; in his budget speech, Jenkins promised 'two years hard slog'.[45] The government also proclaimed a 'nil norm' for wage increases. Another deflationary package followed the November sterling crisis; yet more tax increases were imposed in the budget of April 1969. Then, at long last, when Jenkins was beginning to give up hope, the 'Arctic winter' gave way to a sudden spring.[46] By mid-1969, the monthly figures were showing a surplus on visible trade. The current account surplus for the year as a whole turned out to be £415 million. Funds flowed back into London; and Britain started to repay debt.

However, the political story was one of demoralisation, disaffection and disarray. Rhodesia, the last significant vestige of Britain's African empire, was a running sore that refused to heal. Ian Smith's white supremacist regime announced a unilateral declaration of independence (UDI) in

November 1965. Two much trumpeted sets of negotiations between Smith
and Wilson produced no result, and sanctions were flouted, probably with
the British Government's connivance.[47] In the end, Smith's tenure of office
lasted far longer than Wilson's. Meanwhile, a remarkable switch in Labour's
approach to the European Community came to a sad end. In opposition,
Wilson had been a notable sceptic, but he slowly changed his tune as
experience of office taught him how far British power had declined since
his days in Attlee's Cabinet. Though he covered his tracks with his usual
skill, it seems clear that the trauma of July 1966 turned him into a slightly
reluctant convert.[48]

In early 1967 he and Brown – two Don Quixotes without a Sancho
Panza – embarked on a heroic attempt to batter their way into the EEC in
the face of Cabinet uncertainty and Gaullist obstruction. A 'probe' of the
governments of the Six revealed that de Gaulle's suspicions of Britain were
fractionally less acute than they had been during the Macmillan years.
Unfortunately, the fraction was rather small. When Britain formally applied
to join the EEC in May, de Gaulle responded with a 'velvet veto', proph-
esying 'destructive upheavals' if the application succeeded. Nothing
daunted, Wilson pressed on. De Gaulle, he told Brown, was now 'a lonely
old man', saddened by an 'obvious sense of failure'; though he did not want
Britain in the Community, 'I am not sure that he any longer has the strength
to keep us out.'[49] It was a vivid example of the triumph of hope over
experience, which had been a central theme of Britain's relationship with
the European project since the Schuman Plan. On 27 November, nine days
after sterling was devalued, de Gaulle turned his velvet veto into a real one.

These failures did not stem directly from devaluation, but they fortified
the post-devaluation impression of a government and prime minister drifting helplessly at the mercy of events. Labour's standing in the polls plummeted; by-elections and local government seats were lost on an
unprecedented scale. By December 1967, the Conservatives had a Gallup
Poll lead of 17 per cent. A year later, it was 26 per cent. In the borough
council elections of 1968, Labour's share of the vote was less than 30 per
cent. Long-serving Labour councillors, many of them instinctively loyal to
the party leadership, were swept away by the tide of government unpopularity. They would not have been human if they had not felt aggrieved with
the policy-makers on whose altar they had been sacrificed.

Further blows were the resignations of George Brown in March 1968,
and Ray Gunter, the Minister of Power, in June – both in protest against
the way in which the government was run. Meanwhile, Wilson's popularity
and authority slipped badly. Between December 1966 and December 1967
his approval rating fell from 51 per cent to 34 per cent; by December 1968

it was down to 28 per cent. In moments of crisis, his fascination with political gossip and manoeuvre had often spilled over into fears of plots and plotters. At his private lunchtime meetings with DEA ministers in the months before devaluation, he spent more time on alleged conspiracies against him than on the state of the economy.[50] After devaluation, his dwindling popularity and ebbing authority turned what had been a tiresome habit into a morbid obsession.

A frequent target of his suspicions was Denis Healey, who repaid them with ill-disguised contempt. As Healey recalled later, economic failure led Wilson 'to see enemies in every corner; at worst, he began to behave, in the words of an uncharitable journalist, like "a demented coypu"'.[51] By the spring of 1968, Tony Benn, an admirer of Wilson's in happier days, thought him 'very paranoid and I think he is, in a sense, creating the very thing he is afraid of, namely a plot against himself'.[52] It was a shrewd insight. In the whispering gallery of Westminster, rumours grow with the telling; to dismayed Labour backbenchers, the Cabinet often seemed less a group of colleagues working for a common cause than a snake-pit of rivalrous egos, in which the chief snake was Wilson himself.

The inevitable result was that his fears became self-justifying, as hardy (or perhaps foolhardy) souls on the back benches began to feel that only a change at the top could save the government from disintegration. Imaginary plots turned into real ones, albeit usually with a large element of fantasy about them;[53] these further undermined his authority and self-confidence. The plots got nowhere; heads were counted and intelligence was exchanged, but no action followed. 'All you do,' Crosland complained justly, 'is fucking talk!'[54] In a madcap démarche, Cecil King, effective boss of the then mass-circulation and pro-Labour *Daily Mirror*, signed and published an article calling on Labour MPs to depose their leader. This did Wilson more good than harm. But though he survived, he did not recapture his old authority. By the summer of 1968, the parliamentary party could hardly have been a more unhappy ship.

CASTLE'S STRIFE

By the following spring, unhappiness had begun to verge on mutiny. The causes lay deep in the peculiar structure and culture of the British working-class movement. British trade unions had grown up outside the law and beyond the state. They owed their rights and privileges, not to law, but to hard-won immunities from law. In principle, their leaders were democratic collectivists, committed to state intervention, state planning and even state control. But leaders and led were rooted in the culture of the oldest working class in the world, for which the state had been an enemy more often than a friend. Both were instinctively suspicious of lawyers and the law. Besides, the leaders' political affiliations took second place to their primary role as champions of their members' day-to-day interests in a fragmented labour market, and they were always conscious of the need to carry their followers, and particularly their active followers, with them.

The unions had done their best to comply with the government's prices and incomes legislation, and it had been a better best than critics were willing to admit: the years of standstill and severe restraint in 1966 and 1967 had seen a marked fall in the rate of increase in manual workers' earnings.[55] However, the attempt had run heavily against their grain. Over the long term, a voluntary policy on the lines implied by Brown's Declaration of Intent might have induced a change in trade-union culture, but that possibility had perished in the freezes and squeezes that had followed the 1966 crisis and the 1967 devaluation. By 1968 the unions wanted out – out of anything that smacked of a formal incomes policy; and, above all, out of state interference with industrial relations.

Against this immovable object drove an irresistible force, in the shape of Barbara Castle, whom Wilson promoted to be Secretary of State for Employment and Productivity in April 1968. At fifty-seven Castle was a tireless bundle of passion, determination, charm, courage, eloquence and force. She was an accomplished journalist and a seductive platform orator – one of the darlings of the party conference – yet she found speaking in the House of Commons a nerve-racking ordeal. She was the first woman in British history to break through the glass ceiling that prevented her sex from reaching the heights of politics, yet when the need arose she could use her femininity like a weapon. She was an old Bevanite, and a democratic collectivist *étatiste* through and through; state power, in her eyes, was there to be used and recalcitrant interest groups could not be allowed to stand in its way.

As Minister of Transport she had introduced the breathalyser, extended the 70 mph speed limit trial and required new cars to be fitted with safety belts – all anathema to the powerful motoring lobby. It sometimes seemed that, for her, the trade unions were motorists writ large. Not only was she an activist (a 'button pusher' as the journalist, Alan Watkins, called her),[56] she was an activist in a hurry, impatient for quick results. Like many old Bevanites, she had no special love for the trade unions, whose block votes had sustained the Gaitskellites in the past, often in a peculiarly brutal fashion; and she had no experience whatever of the masculine, not to say sexist world of industrial relations. She had been Wilson's PPS during the

Attlee Government and each had a soft spot for the other. She admired his guile, even when she deplored it; he admired her courage, even when it seemed likely to plunge him into disaster.

The road to disaster was broad, but straight. In 1965, Wilson had appointed a Royal Commission, chaired by Lord Donovan, the Law Lord, to examine the role of trade unions and employers' associations in a modern society. One of the Commission's key members was George Woodcock, a lugubrious, soft-voiced Lancastrian who had been TUC General Secretary since 1960; another was the Warwick professor and doyen of academic industrial relations specialists, Hugh Clegg. The Donovan Report appeared in June 1968.[57] It was a monument to the voluntarist tradition that dominated trade-union thinking and shaped academic scholarship on the subject; Castle thought it had 'George Woodcock's finger prints all over it'.[58] It found that there were two industrial relations systems – one 'formal' and the other 'informal'. The formal system of industry-wide collective bargaining was losing out to the informal one of decentralised factory bargaining, regulated only by custom and practice. The growing gap between formal façade and informal reality was responsible for the inexorable tendency of earnings to run ahead of nationally negotiated wage rates, and thereby for the failure of successive incomes policies. The task was to bring order into the informal system, but because of its very informality that could not be done by legislation. Self-reform was the only hope.

To Castle this seemed a hopeless fudge, characteristic of a bumbling and complacent industrial relations establishment. She replied with a white paper entitled *In Place of Strife*, in a deliberately provocative echo of Aneurin Bevan's tract, *In Place of Fear*. The white paper accepted most of Donovan's proposals, but it explicitly challenged the voluntarist assumptions underlying them and put forward three portentous extensions in the role of government. The Secretary of State would be empowered to order a conciliation pause of up to twenty-eight days for unofficial strikes that seemed likely to damage the economy; to require ballots for official strikes (with the same proviso); and to impose settlements in certain inter-union disputes. Non-compliance would be punishable by fines.

From the vantage point of the twenty-first century these proposals may appear innocuous. In early 1969, coming from a deeply unpopular government, which had exhausted its credit with the unions and ordinary party members, Labour people could be forgiven for seeing them as an abomination. But Wilson was also an instinctive *étatiste* in a hurry and, in another rash gamble, he threw his weight behind Castle. In early January 1969, the draft white paper went to Cabinet. It provoked furious opposition, most notably (and ominously) from Callaghan, an ex-trade-union official in close touch with the major union leaders, and with the voluntarist tradition in his blood. Publication followed later in the month and the most divisive internal Labour Party battle since 1931 promptly ensued.

Constituency parties and the parliamentary party were swept by waves of anger and revolt; stolid party wheel horses, for whom defying the whip had been akin to sacrilege, made it clear that *In Place of Strife* was more than they could stomach. When the Commons debated the white paper at the beginning of March, fifty-three Labour MPs voted against and another thirty abstained. Among those in the 'No' Lobby were the normally ultra-loyal chairman of the Trade Union Group, James Hamilton, and three of the four PLP representatives on the party liaison committee. Three weeks later the fourth also came out against the bill. On 26 March, the Labour Party National Executive decided that it could not accept legislation in favour of all the white paper proposals; Callaghan and three other ministers voted with the majority against government policy. Collective Cabinet responsibility and party discipline – the two great pillars on which British governments rest – had started to fragment. Yet, with the doomed fortitude of the Light Brigade at Balaclava, Wilson and Castle galloped on. In April, the Cabinet decided to bring in a short bill as soon as possible, in the fond belief that speed would throw its opponents off balance. Instead, opposition mounted. The parliamentary party was loud with the noise of anti-Wilson plots and anti-bill cabals, and this time the plotters and caballers meant business. In early May, the chairman of the parliamentary Labour Party, the much loved Douglas Houghton – another former trade-union official, who was working hand in glove with Callaghan and the TUC leadership – made a public statement, warning the government not to risk the disintegration of the Labour Party by pressing on with the bill.

On 8 May 1969, a furious Wilson told the Cabinet that if the government withdrew the bill at the 'dictation of the Parliamentary Labour Party' they would prove the Conservatives were right in claiming that Labour government did not work. Callaghan replied that the loyalty of the PLP and of some ministers had been 'strained to breaking point'; the Cabinet should 'consider how they could withdraw from the brink of disaster'. In his summing-up, Wilson played what he presumably thought was his strongest card – the threat of a dissolution if 'effective Government' became impossible.[59] It was not strong enough: everyone knew that an early election would spell catastrophe both for the Labour Party and for Wilson himself. By June it was clear that the irresistible force had stalled. Tortuous negotiations between Wilson, Castle and assorted trade-union leaders dragged on, but on 17 June, Bob Mellish, the gnarled and foul-mouthed cockney disciplinarian who had become chief whip in late April, told the Cabinet that the PLP would not support the government unless it compromised with the TUC.[60] For all practical purposes that was the end of the story. Jenkins, who had been Castle's most hawkish Cabinet ally and the prime advocate of early legislation, wisely, if shamefacedly, jumped ship. After much embarrassing bluster Wilson and Castle swallowed their pride and agreed to withdraw the proposed legislation in return for a 'solemn and binding' TUC undertaking to do all it could to resolve unofficial disputes.

'Solomon Binding' attracted a good deal of justified mockery, but Wilson recovered his old bounce with surprising speed. However, no one could deny that he had beaten an ignominious retreat, or that his rhetoric of purpose and the purposive had been discredited. In 1967, democratic collectivist *étatisme* had been overwhelmed by the markets. Now it had quailed before an alliance between the unions and the Labour back benches. Callaghan, the canny graduate of the University of Life, had defeated Castle, Wilson and Jenkins, the blithe and cocky graduates of the University of Oxford. Labour MPs had shown that, if they stood their ground, they could defy the Prussian discipline of the whips. The unions had shown that a divided and discredited government could not force unwanted changes down their throats. Attempted coercion had failed, and the Cabinet had fallen back on surrender. The great question for the future was whether democratic collectivist statecraft could find a middle course between the two. The omens were not propitious.

⚬⚬⚬

As the *In Place of Strife* imbroglio entered its critical phase in late April 1969, Richard Crossman went to a party in Kensington full of 'girls and young men with beards', one of whom was the New Left activist and LSE lecturer, Robin Blackburn. 'It is only really in the last five years that the social order has been challenged and undermined,' Crossman noted later, with a slightly forlorn mixture of enthusiasm and regret, 'and this is what makes the life we live interesting and also makes me feel less disconsolate about the failures of the Government.'[61] His comment was both a requiem for old hopes and a portent of new travails.

Labour Members of Parliament were not alone in kicking against the pricks of hitherto unchallenged authority. By the late 1960s, Wilsonian modernisation had lost its glitter. To many it seemed mechanistic, bloodless, even reactionary – the last tremor of a dying old order rather than the harbinger of a new one. The cultural shifts which had undermined the whig imperialist tradition and helped to put Wilson in power had become deeper and more explosive in the following half-decade. Like similar shifts in the 1790s, 1840s and 1930s, they impacted most powerfully on the young. All over North America and Western Europe, so-called 'Baby Boomers' – children of affluent societies, who had grown up during the long post-war boom, who had never been exposed to depression or mass unemployment and who belonged to a self-conscious youth culture with no precedent in earlier periods of history – were in revolt against the seeming materialism, conformism, repressiveness and artificiality of their parents' generation.

May 1968 saw a student rebellion in the Paris suburb of Nanterre spread to the Latin Quarter in the centre of the city, where it helped to precipitate monster demonstrations, clashes with the police and a General Strike that involved 10 million workers. A month earlier, a huge student rally in West Berlin had ended in violent clashes between protesters and the police; a student leader, Rudi Dutschke, had been shot in the head by an indignant right-winger. In Rome there were violent confrontations between left-wing students, fascist students and the police. Students also protested in Geneva, Milan, Brussels, Vienna and Madrid. In the United States a socialist student group, the SDS (Students for a Democratic Society), helped to stimulate demonstrations and sit-ins at campuses across the country. The Berkeley campus of the University of California had been a centre of turbulent student protest since the early 1960s. Now other universities, including Harvard, Michigan, Stanford, North Western, and – most famously – Columbia followed suit. At the Democratic Party Convention in Chicago in August 1968, protesters, not all of them students, were savagely beaten up by the police. At Kent State in 1970, four students were shot dead by National Guardsmen.

The British experience was more muted, and there was a copycat element in the sit-ins and demonstrations that swept through British campuses from LSE to Leeds, and from Bristol to Birmingham. But that does not make them any less significant: it shows that British students felt they belonged to an international movement whose purpose was to change the world. 'Our internationalism,' the post-graduate activist, Sheila Rowbotham, remembered later, 'was implicit and taken for granted.' Foreign students came to Britain, bearing 'information and radical ideas'. 'Friendship and love affairs' cemented the connections with other countries.[62] Only a minority of students took part, and only a small minority identified with the radical *groupuscules* in the van of the movement.[63] But minorities can matter; and the radical students of the 1960s were the advance guard of a new sensibility, whose effects can still be detected at the start of the twenty-first century.[64] They were passionate, intense, impossibilist, desperately sincere, frequently self-righteous and contemptuous of compromise; they were also funny, satirical, and endowed with a keen nose for official humbug and pomposity. (It goes without saying that they were often exceedingly pompous themselves.) The men flaunted long hair and the women short skirts or tight trousers. A vague, delusive air of sexual liberation and even abandon hung over them; some of them talked as if theirs was the first generation in human history to engage in sexual intercourse. How liberated they really were is a moot point. As one Sixties revolutionary remembered later, 'there was an awful lot of sex not happening.'[65] Pot was common, and hard drugs were not unknown – presumably with disastrous consequences for some users' mental health, given what we now know about the connection between cannabis and schizophrenia. The student radicals were, at one and the same time, hyper-individualistic and lyrically communitarian. They would have been at home in the millenarian sects of the 1640s, or dancing around the Liberty tree in the 1790s.

Many of them were Marxists, or thought they were, but it was the early Marx – Marx, the perpetual student radical and scourge of alienation – who inspired them, not the Marx of *Das Kapital*, and, though few of them seem to have realised it, they belonged to a native tradition of democratic republican protest that long pre-dated Marxism and had much deeper roots in Britain's political culture. Most of all they were inspired by the idea of revolution in the abstract: 'workers taking over, the barricades, an actual change of power'.[66] Older Marxists, like the distinguished Communist historian Eric Hobsbawm, viewed them with a mixture of puzzled bene-volence and apprehensive alarm. The rebellious students called for revolu-tion; and revolutionaries were to be supported. On the other hand, they were not *real* revolutionaries. They seemed to have no social ideal. They were inspired by a 'general antinomianism' directed against 'anything that claimed the right and power to stop you doing whatever your ego and id felt like doing'.[67]

To the pure milk of Marxism many student revolutionaries added the enigmatic, sometimes penetrating and sometimes cloudy teachings of the critical theorist Herbert Marcuse, who had emigrated to the United States from Nazi Germany in the 1930s. Like Marx, Marcuse thought alienation and dehumanisation were the inescapable hallmarks of capitalism; so far from mitigating them, he believed, the affluent, technologically advanced welfare state, which was also the 'warfare state', had made them more acute, more subtle and more pervasive. The result was a 'one-dimensional society' in which freedom had been converted into 'unfreedom' and 'waste into need', where even sexuality had become a servant of the system, and where true autonomy was impossible. Unlike Marx, however, Marcuse placed no hope in the working class; prosperity, he thought, had drawn its teeth. The only hope – and it was a faint one – lay in 'the substratum of the outcasts and outsiders, the exploited and persecuted of other races and other colours, the unemployed and the unemployable'.[68] For young people who saw themselves as outsiders, and yearned to make common cause with the exploited and persecuted, it was a heady brew.

Students protested against archaic and illiberal university regulations and what they saw, often with good reason, as heavy-handed, unrepresentative and remote university administrations. Other targets included the relationship between the university and the defence establishment, the cavalier attitude to due process displayed by some university authorities, the alleged influence of big business on research and academic policy, and the use of university premises to propagate opinions – particularly racist ones – that the protesters considered obnoxious or immoral.

A serious confrontation between students and the university authorities at Leeds began with a demonstration against the visit of the Conservative MP and Rhodesia sympathiser, Patrick Wall. The trigger that turned Essex University into one of the most explosive centres of student protest was a projected visit by a speaker from the government's biological warfare research centre at Porton Down. A resonant cause célèbre occurred when students who had raided the Vice-Chancellor's office at Warwick University discovered that the university kept secret records of students' political views. However, the protest leaders also tapped deeper wells than these. For them, domestic questions of university governance were indissolubly linked to the great moral issues that resounded beyond the university walls – racism, nuclear weapons, Rhodesia and, above all, the escalating barbarity of the war in Vietnam.

Liberal-minded people, many of them moderate on other questions, were increasingly appalled by the brutality and ham-fistedness of the Americans' intervention in Vietnam, as revealed in horrifying pictures of the effects of napalm, boasts by American military commanders that North Vietnam would be bombed 'into the stone age' and, most shocking of all, the My Lai massacre in March 1968, when enraged American troops killed hundreds of civilians, most of them women, children, babies and old men. For radical students, however, Vietnam meant more than this. It was a symbol as well as a cause – a symbol of evil; but, at the same time, of redemption and hope. Sheila Rowbotham's memories of watching the television coverage of the Communist Vietcong's brilliantly executed 'Tet' offensive in January 1968 help to explain why. At first she and her friends were incredulous. Then they began to cheer: 'the victims were turning into victors. ... If the Vietnamese could take on the mightiest power in the world, what about us?'[69]

That was not all. Vietnam was the test-bed for a revolutionary struggle by the exploited against the exploiters, a blaze of light in the gloom of systemic repression. Tariq Ali, the Pakistani ex-president of the Oxford Union who had helped to set up the Vietnam Solidarity Committee, was one of the organisers of a 100,000-strong march through London in October 1968. '[R]ed flags and banners,' he wrote later, 'mingled with posters from the French May and anti-capitalist placards in their hundreds. This was much more than a demonstration of solidarity with the struggle of the Vietnamese. It was an assembly of those who regarded the capitalist order in Europe as doomed.'[70] In a penetrating account of the mentality of the student radicals, Colin Crouch, president of the LSE Students' Union during the troubles, argued that Vietnam had become a model of guerrilla warfare and, as such, of a popular cultural revolution through which ordinary people would take control of their own lives, as opposed to the bankrupt, bureaucratic Soviet model of political revolution from the top:

> The guerrilla band is a small face-to-face group. It is, at least in the eyes of romantic young revolutionaries, voluntaristic, autonomous, non-bureaucratic. The fighters are seen as working passionately for a cause in which they believe *and* which represents their own best ideal and material interests. The guerrilla is thus virtually the ideal type of non-alienated man. ...
>
> But the attraction of the guerrilla goes further. Not only does he himself conform to the ideal picture of revolutionary man, but in Vietnam guerrilla bands have been able to tie down, perhaps yet to beat, the most technologically equipped and bureaucratically co-ordinated army the world has ever seen. ... So rich in symbolism is the Vietnam war that it acquires the status of the struggles of the beasts of the Apocalypse.[71]

These attitudes slowly opened up a gulf between moderate student reformers like Crouch himself and the 'romantic' *enragés* who saw the university as a Vietnam in miniature. For the moderates, the demonstrations and sit-ins that swept through the LSE in 1968 served an instrumental purpose. They were designed to bring pressure on the authorities, in order to win tangible concessions. For the 'romantics' the sit-in became an end in itself. As Crouch put it:

> People spoke of the 'community' that had been created during the sit-in; they valued the 'concrete' nature of the immediacy of experience. They placed great stress on 'spontaneity' and on the positive value of mass participative action. It was wrong to talk about tactics, to try to plan what our next moves should be, for that imposed a blueprint, lacked spontaneity and smacked of the calculating world outside; it also meant allowing exogenous factors to impinge on our total autonomy, our total ability to

control our lives. It was more than wrong to do such things; it was treacherous. One was either committed or one had sold out. ... For a week we lived in a world of the eternal present, the heritage of the immediate past being destroyed and the future being left to develop according to the dictates of constant spontaneity.[72]

❧

Some revolutionaries were more autonomous than others. As the painter and former art student, Nicola Lane, remembered them later, the Sixties were 'totally male-dominated. A lot of girls just rolled joints – it was what you did while you sat quietly in the corner, nodding your head. You were not really encouraged to be a thinker. You were there really for fucks and domesticity.' The medical doctor and former New Left ideologue, David Widgery, concurred: in the student left, he remembered, 'men talked and women did the background work.'[73] But not all women were content to roll joints or stay dutifully in the background. As the decade wore on, a 'second wave' of feminism that drew some of its inspiration from the student revolutionaries and their associates, and some from exasperation with their patronising behaviour towards their female comrades, slowly gathered force.

An early swallow in what would become a scorching summer was the Leeds English literature lecturer and future Cambridge professor, Juliet Mitchell. In a much quoted article in *New Left Review*, which appeared in 1966 when the curve of Wilsonian modernisation was on the point of turning down, Mitchell asked an embarrassing question: why did contemporary socialist theory have so little to say to or about women? Her article was scholarly, careful and rather downbeat in tone, and her chief practical recommendation – that the priority for any movement for female emancipation must be 'the entry of women fully into productive industry' – was far from revolutionary, even in the Britain of 1966. But, in spite of the cool tone, her peroration was clearly intended to be a call to arms. Socialism, she wrote, should not mean the abolition of the family, but a diverse range of socially acknowledged relationships:

> Couples living together or not living together, long-term unions with children, single parents bringing up children, children socialised by conventional rather than biological parents, extended kin groups, etc. – all these could be encompassed in a range of institutions which matched the free invention and variety of men and women. ...
>
> The liberation of women under socialism will not be 'rational' but a human achievement, in the long passage from Nature to Culture which is the definition of history and society.[74]

Forty years later this seems unexceptional. The diverse pattern that Mitchell hymned was not very different from the pattern that exists today. But, by an irony that few 1960s feminists could have foreseen and fewer still would have enjoyed, it owes more to the advancing tide of hedonistic market individualism than to any form of socialism.

Student protest and second-wave feminism were only two ingredients in a rich stew of colliding identities. The values that helped to drive them – authenticity, autonomy, spontaneity, community, participation – resounded in other quarters as well. The veteran American observer of British politics, Samuel H. Beer, would later see these values as the stuff of a 'romantic revolt', spreading 'across the political and social spectrum', undermining deference, challenging convention and pitting the local and small-scale against the established and bureaucratic.[75] In the academy, E.P. Thompson's 939-page masterpiece, *The Making of the English Working Class*, and the History Workshops pioneered by the brilliant, disorganised and eloquent Raphael Samuel, a New Left pioneer and tutor at Ruskin College, Oxford, sought to rescue the forgotten and excluded from the 'condescension of posterity'. The *May Day Manifesto*, issued by a group of no-longer-new New Left intellectuals, was another straw in the romantic wind. In language reminiscent of the young Aneurin Bevan, it denounced the 'managed politics' of Westminster, whose atmosphere was 'heavy with rituals' designed to 'confirm a closed circle as against the pressures of a noisy popular world' and to create a 'mellow dusk in which actual power is blurred'. It demanded 'new forms' of ownership to include trade unions, local authorities and co-operative societies; and it called for a 'step-by-step extension of workers' control' as a means towards isolating and ending the power of capital.[76]

Meanwhile, the election of the Spanish civil war veteran, Jack Jones, as General Secretary of the Transport and General Workers' Union, and of the ex-Communist Hugh Scanlon as president of the Engineering Workers, signalled a rebirth of old dreams of industrial democracy among trade-union activists. So did the foundation of the Institute of Workers' Control, headed by the Trotskyite future European Parliament Member, Ken Coates. Less obviously, the accelerating strike wave to which *In Place of Strife* was a response also reflected 'romantic' aspirations. In 1969, nearly 7 million working days were lost in stoppages – the highest figure of the decade. In 1970 the figure was close to 11 million. These figures were due, in part, to the rising expectations associated with full employment and in part to the growing impact of direct taxation on working-class incomes, but economistic explanations cannot catch their full meaning.

Sometimes strikes were directed against union bureaucracies as well as against the employers. Often, they were about power, status, dignity and self-respect as well as bread and butter.[77] (Sometimes they were due to straightforward bloody-mindedness.) In the aftermath of *In Place of Strife*, a pervasive sense of disenchantment and betrayal gave an extra edge to the growing trade-union concern with power, participation and dignity. 'The most effective redistributors of wealth and incomes in the community is not the incomes policy,' warned a delegate to the 1970 Labour Party conference, 'but the militant stand of the Trade Union movement and until we as a movement recognise this, and support the trade unions fully, we will get nowhere.'[78] The warning did not bode well for the future of the democratic collectivist tradition.

Nor did the quintessentially 'romantic' rebirth of nationhood in Scotland and Wales, and of nationalism in Northern Ireland. For most of their history, democratic collectivists had been blind to nationhood, ethnicity and identity. The state in which they put their trust was the British state; they took it for granted that the British state subsumed a British nation and a British identity. They also took it for granted that the state's authority and power were grounded in the familiar doctrine of absolute parliamentary sovereignty. North of the Border, some of them – Tom Johnston, the Secretary of State for Scotland during the Second World War, was one of the most distinguished – occasionally flirted with the notion of Scottish Home Rule, but these were exceptions and their flirtations had no tangible results.

Democratic collectivist centralism rested on bad history. It ignored the complex process through which an overarching 'British' identity had been superimposed on older Irish, Scottish and Welsh identities; and it brushed aside the inconvenient truth that the British state created by the Act of Union in 1707 was multinational, like Austria-Hungary in the nineteenth century, not national, like France. Yet for most of the half-century following Labour's emergence as the main anti-Conservative party in the 1920s, the democratic collectivists' approach to state and nation corresponded with the social and political realities of Scotland and Wales. (Northern Ireland was a different matter.) There were nationalist parties in both countries – the Scottish National Party (SNP) north of the Border, and Plaid Cymru in Wales – but they were little more than sects. The Labour Party dominated Wales, virtually unchallenged. In Scotland it and the Unionists vied for supremacy.

Against a background of comatose constitutional orthodoxy and bland electoral complacency, two alarming thunderbolts then descended on the heads of the Wilson Government.[79] The first came in Wales, where Plaid Cymru's president, Gwynfor Evans, won a by-election in Carmarthen in July 1966, with 39 per cent of the vote to Labour's 33 per cent. The second, more alarming thunderbolt came in Scotland. It fell in November 1967, when Winnie Ewing, the lively and articulate SNP candidate, overturned a Labour majority of 16,000 in a by-election in Hamilton. The immediate sequel was equally alarming. In Wales, Plaid Cymru came within a hair's breadth of winning two of the safest Labour seats in the country; in Scotland, the SNP made unprecedented gains in local elections. In the following general election, Carmarthen and Hamilton each reverted to Labour, but it would soon become clear that there was more to Welsh and Scottish nationalism than a fleeting urge to protest.

There were marked differences between the two. Welsh nationalism had grown out of a struggle to defend a largely rural culture and way of life, centred on the chapel and the Welsh language, from the homogenising pressures of an alien outside world. Scottish nationalism was more complex. It built on old, proud Scottish institutions – the law, the universities and the Kirk – which had survived the disappearance of the separate Scottish state and Parliament in 1707, and had embodied and fortified a distinct Scottish identity ever since. Almost certainly it also reflected a gnawing sense of disenchantment with an inglorious, post-imperial and declining Britain. For the British empire had also been a Scottish empire. Highland regiments had played leading parts in the conquest of India in the eighteenth century. Scottish missionaries had been active in Africa and India; the most illustrious nineteenth-century British missionary-explorer was the Scot, David Livingstone. Scottish immigrants had left an indelible stamp on Canada and New Zealand. Dundee had been the world capital of the trade in Indian jute; Glasgow had probably been the empire's most important shipbuilding centre. Now these glories had vanished. The union no longer gave Scotland a distinctive role in the biggest empire the world had ever seen; many Scots came to feel that it shackled her to a declining and second-rate power, dogged by economic failure and industrial conflict.

But from the London government's point of view the differences between Wales and Scotland counted for less than the similarities. What mattered was that, in both the smaller nations of the British mainland, the British connection was no longer axiomatic – and, on a less elevated level, that valuable Labour fiefdoms were under threat. Wilson responded by setting up a Royal Commission on the Constitution, under the chairmanship of the editor of *The Economist*, Sir Geoffrey Crowther. It remained to be seen what rabbits would emerge from this well-worn hat.

In Northern Ireland two nationalisms were in conflict. Each reflected an ethnic identity buttressed by ancient memories that went back for centuries, as well as by recent experiences.[80] Protestants cherished a belligerent 'British' identity rooted in the disquieting knowledge that, although they were in a majority in Northern Ireland, they were in a minority in the island of Ireland as a whole. Their mentality was shaped by a potent communal myth of resistance to the 'papist' ambitions of James II and to the threat of 'Rome rule' posed during the agitation for Irish Home Rule before 1914. The myth was reinforced by the nagging sense that the (Catholic) Nationalist Party dreamed of submerging them in a united Ireland that would be dominated by one of the most intolerant Catholic Churches in Europe, and by memories of the Irish Republic's ostentatious neutrality during the Second World War, when Britain had been fighting for her life against one of the most evil regimes in human history. Catholics clung to a stubborn 'Irish' identity fuelled by the republican myth of martyrdom at the hands of alien British oppressors, as well as by resentment of the flagrant anti-Catholic discrimination which was part of the texture of the province's life.

These two identities were irreconcilable, but for more than a generation the conflict between them had been contained. London and Dublin had both done their best to forget about Northern Ireland; and the Stormont regime had proceeded undisturbed on its discriminatory way, as though the outside world did not exist. State institutions – notably including the Royal Ulster Constabulary (RUC) and the paramilitary 'B Specials' – were instruments of Protestant supremacy. Constituency boundaries were gerrymandered to bolster the Unionist (in other words, Protestant) majorities, which were in any case inevitable under the first-past-the-post electoral system.

In the mid-1960s, the outside world broke in. In the climate created by the civil rights movement in the American Deep South, the 'Prague Spring' in Czechoslovakia, ANC resistance to apartheid in South Africa and the romantic revolt of the idealistic young all over the developed world, injustices which had seemed irremediable for forty years suddenly seemed intolerable. A civil rights movement took shape, in which civil rights protesters organised marches in territory the Protestants considered their own. There were violent clashes with rival Protestant marchers, and – more seriously – with the RUC. Under pressure from Harold Wilson, the Northern Ireland Prime Minister, Terence O'Neill, promised reforms in local government and in the province's highly discriminatory housing policies. The ensuing Protestant backlash swept O'Neill from power. The rival tribes, which had sullenly co-existed in the days before the Protestant tribe's supremacy was threatened, became increasingly polarised.

The inevitable crisis came in August 1969, with fierce clashes between Catholic rioters and the RUC in Derry, followed by vicious communal violence in Belfast, in which seven people were killed and about a hundred wounded. Ten thousand British troops were despatched to the province to protect the Catholics from what many saw as the threat of a Protestant pogrom. Not surprisingly, the Catholic population gave them an enthusiastic welcome, while the Protestants glowered in dismay. Callaghan, as Home Secretary, was the responsible British minister, and he swept into action with an impressive mixture of energy and aplomb. Reforms were proclaimed, and high-level inquiries into Catholic grievances initiated. For six months or so a superficial tranquillity reigned, while London breathed sighs of relief.

⟨∅⟩

England remained. Unlike its counterparts north of the Border and west of the Severn, English nationalism did not recognise itself as such. There was no English myth of resistance to alien oppression, no specifically English iconography to remind English men and women who they were and no would-be English elite anxious to win a place in the sun. The cross of St George had been absorbed into the Union Jack, where it was virtually invisible; England's nationhood had dissolved in a wider British nationhood. The political class was largely English, of course, but it saw its role, even if not its identity, as British. The English Parliament had become the British Parliament; the English monarchy, the British monarchy. English people often exasperated their non-English fellow citizens by talking as if 'England' and 'Britain' were synonymous. (One of the most spectacular examples was Shakespeare's reference to England as a 'stone set in the silver sea', implying that the frontier with Scotland did not exist.) There was a great deal of poetry about England, some of it haunting and some of it banal. 'England' was intimate, cosy, *home:* the place to be when Browning's April was here. 'Britain' was the place for politics, government and the state. However, a 'Royal Society of St George' had been in existence since 1894, with the reigning monarch as patron; and in 1961 it had provided the venue for one of the most remarkable political speeches of the century.

The speaker was Enoch Powell (John Enoch Powell to give him his full name).[81] He had just returned to office as Minister of Health after three years on the back benches, following his resignation with Thorneycroft and Birch, but he had no intention of sinking back into dutiful and unnoticed loyalty. He was a natural loner, with passionately held views which he was constitutionally incapable of bottling up; and on the still-slumbering but looming questions of nationhood and identity posed by the government's breakneck exit from empire, he and Macmillan were divided by a deep gulf of instinct and style. Macmillan, the guileful whig imperialist, wanted to smooth over the end of empire with emollient words and ambiguous gestures. Britain would be coaxed into post-imperialism without noticing what was happening. The old whig imperialist elite would remain in charge; and the old whig imperialist vision, subtly modified but reassuringly familiar, would continue to guide it.

Powell could be guileful too, but he was not a whig imperialist. His instincts were defiantly tory nationalist; and his contempt for smooth speech and accommodating gestures equalled Salisbury's 100 years before. He wanted to excite, to speak out, to sharpen differences instead of covering them up. Above all, he wanted to force his intellectually sloppy party and his easygoing fellow citizens to face unpalatable truths. He had a brilliant mind, perhaps the most brilliant in the House of Commons, and he used it to become one of the most accomplished rhetoricians of his time. But – ironically, in view of his ferocious patriotism – it was a most un-English mind. His rhetorical mastery stemmed from an extraordinary mixture of resonant language, strangulated emotion and ruthless logic; and he had a terrifying propensity to follow the logic of his argument wherever it led.

Despite exquisite manners, Powell was never fully at home in the metropolitan political elite. He was one of the most highly educated politicians of his generation, but he was also a provincial, proud of his roots. He was born in Stechford, in Birmingham; and he made no effort to lose the harsh accent of the West Midlands. Both his parents were elementary school teachers by profession, though his mother gave up work when he was born. Even in childhood, he was obsessively hard-working and fiercely ambitious, as well as unusually gifted. He won a scholarship to King Edwards School, Birmingham, and another scholarship to Trinity College, Cambridge. At Cambridge he lived a solitary life, dominated by grinding study of the classics; an undergraduate magazine called him 'the Hermit of Trinity'.[82] He won Firsts in both parts of his Tripos; Trinity elected him to a Fellowship when he was twenty-two. At twenty-six he was appointed Professor of Greek at Sydney University in Australia, where his fascination with close and erudite textual criticism earned him the nickname of 'textual pervert'. He enlisted as a private in the Royal Warwickshire Regiment in October 1939, and ended the war as a brigadier.

After four years as a Conservative apparatchik, Powell was elected to Parliament in the vintage Conservative year of 1950. By this time he had taken up hunting and abandoned the atheism that he had learned from Nietzsche to embrace a characteristically idiosyncratic Anglicanism. Eden gave him junior office in 1955, and Macmillan promoted him to be Financial Secretary to the Treasury in 1957. He had spent the closing years of the war in India, where he had been captivated by the romance of the Raj and had studied Urdu and Hindi. The British, he wrote years later, 'were married to India as Venice was married to the sea'.[83] In his days as a party back-room boy he had believed that Britain could and should maintain the Raj by force. But the Attlee Government's withdrawal from India in 1947, and the Churchill Government's withdrawal from Suez in 1954, convinced him that the imperial phase in British history had ended for ever. Post-imperial Britain needed a different role, a different identity and, most of all, a different national Myth.

In his St George's Society speech in 1961 he tried to sketch out the elements of such a Myth. But it was not a British Myth. It was ostentatiously, passionately, uncompromisingly English. The old imperial God had failed; it was time for a new English God to take its place. The power and glory of empire had vanished, he declared, but that was not a reason for despair:

> Herodotus relates how the Athenians, returning to their city after it had been sacked and burnt by Xerxes and the Persian army, were astonished to find, alive and flourishing in the midst of blackened ruins, the sacred olive tree, the native symbol of their country. So we today, at the heart of a vanished empire, amid the fragments of a demolished glory, seem to find, like one of her own oak trees, standing and growing, the sap still rising from her ancient roots to meet the Spring, England herself.

The present generation of the English had 'come home again from years of distant wandering'. Having returned, the travellers had discovered an unexpected affinity with earlier generations, generations before the 'expansion of England', whose inscrutable effigies could be found in England's country churches. Suppose they could talk to us, Powell asked, what would they say? Whatever else it might be, he answered,

> One thing above all they assuredly would not forget, Lancastrian or Yorkist, squire or lord, priest or layman; they would point to the kingship of England and its symbols everywhere visible. The immemorial arms, gules, three leopards or, though quartered of late with France ... and older still the Crown itself and that sceptred awe in which Saint Edward the Englishman still seemed to sit in his own chair to claim the allegiance of all the English. Symbol yet source of power, person of flesh and blood yet incarnation of an idea; the kingship would have seemed to them as it seems to us, to embrace and express the qualities that are peculiarly England's: the unity of England, effortless and unconstrained, which accepts the unlimited supremacy of Crown in Parliament so naturally as not to be aware of it.[84]

That was the essence of Powellism: unflinching, almost masochistic post-imperialism; unshareable and unlimited sovereignty; a romantic Myth of

England and Englishness centred on sacred symbols and half-buried memories; national resurrection through suffering and loss.

Yet the Myth left one nagging question unanswered. Who were the English? Was England's nationhood essentially ethnic, like those of Germany and Ireland? Or was it civic, like those of France and the United States? Powell did not answer that question explicitly, but the tentative outlines of an answer loom through the lines of his beautifully crafted though ambiguous rhetoric. Powell's was a nationalism of soil, not of blood – not surprisingly, since he was himself partly Welsh by descent. But it was, even more, a nationalism of memory and allegiance. By implication at least, Englishness did not embrace all the inhabitants of England, not even all those who had been born on English soil. The English were those who looked back to medieval England before the distant wandering of empire, and who recognised themselves in its rites and symbols. Closely linked with that clouded answer was another. Powell, the former imperialist, had become, not just a post-imperialist, but a strange kind of anti-imperialist.

The equation between the English return to their medieval roots and the Athenians' return to their sacred olive tree carried with it an extraordinary implication: the wandering England of empire, Powell seemed to be saying, was not the true England. It was an aberration, glorious perhaps, but in some profound sense unreal. The central theme of Powell's political career for the next thirty years would lie in a tormented attempt to give substance to the real England of his imagination.

Learned references to Herodotus, Edward the Confessor and the royal coat of arms were not calculated to win a mass following. By the late 1960s Powell had drifted so far from the Heathite Conservatism which now held the reins of party power that he desperately needed a mass following to escape political oblivion. He won it with another speech, one of the most resonant of the second half of the twentieth century, and one of the nastiest. It was delivered in Birmingham in April 1968. The topic was coloured immigration – a throbbing nerve in the body politic that both the front benches in the House of Commons approached with cautious trepidation. Powell had already challenged the broadly liberal consensus that embraced most of the political elite, but in a fairly restrained fashion.

Now he attacked it head-on, with a deadly mixture of populist rage and elitist language. In an astounding passage he compared himself to the 'Roman' who 'seemed to see the River Tiber foaming with much blood'. He quoted a middle-aged, working-class constituent who had told him that he wouldn't be satisfied until his three children were settled overseas, since in Britain the 'black man will have the whip hand over the white man' in fifteen or twenty years' time. He dilated at length on the experiences of an unnamed old lady in Wolverhampton who was now the only white person left in her street, and who was becoming afraid to go out because, when she went to the shops, she was followed by 'charming, wide-grinning piccaninnies' chanting 'Racialist', the only English word they knew. Britain, Powell said, must 'be mad, literally mad, as a nation to be permitting the annual inflow of some 50,000 dependants. . . . It is like watching a nation busily engaged in heaping up its own funeral pyre.'[85]

Heath promptly sacked him from the shadow Cabinet, whereupon 1000 dockers marched from the East End to Westminster in his support. His mail-bag was enormous and virtually all of it came from well-wishers. By early May 1968, he had received more than 43,000 letters, only 800 of which were hostile. Meanwhile, a Gallup poll had shown that 74 per cent agreed with him, while only 15 per cent disagreed. On the most sensitive issue of the time, he had become the tribune of the people. Powell, the provincial populist, had overwhelmed Powell, the intellectually fastidious front-bencher. He had excluded himself from the political elite, and exposed the ugly side of his romantic English nationalism. In doing so, he had made it virtually impossible for anyone else to conduct a searching national conversation about the meaning of the end of empire for England and the English. As we saw in Chapter 4, George Orwell had explored a romantic, revolutionary England of the imagination during the Second World War, but he had no followers. Faced with the prospect of an English nationalism – whether rough or romantic – *bien-pensant* liberals in all parties averted their eyes in shocked distaste. In debates over the future of the multinational British state, there was a hole where England should have been. Part of the explanation lies in the dark shadow of Powellite populism.

ᘓᔕᘎ

When Powell delivered what came to be known as his 'rivers of blood' speech, the Wilson Government was tottering in the aftermath of devalu-ation. It continued to totter for the best part of two years, but in the spring of 1970 its fortunes suddenly and inexplicably recovered. In January 1970, the Conservatives stood at 48 per cent in the Gallup poll and Labour at 41 per cent, yet by May their positions were reversed. Labour's rating was 49 per cent to the Conservatives' 42 per cent. Even in April, when the polls were against him, the incorrigibly optimistic Wilson had wanted an early election. The turnaround in the polls seemed to confirm his instincts. Parliament was dissolved in late May and polling day took place on 18 June, after a campaign of earnest exhortation on Heath's part and bland benevolence on Wilson's. To the astonishment of politicians, pollsters and pundits, the Conservatives won with 46.4 per cent of the popular vote to Labour's 43 per cent, and a majority over all parties of thirty seats.

8

LAST GASP

❖

Do you want a strong Government which has clear authority for the future to take the decisions which will be needed? Do you want Parliament and the elected Government to continue to fight strenuously against inflation? Or do you want them to abandon the struggle against rising prices under pressure from one particular group of workers?

> Edward Heath, television broadcast explaining his decision to call the General Election of February 1974.

[W]e have been living on borrowed time. ... We used to think you could spend your way out of a recession and increase employment by cutting taxes and boosting spending. I tell you in all candour that this option no longer exists, and that insofar as it ever did exist, it only worked by injecting a bigger dose of inflation into the economy, followed by a higher level of unemployment as the next step.

> James Callaghan at the Labour Party conference, October 1976

❖

THE TRAGEDY OF EDWARD HEATH

The 1970 election result was a victory for the Conservative Party, but it was an even greater victory for Edward Heath. He had been the focus for the Conservative campaign, and his scarifying contempt for Wilson's 'cheap and trivial style of government' had suffused the party manifesto, *A Better Tomorrow*.[1] The policies it contained had emerged from an elaborate process of research and discussion, initiated and largely controlled by him. His dogged self-belief and will to win had sustained the party's morale through a buffeting succession of dismal polls and the 'black despair' of some of his closest colleagues.[2] Less obviously, his leadership had been in the balance throughout. Had he lost, as almost all the pollsters and pundits had expected, the Conservative Party would have lived to fight again, but his own career would have suffered a crippling blow. When he kissed hands as Prime Minister, he could have been forgiven for feeling doubly vindicated. Not only had he won; he had been proved right, and the soothsayers and faint-hearted wrong.

However, his victory was not all it appeared to be. The Britain of 1964 had seemed made for Harold Wilson, but the Britain of 1970 – for that matter, the world of 1970 – were alien territory for Heath. His origins were humbler than Wilson's: humbler, in fact, than those of any previous British prime minister apart from Ramsay MacDonald. He was born into the upper working class in the Kentish seaside town of Broadstairs in 1916; John Campbell, his biographer, thought the 'tortured' vowel sounds of his maturity were the legacy of hard-won upward mobility. His father was a skilled carpenter who built up a successful business as a small builder; his mother had been in service with a cosmopolitan and prosperous Hampstead family. Heath won a scholarship to a grammar school in nearby Ramsgate. This was followed by a fee-paying Commonership at Balliol College, Oxford. Though part of the costs were covered by a loan from the local authority, money was very tight until a college organ scholarship of £100 a year (about £4500 in today's money) rescued him from financial hardship.

Unlike his politically quiescent and incorrigibly insular Oxford contemporary, Harold Wilson, he travelled widely on the continent as war approached. Unusually for a Conservative, he sided with the Republicans in the Spanish civil war, visited the Republican forces with an all-party student delegation and narrowly escaped being killed when the cars in which they were travelling were machine-gunned by a Falangist plane. He heard Hitler address a Nazi rally at Nuremberg, and was 'horrified' by the experience;[3] later, he cut short a second visit to Germany days before German forces crossed the Polish border. He threw himself into the famous 1938 Oxford City by-election on the side of the anti-appeasement candidate, A.D. Lindsay, Master of Balliol. He won the presidency of the Union, after successfully moving a vote of no confidence in the Chamberlain Government. Remarkably for a young man from his background at that time, his horizons were already European; despite his mangled French, he was a strong Francophile. He was a Conservative in politics, but his heroes were party dissidents, like Harold Macmillan and Winston Churchill; he thought the mainstream Conservative Party of Baldwin and Chamberlain 'too stuck in the old class system'.[4] He was a disciple of Lindsay, the Labour-voting champion of participatory democracy, and of the Labour churchman, William Temple, then Archbishop of York. He left Balliol in the summer of 1939, torn between the Bar and a career in music.

The war changed his life. He was commissioned in the Royal Artillery, became adjutant to the Heavy Anti-Aircraft Regiment, saw action in France in 1944, and ended the war as a Major with the acting rank of lieutenant colonel, an MBE and a mention in despatches. He was a born adjutant – meticulous, dedicated, popular with his men and 'with a genius for organisation'.[5] He left the army in 1946 and, after a brief spell in the civil service and a fill-in job as news editor of the *Church Times*, he was elected to Parliament in 1950, one of the star-studded Conservative intake that also included Enoch Powell, Iain Macleod and Reginald Maudling. Unlike them, he had few opportunities to win public fame. He became an assistant whip in February 1951; deputy chief whip in 1952 and chief whip in December 1955. Once again, he was essentially an adjutant – first to the chief whip, Patrick Buchan-Hepburn, then to Eden and later to Macmillan – running the whips' office with the same meticulous efficiency that he had displayed in his Army days. Though Macleod and Maudling were ahead of him in public reputation, neither could match his feel for the pulse of the parliamentary party.

In 1959, Macmillan rewarded him with a Cabinet post as Minister of Labour; in 1960 he went to the Foreign Office as Home's second in command, with special responsibility for relations with the European continent. When Britain applied for EEC entry the following year he led the British negotiating team, winning golden opinions for his pertinacity, leadership skills and mastery of detail. As President of the Board of Trade under Home, he pushed through the abolition of resale price maintenance in the teeth of ferocious opposition from his own party. As we saw in the last chapter his victory in the Conservative Party's first leadership election followed hard on the heels of its 1964 general election defeat. His ascent to the party leadership was a tribute to his driving ambition and professionalism, but it was also a sign of a loss of nerve on the part of the old governing class. After Home's defeat, patricians were no longer in demand. The cry went up for classless new men. Heath, the grammar-school boy from Broadstairs, seemed the ideal answer to Wilson, the grammar-school boy from the Wirral.

In some ways, he was, though not in the way his party had expected. He was par excellence a man of government, hopelessly ill suited to the frenetic inconsequence of opposition. In the bearpit of Prime Minister's Questions, Wilson easily outclassed him. Heath's political secretary, the future Foreign Secretary, Douglas Hurd, thought his contempt for Wilson struck

a note of genuine puritan protest, which is familiar in British history, sometimes in one party, sometimes in the other. It is the note struck by Pym against the court of Charles I, by Pitt against the Fox–North coalition, by Gladstone against Disraeli, by the Conservatives in 1922 against Lloyd George. It is the outraged assertion of a strict view of what public life is about, after a period in which its rules have been perverted and its atmosphere corrupted.[6]

The trouble was that he could not make his protest sing. Heath was proud, brave, intellectually honest, intensely patriotic, fiercely competitive and profoundly serious, but he never found a language for his powerful emotions. He was curiously angular, even gauche in personal relationships. In some moods he was companionable and charming; he could also be offensively, sometimes unforgivably, rude. He never married; his emotional life was lived through music. (He found an outlet for his competitiveness in ocean racing.) He had even less time for doctrine than Wilson, but he lacked Wilson's gambling streak and ability to snatch at the unforeseen. He was a problem solver, a rationalist, a believer in forward planning and careful staff work. He inspired devoted loyalty among his subordinates; his Cabinet was one of the most harmonious of the century. But, despite his love of music, he had a tin ear when it came to words. His speeches sounded lifeless and somehow strangulated. Too often, he veiled his deeply felt vision of Britain and her future in a fog of bureaucratic management-speak, leading *Private Eye* to lampoon him as the managing director of 'Heathco', forever bombarding his staff with peppery and linguistically maladroit complaints about slackness and inefficiency.

His vision was not as straightforward as it seemed. As befitted a follower of Churchill and Macmillan, Heath was a whig imperialist of sorts. He did his awkward best to practise a politics of inclusion, reminiscent of Macmillan and even of Baldwin. Power-sharing was one of the central themes of his statecraft. He sought to run the economy through a more explicit form of social partnership, embracing the state, organised labour and the organised employers; in Northern Ireland, he tried to coax the Protestant majority and the Catholic minority to share power in a new system of provincial government. But he was too earnest, too impatient, too much of a technocratic new man, to fit comfortably into the relaxed and reactive whig imperialist tradition.

Beneath the surface, there was a strong streak of democratic collectivist *étatisme* in his make-up. In almost Fabian fashion, he cherished the vision of a professionally run state, sweeping away the obstacles to economic and social progress with rationally determined policies, which rational people would be bound to accept. Heath was no dirigiste. Hugh Dalton's vision of a new society, built from the top by the central state, filled him with horror. As a young man he decided against joining the Labour Party because it preached 'a doctrine of control, centralisation and public ownership'.[7] Like his party, he wanted to give somewhat freer rein to market forces; *A*

Better Tomorrow promised state disengagement from industry, an end to compulsory wage controls, tax cuts, a slimmed-down civil service and far-reaching industrial relations reform.

But, for Heath, there was an unspoken caveat. Modest marketisation was not an end in itself; it was a means to the end of a prosperous, confident, respected nation, in which people from backgrounds like his would live fuller lives. His commitment to it was conditional, not absolute. If market forces failed to deliver the goods, the state would step in. It would be a leaner, keener state than Labour's, employing 'the most modern management, budgeting and cost-effectiveness techniques'.[8] But it would still be the state. The tamed capitalism of the post-war years would stay tamed.

∝§∾

Alas for forward planning. Heath and his colleagues had devised a programme for the 1960s, not for the 1970s. The hallmarks of tamed capitalism were stability, predictability and organisation. Though few saw it at the time, Heath's arrival in office coincided with the protracted and painful birth of a turbulent new phase in capitalist history, marked by volatility, disorganisation, fiercer international competition and tighter constraints on national policy-makers.[9] The post-war golden age, with its steadily rising living standards and increasingly generous welfare states, was petering out. The global monetary system foreshadowed at Bretton Woods, with its combination of exchange-rate stability and managed currency adjustments, had already been shaken by the British and French devaluations of 1967 and 1969, not to mention the German revaluation of 1969. By the early 1970s, an 'exploding' American payments deficit, generated by the inflationary methods used to finance the Vietnam war, had started to put the dollar – the pivot of the whole system – under strain as well.[10] World commodity prices were poised for a boom. Real wages were rising fast, while profits – the engine of capitalist accumulation – were squeezed.[11] The premise of *A Better Tomorrow*'s economic programme was that, given the right policies at the centre, Britain would soon join her competitors in the eternal summer of sustained and rapid growth. Heath's tragedy was that it appeared just after autumn had set in.

At home, a rising tide of hedonistic individualism threatened to sweep away the bonds of family, nationhood, civility and shared morality which had been the ligatures of tamed capitalism in its post-war heyday. During the 1960s the number of children born out of wedlock had soared; it soared again in the 1970s, albeit not as sharply. The same was true of divorce – up from an annual average of nearly 40,000 in 1961–5 to nearly 130,000 ten years later. The late 1960s saw a huge increase in the ratio of abortions to live births, presumably reflecting the impact of the Abortion Act, passed during Roy Jenkins' tenure of the Home Office, but the increase continued through the 1970s and, by 1980, the ratio was almost twice what it had been in 1970.

Recorded crime shot up by 121 per cent between 1957 and 1967, and it doubled again over the next decade.[12] Drug abuse became a serious social problem, affecting prosperous middle-class suburbs and fee-paying schools as well as inner-city ghettoes and state comprehensives. Racial harassment of Afro-Caribbeans and South Asians, as well as sometimes violent conflicts between the police and young blacks, were an ugly counterpoint to official proclamations of racial equality and halting efforts to promote racial integration.[13] Britain had never been as cohesive socially or culturally as the whig imperialist and democratic collectivist visions of democracy implied, and she was still much more cohesive than she would become by the start of the twenty-first century; but the cracks in national unity and civic loyalty were becoming more visible than in the early post-war period or even in the 1930s.

The 'romantic revolt', which had called the Wilson Government's blithe economism into question, acquired a harder edge. So-called 'Free Festivals' promised 'social and political protest, drugs and mass sexual activities',[14] and the self-styled anarchists of the 'Angry Brigade' carried out an assassination attempt on the Employment Secretary, Robert Carr. Less brutally, hippie clothes, frenzied adolescent fans at rock concerts, and episodes such as the six-week-long trial of the magazine *Oz* for obscenity and conspiracy seemed to portend a culture war against the mores of adult society and all forms of authority.[15] The student rebellion fizzled out, as the *enragés* of the 1960s acquired families, mortgages and jobs, yet the after-effects lingered. Malcolm Bradbury's biting and hilarious satire, *The History Man*,[16] threw a cruel light on the process. It told the story of Howard Kirk, a 'small bright, intense, active man, of whom you are likely to have heard, for he is much heard of'. In the early 1960s he had been a dim and withdrawn student at a provincial university. By 1968, he was a junior lecturer and campus activist; in the 1970s, he was not only a fashionable sociologist, whose books urged 'new mores, a new deal for man', but a devious careerist and manipulative sexual predator. *The History Man* was caricature, not reportage, but it was close enough to the bone to evoke many pained half-smiles from former student radicals in university common rooms.

In other spheres, disaffection and direct action spread, as the politics of authenticity and identity took hold. One portentous example was the first National Women's Liberation Conference, which took place at Ruskin College, Oxford, in February 1970. 600 women came – double the figure that the organisers had expected. To many of those involved it seemed 'terrifically exciting', the 'most democratic thing there had ever been'.[17] In November it was followed by an experiment with civil disobedience, in which around a hundred feminist militants disrupted the Miss World competition at the Albert Hall with stink bombs, bags of flour and plastic mice. (Originally they had planned to release real white mice, but at the last moment they changed their minds.)

1970 also saw the publication of Germaine Greer's *The Female Eunuch* – a passionate, exuberant appeal to 'castrated' womanhood to emancipate itself 'from helplessness and need. . . . To stop pretending and dissembling, cajoling and manipulating, and begin to control and sympathise. To claim the masculine virtues of magnanimity and generosity and courage.' It was time to focus less on male sexuality and more on female: 'The cunt must come into its own.' (At that sally, one can almost hear her giggle with delighted glee.) Greer went out of her way to outrage successful women like Barbara Castle; they were like the 'white man's black man, the professional nigger'. As for socialist women, they had wasted their time 'waiting hand, foot and buttock on the middle-class revolutionary males in the movement'. There was no point in step-by-step amelioration designed to achieve equal opportunities. 'The old process must be broken, not made new.'[18] Greer, then a lecturer at Warwick University, was a natural media star – brash, bawdy, glamorous and shameless. Some of her more sober feminist sisters looked at her askance, but her wayward brilliance and pyrotechnic language stirred the blood in a way that few of them could do.

Gradually, the movement took off. In March 1971, women's marches were held in Liverpool and London on International Women's Day, with banners demanding equal pay, equal education and job opportunities, free contraception and abortion on demand, and free twenty-four-hour nurseries. More significant than the banners, Anna Coote and Beatrix Campbell wrote later, was the atmosphere of an 'optimistic, iconoclastic piece of theatre'.[19] Consciousness raising through group discussions, Sheila Rowbotham noted, led to the release of 'an extraordinary energy' as women cramped by traditional female roles 'found one another'.[20] 'Patriarchy', 'male chauvinism' and 'sexism' became favoured terms of abuse; on the wilder shores of the movement the orgasm became a topic of hot debate.

❦

In the long run, militant feminist iconoclasm, wilder shores and all, would help to transform the public culture and private lives. Even in the short run it helped to foster the change in the public mood that led the Heath

Government to introduce a bill outlawing sex discrimination in employment, and the subsequent Labour Government to pass a more far-reaching Sex Discrimination Act. It also offered a non-statist model of political change closer to the democratic republican tradition than to those of mainstream politics.

Yet, at this stage, feminism bulked small in the consciousness of Westminster, Whitehall and the media. Of more concern to all of these was a different assertion of collective identity: the continuing militancy of the trade unions, flushed with their victory over the Wilson Government in 1969 and swept by a heady mood of quasi-syndicalism reminiscent of the early decades of the century. Hard on the heels of the Conservatives' arrival in office came a national dock strike, settled by a pay award that gave the union most of what it wanted. In the autumn of 1970 a strike of low-paid, local-government workers was settled by what Heath publicly called a 'patently nonsensical' award of 14 per cent, recommended by a Court of Inquiry, chaired by 'the arch-conciliator' Sir Jack Stamp.[21] In the winter of 1970, in the face of a crippling work to rule by electricity power workers, the government proclaimed a State of Emergency, and appointed yet another Court of Inquiry, this time chaired by another High Court judge, Lord Wilberforce. The outcome was yet another inflationary award. The scene was set for the most turbulent phase in the history of British industrial relations since 1926.

Non-English nationalism posed a seemingly less urgent, but in the long run more profound, challenge to Heath's statecraft. Nationalist parties in Scotland and Wales lost ground in the 1970 election, but nationalist sentiment continued to grow. In Scotland, it was fuelled by the approaching advent of North Sea oil – 'Scotland's oil', as the SNP provocatively called it. Suddenly, the old unionist argument that Scotland was too poor to break the tie with England was stood on its head. Now it looked as if the Scots could look forward to riches, with the English stuck in relative poverty. In Wales, cultural nationalism was sustained by campaigns to protect the Welsh language and enhance its status. Before long, political nationalism in both countries was once again on a rising curve. In a by-election in once unshakeably Labour Merthyr Tydfil in 1972, Plaid Cymru gained 37 per cent of the vote and came within 4000 votes of winning the seat. In 1973, the safe Labour seat of Glasgow, Govan, fell to the bouncy, charismatic and wayward SNP candidate, Margo MacDonald.

By now, the Royal Commission on the Constitution, set up in the dying days of the Wilson Government, had completed its labours. The original chairman, Sir Geoffrey Crowther, had died suddenly in 1972; his successor was the Scottish judge, Lord Kilbrandon. The Kilbrandon Report was published in 1973. The prose was grey and cautious, but there was dynamite in the recommendations.[22] The majority proposed elected assemblies in Scotland and Wales, the former with legislative powers and the latter with executive ones. Although none of the Commissioners supported outright separation, the majority report thus endorsed the central nationalist claim that Scotland and Wales had distinct identities and interests that deserved special recognition. A minority report by the Labour peer, Norman Crowther Hunt, and the economist, Alan Peacock, advocated a uniform scheme of 'executive devolution' to elected assemblies with 'very substantial powers' in Scotland, Wales and five English regions. Crowther Hunt and Peacock denied that there was anything special about Scotland and Wales, but advocated a far-reaching reconstruction of the British state to overcome growing resentment of over-centralisation and inadequate participation right across the territory of the United Kingdom.

On one central point, the differences between majority and minority hardly mattered. What did matter was that a thoroughly establishment body – embracing distinguished lawyers, prominent politicians, the Moderator of the Church of Scotland, a trio of knights and a brace of prominent academics – had accepted the proposition that British government was too centralised and had given its imprimatur to the principle of devolution. Henceforth the fundamentals of Britain's territorial constitution would be in contention, as they had not been since the battles over Irish Home Rule before and immediately after the First World War.

The research underpinning these reports was as significant as the reports themselves. An attitude survey conducted for the Commission recorded a 'diffuse feeling of dissatisfaction' with the existing system of government. Only 5 per cent of the sample thought it worked 'extremely well'; 49 per cent thought it either needed 'a great deal of improvement' or 'could be improved quite a lot'. In turn, 55 per cent felt 'very' or 'fairly' powerless in the face of government.[23] In a later study a quarter of the sample said that they were prepared to take part in illegal forms of protest, ranging from rent strikes to blocking traffic and occupying buildings, while almost half thought the country was 'run by a few big interests concerned only for themselves'.[24] The potential for protest, the author suggested, was highest among the politically competent, who accepted democratic norms but believed that the political system flouted them. The days when Britain had seemed a model 'civic culture' had long gone. By the middle of the decade the ebullient scholar-politician John Mackintosh, a once and future politics professor as well as an eloquent revisionist Labour MP, was able to report that, at a meeting in a Border village,

Three hundred people were present to protest at a 246 per cent increase in
the local rates. Towards the end of the meeting, in what is a deeply
traditional and conservative rural area, a well-dressed man arose to move
that all those present should refuse to pay rates till certain points had been
met. The motion was later withdrawn but that it was moved at all in such
a community was amazing.

Yet MPs of all parties find themselves going from one meeting to another
where forceful actions or breaches of the law are proposed. In recent
months, the author has been asked to support the Scottish school teachers'
strike, the blockade of ports by inshore fishermen and several suggested
rent and rate strikes.[25]

In his introduction to the volume in which Mackintosh's essay appeared,
Anthony King wrote that, in the 1960s, 'We had got used to the crisis in
our economy. Now we are beginning to wonder whether we are not also
confronted by a crisis in our polity. ... Politically as well as economically,
we in Britain can feel the ground shifting, ever so slightly, under our feet.'[26]

In Northern Ireland, the ground did not just shift; it shook. By the time
Labour left office, the uneasy peace that Callaghan appeared to have imposed
on the province was beginning to unravel.[27] At first the Catholic community
had welcomed British troops as protectors against a possible Protestant
pogrom but, by Easter 1970, Belfast Catholics were pelting the troops with
bottles and stones. After the election, the unravelling speeded up. In July
1970, the British Army commander imposed a thirty-five-hour curfew on
the (Catholic) Falls Road area of Belfast. The troops discovered plentiful
supplies of arms and ammunition, but their discovery came at a high price.
In the eyes of the Catholic community, they were now invaders rather than
protectors.

The chief beneficiary was the intransigently nationalist 'Provisional' IRA,
which draped itself in the mantle of the Fenian tradition and sought to
unite the island of Ireland by force. 'Provo' membership soared from around
a hundred in the early summer of 1970 to nearly 800 by the end of the year.
From then on the province seemed caught in a downward spiral of terroristic
violence and clumsy repression. The death toll mounted inexorably, from
thirteen in 1969 to twenty-five in 1970 to 174 in 1971. In August 1971, the
Northern Ireland government, with the London government's unen-
thusiastic acquiescence, tried to smash the IRA by interning a number of
terrorists without trial. The result was another wave of violence and a
further surge in IRA recruitment. During a riot in the Catholic Bogside of
Londonderry on 'Bloody Sunday', 30 January 1972, British paratroopers
shot thirteen Catholic civilians dead.

The Heath Government decided enough was enough, suspended Stormont and took power to rule Northern Ireland directly. Meanwhile, violence escalated: in 1972, the death toll reached a staggering 467.[28] A brief chink of light appeared in 1973. Thanks largely to the political skill of Heath's Northern Ireland Secretary, William Whitelaw, a new Assembly was elected by proportional representation, with a new power-sharing executive, representing both communities, answering to it. A conference between the main Northern Ireland parties and the governments of the United Kingdom and the Irish Republic, held at the Sunningdale Civil Service College at the end of the year, agreed to set up a Council of Ireland, heavily weighted with symbolism despite its lack of power. Unfortunately, the weight was too much for the Protestant community to bear. Brian Faulkner, the pro-Sunningdale Unionist leader, was repudiated by his party; and by early 1974 the light had faded. When the Conservatives left office, the oldest and bloodiest ethnic conflict in the territory of the British state was as far from a solution as ever.

The implacable presence of Enoch Powell, haunting the government benches like a prophet of doom, posed a different sort of threat. His romantic English nationalism was as intransigent as the romantic Irish nationalism of the Provos; unlike them he coupled his nationalism with a crystalline, passionate and, for many Conservatives, increasingly convincing attack on the Keynesian common sense shared by both front benches. In the 1970 general election, he had called for a Conservative victory, but the themes of his campaign – an immediate halt to immigration, an attack on the bipartisan consensus for EEC entry and a warning that mysterious 'enemies within' were bent on weakening the nation's will[29] – had been deeply offensive as well as embarrassing to the party leadership. Had Heath lost, Powell might have made a bid for the succession. As things were, he could only watch and wait – sustained by his extraordinary forensic skill, his platform magnetism and the knowledge that he had a mass appeal that no other Conservative could rival. An unacknowledged duel between Powell and Heath for the soul of the Conservative Party would become one of the central themes of British politics for half a decade.

❦

The first year of Heath's prime ministership saw one historic success. Despite de Gaulle's second veto in November 1967, the Wilson Government's application to join the European Community had never been withdrawn. After de Gaulle resigned as President of France in April 1969, his successor, the 'crafty Auvergnat' Georges Pompidou,[30] made it clear that he was not, in principle, opposed to British membership. At the end of the year an EEC summit agreed to open negotiations with Britain; by early 1970, Whitehall's preparations were well under way. Had Labour won the election, the chief British negotiator would have been the genial Scottish former Gaitskellite, George Thomson. Instead, the job went to the devoted 'Heathman', Anthony Barber.[31] After Barber's promotion to the chancellorship of the Exchequer, following Iain Macleod's sudden death in July 1970, the shrewd, physically tireless, but engagingly laid-back QC, Geoffrey Rippon, took over. His negotiating brief was, to all intents and purposes, identical with the outgoing Labour Government's.

There was a sharp contrast between the negotiations that followed and those of the Macmillan Government in 1961–2. This time, the British knew perfectly well that they, and not the Community, were the *demandeurs;* that they had to accept the Community system as it stood, including the Common Agricultural Policy and the financial arrangements that the Six had hammered out among themselves; and that the only questions for negotiation were the nature and duration of the transitional period before Britain was subject to the full rigour of Community rules. That left plenty to discuss – the fate of British imports from New Zealand and from Commonwealth sugar producers; the period over which Britain would adapt to the CAP; above all, the British contribution to the Community budget.[32]

But as time went on it became clear that the thicket of detail concealed a much more fundamental question: the ancient, perennial question of Britain's relationship with France. Unlike de Gaulle, Pompidou was not opposed to British entry as such. Yet, though he was prepared, in principle, to let Britain in, he had to be convinced that the British Government shared his view of the European project; that Britain had broken free of her 'instinctive and deep-seated attachments to the outside world'; that she too sought a 'European Europe'.[33] What counted for Pompidou, in other words, were Britain's identity and vocation. Only if he were satisfied about these, would he make sure that the negotiations in Brussels came to fruition.

Heath rose to the challenge as no other post-war British prime minister could have done. Europeanism had been a leitmotiv of his political career – in a sense, of his adult life. Its roots went back to his horrified encounter with Nazi Germany as a young man, and to his experience of war-devastated Germany as a member of the British occupation forces. In his maiden speech he had deplored the Attlee Government's lukewarm response to the Schuman Plan; as the Macmillan Government's chief negotiator over EEC entry in 1961–2, he had acquired a vast range of highly placed continental contacts, among them the 'small, dark, witty' Michel Jobert, later Pompidou's private secretary.[34] As Godkin lecturer at Harvard in 1967, he had proposed that Britain and France should pool their nuclear forces and hold them in trust for Europe – a heresy to the defence establishment in London as well as in Washington.[35] He was not exactly a Gaullist (nor, of course, was Pompidou) but his robustly unsentimental approach to the United States had a strong Gaullist flavour about it. He had no time for romantic Churchillian talk about the 'special relationship' with the United States; for him, Europe came first, and he made sure the Americans and French both knew it.

Heath had to wait until late May 1971, ten months after the formal entry negotiations had started, before he could beard Pompidou. He did so as Pompidou's guest in Paris. Their talks lasted for two intense days, punctuated by glittering banquets and fulsome toasts. They covered a wide range of topics, including the future of the French language in an enlarged Community, the sterling balances and Britain's budgetary contribution.[36] But it was the mood that mattered, not the detail. Heath set out his stall with a slightly clumsy sincerity that obviously endeared him to his host. In his student days in the 1930s, he pointed out, 'the British had always regarded themselves as Europeans. . . . It was only during the past 25 years that it had come to seem as if our natural connection might be with the United States. But we were in fact still part of Europe.' As for the special relationship,

It was sometimes said that Britain only sought partnership with the United States. His frank reply to this was that there could be no satisfactory partnership, even if Britain wanted it, between two powers one of which was barely a quarter the size of the other. In Europe, on the other hand, such a partnership was possible with countries of the same size and within a European Community applying the same rules and working to the same principles. His purpose was to see a strong Europe, which could speak with a single voice after a full discussion. . . . He regarded this of particular importance in the political field. He did not regard it as healthy that world affairs should be settled between themselves between the two Super Powers.[37]

By the end, Pompidou was positively purring. He had, he declared, 'been convinced that the British Government was finally resolved fully to enter the Community and to contribute to its deepening'.[38] At the subsequent press conference, he announced that the mood established during the talks had convinced him that the negotiations would succeed. A month later, Geoffrey Rippon returned to London from Luxembourg with the news that they had done so. It was a triumphant moment for Heath and an epochal one for the British state and Britain's identity.

There was a thorn in the rose. Understandably, Heath and his colleagues had assumed that the Labour opposition would stick to the pro-entry position of the Wilson Government. They had reckoned without the wild mood swing that convulsed the Labour movement after the 1970 defeat. To growing numbers of Labour and trade-union activists, the record of the Wilson Government now seemed shameful at best, and treacherous at worst. Its attempt to join the 'capitalist', 'reactionary', 'inward-looking' EEC became a symptom of ideological turpitude. That mood made it impossible for Wilson to continue the deft manoeuvres which had won him Cabinet support for his EEC entry application. Slowly, inelegantly and with a palpable lack of conviction, he shifted his ground. On 17 July 1971, a month after Rippon's triumphant return from Luxembourg, he told a special Labour Party conference that he opposed entry on the Heath Government's terms; Roy Jenkins, the leader of the Labour pro-Europeans, later compared him to 'someone being sold down the river into slavery, drifting away, depressed but unprotesting'.[39]

Slavish or not, Wilson's formula was endorsed by crushing majorities at Labour's annual conference and in the parliamentary party. That did not prevent a remarkable rebellion by Labour pro-Europeans when the Commons voted on EEC entry on 28 October 1971. In the most momentous parliamentary division since 1940, the House approved the government's decision to join the Community by 356 to 244 votes. In defiance of a three-line whip, and amid angry scenes, sixty-nine Labour MPs voted with the government while another twenty abstained.

But that glory day for Labour Europeanism was followed by a long, dark night. The Treaty of Accession was not signed until January 1972; though the bill giving effect to it eventually reached the statute book, during its passage the government's majority often fell to single figures. A few 'kamikaze' Labour rebels voted with the government in key divisions, but the official party line was Wilson's – opposition to entry on the government's terms, though not to EEC membership in principle. By the time Britain entered the Community in January 1973, Labour was committed to 'renegotiate' the terms on which it did so and to put the results to the British people, either in a general election or in a referendum. What would happen if the 'renegotiations' failed was swathed in embarrassed obscurity.

None of this detracted from Heath's achievement Thanks overwhelmingly to him, Britain was now a full Member State of the Community, with all the rights and obligations that that involved. Community law took precedence over British law; on matters covered by the treaties, the European Court of Justice in Luxembourg outranked all British courts. Community membership, declared Lord Denning in a vivid simile in 1975, 'is like an incoming tide. It flows into the estuaries and up the rivers. It cannot be held back.'[40] The *acquis communitaire* of the preceding fifteen years applied to Britain as much as to the Six; British officials served in the European Commission alongside those of the other Member States; though the Labour Party boycotted it, Conservative MPs sat in the European Parliament, and one or two of them played notable parts in it.

On virtually every weekday, British ministers and officials could be found somewhere in Brussels, taking part in the never-ending process of horse-trading and coalition-building that formed the stuff of Community politics. British interest groups lobbied the Commission and the Parliament as enthusiastically as their continental counterparts; Whitehall gradually acquired a cadre of senior officials with Brussels experience. British foreign trade was gradually reorientated towards the Community; thanks partly to the Common Agricultural Policy, Britain became significantly more self-sufficient in food.

Yet something was lacking. Institutionally and economically, Britain belonged to the Community. Politically and, above all, emotionally, she remained semi-detached. The vision with which Heath had melted Pompidou's heart – the vision of Britain as a fully European nation, collaborating with her partners to develop a united European stance in global politics, and spurning an illusory partnership with the United States – remained unrealised. Part of the responsibility lay with Labour's post-election change of line. So long as the main opposition party refused to commit itself to membership, a question mark was bound to hang over Britain's European vocation – not least in Britain.

But that was only part of the story. In truth, Heath's was a minority vision. He held it himself with passionate, if inarticulate, intensity; so did the Heathmen, the inner core of Labour Europeans and some (though not all) members of pro-European pressure groups like the European Movement and the Labour Committee for Europe. Elsewhere the tom-toms of the special relationship continued to beat. In his stubborn, gawky way, Heath did his best to coax his country out of its old whig imperialist identity and into a new, post-imperial, European one. The verdict of history has to be that his best was not good enough. The vacuum of rhetoric and self-understanding left by the end of empire remained unfilled. The British were still not sure who they were.

⚭

Second only to Community membership among Heath's most cherished causes was reform of industrial relations law, which had become a flagship Conservative policy well before the 1970 election. *A Better Tomorrow* had committed the party to introduce a 'comprehensive Industrial Relations Bill' in the first session of the new Parliament. For Heath, the commitment had a double significance. It symbolised his puritan disdain for Wilson's shilly-shallying: the Conservatives would act where Wilson had wobbled. It appealed both to the whig imperialist and to the democratic collectivist in him. The state, as the custodian of the public interest, would tame obscurantist and selfish private interests as it had done in the battle over resale price maintenance; in doing so, it would lay the foundations for a new form of social partnership. For him, there could be no compromise: statutory reform of industrial relations was 'the centre-piece of our long-term economic programme'.[41]

In October 1971, the new government published a consultative document, setting out the principles that it proposed to carry into law. The details were complex, but the crux was simple: British industrial relations would henceforth be regulated by law instead of by custom. Two innovations lay at the heart of the whole exercise. A National Industrial Relations Court (NIRC) would enforce the law; a new Registrar of Trade Unions and Employers' Associations would become an agent of state intervention in union affairs. A range of specified 'unfair industrial practices' would be actionable, and there would be no immunity for those found guilty of them. Written collective agreements would be legally enforceable unless the parties agreed that they should not be. The Registrar would make sure that the rule books of registered unions protected members' rights and laid down democratic procedures for union governance. Registration would not be compulsory, but failure to register would incur heavy costs. Unregistered unions would liable for damages if their members went on strike. The penalty that the NIRC could impose on a registered union would be limited to £100,000; there would be no limit for unregistered ones. Registration would be a Chinese wall separating the law-abiding and protected sheep from the potentially lawless and unprotected goats. The sheep would have more rights than they had had before. The goats would be thrust back into the legal limbo that the unions had inhabited in the nineteenth century.

Heath and his colleagues were not anti-union. Nor were they perfervid free-market zealots. They said they wanted strong unions, and they meant it. Their objective was an orderly, disciplined, hierarchical trade-union movement, co-operating with management and the state in pursuit of rapid growth. Ironically, their vision was not a million miles away from the corporatist model that prevailed in West Germany. However, it *was* far removed from Jack Jones's confused yearning for a decentralist, participative but union-dominated form of industrial democracy. It also fell foul of a bilious and often xenophobic proletarianism – epitomised by the rasping, chronically disruptive new miners' MP, Dennis Skinner – that seeped into Labour politics in the 1970s.

It was hard to grasp the real nature of this proletarianism then, and it is harder still in retrospect. Skinner and his counterparts were as nihilistic as Alan Sillitoe's Arthur Seaton. In some ways, they harked back to the class warriors of the early 1920s, but there was a curiously formulaic quality about the anger they vented. Though they knew what they were against, they gave little sign of knowing what they were for. After a trade-union dinner where he encountered a much milder form of proletarianism, the renegade bourgeois, Tony Benn, compared it to the American slogan, 'black is beautiful',[42] but this was self-deception. American blacks were a rising group, imbued with the sense that history was on their side. Britain's white working class was already in irreversible decline, squeezed between technological change on the one hand and wider educational opportunities on the other – a dying whale, beached by the tide of history.

Not all union leaders shared Jones's dream, but almost all of them agreed with him that the unions must not 'crawl to the Government'.[43] When the TUC discovered that the fundamental principles of the consultative document were not open to negotiation, it refused to take part in further talks. In February 1971, it organised a monster protest march through London, 140,000 strong. Meanwhile, the parliamentary Labour Party, desperate to purge itself of the Wilson Government's attempt to curb trade-union autonomy, fought the bill clause by clause and night after night, amid frequent scenes. On one notorious occasion, the opposition division lobby resounded to the strains of 'The Red Flag', 'Cwm Rhondda' and 'We Shall Overcome'. After the Division, Labour MPs trooped back into the chamber where they stood in their places, lustily singing the 'Red Flag' while astonished Conservatives threw pennies at them.[44]

Inevitably, these efforts were of no avail; in August 1971 the bill passed into law. But that was not the end of the story; if anything it was the beginning. With the simple device of 'advising' unions not to register, the TUC tore the heart out of the Act. A farcical final chapter followed, with the NIRC, the Court of Appeal and the Law Lords at loggerheads; a hitherto obscure functionary known as the Official Solicitor appearing in the nick of time to save a group of shop stewards from prison; and the NIRC reversing a decision to commit another group of stewards to prison when the government was confronted by a rash of local strikes and the threat of a one-day general strike. By the end of July 1972, the Act had effectively expired, to the manifest relief of all concerned. To militant trade unionists, one moral seemed plain. Labour politicians had tramped through the division lobbies of the House of Commons to no effect, but the strong right arm of the organised working class had won the day. First the unions had defeated a Labour Government. Now they had defeated a Conservative one. It would have been hard to devise a more persuasive argument for militancy.

The Industrial Relations Act was not the only government policy in tatters. The Conservatives had entered office pledged to the 'utter' rejection of compulsory incomes policies, but they had also inherited an alarming wage explosion, with increases running at an annual rate of 15 per cent. They left the private sector to its own devices, but they had to have a policy of some sort for the public sector, if only because its ultimate paymaster was the government. After some havering, and in the wake of the inflationary 1970 settlements mentioned above, they adopted a so-called 'N minus 1' policy, under which each public-sector settlement would be lower than the last. 'N minus 1' worked fairly well in 1971 when a prolonged postal workers' strike ended with a settlement 5 per cent lower than their claim.

In 1972 disaster supervened. The late 1960s had seen rising discontent in Britain's coalfields, due partly to a precipitate rundown in the industry, partly to a steady slippage in the miners' position in the earnings league, and partly to an egalitarian national power-loading agreement, which cut face-workers' incomes in the more prosperous areas. In 1971 the bluff, good-hearted, but unreliable Lancastrian, Joe Gormley, was elected President of the NUM on the ticket of an aggressive wage offensive. The union promptly put in a claim for increases equivalent to 47 per cent and began a national overtime ban.[45] The Coal Board, its hands tied by the government's N minus 1 policy, offered 7 per cent. The NUM proceeded to hold a strike ballot of the membership. On 8 January 1972 it launched the first official nationwide miners' strike since 1921.

The response was extraordinary. The miners liked to think of themselves as the Guards Brigade of organised labour, and they fought for their cause with the pride and self-discipline of an elite regiment. They were fighting the Heath Government, but they were fighting even more for self-respect and for what they saw as justice. In tight-knit mining communities, where group solidarity was a way of life, the atmosphere was that of a nation at war. Natural leaders appeared, as if from nowhere; ordinary miners performed miracles of improvisation and organisation. At the start they picketed the pits, but it soon became clear that there was no point: the miners were solid. In a stroke of genius, picketing was then extended to power stations and ports. At that point, a hitherto unknown Yorkshire miner by the name of Arthur Scargill came into his own. He made no bones about his objectives. As he later explained to Robin Blackburn, 'you will not get real control of the society in which we live unless you commit and convince the working class of *the need to struggle*. ... The issue is a very simple one: it is *them* and it is *us*.' In the 1972 strike,

[W]e took the view that we were in a class war. We were not playing cricket on the village green like they did in '26. We were out to defeat Heath and Heath's policies because we were fighting a government. Anyone who thinks otherwise was living in cloud-cuckoo land. We had to declare *war* on them and the only way you could declare war was to attack the vulnerable points. They were the points of *energy*, the power stations, the coke depots, the points of supply. [Italics in original.][46]

Scargill and his helpers despatched 'flying pickets' to power stations as far away as Great Yarmouth, Ipswich and Bedford; by early February he could claim that virtually all the ports and power stations in Yorkshire and East Anglia had been closed. His most famous coup came in the second week of February when a crowd of between 10,000 and 15,000 pickets, with pipers in attendance, clashed with the police outside a huge coke depot at Saltley in Birmingham, eventually forcing the Chief Constable to close the gates. By now the government had declared a state of emergency (its third since coming to power), and there was talk of sewage flowing in the streets if the strike continued.[47] The Cabinet introduced a three-day working week and appointed a Court of Inquiry, headed by the ever-ready and ever-generous peacemaker, Lord Wilberforce. The Wilberforce Report conceded that the miners had justice on their side and recommended increases amounting to 27 per cent. After a face-to-face meeting with a humiliated Heath, who conceded a long additional 'shopping list' of minor claims and marginal adjustments, the NUM called off the strike. For miners with long memories (and long memories were ubiquitous in mining communities), it was a moment of glory, wiping out the humiliations of 1921 and 1926. No one foresaw that, in the long run, the miners themselves would be the chief victims.

⁂

N minus 1 was dead, but the need for wage restraint was very much alive. As the Employment Secretary, Robert Carr, told the Cabinet immediately after the strike, the miners had won 'because they had great economic power and exercised it almost to the limit. We must now keep the miners as a wholly exceptional case.'[48] This was easier said than done. Heath's first eighteen months as prime minister had seen a sharp rise in unemployment – a belated effect of the deflationary 'hard slog' of the Jenkins years. In 1971, Anthony Barber had tried to bring the figure down with tax cuts of around

£550 million, but to no avail. In January 1972, unemployment reached the unadjusted total of 1 million, then universally seen as a crisis level. (The adjusted total was lower, but for politicians and commentators the headline figure was what counted.) Meanwhile, growth and investment had been disappointingly low. For Heath, the combination of lagging growth and rising unemployment was more than a political threat; it drove a stake through the heart of his whole project. High growth and high investment were necessary corollaries of his vision of Britain as a strong and confident European power, taking her rightful place alongside the leading nations of the Six; he also believed they were essential if British industry were to take advantage of the dynamic market that it was about to enter and to stand up to European competition. When the Conservatives entered office, inflation had been their chief bogey; by early 1972 high unemployment and low growth had taken its place.

Heath, the surface whig imperialist, gave way to Heath, the closet democratic collectivist. This second Heath fulminated endlessly against the private sector's risk aversion and lectured bankers about their failure to emulate the investment behaviour of their German counterparts.[49] In one of his few quotable phrases he declared that the dubious financial operations of the Lonhro group had revealed 'the unpleasant and unacceptable face of capitalism'.[50] More importantly, he also turned Conservative industrial policy upside down. Chinks had already appeared in the disengagement project on which the Conservatives had fought the election: in 1971, the government had nationalised Rolls-Royce and poured money into United Clyde Shipbuilders rather than let them go to the wall. But these were minor aberrations; in general Heath and his colleagues stuck to their election policy. In 1972 they scrapped disengagement altogether in favour of sweeping industrial interventionism, more *étatiste* in conception than the Wilson Government's. An Industry Act gave the Secretary of State power to provide any form of financial aid to any industry or firm when he judged that the economy would benefit. An Industrial Development Advisory Board of business tycoons and an Industrial Development Executive in the Department of Trade and Industry completed the ensemble.

Edmund Dell, a Minister of State under Wilson, was exaggerating a little when he complained that Heath, having marched his troops up the hill to extreme disengagement, was now marching them down to 'selective squandermania ... without precedent and without parliamentary control'.[51] But the exaggeration was forgivable. Under the Industry Act, public money was poured into investment programmes in coal and steel, aid for job creation and regional development. And the Industry Act was not alone. In order to raise the growth rate to an annual rate of 5 per cent, Barber's 1972 budget cut taxes by £1.2 billion and increased the deficit to £2.4 billion. Between them, the Industry Act and the budget gave a powerful boost to inflation, as did a rapid growth in the money supply following the removal of quantitative controls on bank advances in late 1971.

Albeit in a roundabout way, the same was true of the government's decision to let sterling float in June 1972. The decision was taken in the wake of a convulsive, worldwide currency realignment caused by the endemic weakness of the dollar; considered purely as an economic device, it was not inflationary. Its political significance was a different matter. The fixed exchange rate had acted as a reality check on policy-making, forcing ministers to face the consequences of their actions for currency stability. In practice, the check had sometimes been ignored: that was the meaning of the Maudling boom of 1964. But at least it had been there. Floating took it away. There was no longer an unmistakable last ditch in which the custodians of the currency would have to stand and fight. The Treasury had lost its most powerful argument for fiscal continence. Sterling slowly floated down, giving a further push to inflation in the process.

Now began the last act of Heath's tragedy.[52] The inflationary pressures building up in the system were too strong to be left unchecked. The only way to check them without destroying any hope of high growth and low unemployment was to curb wage increases. But, after the miners' victory, 'leaning on the public sector' with some variant of N minus 1 was ruled out. The logic pointed irresistibly to a full-blown, explicit incomes policy of the sort that had come to grief under Harold Wilson, and that the Conservatives had relentlessly pooh-poohed. To win trade-union support for, or at least acquiescence in, such a policy, Heath had to talk to the union leaders. Besides, he *wanted* to talk to them. The left's caricature of him as a hard-faced free-marketeer, deliberately seeking confrontation with organised labour, could not have been further from the truth; when Jack Jones came to write his memoirs he conceded that no prime minister 'could compare with Ted Heath in the efforts he made to establish a spirit of camaraderie with trade union leaders'.[53]

Heath wanted more than camaraderie, however. In an anguished television broadcast immediately after the miners' strike he exclaimed, 'We must find a more sensible way to settle our differences.'[54] He had become – had always been – a corporatist in all but name. In the government's salad days, he had hoped that statutory reform of industrial relations would procure a trade-union movement with the strength and self-discipline to co-operate with the state and the employers in pursuit of the national interest. The unions' decision to boycott the Industrial Relations Act killed that hope. Incomes policy seemed to offer a different route to the same destination.

In the summer of 1972 a 'most courteous' Heath[55] held a series of exploratory talks with the TUC and CBI. Exhaustive, long-drawn-out negotiations over a voluntary incomes policy followed in October and November. For Heath and his colleagues, more was at stake than wage restraint. They sought a new, more muscular and more explicit system of corporatist power-sharing or, in Heath's words to the House of Commons, 'a more sane, rational and peaceful method of organising the whole of our national economy'.[56] But the union leaders lacked the stomach for the responsibilities of Germanic social partnership. In the last resort, they preferred the adversarial jousting that they had grown up with. They shied away, insisting that they could not agree to voluntary wage controls without statutory price controls, as well as a long list of other sweeteners, including renegotiation of the Common Agricultural Policy and the suspension of the Industrial Relations Act. Not surprisingly, Heath broke off the talks. On 6 November 1972, he announced that the government would legislate for an immediate freeze on wages, prices, dividends and rents. It was a black day for him and, as the next ten years would show, an equally black day for tamed capitalism.

✿

The first Conservative backbencher to put a Commons question to Heath after the freeze announcement was Enoch Powell. He was astonishingly brutal:

> Does my Right. Hon. Friend know that it is fatal for any Government, party or person to seek to govern in direct opposition to the principles on which they were entrusted with the right to govern? In introducing a compulsory control on wages and prices, in contravention of the deepest commitments of this party, has my Right. Hon. Friend taken leave of his senses?[57]

Powell's tone was not calculated to win followers on the Conservative benches, even among those who shared his doubts about government policy. But he was not trying to win a following; quite deliberately, he was 'a voice rather than a leader'.[58] He sought to give shape to the suppressed mixture of uneasiness, resentment and unhappiness in the Conservative ranks with fierce, challenging phrases in which the party would recognise its true self.

He could not be accused of failing to vote in line with his voice. In the course of the 1970 Parliament he voted against the government in eighty divisions on European issues, and in more than thirty on other matters.[59]

Although he rarely mustered enough troops to defeat the leadership, he was not totally isolated. Among a handful of others, John Biffen, a future Leader of the House, and Nicholas Ridley, a future Environment Secretary, followed essentially the same line. In any case, what mattered to Powell was the rhetorical war, in which his fortunes steadily improved, not the arithmetical battles that he was doomed to lose. No one who sat in that Parliament will easily forget the sight of Powell uncoiling himself from his seat on the government back benches to assault his leaders with beautifully constructed philippics, delivered, without a note, in the harsh yet curiously captivating tones of the Black Country. The sight of Conservative members listening with uneasy, sometimes almost furtive, attention was equally instructive. As Tony Benn noted, even Labour MPs were mesmerised 'like rabbits caught in a headlamp'.[60]

Powell had delivered plenty of passionate philippics against EEC entry, but to little effect: the moment for Tory nationalism had not yet come. On the economy, however, the mood of the time was beginning to shift in his direction. His case was disarmingly simple. Inflation had nothing to do with the trade unions or with wages. On inflation, the unions were 'as innocent as lambs, pure white as the driven snow'.[61] It followed that an attempt to curb inflation with a prices and incomes policy was 'as absurd as if someone, having dropped a heavy article on his toe, were to say: "I really must get down to altering the law of gravitation".'[62] Compulsion, whether 'exercised by machine guns or by firing CBEs, OBEs and MBEs', could not suspend the laws of supply and demand.[63] Inflation was caused by excessive growth in the money supply, and for that the responsibility lay exclusively with government. The argument was not new; it was a distillation of the quantity theory of money, which had been the orthodoxy of the age before Keynes, and with which Keynes himself had had more sympathy than his more simple-minded disciples imagined.

In 1958, when Powell had resigned from the government along with Thorneycroft and Birch, it seemed quaint, old-fashioned and slightly absurd; vulgar Keynesianism still reigned supreme in Whitehall and Westminster, and more sophisticated forms of Keynesianism in the academy. By the 1970s, however, the Keynesian hegemony had started to break down. In the United States, the Chicago economist, Milton Friedman, had already given new respectability to the quantity theory of old days, and in Britain economists such as Harry Johnson, Alan Walters and David Laidler followed where Friedman had led.

The anti-Keynesian tide was not confined to university economics departments. In 1955, the millionaire chicken farmer, Anthony Fisher, had founded the Institute of Economic Affairs (IEA) to combat Keynesian orthodoxy and propagate the teachings of Friedrich von Hayek, the leading prophet of what became the New Right. It had started slowly, but by the early 1970s it had become a powerhouse of free-market thinking and propaganda, pumping out an increasingly influential flood of pamphlets, articles and public lectures.[64] Meanwhile, the two most brilliant economic journalists of the day – Callaghan's son-in-law, Peter Jay, the economic editor of *The Times*, and Samuel Brittan of the *Financial Times* – added intellectually elegant and politically explosive fuel to the anti-Keynesian flames.

In 1973, as the Barber boom roared ahead, Powellite economics began to find an audience on the government benches. In April 1973, the freeze announced in November 1972 was followed by stage two of the policy, limiting wage increases to £1 a week plus 4 per cent. Stages one and two were remarkably successful. Real wage increases fell quite sharply, despite a rapid reduction in unemployment. There was scarcely a cheep from the unions, and the year saw a dramatic fall in the number of working days lost in strikes.[65] At 6 per cent, the growth rate in the first six months of 1973 exceeded the government's best hopes. Yet all was not well. As measured by the broad M3 definition, which includes bank deposits, the money supply soared to nearly three times the level of 1970–1,[66] helping to generate an explosion in house prices and a speculative frenzy in the City. The pound continued its downward float, while the entire world experienced a surging commodity boom. Not surprisingly, consumer prices in Britain continued to rise, at a faster rate than in 1972.[67]

Keynesian economists were apt to argue that, without the incomes policy, prices would have risen even more, but to growing numbers of unhappy Conservatives such arguments seemed sophistical. The fact was that compulsory wage controls had been in operation, that the unions had respected them and that inflation had still not been checked. Yet Heath and Barber ploughed doggedly on. In March 1973, Barber brought in a neutral budget, designed to maintain the 5 per cent growth rate for another year; preparatory work on a more flexible stage three began in April.

Then came two devastating blows. In July the NUM conference instructed the executive to seek a 35 per cent wage increase in the following year. In mid-October, OPEC, the cartel of oil-producing nations, announced that the posted price of oil would be increased by nearly 70 per cent. (A further increase was announced in December, and by early January 1974 the price had almost quadrupled.) For the time being, at least, the bonanza of cheap energy that had helped to sustain the long post-war boom was over. Developed economies all suffered a double shock – inflation resulting from much higher import prices, and deflation caused by a precipitate cut in demand. Britain, with her poor investment record and lagging competitiveness, seemed destined to suffer more than most. As the Chancellor, Anthony Barber, warned in a Cabinet paper in early December, the country was 'now facing the gravest economic crisis since the end of the war'. 'Substantial' spending cuts were essential; the current spending programme had presupposed GDP growth of 3.5 per cent in 1974, but in fact it was likely to fall.[68]

The assumptions underpinning the government's whole strategy were suddenly out of date. A political genius – a Lloyd George or a Franklin Roosevelt – might have seized the opportunity to redraw the political map and lead the contending interests out of their trenches. But Heath was not a genius. He was simply a brave, honest, stubborn patriot, not particularly fast on his feet. By now, stage three was ready, and he was not the man to abort it. With hideously unfortunate timing he unveiled it on 30 October, just after OPEC had transformed the economic climate that its architects had taken for granted. On 7 November the new limits on wage increases came into effect.

The government spent the best part of the next three months torn between two incompatible imperatives.[69] It was desperately anxious to avoid another battle with the miners, but it was equally anxious to maintain the integrity of its incomes policy. Following secret talks between Heath and Gormley, stage three had been furnished with loopholes designed to allow the miners to win a handsome increase. Nevertheless, it was, by definition, a national policy, applicable to everyone. Ministers were happy for the miners to do better out of it than most other workers: that was why they had constructed it in the way they had. But they feared, with good reason, that it would collapse if the miners openly flouted it and that the government's authority would then be in ruins.

Unfortunately, the miners had no interest in maintaining the integrity of the incomes policy or of the government. Some of them – notably the dour, uncompromising, but eloquent Scottish Communist, Mick McGahey – were eager to bust the policy and Heath with it. Most were indifferent to the policy, and even to Heath, and merely sought to use their bargaining power – now enhanced by the oil crisis – to squeeze all they could out of a government on the run. Heath, the Coal Board and even the TUC scrabbled desperately for a formula that would allow the government to treat the miners as a special case without appearing to do so, but it was a doomed enterprise. To Roy Jenkins it seemed that Heath and his colleagues had been afflicted with 'a reverse Midas touch';[70] the Cabinet Secretary, Sir John Hunt, would later recall that 'the smell of death was around.'[71]

Meanwhile tempers rose. Ineptly, the Coal Board made an offer equivalent to a 16 per cent increase – the maximum allowable under the government's policy – at the outset of its talks with the union, leaving no room for further negotiation. The NUM rejected it and banned overtime. The government declared yet another state of emergency and then imposed a three-day week. There was growing pressure in the Conservative Party for an early election, but Heath resisted it: an election fought on an anti-union ticket would have made nonsense of his vision of corporatist collaboration in the national interest. Then the NUM executive crossed its Rubicon. On 24 January 1974, it decided to hold a pithead ballot in which 81 per cent voted for a strike. On 7 February, Heath announced that Parliament would be dissolved forthwith and a general election held three weeks later. On the same day, Powell denounced the election as 'fraudulent' and declared that he would not be a candidate in it.

THE REVENGE OF ENOCH POWELL

A strange air of unreality hung over the general election of February 1974. Heath sought a new mandate, but he could not explain what it would be for. He hoped to sound a tocsin summoning 'the moderate and reasonable people of Britain' to battle against over-mighty sectional interests, but he was still the same honest, rational, fair-minded man he had always been, and sounding tocsins was not his style. Besides, he knew that if he won, he would once again have to deal with the sectional interests concerned; and he was anxious to avoid inflammatory language that might make his task harder. The result was that his call to arms was limp and anti-climactic. Though he excoriated unnamed 'militants', he carefully eschewed union-bashing; when he was asked how an election victory would help to end the miners' strike, all he could offer was the banal hope that it would create 'a completely different political situation'.[72] Still less could he cope with the two great bombshells of the campaign – Enoch Powell's contorted call for a Labour victory, on the grounds that it offered the only hope of saving Britain from the European embrace; and information from the Pay Board, the policeman of the incomes policy, suggesting that miners' pay was lower than the Coal Board or the government had assumed and that their claim could have been met without breaching stage three.

The end result was a threefold disaster: for Heath, for the nation and for the values and assumptions which had guided British governments since the days of Stanley Baldwin. The Conservatives won 200,000 more votes than Labour, but Labour won 301 seats to the Conservatives' 296. At more than 19 per cent, the Liberals' share of the vote was higher than it had been since 1929, yet they won only fourteen seats. Plaid Cymru won two seats, but less than 11 per cent of the popular vote in Wales; the SNP increased its share of the Scottish vote to a spectacular 21.9 per cent, winning seven seats.

Heath tried to cobble together a deal with the Liberals, but failed. On 4 March, Harold Wilson became Prime Minister at the head of a deeply divided minority government whose overriding objectives were to settle with the miners as soon as possible, to keep on the right side of the unions and to engineer a propitious moment for a second election. It was a government of all the Labour talents – Wilson himself, Callaghan, Jenkins, Healey, Castle, Crosland, Michael Foot, the veteran Bevanite, and Tony Benn, the rising star of the ultra left. It was also one of the weakest and most inconstant governments of the century.

It achieved its first objective with predictable ease. Within days of Wilson's return to office, it settled the miners' strike with an award of 22–32 per cent, at a cost of £103 million. It took its most important step towards its second objective in July 1974, when it repealed the Conservatives' Industrial Relations Act and restored the immunities that the unions had acquired in the halcyon days of 1906. Also in July, Denis Healey, the new Chancellor of the Exchequer, made his contribution to the third objective with a mini-budget, adding £200 million to demand and £340 million to the public sector borrowing requirement (PSBR). 'You must admit,' he boasted to Barbara Castle over lunchtime Stilton and burgundy, 'I am the most political Chancellor you ever had.'[73] His boast was justified. A second general election followed on 10 October, amid record wage increases, falling output and a mounting payments deficit. Heath campaigned for national unity and promised that, if the Conservatives won, he would try to form a coalition government. It was not enough. This time, Labour won a majority of three seats over all parties, but of forty-three over the Conservatives. Heath had now led his party through four general elections, three of which he had lost. A battle for the Conservative leadership was virtually inevitable.

It intersected with a more fateful battle over the party's identity and statecraft. Heath was not the only casualty of the 1974 elections. For the best part of fifty years Conservative governments had sought to ward off the threat of class politics with whiggish accommodation and inclusion. For nearly forty years they had been astonishingly successful, but by the early 1960s inclusion was losing its allure. However, Heath had given it a new gloss and had pushed it further than any of his predecessors. That was the meaning of the Industry Act, the Barber boom, the incomes policy and his doom-laden refusal to play the anti-union card in January and February 1974. For his pains, he had suffered two electoral disasters, to say nothing of three humiliating industrial defeats which had further eroded the depleted authority of Parliament, government and the law.

To a growing number of Conservatives, it seemed that whiggery had backfired. So far from holding class politics at bay, it had played into the hands of Labour's most raucous class warriors; in doing so, it had undermined the structure of authority and consent which it was supposed to protect. The moral seemed clear. The Conservatives had to find an alternative, not just to Heathite corporatism, but to the vision of democracy and democratic politics from which it sprang.

The result was an orgy of Conservative soul-searching, reminiscent of Labour's civil war in the 1950s. The most ostentatious searcher was Sir Keith Joseph, who had been a minister under Macmillan, Home and Heath, and who belonged to a wealthy and distinguished Jewish family. He was a cultivated, charming and wonderfully courteous hereditary baronet and All Souls Fellow; he also possessed a most un-Conservative penchant for doctrinal self-examination, often verging on self-flagellation.[74] After the election he delivered an explosive series of speeches, published in a collection with the ominous title, *Reversing the Trend*. Joseph argued the case for market economics, monetarist policies, lower taxation and higher profits on the lines that Powell and the IEA had made familiar, but he gave it a new rhetorical twist, more reminiscent of Maoist self-criticism than of conventional Conservatism.[75]

Britain's economic and social woes, he insisted, were due to the 'detritus of Socialism' which had accumulated over the thirty years since the Second World War, making Britain the most 'socialist' developed country outside the Communist bloc. Labour was not the only culprit, however. The Conservatives were equally guilty. They had chased after the 'will-o'-the wisp' of the middle ground, which had moved away from them whenever they moved towards it. In doing so, they had connived in the operation of a deadly 'ratchet'. Socialists 'move it up a few notches during their term; at best we leave it still while we are in office. But once the ratchet goes too far, that will be the end of the independent people. We shall be a nation of dependents, a servile nation.'[76] He himself, he added with masochistic relish, was as guilty as the rest of the Conservative Party. For 'it was only in April 1974 that I was converted to Conservatism. (I had thought that I was a Conservative but I now see that I was not really one at all.)'[77] The rhetoric of recantation has rarely been deployed to greater effect.

Powell had already given the languishing tory nationalist strand in the Conservative tradition a kiss of life. Joseph's agonising gave it a more powerful additional boost. Though he devoted the lion's share of his oratory to economics, he saw the economy as part of a seamless web that also included politics, culture and public morality. In language reminiscent of Lord Salisbury 100 years before (and with echoes of Hobbes 300 years before) he conjured up the nightmare of a 'ramifying, hydra-headed ... alliance of destructive forces' that threatened to destroy liberty, private enterprise and the rule of law. Everywhere, authority was under attack. As well as 'deliberate destroyers' on the far left, the hydra included 'excessive permissiveness' in schools; the 'exploitation and glamorisation of violence' in films; 'licensed obscenities' transmitted by the BBC; and an 'inflation' of rights, expectations and laws that mimicked the inflation of money.[78]

Another echo of Salisbury was a warning that, if it continued much longer, the onward march of 'socialism' and its carrier, the class-conscious proletariat, would become irreversible. The bourgeois values of abstinence, deferred gratification and self-improvement, and the property rights on which they depended, were threatened by an 'almost universal pro-letarianization'. The middle classes were 'beginning to learn what they can from the working class; what they learn is militancy, solidarity, put-your-claim-in-and-spend-what-you-have-while-you-have-it'.[79] But there was a portentous difference between Salisbury and Joseph. Salisbury had been content to resist the degeneration he feared. Joseph sought to reverse it. In a pregnant passage he defined a project of Herculean proportions:

> As politicians and economists, our task is to re-create conditions under which the values we cherish can form the cement of our society. Our job is to re-create the conditions which will again permit the forward march of *embourgeoisement* which went so far in Victorian times and even in the much-maligned thirties.[80]

The implications were startling. To restore authority, and return the bourgeoisie to its proper place as the guarantor of the social and moral order, economic change had to go hand in hand with cultural engineering. Who the engineers would be, and how they would set about their mission, remained to be seen.

Joseph swam with an advancing tide. In March 1974 he set up a think-tank, called the 'Centre for Policy Studies' (CPS), to 'convert the Tory Party';[81] with the help of the combative ex-Communist, Alfred Sherman, this became a pacemaker of the tory nationalist renaissance. The renaissance was not all of a piece. The Salisbury Group of Conservative academics and publicists looked askance at Joseph's emphasis on freedom, while outdoing him in lamenting the decline of authority. For Peregrine Worsthorne, the most alarming feature of contemporary Britain was 'not so much the lack of freedom as its excessive abundance; not so much the threat of dictatorship as the reality of something unpleasantly close to chaos.'[82]

That note resounded far beyond the Conservative Party. Among academic social scientists, it became fashionable to argue that 'overload' – a combination of excessive expectations generated in the 'vote market' and empire-building on the part of the bureaucracy – was undermining both the capacity and authority of government.[83] In a seminal article, Samuel Brittan, no tory and still less a nationalist, argued that liberal representative democracy was so menaced by excessive expectations and the disruptive pursuit of group self-interest that it would probably disappear within the lifetimes of people then adult.[84] Peter Jay, Douglas Jay's son and a lifelong Labour supporter as well as a born-again monetarist, foresaw 'another two or three years of phoney crisis' before 'the breakdown of our present political economy'.[85] Andrew Graham, an Oxford economist and future Master of Balliol, who served in Harold Wilson's Policy Unit in 1974 and 1975, later recalled 'a smell of fear in the air as Labour supporters in Whitehall asked each other which side of the barricades they would join – the miners' or the army's'.[86]

The battle over the Conservative leadership took place in late 1974 and early 1975. The atmosphere in the Conservative Party was heavy with recrimination and tinged with hysteria; meanwhile a combination of static output, escalating public spending and soaring inflation added fuel to the tory nationalist fire. At first it looked as if Keith Joseph would be the standard-bearer of the gathering anti-Heath forces, but he withdrew after making an ill-judged speech in which he warned that the nation's 'human stock' was threatened by the propensity of unmarried girls in social classes 4 and 5 to give birth to children they were not fit to bring up. With characteristic daring, the relatively unknown Margaret Thatcher, who had served as Heath's Education Secretary but had no other Cabinet experience, then put her career at risk and announced her candidature. The polls showed that an overwhelming majority of Conservative voters favoured Heath; the bookies gave odds of 5–1 on his re-election. However, Thatcher won 130 votes to Heath's 119 on the first ballot. On the second she was elected with 146 votes out of a total of 276; Whitelaw, the runner-up, scored only 79. Though few saw it then, a revolution in British politics was in the making. It was Powell's revenge.

THE NEMESIS OF JAMES CALLAGHAN

Four more years had to pass before the revolution could get under way. They were not glorious years. When Thatcher won the Conservative leadership election, Harold Wilson had been prime minister for eleven months. At fifty-eight, he was a sadly diminished figure. He was still a smart operator behind the scenes, but he could no longer inspire Labour audiences with futuristic rhetoric or dominate the House of Commons with barbed rep-artee. He had lost his old zest for power; his consumption of brandy had grown; the memory on which he had prided himself was beginning to fail; and he had to devote inordinate quantities of time and energy to the tantrums of his private secretary, Marcia Williams, soon to be ennobled as Lady Falkender.[87] He had no discernible aims beyond staying in office long enough to beat Asquith's record as the longest-serving, twentieth-century prime minister and keeping his fissiparous party together.

The most immediate threat to party unity came from the running Labour sore of EEC membership. Here Wilson displayed his old tactical skill. In opposition, Labour had phrased its 'renegotiation' commitment in bellicose terms, but its bellicosity had concealed a fundamental ambiguity. What precisely did 'renegotiation' mean? Would it be a rerun of the original negotiations, with Britain on one side of the table and the Community on the other? Or would the 'renegotiators' operate within the framework of the Community, of which Britain was now a member?

The first option would almost certainly have guaranteed failure. Britain would have been behaving as though she had left the Community and was applying for membership from outside; in effect she would have been demanding a new Treaty of Accession. A better way of turning the rest of the Community against her would have been hard to find. The second option did not guarantee success, but given reasonable goodwill on all sides it did make it probable. By the summer of 1974 it was clear that this was the option that Wilson and Callaghan, now Foreign Secretary, had chosen: that the Treaty of Accession would stand; and, above all, that the new British government wanted to remain in the Community if it could. Renegotiation ceased to be a drama and became a soap opera – a normal part of the continuing Community process. British ministers on their travels to Brussels discovered that Community decisions were not taken by the 'faceless bur-eaucrats' of anti-market rhetoric, but by largely amiable politicians much like themselves. Little by little, and to the chagrin of anti-market ministers such as Benn and Castle, Labour Britain was sucked into the Community system.[88] Callaghan, in particular, soon seemed indecently at home in it.

The climax came in early March 1975, when Wilson returned tri-umphantly from a Community summit in Dublin with the unsurprising news that the two outstanding issues – Britain's contribution to the Com-munity budget and continued access to the British market for New Zealand's dairy products – had been resolved successfully. At the start of a two-day

Cabinet discussion on the results of the renegotiations, the fervent anti-marketeer, Barbara Castle, passed her neighbour a premonitory note: 'I'm bored before we start'.[89] At the end of the second day the Cabinet voted for continued British EEC membership by 16 to 7. It had been clear for some time that the government would honour its commitment to consult the people with a referendum rather than a general election; and on 5 June 1975 the first (and so far the last) UK-wide referendum in history duly took place.

This too heralded a political revolution of a sort. The referendum was fought by two 'umbrella organisations' – one 'pro' and one 'anti' – that cut across party lines. The 'antis' were a disparate group, ranging from Benn to Powell, whose members had little or nothing in common on other issues. The 'pro' campaign was dominated by a coalition of mostly Heathite Conservatives, Labour revisionists and Liberals, whose members discovered, sometimes to their own surprise, that on a whole range of economic and social issues their differences were paper-thin. For Jenkins and his closest followers, in particular, the whole experience was a liberation. For a blessed few weeks, they could cut loose from the 'tribal loyalties of party' and campaign alongside like-minded colleagues from other parties in a supremely important cause.[90] The end result was one of the most sensational victories in British electoral history. 17,378,581 voted 'yes' to staying in the Community, and 8,470,073 'no' – a majority of more than two to one. The parties returned to their trenches, but in some quarters at least the memory of victorious cross-party collaboration retained a golden glow.

⋘⋙

Compounding Labour's European split was a deeper split over doctrine, purpose and party power. After the 1970 defeat, the gulf between revisionists and fundamentalists, which Wilson had papered over before 1964, had reappeared, in a new and more destructive guise. The leading Bevanites of old had mostly become unacknowledged revisionists. This was certainly true of Wilson himself. Despite her passionate *étatisme*, it was also true of Castle and even of Crossman, the participatory prophet *manqué*. In the devaluation split before 1967 and the greater split over 'In Place of Strife' in 1969, old Gaitskellites had fought alongside old Bevanites on both sides of the question.

However, doctrine returned from the deep freeze to which Wilson had consigned it when Labour returned to opposition. A new wave of fundamentalism, which owed more to the 'romantic revolt' of the time than to the alignments of the past, overwhelmed the revisionist hegemony. The new fundamentalists were harder and more impatient than their predecessors. They were also a lot more aggressive. In the 1950s and 1960s, the revisionists had taken the offensive against defensive fundamentalists. Now roles were reversed. The revisionist prophet, Anthony Crosland, stopped revising. Jenkins and the Labour Europeans were so absorbed in the battle over EEC entry (which, for many, was also a battle for their political lives) that they had no energies to spare.[91] Healey and Callaghan, both revisionists in practice, had never been men for doctrine and were not about to change the habits of a lifetime. The silence of the parliamentary revisionists was matched by an even more resounding silence outside Parliament.

The new fundamentalists were a disparate and amorphous group, but they coalesced around a charismatic leader; and they also found a guru. The leader was Tony Benn – or, to give him the name under which he had first entered politics, Anthony Wedgwood Benn. He belonged to a comfortable, upper-class political family, but the blood of radical dissent ran in his veins. Both his grandfathers had been Liberal MPs. His father, William Wedgwood Benn, had entered Parliament as a Liberal, thrown in his lot with Labour in the 1920s and ended his career as the first Viscount Stansgate. Benn's mother was a prominent Congregationalist and pioneering feminist. After Westminster School and war service in the RAF, he went up to New College, Oxford; at the age of twenty-five he was elected to Parliament for Cripps's old seat in Bristol. His first taste of fame came when his father died in 1960. Against his will, Benn inherited the peerage and was therefore ineligible to sit in the Commons, but he fought and won a brilliant, long-drawn-out campaign for a change in the law and recaptured his seat in 1963. He seemed the epitome of the Wilsonian New Boys of the age and served in the Labour governments of the 1960s, first as Postmaster General and then as Minister of Technology. He was fascinated by gadgetry, an enthusiast for Concorde and in favour of EEC entry.

After the 1970 defeat Benn reinvented himself, becoming to the Labour Party what Enoch Powell and later Keith Joseph were to the Conservatives. Like Powell, he was an instinctive populist, strong outside Parliament but weak within it, engaged in an ultimately forlorn attempt to use his extra-parliamentary following as a battering ram to break into the citadels of established power. Like Joseph, he was a master of the politics of repentance. He was endowed with infectious, boyish charm, indefatigable energy and a formidable capacity for persuasion. Harold Wilson famously said of him that he immatured with age; and it is easy to see why.

In middle age Benn had the eager, sometimes endearing if frequently infuriating enthusiasm of a twenty-year-old. (In old age, as a grand old man of the left, his endearing side would take precedence over his infuriating one. Even so, the change was a long time in the making.) On one level, he was a guileful politician, on another an innocent abroad. He had something in common with the aristocratic Russian Narodniks of the 1860s and 1870s, who 'went among the people' only to be rejected by them. Like many populists he confused the enthusiasms of his own popular constituency with the mood of the people at large. It was somehow characteristic of him that he was the chief author of Labour's commitment to an EEC referendum, which he eventually lost by a crushing margin. For all that, he saw, more clearly than any other Labour politician, that the stable social and economic order of the 1950s and 1960s was vanishing, and that new forces were undermining the political and economic assumptions as well as the social norms of the post-war years.

At the heart of his own politics lay a shifting, incoherent, yet passionately held amalgam of decentralist democratic republicanism, class-war rhetoric and ferocious *étatisme*, with a dash of Marxism about it. He saw himself as an heir of the Levellers and Tom Paine, stressed his debt to the dissenting and Christian Socialist traditions,[92] and mourned the absence of a Marxist tradition in the Labour Party.[93] But, at the start of what became a long journey of intellectual discovery, the Marxism he toyed with was closer to that of the New Left of the early 1960s than to the Communism of earlier decades. In a breathless, but path-breaking 'socialist reconnaissance', set out in a Fabian pamphlet published within weeks of the 1970 election, he argued that the combination of growing international interdependence, increasing economic centralisation and a better-educated and more demanding citizenry had caused the 'social contract' on which parliamentary government depended to break down. Authoritarianism, whether in politics or industry, no longer worked. The only solution was to renegotiate the contract, on the basis of a far-reaching diffusion of power.

Socialists should make dignity and diversity their watchwords, in place of the economism of the past. This would entail workers' control in industry, open government and popular referendums. Above all, it would entail a new approach to leadership. 'New-style' political leaders would have to establish a new relationship with the people:

> They will have to be leaders, rather more in the Moses tradition, drawing their power less from the executive authority they have acquired by election and more from influence, helping people to see what they can achieve for themselves. ... No one could possibly be wise enough, or knowledgeable enough, or have the time and skill to run the world today even if he had all the authority and all the expert advice he asked for to do the job. Individual people have got to do it themselves and argue it out as they go along.[94]

This was not remotely a project for government, but given patience and time it might have provided a fruitful basis for a redefinition of democratic citizenship and the democratic state on pluralistic and participatory lines.

Benn's tragedy was that he never found the time. Increasingly, he was carried along by the eager enthusiasm of his activist audiences, and they hungered for stronger meat than an exploratory reconnaissance. His increasingly rigid *étatisme* soon swallowed up his decentralism. He still championed workers' control and worker co-operatives, but his attention switched from Mosaic leadership and the diffusion of power to the more familiar theme of public ownership.[95] Heavily influenced by the guru of the new fundamentalism – Stuart Holland, a Sussex University economist still in his early thirties – he became the chief pathfinder for a new assault on Aneurin Bevan's commanding heights.

The familiar distinction between macroeconomics and microeconomics, Holland taught him, had been superseded by the growth of a new 'meso-economy' of giant, often multinational firms, which Keynesian techniques were powerless to regulate. The whole revisionist project, which had pre-supposed the continuing success of Keynesian management, was therefore in ruins. The path to socialism now lay through direct state intervention in the meso-economy, partly by new forms of public ownership centred on a state-holding company, and partly by planning agreements to give the government effective control over the meso-economic companies that remained in private hands.[96] It does not seem to have occurred either to Holland or to Benn that, if the giants of the meso-economy were as strong as the new fundamentalism presupposed, they would be unlikely to lie back and allow a Labour Government to clip their wings.

First as party chairman, and then as chairman of its home policy committee, Benn became the conduit through which Hollandism flowed into Labour policy-making. The end result came in the general election of February 1974, which Labour fought on the most radical manifesto since 1945. The government, Labour promised, would take over 'profitable sections or individual firms' in a range of industries, set up a powerful National Enterprise Board to foster industrial development and exports, and institute planning agreements between government and major private companies to the same end.[97] The ports, shipbuilding, marine engineering and the manufacture of airframes and aero-engines would be nationalised outright. That was only one prong of a two-pronged programme. As well, Labour fought the 1974 elections on the ticket of what it chose to call the 'social contract' – a vague agreement between the parliamentary leadership, the National Executive and the most powerful trade-union leaders designed to show that Labour could deliver the industrial peace which had eluded the Conservatives.

Unfortunately, the agreement was neither social nor a contract. In place of Heath's attempted tripartite corporatism, it offered economic bipartism. It was an agreement between one political party and one particularly powerful sectional interest, neither of whom could speak for society as a whole. It bound the party leadership to bring in a wide range of costly measures, including food and transport subsidies, permanent price controls, an end to charges in the welfare services, a big hike in old-age pensions, redistribution of wealth and income and an extension of industrial democracy. The unions made no commitments in return, beyond a pious declaration that they looked forward to a 'wide-ranging agreement' with the next Labour government covering 'all these aspects of our economic life'.[98] There was no mention of wages and, at the top of the Labour Party, support for an incomes policy became a sin that dared not speak its name. At a meeting with TUC leaders shortly before the February election Wilson conceded, 'What we need is more the creation of a mood than a compact.'[99] The consequences were nicely summarised in a comment by Joel Barnett, a chirpy and diminutive Mancunian accountant who served as a Treasury minister from 1974 to 1979. 'The only give and take in the contract,' he wrote, 'was that the Government gave and the unions took.'[100]

The combination of fundamentalist industrial intervention and an unenforceable bargain with the unions offered pitifully inadequate protection from the most ferocious economic storms since the Korean war. When Labour entered office in February 1974 the international economy in general, and the British economy in particular, were spinning out of control.[101] Unemployment had fallen in 1973 but was now beginning to rise. Prices, wages and public spending were soaring. The still-predominant Keynesians in the Treasury had no solution to offer; they persuaded themselves that it was more important to fill up the hole in demand that the oil-price hike had brought in its train than to curb its inflationary effects. In any case, the social contract ruled out solutions that smelled, however faintly, of deflation, as any solution worthy of the name would have been bound to do. As the tough, outspoken, unillusioned, Salford-born Treasury mandarin, Leo Pliatzky, would put it later, a year of collective madness ensued. In accordance with the social contract, ministers piled new increases in public spending on to the bloated totals bequeathed by Barber. Between 1973–4 and 1974–5, the ratio of public expenditure to GDP shot up from less than 39 per cent to 45 per cent.

Ministerial obeisance to the unions had no observable effect on their behaviour. In the 1974–5 wage round, earnings rose by 27 per cent.[102] By

April 1975 inflation was running at 22 per cent – more than double the figure for December 1973, and the highest in the developed world.[103] Meanwhile, the balance of payments plunged further into the red, resulting in a current-account deficit of more than £3 billion for 1974.[104] In a Hobbesian war of group against group, unions struggled to protect their members against the inflationary effects of past wage increases by making ever-larger claims. According to the Kilbrandon Report, trade unions were thought to have more influence on the country's future than Cabinet ministers or the civil service.[105] Not surprisingly, unorganised workers hastened to join unions to protect themselves; by 1978, 53 per cent of the labour force belonged to trade unions, as against less than 46 per cent in 1970. Since the oil-producing countries deposited much of their swollen surpluses in London, the pound remained strong, masking the full horror of the country's economic travails and allowing the government to go on bribing the unions with borrowed money.

Nemesis was inevitable, but it was postponed for a surprisingly long time. Healey's 1975 budget was mildly deflationary, with increases in income tax and VAT, and a slowdown in the rate of increase in public spending. In response to an alarming fall in the exchange rate in May and June, the taboo on talk of an incomes policy was lifted. The Treasury tried to bounce the Cabinet into a statutory policy, but failed.[106] Instead, ministers managed to win TUC agreement to a voluntary policy limiting wage increases to a flat rate of £6 a week for those earning less than £8000 a year. Half hidden in the wings was the spectre of statutory controls if the voluntary policy failed. By dint of deft footwork, Wilson managed to blunt the edge of the Benn–Holland industrial policy, in the teeth of a furious public campaign on Benn's part.

After the crushing defeat of the 'no' campaign in the European referendum, Benn was demoted from Industry Secretary to Energy Secretary. The National Enterprise Board was set up, but it was a pale and respectable shadow of the share-acquiring, company-swallowing, socialist behemoth which had been envisaged in the party manifesto and had made the CBI's flesh creep. Most of its funds were pledged to adjustment aid for failing companies – precisely what Holland's proposed state holding company had been supposed not to do. The legislation provided for planning agreements, but they were to be voluntary, not compulsory, effectively nullifying the purposes that they were originally intended to serve. In the inner recesses of the Treasury, Healey and his officials prepared new and more rigorous spending cuts.

Disaster finally struck in 1976. In February the government published a white paper committing it to spending cuts of £1.6 billion in the previously planned total for 1977-8 and of £3 billion in the total for 1978-9. On 10 March, at the end of a Commons debate on the white paper, abstentions by backbench Labour rebels helped to procure a government defeat by 28 votes, while a purple-visaged Healey traded robust insults with his tormentors. Although the government carried a confidence motion the following day, everyone could see that Healey's attempt to force fiscal rectitude down his colleagues' throats would encounter formidable opposition, perhaps amounting to a veto, from his own party.

Five days later, to the astonishment of most of the political world, Wilson resigned as prime minister. Though he had always intended to resign around two years after his return to Downing Street in February 1974, he had kept his plans secret from all but a handful of intimates; wrongly, but understandably, it was widely assumed that he was leaving in order to flee some new economic disaster. The parliamentary Labour Party then embarked on a leisurely leadership election, with three ballots. On 5 April, Callaghan won, with 176 votes to Michael Foot's 137 – Jenkins, Healey, Crosland and Benn having been eliminated in the first two rounds.

On the same day, Sir John Hunt, the Cabinet Secretary, warned him that the medium-term economic prospect was one of 'serious imbalance', but added that the uncertainties were so great that ministers should avoid radical changes of economic policy during the next few months.[107] The uncertainties dissolved all too soon. Market confidence in sterling had begun to slip at the beginning of March. The slippage accelerated during April and May; by early June the sterling–dollar rate stood at a fraction more than $1.70, a fall of twenty cents in three months. There was a break in the clouds later in June when Healey obtained a six-months stand-by credit from an assortment of foreign banks, yet in spite of TUC support for a lower wage norm the respite was short-lived. By the end of September, the pound had sunk to nearly $1.60. Healey applied to the IMF for a credit of $3.9 billion – the biggest ever requested.

The Cabinet, the Labour Party, the trade unions and the democratic collectivist assumptions which had shaped their politics for as long as anyone could remember all faced a moment of truth. Britain had no automatic right to a credit of that size. The IMF was bound to impose conditions, and the conditions were bound to include more spending cuts. Yet many Cabinet members, including the paladin of 1950s revisionism, Tony Crosland, believed there was no economic case for cuts and imagined that they could bludgeon the IMF into agreeing with them. Those who thought otherwise, Crosland wrote characteristically, were 'illiterate & reactionary'.[108] Seemingly endless negotiations ensued – between Healey, Callaghan and the IMF team; between Callaghan and Healey; between

Callaghan and Healey together and the rest of the Cabinet; and between Callaghan and two foreign heads of government, Helmut Schmidt, the German Chancellor, and President Ford of the United States.

The atmosphere was suffused with hysteria, paranoia, wishful thinking and, on the government's part, a macho belligerence inadequately masking pained resentment and a sense of humiliation. At one point, Healey threatened, Lear-like, that if the IMF asked for more cuts than the government was willing to offer, it would call a general election on the ticket of 'the IMF versus the people'. (He did not add that this would almost certainly have been a recipe for a precipitate collapse of sterling, followed by a crushing Conservative victory.) For his part, Crosland talked wildly of winding down Britain's defence commitments and introducing a siege economy.[109] Bernard Donoughue, a former LSE political scientist who now ran the Prime Minister's policy unit, smelled treason in the Treasury, some of whose officials were said to be colluding with the IMF team behind ministers' backs.[110]

On 1 December, Callaghan told the Cabinet that neither the West Germans nor the Americans were willing to bring pressure on the IMF on Britain's behalf, and warned that without an IMF loan there would be no chance of borrowing from elsewhere. The Cabinet's wishful thinkers were unabashed. Benn called for 'self-reliance', involving import controls, exchange controls, control of bank advances and reserve powers to introduce planning agreements. 'Not to have even attempted to agree such a set of policies internationally would be inexplicable to the Labour movement.' Peter Shore, once a docile Wilson protégé and now Environment Secretary, complained that the Treasury's deflationary policy 'would be [a] political tomb for the Government'. Anthony Crosland, formerly the hero of the Gaitskellite revisionists, saw no case for a change of policy of any kind. If the IMF pushed the government too far, 'it would become necessary for the Prime Minister to state publicly that the only alternative to such a course would be a siege economy'. Germany and the United States would then ensure an IMF change of course.[111]

In the end, however, a majority of the Cabinet fell into line behind the Callaghan–Healey policy: agreement with the IMF to cut spending by £1 billion in 1977–8 and by £1.5 billion the following year, coupled with the sale of £500 million of government shares in BP. Britain got the $3.9 billion credit that the government had asked for, and thereby a good housekeeping seal, which probably did more to rally the markets than the cash. Helped by the arrival of North Sea oil and the prospect of much more to come, sterling bounced back; the balance of payments moved into surplus. Thanks, in part, to a new system of public expenditure control, based on an annual cash limit for each spending programme and launched before the 1976 crisis broke, public spending fell further and faster than either the Treasury or the IMF had expected; by 1977–8 its ratio to GDP was below 40 per cent. The inflation rate also fell, as did the rate of increase in earnings.

In the Labour Party and the trade unions, storm clouds were gathering. The new fundamentalists gained ground in the constituency parties, and trade-union growls against the incomes policy grew in volume. Nevertheless, when the time came for Healey to introduce his 1977 budget, it looked as if the economy, at least, had turned the corner. Yet, in spite of a moderately happy ending, it had been a sorry tale. Healey fought bravely to win the Cabinet's acquiescence in policies that it hated, but the fact that he had to fight at all was an indictment of his previous policies. It was an even more serious indictment of the mixture of fundamentalist economics and industrial appeasement on which he and his colleagues had fought the 1974 elections, and of the self-destructive myopia of the trade unions that they had appeased.

As in the crises of the 1940s and 1960s, however, the true villain of the piece was the democratic collectivist vision itself. The most striking feature of the Cabinet discussions of November–December 1976 is that virtually all the protagonists appeared to think that they had been morally entitled to ignore the foreign exchange markets before the crisis broke, and were now morally entitled to costless foreign loans to save them from the consequences of having done so. This was as true of revisionists who claimed to accept the mixed economy as of fundamentalists who dreamed of superseding it. Crosland's wild talk of running down Britain's troop commitments, Healey's wilder threat of an anti-IMF election and Donoughue's indignation when he discovered that Treasury officials had had the effrontery to talk to members of the IMF team came from the same emotional stable as Benn's advocacy of an economic Fortress Britain.

That stable was built on an element in the democratic collectivist tradition which had been present from the beginning, but had often been forgotten. From Sidney Webb to Evan Durbin to Anthony Crosland to Stuart Holland, democratic collectivists had thought in terms of the *nation*, in isolation from the outside world. Even Holland, who took more account of the international economic environment than his predecessors, wished to hold it at bay. In 1976 – as in 1931, 1947, 1949 and 1967 – the outside world took its revenge. The story has another meaning as well. In a pregnant comment some years later, Benn said that social-democratic revisionism had been 'killed, not by the left, but by the bankers'.[112] He was right, but he could not bring himself to see that his version of socialist fundamentalism had also received a death blow. Never again would the new fundamentalism or the old revisionism shape the policies of a British government.

༄

Oblivious of the fate in store for them, Callaghan and his colleagues soldiered on, for most of the time in remarkably good fettle. Callaghan himself projected an image of eirenic, avuncular authority; Healey basked in a glow of unfamiliar success. By the end of 1977, the sterling–dollar rate was back to $1.90, and inflation was down to 10 per cent. September 1977 saw a record current account surplus. In 1978, economic growth resumed, and unemployment began to fall. A moderately reflationary budget in 1977 was followed by a much more reflationary successor in 1978. In early 1977, by-election losses deprived the government of its overall majority, but it negotiated a pact with the Liberals, insuring it against defeat on confidence votes for the following twelve months.

Yet the government had a curiously zombie-like air about it. At first sight, it seemed alive and well, but it no longer had a moral or intellectual soul. Repeated cuts had discredited the old Crosland doctrine that Labour's purpose was to procure ever-higher levels of public expenditure, financed by the fiscal dividend of economic growth. The growth of transnational economic interdependence, and the uncontrollable capital flows that it had brought with it, had undermined the Keynesian system on which Crosland had based his hopes. The trade unions' fatal combination of sectional intransigence and social irresponsibility had called into question the fundamental premise of Labour politics: that the party of the working class could be an effective instrument of government.

Residues of Bennite fundamentalism remained; the shipbuilding and aerospace industries had been nationalised in the *annus horribilis* of 1976, and British Aerospace and British Shipbuilders duly came into existence in 1977. But these were the end of an old song. The only significant new departure in the economic and industrial domains – the report of a Royal Commission on industrial democracy, chaired by the eminent Oxford historian Alan Bullock – led nowhere. In deference to the unions, Bullock's proposals fell far short of Germanic co-determination: employees would sit on company boards, but as union representatives, not as representatives of the entire labour force. Even this patently undemocratic concession to the trade-union establishment was too little for certain unions, whose leaders feared that any step towards industrial power-sharing, however modest, would compromise their role as wage bargainers. The Commission's proposals were smothered by an unholy alliance between industrial conservatives in the unions, the CBI and the Cabinet.[113] Bullock joined Alfred

Mond, George Brown and Edward Heath in the museum of failed attempts to nudge Britain's fragmented and ill-disciplined trade unions and employers' organisations towards her own version of central European capitalism.

Industrial conservatism went hand in hand with constitutional radicalism. It was an unconvinced and unconvincing radicalism – the product of an opportunistic near-deathbed conversion – but it showed that the foundations of the 270-year-old union state were beginning to tremble. In the October 1974 election, the SNP's share of the Scottish vote had shot up to 30 per cent – 8 per cent more than in February. It won only eleven out of the seventy-one Scottish seats, but it came second in forty-two of them. Scotland now had a four-party political system, with the SNP breathing heavily down Labour's neck. Since its emergence as a serious contender for state power, the Labour Party had been predominantly unionist: democratic collectivists had taken it for granted that the existing British state was the only possible vehicle for their dreams. The SNP advance had forced a reluctant rethink.

In February 1974, Labour's manifesto had said nothing about Scotland or Wales; in October it promised 'elected assemblies' for both.[114] The pace was slow; not until December 1975 did the government publish a white paper setting out firm proposals for legislation. Another year went by before it introduced the Scotland and Wales Bill, clothing the white paper's skeleton with legislative flesh. The bill had many enemies and few convinced friends. It was too restrictive to please devolutionists and went too far to please sceptics, while the fact that it had been introduced at all outraged unionists of all political stripes and in all three nations. Although thirty Labour members voted with the Conservatives against it, it received a second reading in December 1976, but a guillotine motion in February 1977 was lost by 29 votes, twenty-two Labour rebels having voted with the opposition.

The government now found itself on a political rack. The mood of English Labour MPs varied from indifference to dismay; many Northern Labour MPs, fearing that Scottish devolution would disadvantage the Northern Region economically, were positively hostile. Among their Scottish colleagues, only John Mackintosh was a committed, long-standing devolutionist. Tam Dalyell, the magnificently unbiddable Old Etonian MP for West Lothian, saw devolution as a first step to outright separation. He fought it with passion and flair. Scottish MPs at Westminster, he repeated ad nauseam, would not be able to vote on internal Scottish matters if devolution were carried, yet they would be allowed to vote on internal English matters – an anomaly that became known as the 'West Lothian Question'.[115]

Dalyell was joined by the equally unbiddable George Cunningham, an expatriate Scot who sat for an inner-city London constituency and had become one of the most formidable parliamentarians of his political generation. Yet the government dared not draw back. Bruce Millan, Callaghan's colourless Secretary of State for Scotland, declared in the autumn of 1976 that if the government reneged on devolution, the Labour Party would not be a 'credible force' in the next election.[116] That less than inspiring argument continued to shape the government's policy. In November 1977, it brought in two separate devolution bills – one for Scotland and one for Wales. After seemingly endless debates, both passed into law in July 1978.

However, there was a nasty sting in the tail. To get the legislation through, the government had had to accept amendments erecting two hurdles in the devolutionist path. The first was straightforward: referendums would have to be held in Scotland and Wales before the Acts came into force. The second, the brainchild of George Cunningham, was much more ingenious. Not only would devolution have to win a majority of the votes cast; it would also have win the support of 40 per cent of those eligible to vote. The referendums eventually took place on 1 March 1979. The Welsh, divided by language and culture, voted against devolution by a huge majority. A narrow majority of the Scots voted for. But though the 'yes' campaign won 51.6 per cent of the total vote in Scotland, it won only 30.78 per cent of the electorate, well below the 40 per cent threshold. The Cunningham amendment had scuppered devolution. The only remaining question was whether it had scuppered the government as well.

༺༻

By now the fight had gone out of Callaghan. In 1977 and the first half of 1978 he had presided over an encouraging economic upturn, but he had been impatient for more. In a heroic but doomed attempt to vanquish inflation once and for all, the government had proclaimed a 5 per cent pay norm in July 1978. Although a general election was due at the latest in October 1979, most of the political world had taken it for granted that Callaghan would exploit good economic news to the full and go to the country in the autumn of 1978. After an August of careful deliberation, however, he decided to disappoint these expectations; though the electoral omens were better than they had been for a long time past, they were not good enough.

Unfortunately, he failed to reckon with the swelling resentment of pay restraint among rank-and-file trade unionists. In the cold 'winter of discontent' of 1978–79, a wave of mainly unofficial strikes, mostly in the public sector and often accompanied by violence on the picket lines, paralysed the country and demolished Labour's claim to have discovered the secret of industrial peace. Not surprisingly, the government's standing in the polls plummeted; in February 1979, Gallup recorded a 20 per cent Conservative lead over Labour.[117] Callaghan's authority and self-confidence plummeted as well; as his biographer put it long afterwards, he seemed 'shrunken and inert'.[118]

It was thus a battered and demoralised figure who had to determine the government's reaction to the Scottish referendum result. The SNP insisted that the government persist with devolution, but Callaghan refused. He also rejected various ingenious wheezes to postpone a Commons debate. As the Secretary for Prices and Consumer Protection, Roy Hattersley, wrote later, 'Jim was going to go down like a noble Roman.'[119] On 28 March, the government was defeated by one vote on a Conservative no-confidence motion; the SNP, the Liberals and most Ulster Unionists voted with the opposition. Parliament was dissolved on 7 April and a general election took place on 3 May. The Conservatives started with an average poll lead of 11 per cent, although the campaign saw a swing back to Labour.

In a much-quoted exchange not long before polling day, Bernard Donoughue told Callaghan that he thought Labour might 'squeak through'. Callaghan replied quietly, 'You know there are times, perhaps once every thirty years, when there is a sea-change in politics. It then does not matter what you say or do. ... I suspect there is now such a sea-change – and it is for Mrs Thatcher.'[120] On 3 May, the Conservatives won a majority of forty-three seats over all parties and of seventy over Labour. Slowly and hesitantly, the political counter-revolution heralded by Thatcher's election as Conservative leader got under way. As a serious contender for power, the old Labour Party was no more. A decade and a half would pass before Labour people were willing to admit that it had died by its own hand.

PART III
TAMING DEMOCRACY

9

WARRIOR QUEEN

✣

I'm a plain straightforward provincial. I've got no hang-ups about my background like you intellectual commentators in the south-east.
Margaret Thatcher in conversation with Anthony Sampson, 1977

Just rejoice at that news. . . . Rejoice.
Margaret Thatcher replying to journalists after British forces had recaptured South Georgia during the Falklands war, 1982

[T]oo many people have been given to understand that if they have a problem, it's the government's job to cope with it. . . . They're casting their problem on society. And, as you know, there is no such thing as society. There are individual men and women and there are families, and no government can do anything except through people, and people must look to themselves first.
Margaret Thatcher in *Woman's Own*, 1987

No. No. No.
Margaret Thatcher in the House of Commons on Jacques Delors's vision of European integration, 1990

✣

TRIUMPH

The Britain that chose Margaret Thatcher as its prime minister was a perplexed and discontented place, but its mood was far from revolutionary. The voters were more anxious to punish Labour than to reward the Conservatives; they hoped for more competent management of the familiar post-war order, but few dreamed of a new one. Essentially the same was true of the nation's elites. The horrors of the three-day week under Heath, the soaring inflation under Wilson, the IMF crisis and the winter of discontent had shaken them badly, but they had lived through too many false dawns to believe that a new order was possible. They would not have been surprised if the new government had made a few radical gestures; they had seen plenty of those from incoming governments in the past. However, if they had been told that the contours of their world would change utterly during the next ten years, they would have been incredulous.

They mistook their woman. By temperament, Thatcher *was* a revolutionary, albeit of a highly unusual kind. Shimmering on the horizon of her mental universe was the vision of a lost golden age, when authority was respected and rules were obeyed. But though her utopia lay in the past, not the future, she was as eager to break with the post-war era as any Bennite socialist. Though this had not always been apparent during her rise to the top, her political reflexes were tory nationalist. Unlike most previous exemplars of the tory nationalist mentality, however, she was not content to defend authority and order against the threat of disintegration. As she saw it, disintegration had gone too far for that. It was no longer a menacing spectre, but an omnipresent reality, manifested in a crisis of the state as well as of the economy. The task now was to restore authority, not to preserve it in its shrunken condition; and all her instincts told her that it could be restored only through far-reaching change.

In spirit (if not in deed), she was closer to the Ulstermen who flirted with armed resistance before the First World War than to the stand-pat Salisbury or Eldon. Her tory nationalism ran alongside a superficially incongruous and largely unrecognised streak of democratic republicanism. Thanks, perhaps, to her provincial, nonconformist upbringing, she had a Paineite contempt for the old, metropolitan establishment and would have been more at home in Cromwell's New Model Army than any prime minister since Lloyd George. She swept through the closed garden of the old order like a force of nature. More than any of her counterparts in other countries, more even than Ronald Reagan in the United States, she came to personify the capitalist renaissance that dominated world history in the 1980s. If she had never lived, Britain and conceivably the world would be different places today.

Yet when she became Prime Minister in the spring of 1979 she did not know where her search for the golden age would take her, nor how far it would go. She was an intuitive politician, like Lloyd George, not a cerebral one like Heath or Joseph. She felt her way, sensing when it was time to strike; and she often held back longer than her more ardent followers would have wished. But when she thought it was time to act, her mind locked on to the decision, leaving no scope for hesitations or second thoughts. More strongly than all but a handful of her colleagues, she sensed that the post-war order, which had framed her political life until the Heath Government's fall, had broken down in the chaos of the 1974 miners' strike, the 1976 crisis and the terrible winter of 1978–9; that the question for the future was not how to revive it, but what to put in its place; and that it was up to her to seize the opportunity for radical change.

One of the great mysteries of twentieth-century British history is where that sense came from, and how she developed the mixture of guile, will, passion and panache that made it the driver of a decade of change. She was not an intellectual; she engaged in no Keith Joseph-like agonies of public introspection, and she constructed a biography for herself that concealed as much as it revealed. The 'straightforward provincial' was far from straightforward, and dubiously provincial.[1] Famously, she was born in Grantham to austerely Methodist parents, who kept a grocer's shop and lived sober lives, dominated by religion, local politics and the work ethic. From humble beginnings, her father, Alfred Roberts, rose to become one of the town's leading citizens as JP, alderman and mayor; there is little doubt that his combination of moral earnestness, ambition and tireless public spirit left an indelible impression on her. But the myth of the grocer's daughter that she would burnish in later years told only part of the truth.

In a passage in her memoirs heavy with filial piety she wrote that her '"Bloomsbury" was Grantham – Methodism, the grocer's shop, Rotary and all the serious, sober virtues cultivated and esteemed in that environment'.[2] In some ways it was. Yet the young Margaret Roberts escaped from Grantham as soon as she could and never looked back. After Somerville College, Oxford, and a job as a research chemist in Colchester, she married Denis Thatcher, the dashing and decidedly unprovincial managing director of a family firm. She abandoned science and qualified as a barrister; in 1959, by now the mother of twins, she was elected Conservative MP for Finchley, in North London. Somewhere on the way she acquired a slightly rebarbative genteel accent, with no trace of the East Midlands about it.

From the age of seventeen she spent her working life in the South-East; from the age of twenty-six she belonged to the comfortably-off business middle class of London and the home counties, whose lifestyle and instincts she shared. But, at the same time, she was a highly professional, fiercely ambitious and ferociously hard-working politician, determined to make her way in what was still a male club. It was her gender, her self-belief, her willingness to take risks and her formidable courage and will, far more than her social or geographical origins, that differentiated her from her former colleagues in Heath's Cabinet.

Gender mattered in a thousand ways. For one thing, it meant that she escaped the male bonding that went with active service. Unlike First World War subalterns like Eden and Macmillan, and their Second World War counterparts like Heath and Whitelaw, she was never taught that good officers look after their men. Nor, of course, could she take part in the male

bonding of the House of Commons – in those days, a crucial element in
the working of the parliamentary machine. The laid-back, anti-Thatcherite
Conservative MP, Julian Critchley, painted a vivid picture of Thatcher's
arrival at a convivial (and clearly male) lunch-table in the Members' dining
room, preceded by her PPS, Ian Gow. 'Suddenly you look up and the first
thing you see is the sight of Ian Gow with the sunlight glinting from his
spectacles, and you knew that this was the harbinger of trouble. And then
in she would come and everybody would stop talking and she'd look at you
and say, "Julian, what are your views on the money supply?"'[3]

She was doubly an outsider to the political elite. She had held none of
the great offices of state and had less Cabinet experience than any prime
minister since Ramsay MacDonald in 1924. Thanks to her gender she
remained an outsider even when she held the highest office in the land.
Simply by being female, she stood out from the suits. She radiated an
indefinable sexual allure, a compound of power and beauty captured in a
double-edged remark by François Mitterrand, the Socialist President of
France in the 1980s: Thatcher, he said, had 'the eyes of Caligula and the
mouth of Marilyn Monroe'.[4] And, like Barbara Castle, she used her femininity as a weapon. She wept on television when she remembered how the
Labour group on Grantham Council had deprived her father of his position
as alderman; and in one of her most celebrated speeches she answered the
Soviet Army newspaper's jibe that she was 'the Iron Lady':

> Ladies and Gentlemen, I stand before you tonight in my green chiffon
> evening gown, my face softly made up, my fair hair gently waved. . . . The
> Iron Lady of the Western World. Me? A cold war warrior? . . .
>   Well, yes, if that is how they wish to interpret my defence of values and
> freedoms fundamental to our way of life.[5]

Thatcher was also an outsider to the professional middle class that staffed
Whitehall, the universities, the Church of England, the top echelons of the
Health Service and the BBC, the Inns of Court and the serious press. She
aroused a special, sometimes virulent loathing among its female members.
The novelist, Angela Carter, hated her accent, which she thought reminiscent 'not of real toffs but of Wodehouse aunts'. Lady Warnock, the
philosopher and educationalist, also detested her 'elocution accent' and
found the way she dressed on television 'not exactly vulgar, just *low*'.[6] In a
donnish put-down, the normally kindly Dame Janet Vaughan, Principal
of Somerville when the young Margaret Roberts was an undergraduate,
remembered later that 'nobody thought anything of her. She was a perfectly
good second-class chemist, a beta chemist.'[7]

Thatcher's biographer, John Campbell, thought such comments snobbish, but there was more to them than that. A chasm of culture and values divided the business middle class, to which Thatcher had belonged since her marriage, from the professional middle class that disdained her. To professionals, the philistine, golf-playing, cocktail-cabinet-owning, Jaguar-driving business class *was* vulgar – just as the business class thought professionals effete, parasitical and self-indulgent.

Finally, Thatcher was an outsider in the top echelons of her own party. She owed her election as Conservative leader to a 'peasants' revolt' of backbenchers and former junior ministers against the largely Heathite shadow Cabinet. When she first became Prime Minister, more than two-thirds of her Cabinet were old Heathmen, tempted, when the going got rough, to drink to the king over the water. A year before, she had told the astonished British Ambassador to Iran that she saw Conservatives who believed in consensus politics 'as Quislings';[8] and she knew only too well that there were many such among her ministers. Even when the Cabinet consisted largely of her own appointees, as it did later in the 1980s, she viewed most of its members with wary distrust.

No prime minister since Lloyd George had defied the norms of Cabinet collegiality as shamelessly as she did. She bullied her ministers unmercifully and used her faithful press secretary, the redoubtable Yorkshireman, Bernard Ingham, to brief against them on the frequent occasions when she thought they needed cutting down to size. By the end of her term of office, her private secretary, Charles Powell, probably had more influence on her than any minister. Jokes about her bossy ways were legion. (In one of the best, Thatcher orders a meal in a restaurant with her Cabinet in tow. 'I'll have the steak.' 'And the vegetables?' 'They'll have the same as me.')[9] She had occasional, usually short-lived favourites – the boyishly good-looking John Moore, whom she sacked; the former businessman, David Young, who left the Cabinet voluntarily after five years; and the rather oleaginous Cecil Parkinson, who remained loyal to the end. But none of these was remotely a political heavyweight.

Her position as an outsider was her greatest asset. One of the central themes of her prime ministership was a culture war between the business and the professional middle classes; she became a heroine for the former partly because she was a *bête noire* for the latter. Much the same was true of her ambivalent relationship with the political and administrative elite. No male politician, formed by the tacit conventions of Westminster and Whitehall, could have defied them with her brazen élan. In 1970s and 1980s Britain, resentment of the political class and political institutions hung in the air like a noxious smog. With an adroit mixture of effrontery, panache and guile, Thatcher managed to appeal to it, despite being head of the government.

In part this was a matter of vocabulary. Her language was 'insistently, aggressively demotic', as the literary critic, Jonathan Raban pointed out, with none of the 'airs and graces of the traditional Establishment'.[10] But there was more to it than that. She behaved almost as if she were Prime Minister, Leader of the Opposition and tribune of the people rolled into one. Like Lloyd George, she was a populist both by temper and by necessity. She understood instinctively that in a fluid society – where political parties were increasingly disconnected from the public and the social interests which had once sustained them were beginning to fragment – traditional parliamentary methods of mobilising support no longer sufficed. In any case, she was ill at ease with institutions, even with the institutions over which she presided. They hemmed her in; they threatened to water down the pure milk of her message; and they were inescapably tainted with the legacy of the cowardly, defeatist past in which they had taken root. Given half a chance they would capture her ministers and divert them from the true path.

In a phrase that speaks volumes about her political style she once told Simon Jenkins that 'socialism is never defeated'.[11] She saw it lurking in the most surprising places, including the breasts of Conservative Cabinet ministers. To have any hope of extirpating it, she had to appeal over the heads of the institutions to the 'sensible, decent and honourable' people of Britain.[12] She was the Lionheart of what became a Tory nationalist crusade, powered by a fusion of the popular will and her own.

⊷

It was a crusade of the heart rather than of the head. Thatcher enjoyed the company and talk of favoured intellectuals of the right, such as the historian, Norman Stone, the philosopher and polemicist, Roger Scruton, and the theologian, Edward Norman. She liked argument; and she revered Hayek, or at any rate claimed to do so. (How far she understood him is a moot point.) But her cast of mind was religious, not critical. On one side was Truth and on the other, Falsehood; her task was to confute Falsehood and proclaim Truth. The journalist Bruce Anderson caught her argumentative style perfectly. 'Eyes flashing, finger wagging,' he wrote, she would 'explain why Socialism is *evil*'.[13] The arguments she enjoyed were battles, not conversations: she wanted to pulverise her opponents, not to persuade them. Her Hayek was a latter-day Moses, bringing down the tablets of stone from Sinai, not one of the most subtle and original thinkers of the age. ' *This* is what we believe,' she declared on one occasion, taking a well-worn copy of his *Constitution of Liberty* from her handbag and banging it down on the table.[14] She had powerful emotions – the hatreds were more powerful than the loves, it sometimes seemed – and passionate convictions. Others supplied the intellectual and doctrinal cladding for them.

Her personal vision had a fearful purity about it. Like her exemplary tory nationalist predecessors, Lord Salisbury and Enoch Powell, she stood above all for authority in society and the state; like them, she believed that authority at home was inextricably entangled with assertive nationhood abroad. She knew that the British empire had vanished but, as Shirley Letwin, one of her most perceptive followers, put it, she yearned for Britain's revival as 'an independent island power'.[15] The present generation could not 'create a new empire', she conceded at the start of her prime ministership, but it could end 'what Churchill called "the long dismal, drawling tides of drift and surrender"'.[16] She had no doubt that drift and surrender were the hallmarks of collectivism, and she assumed that economic liberalisation would put an end to them. It did not occur to her that insular independence might be impossible for a medium-sized nation with an open market economy unprotected from the gales of global competition.

The same was true of her domestic ambitions. The disasters of the 1970s had taught her that the overextended state of the post-war years was the enemy of order, property and nationhood as well as of freedom (not that she needed teaching). The immediate priorities were economic – to squeeze inflation, the product of 'dishonest money', out of the system; to restore profitability and incentives; to make saving worth while again; and, more generally, to replace the interventionist whims of governments and the anarchic usurpations of the unions with the impersonal disciplines of the competitive market. These, however, were means to a much greater end. Collectivism produced 'moral cripples'.[17] Worse still, the organised interests that it sustained undermined the authority of the state on which they battened. The renewed disciplines of the market-place would foster social discipline and, most of all, self-discipline. If she had been told that the hedonistic individualism of the market-place might undermine social discipline instead of bolstering it, she would have been incredulous.

'Economics,' Thatcher told the *Sunday Times* in 1981, 'are the method; the object is to change the heart and soul.'[18] The changed souls would harbour what Letwin called 'the vigorous virtues': the qualities of the 'upright, self-sufficient, energetic, adventurous, independent-minded' who were 'loyal to friends and robust against enemies'.[19] They would, in fact, be rather like the souls that Thatcher remembered from her Grantham childhood, when she had absorbed the 'Victorian values' that were also 'eternal truths':

You were taught to work jolly hard, you were taught to improve yourself, you were taught self-reliance, you were taught to live within your income, you were taught that cleanliness was next to godliness. You were taught self-respect, you were taught always to give a hand to your neighbour, you were taught tremendous pride in your country, you were taught to be a good member of your community. All these things are Victorian values.[20]

Nigel Lawson, Thatcher's Chancellor of the Exchequer for most of the 1980s, spelled out the implications in a striking phrase. Thatcher and her ministers, he recalled in his memoirs, were seeking 'to change the entire culture of a nation'.[21] Nothing quite as ambitious had been attempted in Britain since the rule of the Saints during the English civil war.

᪵᷈᷈

Four insistent themes dominated the Thatcher era. She and her fellow crusaders sought to free tamed capitalism from its cage and return it to the wild: to give freer rein to market forces, to restore sound money and to break the grip of the unions; to sweep away the residues of quasi-corporatism, vulgar Keynesianism and partial collectivism; and to squeeze out the inflation that they were supposed to have bred. Secondly, they wished to reassert and celebrate nationhood, particularly English nationhood; to realise a new version of the old dream of insular liberty; and to revive national self-confidence and pride in the way that de Gaulle had done in France. Thirdly, they were determined to stamp out what they termed the 'dependency culture', to win the war of the business class against the professional class, to humble the institutions in which professional values were embedded and to re-create the seamless web of state authority and market competition that the long descent into welfarism and collectivism had destroyed. Finally, they tried to construct a new and victorious social coalition based on upward mobility, widening property ownership, economic dynamism in successful sectors and regions, and a powerful rhetoric of individual success and clamant nationalism.

The first theme was uppermost for most of the government's initial three years. In general, they were years of pain, confusion and division, but there was one great exception. The 1980 Housing Act, passed in the teeth of furious Labour opposition, gave council tenants the right to buy their homes at a substantial discount. Culturally, politically and psychologically, this was a revolutionary measure. By 1990 around 1,200,000 council houses had been sold. The proportion of the population living in owner-occupied houses had risen from 55 per cent to 67 per cent in the course of the decade (not, of course, thanks solely to council house sales).[22] Hundreds of thousands of working-class people had been enriched. More importantly, they had also been enfranchised. They were no longer dependent on council housing departments for repairs or redecoration. They could refurbish their houses to their own tastes, with no bureaucratic diktats to prevent them. In grey, once-uniform estates, new homeowners would sport new front doors, with massive brass door knockers, to show that they had moved up in the world. They were beneficiaries of the single most important step towards *embourgeoisement* taken during Thatcher's reign.

In other respects, misery prevailed. It was accompanied by an iron resolution – insane or magnificent according to taste – on the part of Thatcher and her deceptively mild-mannered Chancellor, Sir Geoffrey Howe. Howe was a lawyer, not an economist, and he had a lawyer's respect for rules. In the early 1970s he had been one of the chief architects of the Heath Government's Industrial Relations Act and a loyal Heathman, yet he had been converted to the new, quintessentially rule-centred, monetarist faith when he went into opposition. Although Welsh by origin, he was ostentatiously bereft of Celtic fire. He was careful, prosaic and maddeningly deliberate; in a phrase that went the rounds, Denis Healey likened an attack from him to being 'savaged by a dead sheep'.[23] In truth, Howe was more like an elephant than a sheep. Once he had made up his mind, he proceeded on his way with an affable, ponderous imperturbability that no criticism could shake.

This unlikely revolutionary had charge of the most dramatic switch in economic policy since the war. Thanks partly to North Sea oil, and partly to the deflation imposed by the IMF, the outgoing Labour Government had bequeathed him an improving balance of payments, but that was the only chink of light in a darkening sky. Earnings, inflation and public expenditure were all rising ominously. Given the sorry record of the 1970s, it seemed all too likely that inflation would become endemic.[24] But the Government was unswervingly hostile to the well-worn panaceas of the recent past. To signal its determination to break with post-war collectivism, Howe cut the standard rate of income tax from 33 per cent to 30, and the top rate from Healey's penal 83 per cent to 60. To compensate for the cut in direct taxation, he increased VAT from 8 per cent to 15 per cent. To roll back the frontiers of the state and contain the growth in the PSBR, he cut public spending by £1.5 billion. To curb inflation, bank rate was increased from 12 to 14 per cent; in November 1979 it was raised again, this time to 17 per cent – the largest one-day increase in history.

Keynesian economic management had perished under Healey, but the Labour Government had been unwilling to advertise its death. Now it was publicly buried, with the whole paraphernalia of wages policies, official

norms, price controls and corporatist deals alongside it. An equally portentous shift was the abolition of exchange controls in October. Britain was
now irrevocably locked into the global capital market, to the great benefit
of her competitive and dynamic financial services sector and of capital
owners who could now invest wherever the returns were highest. British
stock markets became more closely integrated with foreign ones, and over
time British investment overseas increased substantially.[25] The social and
political implications were equally profound. The balance of economic
power shifted in favour of mobile capital and against immobile labour; the
Holland–Benn dream of an autarchic Britain, building a socialist New
Jerusalem in isolation from a wicked capitalist world, was laid to rest. Less
obviously, the tacit economic nationalism of Labour's revisionist wing had
also suffered a crippling blow.

1979 was comparatively painless, but pain mounted steadily in the
next three years. North Sea oil had turned sterling into a petro-currency;
and another threefold increase in oil prices in 1979 and 1980 automatically
boosted its value. Tight money had the same effect. By October 1980
the exchange rate had soared to $2.43 to the pound. British manufactur-
ing, never conspicuous for adaptability or competitiveness, was cruelly
squeezed by the combination of high interest rates and a rising pound.
(Contrary to much contemporary mythology, the former had a far bigger
impact than the latter.)[26] The Director General of the CBI threatened a
'bare-knuckle fight' with the government; mutterings from Cabinet
dissenters became more and more audible. By December 1980 unemployment totalled 2,100,000 and rising, compared to 1,300,000 a year
before.

As in the interwar years, the old industrial regions suffered far more than
the South. In April 1981, when unemployment averaged 10 per cent in the
country as a whole, it was 7 per cent in the South-East, 12 per cent in the
North-West, 13 per cent in the Northern Region and 16.4 per cent in
Northern Ireland. In the most hard-hit regions, the psychological wounds
may have gone deeper than they had done fifty years earlier. When talking
to surviving victims of mass unemployment in the 1930s, reported the
dramatist and journalist, Jeremy Seabrook,

> they evoke the idle machinery, the eerie silence over shipyard and pithead.
> Unemployment impaired their sense of worth, assailed their dignity, denied
> them and those they loved adequate food and comfort. But it didn't rob
> them of the skills themselves. Now ... there is a terminal sense of the
> extinction of work itself. Something elusive and despairing pervades those
> towns and cities which were built only for the sake of their purposes in the

old industrial processes. It is as though the working class were being wounded in its very reason for existence, work itself.[27]

The socialist feminist, Beatrix Campbell, noticed the same despair, but she gave it a less sympathetic gloss. Commentators did not deplore redundancy as such, she wrote. It was male redundancy that seemed 'a special tragedy. What a terrible thing to happen to a *man*! Because, of course, work is one of the places in which men are made, it sorts the boys into men. Cut them off from work and there's a collective panic that they'll be no different from women.'[28]

A haunting counterpoint to Campbell's feminist analysis was Peter Cattaneo's gripping comic film, *The Full Monty*. It did not appear until 1997, but it belongs emotionally to the 1980s. It depicts the human meaning of the collapse of heavy industry and male employment with a savage mixture of harsh, unsentimental realism and black humour. It tells the story of a group of unemployed Sheffield steelworkers who form an amateur striptease group to supplement their meagre incomes, and go the 'full monty' to total nudity. In doing so it portrayed the damage that mass redundancy did to male self-respect and the culture of industrial Britain more powerfully than any written reportage had done.

There was much talk of a new underclass, hopeless, alienated and fatalistic, closer in mentality to Marx's *lumpenproletariat* and to the 'residuum' that had figured in the debates over the 1867 Reform Act than to the (male) industrial working class for which social democratic parties had traditionally claimed to speak.[29] However, a wave of riots and lootings that spread from Brixton in South London to a number of northern cities in the spring and summer of 1981 cast doubt on the widespread belief that the victims of mass unemployment were too alienated and apathetic to pose a threat to the system. There was a strong racial element in the riots, born of black resentment of racial discrimination in general and of racist police harassment in particular.[30] 'I'm here to see the pigs get theirs', said an unemployed black youth during the Moss Side riot in Manchester. 'They've done this for years. Now they know what it's like to be hit back. We had the bastards in there [the local police station] shitting themselves. We nearly got a couple of them before they shut up the shop and screamed for help.'[31] But racial prejudice and discrimination were not the only factors, as a poem by 'an unemployed mother of two' after the Toxteth riot in Liverpool bears witness:

> You can see through the riot-shields made of polythene
> the police are angry and vicious

> the people are angry and happy
>   swinging their power like a lantern in the night[32]

cᶺᵒᵟᵒᶺ

With awesome obstinacy, Howe and Thatcher stuck to their chosen course. In the most famous phrase of her career Thatcher told the 1980 Conservative Party conference, 'You turn if you want to. The Lady's not for turning.' Nor was she. In March 1980 the government had committed itself to a year-by-year decline in monetary growth and public borrowing over four years, set out in a deliberately inflexible Medium Term Financial Strategy (MTFS). When the time came to frame the 1981 budget, that was still Howe's lodestar. In the midst of the deepest recession since the 1930s, he did his best to cut the borrowing requirement in line with the MTFS commitments and raised taxes by £4 billion to do so.

Twenty-five years later it is hard to appreciate the bold enormity of these measures. The 1981 budget did not just break with Keynesian orthodoxy, it stood it on its head. The Cabinet dissenters – mostly old Heathmen whom Thatcher derisively (and justly) dubbed 'wet' – spluttered indignantly, but failed to mount a rebellion or even to offer an alternative. July 1981 saw an abortive Cabinet revolt against further spending cuts, in which the wets were joined by heterodox monetarists such as the thoughtful sometime Powellite, John Biffen. Its only result was to provoke Thatcher into a show of force. In a September reshuffle she scattered the wets with carefully chosen sackings, sideways moves and demotions. She also brought two outstanding loyalist protégés – both of whom would play leading roles in her crusade – into the Cabinet. One was the cockney former airline pilot, Norman Tebbit; the other was the former financial journalist, Nigel Lawson. For the time being, at least, her ministerial flank was secure.

It was a different story beyond the narrow confines of Westminster and Whitehall. Within weeks of the 1979 election the government's standing in the polls fell behind Labour's; as unemployment rose, its rating plummeted. By the time of the 1981 budget its Gallup score was 30 per cent. By December 1981 it was down to 23 per cent – lower than Labour's during Wilson's worst days in the 1960s. Thatcher was the most unpopular prime minister since opinion polling began.[33] From the government's point of view, these raw figures were less alarming than the political upheaval they reflected. In early 1981 four former Labour Cabinet ministers – Roy Jenkins; David Owen, Callaghan's Foreign Secretary; Shirley Williams, his Education Secretary; and William Rodgers, his Transport Secretary – had broken with the Labour Party to set up a new Social Democratic Party (SDP) committed to a realignment of politics. In the summer of 1981 the SDP and the Liberal

Party formed an 'Alliance' which soon overtook both the big parties in the polls and performed spectacularly well in by-elections. By December 1981 its poll rating was an astonishing 50 per cent, higher than that of the Conservative and Labour parties put together.

The Alliance – and more particularly the SDP – were more complex creatures than most commentators realised. Though most of the SDP's founders came from the Labour Party, it was not a Labour breakaway. An overwhelming majority of its members had never belonged to a political party before. The SDP drew as many votes from the Conservatives as from Labour.[34] It won the two sensational by-election victories of its first year – at Crosby, which Shirley Williams won in 1981, and at Hillhead, which Jenkins captured in 1982 – in previously Conservative seats. The rise of the SDP, like the sudden Liberal revival in the mid-1970s, reflected a growing mood of disenchantment with the existing political system, and not just with Labour.

Former Labour SDPers had broken away in the first place because a violent swing towards the new fundamentalism of Tony Benn and his followers – by now strongly tinged with a quasi-Trotskyite revolutionary socialism, utterly at odds with the party's traditional commitment to parliamentary government[35] – had followed Labour's 1979 defeat. When Callaghan retired from the leadership in 1980, the parliamentary party had elected Michael Foot, the sometime lion of Bevanite fundamentalism, as his successor, with a majority of 10 votes over Healey, whose uncharacteristically cautious campaign had verged on the comatose. But at sixty-seven Foot had lost his roar.[36] The revisionist wing of the party still distrusted him; the new fundamentalists saw him as an apostate who had connived in reactionary wages policies and expenditure cuts. He was powerless to halt the bitter factional infighting that was tearing his party to pieces, or to stem the surging militant tide in the constituency parties. However unpopular Thatcher's Conservatives might be, there was little doubt that, in a head-to-head contest with Foot's Labour Party, they would win. Alliance or no Alliance, Labour had condemned itself to electoral nullity.

Though Thatcher had nothing to fear from Labour, she had a great deal to fear from the Alliance. It stood for the mixed economy, social partnership and a new political style. Its stated ambition was to 'break the mould of politics', but that titillating phrase meant different things to different people. There were strong traces of democratic republicanism in the Alliance's ranks, particularly in its Liberal wing. The decentralisation of government had been dear to Liberal hearts since the days of John Stuart Mill. Partly because of that, the romantic revolt of the 1960s and 1970s had had a bigger impact on the Liberal Party – above all on the Young Liberals – than on the official

Labour Party. Many Liberals saw themselves as radicals, practised what they called community politics, and campaigned for wider participation in decision-making and the empowerment of ordinary citizens.

In similar vein, David Owen, the most original as well as the most combative and wayward of the SDP's founding four, championed industrial democracy and producer co-operatives, invoking G.D.H. Cole and the nineteenth-century French mutualist, P.J. Proudhon, in support.[37] But for most Alliance politicians, 'breaking the mould' meant replacing the polarisation of the 1980s with something closer to the consensual democracy of the German Federal Republic.

In a cruel jibe, Ralf Dahrendorf, the future Liberal Democrat peer, twitted the SDP with offering 'a better past';[38] he failed to add that, in the harsh climate of the early 1980s, a better version of the past seemed highly attractive to many voters. The twin leaders of the Alliance – Roy Jenkins from the SDP and the canny, engaging David Steel from the Liberals – kept their parties' radicalism under wraps. To troubled Conservative voters, alienated by the dogmatism of the Thatcherites but unwilling to vote Labour, and to troubled Labour voters, alienated by their party's lurch to extremism but hesitant about switching to the Conservatives, the Alliance offered a safe haven. If it polled well enough to procure a hung Parliament, as seemed likely in the winter of 1981–2, Thatcher's experiment would be over and her leadership with it.

❧

Relief came from an unlikely quarter. On 2 April 1982, Argentine forces invaded the Falkland Islands – a remote, windswept British colony in the South Atlantic 8000 miles from Britain, but with 1800 inhabitants of British stock as well as countless sheep. The invasion followed a series of provocations by the Argentine military junta, which should have warned the British Government that an invasion was likely yet did not do so. Though ownership of the islands had been in dispute since the early nineteenth century, there was no doubt that they were British territory in international law. However, Whitehall saw them as a burden and would have liked to offload them through negotiations with Argentina.[39] The fact remained that the Falklanders were British, intended to remain British, and were determined to block any negotiated solution remotely acceptable to Argentina. Preliminary talks with Argentina had always broken on the rock of the islanders' refusal to compromise their British identity.

Once the Argentine force landed on the Falklands, past history ceased to count. All that mattered was that British territory had been illegally invaded by a foreign power. The House of Commons met the day after the invasion

(a Saturday), in a mood of fierce, united and justified patriotic outrage.
Michael Foot spoke for the whole House when he declared that Britain had
'a moral duty, a political duty and every other kind of duty' to sustain the
islanders' determination to remain under British rule.[40] Thatcher could not
have defied that mood even if she had wished to do so; in fact she not only
shared it to the full, but personified it as no other contemporary politician
could have done. The result was one of the most astonishing episodes in
twentieth-century British history. In the Commons, Thatcher announced
that a 'large' task force would sail for the Falklands as soon as possible. By
7 April, its first elements were under way. For the country, for the government and most of all for Thatcher personally, it was an enormous
gamble. The naval chiefs assured her that it was possible to assemble a task
force, but they could not be sure of victory in a war fought 8000 miles
away, with the South Atlantic winter approaching, against an enemy with
a much shorter supply line. Defeat would destroy her, but a compromise
that appeared to validate Argentina's claim to the islands would be scarcely
less damaging. Once the ships had left port, only victory would suffice; and
the odds on victory were far from overwhelming.

For six nail-biting weeks, Thatcher embodied the national will. The
unyielding intransigence that had seemed harshly insensitive before 2 April
now made her an icon of reborn patriotic pride. Assertive nationhood, the
second great theme of her reign, drowned out the divisive economism which
had dominated her first three years in power. Even General Haig, the
American Secretary of State, was moved by the 'reawakening of the spirit
of the Blitz' as 100 ships and 28,000 men steamed 'under the British ensign'
towards the Falklands.[41] For the British themselves the war also evoked a
host of deeper, half-buried memories of resistance to foreign aggressors. It
was a war for honour, not territory; for justice, not gain. At least for a
moment, it overwhelmed the nagging sense of national decline generated
by decades of withdrawal and economic failure.

Thatcher was the focus for these swirling emotions. Having been the
most partisan prime minister of the century, she became a national leader.
When she reminded the Conservative Women's Conference at the height
of the war that 'Right and wrong are not measured by a head-count'[42] she
spoke for the country, not just for her party. The war brought out the
best in her: courage, resolution and conviction, combined with impressive
executive competence. She ran it through a small War Cabinet that met at
9.30 every morning and reported regularly to the full Cabinet. Unlike
Churchill she did not try to second-guess the military. When they needed
hard decisions she took them; otherwise, they knew they had her support.

The most spectacular case in point came when the War Cabinet unhesitatingly gave permission for the British nuclear submarine, the *Conqueror*, to torpedo the Argentine cruiser, the *General Belgrano*, even though it was outside the Exclusion Zone around the islands. (It later emerged that the *Belgrano* was steaming away from the Zone, but neither Admiral Woodward, the Commander of the task force, nor the Cabinet knew this at the material time.)[43] Much liberal opinion was shocked, but there was no room for liberal doubt in Thatcher's crystalline mental universe. It was enough for her that the commander on the spot thought that the *Belgrano* posed a threat to the British forces. When the Union Jack was raised over Port Stanley on 15 June, it was a victory for the military chiefs and the men and women under their command, but it was also a victory for her unflinching will.

She milked it for all it was worth – taking the salute at a victory parade through the city, sweeping into the Conservative Party conference to the strains of 'Rule Britannia', and insisting again and again that Britain had 'found herself again in the South Atlantic'.[44] It is hard to tell what difference such carefully choreographed evocations of Falklands glory made to the political climate. What is certain is that a dramatic turnaround in the government's standing took place in the closing stages of the war. May 1982 saw the Conservative Party in the lead for the first time since the summer of 1979; it stayed there for another two years. Also in May 1982, Thatcher's approval rating in the Gallup poll shot up to 42 per cent. In June, it rose to 48 per cent.

One reason was that Howe's policies were at last bearing fruit. During the next twelve months inflation fell faster than the Treasury expected; by the time Howe rose to make his 1983 budget speech, it had plunged to an astonishing 3.7 per cent – in part thanks to a fall in world commodity prices. Interest rates also fell; living standards for those in work rose; and there was even a slight increase in employment.[45] Yet when all the caveats have been entered, there is not much doubt that the 'Falklands Factor' was a crucial ingredient in the government's recovery. The courage and resolution displayed by Thatcher, the warrior queen, retrospectively vindicated Thatcher, the scourge of monetary incontinence and social indiscipline. When she held a general election in June 1983, the Conservatives were easily the favourites to win.

◌◌◌

Few predicted the scale of their victory. They won 42 per cent of the vote, but 397 seats – an overall majority of 144. It was the best Conservative result since 1935. Labour was led by the charming, civilised but politically inept Michael Foot, and fought on a manifesto known to the irreverent as 'the longest suicide note in history'. For its pains, it won 28 per cent of the vote and 209 seats. At 25 per cent, the Alliance's share of the vote was the highest won by a third party since 1923, but it won only twenty-three seats. In the polling booths, Britain now had a three-party system, but in Parliament the fifty-year-old, two-party duopoly was hardly dented. And of the duopolists, the Conservatives were easily the stronger. Contrary to the apprehensions of the wets and the hopes of the Alliance and Labour parties, the enduring tory nationalist strand in the political culture had turned out to be as vigorous as it had been under Lord Salisbury.

Thatcher was now free to construct a Cabinet in her own image, but her cautious side prevailed. She settled only one old score and made only two significant changes. Francis Pym, the Foreign Secretary, whom Thatcher detested both as a conspicuous wet and as 'a gloomy Whig',[46] was unceremoniously sacked. Howe became Foreign Secretary in his place. Nigel Lawson, Energy Secretary since the 1981 reshuffle, became Chancellor of the Exchequer, the best-qualified holder of the post since Jenkins, and perhaps since Gaitskell. He had been City editor of the *Financial Times* and editor of the *Spectator* before his election to Parliament in 1974. He was the kind of man Thatcher liked: brash, clever, attractively unpompous and slightly louche. In the early 1980s he wore his hair defiantly long and looked more like a pop star than a conventional Conservative politician. There was an engaging touch of impudence about him, and he was willing to take risks – sometimes more so than Thatcher. He was also a bit of a know-all, with a bump of self-belief as big as Thatcher's own. He had been an early convert to monetarism and an effective Wilson-baiter in the dismal Parliaments of 1974. He had also been the chief author of the abolition of exchange controls in 1979. He knew far more economics than Thatcher did; and he had a far more creative mind. Unlike the patient Howe, he could not be bullied. He wanted what she wanted: low inflation; low taxes; an 'enterprise culture'; a free market undistorted by special interests. But he was not prepared to let her dictate the route or the tempo of the march.

For the moment, all was harmony. The 1979 Parliament had been dominated by the battle against 'dishonest money', the public burial of Keynesian economic management and the crushing of the wets. Most of the institutional citadels of collectivism – the nationalised industries, the trade unions, the health and education services and local government in the Labour heartlands – had suffered only minor damage. The government had sold off a miscellany of state-owned assets, but the only big privatisation was the sale of 51 per cent of Britoil. Changes in employment law had trimmed trade-union immunities and opened union funds to civil damages when their officials were judged to have acted unlawfully.

These weakened the unions a little, but organised labour still had sharp teeth. A prolonged steel strike was defeated in 1980, though at the cost of a much higher settlement than the employers had offered at the start. But in 1981 Thatcher raised the Coal Board's borrowing limit to buy off a threatened miners' strike against pit closures – in Lawson's eyes an 'abject surrender'.[47] The health and education services had seen no significant changes. As for local government, current local authority spending had actually increased, despite cuts in grants from the centre.[48] Ultra-left councils in Greater London and old industrial cities such as Liverpool and Sheffield breathed defiance.

After the 1983 election, Thatcher's crusade shifted to a higher gear. Publicly owned assets were the softest target and, thanks partly to Lawson's enthusiasm, privatisation now became the government's policy flagship. (It had figured in the party's 1983 manifesto, but in a distinctly low-key way.) The 1983 Parliament saw two huge and immensely complicated examples: the privatisation of British Telecom in 1984 and of British Gas in 1986. The total yield for the two taken together was more than £8 billion – more than four times the figure for the whole of the government's first term. Altogether, the yield over the four years 1983–87 was more than £10 billion. The following Parliament saw privatisation yields reach a staggering £24 billion.

The economic and political effects were ambiguous, even perverse. Whilst Lawson took it for granted that privatisation made the economy more efficient, the evidence is inconclusive. The nationalised industries had been less efficient than privately owned ones, but it did not follow that privatisation was a magic bullet, automatically improving efficiency in the industries affected by it. Many privatised concerns were effectively immune to the threat of bankruptcy and the pressures of competition – two of the most powerful spurs to efficiency in the rest of the private sector.[49] Another objective was to give birth to a 'people's capitalism', based on much wider share ownership. To that end, publicly owned concerns were sold at bargain basement prices: 'Tell Sid', the advertising slogan for gas privatisation, had a distinctly spivvish ring to it. But, though numerous 'Sids' bought, most of them quickly sold again to cash in their winnings.[50] The number of shareholders in Britain rose substantially (only partly because of privatisation), yet the percentage of the UK equity market owned by individuals plummeted.

The most striking perversity was that the dead hand of the state pressed at least as heavily on the market as it had done before. So far from shrinking, the government's capacity to intervene in the economy grew. The privatised companies enjoyed too much market power to be left to their own devices. A substitute had to be found for the competitive pressures they escaped.

The substitute was regulation; and the regulators were bound to be state officials, appointed and instructed by ministers. Nicholas Ridley, a staunch member of Thatcher's ministerial praetorian guard and a zealous free marketeer, actually boasted that when nationalised industries were moved into the private sector, they were easier to control than they had been before.[51] Yet privatisation was the single most important emblem and embodiment of the Thatcher revolutions. Though its economic effects were ambiguous, its effects on the intellectual, political and moral climate were profound.

As we saw in Chapter 5, the nationalisation measures of the post-war Labour Government had had a mixed ancestry and confused results, but they had embodied a common sense that reigned for a generation. Simply by existing, nationalised concerns conveyed the message that, even in a capitalist economy, state ownership might serve the public interest better than private ownership. The sweeping privatisations of the 1980s entrenched a diametrically opposed common sense – that private firms are always more efficient than governments; that private-sector managers necessarily perform better than state officials; and that private property rights are so fundamental to freedom and efficiency that, wherever possible, public property should be sold off in order to create them. As we shall see, the new common sense was soon entrenched as firmly in the Labour Party as it was in other social institutions.[52] Eventually, it conquered most of the rest of the world and, at the start of the twenty-first century, it is still virtually unchallenged – the most successful British export of the last half-century.

◦⊱⊰◦

1984, the year of the first big privatisation, also saw the beginning of a life-or-death struggle with the NUM – the union with the sharpest teeth of all. The hawks in Thatcher's inner circle had been preparing for this struggle for years. As far back as 1978, Nicholas Ridley had drawn up a battle plan to ensure that in a future struggle between a Conservative Government and the miners, the former would win.[53] In 1982, hard on the heels of Thatcher's 1981 surrender, Arthur Scargill, the hero of the 1972 Saltley confrontation, was elected President of the NUM by a crushing majority. From Thatcher's point of view, Scargill was an enemy made in heaven. He was unimpressive to look at; Anthony Sampson described him as 'a small, neatly dressed figure with bright eyes and a high-pitched Yorkshire voice'.[54] He was also an avowed Marxist-Leninist revolutionary; the son of a Communist father; a graduate of the Young Communist League, schooled by the Communist Party theoretician, James Klugman; a master of the arts of self-promotion; an agitator of genius; and a believer in the crudest Stalinist version of the Marxist doctrine of the class war.

Like many of the far-left quasi-Trotskyites then seeking to take over the Labour Party, he believed that the war was reaching the point of crisis. Half-measures, deft manoeuvres and compromise with the class enemy – for which in any case he had no taste – were therefore tantamount to treachery. He had no time for industrial democracy or trade-union participation in management, he declared; they were 'the apologists' alternative to socialism'. It was time for a head-on assault on the enemy; and the role of the NUM, the vanguard of the working class, was to lead it. How much Scargill cared about the miners he led can never be known. To judge by his tactics he must have viewed them much as Douglas Haig viewed the infantrymen he poured into the killing fields of the Somme. What is certain is that he demanded 'total support' from them. What is also certain is that – in his own Yorkshire coalfield and among the tough young miners whose bitterness and resentment he voiced – he became an emblem of class defiance and pride. They sang, 'Arthur Scargill, Arthur Scargill, we'll support you ever more,' to the tune of 'Cwm Rhondda' and 'Arthur Scargill walks on water' to the tune of 'Deck the Walls'.[55]

Like Salisbury 100 years before, though less obviously, Thatcher saw politics in class terms; more importantly, she also had a bleak, unsentimental, Salisbury-like grasp of the realities of power. She knew as well as Scargill did that the NUM was the *corps d'élite* of organised labour, and that she would have to crush it if her attempt to restore authority and revive individualism were to succeed. Also like Scargill, she had nothing but contempt for well-meaning sentimentalists, forever seeking compromise where there was no room for it. She had hated the retreat forced on her in 1981; and she was determined to fight the next conflict with the miners to a finish. Coal was unobtrusively stockpiled at power stations, and wherever possible they were converted from coal to oil. In 1983, the 61-year-old, offensively hard-boiled Scottish-American manager, Ian MacGregor, became Chairman of the NCB. (David Jenkins, the Bishop of Durham, called him 'an imported elderly American'.)[56]

He had just presided over wholesale redundancies in the overmanned steel industry, and made it clear that coal could survive in an increasingly difficult energy market only by taking the same medicine. Production would have to be cut. Up to twenty uneconomic pits and 20,000 jobs would have to go. Scargill was bound to resist, just as MacGregor was bound to insist; and by late March 1984 one of the nastiest and most tragic strikes in British history was under way. Technically, it was not a national strike. Under NUM rules a national strike could take place only after a ballot, and Scargill was unwilling to call one in case he lost it. Instead, it was a series of Area strikes, each Area striking in accordance with its own rule books, many of which did not prescribe a ballot. Fatally for Scargill, however, the traditionally moderate Nottinghamshire Area did require a ballot; and the Notts miners voted by 70 to 30 per cent to go on working.

With the Notts coalfield working, coal stocks ample and the summer approaching, Scargill's chances of winning were slim. His negotiating stance reduced them to zero. There was no such thing as an uneconomic pit, he insisted; pits should be closed only when no more coal could be got from them. The costs of production were irrelevant. Losses should be accepted 'without limit'; the investment that the miners had made in the industry outweighed mere economics.[57] In effect, miners' jobs were property rights – sacrosanct until Britain's coal reserves were exhausted. It was not a proposition for which workers in other industries would be likely to sacrifice themselves, and though other unions contributed money to the miners, sympathetic industrial action was conspicuous by its rarity.

To Thatcher's horror there was a brief moment in July 1984 when it looked as if a compromise might settle the dispute after all, but Scargill refused to seize it. Another nail in his coffin was that picketing – the weapon with which he had made his name – was more violent than in the 1970s, in some cases shockingly so. Many of these cases were in Nottinghamshire, where working miners, backed by an overwhelming majority in their Area ballot, had to run the gauntlet of pickets despatched by an increasingly resented union leadership in Yorkshire. Again and again the nation's television viewers were treated to the spectacle of violent clashes between police in riot gear or on horseback, and pickets armed with bricks, stones and other projectiles. The ugliest confrontations occurred at the end of May 1984 at the Orgreave coke depot near Sheffield, where daily battles between pickets and police lasted for three weeks. Public sympathy with the NUM had been low to start with, and fell steadily as the strike went on. By December 1984, 88 per cent of those questioned disapproved of the miners' methods, compared with 7 per cent who approved.[58]

Little by little, striking miners scenting defeat dribbled back to work, and in March 1985 the strike was officially called off. Its chief victims were those miners who had heeded the strike call with doomed, ultimately self-destructive solidarity, and their families and communities. The rundown of the mining industry accelerated. The way of life that had grown up around it, and the mutual loyalties and communal pride that it had helped to engender, became little more than a memory. The costs to the national exchequer were considerable: £2.75 billion in public expenditure and a 1 per cent drop in national output.[59] From the government's point of view it was money well spent. The NUM was broken, its leadership's claim to be the irresistible vanguard of the working class exposed as empty boasting. Over the next five years its membership fell from 200,000 to less than 40,000, and it also had to contend with the breakaway Union of Democratic Miners (UDM) in Nottinghamshire. Scargill ceased to be a bogey and became a buffoon.

The demonstration effect on the rest of the Labour movement was even more important. Thatcher was much criticised for calling Scargill and his comrades 'enemies within', equating them with the 'enemies without' in the Argentine junta. But though her language was unseemly, she was right about the substance. Scargill and the inner core of the NUM leadership *were* enemies of the British state and they made no secret of the fact. By the same token, their crushing defeat encompassed far more than the NUM. The syndicalist myth of a heroic proletariat taking direct industrial action to destroy the capitalist state, and the Leninist myth of a disciplined elite leading the rest of the working class to victory, had been comprehensively discredited. Not only had Thatcher avenged Heath's three-day week and Callaghan's winter of discontent, but in doing so she had stamped out the fever which had helped to cause them.

The NUM was not the only union to go down to defeat. Early in 1986 a bitter dispute between the print unions and Rupert Murdoch's News International over the latter's move from Fleet Street to Wapping led to violent picketing and clashes with the police; once again the management, backed by a resolutely supportive government, won hands down. But the Wapping dispute was the end of an old song, not the beginning of a new one. The miners' defeat was a climacteric. With the NUM crushed and most of the trade-union movement cowed, the government was free to remodel industrial relations as it wished. While the strike was still in progress, it put through the 1984 Trade Union Act requiring secret ballots for strikes, elections to union executives and the establishment of political funds. On balance, this did the unions more good than harm, but more deadly measures followed.

The next ten years saw a cascade of legislation weakening unions, strengthening employers and hobbling collective action at the workplace. The government deregulated swathes of the labour market; effectively abolished closed shops; protected trade-union members from disciplinary sanctions against crossing picket lines; gave employers the right to dismiss unofficial strikers; and removed legal immunities for industrial action in support of workers so dismissed.[60] It was not always clear whether the government wanted to destroy trade unionism or to foster a 'new unionism' co-operating with ministers, on the model of Eric Hammond's electricians.[61] However, the central theme of its policy was not in doubt. It hoped, through carefully judged salami tactics, to substitute individual rights for group rights and an individualistic employment culture for a collectivist one.

It was astonishingly successful. Trade-union membership fell from nearly 13.5 million in 1979 to a fraction more than 9.5 million in 1991. Over the same period, the percentage of the labour force in unions plummeted from 53 per cent to 34.4 per cent – a lower figure than in any previous post-war year. In 1979 (admittedly the year of Callaghan's nemesis at the hands of unofficial strikers) a total of almost 30 million working days had been lost in strikes; in 1991 the figure was just over half a million.[62] Where Heath's attempts at Whiggish inclusion had failed to tame the unions, Thatcher's tory nationalist blunderbuss had succeeded. Trade-union leaders were no longer powers in the land; the dream of industrial citizenship at the point of production, which had flickered intermittently in the psyche of the Labour movement for the best part of a century, faded away.

Deeper forces drove in the same direction. The time-honoured 'productivist' assumption that real, lasting wealth came from manufacturing and not from services could still be detected in Labour and trade-union rhetoric, but it rang increasingly hollow. Since the early 1950s, manufacturing had been in decline while the service sector of the economy burgeoned. Repeated attempts to halt or reverse this process of 'de-industrialisation' through industrial policies, regional policies and tax changes had come to nothing – not surprisingly, since it was one of the hallmarks of a mature economy.[63] True to their laissez-faire principles, the Thatcher governments did not even try to reverse it; and from 1980 to 1990 employment in manufacturing fell from 7 million to around 5 million. (In 1966 it had been almost 9 million.)[64]

The inner meaning of this extraordinary transformation was often misunderstood. Charges that Thatcher and her colleagues were wicked or supine in allowing it to take place were wide of the mark. Industrial workers were to Britain what peasants had been to France: victims of a process of economic restructuring that no democratic government could have stopped for long. The real charge against the Tory nationalist crusaders is not that they helped Britain to become one of the pacemakers of the post-industrial economic order which now embraces most of the developed world. It is that they did too little to alleviate the accompanying pain. The chief casualties were the industrial workers who lost their jobs and, in many cases, their self-esteem, but the classical trade-unionism of the movement's great days, with its collectivist ethos and its sometimes truculent class-consciousness, was a casualty as well.

As with privatisation, the moral and cultural effects were as profound as the economic ones. The old industrial culture, particularly in the old industrial regions, had been paternalist, solidaristic and defiantly macho. As de-industrialisation spread, new values came to the fore, particularly in the services with the highest added value: self-reliance, nimbleness and adaptability. The widely held notion that there was no room for collective action in a post-industrial economy was baseless, but the heavy-handed, slow-moving, male-dominated collectivism of the industrial era had become a museum piece.

HUBRIS

Privatisation was straightforward. The government decided which assets to sell and duly sold them. It found it harder to tame the unions, but it overcame the difficulties more easily than most people had expected in 1979. Local government, the third great collectivist citadel, was a more formidable barrier to the tory nationalist advance. Legally, local authorities were creations of the absolutely sovereign Crown-in-Parliament, but custom and practice had given them autonomy in their own sphere. Since the war, successive governments, with the Attlee and Wilson governments in the van, had pushed back the frontiers of local autonomy. Yet, in a vague and muddled way, the notion that there ought to be a frontier of some sort had survived.

One of the central themes of the Thatcher regime was an increasingly formidable assault on that notion. Though Labour had cash-limited the local authorities' capital spending and the rate support grant they received from the centre, the government still had no control over their total current spending. In the early 1980s, Thatcher and her colleagues decided that they would have to close that gap in the fabric of central financial control if Howe's battle to curb public spending were to succeed. As unemployment mounted, a growing number of local authorities fell to an increasingly militant Labour Party. 'Municipal socialists' of varied hues sought explicitly to use the spending power of the 'local state' to negate the policies of the central state. The young, blind and drivingly ambitious David Blunkett of Sheffield set out a programme of breathtaking scope. In manifest defiance of government policy, a 'decentralized municipal socialism' would draw together 'business, commerce, trade unions, community groups and workers to save the declining steel and engineering industries'.[65]

The Greater London Council (GLC) was even more obnoxious to ministers. The leader of the Council was the supposedly far-left Ken Livingstone, whose allies had carried out a successful coup against the moderate Andrew McIntosh immediately after the 1981 council election. Under Livingstone's leadership, the GLC subsidised a 32 per cent cut in London Transport fares, brilliantly packaged as 'Fares Fair', which was eventually struck down by the Court of Appeal. It also set up a Greater London Enterprise Board to promote worker participation and plan London's economy, and for good measure paid out 'a cornucopia of grants' to minority groups ranging from welfare claimants to gays, and from peace campaigners to feminists.[66] Livingstone himself – perky, crafty, telegenic, sometimes funny, sometimes zany and always outrageous – ranked second only to Scargill as a hate-figure for the Conservative tabloids.

It did not take long for an outraged government to revenge itself.[67] Its first move was to cut central grants. That led Labour councils to raise the rates – secure in the knowledge that large number of Labour voters paid none. The government then substituted a block grant for the old rate support grant, and decreed that councils which spent more than the government laid down for them would see their grants cut. Obstreperous councils piled on yet more spending and yet more rate increases. The government retaliated with two draconian measures, designed to show, once and for all, who was boss. In 1984, it took power to limit local spending by 'capping' the rates – a revolutionary measure overturning a 400-year-old tradition that gave local authorities freedom to determine their own rates. In 1985, it passed a Local Government Act abolishing the GLC and the Metropolitan counties.

Livingstone ran a slick, costly and highly effective campaign against GLC abolition, with the slogan 'Say No to No Say', but the government's eventual victory was inevitable. It was the same story with rate-capping. Blunkett, by now a member of the Labour Party national executive, led a doomed campaign of defiance, reminiscent of the trade unions' doomed recourse to direct action sixty years earlier. Socialism, he declared, would 'not come from parliamentary action alone. Socialism will come from the fight in the trade unions and the community.'[68] However, the campaign collapsed in humiliation and confusion, with the 'local state' crushed, the central state more dominant than ever and municipal socialism in ruins.

The government's centralist appetite grew with feeding. In the general election of June 1987, the Conservatives won an unprecedented third term, with a fraction more than 42 per cent of the popular vote. They won an overall majority of 102 – bigger than any other post-war Conservative majority apart from the crushing 144 of 1983. There was a swing to Labour in Scotland, Wales and Northern England, but London swung to the Conservatives, while in the Midlands and the rest of the South-East their vote was undented. Three-quarters of Labour's seats were in its old industrial redoubts. London apart, it had only three seats in the South. The Alliance share of the vote fell by 3 per cent, and Labour's share rose by the same amount. But though Labour was now well ahead of the Alliance, the

Thatcher coalition embracing the business class, small employers, the self-employed and the aspirant, individualised 'new' working class, seemed invulnerable.

In the country as a whole, the Conservatives won 36 per cent of the working-class vote, its highest post-war share, and came ahead of Labour among skilled workers. In the South it won 40 per cent of the total working-class vote, compared to Labour's puny 28 per cent. By common consent, Labour had run a more professional campaign than the Conservatives. Its eloquent and still youthful leader, Neil Kinnock, had fought doughtily against the quasi-Trotskyite Militant Tendency. Its manifesto had been purged of the most extreme far-left excrescences of four years before. Survey evidence showed that a majority of the electorate preferred high social spending, even with higher taxation, to low spending with low taxes. And still Labour's share of the vote was 11 per cent behind the Conservatives'. It seemed irrevocably destined to be the party of declining areas, declining occupations and a declining culture: a relic of the age of steam hobbling into the age of the computer.

Thatcher would not have been human if she had not felt a twinge of hubris, and she had never been good at hiding her feelings. Her interpretation of the result soon became notorious. In the inner cities, she declared, the Conservatives had 'a big job to do ... to help the people get more choice.'[69] Decoded, that signalled a policy mutation that continued under her 'New' Labour successors at the start of the twenty-first century. The third theme of the Thatcher crusade – a campaign to root out the dependency culture; to humble the intermediate social institutions that stood between the individual and the state, and that generations of whig imperialists had cherished; and to exalt business values over professional ones – took centre-stage.

Collectivist local government was still a prime target, but the education and health services, and the professionals who ran them, came a close second. Functions previously performed by elected councillors were farmed out to more reliable bodies – in some cases, to private firms; in some to nominated bodies known as 'quangos' (quasi non-governmental organisations), appointed by ministers; and in some to central government itself. At the same time, ministers did their best to remodel the public services along market lines. The result was a slow, uneven, but radical transformation of the public culture and of the relationship between society and the state. Central government extended its reach and tightened its grasp. The business class was exalted and the professional class demeaned. Unelected appointees increasingly replaced elected persons. Social institutions that countervailed the central state were shackled or marketised or both. There was no master plan, but a vision gleamed through the detail: political power would be concentrated in the hands of ministers and officials at the centre and their agents; market principles would reign supreme elsewhere, except in the private sphere of friendship and family.

In areas most in need of regeneration, centrally appointed quangos called Urban Development Corporations took over the planning, compulsory-purchase and transport powers previously exercised by local councils. By the end of the decade, unelected housing associations, financed by another quango – the Housing Corporation – were carrying out most housing starts. A Local Management of Schools initiative devolved budgets from the local authorities to the schools. The 1988 Education Reform Act transferred control of polytechnics from local to central government, enabling schools to opt out of local authority control – and thereby into central government control instead. Two years later, a National Health Service Act created a so-called 'internal market', in which providers (in other words, hospitals) were supposed to compete for custom from purchasers (in other words, general practitioners). Most hospitals became allegedly self-governing trusts whose boards were appointed and dismissible by the Secretary of State. Medical autonomy was eroded, while quangos, 'remote, secretive and subject to political manipulation',[70] proliferated.

The government's lash fell even more heavily on the academic profession – for many of Thatcher's followers, the most offensive of all the institutional obstacles to the enterprise culture. (Its offensiveness was exacerbated by Oxford University's much publicised refusal to award her an honorary degree.) The academic-dominated University Grants Committee, which had disbursed government funding to individual universities since the 1920s, was replaced by a Funding Council, on which academics were required to be in a minority. In one of the oddest proxy markets of a period rich in such creatures, universities were obliged to contract with the Council, in effect a monopoly purchaser, to deliver specified services, of a specified quality, judged by ever more elaborate appraisals. Some university managements went out of their way to mimic the language of the private sector. The jaunty, fashion-conscious Vice-Chancellor of Salford University even referred to its chairmen of departments as 'line managers'.[71] Everywhere, academics seeking research funding or applying for jobs boasted of their 'entrepreneurial' spirit. The Education Reform Act effectively abolished academic tenure, historically the chief safeguard for academic autonomy, though a clause protecting academic freedom was inserted in the House of Lords, in the teeth of violent ministerial opposition.

Other notably suspect institutions were the BBC, the higher civil service and the Church of England (once known to the disrespectful as the 'Tory

Party at prayer'). Their fates differed. Thatcher stuffed the BBC's board of governors with supporters, but in spite of frequent bullying by ministers and a determined attempt to subject it to market disciplines, the Corporation managed to retain its independence. Her approach to the civil service was more subtle. For many Tory nationalists, bureaucracy was one of the chief drivers of authority-sapping collectivism, and Whitehall a nursery of national defeatism.

Here, however, Thatcher the guileful politician took over from Thatcher the militant crusader. To the chagrin of some of her inner circle, she did not launch a head-on attack on the whole institution.[72] Instead, she did her best to turn it into a committed instrument of her will, and to replace its ethos of dispassionate professionalism with a simulacrum of private-sector managerialism. She savaged civil servants whom she thought waffling or obstructive, and took a closer interest in promotions than any previous prime minister. In a narrow party sense, charges that she politicised the service were wide of the mark; some of those who benefited from her patronage were Labour in politics. But she undoubtedly changed the culture of Whitehall. To use a phrase coined by Lord Bancroft, whom she sacked as head of the civil service at the start of her reign, its 'grovel count' rose,[73] as ambitious officials discovered that it was no longer healthy to tell the truth to power.

A decade later, a much more ferocious new wind was beginning to blow through Whitehall, under the anodyne rubric, *Next Steps*. The aim was to separate responsibility for policy from operational responsibilities. The former would remain with government departments; the latter would be hived off to agencies at arm's length from ministers. To those undazzled by the fashionable rhetoric of public-service management, it seemed a flawed enterprise. In the real world the distinction between policy and operations was hard to maintain, and sometimes almost invisible. Flawed or not, however, *Next Steps* had two far-reaching consequences, both of which struck at the heart of the British version of democracy. Ministerial accountability to Parliament and the people, one of the core values of the old constitution despite the frequency with which it was ignored in practice, was weakened still further. At the same time, the managerial culture of the private sector began to displace the professional ethic which had been fundamental to the higher civil service since the demise of 'Old Corruption' in the second half of the nineteenth century.[74]

The Church of England was the institution that got away. Robert Runcie, the Archbishop of Canterbury for most of Thatcher's term, was for her a peculiarly egregious *bête noire*. He was no wimp. He had served in the Scots Guards during the war; and had won an MC for wiping out a German gun emplacement while under heavy fire. However, that made his conduct at the St Paul's thanksgiving service after the Falklands war all the more outrageous in Thatcherite eyes. Not only did he pointedly refrain from the triumphalism which had become one of Thatcher's favourite political weapons, but he had the temerity to remind the congregation that the Argentines were also mourning their dead and that war was a terrible thing.[75]

Still more outrageous from the government's point of view was a notable report on 'Faith in the City' issued by a Church of England Commission, with representation from the universities, the trade unions and private business as well as the Church itself, and published in 1985.[76] It referred favourably to Marx's insight that 'evil is to be found, not just in the human heart, but in the very structure of economic and social relationships'. It also pointed out that social justice was a recurrent theme of the Old Testament and insisted that 'a long Christian tradition' rejected 'the amassing of wealth unless it is justly obtained and fairly distributed'.[77]

Its recommendations ranged from an increase in Child Benefit to an expanded programme of publicly provided housing, but its critique of the assumptions underpinning Thatcherite statecraft mattered more than its specific proposals. Across the country as many as 20 or even 25 per cent of the population, the Commission found, was 'excluded by poverty or powerlessness from sharing in the common life of our nation'.[78] And this had not happened by accident. It was the result of a 'crude exaltation of the alleged benign social consequences of individual self interest and com-petition',[79] and of the individual and social choices that had resulted. In the eyes of the Church, it seemed, the vigorous virtues were not virtues at all.

Faith in the City struck at the moral heart of Thatcher's vision. She fumed inwardly. Some of her colleagues fumed outwardly as well: one unnamed minister insisted that the report was 'pure Marxist theology'.[80] But neither she nor they could bring the Church to heel. The implications were more complex than either Thatcher or her largely irreligious political opponents were happy to acknowledge. As befitted the oldest institution in the land, the Church of England still mattered, even in a supposedly secular society. No secular institution – not the universities, not the media, not the pro-fessions and certainly not the civil service or the trade unions – had as much moral authority. And because the Church mattered, *Faith in the City* proved that, in spite of all their efforts, the Tory nationalist crusaders had not achieved the cultural hegemony that they sought.

৵৵

Seemingly, however, they *had* achieved political dominance; 1987 and 1988 were their glory years. While they basked in the glow of their third election victory, the Alliance disintegrated, and Labour embarked on a policy review that presaged the final demise of socialism as a political force. Whatever carping clerics might say, their crusade had been astonishingly successful already and seemed set for further advance. The already dying embers of vulgar Keynesianism had been doused. The trade unions had been cowed. A huge swathe of nationalised industries had been sold off; others were about to be sold off. Central government had drawn the teeth of local government. Even in Eastern Europe, the tide seemed to be running in the same direction. Widening cracks were fracturing the once-monolithic Soviet bloc. In the Soviet Union itself, Mikhail Gorbachev's reforms were beginning to undermine the institutional and ideological foundations of the regime. In Poland, 'Solidarity' – part trade union and part social movement – challenged the edifice of Soviet power. In Hungary the regime was moving cautiously towards something suspiciously like a market economy. At the end of the decade the slow meltdown of the Communist system suddenly culminated in the fall of the Berlin Wall and the 'velvet revolutions' that drove the Communists from power all over central and Eastern Europe.

Thatcher could not claim the credit for this extraordinary transformation. She could fairly claim to have been one of its most insistent champions, however – partly because she had been one of the West's harshest critics of Communist totalitarianism during the second Cold War of the early 1980s, but also because she was surprisingly flexible when the Soviet system began to change. With uncharacteristic open-mindedness, she had seen that Gorbachev was a man she 'could do business with' even before he became the ruler of the Soviet Union. East of the old iron curtain she became a heroine. On a visit to Moscow in 1987 she gave an unprecedented, fifty-minute, unedited television interview and aroused so much enthusiasm on a walkabout around a housing estate that an eyewitness felt that she might have been 'fighting a by-election in Moscow North'.[81] When she visited the Gdansk shipyard in Poland eighteen months later to express her support for the still-illegal Solidarity, a crowd of several thousand greeted her with the chant, 'Vivat Thatcher.'

At home, the economy boomed, real wages rose, house prices soared, the growth rate reached higher levels than in France or Germany and unemployment started to fall. Income taxes were cut – the standard rate to 25 per cent and the top rate to 40 per cent.[82] The 1986 'Big Bang' had already opened up the City to a flood of foreign firms and consolidated London's role as a key player in global capital markets. Together with the deregulation of financial services the following year, it helped to procure a culture of feverish speculation and conspicuous consumption that spread well beyond the Square Mile.[83] City dealers seemed to inhabit a bedlam of crudity and loutishness. A visiting reporter from the Midlands painted a particularly vivid picture of the atmosphere:

'Eh! Oi!, Oi!, Oi!, Oi!, Aht, aht', bawled one, as the buyers went into something resembling the feeding frenzy of sharks. There were millions being made and lost here, by boys in ridiculous-looking jackets, shouting and bawling in conditions of complete chaos.

Many of the boys concerned came from working-class homes in the East End: 'The barrow-boy type', said one commodity broker, 'is best at this game.'[84] But the widespread notion that the City had been taken over by upwardly mobile and sharp-elbowed cockneys was wide of the mark. One of the most noteworthy signs of the times was the growing attraction of City careers for professional-class Oxbridge graduates lured by the prospect of dizzy rewards: according to one estimate, the 380,000 people working in the City had a total after-tax disposable income of £4.5 billion by the late 1980s.[85]

Stories of champagne-guzzling yuppies were rife. 'Loadsamoney', originally a character in a sketch by the alternative comedian Harry Enfield, was taken up by the *Sun* and soon became part of the argot of the times. The housing market was awash with capital gains. Fuelling the boom was a huge upsurge in borrowing. Credit control effectively ended, and banks and building societies – by now virtually indistinguishable from each other – fell over themselves to lend. Advances for house purchases rose from £17 billion in 1984 to almost £30 billion in 1987, while in 1987–8 personal borrowing of all sorts rose by £40 billion, according to Lawson ten times the total that his tax cuts pumped into the economy.[86] The rewards were distributed very unevenly. In 1989, more than 40 per cent of total disposable income went to the richest 20 per cent of households, and only a little more than 7 per cent to the poorest 20 per cent. The pay of leading company directors rose four times as fast as average wages.[87] But Thatcher and Lawson saw nothing wrong in that: they had never been egalitarians.

The moral and cultural effects of the boom were a different matter. In the early 1990s the social critic David Selbourne chronicled the rise of a new, coarse, 'plebian' culture, which was particularly obtrusive on package holidays:

Moving in groups and often sporting the colours of national and football allegiance, drunken jollity and (more commonly) drunken sullenness and unease can swiftly turn to pack vandalism and violence. The plebian dog-in-the-manger ... bares his teeth ('the Spanish are shit, I hate them') at the local citizen. He bawlingly expresses his feigned contempt for the youth of the place, and above all for its passing women; then picks his fights and smashes his surroundings, often with female British plebians egging on, or even joining, the mayhem, until violent desire is sated.[88]

Selbourne's plebians were not as new as he implied. They were the 'roughs' of the 1860s in 1980s dress. But there was a big difference between the new roughs and the old ones. The old ones had been poor; the new ones were affluent enough to afford package holidays, not to mention cars, colour televisions and a range of consumer durables. The real significance of Selbourne's 'plebian' culture was that its embrace extended well beyond the victims of economic change to some of the beneficiaries; that, as old restraints dissolved, roughness was moving up the income scale.

In a different sphere, the lure of easy money provoked at least two spectacular cases of fraud – one leading to the collapse of the Bank of Credit and Commerce International (BCCI), and the other to the conviction of four Guinness directors for conspiring to force up the price of Guinness shares during a takeover battle for the drinks company Distillers – as well as excessive borrowing by householders all over the country. In the feverish, coarse-grained, casino-like economic climate of late-1980s Britain, the inescapable tension between Thatcher's free-market economics and her small-town ethics became painfully acute. Upwardly mobile entrepreneurs, willing to take risks and with an eye for new opportunities, sometimes made fortunes, and those in work were better off than they had ever been. But there was no sign of a miraculous rebirth of the puritanical, abstinent, authority-respecting values that had reigned in Alderman Roberts' corner shop. There was plenty of vigour about, but not much virtue. As we shall see in the next chapter, the tension between the two would begin to trouble thoughtful Conservatives in the following decade, but so long as the boom continued doubts were easily stilled.

ᴄᴊᴏ

The good times did not last. (They never do.) By 1989, the *annus mirabilis* that saw the retreat of communism in Eastern Europe turn into a rout, growth in Britain was turning down. Sterling was once again in trouble and inflation was rising again. Far more damagingly in the long run, a profound schism appeared in the crusaders' camp. To understand why, we must retrace our steps and examine the curious story of Lawson's apostasy. When Thatcher promoted him to be Chancellor in 1983 she had seen him as a kindred spirit. But, as noted earlier, he was his own man. Before his promotion to Chancellor, he had been one of the leading prophets of the monetarist faith, yet once in the Treasury he developed symptoms of heterodoxy. He discovered that the fundamental tenet of monetarism – that control of the money supply was the cure for inflation – could not be made operational in practice.

There was a protean, almost metaphysical, quality about money. It eluded precise definition, and its behaviour baffled its would-be controllers. The relationship between the price level and the money supply – however defined – was unstable, even capricious.[89] Using the money supply as the lodestar of anti-inflationary policy was equivalent to flying blind. Lawson cast around for an alternative to orthodox monetarism and eventually found one: Britain would join the Exchange Rate Mechanism (ERM) of the European Monetary System, set up shortly before the Conservatives entered office to create a zone of currency stability in Europe. For Thatcher this was not just heresy; it was close to blasphemy. The very idea that a group of governments should (or could) stabilise exchange rates made her bristle. The only 'right' exchange rate was the rate set by the market; to believe otherwise was to fall into a 'pre-capitalist' trap.[90]

Her opposition had deeper roots as well. A floating rate meant bowing to the sovereignty of the market, but that held no terrors for a good Hayekian. Entering the ERM would mean infringing the political sovereignty of the British state, and make nonsense of the dream of Britain as an independent island power; for Thatcher that was unthinkable as well as intolerable. She vetoed Lawson's proposal, telling her Cabinet that if they joined the ERM they would have to do so without her.

Balked of ERM membership, Lawson eventually fell back on subterfuge. Sterling would shadow the deutschmark, the hardest major currency in Europe. However, this was not a panacea either, not least because Thatcher did her best to sabotage the policy; and, after much delay, Lawson, strongly backed by Howe, returned to the ERM charge. With great difficulty, the two contrived a confrontation with Thatcher on the eve of a European summit in Madrid in June 1989, and threatened to resign unless she committed Britain to ERM membership by 1992. They won a partial victory. At the summit Thatcher declared that Britain would indeed join the ERM, subject to certain achievable conditions, though without giving a date. But she soon took her revenge. The following month, she reshuffled Howe out of the Foreign Office and into the Leadership of the House of Commons. Three months after that Lawson resigned of his own accord, driven to distraction by semi-public sniping from Thatcher's personal economic adviser, Alan Walters, an unreconstructed monetarist and an unyielding opponent of the ERM.

DOWNFALL

More was at stake in Thatcher's dispute with Lawson and Howe than met the eye. In her eyes, her uppity ministers were not just schismatics. They were very nearly traitors – and to their country as well as to her. In her early days as leader, her passionate nationalism had gone together with low-key support for British membership of the European Community. As Prime Minister, she had fought a long-drawn-out battle to cut Britain's contribution to the Community budget, but after winning most of what she wanted she became a co-operative Community citizen. She supported the ambitious project of Community-wide deregulation and trade liberalisation put forward by the Commission President, Jacques Delors, under the rubric of the 'single market'; she also agreed to the proto-federalist 1986 Single European Act eliminating national vetoes from a wide range of policy areas.

That, however, was the high water mark of her Europeanism. To her bitter chagrin she discovered that, for Delors and most member governments, the single market was the beginning of a new European journey, not the end of an old one. They believed that economic liberalisation should go hand in hand with social protection, and that the single market logically implied a single currency. To Thatcher, such notions were hateful. The first spelled corporatism, 'socialism' and, in some of her more fire-eating moments, Marxism. The second spelled the end of Britain as a sovereign state. Everything she had tried to achieve – the untaming of capitalism; the regeneration of nationhood; the enterprise culture; the reassertion of authority – seemed under threat.

Her gorge rose. In the most remarkable speech of her career, delivered at Bruges in 1988, when the sun of the Lawson boom still shone, she raked her new enemies with two defiant broadsides, one near the beginning and one at the end:

> We have not successfully rolled back the frontiers of the state in Britain only to see them reimposed at a European level, with a European superstate exercising a new dominance from Brussels. . . .
>   Let us have a Europe which plays its full part in the wider world, which looks outward, not inward, and which preserves that Atlantic Community – that Europe on both sides of the Atlantic – which is our noblest inheritance and our greatest strength.[91]

In short, no social Europe; no supranational integration; and no distinctive European identity. The implications were stark. If the other member states insisted on taking the path that Delors had sketched out, they would do so without Britain.

In the 1970s, the European issue had split the Labour Party. After the Bruges speech it began to split the Conservatives. For the next two years, Thatcher's heart was at war with her head. She developed a visceral loathing for Delors and all he stood for. She felt hemmed in by aggressive federalists on the continent and shilly-shallying compromisers in her own Cabinet. She yearned to lash out, but she dared not do so. That explains her tortuous conduct in 1989 when she succumbed to the Howe–Lawson blackmail over the ERM, only to manoeuvre Howe out of the Foreign Office and allow Lawson to leave the Treasury in dudgeon.

In 1990 tortuousness gave way to torment. Less than a year after Lawson's resignation, his successor as Chancellor, the amiable, hard-working but inexperienced John Major, persuaded her that Britain should join the ERM after all. In her memoirs she explained that she had too few Cabinet allies to continue her resistance. Not even 'the most determined democratic leader', she wrote ruefully, can 'stand out against what the Cabinet, the Parliamentary Party and the press demand'.[92] Her price was a cut in interest rates, which helped to win her a rapturous reception at the Conservative Party conference in October. But it is hard to believe that that assuaged the sense of humiliation she must have felt.

☙❧

Much more humiliation was in store. Through all the squabbles over anti-inflation policy and ERM membership, a ticking bomb had lurked in the background.[93] It had been put in place in the early months of 1985, while the battle over rate-capping was reaching a crescendo, but its history went much further back. In the October 1974 election, Thatcher, then the Conservatives' shadow Environment Secretary, had committed the party to abolish domestic rates. After the 1979 victory, backbench Conservative pressure led the Environment Department to inquire into possible alternatives, but it concluded that the rates should stay. The same thing happened after the victory of 1983. A white paper published soon after the election rehearsed the arguments for and against a variety of local taxes yet again; yet again the conclusion was that rates should continue.

Then, for no obvious reason, policy switched. Another inquiry started in the autumn of 1985, led by two ambitious, originally damp junior ministers, the plump Kenneth Baker and the lean William Waldegrave. Both were eager to prove that they had purged themselves of their Heathite heresies. Both soon became more Thatcherite than Thatcher. Rates, they concluded, were a thoroughly bad tax. Since only a minority of voters paid them, they allowed local councils to escape electoral punishment for extravagant spending decisions. They bore as heavily on little old ladies living alone as on large households in similar properties, and were therefore unfair; worse still, they helped to promote the 'growing anarchy' in high-spending far-left authorities. The cure for these evils was to introduce a per capita tax falling equally on all consumers of local authority services. An initially cautious Thatcher was soon converted. With the signal exception of Nigel Lawson, so was the Cabinet. At an enthusiastic Conservative Party conference in October 1986, Nicholas Ridley, now Environment Secretary, announced that the proposed per capita tax, now known officially as a 'community charge' and unofficially as a 'poll tax', would be 'at the very top of our agenda'. Legislation to introduce a poll tax in Scotland passed into law not long before the 1987 election. Similar legislation for England and Wales reached the statute book in July 1988. In 1990 it came into effect.

The result was a nationwide explosion of indignation, of astonishing ferocity. In part this was due to the wild variations between the charges levied by different authorities. To take only one striking contrast, Wandsworth's charge was £148 a year; Haringey's, £554. More damaging to the government was a yawning gap between its initial forecasts of the average charge and the outcome. In the Baker–Waldegrave studies in 1985, the average was projected to be £140. In the event it was £363. More damaging still was that there were more losers and fewer winners than the government had expected, and that the hardest hit were the skilled workers and lower middle classes that supplied the foot soldiers of the Thatcher coalition. However, the really fatal feature of the charge was that – like all poll taxes – it was regressive by definition; and that this outraged a deep-seated, cross-class sense of fairness which had survived all the government's attempts to implant market values in the public culture.

Like many populists, Thatcher was not particularly popular. The voters returned her to office with thumping majorities because she was feisty, gutsy and decisive, not because they shared her values. Indeed, public attitudes were less Thatcherite at the end of the 1980s than they had been ten years before.[94] Stories of working-class families facing bills of more than £1000 while wealthy individuals found themselves £10,000 a year better off shocked middle-aged and middle-class Conservatives as much as rebellious working-class youths. More than 70 per cent of the electorate opposed the community charge, and the nationwide demonstrations against it included plenty of respectable citizens as well as habitual militants. The end of March 1990 saw a violent anti-poll tax riot in central London, but this was the work of a small minority who had piggybacked on a good-natured and peaceful demonstration of between 50,000 and 100,000.

In any case, the public delivered its most telling messages from the polling booths, not the streets. In March 1990, Labour captured the safe Conservative seat of Mid-Staffordshire with a swing of 22 per cent. In the local elections in May, the Conservatives suffered heavy losses. In October, the Liberal Democrats overturned a Conservative majority of 17,000 in Eastbourne. Panic swept the Conservative benches in the Commons as Thatcher, the erstwhile heroine, began to look suspiciously like an electoral albatross.

By now, the forces that would bring her down the following year were beginning to muster. In November 1989, Sir Anthony Meyer, a mild-mannered, slightly eccentric, long-serving Conservative backbencher and a committed European federalist, stood against her for the party leadership. He won only 33 votes, but there were 27 abstentions – hardly a ringing endorsement of her position. Meanwhile, a much bigger beast than Meyer was on the prowl. In early 1986, Michael Heseltine, by this time Defence Secretary, had resigned from the Cabinet in protest against Thatcher's refusal to back a European rather than an American link-up to save the failing Westland helicopter firm, and (even more damagingly) against her disdain for the normal rules of Cabinet government. He behaved with ostentatious decorum thereafter. He assiduously courted Conservative constituency associations, but no public criticism of Thatcher passed his lips. Yet he was a focus for discontent, a living indictment of Thatcher's leadership style and – most damagingly of all – a reminder that there were other Conservative traditions besides hers, with different implications for statecraft and national identity.

The end was brutal. Although the story is etched deep in the public memory, the broad outlines bear retelling. At a European Summit in Rome at the end of October 1990, Thatcher found herself in a minority of one in opposing a timetable for monetary union. She left Rome seething with barely suppressed anger, but her Commons statement on the Summit was comparatively restrained. However, the dam holding back her surging emotions broke when she had to answer a needling question from Kinnock. In one of the most astonishing outbursts of raw fury in recent parliamentary history, she alleged that Delors had said he wanted the Commission to be the European executive, the European Parliament to be its democratic body and the Council of Ministers to be its Senate, and then shouted the immortal words, 'No, No, No' – 'her eye,' as Hugo Young put it, 'seemingly directed to the fields and seas, the hills and the landing-grounds, where the island people would never surrender'.[95]

'Up Yours, Delors' the *Sun* inimitably rejoiced next day. It was premature. For two years Thatcher had treated Howe, her most faithful lieutenant in the crucial first Parliament of her reign, with open contempt. For him, her 'No, No, No' was the last straw. He resigned from the government, to deliver an icy, beautifully constructed and devastating resignation statement a few days later. Next day, Heseltine announced his candidacy for the Conservative leadership. Thatcher won a majority on the first ballot, but thanks to the Byzantine complexity of the Conservative Party's election rules she had too few votes for immediate victory. Cabinet minister after Cabinet minister then fled her sinking ship, forcing her to withdraw from the contest. She threw her weight behind John Major, who was duly elected with 185 votes to Heseltine's 131 and Douglas Hurd's 56. Less than two months after her delirious reception at her party conference, she was out of office, never to return. Not for the first or the last time, charisma had evaporated, while centralist populism had boomeranged.

Thatcher was the victim of a double crisis – of identity and, still more, of authority. Her vision of post-imperial Britain as an independent island power, sufficient unto herself, was out of joint with the realities of the integrating Europe on her doorstep and the interdependent world in which the British were increasingly enmeshed. The assertive individualism that she fostered in the economy and society depleted the authority of the state on which her whole project depended, and which it had been her prime purpose to bolster. Like the Attlee Government after the war her governments changed the face of Britain, but not in the way they had originally intended to do. Yet, at the start of the twenty-first century, her legacy is everywhere. Judged by deeds rather than words, she was the most radical prime minister of the century – far more so than Attlee or even than Asquith or Lloyd George.

Under her, and to a large extent because of her, the tamed capitalism of Baldwin, Attlee, Macmillan, Wilson and Heath perished. A new species of untamed capitalism appeared in its place. The political economy, the British version of democracy, the structure of the state, the operating assumptions of its officials and its relationship to society were all transformed – so much so that, in some cases, it was hard to realise that the Britain of 1990 was the same country as the Britain of 1979. Thatcher was not the sole author of this transformation. Privatisation owed more to Lawson than to her; Heseltine deserved as much credit for council house sales as she did; Kenneth Baker was a more determined enemy of local democracy and diversity than she was. Despite her disdain for the traditional civil service ethos of dispassionate political neutrality, the transformation of British governance – which was one of her most important bequests to her successors – owed at least as much to civil servants as to politicians. And, notwithstanding her frequent unpopularity, she was right in thinking that her intransigent Tory nationalism chimed with the instincts of millions of her fellow countrymen and women, in all social classes. They were the foot soldiers of her crusade; without them, 'Thatcherism' would have been impossible.

The fact remains that the crusade was hers. Similar changes took place right across the developed world, from the Antipodes to North America to Western Europe and even, in some degree, to what had once been the Communist bloc, but Thatcher's aggression, willpower and élan gave the British version of the transformation a special flavour that long survived her ejection from office. Since her fall, British politics have been conducted in her monstrous shadow. No serious contender for power seeks to undo her work: the only question is how best to come to terms with it.[96] For better or worse, twenty-first-century Britain is her monument.

TURNING TIDE

✣

We have had less freedom than we believed. That which we have enjoyed has been too dependent on the benevolence of our rulers. Our freedoms have remained their possession, rationed out to us as subjects rather than being our own inalienable possession as citizens.

Charter 88, 1988

Scotland faces a crisis of identity and survival. It is now being governed without consent.

The Scottish Claim of Right, 1988

Deep in the inaccessible nooks and interstices of the fabric, the death-watch beetle bides its time.

Ferdinand Mount on the British constitution, 1992

✣

INHERITANCE

The dramatic suddenness of Thatcher's fall had had no post-war precedent. At one moment, she had been the most commanding prime minister since 1945; at the next she had been cast, Lucifer-like, into an abyss of resentful bitterness. The most recent parallel was Chamberlain's fall in 1940, or even Lloyd George's in 1922. But in 1940 and 1922, the change of prime minister had ushered in a change of regime; in 1990, the death of the old order was followed by half a decade of ambiguity, confusion and schism. For embittered former Thatcherites, John Major quickly became the scapegoat, but in truth his position was impossible from the start. He had won the leadership election both as Not Thatcher and as Son of Thatcher: both as the vehicle of change and as the guardian of continuity. He had been Thatcher's candidate, the latest embodiment of the tradition that went back, through her, to Joseph, Powell and the majestically remote Lord Salisbury. Yet he had to show that he was his own man, with a different approach from hers; after all, there would have been no election for him to win had she not seemed a liability to many of her colleagues and followers.

In any case, he *was* different from Thatcher – more different, perhaps, than he realised himself and far more different than she realised. He had risen to the topmost rungs of the Cabinet through her patronage, but there was no warrant for her assumption that he was 'one of us'. In truth, there was no warrant for any assumptions about his beliefs: no one knew what he stood for, nor if he stood for anything. He had carried out his assignments dextrously and without fuss; the well-worn cliché, 'a safe pair of hands', might have been coined for him. But that was all that anyone really knew about him.

In Thatcher's eyes, his humble social origins were a certificate of existential virtue. He had 'fought his way up from the bottom', she told Woodrow Wyatt, the former Labour politician and ardent Thatcherite. He was 'in tune with the skilled and ambitious and worthwhile working classes' and could therefore be relied on not to 'go back to the old complacent, consensus ways'.[1] However, she did not know what he really believed and had taken no trouble to find out. The only certainty was that, in temperament (and temperament was at least as potent a driver of the Tory nationalist crusade as was doctrine), he could hardly have been less like her. He enjoyed people, collected people and studied people – not least by scrutinising their body language with devoted care. He relished the human interaction involved in negotiation and deal-making, earning high marks for his negotiating skills from officials and foreign leaders alike.[2] He was a consolidator, not an innovator; a compromiser, not a crusader. Above all, he had little of Thatcher's astonishing self-belief or passionate élan, and none of the guileful populism that she had displayed in her great days.

His origins were not as unmixed a blessing as Thatcher believed.[3] He was born in 1943 in a solidly suburban area of South London, where his 64-year-old father, originally known as Tom Ball, ran a business making garden gnomes and other garden accessories. But Ball was not as sedate a character as that implies. Before settling down, he had had a varied career in show business, notably as a trapeze artist. His stage name was Major, and by the time his son, John, was born, he was known as Major-Ball. The young John Major-Ball passed the eleven-plus to Rutlish, a nearby grammar school. Perhaps because his father's business did so badly that the family had to sell their bungalow and move to desperately inadequate rented accommodation, his academic work was poor. He left school at sixteen, with an unknown number of O-levels, no A-levels and little self-esteem; he had dropped the 'Ball' from his surname to escape the jibes that it had earned him from schoolmates and even from teachers. He drifted from one dead-end job to another, until he was taken on by the District Bank at the age of twenty-two.

Then his fortunes turned up, partly because his self-confidence was boosted by a relationship with a divorcée, Jean Kierans, thirteen years older than he was. He had a spell in Nigeria, working for the Standard Bank; in 1968, with some years as an enthusiastic Young Conservative under his belt, he was elected to Lambeth Council for a normally Labour ward, with a majority of seventy. Eleven years later he was Conservative MP for the solidly Tory seat of Huntingdon. Eleven years after that, he became the youngest prime minister since Lord Rosebery in 1894, having served both as Foreign Secretary and as Chancellor of the Exchequer.

Major's career was, in fact, a shining example of the well-worn Conservative themes of grit, self-help and upward mobility. Yet he was clearly embarrassed by, perhaps even ashamed of, his early failures. His O-level results, for example, were a closely guarded secret. He had reinvented himself in his twenties and had done his best to bury the memory of the wasted years at Rutlish and the aimless drifting that followed. He was an exceptionally nice man – perhaps the nicest prime minister of the twentieth century – modest, friendly and considerate. Yet beneath his kindness and affability lay a throbbing vein of insecurity. He flourished when things went well, but when they went badly he fretted absurdly, telephoning colleagues at inconvenient times to complain obsessively of unfair newspaper comment and driving his political secretary, Judith Chaplin, to distraction.[4] Press attacks, cartoonists' mockery and even harmless media investigations of his early life hurt him deeply; and he was quick to see criticisms from former colleagues and followers as disloyal.

For most of the time, he seemed cool under fire, but it was a false coolness, bought at a high price in inner tension. In a notorious outburst to a television interviewer, mistakenly taped when he thought he was having a private conversation, he complained of the 'poison' disseminated by ex-ministers opposed to his European policy and described them as 'the bastards'.[5] The note of indignant self-pity was characteristic. Inevitably, it invited more 'poison'. Rather like Harold Wilson, another fundamentally nice man with too thin a skin for the job, Major inadvertently encouraged the plotting that he constantly bemoaned.

These were unfortunate characteristics for a Conservative leader in the 1990s, obliged to manage a party traumatised by Thatcher's fall and deeply divided over her legacy. On one level, her fate was an accident. If Howe had made his deadly resignation statement a month later, the moment for a leadership ballot would have passed. Heseltine's dagger would have stayed in its sheath; Thatcher would have stayed in office; the poll-tax fever might have subsided; and her Commons outburst after the Rome Summit would probably have been forgotten. But her defenestration was not due to contingency alone. It also reflected a growing sense of unease in the Conservative Party, stemming from a contradiction at the heart of the Tory nationalist crusade that became fully apparent only in Thatcher's third term. She and her ministers sought what they called an 'enterprise culture', but as we saw in the last chapter the notion had always had two dimensions, not one. In the enterprise culture, dynamism, risk-taking and individual initiative would flourish, but these would foster the classic bourgeois values of self-restraint, deferred gratification and, above all, respect for authority. By the same token, it would be embedded in a robust and cohesive civil society, suffused with these values and standing at arm's length from the state. Unfortunately, the project was soon ensnared in a thicket of unintended consequences. Late-1980s Britain was more dynamic, more individualistic and less risk-averse than the Britain of ten years before, but its very dynamism helped to undermine self-restraint and to make the whole idea of deferred gratification seem boring and old-hat. Whatever Thatcher herself might say or hope, her Britain was no friend to respect – either of traditional authorities or of traditional values.

The British remained a law-abiding people, but they became less, not more, law-abiding during the Thatcher years. Survey evidence revealed a fourfold increase in the number of people who had taken part in a protest or demonstration between 1983 and 1989, and a 10 per cent increase in the number who said they might be prepared to break a law to which they were opposed.[6] The absolute figures were still low, but the trend called into question some of the key assumptions of the Thatcher revolution. Even more alarmingly for Conservative politicians, a later survey carried out in 1991 revealed a precipitous decline in public support for the political system since the early 1970s. In the early 1970s the Kilbrandon Commission had discovered that only about half the population thought it worked well, while half thought it needed improvement. Twenty years later, the proportion who thought it worked well had plummeted to 33 per cent. A formidable 62 per cent, nearly two-thirds of the sample, thought it needed improvement.[7] Under Thatcher the central state had accumulated power on a scale without precedent in time of peace, yet its authority was dribbling away.

Meanwhile, the ties of family and shared morality – crucial components of the lost golden age that the Thatcher crusade was supposed to restore – continued to fragment. The abortion ratio no longer soared, as it had done in the 1970s, but it went on rising steadily. The number of live births outside marriage, which had stood at 70,000 in the year when Thatcher became Prime Minister, reached 211,000 in the year after her fall.[8] The number of divorces per year rose by almost one-fifth between 1981 and 1993; by the late 1980s the divorce rate was substantially higher than in any other European Community country, apart from Denmark.[9] According to a MORI survey, around half the population thought drink, drugs and poverty were chiefly to blame.[10] Cohabitation waxed, while marriage waned; by 1996 twice as many women aged between twenty-five and thirty-four were cohabiting as were married.[11]

Traditional social bonds decayed in uglier ways as well. Though there was a slight drop at the end of the decade, the number of notifiable offences per 1000 of the population doubled during the 1980s. There was significantly more robbery with violence, and more household burglary.[12] Drug trafficking almost doubled between 1981 and 1988; the total number of drug offences rose by more than 50 per cent.[13] Prosecutions for rape trebled between 1977 and 1988 – partly, no doubt, because victims grew more willing to come forward.[14] Football hooliganism became a serious stain on the nation's reputation.

It was an old British tradition, but it had been on a falling trend in the post-war years. The curve of violence moved up again in the 1960s, however. By the 1980s many football fans seemed to get more satisfaction from intimidating rival gangs of supporters than from watching the players. The tragedy at the Heysel stadium in Belgium in May 1985, when a stampede by Liverpool fans ended in the death of thirty-nine Italians and Belgians, was a peculiarly harsh commentary, not just on the macho aggression of the terraces, but on the coarsening of the culture that lay behind it.[15] It was simplistic to lay these trends at Thatcher's door, as her opponents often did; governments rarely have as much impact on long-term cultural shifts as politicians or journalists imagine. In truth, the tory nationalists of the 1980s, like their democratic collectivist predecessors in the 1940s and 1960s, had grossly overestimated the state's capacity to reshape the culture of a complex modern society. That, however, was scant consolation to troubled Conservatives, wondering what kind of country they were living in after ten years of Thatcher's rule.

There was another side to the coin. The 1980s saw a marked increase in volunteering and charitable giving. The number of blood donations rose; Oxfam's income doubled.[16] Cinemas, museums and theatres all had higher attendances than football matches.[17] While mass culture coarsened, high culture flourished. Two haunting historical novels, A.S. Byatt's *Possession* and Nicholas Mosley's *Hopeful Monsters*, appeared at the tail end of the Thatcher years. More spectacular reputations were made by the still-young novelists, Ian McEwan and Martin Amis, both of whom consolidated their early promise during the 1980s. In the middle of the Thatcher decade,

ABOVE: Harold Macmillan with his Nemesis, Charles de Gaulle, November 1961.

LEFT: Imperial dusk: the Duke of Edinburgh with Jomo Kenyatta, Kenya Independence Day, December 1963.

CLOCKWISE FROM TOP LEFT
The rage of the righteous: anti-Vietnam War demonstration, Grosvenor Square,
March 1968. European duo: Edward Heath with President Pompidou, November
1972. White racism versus black pride, May 1968. 'Arthur Scargill Walks on
Water': Scargill orating to a miners' rally, 1984.

ABOVE: 'The eyes of Caligula and the mouth of Marilyn Monroe'. Margaret Thatcher with François Mitterrand, January 1986.

LEFT: Vigorous virtues? Foreign exchange dealers, January 1993.

ABOVE: *Fatwa*: Muslim anti-Rushdie marchers praying on Westminster Bridge, May 1989.

RIGHT: Alex Salmond, SNP leader, with deputy leader Nicola Sturgeon and Scotland's first Asian MSP, Bashir Ahmad, after taking their oath in the Scottish Parliament, May 2007.

ABOVE: Special relations: Tony Blair and George W. Bush at the White House, July 2003.

ABOVE RIGHT: At last! Gordon Brown and his wife Sarah on the threshold of Number 10, 27 June 2007.

RIGHT: Strange bedfellows: Ian Paisley with Martin McGuinness in Brussels, January 2008.

FAR RIGHT: Forty years on. Street scene in Kingston-upon-Thames, April 2008, forty years after Enoch Powell's 'rivers of blood' speech.

FOLLOWING PAGE: The surveillance society: a Banksy graffiti in central London, April 2008.

Merchant Ivory films produced at least two masterpieces, *The Bostonians* and *Room with a View*, both scripted by Ruth Prawer Jhabvala, and both more subversive than they seemed at first sight.

Alan Bennett's wry genius flourished as well, though his poignant *The Madness of George III* did not appear until 1991, just after Thatcher's fall. Michael Frayn's farce, *Noises Off*, perhaps the funniest British play to appear since the Second World War, was a joyous counterpoint to Bennett's melancholy compassion. In the academy, Quentin Skinner's sensitivity to cultural and historical context helped to revolutionise the once-arid study of political thought. Meanwhile Eric Hobsbawm's *The Age of Empire* brought his trilogy on 'the triumph and transformation of capitalism' from the French Revolution to the outbreak of the First World War to an appropriately triumphant conclusion (later capped by his history of the short twentieth century, *The Age of Extremes*). Most novelists, playwrights, artists and intellectuals loathed Thatcher and all her works, but their loathing may have been a stimulus to creativity.

All the same, the xenophobic, homophobic, mildly pornographic and ostentatiously vulgar hedonism of the *Sun* – with its endless stream of stories about 'bonking', its glorification of greed and its readership of more than 11 million – seemed a better guide to the mentality of upwardly mobile, skilled and white-collar workers than Thatcher's talk of Victorian values or her guru Hayek's evocation of the ethos of the Great Society. It was certainly a more potent enemy of hierarchy and tradition than any number of nuclear disarmers or Bennite fundamentalists.

As the decade wore on, the tory nationalist crusaders began to look rather like latter-day versions of the Sorcerer's Apprentice, desperately trying to undo the spell that he had purloined from his master. Far from bolstering authority and self-discipline, the onward rush of market individualism seemed to be overwhelming them. The relationship between the enterprise culture, the state and intermediate social institutions was equally remote from the hopes that had inspired the revolution when it began. As we saw in the last chapter, the 'social Thatcherism' of the middle and late 1980s was far more centralist, and entailed a far more ruthless assault on recalcitrant institutions and elites, than anything attempted by the democratic collectivist or whig imperialist governments of the past. Yet it had failed to repair the damage that resurgent capitalism had inflicted on social cohesion, or to mitigate the indignity and deprivation stemming from the collapse of old industries and the death of the communities they had sustained. Not the least of the forces that drove Thatcher from office was a muddled feeling among Conservatives that the crusade had gone too far, or even that it had taken the wrong turning.

BACKLASH

That feeling was not confined to the discomfited wets whom Thatcher had
exiled early in her reign. They no longer mattered. The battle over economic
management was over, and they had lost. Their elegantly caustic high priest,
Ian Gilmour, produced two pungent critiques of Thatcherite 'dogma', but
both were written in the spirit of the discredited Keynesian orthodoxy of
the 1960s and neither cut much ice in the Conservative Party or, indeed,
elsewhere.[18] Michael Heseltine was a more formidable critic of Thatcher's
project. He was no wet, but no ordinary dry. After his resignation, he
contrived, with immense political skill, to argue the case for a corporatist
'caring capitalism', while steering clear of outright rebellion.[19] Yet even
Heseltine was an émigré from the Thatcher regime, a Conservative equivalent of the White Russians who fled Lenin's Russia. So long as the
revolutionaries controlled the Downing Street Kremlin, his criticisms could
be discounted as sour grapes.

The real battle was over identity, community and the boundaries of the
market-place; and here uneasiness was harder to dismiss. At the height of
the Lawson boom in 1988, Douglas Hurd, Heath's old political secretary
and now Home Secretary, proclaimed the need to 'bring back greater social
cohesion', and insisted that the 'diffusion of power' was 'the key to active and
responsible citizenship' for which Conservatives had traditionally stood.[20]
Christopher Patten, Minister of Overseas Development and a future European Commissioner, struck a more belligerent note, calling for an 'enduring
English version of Christian Democracy', based on a fusion of market
economics and 'our more traditional generosity of spirit'.[21]

Outside formal politics, the backlash against the Thatcher governments
was more vigorous. One of its most effective proponents was the torrentially
eloquent and indomitably original political theorist, John Gray, whose
intellectual journey from Thatcherite champion to scarifying enemy of
market fundamentalism reached its mid-point at the end of the 1980s.
Soon after Thatcher's fall, he published a collection of essays offering a
communitarian critique of the enterprise culture. Hayek's vision of a society
held together solely by market exchanges, Gray declared, was 'at best a
mirage, at worst a prescription for a return to the state of nature'. The
task of conservative government was 'to concern itself with those cultural
continuities to which the market is bound to be indifferent, but upon which
its strength finally depends'; hence, the Conservative Party could never be
'solely or exclusively' the party of capitalism.[22]

Ferdinand Mount's subtle and elegant attack on the prevailing 'shrivelled
and corrupted understanding of the British Constitution' was, in some

ways, more subversive. Mount was editor of the *Times Literary Supplement*, but he had served for a while as head of Thatcher's Policy Unit. His Conservative credentials were impeccable, and he had seen government from the inside. His chief target was the allegedly hallowed doctrine of parliamentary supremacy, on which the whole edifice of Thatcherite centralism was based, and which he debunked as the tendentious product of time-bound ideological preoccupations. It had always rested on dubious history, he argued, and thanks to membership of the European Community, the jurisprudence of the European Court of Human Rights, ecological imperatives and the chaotic state of central-local relations, its time was now running out. Constitutional reform was no longer a 'middle-class hobby irrelevant to real politics', rather like growing organic vegetables. For Britain could no longer be seen as a 'ramshackle but pleasant old house, in a sheltered inland spot':

> We are right out on the promontory, at the mercy of wind and tide. And it is the strength of these tides that forces us to look at our constitutional arrangements in a quite different spirit from that of the later Victorians. ... [T]he fact that the huge and agonising adaptations they made to the system – the wholesale widening of the franchise over fifty years, the forty-year struggle for Irish Home Rule and eventually Irish independence – eventually created a fresh platform of stability should not lure us into thinking that this platform is therefore destined to last out the impending storm.[23]

Evolutionary whiggish gradualism, Mount was saying, was no longer enough. Still less so was tory nationalism.

❧

The great question for Major was how to accommodate the feelings behind the backlash without betraying his predecessor, spurning her legacy and outraging her still-numerous devotees. Few incoming prime ministers have faced a harder test. Despite the eloquent prose and intellectual distinction of its proponents, the backlash raised more questions than it answered. The traditions to which it appealed, and even the style in which it was couched, were essentially whig imperialist, though without the imperialism. (It was not an accident that Hurd, the cultivated, gravely voiced Old Etonian son of one Conservative MP and grandson of another, was now the nearest thing to a Burkean gentleman at the top of the Conservative Party. Nor was it an accident that when he stood for the party leadership after Thatcher's fall, he seemed acutely embarrassed by his Etonian past.)

In essence the backlash was a cry of protest on behalf of the Age of Macmillan against the crudity and dogmatism of the Age of Thatcher. The trouble was that the Age of Macmillan had passed – not just because of the policy failures of his last years in office, but because the old governing class, which had carried relaxed and responsive Whiggery in its genes, had virtually ceased to exist. By 1997, only 9 per cent of Conservative MPs had been to Eton or Harrow, against 31 per cent in 1951.[24] A diary entry by the rich, louche, joyously reactionary middle-rank minister, Alan Clark, said it all. Brooding on the fate of the 'OE mafia' which had run the country under Macmillan, he agonised:

> Profumo exposed their essential rottenness. The few who remain – Gilmour, Whitelaw, Carrington – are impossibly defeatist. With the exception, I think the *sole* exception, of Robert Cranborne, the real toffs have opted out.[25]

Peregrine Worsthorne, a more dispassionate observer of Conservative high politics, offered a different interpretation of the same process. In times past, he argued, the old governing class had been imbued with an ethic of public service and *noblesse oblige*. But the triumphant capitalism of the 1980s had no need of the former and scorned the latter. Its message to the old elite was, '*get your snouts into the trough with the rest of us.*' (Italics in the original.) The offer, Worsthorne thought, was irresistible. The gentlemanly aristocracy of old days had abandoned public service to join the greedy and deracinated 'new international plutocracy'.[26]

Not only did the old ruling class disappear, but no successor took its place. In Salisbury's day, the patrician elite had run the Conservative Party and enrolled the so-called 'villa Tories' under its banner. Now the party was run by twentieth-century equivalents of the 'villa Tories' – upwardly mobile new men and women like Major; Tebbit; Michael Howard, Major's Employment Secretary and later Home Secretary; Kenneth Clarke, Health Secretary and later Chancellor; Michael Portillo, arch-Thatcherite and future Defence Secretary; and, not least, Thatcher herself.[27] The complex structure of authority, deference and social control that Conservatives had defended for so long was crumbling. Many of the institutions which had been central to it – the older universities, the liberal professions, the senior civil service, even the Church of England – had been the targets of populist rage, much of it stimulated by the government.

The Conservatives had lost the priceless asset of being the 'stupid party', the party of instinctive social and cultural allegiances, bred in the bone and beyond argument. They were becoming a party of 'notions', just like the

Labour Party or the Liberal Democrats (the descendants of the SDP-Liberal Alliance) – a party of doctrines, of theories and even, in the case of Thatcher and her strongest supporters, the party of a Utopia. Also like the Labour Party and the Liberal Democrats, the Conservative Party was divided, sometimes deeply, about which ideas to espouse.[28] The anti-Thatcher backlash reflected the mood of party traditionalists, but for every Conservative who thought the crusade should be reined in, there was another who thought it should go further.

No one would have found it easy to transcend these divisions. Major was peculiarly ill equipped to do so. The cast of his mind could hardly have been less utopian. At the start of his prime ministership, he made a modest bow in the direction of the backlash. His aim, he declared from the steps of 10 Downing Street, was to build 'a country that is at ease with itself'[29] – clearly implying that it was not at ease with itself after eleven years of Thatcher's rule. But he did not, and perhaps could not, explain how his vision of Britain's future differed from hers. Famously, Major offered 'Thatcherism with a human face' – a phrase that epitomised his statecraft. Another way of putting it might have been 'Thatcherism and water'. Unfortunately, Thatcherism did not go with water. It had to be taken neat or not at all. The tory nationalist crusade could never reach completion. There was no logical end point, after which the crusaders could sit back and relax. Jerusalem could never be taken. There were always new enemies to defeat and new threats to overcome. Authority was always in danger from subversive malcontents; free-market individualism could never be safe from actual or potential producer cartels.

Even (perhaps especially) to Thatcherite true believers, the hard-won achievements of the Thatcher years seemed as fragile as they were magnificent. The threat of disintegration had only been held at bay, not eliminated; the bad old days of consensus and collectivism might yet return. To remain true to Thatcher's legacy, it was not enough to stand still. But 'Thatcherism with a human face' implied standing still, or at the very least finding a new route for advance, different from Thatcher's. However, Major had no new route to offer. All he could think of was to plod doggedly along the trail that Thatcher had blazed. In effect, he was condemned to pursue her Utopia. But his was a grey, wan version of the original, with none of the romance and glitter that had captivated Thatcher's admirers.

Compounding Major's troubles was an increasingly bitter split over Britain's role in the rapidly integrating European Community – the issue which had precipitated Howe's resignation, and which had therefore been the proximate cause of Thatcher's undoing. It was not easy to understand the nature and causes of this split at the time, and it is no easier now. For most of the time, the protagonists talked past each other. On one side were men of government, quintessential insiders, defending the national interest as they saw it through the accepted Community processes of bargaining and compromise, and defending their policies in the language of diplomacy and statecraft. On the other were outsiders, nature's irreconcilables, carried along by a mounting tide of passionate negation which they misleadingly called 'Euroscepticism'. For much of the time, the issues at stake seemed technical and rather tedious, but at bottom the quarrel was over the explosive questions of identity and nationhood. However, the identity in question was essentially, even uniquely, English. Ostensibly, the irreconcilables fought to save the British state and Britain's identity from an encroaching continental embrace, but when they spoke of Britain they meant England. Their rhetoric had little resonance in Scotland or Wales, and no real counterpart in most of continental Europe.

They spoke the dry language of sovereignty, national and parliamentary, and rarely evoked literature, or music, or landscape, or cuisine, or religion, or even a way of life. It was almost as if their England–Britain existed only by virtue of the state; as if the English people would cease to be English if they no longer had a sovereign and indefeasible state to embody their national will. However, the dryness was only superficial. No one made the language of sovereignty sing, in the way that Powell had done in his exalted St George's Day speech in 1961. Yet the emotions he had tapped when he spoke of the 'sceptred awe' of Edward the Confessor were easy to discern in the less elevated language of the 'Eurosceptics' of the 1990s. When William Cash, the gangling, charming and obsessionally Eurosceptic MP for Stafford, subtitled an anti-federalist tract 'the Battle for Britain',[30] or when Norman Tebbit evoked the memory of Great Britain and Northern Ireland standing alone, 'isolated, unwilling to accommodate what almost all the rest of the world regarded as the inevitability of defeat', the emotional charge was unmistakable.[31]

Most (though by no means all) Eurosceptics had swallowed the extensive loss of sovereignty enshrined in the Single European Act of 1986, largely because Thatcher had not only swallowed it too, but saw herself, with some justification, as one of its authors. But her Bruges speech, the Rome Summit and her ejection from office signalled a profound change in her stance, and in the dynamics of the Conservative Party's Euro-politics. She was right in thinking that the pace of integration was speeding up: that the Delors Commission, backed by the major states of continental Western Europe, had rescued monetary union from the status of distant dream and was bent on turning it into a realistic prospect. She was also right that the prevailing continental assumption that economic integration ought to go hand in hand with social protection was utterly at odds with her government's social philosophy. Where she was wrong was in assuming that she could bounce her leading colleagues into outright opposition to the Delors project and the governments that backed it.

Enoch Powell, the old maestro of Tory nationalism, was quick to offer his own exegesis of what he called the 'the declaration of Bruges'. It was, he pointed out, 'totally incompatible with the European Communities Act of 1972', which had renounced Parliament's overriding authority over legislation and taxation, and for which Thatcher had herself voted.[32] There was truth in that, but, as so often with Powell, it was an irrelevant truth. What mattered now was how to respond to the integrationist momentum which was building up on the other side of the Channel. Here, Thatcher's role was crucial. Having headed the most formidable peacetime government of the century, she too was now an outsider. For a growing number of Eurosceptics she became the tragic yet glorious heroine of sea-girt nationhood – a victim of treachery among her colleagues and of plotting by the continentals. As such, she was also a rallying point for patriots, a cross between Cassandra and Boadicea.

The Eurosceptics who clustered in her shadow ceased to give their government the benefit of the doubt in matters European, as most of them had done while she was at Number Ten. Increasingly, their rhetoric was marked by a mixture of paranoia and resentment. There was a 'defeatist, compromising streak' even in the Conservative Party, Tebbit declared; Delors had helped to engineer Thatcher's downfall, opined Russell Lewis.[33] The historian, Lord Thomas of Swynnerton – once (as Hugh Thomas) a leftist hammer of the establishment and now a Conservative peer – was accused by a fellow Conservative of being a 'Pétainist'.[34] In Eurosceptic eyes, European integration had become a ratchet, as 'socialism' had been for Keith Joseph.[35] The Eurosceptic MP, Christopher Gill, spoke for many when he denounced a 'one-way drift to federalism'.[36] For him and those who thought like him, Britain was losing her sovereignty piecemeal because each new sacrifice seemed too trivial to be worth fighting.

Another reason was that governments had refused to tell Parliament and people the truth; from Heath onwards the governing elite had refused to come clean. The British had joined the Community in the first place, and had voted to stay in it in the referendum, because they had been told that their sovereignty was not at stake, that EEC membership was a matter of freer trade and nothing more. Even Cash confessed that he had voted 'yes' in the 1975 referendum, and that it was only after joining the Commons Select Committee on European Legislation that he had realised that 'the Community was in danger of rapidly becoming a political federation'.[37] But now, Eurosceptics insisted, the scales had fallen from their eyes. Thanks to Thatcher's Bruges speech and her 'no, no, no' to monetary union, the true nature of the federalist conspiracy on the other side of the Channel was plain for all to see.

Faced with these impassioned certainties, the men of government who dealt day by day with the realities of Community politics took refuge in a tepid, uninspiring pragmatism. Hurd and Heseltine were old Heathmen and had been enthusiasts for Community entry in Heath's great days. Like Heath they failed to clothe their enthusiasm in a compelling rhetoric, or to offer a European vision of Britain and Britishness with the emotional power of the global, whig imperialist vision of the previous 150 years. In a ringing phrase just after becoming Prime Minister, Major declared that he wanted to see Britain at 'the very heart of Europe'.[38] But he did not say why he wanted her to be there, nor what he wanted her to do once she got there. He and his governmental colleagues defended Britain's Community role in terms of *realpolitik*, of economic advantage and political influence, but they could not – or at least did not – fight on the Eurosceptics' terrain of identity and nationhood. They had no story to tell, no drama to unfold. They did not counter the Eurosceptic narrative of insular self-sufficiency with a narrative of continental involvement; still less did they explain why such a vocation was as worthy of patriotic pride as the imperial vocation of past centuries.

As a result, they were forced on to the defensive. They had no answer to the charges of Pétainism and defeatism beyond the negative claim that the Community was not integrating as fast as the Eurosceptics alleged, and that federalism was not on the cards. Though they fought their corner with tactical skill, their strategy was fatally backward-looking. They played down the significance of the step-change which was taking place in Community politics, and in doing so they made it easy for the Eurosceptics to play it up. Above all, they spoke to the head, while the Eurosceptics spoke to the heart. And in the confused and emotionally battered Conservative Party of the early 1990s, the heart was what counted.

CHALLENGES

Major and his colleagues also faced more complex challenges of mood and doctrine. In its early years the Thatcher revolution had crushed its opponents with almost contemptuous ease. Municipal socialism and militant trades unionism had been trampled underfoot; the Labour Party had been forced back into its decaying industrial fastnesses. The rhetoric of individualism, managerialism and the free market seemed omnipresent and impervious. As the decade wore on, however, there were signs of a reaction. Critical voices slowly began to make themselves heard in the nooks and crannies of a society slowly recovering from a decade of state-imposed upheaval. They did not come from established politicians, and ignored the dividing lines of formal politics. They were fiercely anti-Thatcher, but they did not display much enthusiasm for the opposition parties.

No neat summary can do justice to the turbulent complexity of this reaction. Swirling currents of thought and action stemmed from different preoccupations and flowed in different directions. Yet certain unifying themes stand out. The critics had something in common with the romantic voices of twenty years earlier, but they were sadder, wiser and usually older than the *enragés* of those days. Albeit in widely different forms, they expressed a widely held feeling that Thatcher's counter-revolution, the collapse of Communism and the global capitalist renaissance had, between them, created a new social world, with which only a new politics could cope. Most of them shared a broadly democratic-republican conception of politics and the good life, as distant from conventional Labour *étatisme* as from Thatcherism. Their chief target was the British state tradition and its impact on the economy and society. They did not agree about what to put in its place, but they were all groping for richer, more inclusive and more pluralistic forms of democratic citizenship and the public realm.

Their approach to the political economy eluded the pigeon-holes of Westminster politics. Like the Thatcherites, they saw that the century-long struggle between capitalism and socialism had ended in the victory of the former, but they rejected the Thatcherite conclusion that Britain's individualistic and increasingly inegalitarian capitalism was the only one on offer. With socialism mortally wounded, they believed, the contest that mattered was between different forms of capitalism; and they thought that, in that contest, British capitalism could and should be beaten. The social theorist, Paul Hirst, proposed a new form of economic governance, based on what he called 'associative democracy' – in essence a late-twentieth-century descendant of G.D.H. Cole's guild socialism.[39] The business economist, John Kay, argued that the authoritarian governance of British and American firms mirrored that of Eastern Europe before the collapse of Communism, and called for a reform of company law to make directors 'trustees' for a wide range of interests, including those of employees and suppliers as well as of shareholders.[40]

The French economist, public servant and business tycoon, Michel Albert, argued that the 'neo-American' model of capitalism found in the United Kingdom and the United States was socially, and even economically, inferior to the 'Rhenish' model of central Europe.[41] Whereas the 'Anglo-American' model was based on individual success and obsessed with short-term profit, the 'Rhenish' model gave pride of place to collective success and concern for the long term. Both models were uncompromisingly capitalist. In both, the means of production were largely in private hands; neither had any truck with state planning or monopolistic trade restrictions. But though 'Rhenish' capitalism was competitive, it was also collaborative. It was far more egalitarian than its neo-American counterpart; it gave a higher priority to social cohesion and consensual adaptation; employees had a much bigger stake in the companies they worked for; and human capital was much more highly valued. For most of the recent past it had been more productive than its American counterpart, and it had also procured more harmonious societies, with higher levels of welfare and less injustice.

In a passionate best-seller, *The State We're In*, the burly, bearlike and infectiously optimistic Will Hutton, then economic editor of the *Guardian*, took Albert's analysis a stage further.[42] Unlike Albert, he focused almost exclusively on Britain, but what he lost in scope he made up in depth. His analysis was post-Thatcherite, but also post-socialist. He followed Albert's description of the shortcomings of British capitalism but, in an intriguing echo of Tom Paine and the Chartists, he argued that they stemmed from the culture and institutions of the state as much as from the economy as such. The state embodied the values of the community over which it presided. In Britain, the sovereignty of the Crown-in-Parliament mirrored and reinforced the sovereignty of the shareholder, while the rentier values that dominated in the economy also shaped the culture of the state. What Britain needed was 'a *republican* attitude to its culture and institutions' from which would spring a new kind of 'stakeholder capitalism'. Workers would be 'members of firms' rather than items on a balance sheet; individuals would be 'citizens of the state' rather than subjects; regional public banks would complement elected regional authorities; the world's anarchic financial markets would be brought to heel.

> A written constitution; the democratisation of civil society; the republicanisation of finance; the recognition that the market economy has to be managed and regulated, both at home and abroad; the upholding of a welfare state that incorporates social citizenship; the construction of a stable financial order beyond the nation state. These feasible and achievable reforms must be accomplished if the dynamism of capitalism is to be harnessed to the common good.[43]

Hutton and the other champions of stakeholder capitalism cast their net too widely for the good of their cause. Sometimes, they seemed to be saying that British capitalism was less productive than its central European counterparts; sometimes that it was less just or less democratic or both; and sometimes that it was less productive *because* it was less just and less democratic. Muddled up with all these accusations was an unfortunate residue of the traditional Labour belief that manufacturing was, for some mysterious reason, socially and economically superior to services. As a result, arcane disputes over comparative growth rates and returns on capital were apt to mask the crucial moral and political dimensions of the stakeholder case. The Commission on Wealth Creation and Social Cohesion, set up by the Liberal Democrat leader, Paddy Ashdown, and chaired by Ralf Dahrendorf, sought to redress the balance. Wealth was more than GDP, the Commission argued. It was 'the sum of what people value in their social lives'. It followed that conventionally measured economic growth was not an end in itself; development had to be socially, as well as environmentally, sustainable.[44] Tragically, the insight was left hanging in mid-air, a pointer to further debate which never came.

⁕

Hutton's critique of the British state was widely echoed. Spurred on by contact with dissident movements in Eastern and central Europe, some left intellectuals began to question the heavy-handed statism which had been as central to social democracy as to Marxist Leninism. Many rediscovered the old notion of civil society as a precious entity, that needed protection from state incursions even when the state in question was under ostensibly left control. Nearer home, the Thatcher governments had discredited both evolutionary Whiggism and *étatiste* democratic collectivism. Determined ministers, it seemed, could put what previous generations had seen as evolutionary progress into reverse. Meanwhile, *étatisme* had turned traitor. Thatcher had shown that the engine of autonomous executive power controlled by British governments could savage the political left as readily as the right. A few brave souls on the left began to suspect that British constitutional tradition was not as good a friend to freedom and justice as they had been brought up to think. Some even concluded with Neal Ascherson, the journalist and historian, that it was no more possible to build democratic socialism with the 'Ancient British State' than to 'induce a vulture to give milk'.[45]

The reaction against untrammelled *étatisme* came first from the heart of the legal profession. In his magisterial Hamlyn Lectures for 1974, Leslie Scarman (then a judge of the appeal court and later a much revered Law

Lord) argued that the traditional English combination of common law and parliamentary statute could no longer serve the purposes that traditionalists thought it served. It could not cope with two great challenges – the world-wide movement for Human Rights, whose monuments were the UN Declaration of Human Rights and the European Human Rights Convention, and the growth of the welfare state at home. In signing the Human Rights Convention, Britain had accepted an obligation to protect fundamental rights, even if they conflicted with Acts of Parliament. But the traditional British doctrine of parliamentary supremacy made it impossible for British courts to honour that obligation. The result was a contradiction at the heart of the British legal system, as legal doctrine and international obligations pulled in opposite directions. At home, the growth of social welfare had created a host of new entitlements, and a corresponding potential for conflict between individual citizens and the state, which the common law could not handle. Unless this growing area of social life were subjected to the rule of law, legal safeguards against the abuse of power would wither.

In an astonishing echo of Tom Paine in the 1790s and the Levellers in the 1640s, Scarman concluded that these international and domestic challenges could be met only through a 'new constitutional settlement'. The settlement would have to include a Bill of Rights, which the courts would be duty-bound to uphold, 'even against the power of Parliament itself'. Only then would the citizen be protected from 'instant legislation, conceived in fear or prejudice, and enacted in breach of human rights'.[46] The structure of Scarman's argument was reassuringly whiggish. He did not argue that the existing system was wrong in principle, only that it could not keep pace with the social and cultural changes of the time. Yet his conclusions were explosively radical. With disarming punctiliousness he had launched one of the century's most damaging assaults on British constitutional doctrine and practice. The fact that it came from the epicentre of the establishment made it all the more resonant.

Scarman had followers in surprising places. In his 1976 Dimbleby Lecture, Lord Hailsham famously described the British combination of majoritarian democracy and parliamentary sovereignty as an 'elective dictatorship'. In reply to critics who suggested that the notion was a contradiction in terms, he pointed out that the forms of democracy might continue after the reality had disappeared. This, he thought, was now happening in Britain. The chief culprit was the 'absolute legislative power confided in Parliament' and concentrated in 'a government armed with a Parliamentary majority'. He offered two main remedies: a second chamber, elected by proportional representation, with more powers than the existing House of Lords; and the constitutional entrenchment of fundamental laws and liberties.[47]

Hailsham was a party politician. He had been Lord Chancellor under Heath and would soon hold the same office under Thatcher. But he was also a distinguished lawyer, whose professional eminence gave his critique a persuasive force that no ordinary politician could have emulated.

However, his reforming zeal cooled when he returned to office. The opposition parties did not redress the balance. Though the SDP-Liberal Alliance toyed with far-reaching constitutional reform, including entrenched rights and proportional representation, most Labour politicians clung, with wistful atavism, to the old democratic collectivist faith in parliamentary supremacy and majoritarian democracy. It was not until after Thatcher's third victory in 1987 that the mood changed, and even then the official Labour Party lagged well behind the movement of opinion outside Parliament. The first serious attempt to mobilise public support for Scarman's call for a new constitutional settlement came from outside the political class. In 1988 a diverse group of left intellectuals, led by Stuart Weir, the then editor of the *New Statesman*, published a manifesto entitled 'Charter 88'. Among other things, it called for a Bill of Rights on Scarman lines, freedom of information, proportional representation, an elected second chamber and a written constitution 'anchored in the ideal of universal citizenship'.[48] The Charter recalled the dissident Czech manifesto, 'Charter 77', as well as two renowned British forerunners – the 'People's Charter' of 1838 and 'Magna Carta' of 1215. It struck a powerful chord. By 1994 the original 348 signatories had swollen to 44,000, growing at a rate of between 500 and 1000 a month. Its director, Anthony Barnett, had been a typical 'romantic' rebel in the heyday of the New Left, but he turned out to be a natural social entrepreneur, as well as a dynamo of energy and enthusiasm.

Under his leadership, Charter 88 was part social movement, part pressure group and part secular dissenting chapel. The atmosphere of slightly earnest goodwill would not have surprised the debaters in Putney Church in 1647 or the corresponding societies of the 1790s. It formed local groups of activists, in places as disparate as Sheffield, Bristol, Norwich and Brighton; held vigils in St Martin's-in-the-Fields; organised a series of 'Sovereignty Lectures'; published a newsletter; set up a Democratic Audit in conjunction with the Human Rights Centre at Essex University; and held a 'Democracy Day' of public debate in a range of constituencies when the general election came in 1992. There were plenty of campaigning movements in 1980s Britain, but in England, at least, none of them challenged the entire political order as comprehensively or with the same panache. (As we shall see, Scotland was a different matter.) Charter 88 stood, not just for piecemeal reforms to remedy particular grievances, but for a total overhaul of the constitution, based on an explicit commitment to inalienable human rights.

Its methods were comparatively decorous, but the blood of the British Jacobins and the Levellers ran in its veins.

Its great achievement was to distil a reform agenda that established politicians could not afford to ignore. The Charter challenged both the major parties, but the Conservatives were a lost cause for constitutional reformers, and the challenge to Labour was the one that mattered. It cut deep. The charter's conception of democracy was law-based, rights-centred, pluralistic and, at least by implication, participatory. However, Labour was congenitally suspicious of law, lawyers and the courts. Though the 1945 Labour Government had ratified the European Convention on Human Rights, that was the exception that proved the rule. Since the First World War, with only a brief interlude shortly before the fall of the second Labour Government, Labour's conception of democracy had been resolutely majoritarian. Despite the fact that it was in a minority more often than not, it saw no need for protection against the possible tyranny of the majority.

In a wounding comparison, Ronald Dworkin, one of the most fecund jurists of the age, pointed out that Labour's approach was uncomfortably close to the 'pure statistical concept of democracy', which held that democratic governments were entitled to oppress minorities, and had often been prayed in aid by tyrannical Communist regimes that claimed to govern in the interests of the masses.[49] However, Dworkin's taunt left Labour unmoved. It was for single-party government, in a Parliament as close as possible to uni-cameralism. Checks and balances limiting the power of the central executive were anathema. Aneurin Bevan's cavalier way with local democracy during the battle over hospital nationalisation was emblematic: social citizenship, delivered by an enlightened state, easily trumped political citizenship. Outcomes were what mattered; process was for finicky legal pedants, probably biased against the working class. Few stopped to ask how unjust processes could produce just outcomes. All this reflected the utilitarian disdain for human rights which had been part and parcel of the democratic collectivist world-view since the days of Ramsay MacDonald and Sidney Webb.

Despite the humiliating failures of the *étatiste* programmes of the 1960s and 1970s, this remained the dominant mood in Labour circles. Kinnock and his Deputy Leader, Roy Hattersley, had an improbably Bourbon air about them. Hattersley – a likeable mixture of Yorkshire card, machine politician and compulsive writer, endowed with a roguish grin – saw himself as the keeper of the egalitarian Crosland flame. But his one venture into political theory added little to Crosland's by now hoary legacy.[50] Kinnock had abandoned the fundamentalism of his youth, but it was not clear what he had put in its place. Like Wilson in the 1960s and MacDonald in the

1920s, he and Hattersley talked repeatedly of change. A party document summarising the results of a two-year policy review launched after the 1987 defeat was bravely entitled *Meet the Challenge, Make the Change.*[51] But when it came to specifics, Labour's leaders looked back rather than forward. They slowly cajoled their party out of the fundamentalism of the early 1980s, but their alternative was a slightly modified version of the revisionism of the 1950s and 1960s.

Though Labour also committed itself to freedom of information, a right to privacy and stronger laws against sex or race discrimination, it prevaricated endlessly on human rights and electoral reform. After repeated contortions, it proposed an elected second chamber, 'charged with the protection of liberties' and empowered to delay legislation infringing them, as an alternative to a justiciable Bill of Rights. Electoral reform was referred to a working party chaired by the eminent political philosopher, Raymond Plant, who later became a Labour peer.[52] The early 1990s saw a new twist to the saga. John Smith, Kinnock's successor as party leader, committed his party to a referendum on electoral reform and promised that it would incorporate the European Human Rights Convention into British law. It was not quite a deathbed conversion, but sceptics could be forgiven for wondering how deep it went.

⋘⋙

North of the Border, the reaction against the Thatcher regime went further and faster. One reason was that the democratic republican tradition of civic engagement and popular sovereignty had always had deeper roots in the Presbyterian soil of Scotland than in England; another, that Thatcher's mixture of clamorous English nationalism, free-market messianism and Westminster absolutism grated on Scottish ears in a peculiarly abrasive fashion. For she and her circle seemed almost insultingly ignorant of the distinctive features of Scotland's history and moral economy. They seemed unaware that the British state had always been multinational, not national, and even less aware that Scotland had been an independent, sovereign state until it decided, of its own volition, to join in a union with the sovereign English state. They knew, of course, that the Act of Union had created a single Parliament, inevitably dominated by the English members, but they forgot (or perhaps had never learned) that Scotland's three great autonomous national institutions – the law, the Kirk and the universities – had continued to embody a distinct Scottish identity, as well as forming the nation's professional elites. By the same token, they did not know (or perhaps did not care) that the doctrine of absolute parliamentary sovereignty that legitimised their unyielding centralism had never been fully accepted north of the Border. Still less did they realise that to both the great religious traditions of Scotland – Calvinism and Catholicism – the whole idea of an 'enterprise culture' centred on unfettered economic individualism was alien, even abhorrent.

Thatcher's rhetoric might have been designed to advertise her indifference to Scottish sensibilities. The peroration to her address to the Conservative Women's Conference at the height of the Falklands war in May 1982 was a particularly telling example. At first she had spoken of 'we British', but she ended with a rousing trope from Shakespeare: 'And let our nation, as it has so often in the past, remind itself and the world: "Naught shall make us rue/ If England to herself do rest but true".'[53] South of the Border that would have seemed unexceptional. In Scotland, particularly when Britain was at war, the unconscious slide from 'British' to 'England' was a gratuitous reminder that, in the eyes of its current rulers, the British state was an English state, and English patriotism indistinguishable from British patriotism. A more offensive example came six years later when she treated the General Assembly of the Church of Scotland to a homily in favour of wealth creation and free choice. It was given in the Church Assembly Hall, which stands on a hill in Edinburgh known as the Mound, and the irreverent Scottish press soon dubbed it the Sermon on the Mound. 'St Paul,' she declared, had written in his epistle to the Thessalonians, '"If a man will not work he shall not eat".' 'No one took away the life of Jesus,' she added; 'he *chose* to lay it down.'[54] It would have been hard to devise a better way to outrage the assembled Presbyterian divines. Worse still, in Scottish eyes, rhetoric marched with policy. The recession of the early 1980s cut as deep in industrial Scotland as in industrial England and much deeper than in the English South-East; Scottish local authorities were rate-capped along with their English counterparts; Scotland was a test-bed for the poll tax before it was introduced in England.

In the days of the whig imperialist ascendancy between the wars and in the early 1950s, Scotland's voting behaviour had not been very different from England's. In 1924, 1931 and 1935, and again in 1955, the Conservatives (strictly speaking, Unionists) won majorities north of the Border. By the 1960s, the scene had changed; in 1979 the bedraggled Labour Party won twice as many Scottish seats as the Conservatives. In the 1980s, Scottish Conservatism collapsed. In 1987, the Conservatives won only ten Scottish seats to Labour's fifty. The more it collapsed, the less legitimate seemed the London government. To a widening swathe of Scottish opinion, crucially including the elites in the churches, the universities, local government and the liberal professions, it seemed that the British state was forcing the Scots to swallow an alien ideology, which they had decisively rejected at the polls.

Canon Kenyon Wright, the General Secretary of the Scottish Churches Council, spoke for many when he wrote that there were two reasons for the 'astonishing' animosity that Thatcher aroused in Scotland:

> First we perceived that she was imposing on Scotland . . . an alien ideology that rejected community and expressed itself as an attack on our distinctive systems of education and local government. This behaviour was seen in Scotland as a moral or ideological issue and not simply as a series of unpopular policies.
>
> The second reason was even deeper – the grim centralisation of power, the determined attack on all alternative sources of real corporate power in local government and elsewhere. . . . All this made us see with a clarity that we had never had before, that we could never again rely on the British state or live comfortably with its constitutional doctrines of the absolute authority of the crown in parliament.[55]

The outcome of the 1979 devolution referendum had been a bitter blow for Scottish devolutionists. The Scottish people had voted for devolution, albeit by a narrow margin, but arcane Westminster manoeuvres had then denied them what they had voted for. In response to the hammer blows that the Thatcher Government inflicted on Scotland's culture and moral economy, however, devolutionist sentiment gradually recovered from the inevitable dip. 1980 saw the foundation of a campaign for a Scottish Assembly (CSA), which issued a consultative paper on a Scottish Constitutional Convention in 1985, and the much more explosive *A Claim of Right for Scotland* in 1988. The *Claim of Right* was drafted by Jim Ross, a retired Scottish civil servant, formerly in the Scottish Office, where he had been in charge of devolution in the 1970s. It was one of the most remarkable political documents to appear in Britain in the twentieth century.

The title recalled two of the most resonant dates in Scottish history – 1689 when a Claim of Right declared that James VII (James II of England) had forfeited the Scottish Crown; and 1842 when a second Claim of Right demanded complete spiritual independence for the Scottish Church. The contents lived up to the title. In elegant, lucid, occasionally almost majestic prose, the 1988 *Claim of Right* set out an uncompromising case for an elected Scottish Assembly and, in doing so, struck at the heart of the existing union state.[56] The Scots were a nation, with a culture 'reaching back over centuries and bearing European comparison in depth and quality'; before 1707 they had possessed a state. The Treaty of Union had recognised the special peculiarities of Scotland's culture and identity, and had guaranteed the institutions and policies that had embodied them at that time. But the guarantees had turned out to be worthless. Many treaty provisions had been violated, while the huge areas of government which had developed since had never been affected by it. As a result, 'The say of Scotland in its own government has diminished, is diminishing and ought to be increased.' The conclusion was inescapable:

> Scotland, if it is to remain Scotland, can no longer live with such a constitution and has nothing to hope for from it. Scots have shown it more tolerance than it deserves. They must now show enterprise by starting the reform of their own government. They have the opportunity, in the process, to start the reform of the English constitution; to serve as the grit in the oyster which produces the pearl.[57]

The grit was not long in coming (The fate of the pearl belongs in the next chapter.) After much careful lobbying by the CSA, a Constitutional Convention was set up to decide how to achieve the objectives set out in the *Claim of Right*. It represented virtually all shades of Scottish opinion, apart from the Conservatives at one end of the spectrum and the SNP at the other. The Scottish Labour Party, the Liberal Democrats and the Communist and Green parties all took part; equally importantly, so did a wide range of social institutions of all kinds, including the Scottish TUC, the vast majority of the country's local authorities, the churches, the Scottish Convention of Women and representatives of ethnic minorities. Kenyon Wright, who chaired its executive committee, distilled its purpose in a brilliant soundbite: 'What happens when that other voice we know so well responds by saying, "We say No, We are the State." Well, We say Yes and We are the People.'[58] Inevitably, there were some tense moments, but the popular momentum behind the broad aim of Home Rule was too strong to be gainsaid. On St Andrew's Day 1990 (30 November), the Convention unveiled proposals for a Scottish legislature, elected by proportional representation, and responsible for virtually all policy areas apart from foreign affairs, defence and macro-economic management.

Much remained to be done, but the road to the most far-reaching reconstruction of the British state for nearly three hundred years was open. Although the Scottish Labour and Liberal Democrat parties had played a crucial part in the process and were committed to the result, the lion's share of the credit belonged to Scotland's rich network of democratic republican civic institutions, not to the political class.

British political leaders had been familiar with the ethnic diversity of the British archipelago for centuries. For whig imperialists, in particular, the management of diversity had been one of the central tasks of statesmanship. But by the end of the Thatcher years, Britain's ethnic mix was richer than it had ever been before. New ethnic groups had begun to challenge the assumptions of the British state in unfamiliar and alarming ways. At the heart of the challenge lay two pressing questions. Could that state accommodate minority cultures of a quite novel kind? What did it mean to be British now that the British empire had disappeared, and once-subject peoples had settled in Britain in substantial numbers? These questions were not new. In one form or another, the first had been part of the stuff of British politics ever since the Act of Union. The second had loomed in the background since the 1960s and helped to account for the extraordinary bitterness of the Conservative split over European integration. But in the 1980s and 1990s they assumed new forms, with which British politicians and the British public found it extraordinarily hard to come to terms.

According to the 1991 census, so-called 'ethnic minority' communities – in other words, non-white communities – totalled 3 million, or about 5.5 per cent of the whole population. Of these minority communities, around half a million belonged to the Black Caribbean community and around 1.5 million to the three South Asian ones – the Indians, Pakistanis and Bangladeshis. (Most of the rest were classified as 'Black African', 'Black Other' and 'Chinese'.) However, the minority communities were heavily concentrated in the big conurbations of Greater London, the Midlands and the North. Though certain areas in certain big cities could fairly be described as multi-ethnic, perhaps even as multicultural, Britain was still an over-whelmingly white society.

Her mass culture was heavily tinged with the racism which had been inseparable from empire, and owed little to minority influences, except perhaps in ethnic restaurants, popular music and on the football field. With the possible exception of the 150,000-strong Chinese community, all the ethnic minorities suffered discrimination in the labour market and all of them were targets for racial prejudice and sometimes for racial hatred. The Indian community, much of which originated in East Africa, suffered least. It was less proletarian than the others, more mobile socially and adapted more successfully to British life. In contrast the unemployment rate among Pakistanis and Bangladeshis was about double the national average; among Black Caribbean men it was more than double.[59]

The main minority communities differed sharply from each other in economic status, in culture, in family structure and, not least, in religion. British liberals viewed what they saw as 'race relations' through a prism derived from American experience, but the widely held notion that a 'white' majority was confronted by a more or less homogeneous 'black' minority, analogous to the 'black' population of the United States, was dangerously misleading. Indians, Pakistanis and Bangladeshis did not think of themselves as black; among the last two, the Islamic faith was overwhelmingly the most important element in group identity. The result was a cruel irony. Liberal-minded champions of the underdog knew where they were with race, but when it came to religion they were baffled and suspicious. The Muslim communities of East London and the North were undeniably underdogs. They were poor; they were victims of racial discrimination; and they had to run the gauntlet of racist taunts, often escalating into violence. However, their racial identity was imposed on them from the outside. Race had no meaning for their inner selves; what mattered was religion and the communal way of life to which it was central.[60] But to liberal-minded whites, religious identities were barely comprehensible, and were in any case symptoms of backwardness and ignorance.

A second irony compounded the first. Though Britain's mass culture was virtually impervious to minority influences, intellectuals from the South Asian diasporas made spectacular contributions to her high culture, above all to her universities and her literature. Amartya Sen, future Nobel Prize-winner and future Master of Trinity College, Cambridge, was Drummond Professor of Political Economy at Oxford for most of the 1980s, before he moved to Harvard. V.S. Naipaul, a Trinidadian of Hindu descent, who had been a star in the British literary firmament since the early 1960s, was knighted in 1990. (He too was a future Nobel Prize winner.) The publication of Vikram Seth's almost Tolstoyan epic of Indian family life, *A Suitable Boy*, in 1993 was a notable milestone in the development of another glittering talent of Indian provenance.

The novelist and playwright Hanif Kureishi probably had more public impact. Unlike Naipaul and Seth, Kureishi – the son of a Pakistani father and an English mother – was born in Britain. He explored the pains and tensions of second-generation British Pakistanis, torn between their parents' country, which they hardly knew, and the cool, damp, emotionally starved land of their birth, which did not fully accept them. One captivating example was his funny, touching, autobiographical novel, *The Buddha of Suburbia*, but his caustic, sometimes savage screenplay for Stephen Frears' film, *My Beautiful Laundrette*, explored a darker and more disturbing aspect of the same theme. It told two interwoven stories – one of a gay love affair between an ambitious and good-looking youth of Pakistani extraction and a white working-class petty criminal, and the other of brutal racist harassment by quasi-Fascist, working-class thugs. The English characters were semi-literate morons, barely able to speak their own language, while the Pakistanis were clever, warm and likeable. With good reason, they despised their white tormentors at least as cordially as their tormentors despised them. Yet not everything about Kureishi's fictional Pakistanis was calculated to please the real Pakistani community. They drank whisky, took drugs and sailed close to the law; many of them were sexually promiscuous. Their attitude to Islam was summed up in a memorable line from the hero's uncle. Pakistan, he said, had been 'sodomised by religion'.

Any offence that Kureishi may have given the Pakistani community was soon eclipsed by the wanton brilliance of the diaspora's most audacious writer, Salman Rushdie – a lapsed Muslim, born in Bombay in 1947, but educated at Rugby and Trinity College, Cambridge. He was a champion of racial equality and an opponent of the Thatcher Government. He was also the prose poet of marginality. Like Kureishi, he was torn between two worlds and fully at home in neither. But whereas Kureishi explored the tensions of marginality with brutal realism, Rushdie did so elliptically, with a rich (for some tastes, too rich) mixture of fantasy, fable and magic, coated with extraordinary verbal exuberance. He had made his name with *Midnight's Children*, a complex allegorical satire debunking India's national myth and the government of Indira Gandhi.

In 1988 he published *The Satanic Verses*, in which he turned his attention to Islam. The result was an explosion of outrage among British Muslims, on a scale that had never been seen before on British soil, and would not be seen again until the Iraq war in 2003. *The Satanic Verses* is a fantastic, even phantasmagorical collage, weaving together overlapping tales of rejection, alienation, sexual transgression, psychosis and suicide. There is plenty of black humour, and the verbal inventiveness is always astonishing. However, the overriding impression is one of pain. Whatever Rushdie's intentions may have been, it is a novel of loss – of lost faith, lost identity and lost meaning. It is also a novel of subversion. It lampoons both the Prophet Muhammad, for Muslims the messenger of God, and the Qur'an, the word of God. It also exhumes an ancient story to the effect that certain Qur'anic verses were written by Satan – a story that undermines the crucial Muslim belief that the Qur'an was dictated to Muhammad by God. Intentionally or not (and it is hard to believe that he had no idea how believing Muslims would react), Rushdie had violated some of Islam's most sacred taboos.

The Satanic Verses was burned in Bradford, banned in most Muslim countries, and provoked the Ayatollah Khomeini, the leader of Iran, into issuing a *fatwa* ordering Rushdie's death. All over the world, bookshops alleged to be stocking *The Satanic Verses* were firebombed. Rushdie's Japanese translator was stabbed to death; the Italian translator was seriously wounded.

Rushdie went into hiding; the Thatcher Government, against which he had directed much mockery in the past, gave him police protection. In May 1989, London was the scene of an anti-Rushdie march, vividly depicted by the journalist Malise Ruthven:

> They came in their thousands from Bradford and Dewsbury, Bolton and Macclesfield, the old industrial centres; from outer suburbs like Southall and Woking; from Stepney and Whitechapel in London's East End, from the cities of Wolverhampton, Birmingham, Manchester and Liverpool. They wore white hats and long baggy trousers with flapping shirt tails. Most of them were bearded; the older men looked wild and scraggy with curly, grey-flecked beards – they were mountain men from Punjab, farmers from the Ganges delta, peasants from the hills of Mirpur and Campbellpur. After decades of living in Britain, they still seemed utterly *foreign*. ... They were not sophisticated, suave metropolitans like the blacks – the Afro-Caribbeans – with whom the racists and anti-racists banded them; they seemed like men from the sticks, irredeemably provincial.[61]

Not only did they seem provincial to British secular liberals, they also seemed fanatical, bigoted and threatening. For they were not marching against poverty, deprivation, social injustice or even racial prejudice and discrimination. They were marching against insults to their faith and assaults on their community and their honour. Almost without exception, secular liberals rallied to Rushdie and the cause of free speech, shades of Voltaire hovering in the background. Two absolutisms were in conflict: the Islamic absolutism of the marchers, and the secularist absolutism of the *Guardian*- and *Independent*-reading intelligentsia, to which Rushdie and Kureishi both belonged. In a thoughtful essay the political theorist Bhikhu Parekh, another distinguished product of the Indian diaspora, detected a downward spiral of mutual incomprehension, with liberal intolerance provoking religious fundamentalism, and religious fundamentalism provoking yet more liberal intolerance. He called on Muslims to reinterpret their religious tradition so as to create an 'autonomous space' for secular values, and on the secular left to appreciate that religious sensibilities could give 'much needed moral and spiritual depth' to an increasingly instrumental society.[62] The clash of cultures that led to the Muslim march through London underlined the need for such a reconciliation, but boded ill for its prospects.

⳥

Slower, more gradual shifts of mentality also challenged the presuppositions of the political class and the visions of democracy that had helped to shape them. Margaret Thatcher's notorious jibe, 'What has women's lib ever done for me?' was a back-handed tribute to the most portentous of these shifts: ten years earlier, it would not have occurred to her to say anything of the sort.[63] When she became Prime Minister, the heroic age of feminism, with its anger, exhilaration and passionate self-discovery, was over. Feminists remembered that women, too, had multiple identities. Thatcher herself was a standing reminder that gender identities could be trumped by others; ironically, so were the Women Against Pit Closures who rallied to the striking miners in 1984–5. Meanwhile, some feminists discovered that the state was more permeable than they had imagined, and concluded that there was something to be said for Whiggish gradualism. 1970, the year of the founding National Women's Liberation Conference in Oxford, was also the year of the Equal Pay Act, making it unlawful to pay women less than men for the same or equivalent work. In 1975, it was followed by the Sex Discrimination Act, making it unlawful to discriminate on grounds of sex in employment, education and the provision of professional services. An Equal Opportunities Commission was set up to police the legislation. The results were mixed. The median earnings of full-time adult women workers rose from 54 per cent of the male figure in 1970 to 66 per cent in 1983 and 75 per cent in 1997, but the most poorly paid women fell back while the most highly paid forged ahead.

In the classic style pioneered by generations of popular radicals, the Sex Discrimination Act had been preceded by demonstrations, mass meetings and endless lobbying and letter-writing. One example occurred in February 1973 when a packed meeting in Caxton Hall, Westminster, was followed by a procession of women carrying lighted torches along Victoria Street to Parliament Square. Mary Stott, the doughty editor of the *Guardian's* woman's page, and the future best-selling novelist, Shirley Conran, left a hastily scribbled message to the Prime Minister, written on a page torn out from a friendly policeman's notebook, at No. 10 Downing Street.[64]

An equally striking example of extra-parliamentary pressure designed to change the system by changing expectations came in 1980, when the parliamentary researcher, Lesley Abdela, founded the all-party '300 Group' to work for equal representation of women in Parliament and to encourage women to seek and hold public office. An early victory for the group was the infant SDP's decision that all shortlists for parliamentary candidate selection should contain at least two members from each sex. The number of women MPs was still only twenty-three in 1983 – four up on 1979, but smaller than the totals in the 1960s. In 1987, however, the figure rose to forty-one, the highest in British history; and by 1992 it had reached sixty. Social attitudes changed markedly over quite a short period. In 1984 more than half those surveyed thought the husband's role was to earn the money and the wife's to look after the home, but by 1989 the proportion that thought so had fallen to a quarter, while around ninety per cent thought men and women were equally suited to the job of councillor or MP. On the other hand, the notorious glass ceiling was still very much in place. In 1995, women provided only 9 per cent of MPs and senior civil servants, 5 per cent of university professors and 3 per cent of company directors.[65]

As early exhilaration faded, divisions within the feminist movement – notably between liberal, socialist and radical feminists – became more obtrusive. 'Liberals' sought equality of opportunity within the existing system; 'socialists' insisted that gender inequality was inseparable from capitalism; 'radicals' replied that patriarchy pre-dated capitalism and could perfectly well survive its passing. Socialist feminists had hitched their wagon to a falling star. With capitalism everywhere triumphant, socialism discredited and the working class shrinking, the argument that women could achieve emancipation only by making alliances with the Labour movement so as to overthrow the capitalist system lost what little plausibility it had once had.

However, liberal and radical feminists both helped to widen the agenda of politics and to transform the public culture, as well as private lives. Radical feminists helped to politicise issues such as rape and pornography; Clare Short's Indecent Displays (Newspapers) Bill, designed to ban *Sun*-style 'page three' semi-nudes, was a notable landmark. Liberal feminists did the same to relative rewards and promotion prospects. Public language, and even everyday language, changed. Sexist jokes ceased to be funny. 'Gropers' were frowned on, even by men. Men, as well as women, gradually ceased to view the public sphere through an exclusively masculine prism; public faces were no longer, by definition, overwhelmingly male. Slowly and haltingly, democracy and democratic participation took on new meanings. The debate over citizenship gradually ceased to be gender-blind: citizens slowly stopped being either men or men in skirts. For sixty years after limited female enfranchisement in 1918, women had been represented in Parliament almost entirely by men. By the end of the Thatcher years, this no longer seemed an irremovable part of the political landscape. Meanwhile women began to question their old assumption that membership of the political class was not for them. Changes on the ground were often slow to come, but by the beginning of the 1990s a revolution of identity and expectation was clearly under way, deepening and enriching British democracy in a way that no one had foreseen as recently as twenty-five years before. And here, as in the campaigns for human rights and the Scottish Parliament, politicians followed where civic movements had led.

The heterogeneous, uncoordinated, but rapidly growing Green movement posed a comparable challenge to existing orthodoxies. Like feminists, Greens came in many guises. 'Ecologists' had something in common with radical feminists. They stood for a total transformation of existing societies, ways of life and ethical systems, and believed that nothing less could save the earth. At their most extreme, they rejected science and the Enlightenment as well as industrialism; occasionally, they gave the impression that they positively disliked the human species as well as all known human societies. An American ecologist, writing under the pseudonym 'Miss Ann Thropy', argued that the potential benefits of AIDS to the environment were 'staggering ... just as the Plague contributed to the demise of feudalism AIDS has the potential to end industrialism'.[66] Environmentalists' were more like liberal feminists. They sought ameliorative, step-by-step changes and believed that piecemeal adaptations of policy and behaviour could, in principle, avert planetary disaster.

Like the different schools of feminist thought, however, Greens had more in common with each other than they were always happy to admit. Virtually all of them were children of the romantic revolt of the 1960s and 1970s; they also drew on a much longer romantic heritage going back to William Morris, Ruskin and Blake. They loathed the materialistic consumerism of late-twentieth-century industrial society, not just because it wasted resources and ravaged the environment, but because it stultified the human spirit: because, as the eminent Green campaigner, Jonathon Porritt, put it, 'We have forgotten our dependence on the biosphere, and we have suppressed the gentler, deeper side of human nature.'[67] For many Greens, 'ecological consciousness' was a matter of self-realisation, predicated on identification with the non-human world. Few went as far as the American Green who wrote approvingly that, when a Nez Perce Native American was asked why he did not plough the land, he would reply, not with an economistic argument about the land's intrinsic value, but with the rhetorical question: 'Shall I take a knife and tear my mother's breast?'[68] But echoes of that mood could be detected in many Greens.

Like feminism, but if anything more radically, the Green movement cut across the familiar boundaries of party, class and tradition. Its ethic of stewardship was conservative, with a small 'C'. Its insistence on the need for far-reaching social change had something in common with socialism. Rights-centred liberalism could easily be married to environmentalism, while the participatory localism of the democratic republican tradition was second nature to most Greens. Even the palest Greens sought to recast political debate and the language in which it was conducted. And Greens of all stripes denounced the obsession with economic growth that had dominated British politics throughout the post-war period and, in some ways, since the Great Depression.

They did so in the name of 'sustainability' – a word that entered the political lexicon in the course of the 1980s and has stayed there ever since. The credit for putting it there belonged, above all, to the World Commission on Environment and Development, set up under United Nations auspices in 1983, under the chairmanship of Gro Bruntland, the former Prime Minister of Norway. 'Sustainability' was the overarching theme of the Bruntland Report.[69] It left many loose ends: one person's sustainable growth might be another's headlong rush to environmental disaster. But that did not detract from its political significance. However vaguely, it implied that economic growth was not necessarily good: that it could subtract from welfare as well as add to it; and that harmful, unsustainable growth should be avoided. In doing so it also implied that the assumptions underpinning the statecraft of virtually all British political leaders – the assumptions encapsulated in the mantra of the American Democrats in the 1990s, 'it's the economy, stupid' – were a dangerous basis for policy-making.

These implications were underlined in September 1988 when Margaret Thatcher, the decade's most unexpected recruit to the Green cause, gave a remarkable address to the Royal Society, warning that greenhouse gases were creating 'a global heat trap' with potentially disastrous consequences for the climate. Meanwhile, campaigning environmental groups grew lustily. Friends of the Earth increased its UK membership from around 15,000 at the end of the 1970s to 190,000 in 1990. The noisier and more controversial Greenpeace had more than 400,000 UK supporters by 1990, compared with 30,000 worldwide in 1979. Activist groups such as animal rights and motorway protesters stirred the pot.

The formal party system was undented. The Green Party, which started life as the People Party and then became the Ecology Party, limped along with a minuscule share of the popular vote until the European elections of 1989, when it suddenly jumped to 15 per cent, only to fall back to 1.3 per cent in the subsequent general election.[70] But here, too, formal party politics mattered less than the Westminster village imagined. The size and growth of the environmental movement called into question some of the key assumptions of Westminster democracy, notably the assumption that political parties were the chief agencies for mobilising opinion and articulating interests. If conservation groups like the Royal Society for the Protection of Birds and the National Trust are taken into account, the total membership of environmental bodies far exceeded that of all the political parties taken together. Greenpeace alone had significantly more members than the Labour Party.

At the same time, the Green agenda challenged the existing distribution of power, both between different levels of government within the United Kingdom and between the British state and supranational or international institutions. It was a truism that environmental pollution – and, still more, global warming – did not respect national boundaries. The Green slogan, 'Think globally, act locally', encapsulated a more complex truism. Remote bodies like the United Nations or the European Commission, or even the nation-state, could propose, but on a wide variety of environmental issues they could not dispose. On questions ranging from the recycling of waste to energy conservation, only a concerned and active citizenry working with strong local governments could translate virtuous aspirations into facts on the ground. That implied an essentially democratic republican conception of politics, which was as foreign to most of the British political class in 1990 as it had been when Richard Crossman berated his colleagues' disdain for participation twenty-five years before.

DISINTEGRATION

Major's prime-ministerial honeymoon lasted for the best part of two years. For most of that time, it was remarkably serene. Collegiality, and even harmony, returned to the Cabinet, to the great relief of ministers who had grown tired of Thatcher's hectoring. In January 1991, only a few weeks after becoming Prime Minister, Major led the country into the Gulf war, provoked by Saddam Hussein's invasion of Kuwait in August 1990. The patriotic fervour and nail-biting tensions of the Falklands war were missing. That had been a people's war; this one was the government's. British territory had not been invaded; British kith and kin were not in danger; ancient memories of insular glory were not (and could not have been) evoked. Few disputed the justice of the cause: Iraq had illegitimately invaded another sovereign state. But it was hard to summon up much enthusiasm for the undemocratic Kuwaiti regime. Besides, the war was an inescapably American-run and American-led affair, albeit one backed by a vast coalition of allies, notably including a number of Arab states, and legitimised by UN resolutions. For what it was worth, however, Major was judged to have had a good war and his already high poll ratings rose.

He also had a good peace. The poll-tax dragon was despatched with reasonable speed, to well-nigh universal applause. In his first budget, in April 1991, Norman Lamont, Major's Chancellor, raised VAT from 15 per cent to 17.5 per cent to fund a £140 cut in poll tax per person. In December 1991, the government brought in a Local Government Finance Bill abolishing the poll tax altogether, and replacing it with a new 'council tax', levied partly on property and partly on persons; it reached the statute book in March 1992. Few noticed that the administrative cost of setting up and dismantling the poll tax had reached the staggering sum of £1.5 billion; that by the end of the saga locally raised taxes covered only 20 per cent of local authority spending; or that Major's 'Thatcherism with a human face' had proved more centralist in practice, even if not in its rhetoric, than Thatcher herself had dared to be.[71]

The final demise of the poll tax was the overture to the most evenly matched general election for nearly twenty years. When the election was called on 11 March 1992, Labour was narrowly in the lead in the opinion polls. Apart from rare aberrations, it remained so throughout the campaign. On the other hand, Major's personal rating was consistently far higher than Kinnock's. On a deeper level, Labour's stance and programme had a curiously brittle, Johnny-come-lately air about them. Kinnock and his allies – notably Peter Mandelson, Labour's brilliant and flamboyant director of communications – had fought long and hard to 'modernise' the party. They had been remarkably successful. By 1992, the insular fundamentalism of the early 1980s was dead and buried; Labour fought as a revisionist, European social democratic party, committed to EC membership and a social-market economy, vaguely reminiscent of the 'Rhenish' capitalism lauded by Michel Albert.

But modernisation is not a doctrine, still less an ideal. To the question, 'Why modernise?' the party leadership had no real answer, apart from the uninspiring one that it desperately wanted to win. The policies set out in its document, *Meet the Challenge, Make the Change*, were driven by opinion research, not by ideas or beliefs. On the whole, they were popular, but that only proved that the party's pollsters were good at reading the runes. It did not prove that Labour had undergone a genuine change of heart, as opposed to a change of electoral clothing. Still less did it prove that Kinnock's change of heart was genuine. In 1992 he was a revisionist. Ten years before, when fundamentalism had ridden high, he had been a fundamentalist. What was to stop him changing again?

Less obviously, the same question could be asked of the Conservatives. In Thatcher's twilight period, they, as well as she, had been bitterly unpopular – not just because of the poll tax, but because of what it symbolised. Now Major offered a different kind of Conservatism: consensual, inclusive and human-faced. Yet he and most of his colleagues had served, with varying degrees of happiness, under Thatcher, the mistress of dissension. Why should their new incarnation be thought more genuine than the old? The election was, in truth, a contest between two Johnny-come-latelies, each telling the electorate what it wanted to hear, but each too pat to be entirely convincing. For both parties, trust was the crux of the campaign. The Conservatives' propaganda was designed to show that Labour could not be trusted with the economy, Labour's to show that the Conservatives could not be trusted with the society.[72]

In the end, the Johnny-come-lately in office seemed less untrustworthy than the one seeking it. Against the poll predictions, against even the exit polls on election day, the Conservatives won a Commons majority of twenty-one over all parties, with only a smidgen less than 42 per cent of the popular vote to Labour's 34.4 per cent. They were far ahead of Labour among routine non-manual workers, while the two achieved level pegging among skilled workers. Only among the dwindling class of unskilled workers did Labour have a decisive lead. Its long night was not yet over. For all its talk of challenge and change, it still seemed shackled to the past.

℘

As so often, fortune had surprises in store. By August 1992, Britain was in the throes of yet another sterling crisis.[73] This time it could hardly be blamed on overheating in the domestic economy. The Lawson boom had given way to a sharp and painful recession, which showed little sign of ending. Unemployment was high and rising; output was stagnant; house prices had collapsed; inflation was low and falling. Interest rates stood at 10 per cent – 5 per cent lower than in 1990, but still very high. Yet the balance of payments was in heavy deficit, as were the public finances. The domestic economy cried out for a stimulus, external pressures ran in the opposite direction. The German Bundesbank, whose chief duty was to keep inflation down, raised German interest rates to counter the inflationary effects of its government's irresponsibly profligate reunification policies. Foreign funds flowed into Germany and away from weaker currencies, sterling among them. By mid-August, sterling had fallen close to its permitted floor within the ERM.

Britain's combination of domestic deflation and balance of payments weakness was a classic pointer to devaluation, as Helmut Schlesinger, the conservative President of the Bundesbank, made no secret of believing. But, for Major and Lamont, that would have been as humiliating a defeat as the devaluation of 1967 had been for Wilson and Callaghan. ERM membership within the parity bands agreed when Britain joined had become their golden calf: a totem of anti-inflationary virtue. Like Wilson and Callaghan, they persuaded themselves that political will could override the markets. In a speech reminiscent of Wilson before the 1967 devaluation, Major declared wildly that the 'soft option, the devaluers' option, the inflationary option, would be a betrayal of our future'.[74] With astonishing ineptitude, Lamont used the opportunity of a meeting of EC finance ministers and central bankers in Bath to try to bully Schlesinger into cutting German interest rates. His failure was as miserable as it was predictable. The Bank of England spent huge sums buying up the sterling that speculators were busily unloading, but it too failed to save the day. On Black Wednesday, 16 September 1992, with the Bank's reserves close to exhaustion, an ashen-faced Lamont announced that British membership of the ERM was suspended.

Although the cost to the reserves was immense, the wider economic consequences were uniformly benign. The effective devaluation of 15 per cent that followed sterling's exit from the ERM gave the economy the boost for which exporters, manufacturers, homeowners and workers had cried out in vain. Unemployment and interest rates fell dramatically, output rose and exports rose even further. Inflation remained low. By the end of 1994 the huge balance of payments deficit that had built up in the 1980s was almost eliminated.[75]

But for once politics failed to mirror economics. For Major, his government and his party, Black Wednesday was a crippling blow that no later successes could undo. In a few hours of hectic selling in the currency markets, the Conservatives had lost their most precious electoral asset – the widespread belief that, however unpleasant their social policies might be, they were more competent at managing the economy than was the Labour Party. Their poll ratings sank to unheard-of depths. In June 1992, they had been 7 per cent ahead of Labour. By November, Labour was 20 per cent ahead of them. Major's rating was lower than Thatcher's at her 1990 nadir, and far lower than Wilson's in the aftermath of the 1967 devaluation. With only trivial oscillations, Labour held its lead throughout the Parliament. It led, moreover, not just on declared voting intentions but on perceived economic competence. In the public mind, the Conservatives had taken Labour's old place as the party that could not run a whelk-stall. No one seemed to notice that whelk sales were doing remarkably well.

❦

The government trudged on for five more years of misery, interspersed with bouts of hysteria and paranoia. In December 1991, a European summit at Maastricht had agreed the text of a treaty setting out the route to a single currency. With great skill, Major had managed to walk the tightrope between British economic nationalism and continental quasi-federalism which had been Thatcher's nemesis. He kept Britain within the framework of what now became the European Union. At the same time, he won her the right to opt out of two crucial treaty provisions – the commitment to join the

monetary union when the preconditions for it were met; and a social chapter
enhancing workers' rights. In words written for him by his press office, he
tempted fortune when the conference was over with the boast, 'Game, set
and match for Britain.' From his own point of view, he was right. Britain
was still, in his terms, at the heart of Europe, but without committing
herself to policies that the Conservative Party could not have accepted.

His euphoria did not last. The hard core of Conservative Eurosceptics
were not content with opt-outs from the Maastricht Treaty. They saw it,
correctly, as an another big step towards a supranational and at least quasi-
federal Europe; and they wanted, not just to draw its fangs, but to destroy
it. When the consequential legislation reached the House of Commons in
late 1992, a bitter, occasionally savage Eurosceptic revolt broke out, aided and
abetted by brutal interventions from Tebbit and Thatcher, now ensconced in
the House of Lords. The legislation went through in the end, but only after
seven months of party civil war in which Major's authority was fatally
wounded, while his followers seemed bent on proving that the Conservative
Party was no longer an instrument of government. By the end of his term
of office, as Denis Kavanagh and Anthony Seldon put it, the 'Cabinet of
chums' that Major had presided over at the start had become a 'Cabinet of
vipers'.[76]

Like a drunk clinging to a lamp-post in order to stay upright, Major
and his ministers stuck, with mechanical rigidity, to their predecessors'
characteristic mixture of marketisation and centralism. The most notable
examples were two privatisation measures from which Thatcher had flin-
ched – one of the now virtually invisible coal industry and the other of the
highly visible railways. The sale of British Coal in 1994 went through with
little fuss; a forlorn protest march took place in London but, as Simon
Jenkins put it, it did little more than mark 'the passing of an age'.[77] Rail
privatisation was a different matter. After long and intricate negotiations in
Whitehall over the shape of the privatised network, ministers finally hit on
a scheme of Byzantine complexity that might have been designed to maxi-
mise the political damage to the government while minimising managerial
accountability and public confidence. Before nationalisation, railway services had been provided by four regionally based, self-sufficient, privately
owned companies. One obvious way to privatise the system would have
been to re-create that structure, as John Major wanted. Another would have
been to sell the entire network to one private company in one fell swoop,
as had happened with British Gas, and as the Board of British Rail advocated.
The government did neither. Instead, ownership of the track went to one
private company, and train services to a number of others.

A complex mass of contracts governed the relationships between the new private companies; regulators oversaw the whole ensemble. It was a recipe for bureaucracy, confusion and buck-passing. Hopes that the changeover would widen the scope of the market and narrow that of the state proved cruelly deluded. The new system bore virtually no resemblance to a genuine market. The fate of the new private companies was determined by government-appointed regulators and government-determined contracts, not by free competition. And, whatever economic theory might say, the political reality was that ministers were blamed for everything that went wrong, therefore putting the government under more pressure to interfere with the railways than it had experienced before. It was a classic case of the great paradox of the Thatcher era. The state intervened more, not less; and in doing so it lost authority instead of gaining it. It was hard to dispute the mordant judgement of the Conservative chairman of the Commons Transport Committee, Robert Adley. The whole enterprise, he declared, was 'a poll tax on wheels'.

That was the most extreme example of Major's dogged pursuit of Thatcher's Utopia, but it was by no means the only one. In 1993, the Trade Union and Employment Rights Act gave individual members of the public the right to apply for injunctions against unlawful industrial action, making strike action more difficult; it also abrogated the inter-union Bridlington Agreement of 1939 that prevented unions from 'poaching' each other's members, weakening trade-union solidarity. More generally, the *Next Steps* initiative had developed a momentum of its own, which ministers would have found hard to stop even if they had wanted to; and, in practice, they were happy for it to continue. *Next Steps* agencies proliferated at a remarkable rate. By the year of Thatcher's fall, fifty such agencies employed a total of 180,000 officials. Six years later, the number of agencies had risen to 134, covering around 400,000 officials.[78]

Centralist quangos multiplied as well. Notable examples included a new Funding Agency for Schools, a Higher Education Funding Council and a Higher Education Quality Council to police teaching quality, all created by Major's first Education Secretary, the former academic John Patten. The National Health Service underwent yet another reorganisation, strengthening the Health Department's grip on the service and eroding medical autonomy. Even the criminal justice system and the police could not escape the onward march of central power. In 1994 the Police and Magistrates Court Act transferred responsibility for magistrates to the Lord Chancellor's department; the white paper preceding it explicitly declared that police priorities would be 'refocused' so as to direct them 'to those things which the *government* considers the police should be tackling'. (My italics.)[79]

Accompanying all this was what LSE's Accountancy Professor, Michael

Power, termed an 'audit explosion'.[80] The police became subject to measurable 'performance targets'. League tables assessed school performance. Academic research was monitored by increasingly complex 'research assessment' exercises (known as RAEs). The results bristled with paradox. Audit was not, as its advocates imagined, a neutral process that improved performance while leaving content unchanged. Auditees adapted their behaviour to the pressures of the audit process rather as managers in the old Soviet Union had adapted theirs to the pressures of Gosplan. Academics adopted research strategies designed to achieve high numerical RAE ratings, irrespective of scholarly excellence; the police concentrated resources on activities that would enable them to hit their targets, irrespective of the benefits to the public. All over the public sector, qualitative judgement became suspect, while the spurious objectivity of quantitative measurement replaced it. As Power put it, the 'auditable process' took precedence over 'the substance of activities'.[81]

The implications were startling. The combination of targets, audits and agencies (portentously known as the New Public Management) marked a victory for a particular, mechanistic conception of management – ultimately derived from the supposedly 'scientific management' developed by the American Frederick Taylor in the 1920s to raise productivity on assembly lines[82] – over professional judgement, professional authority and the professional ethos. Few of Major's ministers shed tears over that, but they failed to see that, albeit indirectly, it also helped to undermine the authority of the state, whose restoration had been the heart and soul of the Thatcher project.

Part of the object of the exercise was to farm out blame from ministers and officials at the apex of the state to service providers lower down. It had the opposite effect. The audit explosion was part product and part author of a culture of mistrust, in which all authority was suspect, and which could not be turned on and off like a tap. If doctors, or teachers, or policemen, or academics failed to satisfy the auditors (and, in the nature of things, some of them were bound to fail), ministers, as well as the auditees concerned, were blamed. The more government insisted that public-sector professionals could not be trusted to perform properly without minute and incessant scrutiny, the more it exacerbated mistrust – and the more its own competence and integrity were called into question. Well before the end of Major's prime ministership, the tory nationalist crusade was petering out amid a flurry of pettifogging managerial changes that negated its original purpose.

Meanwhile, the government was plagued by crushing by-election defeats and a string of scandals. Most of the latter concerned trivial sexual peccadilloes on the part of Conservative ministers, whose discomfiture added to the gaiety of nations but had no political significance. Some were more serious. Two middle-rank ministers, Neil Hamilton and Tim Smith, were accused of asking parliamentary questions in return for cash payments from the owner of Harrods, Mohamed Al Fayed. Smith admitted his guilt and resigned; Hamilton protested his innocence but was eventually sacked. After the government's fall, the newly appointed Parliamentary Commissioner for Standards, Sir Gordon Downey, ruled that both men were guilty. In 1995, Jonathan Aitken, Chief Secretary of the Treasury, was alleged to have violated ministerial rules by staying at the Paris Ritz at the expense of an Arab businessman. He resigned from the government and sued for libel. (Later he was found guilty of perjury and sentenced to a term of imprisonment.) Far more serious than these individual misdemeanours was the Arms for Iraq scandal that surfaced in October 1992 and led to a mammoth judicial inquiry, which revealed that ministers and officials had systematically misled the House of Commons about British arms sales to Saddam Hussein's Iraq in the 1980s. The government escaped censure by the Commons, but by only one vote.

Many Conservative MPs seemed more anxious to display their own doctrinal purity while denigrating that of party opponents than to hold and use power. At one point Major resigned the party leadership in the hope that his presumed re-election would stem the flood of backbiting that threatened to engulf him. He was duly re-elected, yet the flood continued. When the general election came in May 1997, the Conservative Party seemed awash with bile, as well as out of touch with the country that it aspired to govern. Its crushing defeat at the hands of Tony Blair's 'New' Labour Party was no surprise. The crusade was over. How the new government would deal with its legacy remained to be seen.

11

YOUNG LOCHINVAR

O young Lochinvar is come out of the west,
Through all the wide Border his steed was the best;
And save his good broadsword he weapons had none,
He rode all unarmed, and he rode all alone.
So faithful in love, and so dauntless in war,
There never was knight like the young Lochinvar.

Sir Walter Scott, 1808

Our party: New Labour. Our mission: New Britain.

Tony Blair, 1994

Blair's good at the high moral tone. If you want to go into battle with a preacher sitting on top of the tank, that's fine by me. But bear in mind, preacher's one more to carry. Needs rations, needs a latrine, just like everyone else.

'Cheney' in David Hare, *Stuff Happens*, September 2004

BRAVE DAWN

'We ran for office as New Labour,' declared Tony Blair from the steps of No. 10 Downing Street on 2 May 1997, immediately after accepting the Queen's commission to form a government, 'we shall govern as New Labour.'[1] The formula would be endlessly repeated, but it raised more questions than it answered. What *was* New Labour? What did it stand for? What interests would it serve? Did it did stand for anything, or was it just a public relations gimmick? On that magical May morning, when an attractively modest Blair made his declaration to a carefully choreographed crowd waving Union Jacks, no one asked such questions. Blair was Britain's Young Lochinvar. He was eloquent, brave, personable and, at forty-three, the youngest prime minister since Lord Liverpool in 1812. His élan and grace had swept his party off its feet, and now they had done the same to the nation.

Labour had campaigned on a minimalist platform, carefully designed to keep expectations low, but simply by being himself Blair had personified the confused yearnings for change that had helped to destroy the Major Government. Labour's crushing Commons majority was won with only a fraction more than 43 per cent of the popular vote – not much more than it had won in 1970, when Wilson had lost to Heath – but it had transformed the political landscape. In the three months before the election, the Major Government's approval ratings had hovered around 25 per cent. In the three months after it, the Blair Government's averaged more than 70 per cent. The *Guardian* thought there was a chance that the new government might construct 'a modern liberal socialist order' that would catch the imagination of the world, and greeted its victory with 'a congratulation, a cheer and a surge of hope'.[2] That was the mood of the moment. It would have seemed churlish to disturb it.

Yet the questions would not go away. New Labour dilated endlessly on what it was not. It insisted ad nauseam that it was not 'Old Labour', but that was another term of art, baffling to the uninitiated. It denied that it was Thatcherite. It was not Eurosceptic, but it was not in favour of a federal Europe. It had no plans to renationalise the undertakings that the Conservatives had privatised. It was not corporatist. Nor was it socialist in any recognisable sense. Instead it was 'social-ist', a Blair coinage explicitly designed to 'liberate' the party from its history.[3] It professed no ideology. 'What counts,' its election manifesto proclaimed, 'is what works.'[4] It did not identify itself with any class or interest group. With resounding banality, it claimed to stand for 'the many and not the few'. Like virtually all political movements in modern democracies, it was for equality of opportunity, but it was not egalitarian in any stronger sense: Peter Mandelson, one of its main architects, once famously said that it was 'intensely relaxed about people getting filthy rich'.[5] But beyond a cloud of amiable generalities, there was no answer to the question of what New Labour was.

Behind the generalities lay a history. It was a murky history, full of betrayal, anguish and bitterness. New Labour did not emerge easily from the womb of Old Labour. Its roots can be traced back to the feuds that had plagued the party before and after the defeat of 1992. As we saw in the last chapter, Kinnock and his associates had seen themselves as 'modernisers', jettisoning old beliefs in a desperate search for power. His successor – the rather owlish, but witty and forensically deadly Scottish barrister, John Smith – had been at most a lukewarm moderniser. Unlike Kinnock and many of the Kinnockites, he had no embarrassing far-left past to disavow. He had always stood firmly in the social-democratic tradition of Hugh Gaitskell and refused to abandon it. 'If radical change involves the Labour

Party subverting its principles and aborting its mission,' he announced during his campaign for the leadership, 'then I'm conservative.'[6]

Smith was suspicious of the glitzy, fashion-obsessed world of television and public relations in which Kinnock's 'modernisers' seemed all too much at home, and thought that Kinnock's survey-driven change of line had been too blatant to carry conviction. By a whisker, he carried through an important change in the party's procedures, substituting OMOV (one member one vote) for the trade-union block vote in party elections, but 'modernisation' went into cold storage thereafter. The sun of the leader's favour ceased to shine on Kinnock protégés like Mandelson, Charles Clarke, the future Home Secretary, and the tousle-haired Philip Gould, Labour's obsessional, and often manic, focus-group supremo.[7] The modernisers muttered behind their hands, but to no effect.

Smith's sudden death in May 1994, at the age of fifty-six, gave them their chance. There were two potential leaders in the modernisers' camp – Tony Blair and his closest friend in politics, Gordon Brown. New MPs often hunt in pairs, and Brown and Blair had soon become the closest and most formidable pair in the 1983 Labour intake. For a long time they shared an office, and they also shared a growing exasperation with the state of their party. Brown was two years older than Blair and, until shortly before Smith's death, most people saw him as the senior of the two. He had made his mark in Parliament earlier; he knew his way around the Labour movement better; and he was more impressive intellectually. But in the two years between the 1992 defeat and Smith's death, Blair's star had risen, while Brown's had fallen. (Ironically, Blair's famous soundbite, 'Tough on crime and tough on the causes of crime' – one of the chief sources of his soaring reputation – appears to have been suggested by Brown.)[8]

The sequel to Smith's death ruined their friendship. In the days of Brown's ascendancy the two had made a pact not to stand against each other in any future leadership election. With a flash of the steel without which few reach the summit of politics, Blair now made it clear that he was determined to stand, come what might. After much dithering and misery, Brown decided not to enter the race. To salve Brown's wound and, no doubt, to make doubly sure of his acquiescence, Blair promised his rival that he would be Chancellor of the Exchequer if Labour won, with effective control over social as well as economic policy. He may or may not have added that when he gave up the prime ministership, Brown would be his preferred candidate for the succession. For more than a decade, the strange, intense, sometimes co-operative and sometimes sulphurous relationship between Blair and Brown would be the pivot on which New Labour turned.

With Brown out of the way, Blair's march to the leadership was irresistible.

He was elected with a crushing majority in all three sections of Labour's cumbersome electoral college. The modernisers had triumphed, more completely than any of them would have dared to hope only two years before. The label, 'New' Labour, was the symbol and guarantee of their victory over the rest of the party. It was also a symbol of Blair's victory – a blank sheet on which he could write whatever he wished, subject only to the limits imposed by his beady-eyed putative (and later actual) Chancellor. Within a few months of his election, Blair launched a triumphantly successful campaign to excise Clause Four, committing the party to public ownership, from Labour's constitution. It was replaced with an anodyne paragraph extolling the virtues of tolerance, solidarity and mutual respect, with whose sentiments Harold Macmillan and even Stanley Baldwin would have found it hard to disagree.[9] The campaign saw Blair at his best. He took the battle to ordinary members up and down the country, and argued his case with a heady blend of passion and reason. To cap it all, he won where Gaitskell had lost. Henceforth, New Labour's ambiguous history would be an emanation of his equally ambiguous biography.

⁂

There was no ambiguity about the outward facts. Blair was born in Edinburgh in 1953, but grew up in Durham. His father, Leo – the illegitimate son of an actor and actress, brought up by foster parents in a Glasgow tenement – had been a Young Communist in his teens, but had risen through the ranks during the war, ending it as an acting major and a Conservative. He became an academic lawyer and barrister, and sought a career in Conservative politics. The young Tony went to a prestigious Durham prep school, called the Choristers' School, and then to Fettes, a rather grand Edinburgh public school, which thought of itself as the Eton of Scotland. Blair began his Fettes career as a conformist, but in his teens he became a 'rebel without a cause'.[10] He wore his hair too long; was forever questioning school rules; and was caught smoking, drinking and breaking bounds. However, three attributes of the later Blair were already present. He was an accomplished actor, both on the stage and off it; you could never be sure what he was thinking; and he had a certain presence, which made people notice when he came into a room.[11]

Blair began to find himself as a law student at St John's College, Oxford. He played no part in student politics, but he was an enthusiastic member of a lively, leftist and largely Christian discussion circle assembled by the 'spellbinding' Australian theology mature student and Anglican priest, Peter Thomson.[12] At Fettes, Blair had shown no interest in religion, but in his second year at St John's he was confirmed; from then on his Christian faith would play a central part in his life. Through Thomson, he discovered John Macmurray, the once-famous radical Scottish philosopher of personal fulfilment through 'community'. Macmurray's teachings played an important part in Blair's intellectual development, but how far Blair understood them is a moot question: in later years his approach to the same topics was much more authoritarian than Macmurray's.[13] After Oxford, Blair was called to the Bar, where his Head of Chambers was Derry Irvine, a distinguished Scottish QC whom he would later appoint as his Lord Chancellor. He joined the Labour Party in 1975, at the age of twenty-two. Through Irvine, he met another fledgling barrister, Cherie Booth, whom he married in 1980. In 1982, Blair fought the safe Conservative seat of Beaconsfield in a by-election. Despite coming a bad third, he won glowing opinions from Michael Foot, then party leader, and from Neil Kinnock, who would soon become leader in Foot's place.

When the by-election was over he wrote a long letter to Foot, which came to light only in 2006 and helps to bring the shadowy figure of the young Blair endearingly to life. He had just finished Foot's collection of essays, *Debts of Honour*, he wrote, and had been inspired by its 'hope, vigour and something irrepressibly optimistic'. However, there was too little of that in the contemporary Labour Party. Thanks to the association of socialism with Marxism, there was 'a tendency against letting the mind roam free'. He had himself come to socialism through Marxism, he explained, but eventually he had found it 'stifling'. Like Benn, he thought the Labour right was bankrupt. 'Socialism ultimately must appeal to the better minds of the people. You cannot do that if you are tainted overmuch with a pragmatic period in power.' Yet the far left was no better:

> There is an arrogance and self-righteousness about many of the groups on the far left which is deeply unattractive to the ordinary would-be member; and a truly absurd gulf between the subject matter and language of the legion of pamphlets they write and the people for whom the pamphlets are supposed to be written. There's too much mixing only with people with whom they agree. I wonder sometimes whether they would prefer to address a meeting of the converted than the unconverted. I can honestly say that I am at my happiest addressing people that don't necessarily agree but are willing to listen.[14]

The following year Blair was elected as Labour MP for the safe seat of Sedgefield, in his home county. From then on, his ascent was smooth. It took him only eleven years to rise from newly elected backbench MP to

Prime Minister. Of twentieth-century prime ministers, only Major had as short an apprenticeship.

The inner meaning of the story is harder to penetrate. Trying to understand Blair is like trying to catch a moonbeam. Kenneth Clarke, whom he shadowed for a while, claimed that Blair reminded him of the famous lines:

> As I was going up the stair
> I met a man who wasn't there
> He wasn't there again today
> I wish to God he'd go away.[15]

It was a telling jibe. Blair travelled light – existentially and culturally as well as ideologically. In striking contrast to Brown, or Smith, or Kinnock, or Callaghan, or even Wilson, he seemed not to know quite who he was, or quite where he belonged. In one of the most revealing comments he ever made, he told the *Observer* that he had never felt 'very anchored in a particular setting or class'.[16]

He belonged to a great liberal profession, but the culture and ethic of professionalism appeared to mean nothing to him. He was a well-brought-up, English, ex-public-schoolboy, yet he did not fit into the English class system – an asset for a political leader at a time when social classes were dissolving, but another sign of a lack of existential ballast. In the brute terms of electoral politics, he was the best leader the Labour Party has ever had, but he did not seem fully at home in it. Yet that, too, was a priceless asset. 'What gives me real edge,' Blair once told his formidable, foul-mouthed and devoted press secretary, Alastair Campbell, 'is that I'm not as Labour as you lot.'[17] But, though Campbell was disconcerted, there is no doubt that Blair was right. He was the least tribal leader in Labour's history and did more than any of his predecessors to dissolve its inward-looking claustrophobia. Partly because of that, he was its most successful vote-winner.

His attitude to the past was particularly revealing. He was said to regret his own lack of historical knowledge, and there were rumours that Roy Jenkins had become an unofficial historical mentor to him. However, tutorials from Jenkins could not change the unhistorical mentality behind his insistent rhetoric of 'New' Labour, 'New' Britain and the 'Young' Country. He was forever discovering new trends, new eras, new intellectual fashions and, during the second half of his prime ministership, new terrors. To some extent this was a matter of political expediency. Talk of novelty, youth and change offered a way of avoiding potentially divisive doctrinal precision. A characteristic example came during his speech to the Labour Party conference in 1995:

We live in a new age but in an old country . . . .

I want us to be a young country again. With a common purpose. With ideals we cherish and live up to. Not resting on past glories. Not fighting old battles. Not sitting back, hand on mouth, concealing a yawn of cynicism, but ready for the day's challenge. Ambitious. Idealistic. United.[18]

There was more to it than that, however. Blair was ill at ease with history, or at least with British history. He showered praise on the American tradition of individual freedom and opportunity, but his references to British traditions varied from the lukewarm to the hostile. Part of the point of 'New Labour' was to expunge the memory of 'Old Labour'; part of the point of 'New Britain' was to obliterate the Old Britain in which Blair did not fit. His fascination with the fashionable new rich from the worlds of show business, sport and the media told the same story. It was somehow appropriate that one of his greatest achievements as party leader was the successful wooing of the global media tycoon Rupert Murdoch, who was so impressed by Blair that he switched his support from the Conservatives to New Labour. It was also appropriate that he seemed happy to accept hospitality from the crass, ostentatiously rich leader of the Italian right, Silvio Berlusconi.

❧

There were hard, practical reasons for consorting with the wealthy as well as personal ones. By the end of the twentieth century, money talked more loudly than it had done for 100 years, in some ways more loudly than it had ever done. The rootless 'international plutocracy' that Peregrine Worsthorne deplored was a political force everywhere. The newly untamed capitalism of the 1980s and 1990s had created a global class of 'super-rich', detached from nation and place.[19] It included Russian oligarchs, American computer magnates and central European retailers, whose wealth dwarfed Murdoch's and Berlusconi's. According to *Forbes* magazine, the world's five richest individuals in early 2007 were worth $212 billion between them.[20] Only one native-born Briton, the Duke of Westminster, made the *Forbes* list of billionaires. With a fortune of $11 billion he was a minnow compared to the whales at the top of the list, but a whale compared to his middle-income contemporaries.

The tension between capitalism and democracy, prefigured in the debates in Putney Church in 1647, had become more acute than at any time since the coming of manhood suffrage. In the non-Communist world, private capital and the state had always been inextricably entangled, but the capitalist renaissance of the last quarter of the twentieth century had changed the terms of the trade between them. The rich still courted politicians, but politicians now needed the rich more than the rich needed them. One reason was that wealth had become more slippery than it had ever been, so that governments were haunted by the fear that the rich might disappear to more friendly shores, taking their capital with them. Another was the steady escalation in the costs of winning power in democracies where the ties of class and doctrine were eroding and electorates were becoming increasingly volatile.

As elections became more costly, the hunt for rich donors became more intense. In November 2006 Lord Sainsbury, Blair's minister of science, was reported to have given a total of £12 million to the Labour Party in the twelve years of Blair's leadership. Between 2005 and 2007 Lakshi Mittal gave it £5 million. Lesser donors included the publisher Lord Hamlyn, who gave it £2 million, and the private-equity tycoon Sir Ronald Cohen, who donated £1.3 million.[21] Charges of 'sleaze' were inevitable. In 1997, Conservative sleaze had been a central theme of Blair's election campaign. By 2006, his government looked more sleazy than Major's had ever done.[22] Scotland Yard investigated charges that peerages had been promised in exchange for undisclosed loans to the Labour Party. Lord Levy, Blair's fundraiser and special envoy to the Middle East, and Ruth Turner, Number Ten's head of government relations, were both arrested, apparently on suspicion of perverting the course of justice. Blair himself was twice interviewed by the police, the first prime minister in history to suffer such an indignity. In the end the Crown Prosecution Service decided there was insufficient evidence to justify a prosecution, but the affair left an acrid cloud of suspicion behind it.[23]

Money hunger went with populist politics. Blair was a natural populist. He was a superb communicator, in virtually any medium, with an uncanny feel for public moods. Initially sceptical audiences warmed to his self-deprecating wit, his combination of passion and forensic skill and, above all, his apparently heartfelt sincerity. In the early years of his prime ministership, he seemed a microcosm of the nation. By belonging nowhere he belonged everywhere. William Hague, Leader of the Opposition in Blair's first term, noticed that in the Labour Party magazine Blair claimed that his favourite food was fish and chips, while in the *Islington Cook Book* he preferred 'fresh fettuccini garnished with an exotic sauce of olive oil, sun-dried tomatoes and capers'.[24]

Many noticed that, particularly in moments of stress, the glottal stops of Estuary English seeped into his speech. In some ways, his populism was reminiscent of Thatcher's, but there were profound differences between them. Thatcher's populism was harsh, abrasive and belligerent, the vehicle of her crusade and the servant of her crystalline vision. In domestic politics, at least, Blair was a consolidator, not a crusader. Whereas Thatcher had sought to extirpate the legacy of Macmillan, Wilson and Heath, Blair sought to root Thatcher's legacy in the nation's soul by softening its hard edges and making it less divisive. The most frequently used word in his speeches was 'we'.[25]

His overriding aim was to construct a new social coalition, analogous to Thatcher's but with a much wider reach. At its heart, wrote Philip Gould, the prophet of Blairite populism, would be 'the new middle class' – the 'aspirational working class in manual occupations, and the increasingly insecure white-collar workers with middle- to low-level incomes'.[26] But the coalition would extend downwards to the poor and the inner cities, and upwards to the suburbs and the business class. Blair's 'big tent' had room for everyone – employers and employed, readers of the *Sun* and of the *Guardian,* Diane Abbott's Hackney constituency as well as Gisela Stuart's in Birmingham, Edgbaston. For the central premise of his statecraft was that society was naturally harmonious: that apparent differences of interest or belief could always be compromised or transcended.

His blandness sometimes verged on the mawkish. The supreme example was his reaction to the death of Princess Diana. When the news of her death came through, Blair famously dubbed her 'the people's Princess'; at her funeral he gave a reading from the Book of Corinthians, in a voice trembling with emotion that would have done credit to a professional actor.[27] However, the mawkishness served a purpose. It epitomised the popular mood, and enabled Blair to symbolise it.

He did not rely on eloquence and intuition alone. To use a term of Richard Rose's, Blair's populism was far more tightly 'managed' than Thatcher's.[28] Like her, he believed that he could speak to and for the ordinary people of Britain over the heads of Cabinet, Parliament and party. Like her, he sought to mould the popular will for which he thought he spoke. The ubiquitous Philip Gould used sophisticated opinion research to track the shifting moods behind the numbers in opinion surveys. By Order in Council – an exercise of the Royal Prerogative immune from parliamentary scrutiny or debate – Blair gave Alastair Campbell authority over civil servants. (Blair privileged his chief of staff, the comparatively shadowy Jonathan Powell, in the same way.) So long as he worked in Downing Street, Campbell was a constant presence at Blair's side. He spent more time with Blair than did anyone else. When Blair first visited Bush, Campbell was with him. He was present at the notorious Azores meeting between Blair, Bush, Aznar of Spain and Barroso of Portugal just before the Iraq war. Though a personal appointee, whose sole loyalty was to his master, he effectively outranked most, if not all, of the professional civil service, which had traditionally provided the British system's most effective check against ministerial abuse of power. He sat in on Cabinet and Cabinet committee meetings and (far more importantly) on the informal, fluid, often unminuted, ad hoc meetings through which Blair worked whenever possible.

In form, Campbell's job was to manage the government's communications with the outside world and, above all, with the media; at first he did this with brutal skill. In fact, his remit went much wider than that. He was not only the Prime Minister's spin doctor; he also had a strong influence on the content of what he spun. Blair saw him as one of the main architects of the whole New Labour project and valued him not just as a conduit for briefing, bullying and rumour-mongering, but as a political strategist. Campbell and Gould worked on the principle laid down by Dick Morris, President Clinton's notorious spin doctor: 'Any leader whose poll ratings have fallen below 50 per cent is functionally out of office.'[29] Policy ideas were market-tested in focus groups. Government speeches and initiatives were tailored to the fears and hopes revealed in opinion research. A strange, three-cornered form of Chinese whispers came into being. Media storms fed into the focus groups; focus-group discussions fed into the Prime Minister's office; and ministerial reactions fed back into the media. Governments had always tried to present their policies as attractively as possible but, under Blair, policy, presentation and reception were a seamless web.

In the later stages of Blair's reign, Sir Christopher Foster, an experienced consultant and former ministerial adviser, painted a vivid picture of the way in which Downing Street wove the web. One observer, he wrote, remembered Blair and some of his advisers lying about 'on sofas and chairs' as they watched a policy slide-show. 'Occasionally he or one of his advisers would interrupt with a comment like "That won't play well", or "Can't see that going down well in the tabloids" .... It seemed more like a production team pondering, not very enthusiastically, whether something was a good idea for a programme than a government.'[30]

✼

Managed populism sustained what Peter Hennessy, the doyen of academic Whitehall watchers, called a new 'governing norm'.[31] The roots of this new norm lay in the schisms, caballing and backstabbing of Labour's years in opposition, when Blair and his circle had learned their trade. Like the Bolsheviks who suddenly found themselves in control of a great empire after spending most of their adult lives in a clandestine twilight, they brought into government the conspiratorial reflexes that they had acquired in their struggle for power. They were a small, intense group, closely knit, who had learned to trust each other and to distrust outsiders. They viewed career civil servants and even the rest of the Labour Party with corrosive suspicion. Their emotional bonds with each other quickly gave way to wariness and even loathing when one of their number fell out of line or seemed about to do so. Number Ten's hostile briefing against the originally Blairite Mo Mowlam after she lost her job as Secretary for Northern Ireland was an egregious example,[32] but it was trivial in comparison with the endless briefing wars between Blair's office and Brown's.

The reflexes of opposition also helped to shape Blair's relations with his ministers. Brown apart, none of them could stand up to him, or rival his extraordinary combination of guile, charisma, political *nous* and histrionic ability. It was easy for him to sideline them, and he did so even more thoroughly than Thatcher had done. In theory, they were still responsible to Parliament for the policies of their departments. In reality, their role was to execute, and take the blame for, decisions reached in Number Ten, where invisible and unaccountable prime ministerial advisers often mattered more than they did. Cabinet meetings were short and perfunctory, and played virtually no part in decision-making. Blair and his aides made no secret of finding them a waste of time. Peter Stothard, former editor of *The Times*, spent a month before the Iraq war as a fly on the wall in Number Ten. In a memorable account of his experiences, he painted a vivid picture of the Blair office's reaction to a 'Cabinet day':

> The arrival of some twenty-five men and women from various government departments, however regular on a Thursday morning, is not welcomed with joy at Number Ten. Cabinet days are like Christmas at a great country house, when all the relatives who think they own the place – who do in certain circumstances own the place – descend for their share of the inheritance. The master and his servants greet the guests cheerfully enough; they can hardly turn them away, but they are mightily pleased when they are gone.[33]

The Cabinet day that Stothard described took place at a moment of acute crisis, but there is no reason to believe that Number Ten's reaction to it was untypical. Blair hated large, structured, impersonal meetings and preferred small, informal groups, that often met without papers or note-takers. During a particularly frenzied two weeks in the summer of 2003, when Number Ten was desperately trying to fend off the charge that it had 'sexed up' an intelligence dossier published during the run-up to the Iraq war, an average of seventeen meetings a day took place in Downing Street, only three of which were minuted.[34] Whenever possible, Blair dealt with his ministers bilaterally, person to person, giving full scope to his charm and persuasive powers. His dealings with Brown – the only minister with an independent power base and, as such, the only one he feared – followed the same pattern. Though their decisions were the fuel on which the government ran, their innumerable tête-à-tête meetings took place in private.

Civil service professionalism fared as badly as Cabinet collegiality.[35] Some civil servants joined the innermost circle around Blair: a notable example was David Manning, one of his Foreign Office advisers. But those who did so had more in common with Blair's personal appointees than with the public servants of old days. Towards the end of his second term, his predilection for 'sofa government' earned him an astonishing public rebuke from Lord Butler, a normally tight-lipped mandarin who had served as Cabinet Secretary under Thatcher, Major and, for a short time, under Blair himself. Butler had chaired an inquiry into the role of intelligence in the prelude to the Iraq war, and had been appalled by what he saw of Blair's governing style. His committee's report had included a paragraph criticising Number Ten for 'reducing the scope for informed collective political judgement' in the run-up to the war, but the language was so Delphic that readers unversed in the ways of Whitehall would have been hard put to understand it.[36] In a subsequent *Spectator* interview, Butler was somewhat less Delphic. 'It isn't wise to listen only to special advisers, and not to listen to fuddy-duddy civil servants,' he declared with an icy disdain only half concealed with feigned moderation. 'Good government,' he added, 'means bringing to bear all the knowledge and all the arguments you can from inside and outside, debating and arguing them as frankly as you can.'[37]

Butler's critique cut deeper than those who read it in the *Spectator* may have realised. In some ways it cut deeper than he seemed to realise himself. Men and women of power have always been apt to inhabit halls of mirrors that reflect their own preconceptions and prejudices back to them. As Butler implied, Blair's indifference to the conventions of Cabinet government, and his disdain for disinterested professional advice, might have been designed to insulate him from the outside world and to buttress the hubris to which all leaders are prone. Yet Butler's critique told only half the story. He did not pay due attention to the rising grovel-count among officials, which Lord Bancroft had identified at the start of the Thatcher era. He appeared to think that ministerial appointees were alone in succumbing to the temptation to soft-pedal unwelcome opinions: that 'fuddy-duddy' civil servants were immune to the pressures of group-think.

Solid facts are hard to come by but, to put it at its lowest, Butler's faith in his old colleagues squares badly with the little we know about the conduct of professional public servants in the weeks before the Iraq war. As an anonymous source told Peter Hennessy, an unacknowledged prime minister's department had come into existence. 'Almost all the people in this structure hold office at the pleasure of the PM. It is *sui generis* – a case apart from the rest of the Whitehall machine. The centre is not just a person, the Prime Minister, and a small staff – it is a machinery around him.'[38] The machinery did not consist only of Blair and his personal appointees. Civil servants belonged to it as well.

The end result was an extraordinary form of bicephalous personal rule. Like a Renaissance prince, Blair presided over a court, in which underlings great and small jostled for the ruler's ear, while favourites rose and fell. But his writ did not run throughout his realm Brown also had a court. It was smaller than Blair's, but it could call on the resources of the Treasury, the most formidable department in Whitehall. And Brown defended its autonomy with unsleeping vigilance.

HIGH NOON

It took a long time to grasp the full implications of this combination of wealthy patrons, sofa government, Cabinet irrelevance and managed populism. Blair's New Labour Party, and the regime that it procured, baffled conventional commentators. The forms of parliamentary government were preserved, but the underlying reality was transformed. Representative democracy depends on political parties and on open debate between alternative governing philosophies. Managed populism was designed to smother debate: to sieve out alternatives that might offend key groups of voters. By the same token, New Labour was less a political party than a costly and, for many years, an astonishingly successful vehicle of plebiscitary personal rule. It was almost as rootless as its leader. The elites that had sustained the old Labour Party – the expert professionals on whom Shaw and the Webbs had pinned their hopes for justice and rationality; the trade-union barons; and the Labour satraps in local government – were shadows of their former selves. As for its ordinary members, their only significant role was to applaud in the right places at its carefully stage-managed conferences.

Blair and his associates had been catapulted into party power by the accident of Smith's death at the ideal moment for them. Thanks to Blair's political genius, and still more to the Conservatives' ineptitude, they had then converted party power into national power. In 1997, they had driven the Conservative Party into the margins of politics, and they kept it there in 2001 with almost contemptuous ease. The journalist Jackie Ashley summed up the inner meaning of their success in a telling phrase. New Labour, she wrote, was 'a top-down, permanent coup'.[39] Some New Labour paladins looked forward to what they called a 'progressive century': in other words, a century that they and their political heirs would dominate.[40] For most of Blair's first two terms, it looked as if they were right. In 1922, Baldwin had put paid to Lloyd George's Caesarism. Seemingly, it had now returned in a new, more emollient and far more successful guise.

Yet no one could be sure what route the legions would follow. From Clinton's 'New Democrats' in the United States, Blair picked up the musty notion of a 'Third Way', championed by Harold Macmillan, in the guise of a 'Middle Way', nearly sixty years earlier.[41] But, in spite of heroic efforts to give the notion an intellectual spine, led by the indefatigable LSE Director and future Labour peer, Anthony Giddens,[42] it was too nebulous to steer by, and it soon faded away. It should be seen as a reflection of Blair's baffling, post-modern indeterminacy, not as a guide to action.

For he was a bewildering mass of contradictions. He was a conservative in radical clothes. He mingled high principles with low cunning. He was sustained by a deep Christian faith, but the jealous God of the Old Testament appeared to mean more to him than the merciful God of the New. He concentrated power in his own hands, but seemed not to know how to use the powers that he amassed. He was sometimes called a chameleon, but a better word is 'protean', from the sea god, Proteus, who could assume any shape he wished. Like Franklin Roosevelt, Blair was, in Machiavelli's language, both a lion and a fox.[43] He was courageous, indomitable and inspiring. He was also tricky, devious and disloyal. All four of the political traditions discussed in this book came together in him and, therefore, in his government. With part of his mind, he was a decentralist democratic republican, with another part a centralist democratic collectivist. In some ways he was an unusual kind of whig imperialist, in others an equally unusual tory nationalist.

For most of his first term, his and his party's democratic republican side was uppermost. Labour came into office committed to a programme of constitutional change broadly in line with that of Charter 88 and the Scottish Claim of Right, and more radical than any seen in Britain since 1914. The centrepiece was a commitment to devolution in Scotland and Wales, but Labour also promised reform of the House of Lords, freedom of information, a referendum on proportional representation, directly elected mayors and statutory protection of human rights. Within a few months of Blair's landslide victory, legislation providing for referendums on a Scottish Parliament and a Welsh Assembly reached the statute book. Those referendums took place in September 1997. The Scots voted by three to one in favour of a Scottish Parliament, and by two to one in favour of giving it power to vary taxation. The Welsh referendum recorded a minuscule majority (51 per cent to 49 per cent) in favour of a Welsh Assembly.

The Scotland Act and the Government of Wales Act giving effect to these results were passed with what previous political generations would have thought breakneck speed. They were very different. The Scottish Parliament was empowered to pass primary legislation on most internal Scottish matters. The Welsh Assembly was a humbler creature, competent only to pass secondary legislation. But, for the moment at least, the legal differences mattered less than the political similarities. By the summer of 1999, a Scottish Parliament was sitting in Edinburgh for the first time since 1707, while a Welsh Assembly sat in Cardiff for the first time in history. The territorial constitution of the United Kingdom had been transformed, with unforeseeable consequences for British democracy and the multinational British state.

The Scottish and Welsh Questions were recent additions to the agenda of Westminster politics. The Irish Question had baffled British politicians for centuries. For most of the twenty-odd years between the failure of the Sunningdale Agreement in the 1970s and Blair's arrival in office, it had taken the form of a bitter, bloody but inconclusive struggle between the Provisional IRA on the one hand and the British Army and security services on the other. 'Provo' terrorist exploits had included an only just unsuccessful attempt to kill most of the British Cabinet by planting a bomb in the Grand Hotel in Brighton during the 1984 Conservative Party conference, and a subsequent mortar attack on No. 10 Downing Street while John Major's Cabinet was in session. However, most IRA terrorism had taken place in Northern Ireland. The same was true of the answering terrorism of self-styled 'loyalist' paramilitaries. A brief chink of light appeared in 1985 with the so-called Anglo-Irish Agreement between the Thatcher Government and the Government of the Republic of Ireland, but it did not last. The Provisionals dreamed of uniting the island of Ireland, against the wishes of the Unionist community in the North, by breaking Britain's will to resist them. So long as they thought they had a chance of success, no lasting peace was possible.

By the late 1980s, however, leading figures in Sinn Fein – the political wing of the IRA – were beginning to realise that their strategy was failing. Tentative, shadowy, deniable contacts took place between the hard-line republicans in Sinn Fein and the moderate nationalists of the SDLP (Social Democratic and Labour Party), between the Dublin Government and the SDLP, and even between Sinn Fein and the British. Slowly, warily and often with mixed feelings, the protagonists edged their way towards all-party peace negotiations. Under John Major the pace warmed up. Early in 1993, the IRA let the British Government know that it wanted to end the armed struggle, but needed help to do so. At the end of the year the British and Irish governments signed the so-called Downing Street Declaration, committing them to work for an agreement covering 'the totality of relationships' between all the people of Ireland. In August 1994 the IRA announced a ceasefire.

Progress towards the Declaration goal was tortuous, halting and interspersed with bitter charges of bad faith. The various Unionist factions circled around each other like suspicious fighting dogs, while Sinn Fein and the SDLP jostled for position in the nationalist community. After seventeen months, the IRA renounced its ceasefire and proceeded to carry out two bloodthirsty atrocities on the British mainland, one in London's Canary Wharf, and one in Manchester city centre. Yet by the time Major left office in the spring of 1997, the skeleton of a future agreement was in being. More convoluted comings and goings took place before the skeleton acquired flesh but, less than a year after Blair's arrival in office, the Good Friday Agreement of 10 April 1998 was signed in Belfast.

Judged against the background of the previous 300 years of British history, this was an astonishing document.[44] It was far more innovative than the devolution statutes for Scotland and Wales and departed far more radically from cherished British constitutional principles. It provided for an elected Assembly, with legislative powers over a wide range of matters, and for a power-sharing executive composed of representatives of the two communities in Northern Ireland, in proportion to their strength in the Assembly. That much was straightforward enough, though the provision for the power-sharing executive had nothing in common with the Westminster model. Other crucial elements in the package were not straightforward at all. For controversial legislation and 'key' decisions, simple majorities would not be enough. They would need concurrent majorities in both communal blocs. In the jargon of political science, Northern Ireland's democracy would be 'consociational', not 'majoritarian'. The guiding principle would be one community, one veto; not one person, one vote.

As though that were not enough, the Agreement would come into force only if it were approved by referendums in the Irish Republic as well as in Northern Ireland. It would be embodied in an agreement (effectively a treaty) between the Irish and British governments. Irish ministers would sit alongside ministers from Northern Ireland in a North–South Ministerial Council to develop and oversee cross-border co-operation on a wide range of matters. A British Irish Council would bring together representatives from the governments of the Irish Republic, Northern Ireland, the United Kingdom, the Channel Islands and the Isle of Man. Crucially, all parties to the Good Friday Agreement acknowledged the right of the people of Northern Ireland to determine their constitutional future by majority vote. The Irish committed themselves to remove the Republic's irredentist claim to Northern Ireland from its constitution. The Agreement also provided for enhanced human rights protection and an independent human rights commission.

The implications were startling. Hard-edged, monolithic British notions of sovereignty – both national and parliamentary – had given way to soft, porous ones. The sovereign British state had agreed to give the sovereign Irish state a role in the governance of part of the United Kingdom. On the crucial question of Northern Ireland's constitutional future, popular sovereignty – exercised by the people of the Republic as well as by the people of Northern Ireland itself – had effectively replaced the sovereignty of the (British) Crown-in-Parliament. The Irish Government had abandoned the long-standing Republican claim to be the sole repository of the will of the Irish people. The British Government had formally agreed that, if they wished, the people of Northern Ireland could exercise their right to self-determination by seceding from the United Kingdom. The new Northern Ireland constitution was not just consociational. It was also communitarian, implicitly confederal and post-modern.

Marjorie ('Mo') Mowlam, the Northern Ireland Secretary, drew an appropriately subtle moral. 'Everyone's political and cultural identity is respected and protected by this deal,' she told the House of Commons. 'Northern Ireland politics, for so long, has been a zero-sum game. This agreement demonstrates the potential for the people of Northern Ireland to move beyond that, into a new type of politics.'[45] The new politics took longer to arrive than Mowlam had expected. There were bitter disputes over decommissioning the IRA's stocks of weapons and the arrangements for policing the province. An interlude of devolved government was followed by another period of direct rule. By early 2007 the prospects for a return to the Good Friday constitution looked better than they had ever been. In March 2007 Ian Paisley's DUP (the most extreme of the Unionist parties) won thirty-six seats in the new Assembly elections. Sinn Fein, the most extreme in the Nationalist community, won twenty-eight. The previously unthinkable then came to pass. In May 2007 the hardest of the hard on both sides of the divide formed a power-sharing government, with Ian Paisley as First Minister.

Many deserved a share of the credit – Major, Clinton, Gerry Adams, the Sinn Fein leader, David Trimble, the Ulster Unionist, John Hume of the

SDLP, the Irish Taoiseach, Bertie Ahern, and the civil servants in the Irish Department of Foreign Affairs, among others. But though Blair was not solely responsible for the Agreement, his role in the negotiations was second to none. Alastair Campbell's depiction is compelling as well as vivid. Blair, Campbell wrote,

> was at his infuriating best. Once he got the bit between his teeth, and decided to go for it, he always knew best, there was no one else could put a counter-view, he was like a man possessed. He would ask to see someone and then ten seconds later shout out 'Where the fuck are they? I need them here NOW.' He would pace up and down, go over all the various parts of the analysis, work out who was likely to be saying what next, work out our own next move . . . . As the days wore on, he started to take on a grey-green tinge, and looked exhausted, but he was brilliant throughout.[46]

It was Blair's finest hour.

◈

There was more. The devolution statutes laid down that elections to the Edinburgh Parliament and the Cardiff Assembly should be by proportional representation. The government also introduced proportional representation for European Parliament elections. Thanks to Blair's personal enthusiasm, New Labour's election manifesto had contained a commitment to give London a directly elected executive mayor, scrutinised by an Assembly also elected by PR, provided the proposal were approved in a London-wide referendum. In 1998, in a low poll, Londoners approved the proposal by 72 per cent to 28 per cent; the necessary legislation was passed the following year.

The government was also committed to hold a referendum on proportional representation for Westminster elections; Roy Jenkins, now Lord Jenkins, was appointed to head a non-party Commission to prepare proposals for submission to the voters. In 1998 it produced an elegantly written report, patently emanating from its chairman's pen. The report advocated a hybrid scheme, combining the Alternative Vote for the great majority of seats in Parliament with regional list elections for the rest. It fell short of complete proportionality, but would have made the system substantially more proportional than it was. Jenkins had framed it with an eye to Blair's likely reaction, and he believed that the government would put it to a referendum before long.[47] In addition, 1998 saw the passage of the Human Rights Act, effectively incorporating the European Human Rights Convention into British law.

It was not difficult to spot holes in this package. The logic of devolution was federalist, or at least proto-federalist. There were now three power centres in the United Kingdom in addition to the Westminster Government. Each represented a distinct political community, with a distinct culture, identity and interests. Scotland's relationship with Westminster was now much closer to Bavaria's with Berlin than to the relationship it had had with Westminster before devolution. However, Blair and his colleagues bent over backwards to deny the logic of their own intentions. Northern Ireland, Scotland and Wales were treated differently. England was not treated at all. The Scotland Act contained a clause expressly entrenching the supremacy of the Westminster Parliament over the Edinburgh Parliament – even though, as Vernon Bogdanor pointed out in a now-classic study, it was almost inconceivable that any future United Kingdom Government would seek to overturn the Scottish Government's decisions.[48]

The incorrigible British love of halfway houses was a rich source of future trouble. Though the Welsh had voted for devolution by the narrowest of margins, they seemed certain to demand parity with Scotland sooner or later. The Welsh problem was trivial in comparison with the English one. Gibbering in the wings was the West Lothian Question with which Tam Dalyell had tormented the Callaghan Government twenty years before: how could it be right for Scottish MPs to vote on English questions when English MPs would no longer be allowed to vote on Scottish ones? Some ministers hoped to defuse the issue by setting up elected regional governments in England, but in a referendum on a proposed elected authority in the Northern Region the voters rejected the idea by 78 per cent to 22 per cent on a poll of less than 50 per cent. The logical answer was a federation, with England as one of the constituent states, but that required a leap of imagination that British politicians would be unlikely to make unless a political crisis forced them to do so.

The financial arrangements were equally rich in unexploded bombs. The tax-varying powers granted to the Scottish Parliament were minimal; after devolution as before it, a block grant from the UK Government in London funded public spending in Scotland. Unfortunately, spending per head on devolved services in Scotland was higher than the equivalent figure for the same services in England. Before devolution no one had noticed. Now that there was a Scottish Parliament sitting in Edinburgh, and an elected Scottish Government spending the money that it received from central government, the coarse question of who got what from whom hovered menacingly on the political horizon.

The Human Rights Act was another halfway house. In form, it too left parliamentary supremacy intact. It did not empower the courts to strike down Acts of Parliament, as Scarman and Hailsham had advocated twenty years earlier. But the formal survival of parliamentary supremacy was only half the story. If the courts believed that a statute conflicted with the Act, they could issue a declaration of incompatibility; and there was a provision for a fast-track procedure for amending the offending statute. Parliament and the government were free to ignore the declaration if they chose, but aggrieved complainants could still seek redress from the Strasbourg Court of Human Rights, which would presumably find in their favour. Particularly after the Al Qaeda attack on New York's twin towers in September 2001, ministers repeatedly railed against the judiciary for overriding democratically elected politicians. They seemed unaware that the Human Rights Act had, in effect, made the European Human Rights Convention a fundamental law, superior in status to ordinary laws, and that part of the point of the exercise was to create a stronger judicial check on the abuse of executive power.[49] Over human rights, as over devolution, the substance of parliamentary supremacy had vanished, leaving behind only a Cheshire Cat grin. But because the grin survived, ministers often mistook it for the substance.

Yet it would be wrong to make too much of these anomalies and illogicalities. Living constitutions are always anomalous to some degree: political life is itself full of anomalies. The Blair Government's halfway houses were inherently unstable, just as the halfway houses of the nineteenth-century Reform Acts had been unstable. Constitutional reform at the end of the twentieth century, like suffrage reform in the nineteenth, was a process, not a destination. No one could tell when or where the process would end, still less how. What mattered was that it was taking place: that the conceptual and emotional foundations of the British tradition of autonomous executive power were crumbling. However much ministers pretended otherwise, a quiet constitutional revolution was under way. It was Blair's greatest achievement, and his chief claim to a place in history.

⌘

There was a further anomaly, stranger than the others. Blair himself was curiously bashful about his achievement; and curiously unaware of its meaning. Part of the point of his constitutional reforms was to force the central executive to disgorge power – to the courts on the one hand, and to the non-English nations of the Kingdom on the other. Whether Blair realised this is unclear. What is certain is that his enthusiasm for power shedding rapidly cooled in office. Indeed, chill winds began to blow even before he crossed the threshold of Number Ten. In an interview with the *Scotsman* during the 1997 election, he declared that 'sovereignty rests with me as an English MP and that's the way it will stay.'[50] For good measure he added that the Scottish Parliament's proposed tax-varying powers would not be used; and that Labour's pledge that there would be no tax rises for five years applied to Scotland as well as to England. He seemed not to realise that, once a Scottish Parliament and Executive came into existence, the Westminster Government would have no power to decide such matters and that his pledge called into question Labour's commitment to devolution.

More symptoms appeared after the election. In the London mayoral election, Blair spent an inordinate amount of political capital on an unsuc-cessful attempt to stop 'Red Ken' Livingstone from becoming mayor, from which he emerged looking cack-handed, authoritarian and devious all at once.[51] In a similar manoeuvre in Wales, he did his best to stop the ebullient and irreverent Rhodri Morgan from becoming First Minister. The result was an anti-Labour swing in the first Welsh Assembly elections, after which Morgan got the job, while a humiliated Blair retired from the fray.

Later, the Jenkins Report disappeared into the oubliette reserved for embarrassing commitments. Later still, Blair and the government whips between them contrived to block backbench demands for a largely elected House of Lords, even though that was the option favoured by the vast majority of Labour MPs.[52] (By early 2007 a large Commons majority for an entirely elected second chamber seemed to have removed the block.) Central government's dealings with local government told a similar story. Before the 1997 election, Blair had denounced the Conservatives' 'destruction of local government' as 'one of the most foolish – almost wicked – dogmas of the Thatcher years'.[53] New Labour had fought the 1997 election on the ticket of decentralisation, not just through devolution in Scotland and Wales, but by making local government 'less constrained by central governmenet'.[54]

However, the straitjacket that centralist tory nationalism had imposed on local government remained in place, with only minor modifications. Around seventy-five per cent of the local authorities' revenue still came from central government, and Whitehall still treated them as instruments for executing centrally determined policies, not as arenas for civic action or embodiments of local democracy.[55] In 2002, the Democratic Audit carried out by the Essex University's Human Rights Centre found that British practice contravened nine out of thirteen key provisions of the European Charter for Local Self-Government, of which Britain was a signatory.[56]

Blair was often accused of being a 'control freak', and perhaps he was. The emotional violence of his call for rules to 'impose order on chaos' soon after he became party leader suggests that there may have been a link between his insecure, troubled adolescence and his autocratic prime min-istership.[57] But psychological speculation misses the real point. In truth,

Blair the democratic republican was at war with Blair the democratic collectivist. This was not surprising: the same was true of virtually the entire Labour Party. The democratic collectivist tradition was part of Labour's inheritance, as it always had been. Labour people still viewed social and economic change through a determinist prism, as Sidney Webb and Ramsay MacDonald had done at the beginning of the twentieth century; and they still looked instinctively to an enlightened central state to deliver justice and rationality. Blair's claim that he and his colleagues were uniquely able to solve the new problems of a new age echoed Ramsay MacDonald's speeches in the 1920s, Labour's election manifesto in 1945 and Harold Wilson's call for a 'purposive new Britain' in the 1960s. Determinist futurism had been fundamental to the democratic collectivists' world-view since the beginning. It was their answer to the relaxed and genial whiggery of the Baldwins, the Churchills and the Macmillans and, still more, to the tense tory nationalism of the Salisburys, the Powells and the Thatchers.

The same applied to Blair's endlessly repeated insistence that rights went with duties. As we saw in Chapter 3, that quintessential democratic collectivist Ramsay MacDonald had exalted duties, while pooh-poohing rights as the expression of outdated and discredited individualism. Blair did not go quite as far as that, but when he wrote that 'Duty is the cornerstone of a decent society', that 'The rights we receive should reflect the duties we owe', or that the 'libertarian Left' had fostered a dangerous 'social individualism', the echo of MacDonald was unmistakable.[58] When Blair and his colleagues said that they were new, they proved that they were old.

The practical implications of New Labour's determinism *were* new, however. Previous generations of democratic collectivists had assumed that History with a capital 'H' was moving ineluctably and irresistibly towards planning, public ownership and a mixed economy, and perhaps towards a socialised one. Their New Labour successors thought it was moving, also ineluctably and irresistibly, in the opposite direction – towards individualism, consumerism and ever-advancing capitalism. The intellectual ferment of the early 1990s, with its debates over alternative models of capitalism, had had virtually no impact on them; though Blair made a speech on the 'stakeholder economy' in January 1996, he soon dropped the idea in deference to the CBI.

For New Labour, as much as for the Thatcherites, capitalism was capitalism was capitalism. There was no point in trying to redesign the architecture of British capitalism, as Will Hutton and John Kay had urged; the only question was how to adapt to it. Alan Milburn, the born-again Blairite who served for a while as Health Secretary during Blair's second term, epitomised New Labour's determinism in a parliamentary debate. The

Health Service, he declared, 'was formed in the era of the ration book'.

> Today we live in a different world. Whether we like it or not, this is a consumer age. People demand services that are tailored to their individual needs. They want choice and they expect quality – we all do it and we all know it. These changes cannot be ignored, they are here to stay.[59]

It might have been Sidney Webb appealing to the 'inevitability of gradualness'.

As in Sidney Webb's day, the implications were in dispute. New Labour determinists rejected state control in favour of an enabling state, whose task was to widen opportunities, to remove obstacles to personal fulfilment and to rescue the most disadvantaged from the traps of poverty and unemployment.[60] But the enabling state was as interventionist as the controlling state of old days and in some ways more so. The Beveridge revolution had been inspired by a vision of social citizenship and equal rights. It had substituted blanket welfare services, covering the entire society, for the means tests of the past. New Labour stood Beveridge on his head. Though it did not say so in so many words, it sought to replace the welfare state of the past with a 'workfare state' that discriminated in favour of the deserving, and punished the undeserving.[61] The object of the exercise was to help particular, precisely targeted persons to overcome particular handicaps. Benefits were no longer social-citizenship rights, given equally to all. They were instruments of precision social engineering, and as such interventionist (and intrusive) by definition.

Support for workfare of this sort was common ground among Blair's colleagues and followers, but in his second term cracks appeared in the New Labour monolith. Blair himself, his advisers and his most trusted ministers increasingly put their faith in the regenerative powers of 'the great engine of the market'.[62] For them, the individualistic consumerism that the Thatcher and Major governments had fostered, and which Milburn eulogised, was the wave of the future, in all social realms. They believed that the public services should accommodate it, just as the private sector did; and they thought it could do so only through markets or proxy markets. They also believed that they could keep control of the middle ground of politics only by proving, over and over again, that they had the courage to overcome the obstacles to marketisation – above all, those favoured by their own party and the unions. They were often accused of wanting to privatise the public services, but the truth was more complicated. Their aim was to blur the distinction between public and private, and to give profit-seeking private firms a central role in the provision of public goods.

Standing in their way were the public service professionals, and the public service ethic. The result was a long, dragging, confused and sometimes almost subterranean battle, in which Blair and his circle fought to clip the wings of the former and to neutralise the latter. But, in this battle, there were dissenters in New Labour's ranks. They did not all manifest their dissent on the same issues or in the same way, but their presence helps to explain the curiously contorted nature of the argument, and the tone of incredulous exasperation that often marked Blair's contributions to it. In a famous complaint to an audience of venture capitalists, he described the difficulties he had faced in trying to instil entrepreneurship into the public sector:

> People in the public sector are more rooted in the concept that if 'it's always been done this way, it must always be done in this way' than any group I have ever come across. You try getting change in the public sector and public services – I bear the scars on my back after two years in government. Heaven knows what it will be like if it's a bit longer.[63]

It was not just a complaint. It was a battle cry – directed against the Labour Party as well as against the public sector itself.

൧൧

At this point in the story, enter Gordon Brown, the strongest Chancellor of the Exchequer since Cripps and superficially the most successful since Gladstone. Brown was as complex a figure as Blair but, unlike Blair, he was all of a piece.[64] He was rooted in the rocky soil of Scottish Presbyterianism, the Scottish Enlightenment and the Scottish Labour movement. Famously, he was a 'Son of the Manse', a slightly awesome Scottish category with no English equivalent. His father was a devoted minister of the Kirk and a small 'l' liberal who believed in voting for the man, not the party. In striking contrast to Blair, Brown himself was a thoroughgoing intellectual. He and Robin Cook, Foreign Secretary during Blair's first term, were the only members of Blair's Government who could stand comparison with such intellectual heavyweights of Labour's past as Dalton, Cripps, Crosland, Jenkins and Healey. After Kirkcaldy High School Brown had entered Edinburgh University at sixteen. At school he was witty, gregarious and athletic, but too much the son of the Manse for some of his contemporaries. At the start of his Edinburgh career, he had to go into hospital with detached retinas in both eyes, the result of a rugby accident a few months before. One eye was saved, but he lost the sight of the other, and spent his first term lying horizontal in a hospital bed, terrified that he might go completely blind. He emerged from the trauma as gregarious as ever, but it may have contributed to a curious lack of inner confidence, in tension with his driving ambition and consciousness of his own gifts. Like Bevin, he was fiercely loyal to his own circle, but he expected loyalty in return. If he was disappointed, he was unforgiving. That too may have been a product of the fearful isolation of his first university term.

But it did not lessen his ferocious appetite for hard work, reflected in the nickname 'Beaver Brown'. He won a First in history and went on to do research on Scottish Labour politics in the 1920s that earned him a Ph.D. He was also an active student politician. In 1972 he defeated the industrialist Sir Fred Catherwood in the election for University Rector by an overwhelming majority of 2,264 to 1,308. As Rector, he was a source of mounting pain and exasperation to the University establishment. He defeated it in a complicated court case, only to see it avenge its humiliation by denying him a University lectureship for which he was well qualified.

He was intellectually meticulous and frighteningly well read; whereas Denis Healey dropped names, Brown (more endearingly) dropped books. His intellectual influences were philosophically diverse, shocking some of the leftist commentariat.

He admired Adam Smith, whom he saw as a scourge of monopoly and vested interests, and drew on the thinking of the great American social and intellectual historian Gertrude Himmelfarb, whose respect for Edmund Burke and the British enlightenment he shared. In private he was relaxed, funny, stimulating and engaging, with a warm smile that lit up his face. But, as Chancellor, his public persona was dour, buttoned up and faintly menacing. He was, he said, a 'private person'. He patently loathed the glitzy celebrity culture that went to the Blairs' heads; he also lacked the lightness of touch and capacity for ready, if skin-deep empathy that made Tony Blair one of the greatest communicators of the age.

At first sight Brown seemed a classic democratic collectivist, eager to use the central state to make the economy more productive and the society more just. But there was a democratic republican side to him as well. As a young man, his untidiness had been as proverbial as Tawney's, and he retained a certain air of republican austerity, typified by ubiquitous dark suits and scruffy shoes. As Chancellor he even refused to wear evening dress at the Lord Mayor's Banquet (though he would succumb to convention as Prime Minister). As a student he had drawn on the writings of the Italian humanistic Communist, Antonio Gramsci. At the age of 27 he had chaired the Scottish Labour Party's Devolution Committee. In early 1992, he gave a 'sovereignty lecture' for Charter 88, insisting that constitutional change was integral to the nation's future.

By then he had published a sympathetic, but far from hagiographic biography of the beloved idol of the Red Clyde, the congenital rebel James Maxton. It had appeared in 1986 after Brown had been in Parliament for three years. Brown's Maxton was a failure – warm-hearted, loveable and morally inspiring, but with no practical achievements to his credit. But that was not all he was. For Maxton, Brown wrote,

> mankind ... 'was infinitely better than the social system within which it lives'. It was his faith in the capabilities of ordinary people, a faith born of his experiences as a teacher, that led him to advocate a social and economic democracy in making the decisions that mattered. The community, and not simply the capitalist, was capable of running industry and had, in the talents of working men and women, the ability to do so.[65]

That note recurred again and again. One of the driving forces of Brown's politics was a haunting sense of the 'tragic waste of vast reserves of human potential'[66] that echoed Tawney. It was not difficult to imagine him standing up to Cromwell at Putney Church or defying the prosecutors in the Treason Trials of 1794.

More than any other member of the government, Brown had a strategic vision. Like Blair, he saw renascent global capitalism, gross inequalities of reward and increasingly powerful financial markets as givens. No one had to teach him that adverse market sentiment could destroy him, as Dalton, Callaghan, Heath and Healey had been destroyed. Nor did he need anyone to tell him that the markets were bound to be suspicious of incoming Labour governments. He had absorbed these lessons as shadow Chancellor, long before he became the real one. The obvious conclusion, as he saw it, was that he had to convince the markets, by deeds and not by just words, that he was a Labour Chancellor with a difference: that, under him, fiscal rigour and monetary continence would rule, at least as firmly as under the Conservatives. He started before the election with a self-flagellatory pledge that, if Labour won, he would stick to the Conservatives' 'eyewateringly tight' spending plans[67] for his first two years as Chancellor.

A more audacious stroke, signalling the final demise of Britain's post-war economic order, soon followed. Less than a week after entering office, Brown announced that control of interest rates would be handed over to the Bank of England's Monetary Policy Committee. A hunt for a politician-proof system of macroeconomic management had been under way since the horrors of the 1970s. Now a Labour Chancellor, of all people, had found it. The Chancellor would set an inflation target, rigorous enough to satisfy the markets, and the MPC would fix interest rates accordingly. The markets would no longer have any reason to fear that Labour might stray from the path of monetary virtue: it would have to stick to it whether it wanted to or not. Brown had not quite reinvented the gold standard, but he had gone as close to doing so as he could.

In this, Blair and Brown were at one. However, Brown did not share Blair's seemingly limitless faith in market solutions. Nor did he believe, as Blair appeared to do, that redistribution was no longer possible or desirable. Market reassurance was the most important priority of his first term as Chancellor, but it was not the only one. Having offloaded the incubus of short-term economic management on to the Bank of England, he was free to turn the Treasury into a super-ministry of economic and social affairs. Through elaborate 'public service agreements' it laid down a vast range of targets for the spending departments to meet. Above all, it used the power of the purse to redirect the welfare state. A 'windfall tax' on the privatised public utilities financed a 'New Deal' to help the young and the long-term unemployed into work. A minimum wage provided a floor below which incomes from work could not fall. 'Working Families Tax Credits' and 'Child Tax Credits' supported the incomes of poor working families and families with children; by 2004 the cost to the Exchequer was running at nearly £15 billion a year.[68]

In its own terms, the Brownist welfare state was a glittering success. It brought great benefits to the working poor and to poor families with children, and it significantly mitigated inequality at the bottom end of the income range. To be sure, inequality at the upper end was undented. The 'Gini coefficient' – the yardstick for measuring inequality across the board – showed that Britain was a slightly more unequal society at the end of Blair's first two terms than it had been at the beginning.[69] From Brown's point of view, however, that was no failure. He wanted to make life chances more equal, but only within the constraints of the global economic order. He had tried to commit the party to a 50 per cent top rate of income tax before the 1997 election, and had been foiled by Blair, but he had always sought to widen opportunities at the bottom, not to narrow the gap between the middle and the top.

Much the same was true of the Scrooge-like rigour of his fiscal policy. Against Treasury expectations, he honoured his promise to stick to the Conservatives' spending plans for the government's first two years. Gladstonian budgetary rectitude continued to reign even after the two years were over. Public spending grew more slowly during the government's first term than it had done under Major. By 2001 the public finances were massively in surplus and the ratio of public debt to GDP was falling fast. Yet the growth rate of GDP was high, and the inflation rate low. Unemployment was lower than it had been for a generation. The achievement was not Brown's alone. Thanks to the boom stimulated by sterling's departure from the ERM, Clarke had bequeathed him a golden legacy, fortified by global forces. But when the caveats have been entered, Brown's record outstripped those of all previous Labour Chancellors. The one serious flaw was that the spending squeeze was reflected in deteriorating public services and an increasingly decrepit infrastructure, but from Brown's point of view that was a price worth paying for apparently rocklike financial stability, unprecedented in the history of Labour governments.

At the end of the first term, the rock seemed firm enough to justify a spectacular shift of policy. Meanness gave way to munificence. Resources were poured into the public services, notably health and education. The annual increase in health spending was about 50 per cent higher in the government's second term than in the first. Central and local government spending on education rose from £33 billion in the government's first year in office to £46 billion in 2003–4.[70] But Treasury largesse did not bring harmony; it brought the latent differences between Blair and Brown out into the open. Dominating domestic policy-making in the government's second and third terms was a bitter battle between Blairites and Brownites over the shape, boundaries and governing philosophy of the public services. As well as being an intrinsically difficult battle to follow, it was complicated by an increasingly open struggle for position between Blair and Brown; since the differences between the two sides were narrow as well as deep, commentators found it hard to grasp the issues at stake. Brownites and Blairites alike put their faith in the central state and treated local democracy with indifference, verging on contempt. Both were captives of the audit culture that had done so much damage to the professional ethic under Thatcher and Major. But though both camps wanted an obtrusive, domineering state, they wanted to use it in different ways.

Under the banners of 'reform' and 'choice', Blair and his allies fought to subject the public services to the pressures of competition, if need be sacrificing equity in the process. In some (but only some) policy areas, Brown and the Brownites resisted, in the name of equity and citizenship. Brown was no enemy to the market or the private sector. He trumpeted the virtues of free trade and embraced globalisation. He also championed the Private Finance Initiative (PFI), launched by the Major Government to tap private capital for public infrastructure investments, while ensuring that the investments would not count towards the public sector borrowing requirement. But in his usual dogged way he developed a characteristically subtle doctrine to distinguish between areas where markets could serve the public interest, and areas where they could not.[71]

A prime example of the latter was health care; and Brown and his allies frustrated an ingenious attempt by the Blairite Alan Milburn to enable foundation hospitals – in effect, the most successful NHS hospitals – to turn themselves into private companies in all but name. But on higher education, another area where, on Brown's assumptions, equity and citizenship ruled out market solutions, his trumpet gave forth an uncertain sound. He favoured a progressive graduate tax to fund much-needed extra spending on universities, but he shrank from an open battle with Blair; and the regressive Blairite solution of so-called top-up fees prevailed.

It is too soon to evaluate the results of the Government's internal battles over public-service 'reform', yet by late 2007 certain things were clear. Aneurin Bevan's NHS remained in being, albeit with modifications, as it might not have done if Thatcher's crusade had continued into the twenty-first century. In education, the picture was more spotty. Fee-paying schools still flourished, and still provided a disproportionate share of the student body at elite universities. In the state sector, relentless targeting may well have made teaching narrower and more instrumental. Though the content of public policy had changed under Blair, the changes were far less striking than those made under Thatcher. Devolution had shaken Whitehall's grip on the smaller nations of the Kingdom, but in England the structure and operation of the central state had changed surprisingly little since 1997.

SLOW DUSK

Blair the whig imperialist was a more baffling creature than Blair the democratic collectivist. His whiggishness was not very pronounced, but his 'Big Tent' statecraft, with its emphasis on inclusiveness, harmony and apolitical goodwill, was uncannily reminiscent of Baldwin's inclusive whig-gery in the 1920s and 1930s, and even of Churchill's in the 1950s. As we saw in Chapter 3, Baldwin had built a vast, hegemonic, Conservative-dominated coalition that went well beyond the frontiers of the Conservative Party and dominated British politics for more than twenty years. He had managed to depoliticise government, to damp down ideological controversy and class conflict, to marginalise the Labour opposition and to convince the electorate that common sense pointed only in his direction. That was what Blair hoped to do for New Labour. He was not a second Baldwin, but the bland, cross-class ecumenism of the Third Way, and the guileful panache with which he pursued it, were more Baldwinian than its votaries would have been happy to admit.

The imperial strand in whig imperialism was a different matter. It gave

Blair the cause of his life and undid him in the process. He did not see himself as an imperialist and would have denied indignantly that he was anything of the sort, but that only proved that he lived at a time when empire had become a dirty word and imperialist a term of abuse. In truth, his vision of Britain's identity and place in the world harked back to those quintessential whig imperialists Macmillan and Churchill, while his approach to international politics was simultaneously reminiscent of the soft, accommodating imperialism of Gladstone and the harder version encapsulated in Rudyard Kipling's famous plea to the Americans to 'take up the white man's burden'.

Few spotted this lineage at the start of his reign. He was the most 'European' Prime Minister since Heath; not coincidentally, he spoke better French than any since Macmillan. As a young man, he had voted 'yes' in the European referendum of 1975; though he had sailed under an anti-European flag in his early days in Labour politics, he had abandoned it with ease – probably with relief – when the Kinnock–Hattersley leadership changed the party's line. In the 1997 election, he and his party campaigned on a promise to give Britain 'leadership in Europe'; in a characteristically double-edged formula, it insisted that leading meant 'to be involved, to be constructive, to be capable of getting our own way'.[72] But, like Macmillan and Churchill (and unlike Heath), Blair was also a convinced Atlanticist, whose instinct was to fudge any differences between the two sides of the Atlantic if he could, and to back the American side if he could not. There was no need to choose between Europe and the United States, he insisted again and again; Britain was 'the bridge between the US and Europe'.[73] It was a latter-day version of the stance that Bevin and his advisers had adopted in the dying days of the Attlee Government.

Blair's fudge fared as badly as had Macmillan's and Churchill's. By the time he arrived in Downing Street, the Delors plan for European monetary union was well on the way to realisation. This was the most audacious integrationist project since the Single European Act, in some ways since the Rome Treaty. It involved the transfer of one of the most important attributes of national sovereignty from Member States to EU institutions; as such, it was a huge step towards political union. It would not turn the European Union into a federal state, but it would make it much more like a federation than it had been before. The core countries of the EU saw monetary union as their most important policy priority. Thanks to Major's diplomacy at Maastricht, Britain had the right to stand aloof from it if she wished, but if she did she would make nonsense of Blair's hopes of leading Europe.

Blair knew this, and there is no doubt that he was eager to take Britain into the monetary union if he could. The trouble was that the 'if' bristled with personal, political and institutional thorns. One of them was that Labour had committed itself to a referendum before any decision to join could be implemented. More serious was a yawning gulf between Number Ten and the Treasury. For Blair, as for the governments on the other side of the Channel, monetary union was a supremely political question. Privately, Brown may well have agreed, but in their battles with Blair he and the Treasury insisted that it was an economic one; and made sure that Brown controlled it. Fatally, Blair shrank from challenging him.

Euroscepticism was in the official Treasury's blood; and the horror of Black Wednesday had made it even more Eurosceptic than it had been before. Brown was not a Eurosceptic by instinct, but on the single currency he became one by conviction. As he saw it, there was nothing to be gained by joining the euro: his own policies, above all the independent Bank of England and the MPC, were already delivering all the benefits that monetary union could bring. But, on the other side of the ledger, there were risks; and Brown, strongly fortified by Ed Balls, did not intend to run any unnecessary risks. The end result was a long and courtly dance, in which the Treasury and Number Ten circled elegantly around each other, without making contact. The Treasury drew up five conditions, phrased so loosely that they could mean anything or nothing, which would have to be met before euro entry could take place. In 1997, Brown announced that they could not be met during the current Parliament. After the 2001 election, Blair tried to reopen the question, only to be repulsed.

In 2003, after a long-drawn-out technical evaluation, the Treasury came to the predictable conclusion that the tests had not yet been satisfied, and that membership of the eurozone would not be in Britain's economic interests. Brown's Commons statement announcing this conclusion was phrased emolliently. Given 'sustainable convergence' between the British and eurozone economies, the Treasury tests could be met one day, and a 'modern, long-term and deep-seated pro-European consensus' could then be built in Britain. But that day had not yet come.[74]

It was the story of the Schuman Plan, the Messina Conference and the EMS all over again. The British were still in Europe, but not properly of it; Blair's oft-repeated ambition to make Britain 'strong in Europe' had been undone. Brown and the Treasury were the most obvious culprits, but in reality Blair was equally to blame. Once he had conceded Brown's premise that monetary union was an economic issue rather than a political one, he had become a prisoner of the Treasury. It was a failure of leadership, but even more a failure of imagination. Blair wanted Britain to be one of the leading member-states of the EU, and he also wanted her to join the eurozone. Yet even this most European of prime ministers did not understand that, for the core countries of the EU, the euro was not just a logical corollary of the single market or even a step towards political union (though it was both of these things), but an assertion of identity.

In his heart of hearts Blair did not share the identity it asserted. He was for 'Europe', but not for a Europe that transcended national sovereignty and presupposed the primacy of European ties over others. For him, the European Union was a forum in which the British state sought to advance its interests through intelligent co-operation with other states. He did not realise – or perhaps it would be truer to say that he did not wish to realise – that it was both an arena for interstate bargaining and something more than that: a quasi-federation, or perhaps a proto-federation, with a supranational vocation and mystique. That was why he did not fight for euro membership. He might have lost even if he had fought, but by failing to fight he made his defeat certain. At the end of his prime ministership, Britain's identity and role in the world were still swathed in ambivalent ambiguity.

✧

One reason for his reticence was that he had found a grander, all-consuming, global purpose, which gave his life a meaning that it had hitherto lacked, and beside which the technicalities of monetary union must have seemed tedious and almost paltry. His discovery started slowly. In 1998, Britain was alone in joining an American-led bombing campaign against Saddam Hussein's Iraq, designed to punish her for failing to comply with UN resolutions following the Gulf war of 1991 and to degrade her military capability. In 1999, Blair was the leading hawk in the NATO war against Serbian ethnic cleansing in Kosovo. He earned himself an international reputation for his messianic belligerence, and often exasperated his American ally in the process. Pictures of Blair in a refugee camp, surrounded by pitiful, suppliant crowds of homeless and dispossessed Albanians, were flashed across the globe, while the airwaves echoed to his claim that the war in Kosovo was 'a battle between good and evil, between civilisation and barbarity'.[75] How far he deserved the credit for Serbia's eventual climbdown is a moot point, but that hardly mattered. What did matter was that he and his aides believed that British pressure had played a decisive part in persuading the Americans to contemplate using ground troops if air power failed to bring the Serbs to heel and, thereby, in procuring a Serbian withdrawal. What mattered even more was that he thought he had found a unique and noble role for Britain (and, needless to say, for himself) as the outrider of a new kind of moral interventionism, combining pure intentions with robust muscles.

His first sustained attempt to articulate this role came at the height of the war in Kosovo when he gave a lecture in Chicago on the 'doctrine of the international community'.[76] The Chicago lecture saw Blair, the champion of a militant international communitarianism, begin to elbow aside Blair, the emollient prophet of the Third Way. True, the two Blairs overlapped. The lecture contained a long passage about the Third Way; more importantly, the starting point of the whole analysis was the familiar Third Way claim that the world had changed so profoundly that old approaches were obsolete. But the new Blair was much more obtrusive than the old one. He began by evoking the 'unspeakable things' taking place in Kosovo and the 'tear stained faces' of the refugees fleeing from 'ethnic cleansing, systematic rape [and] mass murder'. Then he turned to the wider implications. Many of the security problems facing the international community were the work of 'two dangerous and ruthless men – Saddam Hussein and Slobodan Milosevic'. But the issues at stake were larger than mere individuals:

> We are all internationalists now, whether we like it or not. We cannot refuse to participate in global markets if we want to prosper. We cannot ignore new political ideas in other countries if we want to innovate. We cannot turn our backs on conflicts and the violation of human rights within other countries if we want still to be secure . . . .
>
> The most pressing foreign policy problem we face is to identify the circumstances in which we should get actively involved in other people's conflicts. Non-interference has long been considered an important principle of international order . . . . But the principle of non-interference must be qualified in important respects. Acts of genocide can never be a purely internal matter. When oppression produces massive flows of refugees which unsettle neighbouring countries then they can properly be described as 'threats to international peace and security'. When regimes are based on minority rule they lose legitimacy – look at South Africa.

Having set the scene for a virtually unlimited right of intervention, Blair then retreated. Before intervening, 'we' had to be sure of our case; we had to have exhausted diplomatic options; we had to be prepared for the long term; we had to be sure we could undertake military operations 'sensibly and prudently'; and (incongruously) national interests had to be involved.

However, these caveats counted for little. The real significance of the Chicago lecture lay in its combination of moral absolutism and procedural ambiguity. Blair was calling for a revolution in international relations. In the new, post-Cold-War world, he was saying, morality knew no frontiers and overrode established international law. Foreign intervention in the internal affairs of sovereign states was no longer ruled out. By implication, at least, vicious and ruthless rulers like Saddam Hussein and Slobodan Milosevic had to be punished – not for breaking international law, since they had not broken it, but for evil deeds at home. And there was no doubt that they were guilty. About that, honest people could not honestly differ. Evil was evil, and those who failed to recognise it when they saw it were not honest; they were impeding the course of justice. Yet there was a fatal loose end in Blair's moralism. He had skated over the crucial questions: what *was* the international community? How would its will be revealed, and by whom? Who were the 'we' to whom his caveats applied? He referred in passing to the United Nations, but only to say that its role, workings and decision-making processes should be 'reconsidered'. Yet, if the UN did not represent the international community, who did? As so often with Blair, these unanswered questions would soon come back to haunt him.

Blair was often compared with Gladstone, and it is easy to see why. There are obvious parallels between his attacks on Milosevic and Saddam Hussein, and Gladstone's thunderous philippics against the so-called 'Bulgarian Horrors', perpetrated by the decaying Ottoman empire in 1876. Both men were sustained by a profound Christian faith; both believed that their faith should inform public conduct as well as private life; and both were happier with a vivid contrast between black and white than with the ambiguous greys of ordinary politics. There is no evidence that Blair thought that God had called on him to fulfil a divine purpose as did Gladstone, but he was as convinced of his own rectitude as Gladstone was of his, and as determined to maintain what Gladstone called 'a moral right of interference' when other nations transgressed the norms of civilised behaviour.[77] That was as far as the parallel went, however. While Gladstone was quite prepared to use force to defend Britain's imperial possessions, he did not believe that the unprecedented size and power of the British empire gave it special privileges. The right to intervene was an attribute of what he called the 'Concert of Europe', not of individual states, however powerful; the equality of European nations, 'without distinction of great and small', was a fundamental principle.[78]

Blair started as a latter-day Gladstonian. At first, his 'international community' could plausibly have been seen as a late-twentieth-century version of Gladstone's Concert. But he never believed that all nations had equal rights; and under the pressure of events he gradually abandoned Gladstonian multilateralism in favour of a much bleaker, coarser, Kiplingesque vision of Britain's global duty. Little by little, the 'international community' of the Chicago lecture dwindled into an American-dominated 'coalition of the willing' – in essence, the United States and a group of Western nations, acting as prosecutors and judges in their own cause, with no mandate from any international body, and in defiance of the only organisation with any claim to speak for the international community as a whole. Although Blair lost none of his old moral absolutism, the cause associated with it was tarnished by self-deception, illegality and duplicity, while the language in which he expressed it sounded increasingly delusional.

The first big milestone on the path to delusion came into view in the opening weeks of 2001 when George W. Bush succeeded Clinton as President of the United States. Blair and Clinton had been soulmates, fellow seekers after Third Way truth. Bush could hardly have been less of a soulmate. Not only was he a Republican, but his Administration was sprinkled with so-called 'neo-cons' (neo-conservatives) who exuded an alarming mixture of unilateralism and nationalist swagger. However, Blair was determined to remain true to his bridge philosophy of foreign policy despite the widening gulf between the banks that the bridge was supposed to join. He paid court to Bush with his usual assiduous charm, and with considerable success. The summer of 2001 saw another milestone, when Blair won a second crushing election victory, strengthening his hold on his party and fortifying his belief in his own infallibility.

Against that background came the murderous Al Qaeda atrocities in New York and Washington on 11 September. Though an ugly, knee-jerk anti-Americanism still infected sections of the literary intelligentsia, there was a rush of sympathy for the United States and the American people right across Europe. But no other European leader empathised with the American mood of horror, incredulity and outrage as fully as Blair did. With impressive enthusiasm and considerable political courage, he threw himself into the role of Bush's 'Ambassador at Large', travelling 40,000 miles and meeting fifty-four other leaders over eight weeks to muster support for an attack on the Taliban regime in Afghanistan.[79]

Yet premonitory symptoms of delusion were already beginning to appear. In a speech of blazing eloquence and monumental hubris at the Labour Party conference in October 2001, Blair told his party that the events of 11 September 'marked a turning point in history' and promised the American people, 'We were with you at the first. We will stay with you to the last.' After evoking the evils of the contemporary world, from climate change to poverty in Africa and oppression in Afghanistan, he called on his followers to 'fight for freedom' across the globe:

> The starving, the wretched, the dispossessed, the ignorant, those living in want and squalor from the deserts of North Africa to the slums of Gaza to the mountain ranges of Afghanistan: they too are our cause.
>
> This is a moment to seize. The Kaleidoscope has been shaken. The

pieces are in flux. Soon they will settle again. Before they do, let us reorder
this world around us.[80]

This was Gladstonian interventionism *in excelsis*, but though Gladstone
might well have shared Blair's moral absolutism, it is hard to believe that he
would have shared his fatal exaggeration of the significance of 11 September
or the grandiose ambition that it spawned.

In any event, the Gladstonian Blair had made his last throw. In 2002 the
Kiplingesque Blair took over. A dramatic and ultimately disastrous switch
took place in American policy, with Iraq replacing Al Qaeda as the chief
target for the Administration's rage. Without public qualms (and probably
without serious private ones), Blair followed where Bush led. Unlike Bush,
he did not believe that Saddam's regime was linked to Al Qaeda or that it
had anything to do with the New York atrocities. Almost certainly, he would
have liked to give priority to the 'war against terrorism', and believed that a
war against Iraq would be a diversion from it.

But his differences with Bush were marginal. In at least three crucial
respects, the two men were at one. They shared the apocalyptic belief that
11 September had changed the world. They also shared a Manichaean view
of the tortured complexities of Middle Eastern politics, and cast Saddam as
the leader of the forces of darkness. Finally, they shared a blithe, unhistorical
assumption that the artificial, fissiparous, pre-modern Iraqi state could
somehow be transformed into a stable, Western-style democracy that would
become a model for the rest of the region.

By late 2007 Blair's decision to commit British troops to the Iraq war
had few defenders. Many saw it as calamitously misjudged; some thought
it criminal. But that makes it all the more important to understand why
this consummate politician was prepared to risk his prime ministership
for a cause that most informed independent judges thought hopelessly
misguided even at the time. One explanation, skilfully argued by Peter
Stothard, is that Blair acted as he did because he believed that Bush was
bent on war with Saddam in any event, and that a unilateral American
victory would do more damage to world peace and security than a victory
won with international support.[81] Another is that Blair believed that Britain's
special relationship with the United States had to be maintained at virtually
any cost.

The Campbell diaries show that there is truth in both these explanations.
They are not the whole story, however. They imply that Blair would have
supported the Americans irrespective of what he believed to be the merits
of the case. Perhaps he would have, but the tone of passionate conviction
that ran through his speeches during the run-up to the war, and particularly

through his masterpiece of forensic rhetoric in the Commons debate on the eve of the war, suggests a simpler explanation as well. Given his promise that Britain would stand with the Americans 'to the last', it would have been hard for Blair to detach himself from the hawks' juggernaut that slowly carried American policy-makers towards the Iraq war even if he had disagreed with them. But the overwhelming probability is that he did not disagree. He agreed with them about everything that really mattered. Britain fought alongside the Americans because Blair thought they were right. And because he thought they were right, it became clear that he would support them come what might – ensuring that he had no bargaining power on lesser differences. The dangers of messianic idealism in diplomacy have rarely been more dramatically exposed.

On one point, Blair and Bush did differ. Bush had no qualms about saying that his purpose in going to war was to topple Saddam – regime change, in the jargon of the day. Blair could not afford to say that out loud. War for regime change would break international law and would not win UN approval. If he tried to take Britain into a war fought avowedly for regime change, he would split his party and court defeat in Parliament. From his point of view, it was politically essential to disguise what was in fact a war for regime change as a war to pre-empt an imminent threat. If humanly possible, he also had to win UN support for it. Two consequences followed, each carrying the seeds of Blair's ultimate tragedy. The Americans reluctantly agreed to 'take the UN route' – in other words, to win UN approval for military action against Iraq. At the same time, the British and American governments made public intelligence findings allegedly showing that Saddam possessed, or was in process of developing, weapons of mass destruction (WMD) on a scale to justify military action against him.

The UN route turned out to be a cul-de-sac. After seemingly endless weeks of increasingly bitter exchanges, it became clear that a majority of the Security Council would not endorse war with Iraq. As for the intelligence findings, they convinced few who did not already accept the case for war. As hostilities approached, between 1 and 2 million people took part in the biggest protest march that London had ever seen. Robin Cook, whom Blair had demoted from Foreign Secretary to Leader of the House of Commons, noticed that few marchers were the sort of people who had marched with him against Cruise missiles twenty years earlier. Most were 'ordinary people in their everyday clothes, from every walk of life and every age group in Britain'.[82] On the eve of the war, Cook resigned from the Cabinet. Shortly before, he had received a briefing from John Scarlett, the chairman of the Joint Intelligence Committee, and had concluded that the intelligence suggested that Saddam did not possess weapons of mass destruction in the normal sense of the words.[83]

Despite a powerful resignation statement by Cook, the House of Commons voted for war by a comfortable majority, but 139 Labour MPs rebelled. The Iraq war was opposed by the flower of the establishment including Lords Howe and Hurd; Field Marshal Lord Bramall, former Chief of the Defence Staff; Lord Wright, former head of the Diplomatic Service; Sir Michael Quinlan, former Permanent Secretary at the Defence Department; and Sir Rodric Braithwaite, former chairman of the Joint Intelligence Committee. The consensus among international lawyers was that the war was illegal.[84] Whereas the Suez war (and, for that matter, the Falklands war) had been supported by large popular majorities, the Iraq war was opposed by a majority of the general public before it started, and by a susbtantial minority even after British troops were engaged in battle. Nearly fifty years before, Eden's Suez adventure had split the establishment, but had been supported by the country. Blair united most of the establishment against him, and split the country.

The Kiplingesque Blair marched alongside the tory nationalist Blair. Disguised by his ready smile and his talk of change and progress, Blair held a bleak, even harsh view of the human condition and his own faith. Christianity, he famously declared, was 'judgemental', a 'very tough religion'.[85] (What the Christ of the New Testament would have thought of that, we have no way of knowing.) Though he was child enough of the 1960s and 1970s to tolerate deviant lifestyles, he had a punitive streak in him that became increasingly obtrusive as he aged. Sin was a reality. Punishment was necessary. Judgement was not reserved to the Lord; the morally upright in this world were entitled to pass judgement as well.[86] In language reminiscent of Keith Joseph's a quarter of a century earlier, he cast himself as the defender of the decent verities of ordinary people against the onrush of libertarianism. In a much-publicised speech in 2004 he insisted that it was time to break with the liberal consensus of the 1960s and to build a 'society of respect'.[87] (It did not occur to him that one of the chief enemies of such a society was the celebrity culture of glitz and bling that he succoured.)

All this intersected with a strain of illiberalism that had always lurked in the Labour culture as well as with the authoritarianism implicit in populist politics. Even in Blair's first term, which saw the passage of the Human Rights Act, there was a darker side to the government's legislative programme. The Terrorism Act of 2000 undermined the presumption of innocence, which had always been one of the cornerstones of the rule of law; gave the Home Secretary power to proscribe organisations without having to prove that they had committed an offence; and strengthened police powers to stop and search.

After the 11 September atrocities in New York a stream of illiberal legislation reached the statute book as the politics of fear took hold in Number Ten and the Home Office. The 2001 Anti-Terrorism Crime and Security Act gave the Home Secretary power to imprison foreign suspects indefinitely, without trial. Among other things, later statutes restricted the scope of trial by jury; abolished the double jeopardy rule for serious offences; gave Cabinet ministers powers to make a wide range of restrictive emergency regulations without parliamentary approval; restricted the right to peaceful protest within one kilometre of the Houses of Parliament; made all offences arrestable; and provided for the introduction of identity cards, linked to a national identity register, which would become the world's largest biometric database and on which more than fifty pieces of information about every passport holder would be entered. A gleam of light came in 2004, when the Law Lords struck down the internment provisions of the 2001 Act. In a thunderous opinion, Lord Hoffman declared:

> This is a nation which has been tested in adversity, which has survived physical destruction and catastrophic loss of life. I do not underestimate the ability of fanatical groups of terrorists to kill and destroy, but they do not threaten the life of the nation. Whether we would survive Hitler hung in the balance, but there is no doubt that we shall survive Al Qaeda .... The real threat to the life of the nation, in the sense of a people living in accordance with its traditional laws and political values, comes not from terrorism but from laws such as these. That is the true measure of what terrorism may achieve.[88]

However, a government that had caused British troops to risk their lives in a war of questionable legality was hardly likely to be deterred by Lord Hoffman. Its response to the Law Lords was to substitute control orders – in effect a form of house arrest – for internment. In 2006, it returned to the charge with a Terrorism Act, making the 'glorification' of terrorism an offence and widening the grounds on which allegedly terrorist groups could be proscribed.

The government won a third election victory in 2005, albeit with a reduced majority and only 35 per cent of the popular vote, but the victory could not rescue Blair from the consequences of the Iraq adventure. The Americans and their allies had easily defeated Saddam, but they found no WMD. Much worse, Anglo-American nation-building was a disastrous failure. Iraq slithered relentlessly towards a bloody civil war. Terrorism, complete with all the ghastly appurtenances of the suicide bomber, became commonplace. Bush had proclaimed a great victory soon after hostilities ended, but four years after his proclamation, American and British troops were still bogged down in a counter-insurgency campaign that seemed unwinnable. By September 2007 the Iraqi death toll since the start of the invasion was around 80,000 according to the most cautious estimates; *The Lancet* estimated that increased mortality since the beginning of the war had led to 600,000 'excess' deaths, around half of them due to violence.[89] In all 170 British servicemen and more than 3000 Americans had lost their lives.

Jihadist fundamentalism received an enormous boost, not only in Iraq or even in the Muslim world, but in Europe, and not least in Britain. In July 2005, suicide bombings in the London Underground, carried out by British-born young Muslims, killed more than fifty people. Defying common sense, to say nothing of the findings of the American intelligence community,[90] Blair repeatedly denied that the Iraq war had helped to foster the terrorist upsurge in Europe and the Middle East, yet few believed him.

Meanwhile, charges that the government had distorted intelligence findings to support its case for war had forced Blair to set up two high level public inquiries. Both exonerated him of wrongdoing, but both showed that the relationship between the Joint Intelligence Committee and the Downing Street spin machine had been much too close for comfort and that the former had been over-eager to tell the latter what it wanted to hear.[91] The net effect was to fortify public disquiet about the furtive disingenuousness of the whole Iraq adventure. The failure to find WMD undermined the government's stated justification for the war, while the burgeoning anarchy in post-war Iraq discredited the democratic messianism that had furnished the true rationale for it.

In public, at least, Blair retained the jaunty self-confidence of happier days, but his credibility was fatally damaged. By February 2006 his approval rating stood at 28 per cent, not much higher than Thatcher's at the time of her fall. In September he announced, through clenched teeth, that that month's Labour Party conference would be his last as leader. The magic of happier days still lingered. His speech to the 2006 Labour Party conference, making the announcement, was a masterpiece of political theatre, mingling self-deprecating, ironic wit with occasional pathos and moments of soaring uplift. None of his contemporaries and few of the great Labour orators of the past could have equalled it. But tragedy eclipsed the magic. By any reckoning Blair's first term had been a triumphant success; compared to Wilson's and Callaghan's it had been an astonishing one. The only previous Labour Government that ranked as high in achievement was Attlee's. What went on in the inner recesses of Blair's mind is unknown, and perhaps unknowable: of twentieth-century British prime ministers only Lloyd George was harder to read. But whatever Blair may have thought he was doing, there is not much doubt about what he did or, at least enabled others to do.

His government presided over a reconstruction of the British state, more radical than any since 1707, and in doing so gave a new dimension to British democracy. Outwardly at least, its economic record surpassed those of all its Labour predecessors. Partly because of this, it helped a post-socialist, but at the same time post-Thatcherite, consensus to take root in the national psyche. And then, in a frenzy of self-destructive messianism, Blair dwarfed the achievements of his first term with the ill-fated folly of the Iraq war and all that flowed from it. Like Macbeth's, his first fatal step led him inexorably to his doom. Once he had committed himself to wage war alongside the Americans, he could not disentangle himself. Emotionally and politically, he had become Bush's prisoner. From then on, his best qualities – his stubborn self-belief and indomitable will – conspired with his worst ones to bring him down.

His reasons for taking the first step will offer rich pickings to future historians and we cannot know how their debates will go, but in the final months of 2007 one thing seemed clear. Blair's fatal flaw was not ambition, or deviousness, or disloyalty, although he exemplified all of those things. Still less was it lack of principle; over Iraq he was much too principled for his own and his country's good. The fatal flaw was 'presentism' – his lack of historical sense, his restless search for novelty, his fascination with new ideas simply because they were new, his disdain for the wisdom of experts who had learned the lessons of the past better than he had, and his propensity to overreact to every passing breeze. These were, of course, the hallmarks of the 'New Labour' project that had been his passport to power. By a terrible irony, they were also the hallmarks of the Iraq misadventure and the catastrophic fall in his reputation that followed.

12

EPILOGUE

I ... pondered how men fight and lose the battle, and the thing that they fought for comes about in spite of their defeat, and when it comes turns out not to be what they meant, and other men have to fight for what they meant under another name.

William Morris, *A Dream of John Ball*, 1886

Tony Blair finally left office on 27 June 2007, having resigned as Labour leader three days before. His Chancellor, Gordon Brown, succeeded him in both posts. The exultant euphoria that had accompanied Blair's assumption of office ten years earlier was absent, but even so Brown's first three months as Prime Minister were quietly triumphant. With understated dignity he weathered three unexpected crises – a terrorist attack on Glasgow airport, unprecedented flooding in the West Country and an outbreak of foot-and-mouth disease in Surrey – out of which Blair would have made a drama. At his inevitable tryst with George W. Bush, he was ostentatiously formal and downbeat, manifestly disconcerting his host.

Within days of his arrival at Number Ten, Brown made a statement to the Commons, holding out the prospect of a 'new constitutional settlement' that would curb the government's prerogative powers, enhance parliamentary scrutiny of the executive and explicitly incorporate the 'values, founded on liberty' that defined British citizenship.[1] Rather gingerly, a green paper on the 'Governance of Britain' hinted at a possible Bill of Rights and Duties, and even at a written constitution.[2] There was talk of a nationwide consultation, culminating in a 'citizens' summit' to agree a statement of British values and the principles on which the proposed Bill of Rights and Duties would be based.

The message was clear: Brown could not help being Blair's heir, but he had no intention of becoming a Blair Mark II. The politics of the message were clear too. Brown's aim was to construct a new version of the electoral coalition that had given Labour its crushing parliamentary majorities in 1997 and 2001. But whereas Blair had patently despised the liberal constituency with a small 'L' that had turned against Labour in revulsion from his Iraq adventure and his recourse to the politics of fear, Brown's purpose was to win it back. The exercise had a deeper meaning as well. Peeping out from behind Brown, the democratic collectivist and Treasury micro-manager, was Brown, the democratic republican and sometime Charter 88 lecturer. The great question was how the inevitable tension between the two would play out in practice.

Both Browns had a bleak inheritance. The dynamics of party competition had changed dramatically in Blair's last eighteen months. After the 2005 election, Michael Howard had resigned as Conservative leader. His successor was the charming, eloquent, but untried Etonian, David Cameron.[3] Just thirty-nine, Cameron owed his election to a captivating barnstorming speech at the Conservative Party conference as well as to his ready smile, youthful appearance and steely will. In many ways, he was a throwback to the upper-class whig imperialists of old days. He was the first Burkean gentleman to lead his party since Home, and his statecraft was more reminiscent of Macmillan's than of Thatcher's.

But Cameron was even more reminiscent of the young Tony Blair than of his great whig imperialist predecessors. He had the same winsome grace, the same ability to float affably over the rifts of interest and belief that divided the country he hoped to lead, and the same acute nose for public moods. Like Blair ten years before he seemed made for that mythical political El Dorado, 'Middle England', where swing voters lived and marginal constituencies were located. And, unlike Blair, he was deeply rooted socially and existentially, even if not ideologically.

His roots could hardly have been less representative of twenty-first-century Britain. He was not a true aristocrat, like Home or Churchill, or even a fake one, like Macmillan. His father was a stockbroker; the family were 'county' – rich, God-fearing, public-spirited, utterly conventional and safely unintellectual. Cameron himself delighted in the country pursuits that the great Lord Salisbury had detested: he shot and hunted with enthusiasm, although he does not seem to have fished. He was sent to an exclusive prep school, whose intake included Princes Andrew and Edward as well as John Paul Getty's grandson. Apart from inculcating good manners and respect for authority, its main purpose was to send as many boys as possible to Eton – something that presented no problems in Cameron's case. After Eton, Cameron went up to Oxford, as an Exhibitioner at Brasenose College, a rather modest college for an Etonian. He was elected to the Bullingdon Club, an ostentatiously archaic fraternity of the louche and loutish rich, who disported themselves in quaint uniforms, looked down on their state-school contemporaries and got revoltingly drunk. But in spite of his

Bullingdon escapades, the examiners awarded Cameron a First in Philosophy, Politics and Economics.

From then on his ascent was as smooth as Blair's had been. After a period in the Conservative Research Department, followed by shorter periods as a political adviser – first to Norman Lamont at the Treasury and then to Kenneth Clarke at the Home Office – Cameron became public relations adviser to the rough, tough, ostentatiously Thatcherite boss of Carlton Communications, Michael Green. In 2001, aged thirty-four, he was elected to Parliament as MP for the safe Conservative seat of Witney; he had had virtually no working experience of the world beyond the Westminster and media villages. Four and a half years later, he was party leader. In the interim, the birth of a severely handicapped son had pierced the cocoon of privilege in which he had been brought up, giving him, as a friend put it, a new 'empathy with people whose lives have not gone as they would have liked'.[4]

Empathy was one of the chief hallmarks of his style as leader. In the language of the PR man that he had once been, he sought to 'rebrand' his party as Blair had once 'rebranded' Labour. Like Baldwin, Churchill and Macmillan before him, he developed a rhetoric of inclusion, designed to prove that Conservatives were no longer fixated on the divisive tory nationalist themes of the Thatcher era. (On Europe and immigration the old themes survived, with all their old harshness.) While carefully avoiding policy detail and doctrinal precision, he spoke on a multitude of carefully chosen, unthreatening topics, ranging from climate change to poverty and from Britain's 'broken society' to 'the pain and devastation' caused by slavery.[5] His message was as clear as Brown's was to be: the Conservatives were no longer the nasty party; in Cameron's big tent there was room for liberals with a small 'L' as well as for Conservatives with a big 'C'. He and his colleagues were now swimming in the same crowded post-Thatcherite and post-socialist pool as Labour and the Liberal Democrats.

They swam to great effect – in part, no doubt, because of post-Iraq disillusion with Blair. By the spring of 2007, the Conservatives had a comfortable poll lead over Labour. Labour had a 'Brown bounce' in the polls after Blair's departure, but it came to a juddering halt after a rhetorical tour de force by Cameron at the Conservative Party conference and a promise by the shadow Chancellor to raise the threshold for inheritance tax. When the new parliamentary session opened in November 2007, the Conservatives were well ahead in the polls. Labour still had everything to play for, but as the economic skies darkened the Conservatives were in a stronger electoral position than at any time since the disaster of Black Wednesday.

Meanwhile the unexploded bombs left by the Blair Government's devolution settlement were beginning to tick, faintly but ominously. In May 2007, Labour lost ground badly in the elections to the Scottish Parliament and Welsh Assembly. In Wales, the end result was a coalition between Labour and Plaid Cymru (the Welsh Nationalists); in Scotland, Alex Salmond, the canny, forceful and rhetorically adroit leader of the SNP, formed a minority administration. English complaints about the formula that determined the size of Scotland's block grant from the United Kingdom exchequer, and which enabled the Scottish administration to spend more public money per head than the Westminster Government spent in England, became more scratchy and vociferous.

The 'English Question', which Enoch Powell had invested with exquisitely romantic glamour in his St George's Day speech in 1960, and from which Blair and his colleagues had resolutely averted their eyes, hovered menacingly on the edge of the political agenda. Devolution to Scotland and Wales had procured a remarkable growth of national feeling in England. In 1992 only 31 per cent of people living in England had described themselves as 'English' rather 'British'. In 2007 the authoritative British Social Attitudes survey reported that the proportion had risen to 40 per cent.[6] (In 2003 the proportion of Scots who thought of themselves as Scottish rather than British was 65 per cent, but the figure had hardly changed since 1992.)[7] By 2007 some polls showed 60 per cent support for an English Parliament, compared with only 17 per cent between 1999 and 2003.[8] Also in 2007, the Conservatives announced that they were considering a plan, drawn up by the former Scottish Secretary, Sir Malcolm Rifkind, to set up a Commons Grand Committee, from which Scottish MPs would be excluded, to deal with English bills. There was not much doubt that the ground was shifting beneath the halfway house of asymmetric devolution. For the first time since the Act of Union, England's constitutional future was coming into contention, and with it the fundamental assumptions underpinning the multinational British state.

✿

The emergence of the 'English Question' was new; the steady decline in public confidence in the British version of democracy was only too familiar. This is dangerous territory, full of traps for the unwary. Evidence of declining confidence comes largely from opinion surveys, and their apparent precision ought to have a health warning attached to it The attitudes that they seek to probe are complex and often muddled, and cannot easily be reduced to a simple 'yes' or 'no', or even to a 'don't know'. They tell us how respondents answered inevitably simplistic questions; they cannot tell us how deeply those questioned reflected on what they said or how faithful their answers were to their true feelings.

Besides, democracy means different things to different people, as earlier chapters have sought to show. In the whig imperialist tradition it is, above all, about timely responsiveness on the part of a judicious elite. The democratic collectivist tradition focuses on the mandate given to the justice-seeking rulers of the democratic state through popular election. The democratic republican tradition emphasises self-government by free and active citizens, through open discussion and debate. For tory nationalists, democracy is a potential source of disorder or disintegration, which only a strong, authoritative state can keep at bay. Scraps of all these notions float about in contemporary debates on British democracy like leaves in a high wind, confusing the protagonists rather than enlightening them.

Yet, when all possible qualifications have been made, there was no doubt that, long before Brown crossed the threshold of Number Ten, public disaffection from the British political system had reached alarming proportions. In the early 1970s, as we saw in Chapter 8, research for the Kilbrandon Commission showed that only 5 per cent of those surveyed thought the existing system of government worked 'extremely well' while 49 per cent thought it either needed 'a great deal of improvement' or 'could be improved quite a lot'. By 2004, the proportion who thought it needed improvement stood at 63 per cent. A mere 3 per cent thought the system worked extremely well.[9] By the end of the twentieth century few trusted government, politicians or the civil service to tell the truth, and the early twenty-first century saw a further fall in the trust level.

In 1999, a MORI poll showed that only a fraction more than 20 per cent trusted a government of any party to put the national interest above its party interest.[10] By 2002 just around a third of those polled trusted the government to tell the truth about climate change, radioactive waste and GM food.[11] In 2005, a MORI report found that public confidence in government information had fallen too, and quoted a focus-group participant who complained, 'Everything – there's spin on it. Even when you don't think it has got spin, it has got spin on it.'[12] Party membership slumped. In 1964 the Conservative Party had more than 2 million members and the Labour Party 830,000. By 2006 the Conservatives had fewer than 300,000 and Labour fewer than 200,000.

'All the party machines,' wrote John Major in 2003, 'are moribund, near-bankrupt, unrepresentative and ill-equipped to enthuse the electorate.'[13] Turnout in general elections confirmed his view. Fewer people voted in the 1997 election than in any previous election since the Second World War. The turnout in 2001 was the lowest since 1918. There was a tiny increase in

2005, but only to 61 per cent. Labour won a comfortable majority in the House of Commons with just 35 per cent of the popular vote and 22 per cent of those eligible to vote. Non-voters far outnumbered Labour ones. The Commons Select Committee on public administration spoke for many when it diagnosed a 'civic crisis'.[14]

Many blamed the media, and there was a strong case for doing so. The cultural revolution that had toppled the old elites of inherited status, public service and professional eminence had raised up a new media elite, more arrogant and self-serving, less civilised and far more aggressive than the ones it had replaced. Newspaper proprietors had swaggered about the political stage for more than a century, intimidating politicians and pushing their own, often highly eccentric causes. But in times past, the old elites were still in place, and with all their bombast the press lords were only one term in a complex equation of power. Things were different at the start of the twenty-first century. A new race of rootless, global, multimedia moguls, with no national loyalties, had appeared on the scene. Notoriously, the most powerful and aggressive of them was Rupert Murdoch, the 'eagle swooping down from the sky',[15] whose media empire extended from Australia to Britain and thence to the United States and the Far East. But whereas Murdoch was the only eagle, the sky was full of vultures.

Like Beaverbrook and Northcliffe, Murdoch and lesser moguls – such as the latest Lord Rothermere and (until his disgrace) Conrad Black – sought power without responsibility. They faced fewer obstacles than their predecessors had done. They had no other elites to contend with and, in the fluid cultures of the late-twentieth and early-twenty-first centuries, there was an insatiable appetite for easily digested information, titillation and opinion, the commodities in which they dealt. Their impact on the democratic process was even more insidious than appeared at first sight. It had little to do with party. Though Black's and Rothermere's titles were fiercely Conservative, Murdoch, the leader of the pack, switched from the Conservatives to New Labour – not because he had undergone a damascene conversion to the Third Way, but because he saw in Blair another populist, who could exercise the 'strong' leadership that Murdoch and his courtiers prized above all else. And once Murdoch had endorsed him, Blair became, at least to some degree, Murdoch's prisoner.

No other media predator equalled Murdoch's aggression or his power, but the rest of the new global media elite shared his bleak vision of the world and approach to leadership. Society, as they viewed it, was a Hobbesian jungle, where no one was safe, few were faithful and no one – least of all democratically elected political leaders – could be trusted. That message was conveyed ad nauseam, in a thousand ways and through a multitude of channels. It was the water in which leaders and voters had to swim.

Flanking the media proprietors – and often employed by them – was the commentariat, a loose grouping of columnists, radio and television presenters and interviewers. Their currency was overstatement, often bordering on the hysterical, but they tended to be smoother and more self-righteous than the proprietors. They saw themselves as crusaders for truth and justice, penetrating the obfuscations of the powerful and exposing the buried truths beneath in the name of transparency and accountability. Sometimes, this self-image was justified. At times, the powerful *did* obfuscate; truths *were* sometimes buried. The Arms to Iraq scandal under the Thatcher and Major governments and the Blair Government's tergiversations in the run-up to the 2003 Iraq war were proof of that. But obfuscation and burial were not as common as the commentariat believed – or at least pretended to believe. Irrespective of the merits of the case, its motto was the alleged advice of the famous *Sunday Times* editor Harold Evans: 'always ask yourself, when you interview a politician – why is this bastard lying to me?'[16]

Onora O'Neil, the political philosopher, painted a compelling picture of the results:

> Outstanding reporting and writing mingle with editing and reporting that smears, jeers and sneers, names, shames and blames ... In this curious world, commitments to trust-worthy reporting are erratic: there is no shame in writing on matters beyond a reporter's competence, in coining misleading headlines, in omitting matters of public interest or importance, or in recirculating others' speculations as 'news'. Above all, there is no requirement to make evidence accessible to the reader.
>
> For all of us who have to place trust with care in a complex world, reporting that we cannot assess is a disaster ... If the media mislead, or if readers cannot assess their reporting, the wells of public discourse are poisoned.[17]

Even more damaging than media smearing, jeering and sneering was the atmosphere of perpetual crisis born of media hubris, hype and hysteria. At one moment, a delinquent Home Office was flooding the streets with murderers and sex offenders. At the next, dishonest asylum seekers were taking the bread out of the mouths of honest taxpayers. At the one after that, food was unfit to eat or vaccines unsafe to use. How much notice the public took is impossible to tell. Probably, not much. When real crises struck, as in the London Underground bombings of July 2005, most people reacted with the stoicism and sang-froid that have traditionally been among the most highly prized British virtues.

But whatever may have been true of the public, politicians took a great deal of notice. Each new media-manufactured crisis saw ministers and shadow ministers scuttling from television studio to television studio to offer reassurance or to ratchet up the crisis with more accusations. Accountability is fundamental to democracy of any sort, but genuine accountability is impossible unless those giving the account are prepared to admit mistakes and those to whom it is given are willing to listen without rushing to judgement. It is hard to do either of these things in the middle of a media typhoon.

⌘

Yet it was self-indulgent to lay all the ills of the body politic at the media's door. Some of those who railed against them were reminiscent of Caliban, raging at the sight of his own face in the glass. No law compelled anyone to buy Murdoch's papers, to watch television interviewers harrying public figures or to read news stories that turned every passing mishap into a crisis. The media – even the public service broadcasters of the BBC – operate in a market, or rather in a series of markets, not in a vacuum. They are tied to the public they address by a host of shared tastes, assumptions and values. They help to shape the culture, of course, but they also reflect it. To see them as the sole authors of the malaise that now afflicts British democracy is a classic case of shooting the messenger instead of listening to the message. To get to the root of the trouble we must dig deeper.

A good way to begin is to look again at the story I have tried to tell in this book. It is a story of courage, perseverance, wisdom, selfishness, folly and self-deception, all muddled up. But through all the confusion, one central point stands out. Three of the four traditions whose fates I have tried to trace – whig imperialism, democratic collectivism and tory nationalism – have been tested almost to destruction. The fourth – democratic republicanism – has had considerable influence on social movements, but little on governments. The whig imperialist ascendancy of 1922 to 1945 lasted as long as it did because evolutionary whiggish accommodation was astonishingly successful. The same was true, on a smaller scale, of the whig imperialist regime of the 1950s. Yet the last stand of the whig imperialist tradition, during Heath's ill-fated Government in the early 1970s, was a disastrous failure, despite Heath's manifest patriotism and courage.

Much the same is true of the democratic collectivist tradition. Even under the robust and resilient Attlee regime, centralist *étatisme* bequeathed a more ambiguous legacy than the mythology of later Labour generations implies.

Repeated failures dogged the Wilson Government's version of the same approach in the 1960s, while the Wilson–Callaghan regime of the 1970s ended in near-catastrophe. Although the failures of the Blairite version are less obvious, his government's endless torrent of new initiatives, most of them born of disillusionment with old ones, suggest that its attempts to remodel society by fiat from the centre fared as badly as his predecessors'.

Despite the differences between them, the whig imperialist and democratic collectivist traditions had one crucial feature in common. Both were paternalist. Burkean gentlemen and their latter-day successors were paternalists by definition. They were urbane, tolerant, responsive paternalists, but they decided when to respond and how. They led and the people followed. If the people stopped following, as in 1945, they changed course, but they took it for granted that it was up to them to decide what the new course should be. Democratic collectivist paternalism was less obvious, but equally pervasive. The people spoke on election day, but not afterwards. Once the state was in good, democratic-collectivist hands, the assumption ran, it was entitled to expect popular support in its mighty task of social transformation.

These twin paternalisms steered Britain, on the whole successfully, through the class conflicts of the 1920s, the depression of the 1930s, the most terrible war in British history, the reconstruction of the 1940s and the loss of empire in the 1950s and 1960s. No other large country in Europe could boast a comparable record. But, by the late 1960s, or at the latest by the early 1970s, paternalism was no longer enough. Women, young people, gays, Greens, trade unionists, nationalists, consumers, backbenchers, rate-payers and a myriad other groups were on the march, demanding to be heard. The tory nationalist upsurge that began in the 1970s was a response to the cacophonous crisis of authority that resulted. Yet as Thatcher's downfall showed, tory nationalism is crisis-prone as well. In modern conditions, it depends for its success on an inherently unstable combination of charisma and populism that is likely to implode sooner or later. What is surprising about Thatcher's prime-ministership is not that it ended so soon, but that it lasted so long. Blair's fate drove that moral home.

This inhospitable landscape was the background to Brown's sometimes bold and sometimes hesitant talk of restoring trust in politics, of the values informing British citizenship and of a new constitutional settlement including a Bill of Rights and Duties. He had an obvious party-political purpose. He wanted to recapture the high ground of politics for Labour and prick what he saw as the Cameron bubble. He also wanted to save the Union in its existing, Labour-friendly form. But these were not his only purposes. As we saw in the last chapter, there were traces of democratic republicanism in his better angels. More than any previous Labour leader, he had come to feel that democratic collectivist *étatisme* had become self-stultifying; that its blindness to the ultimate political questions of identity and allegiance had become a threat to the survival of the union state; and that the times called for a 'thicker' and richer conception of democracy than that of the democratic collectivist leaders of the past.

But, as the winter of 2007 approached, he seemed unsure how to make these feelings bite or how to weave them into a coherent narrative. The logic implicit in his constitutional initiatives was democratic republican. In an important speech on the British tradition of liberty, he evoked the memory of Milton, Mill, Tawney and Orwell, stressing that liberty as they envisaged it was more than laissez-faire or hyper-individualism, and linking 'the reinforcement of civic responsibility' to the 'empowerment of the individual'.[18] Yet he said little about the dream at the heart of the democratic republican story – the dream of free citizens, governing themselves through dialogue and debate and empowering themselves in doing so. There was no doubt about his commitment to a democracy of consultation and accountability. Only time would show if he also sought a democracy of participation.

Still, he had had the courage, unprecedented in modern times, to launch a debate whose future course he could neither predict nor control. It was hard to see how a national conversation about British values could fail to touch on the English Question, in all its rich complexity, and thereby on the future of the Union – topics that Brown patently did not wish to raise. (It was equally hard to see how such a conversation could ignore the dark side of the empire, the spread of Islamophobia in the wake of the 11 September atrocities in New York and the growing illiberalism associated with the politics of fear and shared by Brown himself.) Equally, a debate over a possible Bill of Rights and Duties that ignored the European Union's Charter of Fundamental Rights, from which the British Government had negotiated an opt-out, would be a travesty. Consultation is a double-edged weapon. It usually starts from the top, with a troubled elite hoping to halt a drain of legitimacy, but, once it starts, the consulted may take control away from those who do the consulting.

It was impossible to tell if this would happen in twenty-first-century Britain, but two things seemed clear. The first is that in the British state, in which whig imperialists, tory nationalists and democratic collectivists had all put their faith, was in flux – with consequences no one could foresee. The second is that there were green shoots in the inhospitable landscape that I described a moment ago. The 'civic crisis' that the public administration committee discerned did not embrace Britain's civil society – the network of intermediate bodies that stand between the individual and the state. According to the most comprehensive recent study of citizenship in modern Britain, most people had a strong sense of civic duty, even if their deeds did not always live up to their words.[19] Though large majorities distrusted politicians, governments and Parliament, the level of interpersonal trust was comparatively high. Around fifty per cent distrusted politicians, government and the House of Commons, but only 10 per cent distrusted other people.[20]

Despite marketisation, consumerism, overwork, unstable relationships, family breakdown, job insecurity, cultural diversity, gross inequality and other pressures making for an atomised society, there was no significant decline in 'social capital' – in the membership of social networks outside the family, such as Neighbourhood Watch, tenants' or residents' associations, professional groups, Parent–Teacher Associations, sports groups, churches, amenity groups and the like. Only a minority were joiners, but it was a large minority. Of that minority, many participated actively in the groups concerned. (A hard core of 12 per cent spent an average of more than five hours a week on group activity outside the home.)[21] Not surprisingly, the number of people who said they were willing to attend a political meeting fell by around half between 1979 and 2000. In contrast, the proportion who said they would, if necessary, sign or collect a petition rose from 44 per cent to 75 per cent, and the proportion prepared to go on a demonstration from 20 per cent to 33 per cent.[22] Most commentators seem to think that falling party membership and low turn-out in elections are symptoms of sickness, but they can just as well be seen as evidence of health. They may show that ordinary citizens realise that managed populism is a travesty of democracy in any of its varied senses.

As petrol blockades, the Countryside Alliance and, most of all, the huge anti-war demonstration in February 2003 all showed, the ancient British tradition of peaceful protest was alive and well. Devolution in the non-English nations of the Union had not only transformed the territorial constitution; it had created new sites for civic engagement and fostered new, pluralistic forms of democracy, closer to the rest of Europe than to the Westminster Model. The welcoming openness of the Parliament building in Edinburgh and the Senedd building in Cardiff were not just a refreshing contrast to the Victorian pomp of the Palace of Westminster; they symbolised a different conception of the relationship between politicians and people. The extraordinary growth of the internet, from 16 million users worldwide in December 1995 to 1.2 billion in June 2007, told a similar story.[23] Virtual communities of lone individuals, glued to their computer screens, are poor substitutes for groups of real people talking to each other, but on balance the internet was a force for civic engagement. It was also a vehicle for new forms of participation and mobilisation, while 'blogging' countervailed media power and managed populism with a new kind of bottom-up political communication.

Altogether, the picture that emerged from the huge pile of evidence collected by polling organisations and academic social scientists was not one of an inert lump, sunk in apathy or indifference and devoid of civic sense. At the start of the twenty-first century, the British were proud of their country, even if not of their political institutions. They had plenty of public spirit. Large numbers of them were involved in a wide range of voluntary organisations and informal social networks. They had outgrown political paternalism, and they felt cheated by their political system, but they were not isolated from their society or from each other.

This did not mean that they were itching to transform the political order. The servility and snobbery that Tawney had seen as the most contemptible vices of his fellow countrymen were much less obvious than they had been in his day, but the culture of Channel 4's *Big Brother* and Murdoch's *Sun* was not exactly Tawneian. Few paid much attention to what Paine had witheringly called the 'baby cloaths of Count and Duke', but the foppishness that he excoriated had a modern equivalent in lubricious gossip about pop stars and famous footballers. Higher up the social pyramid, the dameships, commanderships and orders of a non-existent empire were still scattered like confetti over the eminent and safe. At the apex of the State, grovelling was more common than in the past. But, with all its gaps and uncertainties, the evidence suggested that Tawney's stolid, pragmatic, unimaginative and somewhat anti-intellectual Henry Dubb was stirring in his sleep – to what effect remained to be seen. The four traditions that had structured British political debate for so long still danced their familiar quadrille. But the beat was changing.

NOTES

1 PROLOGUE

1 Anthony King, 'The Night Itself', in Anthony King et al., *New Labour Triumphs: Britain at the Polls* (Chatham House Publishers, Chatham, New Jersey, 1998), p. 5.
2 Ibid., p. 1.
3 Quoted in Stephen Drive and Luke Martell, *New Labour: Politics After Thatcherism* (Polity Press, Cambridge, 1998), p. 41.
4 Karl Marx, *The Eighteenth Brumaire of Louis Bonaparte,* in Karl Marx and Frederick Engels, *Selected Works in Two Volumes,* vol. 1 (Foreign Languages Publishing Hosue, Moscow, 1951).

2 SACRED FLAME

1 Commons, *Hansard,* 22 May 1917, cols 2134–5.
2 Christopher Hill, *The World Turned Upside Down: Radical Ideas during the English Revolution* (Temple Smith, London, 1972). See also H.N. Brailsford, *The Levellers and the English Revolution* (The Cresset Press, London, 1961); J.G.A. Pocock, *The Machiavellian Moment: Florentine Political Thought and the Atlantic Republican Tradition* (Princeton University Press, Princeton, 1975); Andrew Sharp (ed.), *The English Levellers* (Cambridge University Press, Cambridge, 1998); A.S.P. Woodhouse (ed.), *Puritanism and Liberty: Being the Army Debates (1647–9) from the Clarke Manuscripts with Supplementary Documents* (University of Chicago Press, second impression, London, 1965); Keith Thomas, 'The Levellers and the Franchise', in Gerald Aylmer (ed.), *The Interregnum* (Macmillan, London, 1972), pp. 57–78; and David Wootton, 'The Levellers', in John Dunn (ed.), *Democracy: The Unfinished Journey 508 BC – AD 1993* (Oxford University Press, Oxford, 1993), pp. 71–89.
3 John Milton, *Areopagitica,* in *Milton's Prose Writings* (Everyman's Library, London and New York, 1958), p. 177.
4 Christopher Hill, *Antichrist in Seventeenth-Century England* (Verso, London and New York, 1990), pp. 104–13.
5 Brailsford, *Levellers and the English Revolution,* p. 10.
6 How close is a matter of debate among historians. My interpretation is based on Keith Thomas, 'The Levellers and the Franchise', in Gerald Aylmer (ed.), *The Interregnum,* pp. 57–78.
7 Woodhouse, *Puritanism and Liberty,* p. 83.
8 Ibid., pp. 65–6.
9 Sharp, *Levellers,* pp. 168–78.
10 Brailsford, *Levellers and the English Revolution,* p. 484.
11 *The New Whole Duty of Man Containing the Faith and Doctrine of A Christian Necessary*

for all Families (London, [?1747]), pp. 132–3.

12   Pocock, *The Machiavellian Moment*, p. 373.

13   These quotations are from the Putney debates, quoted in Sharp, *English Levellers*, pp. 102–30, and Woodhouse, *Puritanism and Liberty*, pp. 1–124.

14   Marchamont Nedham, quoted in Wootton, 'The Levellers', p. 73.

15   Sharp, *English Levellers*, p. vii.

16   Pocock, *The Machiavellian Moment*, p. 372.

17   John Milton, 'The Ready and Easy Way to Establish a Free Commonwealth', in Stephen Orgell and Jonathan Goldberg (eds), *John Milton: A Critical Edition of the Major Works* (Oxford University Press, Oxford and New York, 1991), p. 336.

18   Woodhouse, *Puritanism and Liberty*, p. 61.

19   Ibid., pp. 7–8.

20   This account is based on Caroline Robbins, *The Eighteenth-Century Commonwealthman: Studies in the Transmission, Development and Circumstance of English Liberal Thought from the Restoration of Charles II until the War with the Thirteen Colonies* (Harvard University Press, Cambridge, Mass, 1959); Linda Colley, *Britons: Forging the Nation 1707–1837* (Yale University Press, London, 1992); J.P. Cain and A.G. Hopkins, *British Imperialism, 1688–2000* (Pearson Education, second edition, London, 2001); John Stevenson, *Popular Disturbances in England, 1700–1832* (Longman, London, 1992); and Pocock, *The Machiavellian Moment*.

21   For the British reacton to the French Revolution, see Albert Goodwin, *The Friends of Liberty: The English Democratic Movement in the Age of the French Revolution* (Hutchinson, London, 1979), Chapters 4 and 5; and E.P. Thompson, *The Making of the English Working Class* (Penguin Books, reprinted London, 1991).

22   Quoted in Thompson, *Making*, pp. 173–4.

23   Frank O'Gorman, 'The Paine Burnings of 192–1793', *Past and Present*, November 2006, 111–55.

24   Thompson, *Making*, p. 194.

25   Thomas Paine, *Agrarian Justice*, in Mark Philp (ed.), Thomas Paine, *Rights of Man, Common Sense and Other Political Writings* (Oxford University Press, Oxford, 1995), p. 430.

26   Paine, *Rights*, p. 96. Here Paine was quoting the Marquis de Lafayette.

27   Paine, *Rights*, p. 16.

28   Paine *Rights*, p. 224. My remaining quotations from Paine come from Philp's edition of Paine's *Rights of Man*, except where otherwise stated.

29   Paine, *Rights*, p. 271.

30   T.B. Macaulay, *Edinburgh Review*, 1829, reprinted in Jack Lively and John Rees (eds), *Utilitarian Logic and Politics* (Clarendon Press, Oxford, 1978), pp. 120–1.

31   Quoted in Gareth Stedman Jones, 'Rethinking Chartism', in Stedman Jones, *Languages of Class* (Cambridge University Press, Cambridge, 1983), p. 109. My account of Chartism is based largely on this; on Dorothy Thompson, *The Chartists* (Temple Smith, London, 1984); on Mark Hovell, *The Chartist Movement* (Manchester University Press, Manchester, 1918, reprinted 1959); and on James Epstein, *The Lion of Freedom: Feargus O'Connor and the Chartist Movement, 1832–1842* (Croom Helm, London and Canberra, 1982).

32   Dorothy Thompson, *Chartists*, p. 32.

33   *Northern Star*, 4 August 1838, quoted in Stedman Jones, *Languages of Class*, p. 104.

34   Friedrich Engels, *The Condition of the Working Class in England*, in *Marx and Engels on Britain* (Foreign Languages Publishing House, Moscow, 1953), pp. 332–3.

35   Dorothy Thompson, *Chartists*, p. 115.

36 John Morley, *The Life of William Ewart Gladstone* (Macmillan, London, vol. 1, 1905), pp. 758 and 760.

37 F.B. Smith, *The Making of the Second Reform Bill* (Cambridge University Press, Cambridge, 1966), p. 1. My account of the 1867 Reform Act is based on this; on Maurice Cowling, *1867 Disraeli, Gladstone and Revolution: The Passing of the Second Reform Bill* (Cambridge University Press, Cambridge, 1967); and Charles Seymour, *Electoral Reform in England and Wales: The Development and Operation of the Parliamentary Franchise, 1832–1885* (Yale University Press, New Haven, 1915).

38 Quoted in Cowling, *1867*, p. 34.

39 Quoted in Smith, *Second Reform Bill*, pp. 232–3.

40 Eugenio F. Biagini, *Liberty, Retrenchment and Reform: Popular Liberalism in the Age of Gladstone, 1860–1880* (Cambridge University Press, Cambridge), pp. 264–75.

41 Andrew W. Robinson, *The Language of Democracy: Political Rhetoric in the United States and Britain, 1790–1900* (Cornell University Press, Ithaca and London, 1995), p. 168.

42 Thomas Carlyle, *Shooting Niagara: And After?* (Chapman & Hall, London, 1867). My quotations from Carlyle all come from this pamphlet.

43 Paul Smith (ed.), *Bagehot: The English Constitution* (Cambridge University Press, Cambridge, 2001), p. 202.

44 Stefan Collini (ed.), *Matthew Arnold: Culture and Anarchy and Other Writings* (Cambridge University Press, Cambridge, 1993), p. 85.

45 George Eliot, *Felix Holt: The Radical* (Penguin Books, Harmondsworth, reprinted 1977), pp. 618 and 626.

46 Ray (Rachel) Strachey, '*The Cause*': *A Short History of the Women's Movement in Great Britain* (G. Bell & Sons, Ltd, London, 1928), p. 396.

47 In her *A Vindication of the Rights of Woman.*

48 Martin Pugh, *The March of the Women: A Revisionist Analysis of the Campaign for Women's Suffrage, 1866–1914* (Oxford University Press, Oxford, 2000), p. 74.

49 An anti-suffragist campaigner, quoted in Pugh, *The March of the Women*, p. 41.

50 Ibid., pp. 46 and 52–3.

51 Strachey, '*The Cause*', p. 332.

52 Pocock, *The Machiavellian Moment*, p. 547.

53 David Cannadine, *Ornamentalism: How the British Saw their Empire* (Penguin Books edition, London, 2002), p. 54.

54 David Edgerton, 'Liberal Militarism and the British State', *New Left Review* (January–February 1991), 138–69.

55 Sidney Lowe, *The Governance of England* (T. Fisher Unwin, London (revised edition), 1914), p. xxxi.

56 Quoted in Ross Terrill, *R. H. Tawney and his Times: Socialism as Fellowship* (André Deutsch, London, 1974), p. 175.

57 Quoted in Harold Nicolson, *King George the Fifth: His Life and Reign* (Constable, London, 1952), p. 386.

58 Alistair B. Cooke and John Vincent, *The Governing Passion: Cabinet Government and Party Politics in Britain 1885–6* (Harvester Press, Brighton, 1974), p. 22.

59 Aneurin Bevan, *In Place of Fear* (William Heinemann Ltd, London, 1952), p. 6.

3 PRIMEVAL CONTRACT

1 Quoted in David Marquand, *Ramsay MacDonald* (Jonathan Cape, London, 1977), p. 235.

2   J.M. Keynes, *The Economic Consequences of the Peace* (Macmillan, London, 1920), p. 131.

3   S. Maccoby, *English Radicalism: The End?* (George Allen & Unwin, London, 1961), p. 285.

4   Roy Jenkins, *A Life at the Centre* (Macmillan, London, 1991), p. 9.

5   Harold Nicolson, *Public Faces* (Constable, London, 1932), p. 2.

6   See in particular Conor Cruise O'Brien, *The Great Melody: A Thematic Biography and Commented Anthology of Edmund Burke* (Minerva paperback edition, London, 1993); John Morley, *Edmund Burke: A Historical Study* (Macmillan and Co. Ltd, London, 1867); F.P. Lock, *Edmund Burke*, vols 1–2 (Clarendon Press, Oxford, 1998–2006).

7   Edmund Burke, *Reflections on the Revolution in France*, in *The Works and Correspondence of the Right Honourable Edmund Burke* (Francis and John Rivington, London, 1852), vol. 4, p. 186.

8   Ibid., p. 214; Paul Langford (ed.), *The Writings and Speeches of Edmund Burke*, vol. 2, *Party, Parliament and the American Crisis* (Clarendon Press, Oxford, 1981), p, 315.

9   Ibid., p. 283.

10   H.C.G. Matthew, *Gladstone 1875–1898* (Clarendon Press, Oxford, 1995), p. 295.

11   Burke, *Reflections*, p. 255.

12   Ibid., p. 228.

13   Ibid., p. 230.

14   David Bromwich (ed.), *On Empire, Liberty and Reform* (Yale University Press, 2000), p. 39.

15   Ibid., pp. 83–4.

16   Ibid., pp. 295–6.

17   Ibid., p. 310.

18   Ibid., pp. 94 and 18.

19   Burke, *Thoughts*, p. 320.

20   Burke, *Reflections*, p. 200.

21   Ibid., p. 222.

22   Ibid., p. 214.

23   Ibid., p. 280.

24   Burke, *Thoughts*, p. 320.

25   Burke, *Reflections*, p. 355.

26   Matthew, *Gladstone 1875–1898*, p. 90.

27   G.M. Trevelyan, *British History in the Nineteenth Century and After* (Longmans, London, 1937), pp. 225 and 243.

28   L.S. Amery, *Thoughts on the Constitution* (Oxford University Press, paperback edition, Oxford, 1964), p. 21.

29   J.M. Keynes, 'The End of Laissez-Faire', in John Maynard Keynes, *Essays in Persuasion* (W. W. Norton, New York and London, 1963 edition), pp. 312–13.

30   Quoted in Cain and Hopkins, *British Imperialism, 1688–2000*, p. 98.

31   William Dalrymple, *The Last Mughal: The Fall of a Dynasty, Delhi, 1857* (Bloomsbury, London, 2006).

32   G.M. Trevelyan, quoted in David Cannadine, *G.M. Trevelyan: A Life in History* (HarperCollins, London, 1992), p. 112.

33   Sir J.A. Marriott, *England since Waterloo* (Methuen, London, 1954), p. 445.

34   Winston S. Churchill, *A History of the English-speaking Peoples*, 4 vols (Cassell & Co., London, 1956–8).

35   Quoted in Cannadine, *Trevelyan*, p. 123.

36   Marquand, *MacDonald*, p. 118.

37   Robert Roberts, *The Classic Slum: Salford Life in the First Quarter of the Century* (Penguin

Books, Harmondsworth, 1973), pp. 143–4.

38 Bernard Porter, *The Absent-Minded Imperialists: Empire, Society and Culture in Britain* (Oxford University Press, Oxford, 2004).

39 Samuel H. Beer, *To Make A Nation: The Rediscovery of American Federalism* (Belknap Press, Cambridge Mass., 1994), p. 61.

40 Johann P. Somerville (ed.), Sir Robert Filmer, *Patriarchy and Other Writings* (Cambridge University Press, Cambridge, 1991).

41 Thomas Hobbes (ed. John Plamenatz), *Leviathan* (Fontana edition, ninth impression, London 1978), p. 143.

42 Ibid., p. 176.

43 Rose A. Melikan, *John Scott, Lord Eldon, 1751–1838: The Duty of Loyalty* (Cambridge University Press, Cambridge, 1999), pp. 251–5.

44 Lady Gwendolen Cecil, *Life of Robert, Marquis of Salisbury* (Hodder & Stoughton, London, 1921), vol. 1, p. 49.

45 Ibid., p. 170.

46 Paul Smith, *Lord Salisbury on Politics: A Selection from his Articles in the Quarterly Review, 1860–1883* (Cambridge University Press, Cambridge, 1972), p. 88.

47 Ibid. pp. 87–8.

48 Ibid., p. 71.

49 Ibid., pp. 338–76.

50 Ibid., p. 63.

51 Ibid., p. 70.

52 Ibid., p. 42.

53 Ibid., p. 213.

54 Ibid., pp. 190–1.

55 Ibid., p. 67.

56 Ibid., p. 45.

57 Peter Marsh, *The Discipline of Popular Government: Lord Salisbury's Domestic Statecraft, 1881–1902* (Harvester Press, Hassocks, Sussex, 1978).

58 Ibid., p. 374.

59 A.M. Gollin, *Proconsul in Politics: A Study of Lord Milner in Opposition and in Power* (Anthony Blond, London, 1964), p. 157 and pp. 172–222.

60 Sir Edward Carson, quoted in D. George Boyce, entry on Carson, in *Oxford Dictionary of National Biography* (Oxford, 2004), www.oxforddnb.com/view/article/32310.

61 F.M.L. Thomson, entry on Joynson Hicks, in *Oxford Dictionary of National Biography*, May 2006, www.oxforddnb.com/view/article33858.

62 George Bernard Shaw, 'The Transition to Social Democracy' in Bernard Shaw et al., *Fabian Essays* ('Jubilee Edition', London, 1948), p. 169.

63 J.A. Hobson, *The Crisis of Liberalism: New Issues of Democracy* (Harvester Press edition, Brighton, 1974), pp. 76–7.

64 J.R. MacDonald, *Socialism and Government* (Independent Labour Party, London, 1909), pp. 3 and 17.

65 MacDonald, *Socialism and Government*, p. 11.

66 Ibid., p. 47.

67 Hobson, *The Crisis of Liberalism*, pp. 78 and 80.

68 Ibid., pp. 32–3.

69 Sidney Webb, *Socialism in England* (Swan Soonenschein & Co., London, 1890), p. 7.

70 Ibid., p. 116.

71 Quoted in Brian Lee Crowley, *The Self, the Individual and the Community: Liberalism in*

the Political Thought of F.A. Hayek and Sidney and Beatrice Webb (Clarendon Press, Oxford, 1987), p. 123.

72 Ibid., p. 115.

73 Ibid., p. 133.

74 MacDonald, *Socialism and Government*, vol. 2, p. 5.

75 Quoted in Edmund Dell, *A Strange Eventful History: Democratic Socialism in Britain* (HarperCollins, London, 2000), p. 56.

76 Quoted in Crowley, *Self,* pp. 152 and 148.

77 Sidney and Beatrice Webb, *Soviet Communism: A New Civilisation* (Private subscription edition, 1935), p. 1143.

78 Sir Stafford Cripps, 'Can Socialism Come by Constitutional Methods?', in Christopher Addison (et al.), *Problems of a Socialist Government* (Victor Gollancz Ltd, London, 1933), pp. 35–66.

79 Hugh Dalton, *Practical Socialism for Britain* (George Routledge & Sons Ltd, London, 1935), especially pp. 245 and 249.

80 Evan Durbin, *The Politics of Democratic Socialism: An Essay on Social Policy* (Routledge & Kegan Paul, London, reprinted 1957).

81 Elizabeth Durbin, *New Jerusalems: The Labour Party and the Economics of Democratic Socialism* (Routledge & Kegan Paul, London, 1985), p. 185.

82 R.H. Tawney, 'Introduction', in J.P. Mayer (ed.), *Political Thought: The European Tradition* (J.M. Dent & Sons Ltd, London, 1939), p. xviii.

83 Quoted in Terrill, *R.H. Tawney and his Times*, p. 191.

84 Quentin Skinner, *Liberty Before Liberalism* (Cambridge University Press, Cambridge, 1998).

85 John Milton, 'The Tenure of Kings and Magistrates', in Orgell and Goldberg (eds), *Milton*, pp. 279–80.

86 John Milton, 'The Ready and Easy Way to Establish a Free Commonwealth', in Orgell and Goldberg (eds), *Milton*, p. 338.

87 Orgel and Goldberg (eds), *Milton*, pp. 249–50, 252 and 265–7.

88 For a marvellously rich treatment of this point, see Beer, *To Make a Nation*, Chapter 2.

89 Quoted in Asa Briggs, *Victorian Cities* (Odhams Press, London, 1963), pp. 208–9.

90 John Stuart Mill, *Principles of Political Economy with some of their applications to social philosophy* (Longmans Green & Co., London, 1883 edition), pp. 572–3.

91 John Stuart Mill, *Essays on Politics and Culture* (ed. Gertrude Himmelfarb), (Peter Smith, Gloucester, Mass., 1973), p. 186.

92 Ibid., p. 230.

93 A.D. Lindsay, *The Essentials of Democracy* (Oxford University Press, London, 1929), p. 37.

94 Quoted in Logie Barrow and Ian Bullock, *Democratic Ideas and the British Labour Movement, 1890–1914* (Cambridge University Press, Cambridge, 1996), p. 247.

95 Ibid., p. 256.

96 Quoted in A.W. Wright, *G.D.H. Cole and Socialist Democracy* (Clarendon Press, Oxford, 1979), p. 51.

97 Terrill, *Tawney*, pp. 79 and 117.

98 Ibid., p. 138.

99 R.H. Tawney, *The Attack and Other Papers* (Spokesman edition, Nottingham, 1981), p. 182.

100 Ibid., p. 164.

101 Ibid., p. 166.

102 Terrill, *Tawney*, p. 173.

103 Tawney, *Attack*, p. 165.

104 *The New Statesman and Nation*, 22 June 1935.

4 GOLDEN CIRCLE

1   For the coalition and its fall, see Kenneth O. Morgan, *Consensus and Disunity: The Lloyd George Coalition Government 1918–1922* (Clarendon Press, Oxford, 1979).
2   J.M. Keynes, *Essays in Biography* (Rupert Hart-Davis, London, 1951), p. 37.
3   Morgan, *Consensus*, p. 279.
4   Hobson, *Crisis*, p. 12.
5   Quoted in Keith Middlemas and John Barnes, *Stanley Baldwin* (Weidenfeld & Nicolson, London, 1969), p. 123.
6   Philip Williamson, *Stanley Baldwin: Conservative Leadership and National Values* (Cambridge University Press, Cambridge, 1999), p. 31.
7   Ibid., p. 85.
8   Quoted in Roy Jenkins, *Baldwin* (Collins, London, 1987), p. 31.
9   A.W. Baldwin, *My Father: The True Story* (George Allen & Unwin, London, 1956), pp. 100–1.
10 Jenkins, *Baldwin*, p. 30.
11 Williamson, *Baldwin*, p. 230.
12 Ibid., p. 145.
13 Earl Baldwin of Bewdley, *An Interpreter of England* (Hodder &a Stoughton, London, 1939), p. 57.
14 Williamson, *Stanley Baldwin*, pp. 145 and 146. My interpretation of the Baldwin era is heavily based on this.
15 Quoted in Ross Martin, *TUC: The Growth of a Pressure Group, 1868–1976* (Clarendon Press, Oxford, 1980), p. 239.
16 Commons *Hansard*, 6 March 1925, cols 835–41.
17 Quoted in Marquand, *Ramsay MacDonald*, p. 320.
18 Bentley Gilbert, *British Social Policy 1914–1939* (B.T. Batsford Ltd, London, 1970), p. 308.
19 Quoted in Bernard Crick, *George Orwell: A Life* (Secker & Warburg, London, 1980), p. 10.
20 Quoted in Ross McKibbin, *The Ideologies of Class: Social Relations in Britain 1880–1950* (Clarendon Press, Oxford, paperback edition, 1994), pp. 271–2.
21 Ross McKibbin, *Classes and Cultures: England 1918–1951* (OUP, Oxford, 1998), p. 100.
22 Quoted in Harold Perkin, *The Rise of Professional Society: England since 1880* (Routledge, London and New York, 1989), p. 275.
23 Bryan Magee, *Clouds of Glory: A Hoxton Childhood* (Jonathan Cape, London, 2003), pp. 84–5.
24 Quoted in David Cannadine, *Class in Britain* (Yale University Press, New Haven and London, 1998), p. 121.
25 Quoted in McKibbin, *Classes and Cultures*, p. 79.
26 Department of Employment and Productivity, *British Labour Statistics, Historical Abstract 1886–1968*, table 110; Roger Middleton, *Government Versus the Market, The Growth of the Public Sector, Economic Management and British Economic Performance* (Edward Elgar, Cheltenham and Brookfield, 1996), p. 335.
27 Williamson, *Baldwin*, p. 191.
28 Ibid., p. 185.
29 Quoted in D.E. Moggridge, *Maynard Keynes: An Economist's Biography* (Routledge,

London and New York, 1992), p. 431.

30 For the talks, see G.A. McDonald and Howard Gospel, 'The Mond–Turner Talks, 1927–1933: A Study in Industrial Co-operation', *The Historical Journal*, 16: 4 (1973), 807–29.

31 Hilary Marquand, 'Great Britain', in Hilary Marquand (ed.),*Organised Labour in Four Continents* (Longmans Green & Co., London, New York and Toronto, 1939), p. 181.

32 John Gallagher, *The Decline, Revival and Fall of the British Empire* (Cambridge University Press, Cambridge, 1982), p. 96.

33 Middlemas and Barnes, *Baldwin*, p. 593.

34 Quoted in Wm. Roger Louis, 'Introduction', in Judith M. Brown and Wm. Roger Louis (eds), *The Oxford History of the British Empire*, vol. 4, *The Twentieth Century* (Oxford University Press, Oxford and New York, 1999), p. 5.

35 For the struggle, see Brown and Louis, *Oxford History of the British Empire*; Carl Bridge, *Holding Britain to the Empire: The British Conservative Party and the 1935 Constitution* (Envoy Press, New York, 1986); R.J. Moore, *The Crisis of Indian Unity, 1917–1940* (Clarendon Press, Oxford, 1974); D.A. Low, *Eclipse of Empire* (Cambridge University Press, Cambridge, 1991); Bernard Porter, *The Lion's Share: A Short History of British Imperialism*, second edition (Longman, London and New York, 1996); Robert Rhodes James, *Winston Churchill: A Study in Failure* (Weidenfeld & Nicolson, London, 1970); Barnes and Middlemas, *Baldwin;* The Earl of Birkenhead, *Halifax: The Life of Lord Halifax* (Hamish Hamilton, London, 1965); Williamson, *Baldwin*.

36 Quoted in Middlemas and Barnes, *Baldwin*, p. 543.

37 Quoted in Rhodes James, *Winston Churchill*, p. 196.

38 Quoted in Porter, *Lion's Share*, p. 304.

39 Martin Gilbert, *Prophet of Truth: Winston S. Churchill* (Minerva paperback edition, London, 1990), p. 356.

40 Middlemas and Barnes, *Baldwin*, p. 713.

41 Quoted in Martin Gilbert, *Finest Hour: Winston S. Churchill 1939–1941* (Minerva, London, 1989), p. 468.

42 John Charmley, *Churchill: The End of Glory, A Political Biography* (Sceptre, London, 1995 edition), p. 408.

43 Quoted in John Lukacs, *Five Days in London, May 1940* (Yale University Press, New Haven and London, 1999), pp. 182–3.

44 David Reynolds, *From World War to Cold War: Churchill, Roosevelt and the International History of the 1940s* (Oxford University Press, Oxford, 2006), pp. 77–9.

45 George Orwell, 'The Lion and the Unicorn: Socialism and the English Genius', in Sonia Orwell and Ian Angus (eds), *The Collected Essays, Journalism and Letters of George Orwell*, vol. 2, *My Country Right or Left* (Penguin Books, Harmondsworth, 1970), pp. 74–134. My quotations come from this edition.

46 Orwell, 'Lion', pp. 125–6.

47 Peter Clarke, *The Cripps Version: The Life of Sir Stafford Cripps* (Allen Lane/The Penguin Press, London, 2002), pp. 257–370.

48 Peter Howlett, 'The Wartime Economy, 1939–1945', in Roderick Floud and Deirdre McCloskey, *The Economic History of Britain since 1700*, vol. 3 (Cambridge University Press, Cambridge, second edition, 1994), p. 9.

49 Douglas Jay, *Change and Fortune: A Political Record* (Hutchinson, London, 1980), p. 91.

50 For an excellent summary of the evidence, see David Kynaston, *Austerity Britain, 1945–51* (Bloomsbury, London, 2007), pp. 20–59.

51 Sidney Pollard, *The Development of the British Economy, 1914–1980* (Edward Arnold, London, third edition, 1983), pp. 192–234.

52 The phrase is Robert Skidelsky's, *John Maynard Keynes: A Biography*, 3 vols (Macmillan, London, 1983–2000), vol. 3, *Fighting for Britain, 1937–1946*, p. 144.

53 The credit came from Gaitskell: Ben Pimlott, *Harold Wilson* (HarperCollins, London, 1992), p. 78.

54 José Harris, *William Beveridge: A Biography* (Clarendon Press, Oxford, 1977), p. 421.

55 Ibid., p. 420.

56 Alan Booth, *British Economic Policy 1931–1945: Was There a Keynesian Revolution?* (Harvester Wheatsheaf, Hemel Hempstead, 1989); Jim Tomlinson, *Employment Policy 1939–1955* (Clarendon Press, Oxford, 1987); Paul Addison, *The Road to 1945: British Politics and the Second World War* (Jonathan Cape, London, 1975).

57 Robert Skidelsky, *John Maynard Keynes*, vol. 3, p. 145.

58 Quoted in Addison, *Road to 1945*, p. 245.

59 Booth, *British Economic Policy*, p. 70.

60 *Employment Policy*, Cmd 6527, HMSO, London, 1944.

61 Stephen Brooke, *Labour's War: The Labour Party during the Second World War* (Clarendon Press, Oxford, 1992), p. 240.

62 Quoted in Wm. Roger Louis, *Ends of British Imperialism: The Scramble for Empire, Suez and Decolonization* (I.B. Tauris, London, 2006), p. 593.

63 Warren F. Kimball, 'Churchill and Roosevelt', in Robert Blake and Wm. Roger Louis, *Churchill* (Oxford University Press, Oxford, 1994), p. 304.

64 David Reynolds, *The Creation of the Anglo-American Alliance: A Study in Competitive Collaboration*, (University of North Carolina Press, Chapel Hill, 1981), p. 284.

65 John Charmley, *Churchill's Grand Alliance: The Anglo-American Special Relationship, 1940–57*, (Hodder & Stoughton, London, 1995), p. 89.

66 For which, see Booth, *British Economic Policy*, Chapter 5; Richard Gardner, *Sterling-Dollar Diplomacy: Anglo-American Collaboration in the Reconstruction of Multilateral Trade* (Clarendon Press, Oxford, 1956), Chapters I to VIII; L.S. Pressnell, *External Economic Policy since the War*, vol. 1, *The Post-War Financial Settlement* (HMSO, London, 1986), Chapters 1 to 8 and appendices 1 to 18; Reynolds, *The Creation of the Anglo-American Alliance*; and Skidelsky, vol. 3, *Fighting for Britain*.

67 Sidney Pollard, *The Development of the British Economy, 1914–1980*, p. 217.

68 Lords *Hansard*, 18 December 1945, col. 794.

69 Commons *Hansard*, 15 May 1945, cols. 2305–7.

70 Kynaston, *Austerity Britain*, pp. 68–9.

5 PALEST PINK

1 Kynaston, *Austerity Britain*, pp. 75–6.

2 Hugh Dalton, *High Tide and After: Memoirs 1945–1960* (Frederick Muller, London, 1962), p. 3.

3 For the party's view of that task, see *Labour's Call to Labour Voters*, 1945, quoted in Stephen Fielding, Peter Thompson and Nick Tiratsoo, *'England Arise': The Labour Party and Popular Politics in 1940s Britain* (Manchester University Press, Manchester, 1995), p. 94.

4 Reprinted in F.W.S. Craig (ed.), *British General Election Manifestos 1918–1966* (Political Reference Publications, Chichester, 1970), pp. 97–105.

5 Jay, *Change and Fortune*, p. 135.

6 Quoted in Robert A. Dahl, 'Workers' Control of Industry and the British Labor Party', *American Political Science Review,* vol. 41 (1947), 899.

7 The phrase is Geoffrey De Freitas's: Ben Pimlott, *The Political Diary of Hugh Dalton, 1918–40, 1945–60* (Jonathan Cape, in association with the London School of Economics, London, 1985), p. 445.

8 Alan Bullock, *The Life and Times of Ernest Bevin,* 3 vols (Heinemann, London, 1960–83) is still unsurpassed. Sir Nicholas Henderson, one of Bevin's private secretaries at the start of the 1945 government, paints an affectionate and revealing picture of him in his memoir, *The Private Office: A Personal View of Five Foreign Secretaries and of Government from the Inside,* (Weidenfeld & Nicolson, London, 1984).

9 Quoted in Bullock, *Bevin,* vol. 1, p. 379.

10 Edwin Plowden, *An Industrialist in the Treasury: The Post-war Years* (André Deutsch, London, 1989), p. 20; see also Clarke, *The Cripps Version,* notably pp. 479–538.

11 Susan Howson and Donald Moggridge (eds), *The Collected Papers of James Meade,* vol. 4, *The Cabinet Office Diary 1944–46* (Unwin Hyman, London, 1990), p. 115.

12 For a good example, see Alan Milburn, 'Labour's contract for a third term', *Guardian,* 15 January 2005.

13 Rose Macaulay, *The World My Wilderness* (Collins and Book Society edition, London and Glasgow, 1950), pp. 159–83.

14 Kynaston, *Austerity Britain,* p. 111.

15 Ibid., *passim.*

16 *Statistical Material Presented During the Washington Negotiations,* Cmd 6707 (HMSO, London, 1945).

17 National Archives, CAB. 129/1 C.P. (45) 112, 14 August 1945.

18 J.M. Keynes, *The Collected Writings of John Maynard Keynes* (ed. Donald Moggridge), (Macmillan and Cambridge University Press, London and New York, 1971–89), vol. 24, pp. 256–95.

19 Sir Alec Cairncross (ed.), Sir Richard Clarke, *Anglo-American Economic Collaboration 1942–1949* (Clarendon Press, Oxford, 1982), pp. 57–8.

20 For a masterly description, see Skidelsky, *John Maynard Keynes,* vol. 3, Chapter 12.

21 Ibid., p. 434.

22 Dalton, *High Tide and After,* pp. 74–5.

23 Commons *Hansard,* 12 December 1945, cols 468–9.

24 Quoted in Anthony Adamthwaite, 'Britain and the world, 1945–9: The View from the Foreign Officer', *International Affairs* (Spring 1985), 231.

25 Quoted in Partha Sarathi Gupta, 'Imperialism and the Labour Government of 1945–51', in Jay Winter (ed.), *The Working Class in Modern British History: Essays in Honour of Henry Pelling* (Cambridge University Press, Cambridge, 1983), p. 100.

26 Quoted in Bullock, *Bevin,* vol. 3, p. 454.

27 Michael J. Hogan, *The Marshall Plan: America, Britain and the Reconstruction of Western Europe* (Cambridge University Press, Cambridge, paperback edition, reprinted 1995), especially Chapter 3.

28 Dalton's diary, quoted in Pimlott (ed.), *Political Diary of Hugh Dalton,* p. 493.

29 Dalton's diary for 9 March 1946, quoted in Kenneth Harris, *Attlee* (Weidenfeld & Nicolson, London, 1982), p. 299.

30 Quoted in Kenneth O. Morgan, *Labour in Power 1945–1951* (Clarendon Press, Oxford, 1984), p. 193.

31 Pimlott (ed.), *Political Diary of Hugh Dalton,* p. 472.

32 National Archives, CAB 129/7. CP (46) 58.

33 Margaret Gowing, *Independence and Deterrence: Britain and Atomic Energy 1945–52*, vol.
    1, *Policy Making* (Macmillan Press, London and Basingstoke, 1974), p. 183.

34 *Statement Relating to Defence*, HMSO, February 1947, Cmd 7042.

35 L.V. Scott, *Conscription and the Attlee Governments: The Politics and Policy of National
    Service 1945–1954* (Clarendon Press, Oxford, 1993), pp. 46 and 277.

36 For the phrase 'nebulous but exalted', see Sir Alec Cairncross, *Years of Recovery: British
    Economic Policy 1945–51* (Methuen, London, 1985), p. 303.

37 My account is based on Charles Webster, *The Health Services since the War*, vol. 1, *Problems
    of Health Care: The National Health Service before 1957* (HMSO, London, 1988), chapter
    4.

38 National Archives, CAB 128/1 CM (45) 43rd meeting.

39 National Archives, CAB 128/1 CM (45) 65th meeting.

40 Webster, *Health Services*, pp. 458 and 390.

41 Sir Norman Chester, *The Nationalisation of British Industry, 1945–51* (HMSO, London,
    1975).

42 Quoted in Samuel H. Beer, *Modern British Politics: A Study of Parties and Pressure Groups*
    (Faber & Faber, London, 1965), p. 134.

43 David Edgerton, *Warfare State: Britain, 1920–1970* (Cambridge University Press, Cam-
    bridge, 2006), pp. 96–7.

44 Quoted in Cairncross, *Years of Recovery*, p. 485. For the broader effects of nationalisation,
    see Jim Tomlinson, *Democratic Socialism and Economic Policy: The Attlee Years 1945–1951*
    (Cambridge University Press, Cambridge, 1997), Chapter 5.

45 For the story of how it came to do so, see Richard Toye, *The Labour Party and the Planned
    Economy 1931–1951* (The Royal Historical Society, The Boydell Press, Woodbridge, 2003).

46 Interview with James Meade, December 1993.

47 Quoted in John Campbell, *Nye Bevan and the Mirage of British Socialism* (Weidenfeld &
    Nicolson, London, 1987), p. 207.

48 Note by Secretary to the Cabinet, 12 December 1945, National Archives, T 273/298.

49 *Economic Survey for 1947*, Cmd 7046.

50 A point powerfully made by Sir Alec Cairncross, *Years of Recovery*, pp. 309–10.

51 National Archives, CAB 129/8. C.P. (46) 148, 10 April 1946.

52 Note by Isaacs, National Archives, PREM 8/1568 (1).

53 My account is based on Cairncross, *Years of Recovery*; Cairncross (ed.), Clarke, *Anglo-
    American Economic Collaboration*; and Morgan, *Labour in Power*.

54 For the details, see Alex J. Robertson, *The Bleak Midwinter 1947* (Manchester University
    Press, Manchester, 1987).

55 Cairncross, *Years of Recovery*, p. 131.

56 Quoted in Peter Hennessy, *Never Again: Britain 1945–1951* (Jonathan Cape, London,
    1992), p. 290.

57 John Fforde, *The Bank of England and Public Policy 1941–1958* (Cambridge University
    Press, Cambridge, 1992), pp. 152–60.

58 Morgan, *Labour in Power*, p. 347.

59 The phrase was Dalton's: Jim Tomlinson, *Democratic Socialism*, p. 222.

60 Quoted in J.C.R. Dow, *The Management of the British Economy, 1945–60* (Cambridge
    University Press, Cambridge, 1964), p. 34.

61 Philip Williams (ed.), *The Diary of Hugh Gaitskell 1945–1956* (Jonathan Cape, London,
    1983), p. 56.

62 Ina Zweiniger-Bargielovska, *Austerity in Britain: Rationing, Controls and Consumption,
    1939–1955* (Oxford University Press, Oxford, 2000), Chapter 5.

63 For 'masculinism', see Martin Francis, *Ideas and Policies under Labour 1945–51: Building a New Britain* (Manchester University Press, Manchester and New York, 1997, Chapter 8.

64 Quoted in Francis, *Ideas and Policies*, p. 217.

65 Zweiniger-Bargielovska, *Austerity in Britain*, p. 45.

66 National Archives, CAB 129/16. C.P. (47) 20, 7 January 1947.

67 Fielding, Thompson and Tiratsoo, *'England Arise'*, p. 171.

68 Quoted in David Pryce-Jones, 'Towards the Cocktail Party', in Michael Sissons and Philip French (eds), *The Age of Austerity 1945–1951* (Oxford University Press, paperback edition, 1986), p. 206.

69 Quoted in Peter Clarke, *The Cripps Version*, p 511.

70 Cairncross (ed.), Sir Richard Clarke, *Anglo-American Economic Collaboration*, p. 83.

71 Susan Cooper, 'Snoek Picquante', in Sissons and French (eds), *Age of Austerity*, pp. 21–42.

72 Morgan, *Labour in Power*, pp. 366–7.

73 The second and last such document was the National Plan of 1965.

74 Memorandum by Harold Wilson, *The State and Private Industry*, National Archives, PREM 8/1183; see also Pimlott, *Harold Wilson*, Chapter 7.

75 My account is based on Cairncross, *Years of Recovery;* Morgan, *Labour in Power;* Dow, *Management,* Tomlinson, *Democratic Socialism;* and Alec Cairncross and Barry Eichengreen, *Sterling in Decline: The Devaluations of 1931, 1949 and 1967* (Blackwell, Oxford, 1983).

76 Commons *Hansard*, 18 April 1950, cols 39–40.

77 Cairncross, *Years of Recovery*, p. 322.

78 Hogan, *Marshall Plan*, p. 49.

79 For Bevin and the Marshall Plan, see Bullock, *Bevin*, vol. 3, Chapter 10; Hogan, *Marshall Plan, passim;* Morgan, *Labour in Power*, Chapter 6; Alan S. Milward, *The Reconstruction of Western Europe, 1945–51* (Methuen, paperback edition, London, 1987); and Geoffrey Warner, 'The Labour Governments and the Unity of Western Europe, 1945–51', in Ritchie Ovendale (ed.), *The Foreign Policy of the British Labour Governments, 1945–51* (Leicester University Press, Leicester, 1984), pp. 61–82.

80 Quoted in Ovendale, *Foreign Policy,* p. 113. Jebb was quoting Arnold Toynbee.

81 National Archives, CAB 128/12 C.M. (48), 2nd meeting.

82 Bullock, *Bevin*, vol. 3, p. 759.

83 Hogan, *Marshall Plan*, p. 250.

84 Ibid., Chapters 6–7.

85 Scott Newton, 'The 1949 Sterling Crisis and British Policy towards European integration', *Review of International Studies*, 11 (1985), 177.

86 Dean Acheson, *Present at the Creation: My Years in the State Department* (Hamish Hamilton, London, 1970), p. 387.

87 Newton, '1949 Sterling crisis', 178.

88 Quoted in Wright, *Cole and Socialist Democracy*, p. 132.

89 Pimlott, *Wilson*, pp. 129–32.

6 LONG RECESSIONAL

1 Quoted in Peter Hennessy, *Having It So Good: Britain in the Fifties* (Penguin Books, London, 2007), p. 187.

2 Cairncross, *Years of Recovery,* p. 239.

3   Lord Butler, *The Art of the Possible: The Memoirs of Lord Butler* (Hamish Hamilton, London, 1971), p. 28.

4   Ibid., p. 157.

5   See the papers in National Archives, T236/ 3240; Cairncross, *Years of Recovery;* Edmund Dell, *The Chancellors: A History of the Chancellors of the Exchequer 1945–90* (HarperCollins, London, 1996), Chapter 5; Donald MacDougall, *Don and Mandarin: Memoirs of an Economist* (John Murray, London, 1987); Plowden, *An Industrialist in the Treasury.*

6   Note by Edwin Plowden, 13 February 1952, National Archives, T269/3240.

7   National Archives, T236/3240.

8   Butler memoranda in National Archives, T236/2340.

9   Lord Cherwell to Churchill, 18 March 1952, National Archives, PREM 11/137.

10   See David Cannadine, *The Decline and Fall of the British Aristocracy* (Yale University Press, New Haven and London, 1990), Chapter 14; and Harold Perkin, *The Rise of Professional Society: England since 1880* (Routledge, London and New York, 1989), Chapters 8 and 9.

11   For an illuminating account, see Hennessy, *Having It So Good,* pp. 97–100.

12   The phrase was Princess Margaret's. Quoted in Ben Pimlott, *The Queen: A Biography of Elizabeth II,* (HarperCollins, London, 1996), p. 193.

13   Edward Shils and Michael Young, quoted in Robert Hewison, *Culture and Consensus: England, Art and Politics since 1940* (Methuen, London, 1995), p. 68.

14   Evelyn Waugh, *The Ordeal of Gilbert Pinfold* (Chapman Hall, London, 1957), p. 1.

15   Julia Namier, *Lewis Namier: A Biography,* (Oxford University Press, London, 1971), pp. 186–7.

16   Sir Ivor Jennings, *The Law and the Constitution* (University of London Press, London, fifth edition, 1964), pp. 8–9.

17   Harry Eckstein, 'The British Political System', in Samuel H. Beer and Adam B. Ulam, *Patterns of Government: The Major Political Systems of Europe* (Random House, New York, 1962), p. 90.

18   Gabriel Almond and Sidney Verba, *The Civic Culture: Political Attitudes and Democracy in Five Nations* (Princeton University Press, Princeton, New Jersey, 1963).

19   Michael Oakeshott, 'Political Education', in Michael Oakeshott (ed.), *Rationalism in Politics and Other Essays* (Methuen, London, 1962), p. 127.

20   Ibid, p. 133.

21   Noel Annan, *Our Age: Portrait of a Generation* (Weidenfeld & Nicolson, London, 1990), pp. 387–401.

22   For the economic climate, see Sidney Pollard, *The Development of the British Economy, 1914–1980* (Edward Arnold, London, third edition, 1983); Alec Cairncross, *The British Economy since 1945* (Blackwell, Oxford, 1992); Middleton, *Government versus the Market,* chapter 10; Dow, *The Management of the British Economy 1945–60,* Chapters 1 to 5; G.D.N. Worswick and P.H. Ady (eds), *The British Economy in the Nineteen-fifties* (Clarendon Press, Oxford, 1962); and Roderick Floud and Donald McCloskey (eds), *The Economic History of Britain since 1700* (Cambridge University Press, Cambridge, 1981), vol. 2.

23   C.A.R. Crosland, *The Future of Socialism* (Jonathan Cape, London, 1956), p. 380.

24   Keith Middlemas, *Power, Competition and the State,* 3 vols (Macmillan, Basingstoke, 1986–91); and *Politics in Industrial Society: The Experience of the British System since 1911* (André Deutsch, London, 1979), Chapter 14.

25   Quoted in Beer, *Modern British Politics,* p. 237.

26   Anthony Seldon, *Churchill's Indian Summer: The Conservative Government 1951–1955* (Hodder & Stoughton, London, 1955), p. 202; for Monckton, see Lord Birkenhead,

Walter Monckton: The Life of Viscount Monckton of Benchley (Weidenfeld & Nicolson, London, 1969).

27 Dell, *Chancellors*, pp. 161–2.

28 Quoted in Kyle, *Suez* (Weidenfeld & Nicolson, London, 1991), p. 43.

29 Quoted in Kenneth O. Morgan, *The People's Peace: British History 1945–1989* (Oxford University Press, Oxford, 1990), p. 147.

30 Kyle, *Suez*, p. 76.

31 For the whole story, see Kyle, *Suez*; John Darwin, *Britain and Decolonisation: The Retreat from Empire in the Post-War World* (Macmillan Press, Basingstoke, 1988), pp. 206–14; Robert Rhodes James, *Anthony Eden*; (Papermac edition, London, 1987); David Carlton, *Anthony Eden: A Biography* (Allen Lane, London, 1981); Alistair Horne, *Macmillan 1894– 1956*, vol. 1 of the official biography (Macmillan, London, 1988); Avi Shlaim, *The Iron Wall: Israel and the Arab World* (Allen Lane, London, 2000, chapter 4); and Hennessy, *Having it So Good*, Chapter 9.

32 Kyle, *Suez*, p. 136.

33 The phrase is R.A. Butler's. Lord Butler, *Art of the Possible*, p. 190.

34 Anthony Head, the Defence Secretary, quoted in Horne, *Macmillan*, vol. 1, p. 442.

35 Alistair Horne, *Macmillan 1957–1986*, vol. 2 of the official biography (Macmillan, London, 1989), p. 5.

36 John Campbell, *Nye Bevan and the Mirage*, p. 122.

37 Anthony Sampson, *Anatomy of Britain* (Hodder & Stoughton, London, 1962), Chapters 10 and 11.

38 W.L. Guttsman, *The British Political Elite* (MacGibbon & Kee, London, 1963), p. 336.

39 Nigel Dennis, *Cards of Identity* (Weidenfeld & Nicolson, London, 1955), pp. 151–2.

40 Kenneth Tynan, *Observer*, 13 May 1956, quoted in John Osborne, *Look Back in Anger* (Faber & Faber edition, London, 1996).

41 Osborne, *Look Back in Anger*, pp. 14–15.

42 Ibid., p. 89.

43 Ibid., p. 11.

44 John Osborne, 'They call it cricket', in Tom Maschler (ed.), *Declaration* (MacGibbon & Kee, London, 1957), pp. 75–6.

45 Quoted in Hennessy, *Having It So Good*, p. 458.

46 Harold Macmillan, *Riding the Storm 1956–1959* (Macmillan, London, 1971), p. 197.

47 Horne, *Macmillan*, vol. 2, p. 269. The two volumes of Horne's biography are indispensable for Macmillan. See also Anthony Sampson, *Macmillan: A Study in Ambiguity* (Allen Lane, the Penguin Press, London, 1967); John Turner, *Macmillan* (Longman, London, 1994), and H.C.G. Matthew's entry on Macmillan in the *Oxford Dictionary of National Biography*, online edition, www.oxforddnb.com/view/article 40185.

48 The phrase is Macmillan's own. Macmillan, *Riding the Storm*, p. 197.

49 Personal information.

50 Quoted in Anthony Sampson, *Macmillan*, p. 61.

51 For the continuities between Macmillan's views in the 1930s and after the war, see E.H.H. Green, 'Searching for the Middle Way: the Political Economy of Harold Macmillan', in E.H.H. Green, *Ideologies of Conservatism: Conservative Political Ideas in the Twentieth Century* (Oxford University Press, Oxford, 2002), pp. 157–191.

52 Peter Hennessy, *Having It So Good*, p. 556.

53 Quoted in ibid., p. 557.

54 Ibid, p. 16.

55 Kyle, *Suez*, p. 467.

56 Horne, *Macmillan*, vol. 2, p. 50.

57 For the gulf between British and American attitudes, see Richard E. Neustadt, *Alliance Politics* (Columbia University Press, New York and London, 1970), Chapter 3, pp. 30–55.

58 Horne, *Macmillan*, vol. 2, p. 85.

59 Darwin, *Britain and Decolonisation*, Chapters 5 to 8.

60 Turner, *Macmillan*, p. 200.

61 Harold Macmillan, *At the End of the Day 1961–1963* (Macmillan, London, 1973), p. 311.

62 Robert Shepherd, *Iain Macleod: A Biography* (Hutchinson, London, 1994) pp. 225–6.

63 Horne, *Macmillan*, vol. 1, p. 319.

64 For the story see Miriam Camps's now classic *Britain and the European Community, 1955–1963* (Oxford University Press, London, 1964); Hugo Young, *This Blessed Plot: Britain and Europe from Churchill to Blair* (Macmillan, London and Basingstoke, 1998); Horne, *Macmillan*, vol. 2; Turner, *Macmillan*; and Harold Macmillan, *Pointing the Way, 1951–1961* and *At the End of the Day 1961–1963* (Macmillan, London, 1972 and 1973).

65 Macmillan to Thorneycroft, July 1957, quoted in Turner, *Macmillan*, p. 215.

66 Quoted in Young, *This Blessed Plot*, p. 117.

67 For these remarks, see Horne, *Macmillan*, vol. 2, pp. 113 and 256; and Young, *This Blessed Plot*, p. 118.

68 National Archives, CAB 128/35, CC(61), 42nd Conclusions, July 1961.

69 N. Piers Ludlow, *Dealing with Britain: The Six and the First UK Application to the EEC* (Cambridge University Press, Cambridge, 1997).

70 So, at least, de Gaulle told his Cabinet. Hugo Young, *This Blessed Plot*, p. 137.

71 Camps, *Britain and the European Community*, pp. 478–9; Ludlow, *Dealing with Britain*, pp. 206–8

72 For the details, see Green, *Ideologies of Conservatism*, pp. 192–213; and Dell, *The Chancellors*, pp. 223–41.

73 Horne, *Macmillan*, vol. 2, p. 140.

74 Quoted in Robert Taylor, *The Trade Union Question in British Politics: Government and Unions since 1945* (Blackwell, Oxford, 1993), p. 101.

75 Alan Sillitoe, *Saturday Night and Sunday Morning* (Pan Books edition, London, 1960), pp. 21 and 144.

76 John H. Goldthorpe, David Lockwood, Frank Bechhofer and Jennifer Platt, *The Affluent Worker* (Cambridge University Press, Cambridge, 1968), especially vols 1 and 2.

77 The phrase is Robert Hewison's, quoted in Kenneth O. Morgan, *The People's Peace*, p. 207.

78 Quoted in Humphrey Carpenter, *That Was Satire That Was: The Satire Boom of the 1960s* (Victor Gollancz, London, 2000), p. 103.

79 C.H. Rolph (ed.), *The Trial of Lady Chatterley: Regina v. Penguin Books Limited* (Penguin Books, Harmondsworth, 1961).

80 The best account is Michael Kenny, *The First New Left: British Intellectuals after Stalin* (Lawrence & Wishart, London, 1995).

81 Editorial in *Universities and Left Review* (Spring 1957), quoted in Hewison, *Culture and Consensus*, p. 108.

82 E.P. Thompson, 'Outside the Whale', in E.P. Thompson (ed.), *Out of Apathy* (Stevens & Sons, London, 1960), pp. 184–5.

83 Quoted in Christopher Driver, *The Disarmers: A Study in Protest* (Hodder & Stoughton, London, 1964), p. 55.

84 A.J.P. Taylor, *A Personal History* (Hamish Hamilton, London, 1983), p. 227.

85 Quoted in Hewison, *Culture and Consensus*, p. 78.

86 Hugh Thomas, 'The Establishment and Society', in Hugh Thomas (ed.), *The Establishment* (Anthony Blond, London, 1959), pp. 9–20.

87 Thomas Balogh, 'The Apotheosis of the Dilettante', in Thomas (ed.), *The Establishment*, pp. 83–126.

88 For these quotations, see D.E . Butler and Anthony King, *The British General Election of 1964* (Macmillan, London, 1965), pp. 32–3.

89 Michael Shanks, *The Stagnant Society* (Penguin Books, Harmondsworth, 1972 edition), p. 232.

90 John Vaizey, 'The Public Schools', in Thomas (ed.), *The Establishment*, pp. 23–46.

91 Anthony Sampson, *Anatomy of Britain Today* (Hodder & Stoughton, London, 1965), p. 680.

92 For the scandal, see Horne, *Macmillan*, vol. 2; Kevin Jeffery, *Finest and Darkest Hours: The Decisive Events in British Politics from Churchill to Blair* (Atlantic Books, London, 2002), pp. 113–37; and Wayland Young, *The Profumo Affair: Aspects of Conservatism* (Penguin Books, Harmondsworth, 1963).

93 Quoted in Jefferys, *Finest and Darkest*, p. 125.

94 Quoted in Young, *Profumo*, p. 52.

95 Horne, *Macmillan*, vol. 2, p. 484.

96 Young, *Profumo*, pp. 111–12.

97 Macleod's position has been disputed, but in my view the weight of evidence suggests that he was for Butler.

98 Quoted in Dick Leonard, *A Century of Prime Ministers: Salisbury to Blair* (Palgrave Macmillan, Basingstoke and New York, 2005), p. 228.

99 Quoted in Ian Gilmour and Mark Garnett, *Whatever Happened to the Tories: the Conservatives since 1945* (Fourth Estate, London, paperback edition 1998), p. 197.

100 Iain Macleod, 'The Fight for the Tory Leadership', *Spectator*, 17 January 1964, pp. 65–7.

7 SECOND CHANCE

1 A.H. Halsey and Josephine Webb (eds), *Twentieth-Century British Social Trends* (Macmillan Press, Basingstoke, 2000), Chapters 4, 7 and 8.

2 Sampson, *Anatomy of Britain Today*, Chapter 37.

3 Harold Wilson, *Purpose in Politics* (Weidenfeld & Nicolson, 1964), p. vii.

4 Quoted in Butler and King, *The British General Election of 1964*, p. 110.

5 Ibid., p. 297.

6 Crosland, *The Future of Socialism;* Martin Francis, 'Mr Gaitskell's Ganymede? Re-assessing Crosland's *The Future of Socialism*', *Contemporary British History*, 11: 2 (summer 1997), 50–64.

7 Bevan, *In Place of Fear*, p. 45.

8 Barbara Castle, quoted in Ben Jackson, 'Egalitarian Thought on the British Left', Oxford University D. Phil. thesis, 2003), p. 234.

9 Speech by Aneurin Bevan, quoted in John Campbell, *Nye Bevan*, p. 363.

10 R.H.S. Crossman, 'The Lessons of 1945', in Perry Anderson and Robin Blackburn (eds), *Towards Socialism* (Cornell University Press edition, Ithaca, New York, 1966), p. 157.

11 Richard Crossman, *The Diaries of a Cabinet Minister*, vol. 2, *Lord President of the Council and Leader of the House of Commons, 1966–68* (Hamish Hamilton and Jonathan Cape, London, 1976), entry for 24 September 1966.

12 Philip Ziegler, *Wilson: the Authorised Life of Lord Wilson of Rievaulx* (Weidenfeld &

Nicolson, London, 1993), p. 117.

13 (Sir James) Harold Wilson, *Memoirs: The Making of a Prime Minister* (Weidenfeld & Nicolson and Michael Joseph, London, 1986), p. 35.

14 Roy Jenkins, entry on Harold Wilson in the *Oxford Dictionary of National Biography*, 2004, www.oxforddnb.com.

15 Wilson, *Purpose in Politics*, pp. 17–18 and 27–8.

16 Perry Anderson, 'Critique of Wilsonism', *New Left Review* (September-October 1964), 3–27.

17 For whom, see Denis Healey, *The Time of My Life* (Michael Joseph, London, 1989); Edward Pearce, *Denis Healey: A Life In Our Times* (Little Brown, London, 2002); and Giles Radice, *Friends and Rivals: Crosland, Jenkins and Healey* (Little Brown, London, 2002).

18 Pimlott, *Harold Wilson*, p. 267.

19 For these, see F.T. Blackaby (ed.), *Economic Policy 1960–74* (Cambridge University Press, Cambridge, 1978); Wilfred Beckerman (ed.), *The Labour Government's Economic Record: 1964–1970* (Duckworth, London, 1972); Samuel Brittan, *Steering the Economy* (Penguin, Harmondsworth, 1971); Cairncross, *Sterling in Decline*; Alec Cairncross, *The Wilson Years: A Treasury Diary 1964–1969* (Historians' Press, London, 1997); Dell, *The Chancellors*; Floud and McCloskey, *The Economic History of Britain;* Jacques Leruez, *Economic Planning and Politics in Britain* (Martin Robertson, London, 1975); Macdougall, *Don and Mandarin*; and Michael Stewart, *The Jekyll and Hyde Years: Politics and Economic Policy since 1964* (Dent, London, 1977).

20 Dell, *The Chancellors*, p. 306.

21 National Archives CAB 128/ 39; CC1 (64), 19 October 1964.

22 For a full discussion, see Tim Bale, 'Dynamics of a Non-Decision: the "Failure" to Devalue the Pound, 1964–7', *Twentieth Century British History*, 10: 2 (1999), 192–7.

23 Ziegler, *Wilson*, p. 191.

24 Harold Wilson, *The Labour Government, 1964–70: A Personal Record* (Penguin Books, Harmondsworth, 1974), pp. 27–8.

25 Bale, 'Dynamics of a Non-Decision', p. 202.

26 Quoted in Ziegler, *Wilson*, p. 190.

27 Ibid., p. 222.

28 Clive Ponting, *Breach of Promise: Labour in Power 1964–70* (Hamish Hamilton, London, 1989), especially Chapter 3; Ziegler, *Wilson*, especially Chapter 11; J.H.B Tew, 'Policies Aimed at Improving the Balance of Payments', in Blackaby, *British Economic Policy*, pp. 304–53.

29 Christopher Clifford, 'The Rise and Fall of the Department of Economic Affairs 1964–69: British Government and Indicative Planning', *Contemporary British History*, 11: 2 (Summer 1997). I have also drawn on the recollections of my wife, Judith Marquand, who served as an 'irregular' civil servant in the DEA.

30 Brittan, *Steering the Economy*, p. 317.

31 Denis Barnes and Eileen Reid, *Government and the Trade Unions: The British Experience 1964–79* (Heinemann Educational, London, 1980), p. 61.

32 *The National Plan*, Cmnd 2764, HMSO, London, 1965.

33 Roger Opie, 'Economic Planning and Growth', in Beckerman (ed.), *The Labour Government's Economic Record*, p. 163.

34 National Archives, CAB 128/ 39 CC (66), 35th Conclusions, 12 July 1966.

35 George Brown, *In My Way: The Political Memoirs of Lord George-Brown* (Victor Gollancz, London, 1971), p. 114.

36 Kenneth O. Morgan, *Callaghan: A Life* (Oxford University Press, Oxford, 1997), p. 245.

37 Barbara Castle, *The Castle Diaries 1964–70* (Weidenfeld & Nicolson, London, 1984), entry for 19 July 1966. Some devaluationists, Castle among them, favoured floating rather than devaluation to another fixed rate.

38 Morgan, *Callaghan*, p. 246.

39 Ibid., p. 257.

40 Alec Cairncross, *The Wilson Years: A Treasury Diary*, entries for 18 September and 4 November 1967.

41 Castle, *The Castle Diaries 1964–70*, entry for 16 November 1967.

42 Roy Jenkins, *A Life at the Centre* (Macmillan, London, 1991), p. 324.

43 Ibid., p. 220.

44 Jeffery Pickering, 'Politics and "Black Tuesday": shifting power in the Cabinet and the decision to withdraw from east of Suez, November 1967–January 1968', *Twentieth Century British History*, 13: 2 (2002), 144–70.

45 Barnes and Reid, *Government and the Trade Unions*, p. 105.

46 Dick Taverne, 'Chancellor of the Exchequer', in Andrew Adonis and Keith Thomas (eds), *Roy Jenkins: A Retrospective* (Oxford University Press, Oxford, 2004), p. 88; Jenkins, *A Life at the Centre*, pp. 276–8.

47 Ponting, *Breach of Promise*, pp. 249–56.

48 Helen Parr, 'The Foreign Office and Harold Wilson's Policy', in Oliver J. Haddow (ed.), *Harold Wilson and European Integration, Britain's Second Application to join the EEC* (Frank Cass, London, 2003), pp. 75–94.

49 Ziegler, *Wilson*, p. 335.

50 Dell, *The Chancellors*, p. 342.

51 Healey, *The Time of My Life*, p. 336.

52 Tony Benn, *Office Without Power: Diaries 1968–72* (Arrow Books, London, 1989), p. 63.

53 I write as a former plotter.

54 Ziegler, *Wilson*, p. 295.

55 Derek Robinson, 'Labour Market Policies', in Beckerman (ed.), *The Labour Government's Economic Record*, pp. 312–13.

56 Barbara Castle, *Fighting All the Way* (Macmillan, London, 1993), p. 402.

57 For the Commission and its sequel, see Taylor, *The Trade Union Question;* Barnes and Reid, *Government and the Trade Unions;* and Peter Jenkins, *The Battle of Downing Street* (Charles Knight & Co. Ltd, London, 1970).

58 Castle, *Fighting All the Way*, p. 413.

59 National Archives, CAB 128 CC (69) 22, Minute 1, 8 May 1969.

60 Castle, *Diaries 1964–70*, p. 673.

61 Crossman, *The Diaries of a Cabinet Minister*, vol. 3, entry for 21 April.

62 Sheila Rowbotham, *Promise of a Dream: Remembering the Sixties* (Allen Lane, The Penguin Press, London, 2000), p. 172.

63 Nick Thomas, 'Challenging myths of the 1960s: the case of student protest in Britain', *Twentieth Century British History*, 13: 3 (2002), 277–97.

64 For this see, in particular, Samuel H. Beer, *Britain Against Itself: The Political Contradictions of Collectivism* (Faber & Faber, London, 1982), Chapter 4.

65 Quoted in Jonathon Green, *Days in the Life: Views from the English Underground 1961–1971* (Heinemann, London, 1988), p. 426.

66 David Widgery, quoted in Jonathon Green, *Days in the Life: Voices from the English Underground 1961–1971* (Heinemann, London, 1988), p. 256.

67 Eric Hobsbawm, *Interesting Times: A Twentieth-Century Life* (Allen Lane, The Penguin

Press, London, 2002), pp. 249–50.

68 Herbert Marcuse, *One-Dimensional Man: Studies in the Ideology of Advanced Industrial Society* (Routledge & Kegan Paul, London, 1964), p. 256.

69 Rowbotham, *Promise of a Dream*, p. 164.

70 Tariq Ali, *Street Fighting Years: An Autobiography of the Sixties* (Verso edition, London, 2005), p. 304.

71 Colin Crouch, *The Student Revolt* (The Bodley Head, London, 1970), pp. 23–4.

72 Ibid., p. 56.

73 Green, *Days in the Life*, pp. 403 and 407.

74 Juliet Mitchell, 'Women: the Longest Revolution', reprinted in Juliet Mitchell, *Women: The Longest Revolution: Essays on Feminism, Literature and Psychoanalysis* (Virago, London, 1984), p. 54.

75 Beer, *Britain Against Itself*, p. 130.

76 Raymond Williams (ed.), *May Day Manifesto 1968* (Penguin Books, Harmondsworth, 1968), especially pp. 133–68.

77 James E. Cronin, *Industrial Conflict in Modern Britain* (Croom Helm, London, 1979), pp. 143–5.

78 Robinson, 'Labour Market', in Beckerman (ed.), *The Labour Government's Economic Record*, p. 332.

79 For these thunderbolts and their origins and sequel, see Alan Butt Philip, *The Welsh Question: Nationalism in Welsh Politics* (University of Wales Press, Cardiff, 1975); Kenneth O. Morgan, *Rebirth of a Nation: A History of Modern Wales* (Oxford University Press, paperback edition, Oxford, 1982); Christopher Harvie, *Scotland and Nationalism, Scottish Society and Politics 1707–1977* (George Allen & Unwin, London, 1977); and Tom Nairn, *The Break-up of Britain: Crisis and Neo-Nationalism* (NLB, London, 1977).

80 For the Northern Ireland story in this period, see J.J. Lee, *Ireland 1912–1985* (Cambridge University Press, Cambridge, 1989), Chapter 6; and Morgan, *Callaghan*, pp. 345–56.

81 For whom, see Simon Heffer, *Like the Roman: The Life of Enoch Powell* (Phoenix Giant edition, London, 1998); and Robert Shepherd, *Enoch Powell: A Biography* (Hutchinson, London, 1996).

82 Ibid., p. 19.

83 Ibid., p. 98.

84 J. Enoch Powell, *Freedom and Reality* (ed. John Wood), (Elliott Rightway Books, paperback edition, Kingswood, Surrey, 1969), pp. 338–9.

85 Heffer, *Like the Roman*, pp. 450–9.

8 LAST GASP

1 'The Conservative Manifesto 1970', in F.W.S. Craig (ed.), *British General Election Manifestos 1900–1974* (Macmillan Press, London and Basingstoke, 1975), pp. 325–44.

2 James Margach, quoted in John Campbell, *Edward Heath: A Biography* (Pimlico paperback edition, London, 1994), p. 269. See also Leonard, *A Century of Premiers*, Chapter 16.

3 Edward Heath, *The Course of My Life: My Autobiography* (Hodder & Stoughton, London, 1998), p. 44.

4 Ibid., p. 29.

5 His Quartermaster, Major Harrington, quoted in Campbell, *Edward Heath*, p. 44.

6 Douglas Hurd, *An End to Promises: Sketch of a Government 1970–74* (Collins, London, 1979), p. 14.

7   Heath, *The Course of My Life*, p. 28.

8   Craig, *Manifestos 1900–1974*, p. 330.

9   Claus Offe, *Disorganized Capitalism: Contemporary Transformations of Work and Politics* (MIT Press, Cambridge, Mass., 1985); Michael J. Piore and Charles F. Sabel, *The Second Industrial Divide: Possibilities for Prosperity* (Basic Books, New York, 1984); Philip Armstrong, Andrew Glyn and John Harrison, *Capitalism since World War II: The Making and Breakup of the Great Boom* (Fontana Paperbacks, London, 1984), Chapters 11 and 12.

10 John Williamson, *The Failure of World Monetary Reform, 1971–74* (Thomas Nelson & Sons, Sudbury-on-Thames, 1977), p. 15.

11 Richard Coopey and Nicholas Woodward, 'The British Economy in the 1970s: An Overview', in Richard Coopey and Nicholas Woodward (eds), *Britain in the 1970s: The Troubled Economy* (UCL Press, 1996), p. 4.

12 Halsey and Webb, *Social Trends*, Chapters 2 and 20.

13 John Solomos, *Race and Racism in Britain*, second edition (Macmillan Press, Basingstoke, 1993).

14 Richard Clutterbuck, *Britain in Agony: The Growth of Political Violence* (Faber & Faber, London and Boston, 1978), p. 166.

15 Stuart Ball, 'The Conservative Party and the Heath Government', in Stuart Ball and Anthony Seldon, *The Heath Government 1970–74: A Reappraisal* (Longman, London and New York, 1996), pp. 315–50.

16 Malcolm Bradbury, *The History Man*, first published 1975 (Arrow Books edition, London 1977).

17 Joanthon Green, *Days in the Life*, p. 407.

18 Germaine Greer, *The Female Eunuch*, first published 1970 (Paladin edition, London, 1971), pp. 315–31.

19 Anna Coote and Beatrix Campbell, *Sweet Freedom: The Struggle for Women's Liberation* (Basil Blackwell, Oxford, 1987 edition), Chapter 1.

20 Sheila Rowbotham, *The Past Is before Us: Feminism in Action since the 1960s* (Pandora Press, London, 1989), p. 5.

21 Heath, *The Course of My Life*, p. 336; Robert Taylor, *The Trade Union Question*, p. 188.

22 *Royal Commission on the Constitution*, vol. 1, *Report*; vol. 2, *Memorandum of Dissent*, Cmnd 5460 and 5460–I, HMSO, London, 1973.

23 Ibid., vol. 2, pp. 14–17.

24 For the details, see David Marquand, *The Unprincipled Society: New Demands and Old Politics* (Fontana edition, London, 1988), pp. 191–2.

25 John P. Mackintosh, 'The Declining Respect for the Law', in Anthony King (ed.), *Why is Britain Becoming Harder to Govern?* (British Broadcasting Corporation, London, 1976), p. 74.

26 Anthony King, 'Foreword', in King, *Why is Britain Becoming Harder to Govern?*, p. 6.

27 For the unravelling, see Martin Wallace, *British Government in Northern Ireland: From Devolution to Direct Rule* (David & Charles, Newton Abbot, 1982); Richard Rose, *Governing without Consensus: An Irish Perspective* (Faber & Faber, London, 1971); John McGarry and Brendan O'Leary, *The Future of Northern Ireland* (Clarendon Press, Oxford, 1990); F.S.L. Lyons, *Ireland since the Famine* (Fontana, London, 1973), pp. 760–80; and Campbell, *Heath*, Chapter 22.

28 For the death toll, see McGarry and O'Leary, *The Future of Northern Ireland*, p. 319.

29 Heffer, *Like the Roman*, pp. 555–65; David Butler and Michael Pinto-Duschinsky, *The British General Election of 1970* (Macmillan, London, 1971), *passim*.

30 The characterisation was coined by Christopher Soames, British Ambassador to

Paris. Soames to Sir Alec Douglas-Home, 9 June 1971. PREM 15/372;
www.margaretthatcher.orgi/archives/arcdocs/710609.

31 For Heathmen, see Andrew Roth, *Heath and the Heathmen* (Routledge & Kegan Paul,
London, 1972).

32 Christopher Lord, *British Entry to the European Community under the Heath Government
of 1970–4* (Dartmouth, Aldershot, 1993), pp. 16–74.

33 Sir Christopher Soames to Sir Denis Greenhill, 21 April 1971), PREM 15/371,
www.margaretthatcher.org/archives/arcdocs/710421.

34 The description is Douglas Hurd's: Hurd, *An End to Promises*, p. 63.

35 Edward Heath, *Old World, New Horizons: Britain, the Common Market and the Atlantic
Alliance* (Oxford University Press, London, 1970); Sir Bernard Burrows, 'European Secur-
ity', in Max Kohnstamm and Wolfgang Hager, *A Nation Writ Large?: Foreign Policy
Problems before the European Community* (Macmillan, London, 1973), pp. 128–52.

36 PREM 15/372, www.margaretthatcher.org/archive/arcdocs/710521.

37 www.margaretthatcher.org/archives/arcdocs/710520.

38 www.margaretthatcher.org/archives/arcdocs/710521.

39 Jenkins, *A Life at the Centre*, p. 320.

40 Quoted in Anthony Sampson, *Who Runs This Place?: The Anatomy of Britain in the 21st
Century* (John Murray, paperback edition, London, 2005), p. 367.

41 Heath, *The Course of My Life*, p. 334; see also Michael Moran, *The Politics of Industrial
Relations: The Origins, Life and Death of the 1971 Industrial Relations Act* (Macmillan,
London and Basingstoke, 1972), especially pp. 82–96; Robert Taylor, *The Trade Union
Question*, pp. 177–93.

42 Benn, *Office Without Power*, p. 337.

43 Jack Jones, *Union Man: The Autobiography of Jack Jones*, (Collins, London, 1986), p. 229.

44 Tony Benn, *Office Without Power*, p. 328; Eric Heffer, *The Class Struggle in Parliament: A
Socialist View of Industrial Relations* (Victor Gollancz, London, 1973), p. 231.

45 Robert Taylor, 'The Heath Government and Industrial Relations', in Ball and Seldon,
The Heath Government 1970–74, pp. 161–90. See also John Campbell, *Edward Heath*,
Chapter 21; and Clutterbuck, *Britain in Agony*, Chapters 3 and 4.

46 Clutterbuck, *Britain in Agony*, p. 59.

47 John Campbell, *Edward Heath*, p. 417.

48 National Archives, CAB 129/161/22, CP (72) 22.

49 John Campbell, *Edward Heath*, pp. 526–7.

50 Ibid., p. 528.

51 Quoted in Robert Taylor, 'The Heath Government', in Ball and Seldon, *The Heath
Government*, p. 152.

52 For which, see John Campbell, *Edward Heath*, Chapters 25 and 28–32; Stewart, *The Jekyll
and Hyde Years*; Barnes and Reid, *Governments and the Trade Unions*; Robert Taylor, *The
Trade Union Question*; and Keith Middlemas, *Power, Competition and the State*, vol. 2,
Threats to the Postwar Settlement: Britain 1961–74 (Macmillan Press, Basingstoke, 1990),
Chapter 10.

53 Jack Jones, *Union Man*, p. 259.

54 John Campbell, *Edward Heath*, p. 420.

55 Jack Jones, *Union Man*, p. 256.

56 John Campbell, *Edward Heath*, p. 477.

57 Quoted in Shepherd, *Enoch Powell*, p. 427.

58 Richard Rose, quoted in Shepherd, *Enoch Powell*, p. 406.

59 Philip Norton, *Conservative Dissidents: Dissent within the Conservative Parliamentary Party,*

1970–74 (Temple Smith, London, 1978), pp. 80–1.

60 Tony Benn, *Against the Tide: Diaries 1973–76* (Hutchinson, London, 1989), entry for 23 July 1973.

61 J. Enoch Powell, *Still to Decide*, (ed. John Wood), (B.T. Batsford, London, 1972), p. 149.

62 Quoted in Heffer, *Like the Roman*, p. 621.

63 Ibid., p. 658.

64 Richard Cockett, *Thinking the Unthinkable: Think-Tanks and the Economic Counter-Revolution, 1931–1983* (HarperCollins, London, 1994), Chapters 4 and 5.

65 R.J. Flanagan, David Soskice and Lloyd Ulman, *Unionism, Economic Stabilisation and Incomes Policies: European Experience* (The Brookings Institution, Washington DC, 1983), p. 370.

66 Blackaby (ed.), *British Economic Policy*, p. 278.

67 Ibid., p. 368.

68 National Archives, CAB 129/173/19, CP (73) 139.

69 John Campbell, *Edward Heath*, Chapter 31; Barnes and Reid, *Governments and the Trade Unions*, pp. 174–88; Robert Taylor, *The Trade Union Question*, pp. 206–14; Clutterbuck, *Britain in Agony*, Chapters 7 and 8.

70 Personal recollection.

71 John Campbell, *Edward Heath*, p. 577.

72 For the election, and these quotations, see David Butler and Dennis Kavanagh, *The British General Election of February 1974* (Macmillan Press, London and Basingstoke, 1974).

73 Clutterbuck, *Britain in Agony*, p. 85.

74 Andrew Denham and Mark Garnett, *Keith Joseph* (Acumen, Chesham, 2001).

75 Sir Keith Joseph, Bt, MP, *Reversing the Trend* (Barry Rose, Chichester and London, 1975).

76 Ibid., pp. 60 and 61.

77 Ibid., p. 5.

78 Commons *Hansard*, vol. 877, cols 1837–8, 25 July, 1974.

79 Keith Joseph, *Reversing the Trend*, p. 57.

80 Ibid., pp. 55 and 57.

81 Keith Joseph, quoted in Cockett, *Thinking the Unthinkable*, p. 237.

82 Peregrine Worsthorne, 'Too Much Freedom', in Maurice Cowling (ed.), *Conservative Essays* (Cassell, London, 1978), p. 147.

83 A classic statement of the case is Richard Rose and Guy Peters, *Can Government Go Bankrupt?* (Macmillan, London, 1979).

84 Samuel Brittan, 'The economic contradictions of Democracy', *British Journal of Political Science*, 5 (1975), p. 128.

85 Peter Jay, 'A General Hypothesis of Employment, Inflation and Politics' (Institute of Economic Affairs, London, 1976), p. 32.

86 The phrase is Kathleen Burk's: Kathleen Burk and Alec Cairncross, *Goodbye, Great Britain: The 1976 IMF Crisis* (Yale University Press, New Haven and London, 1992), p. 14.

87 Bernard Donoughue, *Downing Street Diary: With Harold Wilson in No. 10* (Jonathan Cape, London, 2005), *passim*; Joe Haines, *The Politics of Power* (Jonathan Cape, London, 1977), passim; Ziegler, *Wilson*, Chapters 12 and 13; Pimlott, *Wilson*, Chapters 27 and 28.

88 Benn, *Against the Tide, passim*; Castle, *The Castle Diaries 1974–76, passim.*

89 Castle, *The Castle Diaries 1974–6*, p. 340 (entry for 17 March 1975).

90 Jenkins, *A Life at the Centre*, p. 418.

91 I was one of them. For a fuller discussion of this point, see David Marquand, 'The Welsh

Wrecker', in Andrew Adonis and Keith Thomas (eds), *Roy Jenkins: A Retrospective* (Oxford University Press, Oxford, 2004), p. 114.

92 Tony Benn, *Arguments for Socialism* (ed. Chris Mullin), (Jonathan Cape, London, 1979), Chapter 1.

93 Benn, *Against the Tide*, p. 15 (entry for 30 March 1973).

94 Tony Benn, 'The New Politics: A Socialist Reconnaissance', in Benn, *Office Without Power: Diaries 1968–72*.

95 Benn, *Arguments for Socialism*, Chapter 2.

96 Stuart Holland, *The Socialist Challenge* (Quartet Books, London, 1975).

97 Craig (ed.), *British General Election Manifestos*, p. 403 (from Labour manifesto for February 1974).

98 Barnes and Reid, *Governments and the Trade Unions*, p. 194.

99 Castle, *The Castle Diaries 1974–6*, p. 20 (entry for 4 January 1974).

100 Joel Barnett, *Inside the Treasury* (André Deutsch, London, 1982), p. 49.

101 Burk and Cairncross, *Goodbye, Great Britain*; Edmund Dell, *A Hard Pounding: Politics and Economic Crisis, 1974–1976* (Oxford University Press, Oxford, 1991); Michael Artis and David Cobham (eds), *Labour's Economic Policies 1974–1979* (Manchester University Press, Manchester, 1991).

102 Leo Pliatzky, *Getting and Spending: Public Expenditure, Employment and Inflation* (Basil Blackwell, Oxford revised edition, 1984), p. 125.

103 Burk and Cairncross, *Goodbye Great Britain*, p. 15.

104 Artis and Cobham (eds), *Labour's Economic Policies*, p. 302.

105 *Kilbrandon Commission*, vol. 2, p. 24.

106 Bernard Donoughue, *Prime Minister: The Conduct of Policy under Harold Wilson and James Callaghan* (Jonathan Cape, London, 1987), p. 66.

107 National Archives, PREM 16/908, note by Sir John Hunt, 5 April 1976.

108 Susan Crosland, *Tony Crosland* (Coronet Books, London, paperback edition, 1983), pp. 355–6.

109 Burk and Cairncross, *Goodbye, Great Britain*, pp. 103 and 87.

110 Ibid., p. 244, footnote 51.

111 National Archives, CAB 128/60/13, CM (76) 35th Conclusions.

112 Tony Benn, *Parliament, People and Power: Agenda for a Free Society*, Interviews with New Left Review (Verso Editions and NLB, London, 1982), p. 33.

113 Robert Taylor, *The Trade Union Question*, p. 241; Donoughue, *Prime Minister*, pp. 149–50.

114 For the ensuing devolution saga see Vernon Bogdanor, *Devolution in the United Kingdom* (Oxford University Press, Oxford, 2001); and William Miller, 'The Scottish Dimension', in David Butler and Denis Kavanagh, *The British General Election of 1979* (Macmillan Press, London and Basingstoke, 1980), pp. 98–118.

115 H.M. Drucker and Gordon Brown, *The Politics of Nationalism and Devolution* (Longman, London, 1980), p. 113.

116 Quoted in Miller, 'The Scottish Dimension', p. 107.

117 David Butler and Gareth Butler, *Twentieth-Century British Political Facts 1900–2000* (Macmillan Press, Basingstoke, 2000), p. 274.

118 Morgan, *Callaghan*, p. 664.

119 Ibid., p. 683.

120 Donoughue, *Prime Minister*, p. 191.

9 WARRIOR QUEEN

1   John Campbell, *Margaret Thatcher*, 2 vols (Pimlico paperback editions, London, 2001 and 2004); Hugo Young, *One of Us* (Macmillan, London, 1989).

2   Margaret Thatcher, *The Path to Power* (HarperCollins, London, 1995), p. 565.

3   Young, *One of Us*, p. 245.

4   Quoted in Campbell, *Thatcher*, vol. 2, p. 303.

5   Campbell, *Thatcher*, vol. 1, pp. 354–5.

6   Campbell, *Thatcher*, vol. 2, p. 477.

7   Campbell, *Thatcher*, vol. 1, p. 47.

8   Young, *One of Us*, p. 233.

9   Campbell, *Thatcher*, vol. 2, p. 471.

10 Jonathan Raban, *God, Man and Mrs Thatcher* (Chatto & Windus, London, 1989), p. 4.

11 Simon Jenkins, *Accountable to None: The Tory Nationalisation of Britain* (Hamish Hamilton, London, 1995), p. 8.

12 Quoted in Brian Harrison, 'Thatcher and the intellectuals', *Twentieth Century British History*, 5: 2 (1994), p, 227.

13 Ibid., p. 227.

14 Campbell, *Thatcher*, vol. 1, p. 365.

15 Shirley Letwin, *The Anatomy of Thatcherism* (Fontana, London, 1992), p. 37.

16 Campbell, *Thatcher*, vol. 2, p. 3.

17 Peter Jenkins, *Mrs Thatcher's Revolution, The Ending of the Socialist Era* (Jonathan Cape, London, 1987), p. 66.

18 Quoted in Ian Gilmour, *Dancing with Dogma: Britain under Thatcherism* (Simon & Schuster, London, 1992), p. 105.

19 Letwin, *Thatcherism*, p. 33.

20 Campbell, *Thatcher*, vol. 2, p. 182.

21 Nigel Lawson, *The View from No. 11: Memoirs of a Tory Radical* (Corgi Books, London 1993), p. 64.

22 Butler and Butler, *Twentieth-Century British Political Facts*, p. 357.

23 Ibid., p. 294.

24 Dell, *The Chancellors*, p. 456; for the Thatcher Governments' economic policies, see also Campbell, *Thatcher*, vol. 2, *passim*; Lawson, *The View from No. 11*; Andrew Britton, *Macroeconomic Policy in Britain 1974–87* (Cambridge University Press, Cambridge, 1991); Cairncross, *The British Economy since 1945*, Chapter 6.

25 M.J. Antis and Mark P. Taylor, 'Abolishing Exchange Control: the UK Experience' (Centre for Economic Policy Research, Discussion Paper no. 294, February 1989).

26 Cairncross, *The British Economy since 1945*, p. 232.

27 Jeremy Seabrook, 'Unemployment Now and in the 1930s', in Bernard Crick (ed.), *Unemployment* (Methuen, London, 1981), p. 14.

28 Beatrix Campbell, *Wigan Pier Revisited: Poverty and Politics in the 80s* (Virago Press, London, 1985), p. 170.

29 Ralf Dahrendorf, *The Modern Social Conflict* (Weidenfeld & Nicolson, London, 1988).

30 *The Brixton Disorders 10–12 April 1981, Report of an Inquiry by the Rt Hon. The Lord Scarman OBE*, Cmnd. 8427 (HMSO, London, 1981).

31 Quoted in Michael Nally, 'Eyewitness in Moss Side', in John Benyon (ed.), *Scarman and After: Essays Reflecting on Lord Scarman's Report, the Riots and their Aftermath* (Pergamon Press, Oxford, 1998), p. 57.

32 Ibid., p. 54.

33 David Butler and Denis Kavanagh, *The British General Election of 1983* (Macmillan Press, London, 1984), p. 16.

34 Ivor Crewe and Anthony King, *SDP: The Birth, Life and Death of the Social Democratic Party* (Oxford University Press, Oxford, 1995), especially Chapter 16. I write as a founder member of the SDP and a former Alliance parliamentary candidate.

35 Philip Williams, 'The Labour Party: The Rise of the Left', in Hugh Berrington (ed.), *Change in British Politics* (Frank Cass, London, 1984), pp. 26–55.

36 For an alternative view of Foot, see Kenneth O. Morgan, *Michael Foot: A Life* (HarperCollins, London, 2007).

37 David Owen, *Face the Future* (Jonathan Cape, London, 1981).

38 Peter Jenkins, *Mrs Thatcher's Revolution*, p. 147.

39 Lawrence Freedman and Virginia Gamba-Stonehouse, *Signals of War: The Falklands Conflict of 1982* (Faber & Faber, London, 1990).

40 House of Commons, *The Falklands Campaign: A Digest of Debates in the House of Commons* (HMSO, London, 1982), p. 8.

41 Quoted in Peter Jenkins, *Mrs Thatcher's Revolution*, p. 163.

42 Thatcher Archive: CCOPR 405/82.

43 Freedman and Gamba-Stonehouse, *Signals of War*, Chapter 16.

44 Campbell, *Thatcher*, vol. 2, p. 154.

45 Dell, *The Chancellors*, pp. 484–8; Britton, *Macroeconomic Policy*, pp. 60–6.

46 Campbell, *Thatcher*, vol. 2, p. 135.

47 Lawson, *The View from No. 11*, p. 131.

48 Peter Riddell, *The Thatcher Government* (Martin Robertson, Oxford, 1983), p. 129.

49 Richard Pryke, 'The Comparative Performance of Public and Private Enterprise', in John Kay, Colin Mayer and David Thompson, *Privatisation and Regulation: The UK Experience* (Clarendon Press, Oxford, 1986), Chapter 5; Cento Veljanovski, *Selling the State: Privatisation in Britain* (Weidenfeld & Nicolson, London, 1987), Chapter 7; Matthew Bishop, John Kay and Colin Mayer (eds), *Privatization and Economic Performance* (Oxford University Press, Oxford, 1994), Chapter 1.

50 John Kay, 'Twenty Years of Privatisation', *Prospect* magazine, 1 June 2002.

51 Simon Jenkins, *Accountable to None*, p. 39.

52 A revealing example is Geoff Mulgan, 'Reticulated Organisations: The Birth and Death of the Mixed Economy', in Colin Crouch and David Marquand (eds), *Ethics and Markets: Co-operation and Competition in Capitalist Economies* (Blackwell Publishers, Oxford, 1993), pp. 31–47.

53 Nicholas Ridley, *My Style of Government: The Thatcher Years* (Hutchinson, London, 1991), pp. 67–8.

54 Anthony Sampson, *Changing Anatomy*, p. 66.

55 Martin Adeney and John Lloyd, *The Miners' Strike 1984–5: Loss without Limit* (Routledge and Kegan Paul, London, 1986), Chapter 3.

56 Campbell, *Thatcher*, vol. 2, p. 364.

57 Adeney and Lloyd, *The Miners' Strike*, p. 24.

58 Robert Taylor, *The Trade Union Question*, p. 294.

59 Campbell, *Thatcher*, vol. 2, p. 369.

60 Robert Taylor, *The Trade Union Question*, pp. 298–325.

61 Andrew Gamble, *The Free Economy and the Strong State: The Politics of Thatcherism* (Macmillan Education, Basingstoke and London, 1988), p. 218.

62 Robert Taylor, *The Trade Union Question*, pp. 380–1.

63 R.E. Rowthorn and J.R. Wells, *De-Industrialization and Foreign Trade* (Cambridge Uni-

versity Press, Cambridge, 1987), chapter 10.

64 Cairncross, *The British Economy since 1945*, p. 231.

65 Quoted in Stephen Pollard, *David Blunkett* (Hodder & Stoughton, London, 2005), p. 133.

66 The phrase is Anne Sofer's, quoted in Peter Jenkins, *Mrs Thatcher's Revolution*, p. 243.

67 For the saga, see David Butler, Andrew Adonis and Tony Travers, *Failure in British Government; The Politics of the Poll Tax* (Oxford University Press, Oxford, 1994); Simon Jenkins, *Accountable to None*, Chapter 3; Colin Crouch and David Marquand (eds), *The New Centralism: Britain Out of Step in Europe?* (Basil Blackwell, Oxford, 1989); Peter Jenkins, *Mrs Thatcher's Revolution*, Chapter 10; Campbell, *Thatcher*, vol. 2, pp. 371–84; Lawson, *The View from No. 11*, passim; Stephen Pollard, *Blunkett*, Chapters 6 and 7.

68 Quoted in Pollard, *Blunkett*, p. 145.

69 David Butler and Dennis Kavanagh, *The British General Election of 1987* (Macmillan Press, Basingstoke, 1988), p. 269.

70 Charles Webster, *The National Health Service: A Political History*, second edition (Oxford University Press, Oxford, 2002), p. 198.

71 I worked at Salford University throughout the 1980s.

72 Sir John Hoskyns, 'Conservatism is not enough', *The Political Quarterly*, 55: 1 (January–March 1984).

73 Quoted in Hugo Young, *One of Us*, p. 232.

74 Martin J. Smith, *The Core Executive in Britain* (Macmillan Press, Basingstoke, 1999), pp. 193–9.

75 www.derbydeadpool.co.uk/deadpool2000/obits/runcie.html.

76 *Faith in the City: A Call for Action by Church and Nation, The Report of the Archbishop of Canterbury's Commission on Urban Priority Areas* (Church House Publishing, London, 1985).

77 *Faith in the City*, pp. 52–3.

78 Ibid., p. 359.

79 Ibid., p. 25.

80 Campbell, *Thatcher*, vol. 2, p. 390.

81 Quoted in Campbell, *Thatcher*, vol. 2, p. 298.

82 A good source for the details is Christopher Johnson, *The Economy under Mrs Thatcher 1979–1990* (Penguin Books, Harmondsworth 1991).

83 Cain and Hopkins, *British Imperialism*, pp. 640–4, and the references therein.

84 Quoted in David Kynaston, *The City of London*, vol. 4, *A Club No More* (Chatto & Windus, London, 2001), pp. 720 and 705.

85 Colin Leys, *Market-Driven Politics: Neoliberal Democracy and the Public Interest* (Verso, London, 2001), p. 60; see also Andrew Adonis and Stephen Pollard, *A Class Act: The Myth of Britain's Classless Society* (Hamish Hamilton, London, 1997), Chapter 3.

86 Alan Watson, *A Conservative Coup: The Fall of Margaret Thatcher* (Gerald Duckworth, London, 1991), pp. 111–12.

87 *Social Justice, Strategies for National Renewal* (Report of the Commission on Social Justice, Vintage, London, 1994), pp. 29–30.

88 David Selbourne, *The Spirit of the Age: An Account of Our Times* (Sinclair-Stevenson, London, 1993), p. 219.

89 Britton, *Macroeconomic Policy*, Chapter 8.

90 Margaret Thatcher, *The Downing Street Years*, p. 722.

91 www.brugesgroup. com/mediacentre/index.live?article=92.

92 Thatcher, *The Downing Street Years*, p. 722.

93　For the bomb, and the eventual explosion, see Butler, Adonis and Travers, *Failure in British Government*; Simon Jenkins, *Accountable to None*, Chapter 3; and Campbell, *Thatcher*, vol. 2,

94　Ivor Crewe, 'Has the Electorate Become Thatcherite?', in Robert Skidelsky (ed.), *Thatcherism* (Basil Blackwell paperback edition, 1989), pp. 25–49.

95　Hugo Young, *This Blessed Plot*, p. 368.

96　For a powerful expression of this view, see Simon Jenkins, *Thatcher and Sons: A Revolution in Three Acts* (Allen Lane, London, 2006).

10　TURNING TIDE

1　Thatcher to Woodrow Wyatt, quoted in Campbell, *Thatcher*, vol. 2, p. 745.

2　Hugo Young, *This Blessed Plot*, p. 429.

3　Anthony Seldon with Lewis Baston, *Major: A Political Life* (Weidenfeld & Nicolson, London, 1997).

4　Douglas Hurd, *Memoirs* (Little Brown, London, 2003); Seldon, *Major*, p. 206.

5　Seldon, *Major*, pp. 389–90.

6　Social and Community Planning Research, *British Social Attitudes Cumulative Sourcebook*, (Gower, Aldershot, 1992), pp. A–2 to A–9.

7　Trevor Smith, 'Citizenship and the British Constitution', *Parliamentary Affairs*, 44: 4 (October 1991), 432–7.

8　Halsey and Webb (eds), *Twentieth-Century British Social Trends*, p. 54.

9　Ibid., p. 63; Central Statistical Office, *Social Trends* (HMSO, London, 1990), vol. 20, section 2.14.

10　Eric Jacobs and Robert Worcester, *We British: Britain under the MORIscope* (Weidenfeld & Nicolson, London, 1990), p. III.

11　Halsey and Webb (eds), *Twentieth-Century British Social Trends*, p. 60.

12　Ibid., pp. 681–4.

13　Central Statistical Office, *Social Trends*, vol. 20, Section 12.13.

14　Ibid., Section 12.9.

15　The Sir Norman Chester Centre for Football Research, www.le.ac.uk/footballresearch/resources/factsheets/fsl.html.

16　Halsey and Webb (eds), *Twentieth-Century British Social Trends*, Chapter 17.

17　Jacobs and Worcester, *We British*, p. 131.

18　Ian Gilmour, *Britain Can Work* (Martin Robertson, Oxford, 1983), and *Dancing with Dogma*.

19　Michael Heseltine, *Where There's a Will* (Hutchinson, London, 1987).

20　John Rentoul, *Me and Mine: The Triumph of the New Individualism?* (Unwin Hyman, London, 1989), p. II; Douglas Hurd, 'Citizenship in the Tory Democracy', *New Statesman*, 29 April 1988.

21　Rentoul, *Me and Mine*, p. 10.

22　John Gray, 'A Conservative Disposition', in John Gray (ed.), *Beyond the New Right: Markets, Government and the Common Environment* (Routledge, London and New York, 1993), especially pp. 62–5.

23　Ferdinand Mount, *The British Constitution Now: Recovery or Decline?* (Heinemann, London, 1992), p. 218.

24　Richard Rose, *The Prime Minister in a Shrinking World* (Polity Press, Cambridge, 2001), p. 65.

25 Alan Clark, *Diaries* (Phoenix paperback edition, London, 1993), p. 159.

26 Peregrine Worsthorne, *In Defence of Aristocracy* (HarperCollins, London, 2004), pp. 199–200.

27 Andrew Adonis, 'The Transformation of the Conservative Party in the 1980s', in Andrew Adonis and Tim Hames, *A Conservative Revolution: The Thatcher–Reagan Decade in Perspective* (Manchester University Press, Manchester and New York, 1994), pp. 145–67.

28 For the doctrinal differences at the grass roots of the party, see Paul Whiteley, Patrick Seyd and Jeremy Richardson, *True Blues: The Politics of Conservative Party Membership* (Clarendon Press, Oxford, 1994), pp. 126–60.

29 Butler and Butler, *Twentieth-Century British Political Facts*, p. 296.

30 William Cash, *Against a Federal Europe: The Battle for Britain* (Duckworth, London, 1991).

31 William Cash, *Against a Federal Europe*; Rt Hon. Lord Tebbit of Chingford, 'Address to the 5th Anniversary of the Foundation of the Bruges Group' (Bruges Group, Occasional Paper 15, London, 1994), p. 5.

32 J. Enoch Powell, 'How Not to Oppose Political Union', in Patrick Robertson (ed.), *Reshaping Europe in the Twenty-first Century* (Macmillan Press in association with the Bruges Group, Basingstoke, 1992), pp. 227–9.

33 Tebbit, 'Address', p. 14; Russell Lewis, 'Master Eurocrat – the Making of Jacques Delors' (Bruges Group, Occasional Paper 13, London, 1991), p. 9.

34 Hugo Young, *This Blessed Plot*, p. 401.

35 Jim Bulpitt, 'Conservatives and the Euro-Ratchet', *The Political Quarterly*, 63: 3 (July–September 1992), 258–75.

36 Christopher Gill, MP, 'Speaking Out on Europe' (Bruges Group, Occasional Paper 18, London, April 1995).

37 Cash, *Against a Federal Europe*, p. 3.

38 Hugo Young, *This Blessed Plot*, p. 424.

39 Paul Hirst, *Associative Democracy: New Forms of Economic and Social Governance* (Polity Press, Cambridge, 1994).

40 John Kay, 'The Stakeholder Corporation', in Dominic Kelly, Gavin Kelly and Andrew Gamble (eds), *Stakeholder Capitalism* (Macmillan Press, Basingstoke, 1997), pp. 125–41.

41 Michel Albert, *Capitalism Against Capitalism* (London, 1993; original French edition, Editions du Seuil, Paris 1991).

42 Will Hutton, *The State We're In* (Jonathan Cape, London, 1995).

43 Ibid., p. 326.

44 Commission on Wealth Creation and Social Cohesion, *Report on Wealth Creation and Social Cohesion in a free society (the Dahrendorf Report)*, (London, 1995), especially pp. 33–5. The author served on the Commission.

45 Quoted in Bernard Crick, 'For My Fellow English', in Owen Dudley Edwards (ed.), *A Claim of Right for Scotland* (Polygon, Edinburgh, 1989), p. 160.

46 Leslie Scarman, *English Law: The New Dimension* (Stevens & Sons, London, 1974).

47 Lord Hailsham, *The Dilemma of Democracy: Diagnosis and Prescription* (Collins, London, 1978), Chapters 20 and 21.

48 I write as one of the signatories.

49 Ronald Dworkin, *A Bill of Rights for Britain: Why British Liberty Needs Protecting* (Chatto & Windus, London, 1990), p. 36.

50 Roy Hattersley, *Choose Freedom: The Future for Democratic Socialism* (Michael Joseph, London, 1987).

51 *Meet the Challenge Make the Change: A New Agenda for Britain* (The Labour Party,

London, 1989); Martin Westlake, *Kinnock: The Biography* (Little Brown & Company, London, 2001), Chapter 18.

52 David Marquand, 'Half-way to Citizenship? The Labour Party and Constitutional Reform', in Martin J. Smith and Joanna Speer, *The Changing Labour Party* (Routledge, London, 1992).

53 Margaret Thatcher, *In Defence of Freedom: Speeches on Britain's Relations with the World* (Aurum Press, London, 1986), pp. 72–9.

54 Campbell, *Thatcher*, vol. 2, p. 392.

55 Kenyon Wright, *The People Say Yes, The Making of Scotland's Parliament* (Argyll Publishing, Argyle, 1997), pp. 140–1.

56 For the text, see Edwards (ed.), *A Claim of Right for Scotland.*

57 Ibid., p. 52.

58 Wright, *The People Say Yes*, p. 52.

59 Ceri Peach, Alisdair Rogers, Judith Chance and Patricia Daley, 'Immigration and Ethnicity', in A.H. Halsey with Josephine Webb (eds), *Twentieth-Century British Social Trends* (Macmillan Press, Basingstoke, 2000), Chapter 4.

60 Tariq Modood, 'Religious anger and minority rights', *The Political Quarterly*, 60: 3 (July–September 1989).

61 Malise Ruthven, *A Satanic Affair: Salman Rushdie and the Wrath of Islam* (The Hogarth Press, London, 1991), p. 1. My account of the Rushdie affair is heavily based on Ruthven's.

62 Bhikhu Parekh, 'Minority Rights, Majority Values', in David Miliband (ed.), *Reinventing the Left* (Polity Press, Cambridge, 1994), pp. 101–8.

63 Campbell, *Thatcher*, vol. 2, p. 473.

64 Mary Stott, *Before I Go: Reflections on My Life and Times* (Virago, London, 1985), pp. 6–7.

65 Coote and Campbell, *Sweet Freedom;* Paul Byrne, *Social Movements in Britain* (Routledge, London and New York, 1997), Chapter 7; Halsey and Webb (eds), *Twentieth-Century British Social Trends*, Chapters 7, 8 and 11.

66 Quoted in Andrew Dobson, *Green Political Thought* (Routledge, London and New York, second edition, 1995), p. 62.

67 Jonathon Porritt, *Seeing Green: The Politics of Ecology Explained* (Basil Blackwell, Oxford, reprinted 1986), p. 110.

68 W. Fox, quoted in Dobson, *Green Political Thought*, p. 57.

69 World Commission on Environment and Development, *Our Common Future* (Oxford University Press, Oxford, 1987).

70 Byrne, *Social Movements in Britain*, Chapter 8.

71 Butler, Adonis and Travers, *Failure in British Government*, pp. 170–83.

72 David Butler and Dennis Kavanagh, *The British General Election of 1992* (Macmillan, Basingstoke, 1992).

73 Philip Stephens, *Politics and the Pound: The Tories, the Economy and Europe* (Papermac edition, London, 1997).

74 Seldon, *Major*, p. 312.

75 Stephens, *Politics and the Pound*, pp. 292–3.

76 Quoted in Sir Christopher Foster, *British Government in Crisis, or the Third English Revolution* (Hart Publishing, Oxford, and Portland, Oregon, 2005), p. 113.

77 Simon Jenkins, *Thatcher and Sons*, p. 165.

78 Martin J. Smith, *Core Executive*, p. 194.

79 Simon Jenkins, *Thatcher and Sons*, pp. 175–88; David Marquand, *Decline of the Public: The Hollowing Out of Citizenship* (Polity Press, Cambridge, 2004), Chapter 4.

80 Michael Power, *The Audit Explosion* (Demos, London, 1994).

81 Ibid., pp. 48–9.

82 An insight I owe to Simon Head.

11 YOUNG LOCHINVAR

1 John Rentoul, *Tony Blair: Prime Minister* (Little Brown & Company (UK), London, 2001), p. 323.

2 'A political earthquake', leader article in *Guardian*, 2 May 1997.

3 Tony Blair, *New Britain: My Vision of a Young Country* (Fourth Estate, London, 1996), p. 16.

4 1997 Labour Party manifesto, www.labour-party.org/manifestos/1997/1997–labour-manifesto.shtml.

5 Quoted in Sampson, *Who Runs this Place?* p. 83.

6 John Sopel, *Tony Blair: The Moderniser* (Michael Joseph, London, 1995), p. 135.

7 Philip Gould, *The Unfinished Revolution: How the Modernisers Saved the Labour Party* (Little Brown & Company (UK), London, 1998).

8 Paul Routledge, *Gordon Brown: The Biography* (Simon & Schuster, London, 1998), p. 181.

9 They might not have approved of the wording, however, and they would have blanched at the misleading opening sentence: 'The Labour Party is a democratic socialist party.'

10 Anthony Seldon with Chris Ballinger, Daniel Collins and Peter Snowdon, *Blair* (The Free Press (paperback edition), London, 2005), p. 14.

11 Private information.

12 'Spellbinding' was Blair's word. Rentoul, *Tony Blair*, p. 35.

13 Sarah Hale, 'Professor Macmurray and Mr Blair: The strange case of the communitarian guru that never was', *The Political Quarterly*, 73: 2 (April–June 2002), 191–7.

14 Reprinted in *Daily Telegraph*, 16 June 2006.

15 Sopel, *Tony Blair*, p. 141.

16 Blair, *New Britain*, p. 45.

17 Alastair Campbell and Richard Stott (eds), *The Blair Years: Extracts from the Alastair Campbell Diaries* (Hutchinson, London, 2007), p. 467.

18 Blair, *New Britain*, p. 65.

19 Stephen Haseler, *The Super Rich: The Unjust New World of Global Capitalism* (Macmillan Press, Basingstoke, 2000), pp. 1–26.

20 http://wikipedia.org/wiki/List–of–billionaires–%282007%29.

21 http://politics.guardian.co.uk/funding/Story/O,,1945280,,00.html.

22 Although not as sleazy as the once-prominent Conservative politicians Jonathan Aitken and Jeffrey Archer, both of whom were imprisoned for perjury.

23 www.telegraph.co.uk/core/Content/displayPrintable.jhtml;jsessionid=OK24SLVSQOWFTL

24 Quoted in Sampson, *Who Runs This Place?* p. 81.

25 Rose, *The Prime Minister*, p. 225.

26 Gould, *The Unfinished Revolution*, p. 396.

27 Rentoul, *Tony Blair*, pp. 345–6.

28 Rose, *The Prime Minister*, p. 219.

29 Ibid., p. 88.

30 Sir Christopher Foster, *British Government in Crisis* (Hart Publishing, Oxford, 2005), p. 173.

31   Peter Hennessy, 'The Blair Style and the Requirements of Twenty-first Century Prem-
     iership', *The Political Quarterly*, 71: 4 (October–December 2000), 388.
32   Mo Mowlam, *Momentum: The Struggle for Peace, Politics and the People* (Hodder &
     Stoughton, London, 2002), Chapter 12.
33   Peter Stothard, *30 Days: A Month at the Heart of Blair's War* (HarperCollins, London,
     2003), p. 31.
34   Hutton Inquiry, transcript of evidence for 13 August 2003.
35   Foster, *British Government in Crisis*, Chapter 15.
36   *Review of Intelligence on Weapons of Mass Destruction, Report of a Committee of Privy
     Councillors* (the Butler Report), HC 898 (Stationery Office, London, 2004), para. 67.
37   *Spectator*, 11 December 2004, www.theage.com.au/news/World/Blair-gets-scathing-
     thumbsdown/2004/12/10/11026255.
38   Quoted in Peter Hennessy, 'The Blair Style', p. 388.
39   Quoted in Sampson, *Who Runs This Place?*, p. 60.
40   Gould, *The Unfinished Revolution*, pp. 391–9.
41   Michael Freeden, 'New Labour and Social Democratic Thought', in Andrew Gamble
     and Tony Wright (eds), *The New Social Democracy* (Blackwell, Oxford, 1999), p. 152.
42   Anthony Giddens, *The Third Way: The Renewal of Social Democracy* (Polity Press, Cam-
     bridge, 1998); and *The Third Way and its Critics* (Polity Press, Cambridge, 2000).
43   James MacGregor Burns, *Roosevelt: The Lion and the Fox 1882–1940* (Secker & Warburg,
     London, 1956).
44   It can be read at http://cain.ulst.ac.uk/events/peace/docs/agreement.htm. My account is
     also based on Brendan O'Leary, 'The Belfast Agreement and the Labour Government',
     in Anthony Seldon (ed.), *The Blair Effect 1997–2001* (Little, Brown & Company, London,
     2001); John McGarry and Brendan O'Leary, *The Northern Ireland Conflict: Consociational
     Engagements* (Oxford University Press, Oxford, 2004); and Jonathan Tonge, *Northern
     Ireland* (Polity Press, Cambridge, 2006).
45   Commons *Hansard*, 20 April 1998, cols 479–80.
46   Campbell, *Diaries*, p. 290.
47   Personal information.
48   Bogdanor, *Devolution in the United Kingdom* pp. 287–92.
49   Vernon Bogdanor, 'Constitutional Reform', in Seldon (ed.), *The Blair Effect 1997–2001*,
     pp. 130–58.
50   Quoted in Iain Maclean, 'The National Question', in Seldon (ed.), *The Blair Effect 1997–
     2001*, p. 436.
51   Mark D'Arcy and Rory Maclean, *Nightmare: The Race to Become London's Mayor*,
     (Politico's, London, 2000).
52   Robin Cook, *The Point of Departure* (Simon & Schuster, London, 2003), pp. 274–9.
53   Blair, *New Britain*, p. 220.
54   Labour Party manifesto, 1997 general election, www.labour-party.org.uk/
     manifestos/1997/1997–labour-manifesto.st.
55   Tony Travers, 'Local Government', in Seldon (ed.), *The Blair Effect, 1997–2001*, Chapter 6.
56   David Beetham, Iain Byrne, Pauline Ngan and Stuart Weir, *Democracy Under Blair: A
     Democratic Audit of the United Kingdom* (Politico's Publishing, London, 2002), pp. 263–
     4.
57   Blair, *New Britain*, p. 237.
58   Ibid., pp. 236–8.
59   www.publications.uk/pa/cm200203/cmhansard/cm030507/debtext/30507.
60   Andrew Gamble, 'The Meaning of the Third Way', in Anthony Seldon and Dennis

Kavanagh (eds), *The Blair Effect 2001–5* (Cambridge University Press, Cambridge, 2005), pp. 430–8.

61 Desmond King, *In the Name of Liberalism: Illiberal Social Policy in the United States and Britain* (Oxford University Press, Oxford, 1999), pp. 255–7.

62 Blair, quoted in Rentoul, *Tony Blair, Prime Minister*, p. 533.

63 Ibid, p. 534.

64 Robert Preston, *Brown's Britain* (Short Books, paperback edition, London, 2006); Francis Beckett, *Gordon Brown: Past, Present and Future* (Hans Books London, 2007).

65 Gordon Brown, *Maxton* (Mainstream Publishing, Edinburgh, 1986), p. 313.

66 Labour Party Conference speech, 26 September 2005, www.labour.org.uk/news/ac05gb.

67 The phrase was Kenneth Clarke's, quoted in David Smith, 'The Treasury and Economic Policy', in Seldon and Kavanagh (eds), *The Blair Effect 2001–5*, p. 170.

68 Preston, *Brown's Britain*, Chapter 8.

69 Kitty Stewart, 'Equality and Social Justice', in A. Seldon and P. Kavanagh, *The Blair Effect 2001–5* (Bloomsbury, London, 2006), pp. 306–35.

70 Seldon and Kavanagh (eds), *The Blair Effect 2001–5*, pp. 286 and 274.

71 Wilf Stevenson (ed.), Gordon Brown, *Moving Britain Forward: Selected Speeches 1997–2006*, pp. 140–80.

72 www.labour-party.org.uk/manifestos/1997/1997–labour-manifesto.shtml.

73 Guildhall speech, 11 November 1997, quoted in John Kampfner, *Blair's Wars* (The Free Press, paperback edition, London, 2004), p. 17.

74 Commons *Hansard*, June 2003, cols 407–15.

75 Kampfner, *Blair's Wars*, p. 56.

76 www.number10.gov.uk/output/Page1297.asp.

77 For Gladstone, see Matthew, *Gladstone, 1875–1898*, chapters 1, 2 and 6; for Blair, see Seldon et al., *Blair*, Chapter 34.

78 Matthew, *Gladstone*, p. 123.

79 The phrase is Peter Riddell's: Peter Riddell, *Hug Them Close: Blair, Clinton, Bush and the 'Special Relationship'* (Politico's, London, 2003), p. 161.

80 Tony Blair, Labour Party conference speech, 2 October 2001, www.angelfire.com/home/pearly/htmls1/terror-blair.html.

81 Stothard, *30 Days*, p. 87.

82 Cook, *The Point of Departure*, p. 298.

83 Ibid., p. 299.

84 Louis Blom-Cooper, 'Government and the Judiciary', in Seldon and Kavanagh (eds), *The Blair Effect 2001–5*, p. 253.

85 Quoted in Seldon et al., *Blair*, p. 517.

86 Blair, *New Britain*, pp. 60–1.

87 www.number-10.gov.uk/output/Page6129.asp.

88 Quoted in David Runciman, *The Politics of Good Intentions: History, Fear and Hypocrisy in the New World Order* (Princeton University Press, Princeton and Oxford, 2006), p. 205.

89 www.iraqanalysis.org/mortality/432.

90 Declassified Key Judgments of the National Intelligence Estimate, 'Trends in Global Terrorism: Implications for the United States', April 2006, www.dni.gov.

91 *Report of the Inquiry into the Circumstances Surrounding the Death of Dr David Kelly CMG by Lord Hutton*, January 2004, HC 247; *Review of Intelligence on Weapons of Mass Destruction* (the Butler Report).

12 EPILOGUE

1 www.number10.gov.uk/output/Page12274.asp
2 *The Governance of Britain*, CM 7170, London, July 2007.
3 For whom see Francis Elliott and James Hanning, *Cameron: The Rise of the New Conservative* (Fourth Estate, London, 2007).
4 Ibid., p. 231.
5 The Conservative Party website, www.conservatives/com/tile.do?def=david.cameron.speeches
6 www.natcen.ac.uk/natcen/pages/news_and_media_docs/BSA_%20press_release_Jan07.pdf.
7 Christopher G.A. Bryant, *The Nations of Britain* (Oxford University Press, Oxford, 2006), p. 5.
8 Guy Lodge and Katie Schmuecker, *The End of the Union?*, in *IPPR Public Policy Research*, June-August 2007), p. 93.
9 Joseph Rowntree Reform Trust, Ltd, *State of the Nation Poll 2004*.
10 www.ipsos-mori.com/publications/rd/trust.shtml.
11 www.ipsos-mori.com/polls/2002/uea.shtml.
12 www.ipsos-mori.com/publications/rd/who-do-you-believe.shtml.
13 Quoted in Sampson, *Who Runs This Place?*, p. 45.
14 Quoted in Charles Pattie, Patrick Seyd and Paul Whitely, *Citizenship in Britain: Values, Participation and Democracy* (Cambridge University Press, Cambridge, 2004), p. xvi.
15 Anthony Sampson, *Who Runs this Place?*, p. 232.
16 John Lloyd, *What the Media Are Doing to Our Politics* (Constable, London, 2004) p. 17.
17 Onora O'Neill, *A Question of Trust* (Cambridge University Press, Cambridge, 2002), pp. 90–1. See also Lloyd, *What the Media Are Doing to Our Politics*.
18 www.number10. gov.uk/output/Page13630.asp.
19 Pattie, Seyd and Whitely, *Citizenship in Britain*, pp. 48–56.
20 Ibid., p. 170.
21 Ibid., pp. 87–91.
22 Ibid., p. 83.
23 www.internetworldstats.com/emarketing.htm.

SELECT BIBLIOGRAPHY

Public records in the National Archives, parliamentary debates and records downloaded from the internet are indicated in the Notes.

BOOKS, ARTICLES, CHAPTERS IN BOOKS AND UNOFFICIAL REPORTS

Acheson, Dean, *Present at the Creation: My Years in the State Department*, Hamish Hamilton, London, 1970

Adamthwaite, Anthony, 'Britain and the world, 1945–9: The View from the Foreign Office', *International Affairs*, vol. 61, Spring 1985

Addison, Christopher (et al.), *Problems of a Socialist Government*, Victor Gollancz Ltd, London, 1933

Addison, Paul, *The Road to 1945: British Politics and the Second World War*, Jonathan Cape, London, 1975

Adeney, Martin and Lloyd, John, *The Miners' Strike 1984–5: Loss Without Limit*, Routledge & Kegan Paul, London, 1986

Adonis, Andrew and Thomas, Keith (eds), *Roy Jenkins: A Retrospective*, Oxford University Press, Oxford, 2004

Adonis, Andrew and Pollard, Stephen, *A Class Act: The Myth of Britain's Classless Society*, Hamish Hamilton, London, 1997

Adonis, Andrew and Hames, Tim, *A Conservative Revolution: The Thatcher–Reagan Decade in Perspective*, Manchester University Press, Manchester and New York, 1994

Albert, Michel, *Capitalism Against Capitalism*, London, 1993 (original edition Editions du Seuil, Paris, 1991)

Ali, Tariq, *Street Fighting Years: An Autobiography of the Sixties*, Verso edition, London, 2005

Almond, Gabriel and Verba, Sidney, *The Civic Culture: Political Attitudes and Democracy in Five Nations*, Princeton University Press, Princeton, New Jersey, 1963

Amery, L.S., *Thoughts on the Constitution*, Oxford University Press, paperback edition, Oxford, 1964

Anderson, Perry, 'Critique of Wilsonism', *New Left Review*, September–October 1964

Anderson, Perry and Blackburn, Robin (eds), *Towards Socialism*, Cornell University Press edition, Ithaca, New York, 1966

Annan, Noel, *Our Age: Portrait of a Generation*, Weidenfeld & Nicolson, London, 1990

Armstrong, Philip, Glyn, Andrew, and Harrison, John, *Capitalism Since World War II: The Making and Breakup of the Great Boom*, Fontana Paperbacks, London, 1984

Artis, M.J. and Taylor, Mark P., 'Abolishing Exchange Control: the UK Experience', Centre for Economic Policy Research, Discussion Paper no. 294, February 1989

Artis, Michael and Cobham, David (eds), *Labour's Economic Policies 1974–1979*, Manchester University Press, Manchester, 1991

Baldwin, A.W., *My Father: The True Story*, George Allen & Unwin, London, 1956

Baldwin of Bewdley, Earl, *An Interpreter of England*, Hodder & Stoughton, London, 1939

Bale, Tim, 'Dynamics of a non-decision: the "failure" to devalue the pound, 1964–7', *Twentieth Century British History*, vol. 10, no. 2, 1999

Ball, Stuart and Seldon, Anthony, *The Heath Government 1970–74: A Reappraisal*, Longman, London and New York, 1996

Barnes, Denis and Reid, Eileen, *Government and the Trade Unions: The British Experience 1964–79*, Heinemann Educational, London, 1980

Barnett, Joel, *Inside the Treasury*, André Deutsch, London, 1982

Barrow, Logie and Bullock, Ian, *Democratic Ideas and the British Labour Movement, 1890–1914*, Cambridge University Press, Cambridge, 1996

Beckerman, Wilfred (ed.) *The Labour Government's Economic Record: 1964–1970*, Duckworth, London, 102

Beckett, Francis, *Gordon Brown: Past, Present and Future*, Haus Books, London, 2007

Beer, Samuel H., *Modern British Politics: A Study of Parties and Pressure Groups*, Faber & Faber, London, 1965

Beer, Samuel H., *Britain Against Itself: The Political Contradictions of Collectivism*, Faber & Faber, London, 1982

Beer, Samuel H., *To Make a Nation: The Rediscovery of American Federalism*, Belknap Press, Cambridge, Mass., 1994

Beetham, David, Byrne, Ian, Ngan, Pauline and Weir, Stuart, *Democracy Under Blair: A Democratic Audit of the United Kingdom*, Politico's Publishing, London, 2002

Benn, Tony, *Arguments for Socialism* (ed. Chris Mullin), Jonathan Cape, London, 1979

Benn, Tony, *Parliament, People and Power: Agenda for a Free Society*, Interviews with New Left Review, Verso Editions and NLB, London, 1982

Benn, Tony, *Out of the Wilderness: Diaries 1963–67*, Hutchinson, London, 1987

Benn, Tony, *Against the Tide: Diaries 1976–76*, Hutchinson, London, 1989

Benn, Tony, *Office Without Power: Diaries 1968–72*, Arrow Books, London, 1989

Benn, Tony, 'The New Politics: A Socialist Reconnaissance', in Benn, *Office Without Power: Diaries 1968–72*, Arrow Books, London, 1989

Bevan, Aneurin, *In Place of Fear*, William Heinemann Ltd, London, 1952

Biagini, Eugenio F., *Liberty, Retrenchment and Reform: Popular Liberalism in the Age of Gladstone, 1860–1880*, Cambridge University Press, Cambridge

Birkenhead, Lord, *Walter Monckton: The Life of Viscount Monckton of Benchley*, Weidenfeld & Nicolson, London, 1969

Birkenhead, The Earl of, *Halifax: The Life of Lord Halifax*, Hamish Hamilton, London, 1965

Bishop, Matthew, Kay, John and Mayer, Colin (eds), *Privatization and Economic Performance*, Oxford University Press, Oxford, 1994

Blackaby, F.T. (ed.), *British Economic Policy 1960–74*, Cambridge University Press, Cambridge, 1978

Blair, Tony, *New Britain: My Vision of a Young Country*, Fourth Estate, London, 1996

Blake, Robert and Louis, Wm. Roger, *Churchill*, Oxford University Press, Oxford, 1994

Bogdanor, Vernon, *Devolution in the United Kingdom*, Oxford University Press, Oxford, 2001

Booth, Alan, *British Economic Policy 1931–1945: Was There a Keynesian Revolution?*, Harvester Wheatsheaf, Hemel Hempstead, 1989

Bradbury, Malcolm, *The History Man*, first published 1975, Arrow Books edition, London, 1977

Brailsford, H.N., *The Levellers and the English Revolution*, The Cresset Press, London, 1961

Bridge, Carl, *Holding Britain to the Empire: The British Conservative Party and the 1935 Constitution*, Envoy Press, New York, 1986

Briggs, Asa, *Victorian Cities*, Odhams Press, London, 1963

Brittan, Samuel, *Steering the Economy*, Penguin, Harmondsworth, 1971

Brittan, Samuel, 'The economic contradictions of democracy', *British Journal of Political Science*, vol. 5, 1975

Britton, Andrew, *Macroeconomic Policy in Britain 1974–87*, Cambridge University Press, Cambridge, 1991

Brooke, Stephen, *Labour's War: The Labour Party during the Second World War*, Clarendon Press, Oxford, 1992

Brown, George, *In My Way: The Political Memoirs of Lord George-Brown*, Victor Gollancz, London, 1971

Brown, Gordon, *Maxton*, Mainstream Publishing, Edinburgh, 1986

Brown, Judith M. and Louis, Wm. Roger (eds), *The Oxford History of the British Empire*, vol. 4, *The Twentieth Century*, Oxford University Press, Oxford and New York, 1999

Bryant, Christopher G.A., *The Nations of Britain*, Oxford University Press, Oxford, 2006

Bullock, Alan, *The Life and Times of Ernest Bevin*, 3 vols, Heinemann, London, 1960–83

Bulpitt, Jim., 'Conservatives and the Euro-ratchet', *The Political Quarterly*, vol. 63, no. 3, July–September 1992

Burk, Kathleen and Cairncross, Alec, *Goodbye, Great Britain: The 1976 IMF Crisis*, Yale University Press, New Haven and London, 1992

Burke, Edmund, *Reflections on the Revolution in France*, in *The Works and Correspondence of the Right Honourable Edmund Burke*, vol. 4, Francis and John Rivington, London, 1852

Burns, James McGregor, *Roosevelt: the Lion and the Fox 1882–1940*, Secker & Warburg, London, 1956

Butler, D.E. and King, Anthony, *The British General Election of 1964*, Macmillan, London, 1965

Butler, David and Pinto-Duschinsky, Michael, *The British General Election of 1970*, Macmillan, London, 1971

Butler, David and Kavanagh, Dennis, *The British General Election of February 1974*, Macmillan Press, London and Basingstoke 1974

Butler, David and Kavanagh, Dennis, *The British General Election of 1979*, Macmillan Press, London and Basingstoke, 1980

Butler, David and Kavanagh, Dennis, *The British General Election of 1983*, Macmillan Press, London, 1984

Butler, David and Kavanagh, Dennis, *The British General Election of 1987*, Macmillan Press, Basingstoke, 1988

Butler, David and Kavanagh, Dennis, *The British General Election of 1992*, Macmillan, Basingstoke, 1992

Butler, David, Adonis, Andrew and Travers, Tony, *Failure in British Government: The Politics of the Poll Tax*, Oxford University Press, Oxford, 1994

Butler, David and Butler, Gareth, *Twentieth-Century British Political Facts, 1900–2000*, Macmillan Press, Basingstoke, 2000

Butler, Lord, *The Art of the Possible: The Memoirs of Lord Butler*, Hamish Hamilton, London, 1971

Cain, P.J. and Hopkins, A.G., *British Imperialism, 1688–2000*, Longman, London, 2002

Cairncross, Sir Alec, *Years of Recovery: British Economic Policy 1945–51*, Methuen, London, 1985

Cairncross, Alec, *The British Economy since 1945*, Blackwell, Oxford, 1992

Cairncross, Alec, *The Wilson Years: A Treasury Diary 1964–1969*, Historians' Press, London, 1997

Cairncross, Alec and Eichengreen, Barry, *Sterling in Decline: The Devaluations of 1931, 1949 and 1967*, Blackwell, Oxford, 1983

Cairncross, Sir Alec (ed.), Sir Richard Clarke, *Anglo-American Economic Collaboration 1942–1949*, Clarendon Press, Oxford, 1982

Campbell, Beatrix, *Wigan Pier Revisited: Poverty and Politics in the 80s*, Virago Press, London, 1985

Campbell, John, *Nye Bevan and the Mirage of British Socialism*, Weidenfeld & Nicolson, London, 1987

Campbell, John, *Edward Heath: A Biography*, Pimlico paperback edition, London, 1994

Campbell, John, *Margaret Thatcher*, 2 vols, Pimlico paperback editions, London, 2001 and 2004

Camps, Miriam, *Britain and the European Community, 1955–1963*, Oxford University Press, London, 1964

Cannadine, David, *The Decline and Fall of the British Aristocracy*, Yale University Press, New Haven and London, 1990

Cannadine, David, *G.M. Trevelyan: A Life in History*, HarperCollins, London, 1992

Cannadine, David, *Class in Britain*, Yale University Press, New Haven and London, 1998

Cannadine, David, *Ornamentalism: How the British Saw Their Empire*, Penguin Books edition, London 2002

Carlton, David, *Anthony Eden: A Biography*, Allen Lane, London, 1981

Carlyle, Thomas, *Shooting Niagara: And After?*, Chapman & Hall, London, 1867

Carpenter, Humphrey, *That Was Satire that Was: The Satire Boom of the 1960s*, Victor Gollancz, London, 2000

Cash, William, *Against a Federal Europe: The Battle for Britain*, Duckworth, London, 1991

Castle, Barbara, *The Castle Diaries 1974–76*, Weidenfeld & Nicolson, London, 1980

Castle, Barbara, *The Castle Diaries 1964–70*, Weidenfeld & Nicolson, London 1984

Castle, Barbara, *Fighting All the Way*, Macmillan, London, 1993

Cecil, Lady Gwendolen, *Life of Robert, Marquis of Salisbury*, Hodder & Stoughton, vol. 1, London, 1921

Charmley, John, *Churchill: The End of Glory, A Political Biography*, Sceptre, London, 1995 edition

Charmley, John, *Churchill's Grand Alliances: The Anglo-American Special Relationship, 1940–57*, Hodder & Stoughton, London, 1995

Chester, Sir Norman, *The Nationalisation of British Industry, 1945–51*, HMSO, London, 1975

Churchill, Winston S., *A History of the English-speaking Peoples*, 4 vols, Cassell & Co., London, 1956–8

Clark, Alan, *Diaries*, Phoenix paperback edition, London, 1993

Clarke, Peter, *The Cripps Version: The Life of Sir Stafford Cripps*, Allen Lane/The Penguin Press, London, 2002

Clifford, Christopher, 'The rise and fall of the Department of Economic Affairs 1964–69: British government and indicative planning', *Contemporary British History*, vol. 11, no. 2, Summer 1997

Clutterbuck, Richard, *Britain in Agony: The Growth of Political Violence*, Faber & Faber, London and Boston, 1978

Cockett, Richard, *Thinking the Unthinkable: Think-Tanks and the Economic Counter-Revolution, 1931–1983*, HarperCollins, London, 1994

Colley, Linda, *Britons: Forging the Nation 1707–1837*, Yale University Press, London, 1992

Collini, Stefan (ed.), *Matthew Arnold: Culture and Anarchy and Other Writings*, Cambridge University Press, Cambridge, 1993

Commission on Wealth Creation & Social Cohesion, *Report on Wealth Creation and Social Cohesion in a Free Society (the Dahrendorf Report)*, London, 1995

Cook, Robin, *The Point of Departure*, Simon & Schuster, London, 2003

Cooke, Alistair B. and Vincent, John, *The Governing Passion: Cabinet Government and Party Politic in Britain 1885–6*, Harvester Press, Brighton, 1974

Coopey, Richard and Woodward, Nicholas (eds), *Britain in the 1970s: The Troubled Economy*, UCL Press, 1996

Coote, Anna and Campbell, Beatrix, *Sweet Freedom: The Struggle for Women's Liberation*, Basil Blackwell, Oxford, 1987

Cowling, Maurice, *1867 Disraeli, Gladstone and Revolution: The Passing of the Second Reform Bill*, Cambridge University Press, Cambridge, 1967

Cowling, Maurice (ed.), *Conservative Essays*, Cassell, London, 1978

Craig, F.W.S. (ed.), *British General Election Manifestos 1918–1966*, Political Reference Publications, Chichester, 1970

Craig, F.W.S., *British General Election Manifestos 1900–1974*, Macmillan Press, London and Basingstoke, 1975

Crewe, Ivor, 'Has the Electorate Become Thatcherite?', in Robert Skidelsky (ed.), *Thatcherism*, Basil Blackwell paperback edition, London, 1989

Crewe, Ivor and King, Anthony, *SDP: The Birth, Life and Death of the Social Democratic Party*, Oxford University Press, Oxford, 1995

Crick, Bernard, *George Orwell: A Life*, Secker & Warburg, London, 1980

Crick, Bernard, 'For My Fellow English', in Owen Dudley Edwards (ed.), *A Claim of Right for Scotland*, Polygon, Edinburgh, 1989

Cronin, James E., *Industrial Conflict in Modern Britain*, Croom Helm, London, 1979

Crosland, C.A.R., *The Future of Socialism*, Jonathan Cape, London, 1956

Crosland, Susan, *Tony Crosland*, Coronet Books, London, paperback edition, 1983

Crossman, Richard, *The Diaries of a Cabinet Minister*, vol. 2, *Lord President of the Council and Leader of the House of Commons, 1966–68*, Hamish Hamilton and Jonathan Cape, London, 1976

Crossman, Richard, *The Diaries of a Cabinet Minister*, vol. 3, *Secretary of State for Social Services*, Hamish Hamilton and Jonathan Cape, London, 1977

Crouch, Colin, *The Student Revolt*, The Bodley Head, London, 1970

Crouch, Colin and Marquand, David (eds), *The New Centralism: Britain Out of Step in Europe?*, Basil Blackwell, Oxford, 1989

Crowley, Brian Lee, *The Self, the Individual and the Community: Liberalism in the Political Thought of F.A. Hayek and Sidney and Beatrice Webb*, Clarendon Press, Oxford, 1987

Dahl, Robert A., 'Workers' control of industry and the British Labor Party', *American Political Science Review*, vol. 41, 1947

Dahrendorf, Ralf, *The Modern Social Conflict*, Weidenfeld & Nicolson, London, 1988

Dalton, Hugh, *Practical Socialism for Britain*, George Routledge & Sons Ltd, London, 1935

Dalton, Hugh, *High Tide and After: Memoirs 1945–1960*, Frederick Muller, London, 1962

Darwin, John, *Britain and Decolonisation: The Retreat from Empire in the Post-War World*, Macmillan Press, Basingstoke, 1988

Dell, Edmund, *A Hard Pounding: Politics and Economic Crisis, 1974–1976*, Oxford University Press, Oxford, 1991

Dell, Edmund, *The Chancellors: A History of the Chancellors of the Exchequer 1945–90*, HarperCollins, London, 1996

Dell, Edmund, *A Strange Eventful History: Democratic Socialism in Britain*, HarperCollins, London, 2000

Denham, Andrew and Garnett, Mark, *Keith Joseph*, Acumen, Chesham, 2001

Dennis, Nigel, *Cards of Identity*, Weidenfeld & Nicolson, London, 1955

Dobson, Andrew, *Green Political Thought*, Routledge, London and New York, second edition, 1995

Donoughue, Bernard, *Prime Minister: The Conduct of Policy under Harold Wilson and James Callaghan*, Jonathan Cape, London, 1987

Donoughue, Bernard, *Downing Street Diary: With Harold Wilson in No. 10*, Jonathan Cape, London, 2005

Dow, J.C.R., *The Management of the British Economy, 1945–60*, Cambridge University Press, Cambridge, 1964

Driver, Christopher, *The Disarmers: A Study in Protest*, Hodder & Stoughton, London, 1964

Driver, Stephen and Martell, Luke, *New Labour: Politics After Thatcherism*, Polity Press, Cambridge, 1998

Drucker, H.M. and Brown, Gordon, *The Politics of Nationalism and Devolution*, Longman, London, 1980

Durbin, Elizabeth, *New Jerusalems: The Labour Party and the Economics of Democratic Socialism*, Routledge & Kegan Paul, London, 1985

Durbin, Evan, *The Politics of Democratic Socialism: An Essay on Social Policy*, Routledge & Kegan Paul, London, reprinted 1957

Dworkin, Ronald, *A Bill of Rights for Britain: Why British Liberty Needs Protecting*, Chatto & Windus, London, 1990

Eckstein, Harry, 'The British Political System', in Samuel H. Beer and Adam B. Ulam, *Patterns of Government, the Major Political Systems of Europe*, Random House, New York, 1962

Edgerton, David, 'Liberal Militarism and the British State', *New Left Review*, January–February 1991

Edgerton, David, *Warfare State: Britain, 1920–1970*, Cambridge University Press, Cambridge, 2006

Edwards, Owen Dudley (ed.), *A Claim of Right for Scotland*, Polygon, Edinburgh, 1989

Eliot, George, *Felix Holt: The Radical*, Penguin Books, Harmondsworth, reprinted 1977

Engels, Friedrich, *The Condition of the Working Class in England*, in *Marx and Engels on Britain*, Foreign Languages Publishing House, Moscow, 1953

Epstein, James, *The Lion of Freedom: Feargus O'Connor and the Chartist Movement, 1832–1842*, Croom Helm, London and Canberra, 1982

Faith in the City: A Call for Action by Church and Nation, The Report of the Archbishop of Canterbury's Commission on Urban Priority Areas, Church House Publishing, London, 1985

Fforde, John, *The Bank of England and Public Policy 1941–1958*, Cambridge University Press, Cambridge, 1992

Fielding, Stephen, Thompson, Peter and Tiratsoo, Nick, '*England Arise': The Labour Party and Popular Politics in 1940s Britain*, Manchester University Press, Manchester, 1995

Flanagan, R.J., Soskice, David and Ulman, Lloyd, *Unionism, Economic Stabilisation and Incomes Policies: European Experience*, The Brookings Institution, Washington DC, 1983

Floud, Roderick and McCloskey, Deirdre, *The Economic History of Britain since 1700*, vol. 3, Cambridge University Press, Cambridge, second edition, 1994

Foot, Paul, *The Vote: How It Was Won and How It Was Undermined*, Viking, London, 2005

Foster, Sir Christopher, *British Government in Crisis, or The Third English Revolution*, Hart Publishing, Oxford, and Portland, Oregon, 2005

Francis, Martin, *Ideas and Policies under Labour 1945–51: Building a New Britain*, Manchester University Press, Manchester and New York, 1997

Francis, Martin, 'Mr Gaitskell's Ganymede? Re-assessing Crosland's *The Future of Socialism*', *Contemporary British History*, vol. 11, no. 2 (summer 1997)

Freeden, Michael, 'New Labour and Social Democratic Thought', in Andrew Gamble and Tony Wright (eds), *The New Social Democracy*, Blackwell, Oxford, 1999

Freedman, Lawrence and Gamba-Stonehouse, Virginia, *Signals of War: The Falklands Conflict of 1982*, Faber & Faber, London, 1990

Gallagher, John, *The Decline, Revival and Fall of the British Empire*, Cambridge University Press, Cambridge, 1982

Gamble, Andrew, *The Free Economy and the Strong State: The Politics of Thatcherism*, Macmillan Education, Basingstoke and London, 1988

Gardner, Richard, *Sterling–Dollar Diplomacy: Anglo-American Collaboration in the Reconstruction of Multilateral Trade*, Clarendon Press, Oxford, 1956

Giddens, Anthony, *The Third Way: The Renewal of Social Democracy*, Polity Press, Cambridge, 1998

Giddens, Anthony, *The Third Way and its Critics*, Polity Press, Cambridge, 2000

Gilbert, Bentley, *British Social Policy 1914–1939*, B.T. Batsford Ltd, London, 1970

Gilbert, Martin, *Finest Hour: Winston S. Churchill 1939–1941*, Minerva paperback, London, 1989

Gilbert, Martin, *Prophet of Truth: Winston S. Churchill, 1922–1939*, Minerva paperback, London, 1990

Gill, Christopher, MP, 'Speaking Out on Europe', Bruges Group, Occasional Paper 18, London, April 1995

Gilmour, Ian, *Britain Can Work*, Martin Robertson, Oxford, 1983

Gilmour, Ian, *Dancing with Dogma: Britain under Thatcherism*, Simon & Schuster, London, 1992

Gilmour, Ian and Garnett, Mark, *Whatever Happened to the Tories: The Conservatives since 1945*, Fourth Estate, London, paperback edition, 1998

Goldthorpe, John H., Lockwood, David, Bechhofer, Frank and Platt, Jennifer, *The Affluent Worker*, Cambridge University Press, Cambridge, 1968

Gollin, A.M., *Proconsul in Politics: A Study of Lord Milner in Opposition and in Power*, Anthony Blond, London, 1964

Goodwin, Albert, *The Friends of Liberty: The English Democratic Movement in the Age of the French Revolution*, Hutchinson, London, 1979

Gould, Philip, *The Unfinished Revolution: How the Modernisers Saved the Labour Party*, Little Brown & Company (UK), London, 1998

Gray, John, (ed.), *Beyond the New Right: Markets, Government and the Common Environment*, Routledge, London and New York, 1993

Green, E.H.H., *Ideologies of Conservatism: Conservative Political Ideas in the Twentieth Century*, Oxford University Press, Oxford, 2002

Green, Jonathon, *Days in the Life: Views from the English Underground 1961–1971*, Heinemann, London, 1988

Greer, Germaine, *The Female Eunuch* (first published 1970), Paladin edition, London, 1971

Guttsman, W.L., *The British Political Elite*, MacGibbon & Kee, London, 1963

Haddow, Oliver J. (ed.), *Harold Wilson and European Integration: Britain's Second Application to Join the EEC*, Frank Cass, London, 2003

Hailsham, Lord, *The Dilemma of Democracy: Diagnosis and Prescription*, Collins, London, 1978

Haines, Joe, *The Politics of Power*, Jonathan Cape, London, 1977

Hale, Sarah, 'Professor Macmurray and Mr Blair: the strange case of the communitarian guru that never was', *The Political Quarterly*, vol. 73, no. 2, April–June 2002

Halsey, A.H. and Webb, Josephine (eds), *Twentieth-Century British Social Trends*, Macmillan Press, Basingstoke, 2000

Harris, José, *William Beveridge: A Biography*, Clarendon Press, Oxford, 1977

Harris, Kenneth, *Attlee*, Weidenfeld & Nicolson, London, 1982

Harrison, Brian, 'Thatcher and the intellectuals', *Twentieth Century British History*, vol. 5, no. 2, 1994

Harvie, Christopher, *Scotland and Nationalism: Scottish Society and Politics 1707–1977*, George Allen & Unwin, London, 1977

Haseler, Stephen, *The Super Rich: The Unjust New World of Global Capitalism*, Macmillan Press, Basingstoke, 2000

Hattersley, Roy, *Choose Freedom: The Future for Democratic Socialism*, Michael Joseph, London, 1987

Hayek, F.A., *The Road to Serfdom*, Routledge & Sons, London, 1944

Healey, Denis, *The Time of My Life*, Michael Joseph, London, 1989

Heath, Edward, *Old World, New Horizons: Britain, The Common Market and The Atlantic Alliance*, Oxford University Press, London, 1970

Heath, Edward, *The Course of My Life: My Autobiography*, Hodder & Stoughton, London, 1998

Heffer, Eric, *The Class Struggle in Parliament: A Socialist View of Industrial Relations*, Victor Gollancz, London, 1973

Heffer, Simon, *Like the Roman: The Life of Enoch Powell*, Phoenix Giant edition, London, 1998

Henderson, Nicholas, *The Private Office: A Personal View of Five Foreign Secretaries and of Government from the Inside*, Weidenfeld & Nicolson London, 1984

Hennessy, Peter, *Never Again: Britain 1945–1951*, Jonathan Cape, London, 1992

Hennessy, Peter, *Having it So Good: Britain in the Fifties*, Penguin Books, London, 2007

Hennessy, Peter, 'The Blair style and the requirements of twenty-first century premiership', *The Political Quarterly*, vol. 71, no. 4, October–December 2000

Heseltine, Michael, *Where There's a Will*, Hutchinson, London, 1987

Hewison, Robert, *Culture and Consensus: England, Art and Politics since 1940*, Methuen, London, 1995

Hill, Christopher, *The World Turned Upside Down: Radical Ideas during the English Revolution*, Temple, Smith, London, 1972

Hill, Christopher, *Antichrist in Seventeenth-Century England*, Verso, London and New York, 1990

Hirst, Paul, *Associative Democracy: New Forms of Economic and Social Governance*, Polity Press, Cambridge, 1994

Hobbes, Thomas (ed. John Plamenatz), *Leviathan*, Fontana edition, ninth impression, London 1978

Hobsbawm, Eric, *Interesting Times: A Twentieth-Century Life*, Allen Lane, The Penguin Press, London, 2002

Hobson, J.A., *The Crisis of Liberalism: New Issues of Democracy*, Harvester Press edition, Brighton, 1974

Hogan, Michael J., *The Marshall Plan: America, Britain and the Reconstruction of Western Europe*, Cambridge University Press, Cambridge, paperback edition, reprinted 1995

Holland, Stuart, *The Socialist Challenge*, Quartet Books, London, 1975

Horne, Alistair, *Macmillan 1894–1956*, vol. 1 of the official biography, Macmillan, London, 1988

Horne, Alistair, *Macmillan 1957–1986*, vol. 2 of the official biography, Macmillan, London, 1989

Hoskyns, Sir John, 'Conservatism is not enough', *The Political Quarterly*, vol. 55, no. 1, January–March 1984

House of Commons, *The Falklands Campaign: A Digest of Debates in the House of Commons*, HMSO, London, 1982

Hovell, Mark, *The Chartist Movement*, Manchester University Press, Manchester, 1981, reprinted 1959

Hurd, Douglas, *An End to Promises: Sketch of a Government 1970–74*, Collins, London, 1979

Hurd, Douglas, *Memoirs*, Little Brown, London, 2003

Hurd, Douglas, 'Citizenship in the Tory democracy', *New Statesman*, 29 April 1988.

Hutton, Will, *The State We're In*, Jonathan Cape, London, 1995

Jacobs, Eric and Worcester, Robert, *We British: Britain under the MORIscope*, Weidenfeld & Nicolson, London, 1990

James, Robert Rhodes, *Winston Churchill: A Study in Failure*, Weidenfeld & Nicolson, London, 1970

James, Robert Rhodes, *Anthony Eden*, papermac edition, London, 1987

Jay, Douglas, *Change and Fortune: A Political Record*, Hutchinson, London, 1980

Jay, Peter, 'A General Hypothesis of Employment, Inflation and Politics', Institute of Economic Affairs, London, 1976

Jefferys, Kevin, *Finest and Darkest Hours: The Decisive Events in British Politics from Churchill to Blair*, Atlantic Books, London, 2002

Jenkins, Peter, *The Battle of Downing Street*, Charles Knight & Co. Ltd, London, 1970

Jenkins, Peter, *Mrs Thatcher's Revolution: The Ending of the Socialist Era*, Jonathan Cape, London, 1987

Jenkins, Roy, *Baldwin*, Collins, London, 1987

Jenkins, Roy, *A Life at the Centre*, Macmillan, London, 1991

Jenkins, Simon, *Accountable to None: The Tory Nationalisation of Britain*, Hamish Hamilton, London, 1995

Jenkins, Simon, *Thatcher and Sons: A Revolution in Three Acts*, Allen Lane, London, 2006

Jennings, Sir Ivor, *The Law and the Constitution*, University of London Press, London, fifth edition, 1964

Johnson, Christopher, *The Economy under Mrs Thatcher 1979–1990*, Penguin Books, Harmondsworth, 1991

Jones, Gareth Stedman, *Languages of Class*, Cambridge University Press, Cambridge, 1983

Jones, Jack, *Union Man: The Autobiography of Jack Jones*, Collins, London, 1986

Joseph Rowntree Reform Trust, Ltd, *State of the Nation Poll 2004*

Joseph, Sir Keith, Bt, MP, *Reversing the Trend*, Barry Rose, Chichester and London, 1975

Kampfner, John, *Blair's Wars*, The Free Press, paperback edition, London, 2004

Kay, John, 'Twenty years of privatisation', *Prospect* magazine, 1 June 2002

Kelly, Dominic, Kelly, Gavin and Gamble, Andrew (eds), *Stakeholder Capitalism*, Macmillan Press, Basingstoke, 1997

Kenny, Michael, *The First New Left: British Intellectuals after Stalin*, Lawrence & Wishart, London, 1995

Keynes, J.M., *The Economic Consequences of the Peace*, Macmillan, London, 1920

Keynes, J.M., *Essays in Biography*, Rupert Hart-Davis, London, 1951

Keynes, John Maynard, *Essays in Persuasion*, W.W. Norton, New York and London, 1963

Keynes, J.M., *The Collected Writings of John Maynard Keynes* (ed. Donald Moggridge), vol. 24, Macmillan & Cambridge University Press, London and New York, 1971–89.

King, Anthony, 'The Night Itself', in Anthony King, et al., *New Labour Triumphs: Britain at the Polls*, Chatham House Publishers, Chatham, New Jersey, 1998

King, Anthony (ed.), *Why is Britain Becoming Harder to Govern?*, British Broadcasting Corporation, London, 1976

King, Desmond, *In the Name of Liberalism: Illiberal Social Policy in the United States and Britain*, Oxford University Press, Oxford, 1999

Kohnstamm, Max and Hager, Wolfgang, *A Nation Writ Large? Foreign Policy Problems before the European Community*, Macmillan, London, 1973

Kyle, Keith, *Suez*, Weidenfeld & Nicolson, London, 1991

Kynaston, David, *The City of London*, vol. 4, *A Club No More*, Chatto & Windus, London, 2001

Kynaston, David, *Austerity Britain, 1945–51*, Bloomsbury, London, 2007

Langford, Paul (ed.) *The Writings and Speeches of Edmund Burke*, vol. 2, *Party, Parliament and the American Crisis*, Clarendon Press, Oxford, 1981

Lee, J.J., *Ireland 1912–1985*, Cambridge University Press, Cambridge, 1989

Leonard, Dick, *A Century of Prime Ministers: Salisbury to Blair*, Palgrave Macmillan, Basingstoke and New York, 2005

Leruez, Jacques, *Economic Planning and Politics in Britain*, Martin Robertson, London, 1975

Letwin, Shirley, *The Anatomy of Thatcherism*, Fontana, London, 1992

Lewis, Russell, 'Master Eurocrat – the Making of Jacques Delors', Bruges Group, Occasional Paper 13, London, 1991

Leys, Colin, *Market-Driven Politics: Neoliberal Democracy and the Public Interest*, Verso, London, 2001

Lindsay, A.D., *The Essentials of Democracy*, Oxford University Press, London, 1929

Lively, Jack and Rees, John (eds), *Utilitarian Logic and Politics*, Clarendon Press, Oxford, 1978

Lloyd, John, *What the Media Are Doing to Our Politics*, Constable, London, 2004

Lock, F.P., *Edmund Burke*, vols 1–2, Clarendon Press, Oxford, 1998–2006

Lord, Christopher, *British Entry to the European Community under the Heath Government of 1970–4*, Dartmouth, Aldershot, 1993

Louis, Wm. Roger, *Ends of British Imperialism: The Scramble for Empire, Suez and Decolonization*, I.B. Tauris, London, 2006

Low, D.A., *Eclipse of Empire*, Cambridge University Press, Cambridge, 1991

Lowe, Sidney, *The Governance of England*, T. Fisher Unwin, London (revised edition), 1914

Ludlow, N. Piers, *Dealing with Britain: The Six and the First UK Application to the EEC*, Cambridge University Press, Cambridge, 1997

Lukacs, John, *Five Days in London, May 1940*, Yale University Press, New Haven and London, 1999

Lyons, F.S.L., *Ireland since the Famine*, Fontana, London, 1973

Macaulay, Rose, *The World my Wilderness*, Collins and Book Society edition, London and Glasgow, 1950

Maccoby, S., *English Radicalism: The End?*, George Allen & Unwin, London, 1961

MacDonald, J.R., *Socialism and Government*, Independent Labour Party, London, 1909

MacDougall, Donald, *Don and Mandarin: Memoirs of an Economist*, John Murray, London, 1987

McGarry, John and O'Leary, Brendan, *The Future of Northern Ireland*, Clarendon Press, Oxford, 1990

McGarry, John and O'Leary, Brendan, *The Northern Ireland Conflict: Consociational Engagements*, Oxford University Press, Oxford, 2004

McKibbin, Ross, *The Ideologies of Class: Social Relations in Britain 1880–1950*, Clarendon Press, Oxford (paperback edition), 1994

McKibbin, Ross, *Classes and Cultures: England 1918–1951*, OUP, Oxford, 1998

Macmillan, Harold, *Riding the Storm, 1956–1959*, Macmillan, London, 1971

Macmillan, Harold, *Pointing the Way, 1959–1961*, Macmillan, London, 1972

Macmillan, Harold, *At the End of the Day, 1961–1963*, Macmillan, London, 1973

Macmillan, Harold, *The Middle Way: A Study of the Problems of Economic and Social Progress in a Free and Democratic Society*, E.P. Publishing edition, Wakefield, 1978

MacMillan, Margaret, *Peacemakers: The Paris Peace Conference of 1919 and its Attempt to End War*, John Murray, London, 2001

Magee, Bryan, *Clouds of Glory: A Hoxton Childhood*, Jonathan Cape, London, 2003

Maine, Sir Henry Sumner, FRS, *Popular Government: Four Essays*, John Murray, London, reprinted 1918

Mallock, W.H., *The Limits of Pure Democracy*, Chapman Hall, London, 1918

Marcuse, Herbert, *One-Dimensional Man: Studies in the Ideology of Advanced Industrial Society*, Routledge & Kegan Paul, London, 1964

Marquand, David, *Ramsay MacDonald*, Jonathan Cape, London, 1977

Marquand, David, *Decline of the Public: The Hollowing Out of Citizenship*, Polity Press, Cambridge, 2004

Marquand, David, 'Half-way to Citizenship? The Labour Party and Constitutional Reform', in Martin J. Smith and Joanna Speer, *The Changing Labour Party*, Routledge, London, 1992

Marquand, David, 'The Welsh Wrecker', in Andrew Adonis and Keith Thomas (eds), *Roy Jenkins:, A Retrospective*, Oxford University Press, Oxford, 2004

Marquand, Hilary (ed.), *Organised Labour in Four Continents*, Longmans Green & Co, London, New York and Toronto, 1939

Marriott, Sir J.A., *England since Waterloo*, Methuen, London, 1954

Marsh, Peter, *The Discipline of Popular Government: Lord Salisbury's Domestic Statecraft, 1881–1902*, Harvester Press, Hassocks, Sussex, 1978

Martin, Ross, *TUC: The Growth of a Pressure Group, 1868–1976*, Clarendon Press, Oxford, 1980

Marx, Karl, *The Eighteenth Brumaire of Louis Bonaparte*, in Karl Marx and Frederick Engels, *Selected Works in Two Volumes*, vol. 1, Foreign Languages Publishing House, Moscow, 1951

Maschler, Tom (ed.), *Declaration*, MacGibbon & Kee, London, 1957

Matthew, H.C.G., *Gladstone 1875–1898*, Clarendon Press, Oxford, 1995

Mayer, J.P. (ed.), *Political Thought: The European Tradition*, J.M. Dent & Sons Ltd, London, 1939

Meet the Challenge Make the Change: A New Agenda for Britain, The Labour Party, London, 1989

Middlemas, Keith and Barnes, John, *Stanley Baldwin*, Weidenfeld & Nicolson, London, 1969

Middlemas, Keith, *Power, Competition and the State*, 3 vols, Macmillan, Basingstoke, 1986–91

Middlemas, Keith (ed.), Thomas Jones, *Whitehall Diary*, vol. 1, Oxford University Press, London and New York, 1969

Middlemas, Keith, *Politics in Industrial Society: The Experience of the British System since 1911*, André Deutsch, London, 1979

Middleton, Roger, *Government Versus the Market: The Growth of the Public Sector, Economic*

Management and British Economic Performance, Edward Elgar, Cheltenham and Brookfield, 1996

Mill, John Stuart, *Principles of Political Economy with some of their applications to social philosophy*, Longmans Green & Co., London, 1883 edition

Mill, John Stuart, *Essays on Politics and Culture* (ed. Gertrude Himmelfarb), Peter Smith, Gloucester, Mass., 1973

Milton, John, *Areopagitica*, in *Milton's Prose Writings*, Everyman's Library, London and New York, 1958

Milton, John, 'The Ready and Easy Way to Establish a Free Commonwealth', in Stephen Orgell and Jonathan Goldberg (eds), *John Milton: A Critical Edition of the Major Works*, Oxford University Press, Oxford and New York, 1991

Milward, Alan S., *The Reconstruction of Western Europe, 1945–51*, Methuen, paperback edition, London, 1987

Mitchell, Juliet, *Women: The Longest Revolution: Essays on Feminism, Literature and Psychoanalysis*, Virago, London, 1984

Moggridge, D.E., *Maynard Keynes: An Economist's Biography*, Routledge, London and New York, 1992

Moore, R.J., *The Crisis of Indian Unity, 1917–1940*, Clarendon Press, Oxford, 1974

Moran, Michael, *The Politics of Industrial Relations: The Origins, Life and Death of the 1971 Industrial Relations Act*, Macmillan, London and Basingstoke, 1972

Morgan, Kenneth O., *Consensus and Disunity: The Lloyd George Coalition Government 1918–1922*, Clarendon Press, Oxford, 1979

Morgan, Kenneth O., *Rebirth of a Nation: A History of Modern Wales*, Oxford University Press, paperback edition, Oxford, 1982

Morgan, Kenneth O., *Labour in Power 1945–1951*, Clarendon Press, Oxford, 1984

Morgan, Kenneth O., *The People's Peace: British History 1945–1989*, Oxford University Press, Oxford, 1990

Morgan, Kenneth O., *Callaghan: A Life*, Oxford University Press, Oxford, 1997

Morgan, Kenneth O., *Michael Foot: A Life*, HarperCollins, London, 2007

Morley, John, *Edmund Burke: A Historical Study*, Macmillan & Co. Ltd, London, 1867

Morley, John, *The Life of William Ewart Gladstone*, Macmillan, London, vol. 1, 1905

Mount, Ferdinand, *The British Constitution Now: Recovery or Decline?*, Heinemann, London, 1992

Mowlam, Mo, *Momentum: The Struggle for Peace, Politics and the People*, Hodder & Stoughton, London, 2002

Mulgan, Geoff, 'Reticulated Organisations: The Birth and Death of the Mixed Economy', in Colin Crouch and David Marquand (eds), *Ethics and Markets: Co-operation and Competition in Capitalist Economies*, Blackwell Publishers, Oxford, 1993

Nairn, Tom, *The Break-up of Britain: Crisis and Neo-Nationalism*, NLB, London, 1977

Nally, Michael, 'Eyewitness in Moss Side', in John Benyon (ed.), *Scarman and After: Essays Reflecting on Lord Scarman's Report, the Riots and their Aftermath*, Pergamon Press, Oxford, 1984

Namier, Julia, *Lewis Namier: A Biography*, Oxford University Press, London, 1971

Neustadt, Richard E., *Alliance Politics*, Columbia University Press, New York and London, 1970

Newton, Scott, 'The 1949 sterling crisis and British policy towards European integration', *Review of International Studies*, vol. 11, 1985

Nicolson, Harold, *Public Faces*, Constable, London, 1932

Nicolson, Harold, *King George the Fifth: His Life and Reign*, Constable, London, 1952

Norton, Philip, *Conservative Dissidents: Dissent within the Conservative Parliamentary Party,* *1970–74,* Temple Smith, London, 1978

Oakeshott, Michael (ed.), *Rationalism in Politics and Other Essays,* Methuen, London, 1962

O'Brien, Conor Cruise, *The Great Melody: A Thematic Biography and Commented Anthology of Edmund Burke,* Minerva paperback edition, London, 1993

Offe, Claus, *Disorganized Capitalism: Contemporary Transformations of Work and Politics,* MIT Press, Cambridge, Mass., 1985

O'Gorman, Frank, 'The Paine burnings of 1792–1793', *Past and Present,* November 2006

O'Neill, Onora, *A Question of Trust,* Cambridge University Press, Cambridge, 2002

Orwell, Sonia and Atigus, Ian (eds), *The Collected Essays, Journalism and Letters of George Orwell,* vol. 2, *My Country Right or Left,* Penguin Books, Harmondsworth, 1970

Osborne, John, *Look Back in Anger,* Faber & Faber, London, 1996

Ovendale, Richie (ed.), *The Foreign Policy of the British Labour Governments, 1945–51,* Leicester University Press, Leicester, 1984

Owen, David, *Face the Future,* Jonathan Cape, London, 1981

Owen, David, *The Hubris Syndrome: Bush, Blair and the Intoxication of Power,* Politico's, London, 2007

Paine, Thomas (ed. Mark Philp), *Rights of Man, Common Sense and Other Political Writings,* Oxford University Press, Oxford, 1995

Parekh, Bhikhu, 'Minority Rights, Majority Values', in David Miliband (ed.), *Reinventing the Left,* Polity Press, Cambridge, 1994

Pattie, Charles, Seyd, Patrick and Whitely, Paul, *Citizenship in Britain: Values, Participation and Democracy,* Cambridge University Press, Cambridge, 2004

Peach, Ceri, Rogers, Alisder, Chance, Judith and Daley, Patricia, 'Immigration and Ethnicity', in A.H. Halsey with Josephine Webb (ed.), *Twentieth-Century British Social Trends,* Macmillan Press, Basingstoke, 2000

Pearce, Edward, *Denis Healey: A Life in Our Times,* Little Brown, London, 2002

Perkin, Harold, *The Rise of Professional Society: England since 1880,* Routledge, London and New York, 1989

Peston, Robert, *Brown's Britain,* Short Books, paperback edition, London, 2006

Philip, Alan Butt, *The Welsh Question: Nationalism in Welsh Politics,* University of Wales Press, Cardiff, 1975

Pickering, Jeffery, 'Politics and "Black Tuesday": shifting power in the Cabinet and the decision to withdraw from east of Suez, November 1967–January 1968', *Twentieth Century British History,* vol. 13, no. 2, 2002

Pimlott, Ben, *Hugh Dalton,* Jonathan Cape, London, 1985

Pimlott, Ben, *Harold Wilson,* HarperCollins, London, 1992

Pimlott, Ben, *The Queen: A Biography of Elizabeth II,* Harper Collins, London, 1996

Pimlott, Ben (ed.), *The Political Diary of Hugh Dalton 1918–40, 1945–60,* Jonathan Cape in association with the London School of Economics, London, 1986

Piore, Michael J. and Sabel, Charles F., *The Second Industrial Divide: Possibilities for Prosperity,* Basic Books, New York, 1984

Pliatzky, Leo, *Getting and Spending: Public Expenditure, Employment and Inflation,* Basil Blackwell, revised edition, Oxford, 1984

Plowden, Edwin, *An Industrialist in the Treasury: The Post-War Years,* André Deutsch, London, 1989

Pocock, J.G.A., *The Machiavellian Moment: Florentine Political Thought and the Atlantic Republican Tradition,* Princeton University Press, Princeton, 1975

Pollard, Sidney, *The Development of the British Economy, 1914–1980*, Edward Arnold, London, third edition, 1983

Pollard, Stephen, *David Blunkett*, Hodder & Stoughton, London, 2005

Ponting, Clive, *Breach of Promise: Labour in Power 1964–70*, Hamish Hamilton, London, 1989

Porritt, Jonathon, *Seeing Green: The Politics of Ecology Explained*, Basil Blackwell, Oxford, reprinted 1986

Porter, Bernard, *The Absent-Minded Imperialists: Empire, Society and Culture in Britain*, Oxford University Press, Oxford, 2004

Porter, Bernard, *The Lion's Share: A Short History of British Imperialism*, second edition, Longman, London and New York, 1996

Powell, J. Enoch, *Freedom and Reality* (ed. John Wood), Elliott Rightway Books, paperback edition, Kingswood, Surrey, 1969

Powell, J. Enoch, *Still to Decide* (ed. John Wood), B.T. Batsford, London, 1972

Power Inquiry, The, *Power to the People*, York, 2006

Pressnell, L.S., *External Economic Policy since the War*, vol. 1, *The Post-War Financial Settlement*, HMSO, London, 1986

Pryke, Richard, 'The Comparative Performance of Public and Private Enterprise', in John Kay, Colin Mayer and David Thompson, *Privatisation and Regulation: The UK Experience*, Clarendon Press, Oxford, 1986

Pugh, Martin, *Women's Suffrage in Britain, 1867–1928*, Historical Association, London, 1980

Pugh, Martin, *The March of the Women: A Revisionist Analysis of the Campaign for Women's Suffrage 1866–1914*, Oxford University Press, Oxford, 2000

Raban, Jonathan, *God, Man and Mrs Thatcher*, Chatto & Windus, London, 1989

Radice, Giles, *Friends and Rivals: Crosland, Jenkins and Healey*, Little Brown, London, 2002

Rentoul, John, *Me and Mine: The Triumph of the New Individualism?*, Unwin Hyman, London, 1989

Rentoul, John, *Tony Blair, Prime Minister*, Little Brown & Company (UK), London, 2001

Reynolds, David, *The Creation of the Anglo-American Alliance: A Study in Competitive Collaboration*, University of North Carolina Press, Chapel Hill, 1981

Reynolds, David, *From World War to Cold War: Churchill, Roosevelt and the International History of the 1940s*, Oxford University Press, Oxford, 2006

Riddell, Peter, *The Thatcher Government*, Martin Robertson, Oxford, 1983

Ridley, Nicholas, *My Style of Government: The Thatcher Years*, Hutchinson, London, 1991

Robbins, Caroline, *The Eighteenth-Century Commonwealthman: Studies in the Transmission, Development and Circumstance of English Liberal Thought from the Restoration of Charles II until War with the Thirteen Colonies*, Harvard University Press, Cambridge, Mass., 1959

Roberts, Andrew, *Salisbury: Victorian Titan*, Weidenfeld & Nicolson, London, 1999

Roberts, Robert, *The Classic Slum: Salford Life in the First Quarter of the Century*, Penguin Books, Harmondsworth, 1973

Robertson, Alex J., *The Bleak Midwinter 1947*, Manchester University Press, Manchester, 1987

Robertson, Patrick (ed.), *Reshaping Europe in the Twenty-first Century*, Macmillan Press in association with the Bruges Group, Basingstoke, 1992

Robinson, Andrew W., *The Language of Democracy: Political Rhetoric in the United States and Britain 1790–1900*, Cornell University Press, Ithaca and London, 1995

Rolph, C.H. (ed.), *The Trial of Lady Chatterley: Regina v. Penguin Books Limited*, Penguin Books, Harmondsworth, 1961

Rose, Richard, *Governing without Consensus: An Irish Perspective*, Faber & Faber, London, 1971

Rose, Richard, *The Prime Minister in a Shrinking World*, Polity Press, Cambridge, 2001

Rose, Richard and Peters, Guy, *Can Government Go Bankrupt?* Macmillan, London, 1979

Roth, Andrew, *Heath and the Heathmen*, Routledge & Kegan Paul, London, 1972

Routledge, Paul, *Gordon Brown: The Biography*, Simon & Schuster, London, 1998

Rowbotham, Sheila, *The Past Is before Us: Feminism in Action since the 1960s*, Pandora Press, London, 1989

Rowbotham, Sheila, *Promise of a Dream: Remembering the Sixties*, Allen Lane, The Penguin Press, London, 2000

Rowthorn, R.E. and Wells, J.R., *De-Industrialization and Foreign Trade*, Cambridge University Press, Cambridge, 1987

Runciman, David, *The Politics of Good Intentions: History, Fear and Hypocrisy in the New World Order*, Princeton University Press, Princeton and Oxford, 2006

Ruthven, Malise, *A Satanic Affair: Salman Rushdie and the Wrath of Islam*, The Hogarth Press, London, 1991

Sampson, Anthony, *Anatomy of Britain*, Hodder & Stoughton, London, 1962

Sampson, Anthony, *Anatomy of Britain Today*, Hodder & Stoughton, London, 1965

Sampson, Anthony, *Macmillan: A Study in Ambiguity*, Allen Lane, The Penguin Press, London, 1967

Sampson, Anthony, *Who Runs This Place?: The Anatomy of Britain in the 21st Century*, John Murray (paperback edition), London, 2005

Scarman, Leslie, *English Law: The New Dimension*, Stevens & Sons, London, 1974

Scott, L.V., *Conscription and the Attlee Governments: The Politics and Policy of National Service 1945–1951*, Clarendon Press, Oxford, 1993

Seabrook, Jeremy, 'Unemployment Now and in the 1930s', in Bernard Crick (ed.), *Unemployment*, Methuen, London, 1981

Selbourne, David, *The Spirit of the Age: An Account of Our Times*, Sinclair-Stevenson, London, 1993

Seldon, Anthony, *Churchill's Indian Summer: The Conservative Government 1951–1955*, Hodder & Stoughton, London, 1955

Seldon, Anthony with Baston, Lewis, *Major: A Political Life*, Weidenfeld & Nicolson, London, 1997

Seldon, Anthony with Ballinger, Chris, Collins, Daniel and Snowdon, Peter, *Blair*, The Free Press (paperback edition), London, 2004

Seldon, Anthony (ed.), *The Blair Effect 1997–2001*, Little, Brown, London, 2001

Seldon, Anthony and Kavanagh, Dennis (eds), *The Blair Effect 2001–5*, Cambridge University Press, Cambridge, 2005

Seymour, Charles, *Electoral Reform in England and Wales: The Development and Operation of the Parliamentary Franchise, 1832–1885*, Yale University Press, New Haven, 1915

Sharp, Andrew (ed.), *The English Levellers*, Cambridge University Press, Cambridge, 1998

Shanks, Michael, *The Stagnant Society*, Penguin Books, Harmondsworth, 1972 edition

Shaw, G. Bernard, 'The Transition to Social Democracy' in Shaw, Bernard, *Fabian Essays*, Jubilee Edition, London, 1948

Shepherd, Robert, *Iain Macleod: A Biography*, Hutchinson, London, 1994

Shepherd, Robert, *Enoch Powell: A Biography*, Hutchinson, London, 1996

Shlaim, Avi, *The Iron Wall: Israel and the Arab World*, Allen Lane, London, 2000

Sillitoe, Alan, *Saturday Night and Sunday Morning*, Pan Books edition, London, 1960

Sissons, Michael and French, Philip (eds), *The Age of Austerity 1945–1951*, Oxford University Press, paperback edition, 1986

Skidelsky, Robert, *John Maynard Keynes: A Biography*, 3 vols, Macmillan, London, 1983–2000

Skinner, Quentin, *Liberty before Liberalism*, Cambridge University Press, Cambridge, 1998

Skinner, Quentin, *Visions of Politics*, vol. 2, *Renaissance Virtues*, Cambridge University Press, Cambridge, 2002

Smith, F.B., *The Making of the Second Reform Bill*, Cambridge University Press, Cambridge, 1966

Smith, Martin J., *The Core Executive in Britain*, Macmillan Press, Basingstoke, 1999

Smith, Paul, *Lord Salisbury on Politics: A Selection from his Articles in the Quarterly Review, 1860–1883*, Cambridge University Press, Cambridge, 1972

Smith, Paul (ed.), *Bagehot: The English Constitution*, Cambridge University Press, Cambridge, 2001

Smith, Trevor, 'Citizenship and the British Constitution', *Parliamentary Affairs*, vol. 44, no. 4, October 1991

Social and Community Planning Research, *British Social Attitudes Cumulative Sourcebook*, Gower, Aldershot, 1992

Social Justice: Strategies for National Renewal, Report of the Commission on Social Justice, Vintage, London, 1994

Solomos, John, *Race and Racism in Britain*, second edition, Macmillan Press, Basingstoke, 1993

Somerville, Johann P. (ed.), Sir Robert Filmer, *Patriarchy and Other Writings*, Cambridge University Press, Cambridge, 1991

Sopel, John, *Tony Blair: The Moderniser*, Michael Joseph, London, 1995

Stephens, Philip, *Politics and the Pound: The Tories, the Economy and Europe*, Papermac edition, London, 1997

Stevenson, John, *Popular Disturbances in England, 1700–1832*, Longman, London, 1992

Stevenson, Wilf (ed.), Gordon Brown, *Moving British Forward: Selected Speeches 1997–2006*, Bloomsbury, London, 2006

Stewart, Michael, *The Jekyll and Hyde Years: Politics and Economic Policy since 1964*, Dent, London, 1977

Stothard, Peter, *30 Days: A Month at the Heart of Blair's War*, HarperCollins, London, 2003

Stott, Mary, *Before I Go: Reflections on My Life and Times*, Virago, London, 1985

Strachey, Ray, '*The Cause': A Short History of the Women's Movement in Great Britain*, G. Bell & Sons, Ltd, London,. 1928

Tawney, R.H., *The Attack and Other Papers*, Spokesman edition, Nottingham, 1981

Taylor, A.J.P., *A Personal History*, Hamish Hamilton, London, 1983

Taylor, Robert, *The Trade Union Question in British Politics: Government and Unions since 1945*, Blackwell, Oxford, 1993

Taylor, Robert, 'The Heath Government and Industrial Relations, in Stuart Ball and Anthony Seldon, *The Heath Government 1970–74: A Reappraisal*, Longman, London and New York, 1996

Tebbit, Rt Hon. Lord of Chingford, 'Address to the 5th Anniversary of the Foundation of the Bruges Group', Bruges Group Occasional Paper 15, London, 1994

Terrill, Ross, *R.H. Tawney and His Times: Socialism as Fellowship*, André Deutsch, London, 1974

Thatcher, Margaret, *In Defence of Freedom: Speeches on Britain's Relations with the World*, Aurum Press, London, 1986

Thatcher, Margaret, *The Path to Power*, HarperCollins, London, 1995

The New Whole Duty of Man Containing the Faith and Doctrine of a Christian Necessary for all Families, London, [?1747]

Thomas, Hugh (ed.), *The Establishment*, Anthony Blond, London, 1959

Thomas, Keith, 'The Levellers and the Franchise', in Gerald Aylmer (ed.), *The Interregnum*, Macmillan, London, 1972

Thomas, Nick, 'Challenging myths of the 1960s: the case of student protest in Britain', *Twentieth Century British History*, vol. 13, no. 3, 2002

Thompson, Dorothy, *The Chartists*, Temple Smith, London, 1984

Thompson, E.P., *The Making of the English Working Class*, Penguin Books, reprinted London, 1991

Thompson, E.P. (ed.), *Out of Apathy*, Stevens & Sons, London, 1960

Tomlinson, Jim, *Employment Policy 1939–1955*, Clarendon Press, Oxford, 1987

Tomlinson, Jim, *Democratic Socialism and Economic Policy: The Attlee Years 1945–1951*, Cambridge University Press, Cambridge, 1997

Tonge, Jonathan, *Northern Ireland*, Polity Press, Cambridge, 2006

Toye, Richard, *The Labour Party and the Planned Economy 1931–1951*, The Royal Historical Society, The Boydell Press, Woodbridge, 2003

Trevelyan, G.M., *British History in the Nineteenth Century and After*, Longmans, London, 1937

Turner, John, *Macmillan*, Longman, London, 1994

Veljanovski, Cento, *Selling the State: Privatisation in Britain*, Weidenfeld & Nicolson, London, 1987

Wallace, Martin, *British Government in Northern Ireland: From Devolution to Direct Rule*, David & Charles, Newton Abbot, 1982

Watson, Alan, *A Conservative Coup: The Fall of Margaret Thatcher*, Gerald Duckworth, London, 1991

Waugh, Evelyn, *The Ordeal of Gilbert Pinfold*, Chapman Hall, London, 1957

Webb, Sidney, *Socialism in England*, Swan Soonenschein & Co., London, 1890

Webb, Sidney and Webb, Beatrice, *Soviet Communism: A New Civilisation*, private subscription edition, 1935

Webster, Charles, *The Health Services since the War*, vol. 1, *Problems of Health Care: The National Health Service before 1957*, HMSO, London, 1988

Webster, Charles, *The National Health Service: A Political History*, second edition, Oxford University Press, Oxford, 2002

Westlake, Martin, *Kinnock: The Biography*, Little Brown & Company, London, 2001

Whiteley, Paul, Seyd, Patrick and Richardson, Jeremy, *True Blues: The Politics of Conservative Party Membership*, Clarendon Press, Oxford, 1994

Williams, Philip, (ed.), *The Diary of Hugh Gaitskell 1945–1956*, Jonathan Cape, London, 1983

Williams, Philip, 'The Labour Party: The Rise of the Left', in Hugh Berrington (ed.), *Change in British Politics*, Frank Cass, London, 1984

Williams, Raymond (ed.), *May Day Manifesto 1968*, Penguin Books, Harmondsworth, 1968

Williamson, John, *The Failure of World Monetary Reform, 1971–74*, Thomas Nelson & Sons, Sudbury-on-Thames, 1977

Williamson, Philip, *Stanley Baldwin: Conservative Leadership and National Values*, Cambridge University Press, Cambridge, 1999

Wilson, Harold, *Purpose in Politics*, Weidenfeld & Nicolson, 1964

Wilson, Harold, *The Labour Government, 1964–70: A Personal Record*, Penguin Books, Harmondsworth, 1974

Wilson, (Sir James) Harold, *Memoirs: The Making of a Prime Minister*, Weidenfeld & Nicolson and Michael Joseph, London, 1986

Winter, Jay (ed.), *The Working Class in Modern British History: Essays in Honour of Henry Pelling*, Cambridge University Press, Cambridge, 1983

Woodhouse, A.S.P. (ed.), *Puritanism and Liberty: Being the Army Debates (1647–9) from the*

Clarke Manuscripts with Supplementary Documents, University of Chicago Press, second impression, London, 1965

Wootton, David, 'The Levellers', in John Dunn (ed.), *Democracy: The Unfinished Journey 508 BC–AD 1993*, Oxford University Press, Oxford, 1993

World Commission on Environment and Development, *Our Common Future*, Oxford University Press, Oxford, 1987

Worsthorne, Peregrine, *In Defence of Aristocracy*, HarperCollins, London, 2004

Worsthorne, Peregrine, 'Too Much Freedom,' in Maurice Cowling (ed.). *Conservative Essays*, Cassell, London, 1978

Worswick, G.D.N. and Ady, P.H. (eds), *The British Economy, 1945–1950*, Clarendon Press, Oxford, 1952

Worswick, G.D.N. and Ady, P.H. (eds), *The British Economy in the Nineteen-Fifties*, Clarendon Press, Oxford, 1962

Wright, A.W., *G.D.H. Cole and Socialist Democracy*, Clarendon Press, Oxford, 1979

Wright, Kenyon, *The People Say Yes; The Making of Scotland's Parliament*, Argyll Publishing, Argyle, 1997

Young, Hugo, *One of Us*, Macmillan, London, 1989

Young, Hugo, *This Blessed Plot: Britain and Europe from Churchill to Blair*, Macmillan, London and Basingstoke, 1998

Young, Wayland, *The Profumo Affair: Aspects of Conservatism*, Penguin Books, Harmondsworth, 1963

Ziegler, Philip, *Wilson: The Authorised Life of Lord Wilson of Rievaulx*, Weidenfeld & Nicolson, London, 1993

Zweiniger-Bargielovska, Ina, *Austerity in Britain: Rationing, Controls and Consumption, 1939–1955*, Oxford University Press, Oxford, 2000

GOVERNMENT AND PARLIAMENTARY PUBLICATIONS

Economic Survey for 1947, Cmd 7046

Employment Policy, Cmd 6527, HMSO, London 1944

Report of the Inquiry into the Circumstances Surrounding the Death of Dr David Kelly CMG by Lord Hutton, January 2004, HC 247

Review of Intelligence on Weapons of Mass Destruction, Report of a Committee of Privy Councillors (The Butler Report), HC 898, Stationery Office, London, 2004

Royal Commission on the Constitution, 1969–73, 2 vols, Cmnd 5460 and 5460–I, HMSO, London, 1973

Social Trends, Central Statistical Office, HMSO, London, vol. 20

Statement Relating to Defence, HMSO, February 1947, Cmd 7042

Statistical Material Presented During the Washington Negotiations, Cmd 6707, HMSO, London, 1945

The Brixton Disorders 10–12 April 1981, Report of an Inquiry by the Rt Hon. The Lord Scarman OBE, Cmnd 8427, HMSO, London, 1981

The Governance of Britain, CM 7170, London, July 2007

The National Plan, Cmnd 2764, HMSO, London, 1965

DISSERTATION

Ben Jackson, 'Egalitarian Thought on the British Left', Oxford University D. Phil. thesis, 2003

INDEX